The Why, Who and How of the Editorial Page

D0140633

Fourth Edition

The Why, Who and How of the Editorial Page

Kenneth Rystrom

Virginia Polytechnic Institute and State University

Strata Publishing, Inc.

State College, Pennsylvania

9 8 7 6 5 4 3 2 1

The Why, Who and How of the Editorial Page

Published by:
Strata Publishing, Inc.
P.O. 1303
State College, PA 16804
USA

telephone: 1-814-234-8545
fax: 1-814-238-7222
web site: http://www.stratapub.com

Library of Congress Cataloging-in-Publication Data

Rystrom, Kenneth
    The why, who, and how of the editorial page / Kenneth Rystrom.– 4th ed.
        p. cm.
    Includes bibliographical references and index.
    ISBN 1-891136-09-7 (alk. paper)
        1. Editorials. 1. Title.

 PN4778.R95 2003
 070.4'1–dc2l

                                                            2003050583

Text and cover design, page makeup and composition by Keith McPherson, WhiteOak
Creative.

Cover image: Jack Start/PhotoLink/Getty Images.

Manufactured in the United States of America by Thomson-Shore, Inc.

Credits and acknowledgments appear on pages 367–369 and on this page by reference.

ISBN 1-891136-09-7

To my children, grandchildren and great-grandchildren—
May they enjoy, appreciate and love the written word,
to which I have dedicated myself,
as a reporter, editor and journalism professor,
since receiving a toy printing press at age 8.

Contents

Preface

Since publication of the first edition of *The Why, Who and How of the Editorial Page*, typical assignments for editorial writers have expanded far beyond the traditional unsigned newspaper editorial. Opinion writers these days may be asked to write broadcast editorials, signed columns, interpretive articles, cultural reviews, opinion essays for the Internet and pieces that might be labeled "public journalism."

With each edition, this book has reflected the increasing variety of assignments; yet, the goal of the book remains the same. The suggestion that I write this book came from officers of the National Conference of Editorial Writers, who wanted a textbook that would benefit both college students and professional editorial writers. I had three purposes in mind. First, I wanted to help students and beginning editorial writers learn how to write newspaper and broadcast editorials and a broader array of opinion pieces. Second, I wanted to help them understand what it is like to be an opinion writer today. Third, I wanted to show them not only the practical aspects of opinion writing, but the historical and theoretical as well.

Responses to each edition have encouraged me to keep the book up to date. I am grateful to the journalists and journalism professors who over the years have helped make this book the leading textbook on opinion writing, the first such book to go into a fourth edition. Several editors have told me they require their new editorial writers to study the book before they start writing. Some editorial writers report that they keep their copies of the book in their offices. The book has been widely used in college and university courses with various titles: editorial writing, opinion writing, persuasive writing and feature writing.

In response to comments and suggestions from journalists, journalism professors and students, this edition retains the basic content and format of the previous editions. The book has been updated to reflect current issues and ideas about opinion writing and opinion pages. Responding to requests, I have expanded discussions of specific skills and types of opinion writing. The new edition also has more examples. Most of the examples in this edition are new.

■ DESCRIPTION OF THE BOOK

As the title suggests, the book consists of three main sections.

Part I, "The Why of the Editorial Page," looks at where opinion writing has come from, where it is today and where it might be headed. Chapter 1 provides a more extensive and in-depth account of the history of the American editorial page than previous editions, probably a more extensive and in-depth account than any other publication now in print. It demonstrates that, while some of today's editorial page policies and practices are rooted in the rich, exciting past, the story of the American editorial page is principally that of change—how editors and writers, both in the past and today, face the challenge of political, social and cultural changes. Chapter 2 examines a range of varied editorial approaches—from the "bugle call" to the strictly logical. Historical and recent examples are intended to inspire as well as instruct students and professional writers.

Part II, "The Who of the Editorial Page," describes how people become opinion writers; how they can prepare themselves to become writers, or better writers; and how editorial writers fit into the newspaper organization and the wider community. Included are chapters on relations with publishers and owners, the news staff, the editorial page staff and the community. Over the years, the role of the opinion writer has been changing in all of these relationships. As will become evident in this edition, this role continues to change. In many ways, opinion writers now are better prepared and are being given more responsibility than in the past, but more also is expected of them in terms of knowledge, commitment and integrity.

Part III, "The How of the Editorial Page," is the largest section of the book. It explains how to write opinion pieces and edit opinion pages. It emphasizes how writers and editors can do their jobs better, whether in writing editorials, handling letters to the editor and syndicated features, bringing diverse opinions to the page or attracting readers with innovative designs or new features. I have made a particular effort to expand coverage, reflect current issues and provide more examples, while maintaining the fundamental strengths of this section.

Throughout, the book is extensively illustrated with journalists' ideas, thoughts and experiences (some of them contradictory) about how opinion pieces should be written and opinion pages produced. Principles and guidelines are illustrated with a variety of sample editorials, other opinion pieces, and editorial and op-ed pages.

As I recount some of my own experiences and state my opinions, I hope readers will catch my enthusiasm for opinion page work. I have enjoyed writing my own editorials and editing other people's. I have found pleasure in seeing the results of editing and arranging letters, columns and cartoons on an opinion page. Probably as much as anything, I have enjoyed the life of an editorial writer as a recognized member of, and participant in, a community. I feel confident that, as users of this book read about what writers and editors have said and done, they will conclude that these writers and editors too see their jobs as fun, interesting and stimulating.

■ FEATURES OF THE NEW EDITION

The new edition has been expanded and updated to reflect current issues in the field, as well as suggestions and comments from journalism professors, opinion page writers and students. These efforts have focused especially on five areas: the breadth of opinion writing, examples, innovations, the Internet and comments from working journalists.

Breadth: This edition takes a broader view of opinion writing than earlier editions did. Traditional newspaper and broadcast editorials are thoroughly studied, as in the past, but I have also given more attention to the growing opportunities to write cultural reviews, signed opinion pieces, columns, interpretive articles, "public journalism" articles and Internet contributions.

Examples: This edition contains approximately 100 sample editorials, opinion pieces and excerpts from a wide range of newspapers and other sources—more than in previous editions. Almost all these examples are new to this edition. Thanks to Internet resources, I have been able to include very recent examples.

Innovations: This edition continues the practice of emphasizing new ideas and practices that writers and editors have tried to make their pages more informative, lively and attractive to readers. These innovations include ways of handling letters to the editor, employing columnists and cartoonists, designing opinion pages, encouraging reader and community participation and making use of the Internet.

Internet: The Internet has given rise to many new resources and opportunities, which I have tried to reflect in this edition. Throughout the book, potential sources of information for opinion writers are listed. Some chapters describe how opinion writers and editors are using the Internet to expand the readership of their editorials, encourage reader contributions, offer new types of community forums and conduct opinion polls. The e-mail discussion group sponsored by the National Conference of Editorial Writers makes it possible for members to engage in an ongoing discussion of editorial issues, problems and ideas.

Comments from working journalists: The ideas and opinions of a wide range of editorial page writers, editors and scholars have been incorporated in this edition. Efforts have been made especially to reflect current issues and circumstances by drawing on articles and books that have appeared since the last edition. As in the past, many of the articles that are cited appeared in *The Masthead*, the quarterly publication of the National Conference of Editorial Writers.

ACKNOWLEDGMENTS

Although I had written editorials as a college student at the University of Nebraska–Lincoln, I had assumed that editorial writing was reserved for journalists late in their careers. I was surprised when, at age 28, I was asked by Professor Nathaniel B. Blumberg of the University of Montana whether I would be interested in a job he had heard about. Lauren K. Soth of the *Des Moines Register and Tribune* was looking for a person who would write editorials, edit and lay out the *Tribune*'s editorial page. Soth had recently won a Pulitzer Prize in editorial writing. I immediately applied, and spent five years under his guidance, learning how to write and edit opinion pieces. I suspect that the way I write editorials and teach editorial writing can be traced to what I learned in Des Moines. Much of my understanding of issues grew out of listening to 10 editorial writers sitting around Soth's office every morning at 9 a.m., talking about the affairs of the world. I also learned a lot from being called into Soth's office to discuss my latest editorial effort. The basic message of my Des Moines experience was that you should try to convince readers, not harangue them.

Although you can't expect to learn in five years everything there is to know about editorial pages, I accepted an invitation to become an editorial page editor (and sole editorial page staff member) on the newspaper on which I had been a reporter before I went to Des Moines, the *Columbian*, in Vancouver, Wash. I quickly learned that it was possible to write two editorials a day; handle the letters, columns and cartoons and lay out the page—and still find time to get around the community and have a family and social life. As I look back now, those days seem the most exciting and fulfilling. Much of the reason was that the paper was owned by two brothers, Don and Jack Campbell, who knew what was needed to produce a good newspaper and who were willing to provide the resources, guidance and freedom to produce such a newspaper. They were committed to a strong, independent editorial voice.

As the paper and the community grew, the *Columbian* added a second, and then a third, person to work on the editorial page. While I was there, the other positions were held by Elisabet Van Nostrand, Dennis Ryerson and Mike Heywood, all of whom have had distinguished editorial writing careers. I must acknowledge that, especially during my solo years, I often relied on Erwin O. Rieger, the managing editor, to write the second editorial of the day—and to run the page, in addition to his other duties, when I was out of town. The other staff members taught me as much about editorial pages as I ever taught them.

Before that, my mother, Zella Rae Borland Rystrom, first inspired me and taught me the love of writing. Nathaniel Blumberg, my first journalism professor, in Nebraska, introduced me to the wonders and challenges of journalism. During my first stint on the *Columbian*, managing editor Erwin Rieger forced me to face the rigors of responsible and accurate reporting. On the Des Moines newspaper, Lauren Soth fostered a love of editorial writing in me that, for more than four decades, I have considered to be the highest possible calling for a journalist.

I also had assumed that teaching journalism would come even later in life than writing editorials. At my 20-year mark in working on newspapers, Nathaniel Blumberg introduced me to the possibility of teaching. After serving as a visiting editor for a quarter at the University of Montana, I found myself looking for opportunities to switch careers. A one-year appointment at Washington State University was followed by six years at the University of Redlands and 13 years at Virginia Polytechnic Institute and State University. I am grateful for the support and help that I received from fellow faculty members and students during my 20 years on university campuses.

I also want to express my appreciation to the countless editorial writers and editors with whom I have associated through the National Conference of Editorial Writers. Without the encouragement and contributions from members of NCEW, this book literally would not have been possible. The officers of NCEW have allowed, in fact urged, me to draw as much as I wished upon the rich, varied contents of 55 years of that organization's quarterly, *The Masthead.* During the nearly 40 years that I have been a member of NCEW, Cora Everett, who only recently retired as executive secretary of that organization, has provided friendship, support and assistance in producing all four editions of this book.

I also want to express my appreciation to my friend Patricia Romanov, who has provided support and suggestions, particularly in writing the introduction and deciding on the design of the book.

My thanks also go to the reviewers whose many substantial contributions helped me refine and improve the book. For the first edition, they were R. Thomas Berner, The Pennsylvania State University; Kenneth Edwards, University of Alabama; Robert C. Kochersberger, Jr., State University of New York, College at Cortland; William McKeen, Western Kentucky University, and Robert M. Ours, West Virginia University.

For the second edition, they were Sharon Barrett, University of Montana; David Bennett, Indiana State University; Terry M. Clark, University of Central Oklahoma; Martin L. Gibson, The University of Texas at Austin, and Donald A. Lambert, Ohio University.

For the third edition, they were Joan Atkins, Morehead State University; Sharon Barrett, University of Montana; Eric Bishop, University of LaVerne; Robert H. Bohler, Georgia Southern University; Max Coursen, Pembroke State University; William A. Fisher, Winthrop University; Kate Hastings, Susquehanna University; Mary S. Haupt, State University of New York, College at Binghamton; R.V. Hudson, Michigan State University; Saundra Hybels, Lock Haven University;

Arnold Mackowiak, Eastern Michigan University; Orayb Najjar, Northern Illinois University; Neil Nemeth, Pittsburg State University; John David Reed, Eastern Illinois University; William J. Roach, University of North Florida, and Jerry Reynolds, Humboldt State University.

For the fourth edition, they were Susan J. Albright, Editorial Page Editor, Minneapolis, Minn., *Star Tribune*; Robert J. Caldwell, Editorial Page Editor, Portland *Oregonian*; Dan Radmacher, *Sarasota* (Fla.) *Herald-Tribune*; John J. Breen, University of Connecticut; Lori Demo, University of Kansas; Coke Ellington, Alabama State University; George Fattman, University of Pittsburgh at Johnstown; David Feldman, San Diego State University; William A. Fisher, Winthrop University; Patsy Gordon, University of Texas at Arlington; Tim Hanson, Francis Marion University; Repps B. Hudson, Washington University; Gerald B. Jordan, University of Arkansas; Charity Lyon, Northwestern Oklahoma State University; John McClelland, Roosevelt University; Mike McDevitt, University of Colorado; Deckle McLean, Western Illinois University; Joe Mirando, Southeastern Louisiana University; Philip Potempa, Valparaiso University; John David Reed, Eastern Illinois University; Jerry Reynolds, Humboldt State University; Sam G. Riley, Virginia Tech; Sharon Stringer, Lock Haven University; Brian Thornton, Northern Illinois University, and Liz Watts, Texas Tech University.

In putting out the first edition, as a neophyte to book publishing, I was helped by Mary Shuford, Martha Leff and Kathleen Domenig at Random House. Nearly a decade later, when Kathleen had established Strata Publishing, Inc., she asked me if I would be interested in working with her to publish a second edition. In the preface to that edition I wrote: "The result, from my point of view, has been the smoothest major writing effort with which I had been associated." In the preface to the third edition, I reported that working with Kathleen on that edition was "the smoothest and the most enjoyable." Although as my editor Kathleen often has advised me against unnecessary repetition, in this case "the smoothest and most enjoyable label" must be attached to the fourth edition. Kathleen is a demanding, meticulous, creative editor. She is more than that. After four editions she knows about as much about editorial writing and editorials as I do. She is at least as devoted as I am to producing the best possible book on opinion writing.

Introduction

Can editorial writers compete successfully in today's fierce battle for public attention?

Gone are the days when editorial writers could count on faithful and sympathetic readers. And gone are the days when readers looked primarily to newspapers for opinion. In the face of competition from other popular media, such as television and the Internet, is there still a significant role for those who write opinion pieces for newspapers?

David Shaw, the *Los Angeles Times* press critic, contends that "only rarely does the press help determine what people *think*," but that it can "help determine what people think *about*."[1] In determining what people think, opinion writers today may have three roles in public discussion: helping to set public agendas, creating community forums and providing community leadership.

In seeking meaningful roles for today's opinion writers, is there anything to be learned from looking back at our predecessors, the great editors and writers who were blessed with strong, loyal readers?

When you consider Benjamin Harris, James Franklin, John Peter Zenger and Horace Greeley, you have to admire their spunk and their willingness to run risks. Harris's *Publick Occurrences, Both Foreign and Domestick,* the first newspaper published in this country, was shut down after one day because Massachusetts authorities didn't like what Harris had written. James Franklin (Benjamin's brother) was sent to jail for what he said in his *Pennsylvania Gazette.* John Peter Zenger was charged with sedition and imprisoned for what he dared to print.

As the break from England approached, readers gloried in reading what their favorite Tory, Whig or Radical editor had written. But those who disagreed went so far as to break into newspaper offices, destroy the presses, carry away the type and melt it into bullets.

After the Revolutionary War, the Founders drew up a Constitution and a Bill of Rights that were intended to guarantee the rights, including freedom of press, that they had accused the colonial officials of violating. During the John Adams administration, however, when anti-Federalist editors spoke out vociferously against Adams' anti-French policies, they were jailed under the Alien and Sedition Acts for providing aid and comfort to French revolutionaries. (Thomas Jefferson freed the editors when he became president.) In the 1850s the Populist editors raised such ire that they risked being physically attacked by their competitors as they walked down the street.

The role of editorial writers was clear in those days: Write strong, strident, emotional editorials expressing views that the publishers wanted to propound and that *their* readers wanted to read—never mind that the authorities or other readers might legally or physically attack them.

Stories about thundering editorial writers make exciting reading and no doubt provoke nostalgia for the days of the "Great Editors." From their bravado we can draw inspiration to speak out strongly ourselves when, in an era of one-newspaper towns, many editorials writers feel pressure to temper their tongues. In such towns, editorial writers have opportunities for persuading readers of widely ranging opinions by aggressively pursuing the three roles mentioned above: setting public agendas, creating community forums and providing community leadership.

Setting the public agenda—controlling the subject matter that a community reads about—is no small power. Editorial writers have more freedom than reporters do to decide what they want to discuss and are likely to be more visible now than in recent decades. Today editorial pages offer opportunities for writers to attach their names to signed columns, interpretive articles, Internet essays and other opinion pieces. A photograph or a sketch of the writer, accompanying an article, can bring added recognition for the writer.

Editorial writers also get more opportunities today to affect editorial policy, which increasingly is set by a board composed of editors and editorial writers rather than by the publisher or a single editor. In addition, publishers are looking for more diverse editorial writers in terms of age, sex and racial-ethnic background. As a result, editorial writers have new opportunities to draw on their own ideas and more diverse backgrounds that affect the agenda for discussing public issues.

To be successful and responsible in carrying out this role, opinion writers today must be better educated than ever before. They must work hard to keep up with what is going on in their communities, in this country and around the world. They need to get out into their communities, cultivate knowledgeable and opinionated sources, and travel.

Closely allied to the role of setting the public agenda is providing a public forum. When the editorial column expresses an opinion, it is important to encourage readers with different points of view to express their opinions. Many newspapers today provide more space for readers' comments. Diverse ideas appear regularly on op-ed (opposite the editorial) pages, typically labeled "Commentary," which offer opportunities for lengthier articles.

Newspaper opinion pages may provide the only opportunity for the balanced, reasoned discussion of community issues that is vital in an open, democratic society. Opinion page editors cannot be satisfied with simply reprinting letters that come in the mail. Instead they encourage letter writers to use the telephone, fax and Internet. They solicit contributions from people of diverse views and encourage readers to write on specific topics or respond to important questions. They create boards of contributors, drawing members from the community. In all these efforts, today's editors work harder than most editors of the past to create forums for widely diverse viewpoints.

Opinion pages also can provide leadership in a community. How far news-papers should go in this role, however, has become a matter of disagreement among newspapers and among editors and writers. Some newspapers simply try to increase responses from, and articles written by, readers. Others, however, take an additional step: they organize and encourage readers to attend public meetings, with the goal of helping communities reach consensus on troubling issues. Some newspapers have worked with television stations to mobilize communities in support of causes.

Some editors criticize these efforts at activism—sometimes referred to as "civic journalism"—as going beyond the proper role of a newspaper. They contend that a newspaper's credibility is threatened when it stages public events and promotes causes in its news columns. Other editors believe that newspapers should play a leadership role but that that role should be confined to opinion pages. But whether or not they limit themselves to the editorial page, editorial writers play a community leadership role when they point out flaws in bad ideas, praise worthy projects and propose ideas of their own. As we will see in one of the chapters on editorial writing, they also write editorials promoting as well as praising their communities.

These three roles of the opinion page—setting the public agenda, creating community forums and providing community leadership—will vary from community to community, from one newspaper to another. Every newspaper faces different circumstances. A community with a more sophisticated reader-ship may offer opportunities for more in-depth discussion of issues. Newspapers in state capitals or university towns have easier access to the opinion of experts. Newspapers in business-oriented communities need to make certain that the views of management are balanced with other opinions. Newspapers in strong labor communities have similar responsibilities. Newspapers in economically healthy communities have more opportunities to devote space and resources to build public forums. Newspapers may see their roles differently in communities in which local leadership is weak.

All these elements affect the roles that editorial pages can, and should, play in a community. No one formula can be prescribed. One task for contempo-rary and future opinion writers and editors is to find new and better ways to fulfill these roles and, in doing so, keep the opinion function of the press alive and healthy. The purpose of this book is to help them meet that challenge.

The Why of the Editorial Page

The Editorial Page That Used to Be

Editorial writing is not what it used to be. Now, you may assume that I am comparing today's editorial writers with Horace Greeley or James Gordon Bennett or Charles Dana. And I am. No editorial writer today is blessed with the name recognition or devoted readership of these giants of the days of "personal journalism." But I also have a much more recent comparison in mind. Many of today's editorial writers are different from editorial writers of only a few years ago. They are better prepared for their jobs and better known in their communities than those "anonymous wretches" that one participant described as assembling at the first national meeting of editorial writers in 1947.

Editors no longer thunder in the manner of a Greeley, whose editorials could send a screaming mob to New York's city hall or provoke an ill-prepared Union Army into fighting the Battle of Bull Run. Editors of the first half of the 19th century often spoke with the editorial "I," and when they used "we," they meant "I." Editorials didn't have to be signed; readers knew who wrote the editorials in the papers they read.

Readers usually agreed with editorials in the papers they subscribed to. The large number of newspapers in most cities represented a wide variety of political opinions, and people read the papers they found most compatible with their own views. Consequently, editors could be as dogmatic and vitriolic in their editorials as they wished to be and know that their readers would not only agree with what they said but enjoy every nasty word written against mutual opponents. Editors could find comfort in the fact that, even if they did not know any more about an issue than their own political party's line, they were more knowledgeable than the vast majority of their readers. During the days of the "penny press" (when some papers actually did cost only one penny), many readers were immigrants—new to the country and new to the language—and most of them, as well as readers born in America, were only aware of what they read in their papers.

Those were great days for editors who were sure of what they wanted to say and said it boldly. But in addition to spreading their views, they spread a great deal of misinformation and fear among their readers. You have only to recall how the circulation war between Joseph Pulitzer and William Randolph Hearst whipped up a frenzy that helped ignite the Spanish-American War.

The Greeleys and the Hearsts used their skills to lambaste their competitors. So did other editors. In the little town of Lostine in Eastern Oregon in 1897, W.S. Burleigh let loose with an almost unending diatribe against a neighbor editor, Levi J. Rouse of the *Wallowa Chieftain*. In one editorial, Burleigh said:

It is not our intention to resume our controversy with the *Chieftain* Jassacks again, as we stated last week, but as they still persist in trying to beslime the *Leader* and its correspondents, and belching their fetid bile at the citizens of Lostine, we are, as a matter of duty, obliged to again side-swipe these foul featherless two-legged creatures who neither possess the instincts of man nor ape; whose souls are but the inspiration of a sick buzzard, who are a suppurating sore on the body social; creatures so foul that were Doll Tearsheet their mother, Falstaff their father and Perdition their birth-place, they would shame their shameless dam, disgrace their graceless sire and dishonor their honorless country.[3]

No editor of today has the power that a Greeley or Hearst had over the emotions, and presumably the opinions, of readers. And while they may sometimes wish they had more influence, today's editorial writers are not about to resort to the shenanigans, the (sometimes self-) deception, name-calling and outright lying that those "great editors" engaged in.

Compared to Horace Greeley, today's editorial writers are not well-known to their readers. They rarely sign their names to what they write. Their editorials are the anonymous opinions of "the newspaper." Since today's readers have virtually no choice in their local daily newspapers, modern editorial writers know that those who read what they write hold as many varieties of opinion as exist in the community. This diverse readership is one reason editorial writers no longer roar like Greeley. If writers take a strong stand on a controversial issue, they know they will please those who agree with them but displease those who disagree (if these people read the editorials at all). Today's writers suspect that if they come on too strong in their editorials, they will antagonize the readers they think they have the best chance to influence—those in the middle who have not made up their minds. Expression of a strong editorial opinion also may suggest to readers that the paper is using its news columns to advance that same opinion.

Writers know a lot of their readers are as well-educated as they. Readers may not see another daily newspaper, but they have many other channels of communication through which they can learn what is happening in their communities and the world. Today's public has a far better chance of finding out whether editorial writers know what they are talking about than did readers of a century ago. If an editorial hands out the party line, those who are unfamiliar with the issue at hand may be swayed for the moment. But if the editorial has told only half the story and the readers come across the other half at a later time, they are likely to sway right back again—and will thereafter be warier when the newspaper tries to tell them something.

These are some of the ways in which editorial writing is different now from the way it was in the days of Greeley, Bennett and Dana. How, then, does today's editorial writing differ from that of more recent times?

Personal journalism began to die out in the 1870s. Newspapers became corporately, instead of individually, owned. Publishers became more important than editors. Editorial-writing staffs, at least on larger papers, grew in size. If editorials did not specifically represent the handed-down views of the publisher, they were at least the product of a group rather than the thoughts of an independent editorial writer.

When the group of "anonymous wretches" assembled for the first meeting of the National Conference of Editorial Writers (NCEW) in Washington, D.C., in 1947, the 26 editorial writers, all men, had not previously met one another. The majority had never heard of most of the others. Only a few of the people whose work appeared on editorial pages then were very well-known. Beginning in the early 1930s, editorial page columnists such as Walter Lippmann, David Lawrence, Raymond Clapper and Arthur Krock had gained many readers through interpreting national and international events. Their bylines were displayed prominently, generally on the right side of the editorial page. But the opinions on the left side of the editorial page, those of "the newspaper," almost invariably were left unsigned. These writers were not well-known, and they were not well-paid. If they disagreed with what they were told to write, they could try to find other jobs. Participants at the Washington meeting speculated that they were among the last newspaper groups to form a national organization because their publishers didn't want them to get any ideas about gaining an independent voice.

Since then, editorial writers on many newspapers have carved out for themselves more secure and more prominent positions in relations with their publishers and with their communities. They have adapted to, and helped to change, the conditions in which they work.

Change and adaptation, in fact, have been at work in the evolution of the American editorial page ever since the introduction of the first newspapers on the continent. The changes began long before Greeley, Bennett and Dana appeared on the journalistic scene. The strong editor of personal journalism comes in the third of five general phases through which American newspapers, and editorial pages, have passed since Colonial days. The five phases can be described as follows:

1. During the Colonial era and the period immediately after the Revolutionary War, little effort was made to separate opinion from news. Both appeared intertwined in the columns of the press. Newspapers openly proclaimed that they were partisan voices.

2. With the writing of the new Constitution in 1787 came political parties and the partisan press. Editorials began to appear as distinct forms. Each newspaper was committed to a political party.

3. With the populist ("penny") press that emerged in the 1830s came the strong editor, who initially was concerned with sensationalized news and not with editorials but who, as readers became more literate and sophisticated, began to produce highly personalized editorial pages and better news products as well. Ties to political parties began to weaken.

4. Following the Civil War, and more so following the turn of the century, anonymous corporate editorial staffs began to replace the famous editors. Writing became more bland. Newspapers, while claiming increasing independence, generally remained committed to conservative editorial policies.

5. In recent years, beginning in the politically active 1960s, younger, more pragmatic and sometimes more aggressive editorial writers have started to emerge. Such writers tend to be nonpartisan but committed to a general editorial philosophy. And while many editorials still seem bland, from time to time writers will rise from their comfortable chairs and speak out sharply on issues that affect their communities and beyond.

In each of these phases, newspapers and their editorials have served different purposes according to readers' changing needs. Those papers—and editorials—that changed with the times survived; those that did not perished.

The remainder of this chapter will briefly describe the first four phases. The last phase will be discussed in the following chapter and throughout this book.

■ NEWS MIXED WITH OPINION

During the Colonial period, the first newspapers were heavily influenced by British tradition. The British press was licensed, and printers published under the authority of the Crown. A license could be suspended if the printer published anything that displeased authorities. The publisher of the first newspaper on American soil, Benjamin Harris, quickly learned what would happen if opinions displeased the Colonial officials in Boston. In his *Publick Occurrences, Both Foreign and Domestick*, on September 25, 1690, Harris said the English had postponed attacking the French because their Indian allies had failed to provide promised canoes. If that were not clear enough criticism of Colonial policy, Harris proceeded in his news columns to call the Indians "miserable savages, in whom we have too much confided." Harris also raised another issue that the Colonial authorities did not want talked about, smallpox:

The *Small-pox* which has been raging in *Boston,* after a manner very Extraordinary is now very much abated. It is thought that far more have been sick of it than were visited with it, when it raged twelve years ago, nevertheless it has not been so Mortal. The number of them who dyed in Boston by this last Visitation is about three hundred and twenty, which is not perhaps half as many as fell by the former.

On the pretext that Harris had not obtained the required license, members of the Colonial Council shut the newspaper down. It died after one issue.

For a large part of the Colonial period, American readers were more interested in what was happening in Europe than in the Colonies. Events in the Colonies did not seem very important except as they related to Europe. Consequently, Colonialists primarily looked for news from abroad in their early newspapers.

The first generally recognized American newspaper, the *Boston News-Letter,* was started in 1704—14 years after Harris' first attempt—and was a printed version of what had been a handwritten newsletter circulated by Boston postmaster John Campbell. Not much concerned with politics, Campbell avoided Harris' troubles by publishing with the permission of the government. But he did not hesitate to offer opinions, unpolitical though they were. At the conclusion of a news item about a woman's suicide, he said he hoped that the recounting "may not be offensive, but rather a Warning to all others to watch against the Wiles of our Grand Adversary." The reporting of the whipping of a prisoner who had sold tar mixed with dirt was "here inserted to be a caveat to others, of doing the like, least a worse thing befal (sic) them. . . ."

With the *News-Letter* already in existence, the father of James and Benjamin Franklin thought James was making a mistake in starting the *New England Courant* in 1721. The continent could not support more than one newspaper, he felt. James Franklin not only dared to publish; he dared to publish without the required license. The *Courant,* carrying little news and few advertisements, contained mostly commentary and essays. One of Franklin's targets was a group that advocated smallpox inoculations. He also attacked civil and religious leaders and questioned some of the religious opinions of the day. Franklin so enraged the Rev. Increase Mather that Mather called the *Courant* the work of the devil. If the government did not do something about the paper, he proclaimed from his pulpit, "I am afraid some *Awful Judgment* will come upon this land, and that the *Wrath of God will arise, and there will be no Remedy.*" However, what finally provoked the Colonial Council to charge Franklin with contempt was Franklin's allegation that the government had not done enough to protect Boston from pirates. Franklin was thrown into jail and ordered not to publish again. Subsequent issues were listed as being published by his younger brother Benjamin.

Benjamin Franklin began publishing his own *Pennsylvania Gazette* in 1729. He was not averse to inserting opinions into what he wrote, but, being a skilled writer and diplomat, he was able to avoid the trouble that James had encountered. One device he used to help arouse the Colonies was a drawing of a snake divided into eight parts, representing New England and seven other Colonies, accompanied by the motto "Join or die." It was run with an account of the French and Indian killing and scalping of frontier Colonists in Virginia and Pennsylvania.

In 1734, John Peter Zenger's mixing of comment with news in the *New York Weekly Journal* resulted in his being charged with printing seditious libels that "tended to raise factions and tumults in New York, inflaming the minds of the people against the government, and disturbing the peace." In a story on election results, Zenger claimed that voters had been harassed about their qualifications for voting. In another story, he said that the Colonial governor had allowed the French to spy on Colonial naval defenses. An elegant appeal by Zenger's lawyer, 80-year-old Andrew Hamilton of Philadelphia, convinced the jury to ignore the British common law standard that in matters of libel the jury's only task was to determine whether the alleged words had been published. The jury's verdict encouraged other editors to speak out. Eventually truth became an accepted defense against charges of libel in this country.

More threatening than libel laws to most newspapers was the Stamp Act of 1765, through which the British levied a heavy tax on paper to support their military presence in the Colonies. The tax produced vigorous editorial protests. Franklin suspended the *Gazette* for three weeks, during which time he printed as substitutes large handbills headed "Remarkable Occurrences" and "Stamped paper not to be had." The day after the act took effect, William Bradford III's Pennsylvania *Journal and Weekly Advertiser* ran a black border, usually indicating mourning, in the shape of a tombstone.

As the Revolution approached, Colonial papers generally split into three camps: Tory, Whig and Radical. The Tories championed the status quo, Colonial relations with Britain. One Tory paper, started in 1772, *Rivington's New York Gazetteer or the Connecticut, New Jersey, Hudson's River and Quebec Weekly*

Advertiser, at first tried to give space to all sides. In 1775, however, a party of "Patriot" armed men on horseback broke into the print shop, destroyed the press, carried away the type and melted it into bullets.

The Whigs represented a rising business class that at first was mostly interested in protecting itself from economic harassment by the British. John Dickinson, in a series of articles titled "Letters From a Farmer in Pennsylvania," argued for preservation of property and self-taxation. The articles were printed in the *Pennsylvania Chronicle* and the *Boston Gazette* in 1767.

Isaiah Thomas founded the *Massachusetts Spy* in 1770 as a paper "open to all parties," but when Tories stopped taking his paper he moved into the Whig camp. Then, as issues became sharper, he and some other Whigs joined the Radicals, who were the most critical of the way the mother country was treating the Colonies.

One of the first avowed Radical publications was the *Boston Gazette and Country Journal,* in which publishers Benjamin Eades and John Gill wrote and provided space for anti-British essays as early as 1764. Samuel Adams, who wrote for the *Gazette,* believed that writers could twist and interpret events and facts in the cause of liberty, to help arouse the Colonialists against the British. The authors made a point of distinguishing between facts and comments by printing their opinions in italic. Although historians have since concluded that some of the "facts" were not quite true, the attempt at differentiation between fact and opinion in news columns represented a step toward the editorial as distinct from a news article.

Another Radical writer, more pamphleteer than newspaper writer, was Tom Paine. His *Common Sense,* in early 1776, pleaded the cause of independence with an eye to persuading Whigs who were still on the fence.

▓ THE PARTISAN PRESS

The framers of the Constitution in 1787 thought they had achieved sufficient compromises between large and small states, and between the central government and the states, to eliminate the divisiveness that had characterized the late Colonial period. James Madison expressed the hope in "The Federalist," also known as "The Federalist Papers," that under the new government there would be no need for factions. One reason for nominating George Washington, the leader of the Continental Army and symbol of Colonial resistance, as the first president was to rally all Americans around the new government. The "Federalist Papers" themselves, written by Alexander Hamilton, James Madison and John Jay to support ratification of the Constitution, were first published in a newspaper, the *New York Independence Journal.* They were a mixture of fact, argument and opinion.

Disagreements soon appeared over how strong the federal government should be. Hamilton, as secretary of the Treasury, pushed for an active national administration that favored the business community, specifically for a national bank. Thomas Jefferson and his supporters wanted a weak federal government.

In addition, Jeffersonians tended to be favorably disposed toward the French Revolution. Hamilton and his supporters generally allied themselves with the British.

The two factions eventually formed parties and became known as the Federalists and the Democratic-Republicans.

To foster support for the Washington administration, Hamilton provided the inspiration for the first partisan newspaper, the *Gazette of the United States*, which appeared in 1789 with John Fenno as editor. Another Federal paper, *Porcupine's Gazette and Daily Advertiser*, founded by William Cobbett in 1797, was known for its vitriolic attacks on the opposition. In the following example the object of the verbal assault was the French minister to the United States.

When we see an unprincipled, shameless bully, "A dog in forehead, and in heart a deer," who endeavors, by means of a big look, a threatening aspect, and a thundering voice, to terrify peaceable men into a compliance with what he has neither a right to demand, nor power nor course to enforce, and who, at the same time, acts in such a bungling, stupid manner, as to excite ridicule and contempt in place of fear; when we see such a gasconading, impudent bluff as this (and we do every day), we call him a *Blunderbuss*.

A Federal writer of much milder tone was Noah Webster, of dictionary fame. Webster is credited by historian Wm. David Sloan as writing "the first editorial in the modern sense ever to appear in an American newspaper." Webster published this comment in 1783 under the "Hartford" local column of the *Connecticut Courant*:

. . . when the people, so enlightened as the inhabitants of this State, suffer themselves out of their senses by the foes of our independence and British emissaries, who are scattering the seeds of discord in the regions of tranquility, it seems the design of heaven to punish their blindness by some fatal catastrophe, and harden them, like Pharaoh of old, till they plunge themselves into an ocean of difficulties.

Later, while editing a Federalist paper called the *American Minerva* (founded in 1793), Webster placed editorials under the "New York" local news heading. By 1796 he was placing them under the heading "The Minerva," in the forerunner of what we now call the masthead—a box on the editorial page that carries the name of the paper, the names of the main editorial and business persons and other information about the paper. These new placements represented further steps toward differentiating editorials from news.

Although James Madison had contributed to "The Federalist Papers," he urged Jefferson, as secretary of state, to provide government subsidies to Philip Freneau to start the first anti-Federalist paper, the *National Gazette*, which was published only from 1791 to 1793. The *Gazette* and its successors generally spoke for agricultural interests, the less affluent, the smaller states and Americans who sympathized with the French Revolution.

For most of American history, George Washington generally has been considered beyond reproach. Some anti-Federalist writers had other opinions. One of the most outspoken was Benjamin Franklin Bache, grandson of Benjamin Franklin. Bache founded the *Philadelphia General Advertiser*, widely known as the *Aurora*, in 1790. When he wrote that the nation had been "debouched by Washington," Federalists wrecked his office and beat him. In 1797, when Washington announced he would not seek a third term, Bache saw "cause for rejoicing."

If ever there was cause for rejoicing, this is the moment—every heart, in unison with the freedom and happiness of the people, ought this day beat high with exultation that the name of WASHINGTON from this day ceases to give currency to political inequity and to legalized corruption . . . .

Of Bache, *Porcupine's Gazette* stated: "This atrocious wretch (worthy descendent of old Ben) knows that all men of any understanding put him down as an abandoned liar, as a tool and a hireling. . . . He is an ill-looking devil. His eyes never get above your knees." The long tradition of street encounters between 19th-century editors began when Fenno, of the Federalist *Gazette of the United States*, exchanged blows with Bache.

Bache's *Aurora* was the first, in 1800, to specifically designate its second page as an editorial page. It also used the editorial "we."

Because of their antipathy toward Britain and sympathy for the French Revolution, the anti-Federalists attacked the John Adams administration's inclination to support Britain and oppose France. Their opposition, often expressed in scathing language, helped account for passage of the Alien and Sedition Acts of 1798, which forbade "any false, scandalous and malicious writing . . . against the government of the United States, or either house of the Congress . . . or the President . . . or to excite against them the hatred of the good people of the United States." Excluded from the acts was the vice president, who happened to be Jefferson. The administration of the laws was so unfair—so obviously against anti-Federalist editors—that it contributed to Adams' defeat in his bid for re-election and to Jefferson's election. When Jefferson took office, he pardoned the imprisoned editors. The laws were allowed to expire.

Under Jefferson, the press became less vicious but remained partisan. In 1801, the year Jefferson took office, Hamilton founded the *New York Post*, with William Coleman as editor, to support the Federalists. Hamilton wrote many of the editorials. (Today, the *New York Post* is the longest continuously published newspaper in the country.)

Coleman reluctantly acknowledged that the Louisiana Purchase, one of Jefferson's major accomplishments, was "an important acquisition," but he wasn't convinced when Jefferson reported to Congress that up the Missouri River was a mountain of rock salt:

Methinks such a great, huge mountain of solid, shining salt must make a dreadful glare in a clear sunshiny day, especially just after a rain. . . . We think it would have been no more fair in the traveler who informed Mr. Jefferson of this territory of solid salt, to have added that some leagues to the westward of it there was an immense lake of molasses, and that between this lake and the mountain of salt, there was an extensive vale of hasty pudding, stretching as far as the eye could reach. . . .

Every president from Thomas Jefferson to James Buchanan, who was elected in 1856, had an official newspaper in Washington. Its principal purpose was to serve as the mouthpiece, to spread the official word to the party faithful. An exception was the *National Intelligencer*. Although it was the official paper of the Jefferson administration, under editors Joseph Gales Jr. and William E. Seaton it built a reputation for separating editorial positions from news reports and for providing nonpartisan coverage of Congress.

President Andrew Jackson, who became president in 1829, made the most effective use of an official newspaper. First he relied on the *United States Telegraph,* founded in 1825 by Duff Green. When Green switched his allegiance to Jackson's rival, John C. Calhoun, Jackson called on Francis P. Blair, who had been editor of the Democratic *Argus of Western America* in Frankfort, Ky., to establish the *Washington Globe.* Blair became one of Jackson's "kitchen cabinet." Another *Argus* editor, Amos Kendall, became Jackson's principal writer. Working his "Old Hickory" charm, Jackson gained influence with a substantial number of other newspapers. He appointed many editors to government positions, notably postmasterships.

One paper that shifted its policies to support Jackson was the *New York Evening Post* under William Cullen Bryant, who became editor the year Jackson took office. Bryant was one of the first editors to speak out for the right of free speech for abolitionists and the right of labor to organize. Because Bryant was interested in expanding readership beyond a few thousand politically aware readers and merchants, his editorials tended not to be marked by excessively partisan, shrill tones. He might begin an editorial with poetry or a humorous story. In one 1844 editorial, which has been credited with the idea for New York City's Central Park, Bryant chose a leisurely opening:

> The heats of summer are upon us, and while some are leaving the town for shady retreats in the country, others refresh themselves in short excursions to Hoboken or New Brighton, or other places among the beautiful environs of our city. If the public authorities, who extend so much of our money in laying out the city, would do what is in their power, they might give our vast population an extensive pleasure ground for shade and recreation in these sultry afternoons, which we might reach without going out of town. . . .

The *Post* succeeded in making the transition from party press to populist press. Partisan papers that attempted to remain partisan when the new, growing readership of the country was not much interested in politics did not survive. The Whig Party split apart, then died. The new Republican Party came out of almost nowhere. The Democratic Party split along North-South lines. By the time Abraham Lincoln became president in 1861, most newspaper readership was concentrated in the Populist press; most Partisan papers had died or lapsed into obscurity.

■ THE POPULIST PRESS

The first papers that reflected the nation's interest in something besides party politics were the mercantile dailies, which became prominent in the business community in the 1820s. But like the party papers they found only a few thousand readers sufficiently interested to read them regularly. They offered little editorial comment.

Both party and mercantile press ignored a rapidly growing potential readership that arose partly from immigration, partly from increasing literacy. Such readers may not have been especially interested in party politics, but they were interested in what was going on in their communities. They presented an opportunity for a new kind of newspaper, which would sell to the masses.

Day, Bennett, Greeley and Raymond

The first of the populist papers were called the "penny press" because some of them actually cost only a penny. Others cost two or three cents. In the first years much of the content was crime news and gossip. Courts and the police record were favorite sources for stories, many of them full of sex, blood and drunkenness. The readers loved these new papers, and circulation soared into the tens of thousands.

Editorial pages were slow in working their way into these papers. The first of the penny press papers was the *New York Sun,* founded in 1833 by Benjamin H. Day. He allied himself with no political party and employed no regular editorial writer. His few editorials dealt briefly with the latest sensations, municipal affairs, and morals and manners. One example: "SUDDEN DEATH—Ann McDonough, of Washington Street, attempted to drink a pint of rum on a wager, on Wednesday afternoon last. Before it was half swallowed Ann was a corpse. Served her right." Another example: "DUEL—We understand that a duel was fought at Hoboken on Friday morning last between a gentleman of Canada and a French gentleman of this city, in which the latter was wounded. The parties should be arrested." The *Sun* had only this to say when the 1843 New York Legislature adjourned: "The Legislature of this State closed its arduous duties yesterday. It has increased the number of our banks and fixed a heavy load of debt upon posterity."

The *New York Herald,* founded in 1835 by James Gordon Bennett, offered even more sensationalism than the *Sun.* In the early years, Bennett offered little serious editorial comment, but he loved to flaunt his ego and wit before his readers; they loved his swagger and flippancy. He was the first of the editors noted for "personal journalism." Concerning the *Herald,* he wrote: "Nothing can prevent its success but God Almighty, and he happens to be on my side." Although he liked to attack speculators, pickpockets and competing editors for their "crimes and immoralities," his editorials contained more bombast and personal references than solid opinion. Bennett's famous competitor, Horace Greeley, while perhaps not the most objective of critics, accurately characterized Bennett as "cynical, inconsistent, reckless, easily influenced by others' opinions, and by his own prejudices."

Bennett's biting editorial language and sensational news practices earned him occasional physical abuse. Several times he was horsewhipped in the streets. Usually he took advantage of these attacks to parade his fearlessness before his readers. After James Watson, editor of the *Courier and Enquirer,* had pushed Bennett down some stone steps, Bennett reported that he had suffered only a scratch and three torn buttons, but that Watson's "loss is a rent from top to bottom of a very beautiful black coat, which cost the ruffian $40, and a blow in the face, which may have knocked down his throat some of his infernal teeth for anything I know." He concluded self-righteously: "As for intimidating me, or changing my course, the thing cannot be done. . . . I tell the honest truth in my paper, and leave the consequences to God."

Bennett's ego was never more evident than in an 1840 editorial announcing his engagement." The heading was: "To The Readers of the Herald— Declaration of Love—Caught at Last—Going to Be Married—New Movement in Civilization." The editorial said in part:

I am going to be married in a few days. The weather is so beautiful; times are getting so good; the prospects of political and moral reform so auspicious, that I cannot resist the divine instinct of honest nature any longer; so I am going to be married to one of the most splendid women in intellect, in heart, in soul, in property, in person, in manner, that I have yet seen in the course of my interesting pilgrimage through human life. . . .

I cannot stop in my career. I must fulfill that awful destiny which the Almighty Father has written against my name, in the broad letters of life, against the wall of heaven. I must give the world a pattern of happy wedded life, with all the charities that spring from a nuptial love.

In later years, as readers became more sophisticated and Bennett less flippant, the *Herald* developed a serious and thoughtful editorial page. But it is to Horace Greeley that credit traditionally has gone for making the editorial page a significant and respectable portion of the daily newspaper. Greeley might be credited with establishing the first penny press. He published his first issue on a snowy day in January 1833, but readers could not get out to buy the paper, and he did not sell enough copies to be able to put out a second issue. His second effort, the *New York Tribune,* was founded in 1841.

Tribune editorials, written in a variety of styles but almost always with literary merit, commented on a broad range of topics. They generally followed a consistent editorial policy. Several writers contributed to the thinking behind the editorials and the writing, but readers customarily thought of the *Tribune's* editorial page, if not the *Tribune* itself, as a one-man show. Subscribers read the paper to see what Greeley thought, and they assumed that every word was his. *The New York Weekly Tribune,* in particular, with circulation across the country, was read with devotion.

With Day's and Bennett's papers appealing mostly to Democratic voters, Greeley's *Tribune* was the first of the populist press to have a Whig editorial outlook. But Greeley's philosophy was far more radical than that of most Whigs. He favored high tariffs, as did the Whig party, but not just to protect business; he wanted the creation of an American economy that would benefit merchants, workers and farmers as well. His interest in socialist and utopian ideas reflected the belief that all classes working together in an ideal community could produce wealth and harmony for all. He not only preached this belief in his editorial columns but he traveled the country lecturing to audiences on his ideas.

Greeley strongly believed in Western expansion and supported the march of farmers and merchants westward. But he did not support the method being used to annex Texas. The only New York editor to oppose the Mexican-American War, Greeley said after the Senate in 1845 had voted to annex Texas that Mexicans had "no choice but to resist."

The mischief is done . . . ! We have adopted a war ready made, and taken upon ourselves its prosecution to the end. We are to furnish the bodies to fill trenches and the cash to defray the enormous expense. Mexico, despoiled of one of her fairest provinces by our rapacity and hypocrisy, has no choice but to resist, however ineffectively, the consummation of our flagitious designs.

Greeley was an early advocate of the abolition of slavery. E.L. Godkin, editor of the *New York Evening Post,* concluded that by the early 1860s Greeley had "done more than any other man to bring slaveholders to bay, and place the Northern fingers on the throat of the institution." Godkin perceived that Greeley had "waged one of the most unequal battles in which any journalist ever engaged with a courage and tenacity worthy of the cause, and by dint of biting sarcasm, vigorous invective, powerful arguments, and a great deal of vituperation and personality."[4]

But, for all that, Godkin accused Greeley of treating his opponents with contempt, of being half-educated "and very imperfectly at that." According to Godkin, Greeley had "no grasp of mind, no great political insight"; his brain was "crammed with half truths and odds and ends of ideas which a man inevitably accumulates who scrapes knowledge together by fits and starts on his way through life." Greeley was saved, Godkin said, by his unflagging enthusiasm, an unshakable faith in principles and a writing style virtually unsurpassed in vigor, terseness, clarity and simplicity. But he was known also for his coarse and abusive language. As Godkin wrote: "He calls names and gives the lie, in his leading articles, with a heartiness and vehemence which in cities seem very shocking, but which out in the country, along the lakes, and in the forests and prairies of the Northwest, where most of his influence lies, are simply proofs of more than ordinary earnestness."

Illustrating both Greeley's penchant for name-calling and his devotion to the antislavery movement was an 1854 editorial that metaphorically took Sen. Stephen A. Douglas to task for making concessions to the South in the Kansas-Nebraska Act ("Stephen A. Douglas as the Volunteer Executioner"). Greeley describes a scene in which "a poor, miserable, half-witted and degraded Wretch, who consorted with the negroes," was about to be lynched by a mob.

Greeley wanted desperately to be elected to high political office. He did win one term in Congress as a Whig, but his self-righteous attitude toward his colleagues made him unpopular. Later, he became one of the leaders in forming the Republican Party. Finally, when he was old and the nomination was not worth much, Greeley was nominated for president in 1872 on a coalition Democratic-Liberal Republican ticket. Ulysses S. Grant was elected by an overwhelmingly majority. Greeley died a few weeks later.

Another editor of the populist press era who was interested in holding public office was Henry J. Raymond, who with George Jones founded the *New York Times.* Raymond, like Greeley, helped form the Republican Party when the Whig Party disintegrated. But he was more successful than Greeley in winning office and in fact was nominated and elected lieutenant governor of New York at a time when Greeley hoped to be nominated.

Raymond's goal in establishing the *Times* was to publish a paper that was more objective in its news columns and less emotional in its editorials than were the *Tribune,* the *Herald* and other populist papers. In this goal he succeeded.

The *Times* was less flamboyant and more respectable than its competitors. It was also less exciting to read. Raymond's inability to make up his mind about whether he was more editor or politician also affected the vitality of the *Times.* If he had not been lured into politics, he would have been a better editor, in Godkin's view, "the most successful journalist that has ever been seen." But, to quote Godkin, Raymond had a tendency to hold doubts about his political convictions and lacked the "temper which was necessary to victory" in the

---

STEPHEN A. DOUGLAS AS THE VOLUNTEER EXECUTIONER

. . . . A moment more and there would have gone up in the crowd a cry, "Let him go," but at this moment a person unknown to the crowd was seen to move toward the cart. Springing upon it and rudely seizing the dangling rope, he turned round to the astonished spectators and said: "If none of you will act as hangman, I will. Damn the Abolitionists!" In another instant the fatal cord was adjusted, the cart driven off, and there was suspended between heaven and earth the trembling—the dead— form of an innocent man.

Now who was this hangman? Who was this fierce defender of the peculiar institution? Was he a Southern man? No. Was he a citizen identified with the South? No. It was on the contrary a Northern man, from a free State—in fact, one who had been two days in the place. It seemed as if, suspecting his own principles, revolting in his heart at slavery and afraid that in the excitement of the hour he might next be arraigned, he took this fearful and terrible office of executioner in order to place himself, as he supposed, on "high Southern ground." . . . And here is to be seen reflected the true picture of Mr. Douglas's turpitude. Southern men may have in the madness of the hour conceived such iniquity as is embodied in the Nebraska bill. They may have prepared the halter for the neck of the Missouri Compromise—but the last fatal act would never have been undertaken had not the Senator from Illinois volunteered to act as executioner, had been willing to mount the scaffold, and call down the infamy of murdering liberty upon his own head.

Horace Greeley
New York Tribune

---

political realm. A "sense of the necessities and limitations of his position as a politician" kept him from being the journalist he could have been.

Other Voices

Historians traditionally have described the journalism of the 18th and 19th centuries, and even the 20th century, as the work of white male editors, most of them in New York City or Washington, D.C. But there were other voices as well, including women and African-Americans, some of whom have been recently rediscovered.

A number of strong newspapers run by white males emerged throughout the country in the mid-1800s. In Chicago the *Tribune,* founded in 1847, achieved a formidable reputation after Joseph Medill assumed control in 1855. This paper took a strong anti-slavery stand, promoted the new Republican Party and pushed fellow Illinoisan Lincoln for the presidency. In the Northeast, the *Springfield* (Mass.) *Republican,* founded by Samuel Bowles II in 1824, earned respect for conservative, enlightened, well-written editorials. In 1884, the *Republican* displayed its political independence by switching its support to a Democrat, Grover Cleveland, in the race for president.

As for women editors and publishers, 17 are known to have taken over operations of newspapers following their husbands' deaths during the Colonial period.[5] The first was Elizabeth Timothy, who became publisher of the *South Carolina Gazette* upon the death of her husband in 1738. The first woman to start a newspaper on her own (in 1762), with the help of daughter Mary Katherine and son William (who didn't stay around very long), was Sarah Goddard, of the solidly Whig *Providence* (R.I.) *Gazette.*

Seventy years later, declaring she had "no party, the welfare and happiness of our country is our politics," Anne Royall launched *Peter* Pry, which Ishbel Ross described as containing an occasional "gleam of common sense sift[ing] through the thick layers of fanatical upbraiding."[6] She fought against corrupt officials, for separation of church and state and against the Bank of the United States. According to Ross, when Royall wanted to interview President John Quincy Adams about the bank, she supposedly "sat on his clothes while he bathed in the Potomac River and refused to budge until he had answered her questions." In less flamboyant style, Royall published the *Huntress* from 1836 to 1854, advocating Jacksonian principles, free public education, free speech and justice to immigrants and Indians.

Although not strictly an editorial writer, Margaret Fuller wrote essays, reviews and opinion pieces that advanced radical ideas for Greeley's *Tribune*. From 1846 until her death in a shipwreck in 1850, she wrote for the *Tribune* from Europe as the first U.S. woman foreign correspondent.

In 1870 Victoria Woodhull and her sister, Tennessee Claflin, launched *Woodhull and Claflin's Weekly* to promote "Progress! Free Thought. Untrammeled Lives." But, according to Ishbel Ross, they "plunged [so] boldly into the muckraking field . . . all the banned topics of . . . prostitution, free love, social disease, abortion [that] the very words were shocking to the prim readers of the day."[7]

Using a lighter touch, Kate Field, through the columns of *Kate Field's Washington,* which was published from 1890 to 1896, supported the rights of women and campaigned for Hawaiian annexation, international copyright, temperance, prohibition of Mormon polygamy and dress reform.[8]

The first African-American newspaper in the United States, *Freedom's Journal,* was begun in 1827 by John B. Russwurm and Samuel E. Cornish to answer the *New York Inquirer's* attacks on African-Americans.[9] Most readers were white, as few African-Americans were literate. The paper lasted three years. The second paper, the *Weekly Advocate,* another Cornish paper, lasted from 1837 to 1842, an unusually long time. I. Garland Penn, one of the few historians of African-American journalism, edited the *Lynchburg Virginia Laborer.* Forty more African-American newspapers were founded before the Civil War, but most were short-lived. Most of these publications were more concerned with opinion, advancing the antislavery cause, than with news.[10]

A journalist who was both African-American and a woman was Ida B. Wells-Barnett. The daughter of slaves, she spoke out against racial injustice as part owner and editor of the *Memphis Free Speech and Headlight.* When the newspaper office was burned and she was physically threatened, she fled North, where she continued to write and lecture in the cause of justice for African-Americans. (Today, an Ida B. Wells Award is given annually to people who have displayed exemplary leadership in providing employment opportunities in journalism for minorities. Sponsors are the National Association of Black Journalists and the National Conference of Editorial Writers.)

Abolition and the Civil War

The Civil War and events leading up to it provided editors with plenty of opportunities to express strong and diverse viewpoints. The abolitionist movement began to be popularized with publication of the *Liberator,* founded by William

Lloyd Garrison in 1831. The *Liberator* might have failed in its first year if an African-American preacher named Nat Turner had not led a slave revolt in Virginia that resulted in the death of 57 whites. Although Garrison had no subscribers in the South at the time, his writings were perceived to have induced Turner to riot. Southern editors, who wished to place the blame on abolitionist interference from the North, began reprinting Garrison's writings as examples of inflammatory material. Garrison was immediately thrust into the editorial leadership of the abolitionist movement.

Illustrative of Garrison's work was his 1850 response to President Millard Fillmore's call for new, tougher legislation after abolitionists had defied the Fugitive Slave Act by rescuing a slave from a U.S. deputy marshal in Boston.

Nobody injured, nobody wronged, but simply a chattel transformed into a man, and conducted to a spot where he can glorify God in his body and spirit, which are his!

And yet, how all his friends in the pit are writhing and yelling! Not tormented before their time, but just at the right time. Truly, "devils with devils damned firm concord hold!" The President of the United States is out with the Proclamation of Terror, conveying it to us in tones of thunder and on the wings of the lightning; even as though in the old Bay State chaos had come again, and millions of foreign mymidons [*sic*] were invading our shores! A poor, hunted, entrapped fugitive slave is dexterously removed from the courtroom, and the whole land is shaken! . . . Henry Clay—with one foot in the grave, and just about ready to have both body and soul cast into hell—as if eager to make his damnation doubly sure, rises in the United States Senate and proposes an inquiry into the expediency of passing yet another law, by which everyone who shall dare peep or mutter against the execution of the Fugitive Slave Bill shall have his life crushed out!

Abolitionist editors who spoke out strongly risked their property and their lives. Garrison barely escaped an angry mob in Boston in 1835 by jumping out a window and voluntarily spending a night in jail. The abolitionist editor who became the most honored was Elijah Lovejoy. Anti-abolitionists twice destroyed the offices of his *St. Louis Observer*, forcing it to move from St. Louis to Alton, Ill. When he re-established his paper for a third time, in 1837, a mob destroyed his office and killed him.

One editor whom Garrison helped to launch was Frederick Douglass. Douglass toured the Western states and Europe with Garrison, then went on his way in 1847 to found the *North Star*. The object of the paper, Douglass wrote, "will be to attack slavery in all its forms and aspects; advocate Universal Emancipation; exact the standard of public morality; promote the moral and intellectual improvement of the colored people; and to hasten the day of freedom of our three million enslaved fellow countrymen." He continued to promote the African-American cause in a series of publications until 1875. By then both he and Garrison were widely honored, at least among African-Americans and Northerners.

The *New York Evening Post*, under William Cullen Bryant, defended the right of the unpopular abolitionists to meet and demonstrate as early as 1833. It spoke sympathetically of John Brown at the time of his 1859 raid into Virginia to free slaves and incite insurrection. The *Post* foresaw a growing threat of uprising among African-Americans:

But while the tocsin sounds, the blacks are in arms, their houses are in flames, their wives and children driven into exile and killed, and a furious servile war stretches its horror over the years. This is the blessed institution you ask us to foster and spread and worship, and for the sake of which you even spout your impotent threats against the grand edifice of the Union!

Henry J. Raymond's *New York Times* characteristically took a more moderate stance, opposing abolition until after the Civil War had begun, even though it had strongly supported the election of Lincoln in 1860. James Gordon Bennett's *New York Herald* remained opposed to abolition until after the war was over. It did not favor Lincoln's election and in fact demonstrated sympathy for the South before and during much of the war.

At the extreme end of the Southern political spectrum before the war were the Southern "fire-eaters." Robert Barnwell Rhett of the *Charleston* (S.C.) *Mercury* was ignored in 1832 when he first began writing that the South should secede, but in later years, as he and others gained credence, they helped convince fellow Southerners that the North would let the South go.

When the war began, Northern papers generally supported Union policies, but the *Times* was the only major New York daily (and one of only three or four of the city's 17 dailies) to consistently support Lincoln throughout the war. On April 13, 1861, the day after the bombardment of Fort Sumter, the *Times* editorialized in favor of all-out war.

. . . For the first time in the history of the United States, an organized attempt is made to destroy, by force of arms, the government which the American people have formed for themselves—and to overthrow the glorious Constitution which has made us the envy of the world. The history of the world does not show so causeless an outrage. . . . One thing is certain. Now that the rebels have opened the war, the people will expect the government to defend itself with vigor and determination now. . . . *The South has chosen war, and it must have all the war it wants.* . . .

Greeley ran hot and cold on Lincoln and the war in spite of his strong abolitionist beliefs. Shortly after the attack on Fort Sumter he argued for letting the South secede if that was what the Southern people really wanted. But a few weeks later, the *Tribune* urged immediate action to bring the seceding states back into the Union. As the summer of 1861 approached, the *Tribune*, beginning on June 26, ran a war slogan atop its editorial page every day for a week.

THE NATION'S WAR-CRY!

Forward to Richmond!   *Forward to Richmond!*
The Rebel Congress must not be allowed to meet there on the 20th of July! BY THAT DATE THE PLACE MUST BE HELD BY THE NATIONAL ARMY!

The *Tribune* contributed to the pressures on the Union army to engage in battle prematurely at the First Battle of Bull Run. Casualties were heavy, and the Union troops retreated in disarray to Washington. Although he did not write the slogan himself, Greeley accepted such a heavy personal responsibility for running it that he became physically ill and could not leave his bed for several days after the Bull Run fiasco.

The *Post* supported the administration's efforts to wage the war, but Bryant became increasingly impatient with Lincoln when the president delayed issuing the Emancipation Proclamation, freeing the slaves, until 1863. Bryant also was disgusted with newspapers that professed to support the Union but took every opportunity to criticize it.

Even more critical was the Copperhead press, which spoke for Northern Democrats who openly sympathized with the South. The most prominent Copperhead was Clement Laird Vallandigham, who had become co-owner of an anti-abolitionist magazine, the *Dayton* (Ohio) *Empire*, in 1847. When the governor of Ohio prepared to answer Lincoln's call for troops after Fort Sumter, the *Empire* declared: "Governor Dennison has pledged the blood and treasure of Ohio to back up a Republican administration in its contemplated attack upon the people of the South."

One effect of the Civil War was to put a premium on news. Newspapers that could not afford their own correspondents pooled resources and formed cooperative news services. Because these services provided news to papers of widely differing editorial viewpoints, they had to be careful to report as objectively as possible. Their dependence on the telegraph provided further incentive to keep stories factual and short. As a result, the line between news and editorials became more marked.

After the deaths of Raymond in 1869 and Bennett and Greeley in 1872, Greeley biographer James Parton wrote that "The prestige of the editorial page is done." With the great voices gone, he said, editorials no longer "much influence the public mind, nor change many votes, and . . . the power and success of a newspaper depend wholly and absolutely upon its success in getting, and its skill in exhibiting, the news."[11]

Woman Suffrage, Native Americans and African-Americans

Among the most common editorial topics immediately after the Civil War were woman suffrage, Native Americans (or Indians), the newly emancipated slaves and economic development. Within a few years it became clear, to say the least, that the Civil War had barely disturbed the white male power balance, at the national level or on editorial pages. Editors were more interested in promoting prosperous communities than in sharing power with another race or sex.

Women such as Susan B. Anthony, Lucy Stone and Elizabeth Cady Stanton, who had been working for abolition, expected that after emancipation and voting rights for African-Americans, woman suffrage would come next. A few editorial voices, among them Greeley's, supported their cause, but others argued that women didn't need the vote, since, according to the *New Orleans Crescent*, "they are represented at the ballot box, as well as in the halls of legislation, by their husbands, fathers, and brothers." The *Richmond Whig* saw women's "most effective and irresistible weapon [to be] the artillery of her charms, before which the Columbiad, the Brooke, the Armstrong, and all other guns, 'pale their ineffectual fires.'" Some editors expressed the fear that allowing women to enter the evil world of politics would destroy their traditional superior moral capability, which the St. Louis *Missouri Republican* described as "the aptitude and the habit of the soul to distinguish the finest shades of good and evil, and of what is beautiful and decent."

"It will be a pretty spectacle," wrote an editor for the Memphis *Avalanche,* "to see a strong minded woman haranguing a crowd or squabbling at the ballot box, while her husband is at home darning stockings, making night caps, baking bread and rocking the cradle."

As more and more travelers and settlers headed west after the end of the war, the nation faced difficult choices concerning the Native Americans (Indians) on the Western Plains. A few editors expressed the belief that (in the words of the St. Louis *Missouri Democrat*) "the Indian is endowed with many nobel [*sic*] traits of character, which under proper treatment and training might be rendered highly serviceable to humanity." A few, such as the *Louisville Courier Journal,* questioned the notion that "civilization must be pushed as far as it will go, that Christianity has to be taught the heathen." But most editors seemed to agree with the *Missouri Republican* and condemned "the war-path, murdering, scalping and plundering, spreading terror through various settlements and causing mourning in many families." Forget the peace treaties. "Let the Peace Commissioners stand aside for a few months while Gen. Sherman goes in and thrashes these savages till they cry for peace and will be ready to go upon their reservations and stay there." The *Raleigh Standard* was even more blunt: "Let the war of extermination be commenced and followed up until the Indians are either destroyed or driven beyond the limits of the United States."

Most newspapers in the North, but only a few in the South, supported civil and political rights for the newly emancipated African-Americans. Some papers, like the *Memphis Appeal,* lamented that, with the end of slavery, "there . . . never again will be . . . a body of agricultural laborers, so generally contented, so happy, so prolific, with so little disease and deformity among their children, and so little want of common comforts of life among the adults." Some papers, like the Nashville *Republican Banner* (decidedly not a Republican paper), viewed "the Negro [as] indolent by nature, faithless to all their pledges, false to their engagements, deceitful in their contracts, and thriftless and wasteful [and] insolent." The *Charleston Courier* expressed the opinion of many Southern editors concerning the abilities of African-Americans to exercise political rights: "No negro can be so blind as not to know that white men are to be right rulers in this great Republic. Compared with the whites the negros [*sic*] are as insignificant in numbers as they are deficient in intelligence, and he deceives himself who does not think that intelligence and numbers will not rule."

More sympathy was exhibited toward African-Americans by the relatively few Republican papers in the South and, of course, by the even rarer African-American papers. Responding to concerns similar to those expressed above, the Nashville *Colored Tennessean* said in August 1865: "One set of people declares we won't work, and must be made to. Another is afraid that a war of races will arise. Another thinks we will abandon our Southern homes, and go North. . . . Another thinks we must be made to emigrate. . . ." To all of these, the writer said: "Now, dearly beloved friends, we can solve your problem. A few words will suffice. *Do justly by the Negro, and then let him severely alone.* . . . We are not exceptional beings, we are human. In these dark bodies run the same red running blood."

The *Missouri Democrat,* in spite of its name, was one of the Republican papers that rather consistently espoused the cause of African-Americans. It advised the Southern states to accept the terms of Reconstruction and offer "all Constitutional guarantees," including suffrage, to African-Americans. It warned that "resistance is useless" and that "the attempt to tire out the North will prove suicidal." The suffrage amendment was adopted over the objections of the Southern states. For a time African-Americans and Republicans wielded modest amounts of power and won a few elections in the South. But the *Democrat* was to be proved wrong. It was not long before the Conservatives and the Conservative editors of the South carried the day and returned to power. During this time several editors were accused of being local and even state leaders of the Ku Klux Klan (which of course they denied).

Dana, Godkin and Watterson

American newspapers were approaching the threshold of corporate journalism, the fourth phase in the development of the editorial page. But, even as most editors were lapsing into corporate anonymity, a few recognizable voices spoke out. Among them were Charles A. Dana of the *New York Sun,* E.L. Godkin of the *Nation* and later of the *New York Evening Post,* Henry Watterson of the *Louisville Courier-Journal* and Henry W. Grady of the *Atlanta Constitution.*

Dana quit the *Tribune* in 1862 after disagreeing with Greeley's criticism of the conduct of the Civil War. He felt so strongly about Lincoln's policies that he joined the administration as assistant secretary of war. After the deaths of Raymond and Greeley, Watterson wrote that Dana, then on the *Sun,* was "left alone to tell the tale of old-time journalism in New York." Dana, he said, was as "blithe and nimble" as the young editors in the country and was "no less a writer and scholar than an editor."

During the early days of his editorship, Dana took editorial swings at the corruption of the Tweed regime in New York and waged campaigns for reforms in government. But as the years went by the *Sun* became more cynical toward reform. Turning a good phrase and enticing readership through humorous, clever writing assumed greater importance. Edward P. Mitchell, later editor of the *Sun* himself, recalled that, before he joined Dana's staff as an editorial writer, he had been told, "Dana's a good teacher for condensation and for saying what you want to say, but as to what he generally wants to say!—"

Dana's sarcasm could be so strong that readers sometimes took him at his literal word or failed to understand his references. When an 1870 public campaign to raise money to erect a statue of "Boss" Tweed seemed to lag, Dana wrote an editorial in which he suggested putting the statue on a yacht, a reference to one of the luxurious perquisites enjoyed by Tweed, no doubt at taxpayer expense. ("P. Brains Sweeney" refers to Tweed's lieutenant, Peter B. Sweeney.)

Has Boss Tweed any friends? If so, they are a mean set; it is now a year since an appeal was made to them to come forward and put up the ancillary qualities to erect a statue to Mr. Tweed in the center of Tweed Plaza; but as yet only four citizens have sent in their subscriptions. . . . [T]he hundreds or rather thousands of small-potato politicians whom he has made rich and powerful stand aloof, and do not offer a picayune. . . . [W]e have not decided whether [the statue] shall represent the favorite son of New York afoot or a-horseback.

In fact, we rather incline to have a nautical statue, exhibiting Boss Tweed as a bold mariner, amid the foretop-gallant buttock shrouds of his steam yacht. But that is a matter for future consideration. The first thing is to get the money; and if those who claim to be Mr. Tweed's friends don't raise it we shall begin a rumor that the Honorable P. Brains Sweeney has turned against him, and has forbidden everyone to give anything toward the erection of the projected statue.

Edwin Lawrence (E.L.) Godkin came to the United States to cover the Civil War for English papers. He stayed after the war to found *The Nation* magazine, devoted to discussing political and economic issues. One of his interests was in a more equal distribution of the economic and social benefits of prosperity. Philosopher William James described Godkin as "the towering influence in all thought concerning public affairs" during the 1880s and 1890s.

Godkin's style was complex and carefully written, but, when he so desired, lively, humorous and ironic. Concerning the appointment of Elihu B. Washburne as President Grant's secretary of state, Godkin cited the "general, and apparently well-founded belief" that Washburne's "installation in the State Department would be the commencement of his intimate acquaintance with the precedents and principles of international law."

In describing an anarchists' picnic at which there was a riot, Godkin wrote: "The meeting was a great success in the way of promoting practical anarchy, the rioting being protracted to a late hour in the afternoon. Anarchy, like charity, should always begin at home."

Godkin's successor, Edward P. Mitchell, credited Godkin with being the first editor in New York to hold daily conferences with his editorial writers. Mitchell recounted that every writer was encouraged to propose his own topic and to comment freely on topics proposed by other writers. But Godkin had no mercy on unsound and commonplace ideas. "If the junior editor had nothing worth while to say, Godkin would cut across his flounderings with 'O, there's nothing in that,' or 'We said that the other day,' or 'O everybody sees that.'" But, when a writer came up with a new idea, "Mr. Godkin's eye would kindle with interest, he would lean forward alertly, and catching up the theme, he would perhaps begin to enlarge it by ideas of his own, search its depths with penetrating inquiries, and reveal such possibilities in it that the original speaker had the feeling of having stumbled over a concealed diamond." Sometimes, Mitchell recalled, Godkin became so enthusiastic about the idea that he would decide to write on the subject himself.[12]

One of the strong, extravagant voices after the Civil War was that of Colonel Henry Watterson of the *Louisville* (Ky.) *Courier-Journal*. Watterson had edited a Southern paper during the Civil War but thought that secession was wrong. For half a century (from 1868 to 1918) he preached conciliation between North and South—and both sides listened to him, at least to the extent that either listened.

In 1868, when Kentucky was being criticized for having elected anti-Reconstruction Democrats to office, a Watterson editorial reminded the North that Kentucky had not seceded during the war, that "Kentucky's head was with the Union and her heart was with the South; for it is in the nature of a generous and manly people to sympathize with the weak in its struggle with the strong."

We are perfectly honest, and think we have a right, as free citizens of a free republic, to decide for ourselves. For so doing and so thinking we are denounced as traitors to our country and a despotism is sought to be placed over us by those who claim that we ought to be forced to vote for Republican candidates and Republican measures, and who declare that if we do not, we are guilty of rebellion and should be punished therefore.

Promotion and Prosperity

Watterson of the *Courier-Journal* and Henry W. Grady of the *Atlanta Constitution* have been credited with urging their readers to forget old grievances arising out of the Civil War and to work toward a New South that was more concerned with prosperity than issues. Watterson worked at promoting Louisville, Kentucky and the South through the last third of the 19th century and the early part of the 20th century. He and his fellow editors promoted transcontinental railroads, local and regional railroads, canals, ports, agriculture, paved streets, municipal water supplies, electrical and sewer systems and higher education. In the eyes of the local editor, his community was the one most deserving of success and prosperity—and the railroad.

Grady may have been the preeminent promoter. He preached a New South ("sunshine everywhere and all the time") up and down the Atlantic Coast, mostly promoting Atlanta. A promotional trip to Boston, when he was ill, resulted in an early death at age 49, when he was at the height of his prominence.[13]

Community promotion was not limited to the cities. Hal Borland recalled that his father had used the *Flagler* (Colo.) *News* to editorialize for water, electricity and paved streets.[14] William Allen White of the *Emporia* (Kan.) *Gazette* generally is regarded as the ideal small-town editor, and in fact depicted himself as such in his autobiography, but a later biographer reported that White of the *Emporia* (Kono) *Gazette* worked some deals to promote his community that today would be considered conflicts of interest.[15] White probably is best known for an 1896 editorial in which he took a statewide view. The editorial, which was widely reprinted around the country, was titled "What's the Matter with Kansas?"

. . . Nothing under the shining sun. She is losing wealth, population, and standing. She has got her statesmen, and the money power is afraid of her. Kansas is all right. She has started in to raise hell, as Mrs. [Mary Elizabeth] Lease [a Populist campaign speaker] acknowledged, and she seems to have an overproduction. But that doesn't matter. Kansas never did believe in diversified crops. Kansas is all right. There is absolutely nothing wrong with Kansas. "Every prospect pleases and only man is vile."[16]

Pulitzer and Hearst

For every trend, there is an exception. While most newspapers were headed toward corporate journalism, Joseph Pulitzer and William Randolph Hearst exploded onto the journalistic scene. With the purchase of the *New York World* in 1883, Joseph Pulitzer brought to the East Coast the sensational, aggressive style of news reporting that he had developed with the *St. Louis* (Mo.) *Post-Dispatch* and a strong commitment to the editorial page.

In St. Louis, Pulitzer had campaigned editorially for the middle class at the expense of the wealthy. In New York, he took on the cause of the more numerous poor, including workers and the millions of new immigrants. The irresponsible rich, he said, had "the odor of codfish and not the mustiness of age." The *World's* editorial opinion was that "such an aristocracy ought to have no place in the republic." On May 13, 1883, a week after he had taken over the *World*, Pulitzer printed the following list of governmental goals for social justice that the *World* would pursue:

1. Tax Luxuries.
2. Tax Inheritance.
3. Tax Large Incomes.

4. Tax Monopolies.
5. Tax the Privileged Corporations.
6. A Tariff for Revenue.
7. Reform the Civil Service.
8. Punish Corrupt Officers.
9. Punish Vote Buying.
10. Punish Employers who Coerce their Employees in Elections.

At the end of the list, Pulitzer tacked this notice: "This is a popular platform of 10 lines. We recommend it to the politicians in place of long-winded resolutions."

The *New York World* generally supported Democrats, but it reluctantly backed William McKinley for president in 1896 because Pulitzer thought that the Democratic candidate, William Jennings Bryan, was ignorant on important issues and that the mining and coining of more silver (the "free silver" issue) would not solve the problems of economic depression. But even though he praised McKinley's election, Pulitzer took the occasion to say that some problems that Bryan and the Populists were talking about were real:

There is no doubt that in this Republic, based as it is upon simplicity and ideas of equality before the law, there are growing inequalities of privilege and increasingly offensive encroachments and vulgarities of the rich.

The trust combinations are fostered by tariffs that protect them from foreign competition. They grow every year more arrogant, more despotic, and more oppressive in their exactions. Yet the laws against them are not only not enforced, but no honest effort is made to enforce them. . . .

In the same way the people have seen bargains made in secret between the Treasury authorities and a Wall Street syndicate for the sale of millions of bonds for 15 cents on the dollar less than their open market value. . . .

They have seen State legislatures of both parties dominated by corporations so that no measure of relief from wrong doing by corporations could become law. . . .

In brief, the money is too largely usurping power and influence of manhood.

The New York press was further enlivened when William Randolph Hearst ventured off his home base in San Francisco in 1895 to out-sensationalize Pulitzer with his newly acquired *New York Journal.* Hearst too undertook the cause of have-nots, but his editorial approach was a more simplistic, emotional, entertaining appeal to readers. In 1896, on its first birthday, Hearst was effusive in extolling the virtues of his new *New York Journal.*

What is the explanation of the *Journal's* amazing and wholly unmatched progress? . . . When the paper was purchased by its present proprietor, a year ago today, the work contemplated was at once begun. . . . The *Journal* realized what is frequently forgotten in journalism, that if news is wanted it often has to be sent for . . . .

No other journal in the United States includes in its staff a tenth of the number of writers of reputation and talent. It is the *Journal's* policy to engage brains as well as to get the news, for the public is even more fond of entertainment than it is of information . . . .

To entice readers, some of whom were not very literate, Hearst set editorials in large type, used large headlines, spread editorials over several columns and sometimes published them on page one. Editorial cartoons added further interest to the page.

Arthur Brisbane, one of the many editors and reporters hired away from Pulitzer, became a master at expressing Hearst's views and promoting his causes in clear, direct language that no reader could misunderstand. The *Journal* addressed such topics as "The Existence of God," "What Will 999 Years Mean to the Human Race?" "Crime Is Dying Out," "Have the Animals Souls?" and "Woman Sustains, Guides and Controls the World." Brisbane editorials often had a simple moralistic tone. One example is "Those Who Laugh at a Drunken Man," written during the prohibition movement following World War I.

Both Hearst and Pulitzer had political ambitions. Pulitzer satisfied his ambition with one term in Congress and some service in the Missouri legislature. But it look Hearst a long time to learn that he was not destined for high office. Narrow defeats in races for mayor of New York City and governor of the state did nothing to lessen his efforts to become president. Hearst was a serious contender for the Democratic nomination in 1904, but he deluded himself that he was a possible nominee in the three subsequent presidential elections. Few took him seriously as a candidate in those years.

■ THE CORPORATE EDITORIAL PAGE

The corporate editorial page evolved at a time when newspapers were beginning to earn greater profits. The nation, after recovering from the Civil War, began to attain an economic and political stature that made the United States a major player on the international scene for the first time. The economic

---

THOSE WHO LAUGH AT A DRUNKEN MAN

How often have you seen a drunken man stagger along the street!

His clothes are soiled from falling. His face is bruised. His eyes are dull. Sometimes he curses the boys that tease him. Sometimes he tries to smile in a drunken effort to placate pitiless, childish cruelty.

His body, worn out, can stand no more, and he mumbles that he is going home.

The children persecute him, throw things at him, laugh at him, running ahead of him.

Grown men and women, too, often laugh with the children, nudge each other, and actually find humor in the sight of a human being sunk below the lowest animal.

The sight of a drunken man going home should make every man sad and sympathetic. . . .

That reeling drunkard is going home.

He is going home to children who are afraid of him, to a wife whose life he has made miserable.

He is going home, taking with him the worst curse in the world—to suffer bitter remorse himself after having inflicted suffering on those whom he should protect . . . .

. . . we cannot call ourselves civilized while our imaginations and sympathies are so dull that the reeling drunkard is thought an amusing spectacle.

Arthur Brisbane
New York Journal

forces that changed the character of American newspapers were those that made it possible for the United States to take on Spain in the Spanish-American War, liberate Cuba and take over Spanish colonial possessions, and for President Theodore Roosevelt to send the "White Fleet" around the world and confidently undertake what the French failed to do—build the Panama Canal. The country's economic capability also was a major consideration during World War I, when newspaper editors felt called to write editorials supporting wars to "save the world for democracy," which in an earlier time they would have disdainfully referred to as "foreign wars."

The emergence of newspapers and the country as economic powerhouses coincided, with a few exceptions, with the passing of the famous editors and the emergence of anonymous opinion writers. Dana continued for some years to run the editorial page on the *Sun,* as did Godkin on the *Post,* Watterson on the *Courier-Journal* and Grady on the *Atlanta Constitution.* Most readers knew that Arthur Brisbane wrote the editorials in the Hearst papers and that Irvin S. Cobb wrote them on the *New York World* after Pulitzer's death. On most newspapers, though, readers did not know who wrote the impersonal (and often bland) editorials.

The *New York Times* epitomized the trend toward anonymous and dull editorials. The transition occurred after the *Times* had had a brief moment of glory in exposing W.M. Tweed, boss of New York's Tammany Hall. After several New York editors turned down offers to publish evidence of corruption, the late Henry L. Raymond's partner, George Jones, dared to do so. After the news columns had reported that an obscure carpenter named C.S. Miller had received $360,751.61 for one month's work and a plasterer named Andrew J. Garvey had received $2,870,464.06, the *Times* editorialized: "As C.S. Miller is the luckiest of carpenters, so Andrew J. Garvey is clearly the Prince of Plasterers. His good fortune surpasses anything in the Arabian Nights." (Thomas Nast, with his famous cartoons in *Harper's Weekly,* also helped rouse the public to break up the Tweed Ring and send Tweed to jail.)

"The mistake of the *Times,*" Dana wrote in the *Sun* in 1875, "was in lapsing into the dullness of respectable conservatism after its [Tweed] Ring fight. It should have kept on and made a crusade against fraud of all sorts." Adolph S. Ochs rescued the paper from hard times in 1896, but he was primarily interested in putting out a good news product. Harrison E. Salisbury wrote that "there were those who felt [Ochs] would have been happier had there been no editorial page."[17]

Newspapers in general during this period were closely allied with the growing business and industrial community. The papers became more dependent on advertising for revenue and on increasing circulation to justify higher advertising rates. The business side came to overshadow the editorial side. More will be said about the corporate editorial at the end of this chapter.

The Social Reformers

By the beginning of the 20th century most literary efforts directed toward social reform were confined to magazines and books, which were able to reach a nationwide audience. At the local level, readers interested in hearing about the evils of society were in a minority in the decade or so just before World War I, when the prevalent attitude in America and Western Europe was that the world was making unbroken social and economic progress.

The most prominent platforms for the reform writers, dubbed "muckrakers" by President Theodore Roosevelt, were *McClure's, Cosmopolitan, Collier's* and *Ladies' Home Journal.* The articles that appeared in these magazines, by such writers as Lincoln Steffens, Ida M. Tarbell and Ray Stannard Baker, were part investigative reporting and part editorializing.

One of Steffen's best-known efforts, a series of six articles in *McClure's* on corruption in American cities, was subsequently published as a book, *The Shame of the Cities.* Steffens tried to show that corruption in society came from the top of the economic and social order, and that changes therefore needed to be made at that level. In the introduction to the book, however, Steffens expressed his belief that the same temptations were felt at the personal level.

> The corruption that shocks us in public affairs we practice in our private concerns. There is no difference between the pull that gets your wife into society or for the book a favorable notice and that which gets a heeler into office, a thief out of jail, and a rich man's son on the board of directors.[18]

Upton Sinclair, another muckraker, wrote an exposé of American journalism in a book titled *The Brass Check.* (The "brass check" referred to the piece of metal a cashier gave a customer at a house of prostitution to be given to "the woman upon receipt of her favors.") In the conclusion of the book, Sinclair directed his words to American journalists.

> The Brass Check is found in your pay-envelope every week—you who write and print and distribute newspapers and magazines. The Brass Check is the price of your shame—you who take the fair body of truth and sell it in the market-place, who betray the virgin hopes of mankind into the loathsome brothel of Big Business. And down in the counting-room below sits the "madame" who profits by your shame; unless, perchance, she is off at Palm Beach or Newport, flaunting her jewels and her feathers.[19]

Spanish-American War

The trouble with Spain over Cuba in the late 1890s was ready-made for Hearst in his efforts to overtake Pulitzer. Hearst had a new underdog to champion— the Cuban rebels. Sensationalizing news and editorial comment about Spain and Cuba sold papers, and Hearst's circulation soon caught up with Pulitzer's. Pulitzer responded in kind. The battle between the two to see who could find, or invent, the most grisly revelations about Spanish atrocities helped create the political climate in which President McKinley finally concluded he had little choice but to seek a declaration of war against Spain. Edwin L. Godkin of *The Nation* placed the blame squarely on Hearst's and Pulitzer's "yellow journalism":

> The fomenting of war and the publication of mendacious accounts of the war have, in fact, become almost a special function of that portion of the press which is known as "yellow journals." The war increases their circulation immediately. They profit enormously by what inflicts sorrow and loss on the rest of the community. They talk incessantly of war, not in the way of instruction, but simply to incite by false news, and stimulate savage passions by atrocious suggestions.[20]

Following the sinking of the *U.S. Maine* in Havana harbor on February 15, 1898, the *New York Journal* (while running front-page headlines such as "The Warship Maine Was Split in Two by an Enemy's Secret Infernal Machine") in its editorials pretended to withhold judgment on who was blame. Still, one editorial concluded that, no matter how the investigation turned out, there was no reason not to proceed with freeing Cuba.

To five hundred thousand Cubans starved or otherwise murdered have been added an American battleship and three hundred American sailors lost as the direct result of the dilatory policy of our government toward Spain. If we had stopped the war in Cuba [between Spain and the rebels] when duty and policy alike urged us to do so the Maine would have been afloat today, and three hundred homes, now desolate, would have been unscathed.

It was no accident, they say. Perhaps it was, but accident or not, it would never have happened if there had been peace in Cuba, as there would have been had we done our duty. . . . The investigation into the injuries of the Maine may take a week, but the independence of Cuba can be recognized today. . . . The American fleet can move on Havana today and plant the flag of the Cuban Republic on Morro and Cabanas. It is still strong enough for that in the absence of further "accidents." And if we take such action as that, it is extremely unlikely that any further accidents will appear.

World War I

Although voters responded favorably to President Wilson's 1916 re-election campaign slogan, "He kept us out of war," most newspapers were editorially sympathetic to the Allied cause during the months leading up to the United States' entry of the war. Among the pro-Allies were the *New York Herald*, the *New York Times* and the *New York World*, but the most outspoken of all was Watterson's *Courier-Journal* in Louisville, Ky., as exemplified by a much-cited brief editorial, titled "To Hell with the Hohenzollerns and the Hapsburgs," urging the United States to enter World War I as early as September 1914.[21] (Herman Ridder was a German-American editor.)

The most anti-British and the most opposed to intervention right up to the entrance into the war were William Randolph Hearst's newspapers, notably the *New York Journal*. Hearst's reluctance to send troops abroad was evident in an editorial published April 3, 1917, the day after Wilson called for a declaration of war, in which he said: "It is no secret that we are almost wholly unprepared for real warfare. . . . That is no fault of the Hearst newspapers. We have argued and pleaded for preparedness for twenty years. Most of that our reward was the sneers and the jeers of the unthinking and the foolish." In another editorial, ten days later, he said: "In these circumstances of uncertainty . . . there is only one possible course that is sensible, and that is to keep every dollar and every man and every weapon and all our supplies and stores AT HOME, for the defense of our own land, our own people, our own freedom, until that defense has been made ABSOLUTELY secure. After that we can think of other nations' troubles. But till then, America first!" The two editorials, according to Hearst biographer David Nasaw, roused the "administration's suspicion that [Hearst and his editors] were traitors to the nation."[22]

Among other newspapers reluctant to enter the war were the *New York Evening Mail, Chicago Tribune, Cincinnati Enquirer, Cleveland Plain Dealer, Washington Post, Milwaukee Sentinel, Los Angeles Times, San Francisco Chronicle* and *San Francisco Call*.[23] Once the United States entered the war, however, most of these newspapers fell into line in support of the Allies.

To Hell with the Hollenzollerns and the Hapsburgs

Herman Ridder flings Japan at us. Then he adduces Russia. What does he think now of Turkey? How can he reconcile the Kaiser's ostentatious appeal to the Children of Christ and his pretentious partnership with God—"meinself und Gott"—with his calling the hordes of Mahomet to his aid? Will not this unite all Christendom against the unholy combine? May Heaven protect the Vaterland from contamination and give the German people a chance! To Hell with the Hohenzollerns and the Hapsburgs.

Henry Watterson
Courier-Journal

Between the Wars

In 1920, according to a poll conducted among the nation's leading editors, the papers with the most respected editorial pages were (in a tie for first place) the *New York Times, Chicago Tribune* and *Boston Globe*.[24] According to journalism historians Edwin and Michael Emery, editorial pages at that time gave the proposed League of Nations "good press on the whole, right up to the end," but "Republican politics and Wilson's mistakes killed it" as far the United States was concerned.[25] Coincident with the fight over the League was public reaction to the Russian Revolution (known as the "Red scare"). Offices, including newspaper offices, were raided. Presumed radicals were charged and convicted for what they had said or published. Emery and Emery said, "In general, the newspapers failed dismally to defend the civil liberties of those being questionably attacked." Exceptions included the liberal magazines *The New Republic* and *The Nation* as well as a few newspapers, notably the *St. Louis Post-Dispatch, New York Globe* and *New York World*.[26]

During the 1920s Americans routinely elected Republicans to the presidency (and to other offices) and most American newspapers endorsed them. Many, including the *Chicago Tribune* and the Hearst papers, initially supported Franklin D. Roosevelt (first elected in 1932) in his efforts to deal with the depressed economy, but when implications of the National Recovery Act became evident, most reacted the way Hearst did (although not so flamboyantly). Hearst directed his representative in Washington to "[p]lease tell the President that I consider his proposal to license the press under the NRA in direct violation of the Bill of Rights, that it is an abridgment of the freedom of the press guaranteed by the Constitution, and that I will fight his proposal with every means at my command, even if it means taking it to the Supreme Court of the United States, and even if it costs me every nickel I possess."[27] (Part of Hearst's resentment was based on his growing conservatism on social issues; part on the fact that Roosevelt was not paying as much attention to Hearst as he had in the early days of his administration.)

Faced with an economic and social, if not political, revolution, the country required greater quantities and kinds of information and insights. Most of the nation's anonymous editorial writers were unwilling or unable to provide what readers wanted. Many of their editorial pens were stuck with automatic reactions to the changes going on in Washington. One result was the sudden growth in popularity of bylined columnists, hired by newspapers and syndicated services to explain to readers what was going on, especially in Washington, D.C. The columns, generally interpretive in nature, were usually published on the editorial page. They were more lively and informative than most unsigned editorials that represented the views of the corporate newspapers.

By 1936 U.S. newspapers were almost solidly against Roosevelt's bid for re-election, as they were, to a lesser extent, in the 1940 and 1944 presidential campaigns. The divergence between editorial endorsements and voters' behavior gave rise to growing doubts about the power of the editorial page, certainly about the power of endorsements. (See "What Effects?" section in Chapter 15, "Editorials on Elections.")

World War II

As the U.S. approached World War II, newspapers were divided between isolationists and interventionists. Among the strongest isolationists were Robert R. McCormick and Joseph Medill Patterson's *Chicago Tribune* and *New York Daily News* and the Hearst newspapers. On September 2, 1939, the day after Hitler invaded Poland, McCormick wrote an editorial that made clear his newspaper's stance:

> This is not our war. We did not create the Danzig situation. We did not sign the treaty of Versailles. The peace America made with Germany did not contain another war. The United States did not take spoils. It did not divide up colonies.
>
> This is not our war. We should not make it ours. We should keep out of it.[28]

Probably the most notable editor to support helping the Allies was William Allen White, of the *Emporia Gazette*, who headed the Committee to Defend America by Aiding the Allies.[29] In May 1940, as German tanks were invading France, White argued that sending aid was in the United States' best interest:

> America must spend every ounce of energy to keep the war from the Western hemisphere by preparing to defend itself and aiding with our supplies and wealth the nations now fighting to stem the tide of aggression. . . . It is for us to show the people of England, of France, of Belgium and Scandinavia that the richest country on earth is not too blind or too timid to help those who are fighting tyranny abroad.[30]

As in World War I, once the United States declared war, virtually all newspapers swung into line to support the war. In general the press voluntarily followed government guidelines on what should and should not be published. Coverage of the war by U.S. newspapers and radio, according to Emery and Emery, "was considered by most observers to be the best and fullest the world had ever seen."[31]

The 1950s and 1960s

By the 1950s, most newspapers had shed any formal labels that had tied them to one party (usually Republican), but they continued by wide margins to endorse Republicans for president and, to a lesser degree, for lower-level offices. In 1952 President Harry Truman leveled the charge of "one-party press" at the newspapers for their coverage of the race between Dwight D. Eisenhower and Adlai Stevenson. A subsequent study found that the editorial pages of the nation had backed Eisenhower almost 5 to 1 but that partiality had been evident in the news columns in only 6 of 35 newspapers studied.[32]

In the same era, only a few editorial voices were raised early against "McCarthyism." Sen. Joseph McCarthy, a Republican from Wisconsin, and others, raised emotional and largely unsubstantiated accusations of disloyalty, "communism" and "un-American activities" against American citizens. The accusations eventually proved to be overblown, misleading or wholly fallacious. Only after five years of these attacks did McCarthy's fellow senators finally vote to censure him. Alan Barth of the *Washington Post* was one of the few who spoke out early. The most publicly recognized voice was that of broadcaster Edward R. Murrow, who put together a documented television program on CBS that showed McCarthy for the demagogue that he was. The broadcast helped move public opinion toward eventual support for censure by the Senate.

One looks in vain for many examples of strong editorial leadership in the 1950s and 1960s. If the Eisenhower administration was content to let social issues lie dormant, so was most of the press. If editorial writers responded to John F. Kennedy's challenge of a "New Frontier" in the early 1960s, it may have been more because of their fascination with the personality and glamour of the new administration than because of concern for civil and social justice. The assassinations of John F. Kennedy, Martin Luther King and Robert Kennedy shocked editorial writers, as they did all Americans. One result was that voters and editors rallied around Lyndon Johnson, the new president, and in 1964 overwhelmingly elected him to the presidency. For the first time in the 20th century, more newspapers supported a Democrat than a Republican for president. Still feeling the shock of the assassinations, editorial writers and the public also supported the brief flurry of civil rights and social legislation passed during the Johnson administration.

The high hopes for Johnson's "Great Society," however, proved overly optimistic, partly because funds that might have gone to fight poverty and racial inequality were sent to fight a war in Vietnam. At first, the war seemed within the capability of the United States and its United Nations allies to win, but proved to be a quagmire and a blow to the invincibility of the American economic and military might in which editors had expressed their confidence for 70 years.

■ RECENT BRIGHT AND NOT-SO-BRIGHT SPOTS

The last few decades have produced an array of sterling performances and missed opportunities to display editorial leadership.

Vietnam War

The Vietnam War was one era in which we might have expected to find signs of vigor among U.S. editorial pages. Unfortunately only a few editors early on recognized that the country was unwilling or unable (and unwise) to try to accomplish what it set out to do. The *Washington Post* continued its support of the war until Russell Wiggins was replaced as editorial page editor by Philip Geyelin in 1968. Among early skeptics were Robert Lasch of the *St. Louis* (Mo.) *Post-Dispatch* and Lauren Soth of the *Des Moines* (Iowa) *Register and Tribune*. Lasch won the Pulitzer Prize for several 1965 editorials questioning the U.S. role in Vietnam. One of the editorials was "The Containment of Ideas."[33]

THE CONTAINMENT OF IDEAS

Coming events in South Viet Nam promise for many Americans a profound psychological shock, which a foresighted Administration would be preparing to offset. When the day comes for American forces to leave Viet Nam after 10 years of vain effort to build an anti-Communist bastion there, not only will our national pride be hurt, but some basic assumptions of our postwar foreign policy will be called into question. . . .

We shall improve our position with the developing nations and the world at large not by proving that we can wage endless war in Viet Nam, but by showing, through actual conduct, that the CIA is not enfranchised to swagger around the world setting up governments and knocking them down; that we do not undertake to dictate the form and pace of political change anywhere; that we are prepared to accept revolutions even when we do not approve of them; and that we have enough faith in the ideas of freedom to entrust to them, rather than to arms, the task of containing the ideas of Communism.

Robert Lasch
St. Louis Post-Dispatch

(Soth had won the Pulitzer Prize for editorials in 1956 for expressing a similar faith in relying on ideas in dealing with Communism. He proposed the first exchange of delegations between the United States and the Soviet Union—in this instance, farm delegations.)

Civil Rights Era

In the civil rights era, a few brave voices dared to speak out, some risking physical danger. A glance at the names and dates of Pulitzer Prize winners from World War II to 1970 suggests that editors' awareness of civil rights issues rose belatedly, reached a peak, then declined. The lone winner in the 1940s was Hodding Carter of the *Delta Democrat-Times*, in Greenville, Miss. In 1946, he won the Pulitzer Prize for editorials on racial, religious and economic intolerance. In 1954 came *Brown vs. Board of Education of Topeka, Kansas,* a Supreme Court ruling that ordered desegregation of schools. Between 1957 and 1964 six out of eight prizes were awarded for editorials on school desegregation or other civil rights issues. These prizes went to the *Tuscaloosa* (Ala.) *News, Arkansas Gazette* in Little Rock, *Atlanta* (Ga.) *Constitution, Virginian-Pilot* in Norfolk, *Pascagoula* (Miss.) *Chronicle* and *Lexington* (Miss.) *Advertiser.* In the award-winning editorial in the *Virginian-Pilot,* Lenoir Chambers criticized the state of Virginia's decision to shut down nine schools to avoid court-ordered integration.

Substantial civil rights legislation was passed during the early years of the Johnson administration, from 1964 to 1966, when award-winning civil rights editorials began to come less frequently. Between 1969 and 1972, Pulitzer Prizes were awarded to three newspapers for editorials on civil rights issues: the *Pine Bluff* (Ark.) *Commercial, Gainesville* (Fla.) *Sun* and *Bethlehem* (Pa.) *Globe-Times.* The next civil rights recognition went to the *Miami Herald* in 1983 for editorials about Haitian immigrants.

THE YEAR VIRGINIA CLOSED THE SCHOOLS

So far as the future histories of this state can be anticipated now, the year 1958 will be best known as the year Virginia closed the public schools.

This was the year when the automatic operation of Virginia law, moving precisely as the state's governmental leadership and its General Assembly had provided, reached out to shut and lock the doors of a Warren County high school in Front Royal, of two schools in Charlottesville, and of three junior high schools and three high schools in Norfolk.

By the same act the state denied nearly 13,000 boys and girls, some 10,000 in Norfolk, the kind of education which the people of Virginia had in mind when they wrote into their Constitution with wide approval and great confidence these words:

"The General Assembly shall establish and *maintain* an efficient system of public free schools *throughout the state*."

The year that has run out has carried Virginia, and especially Norfolk, where the penalty exacted has been the heaviest, far down a defeatist road. We cannot continue this way. The state is bound by every obligation of governmental principle and human dignity and decency and its own self-interest to find a better way than the one we live under. . . .

Lenoir Chambers
Virginian-Pilot

Watergate-Nixon Era

Editorial writers returned to supporting Republicans in the 1968 presidential election, when Richard Nixon barely defeated Hubert Humphrey. Even though much of the press and the public had grown weary of the Vietnam War and had become convinced that it could not be won, the war dragged on throughout Nixon's first term. Much of the press eagerly endorsed Nixon for a second term in 1972, even though revelations of the scandal later known as "Watergate" had been published during the campaign.

The documented details of Watergate eventually emerged, and Nixon resigned from the presidency—nearly two years after the break-in at the Watergate complex. A few newspapers, notably the *Washington Post*, deserved credit for the early revelations and for keeping public attention centered on the affair. But the Watergate story was essentially a news story, not an editorial page accomplishment. In 1974, the *Chicago Tribune*, a staunch supporter of Nixon and Republicans in general, was one of the first major newspapers to call for Nixon's resignation.

In the same era, the *New York Times* and *Washington Post* won much-deserved credit for daring to publish "The Pentagon Papers," in the face of the Nixon administration's efforts to keep the real story of the Vietnam War under cover. Again, though, the effort was primarily on the news side.

Reagan Era to the Present

During Ronald Reagan's two terms as president (1981–1989) neither editorial pages in particular nor newspapers in general took the lead in crusading for national or international causes. They played no significant role in smoking out the "Irangate" affair, in which Iran paid cash for U.S. military arms that then were sent to support "contra" forces in Nicaragua. During the George H.W. Bush administration (1989–1993) the press generally applauded the military action in the Iraq "Desert Storm" war and did no more than reiterate voters' concerns over the "no new taxes" promise that Bush proved unable to keep.

During Bill Clinton's administration (1993–2001) the press did little more than pass on the rumors and gory details that came its way (often from the pages of the nation's sensational tabloids).

In the aftermath of the attacks on the Pentagon and the World Trade Towers on September 11, 2001, most editorial writers and cartoonists expressed support for the George W. Bush administration's response to the tragedy and its subsequent efforts to wage war against terrorism. Still, a few voices expressed doubts. Among columnists who questioned President Bush's leaving Washington immediately after the attacks were William Safire,[34] Maureen Dowd[35] and Frank Rick,[36] all *New York Times* staff members, and Dan Guthrie of the *Daily Courier* in Grants Pass, Ore. The *Times* writers kept their jobs, but Guthrie was fired for describing "Bush hiding in a Nebraska hole" as "an embarrassment" with "the president's men . . . frantically glossing over his cowardice."[37]

Five months later, Scott Stantis of the *Birmingham* (Ala.) *News,* president of the Association of Editorial Cartoonists, said that 85 percent of the nation's cartoonists had done "extraordinary" work in responding to events. He noted that most had backed the Afghanistan war but had not been "lackeys of the government"; they had also questioned military tribunals and other new threats to civil liberties.[38] Jim Borgman of the *Cincinnati Enquirer* raised some readers' hackles in a cartoon labeled "Choose the patriot," which showed a driver in a fuel-efficient car and another driver in a gas-hog SUV flying American flags. Steve Benson of the *Arizona Republic* in Phoenix drew protests for cartoons that questioned a wave of super-patriotism.[39] Mike Marland of the *Concord* (N.H.) *Monitor* provoked his editor to write a public apology for a cartoon that showed a plane labeled "Bush Budget" slamming into two towers labeled "Social Security."[40]

Recent years have been marked by increasing concentration of ownership of daily and non-daily newspapers by fewer and fewer groups. For some of these groups, newspapers represent only a part, even a minor part, of their total investments. To meet group demands for fixed profit levels, emphasis has been placed at the local level on increasing advertising, tightening budgets and reducing staffs. "In a nutshell," Gilbert Cranberg wrote in summarizing a University of Iowa study, "the problem is that stock price becomes an overwhelming preoccupation of the companies, and people who have no interest in quality journalism are in positions to influence the price" and the quality of the journalistic product.[41] This trend will be discussed further in Chapter 9, "Relations with Publishers," which explores some ideas on how editors and editorial writers might cope in an era of corporate journalism.

■ HISTORICAL SUMMARY

In the nearly three centuries in which editors on the North American continent have been commenting on public issues, opinion has taken different roles. For the first century or so, editorial comment was sparse and generally intermixed with (often highly personalized) accounts of news. Then, as tension mounted between the Colonies and Great Britain, editors began to be called to comment on the issues. As the Revolutionary War approached, journals were increasingly filled with opinion.

In the first decades following the ratification of the Constitution, in 1787, any newspaper, including its editorial page, served as a mouthpiece for a political party. The function of editorials, which began appearing during this era on designated editorial pages, was to argue the party line as forcefully as possible for the party faithful. The stronger and more emotional the tone of an editorial, the more likely it was to please the reader.

Beginning in the 1830s, the new populist press began appealing to a much broader and less political group of readers. At first these penny papers offered mostly crime, sex and gossip. Unsophisticated readers were not interested in editorial comment. But as readers became more literate and editors more concerned about issues, the populist press became more serious. In the two decades before the Civil War the major issues facing the nation got a thorough, if highly emotional and personalized, airing in the editorial columns. Editors did not hesitate to put into print their concerns about the conduct of the Civil War.

The Civil War brought new interest in news, and the day of the great personalized editorialist began to wane. A few voices still spoke out. Writers such as Charles Dana, E.L. Godkin, William Randolph Hearst and Joseph Pulitzer raised a ruckus in the late 19th and early 20th centuries. But the trend was clear: Editorial writers were retreating into anonymity on conservative newspapers owned by corporations.

In the waning years of the 19th century newspaper writers and editors, notably William Randolph Hearst and Joseph Pulitzer, spoke out strongly for going to war with Spain, but most (with the possible exception of Pulitzer) left the war on social and economic injustice to the muckraker writers for magazines. As the nation approached World War I and World War II, few editorial writers expressed enthusiasm for getting involved in "foreign wars," but as soon as war was declared they lost no time in volunteering their enthusiastic support.

Rare were the writers with the wisdom and foresight of Alan Barth of the *Washington Post,* who fought against "McCarthyism," or Robert Lasch of the *St. Louis* (Mo.) *Post-Dispatch,* who argued that the war in Vietnam was wrong and likely to prove self-defeating.

A few editorial writers in the South (Lenoir Chambers of the *Virginian-Pilot,* for example) were given much deserved recognition in the late 1950s, 1960s and early 1970s when they risked lives and property to convince hostile readers that the U.S. Supreme Court meant what it said about desegregating schools.

The next chapter will look at more recent examples of what editorial writers and their newspapers are doing and at what editorial writing could, and should, be.

▨ QUESTIONS AND EXERCISES

1. Why did writers for the Colonial press see little reason to make a distinction between news and opinion?
2. What brought about the decline and eventual demise of the partisan press during the 1840s and 1850s?

3. Why were Benjamin Day and James Gordon Bennett not interested in editorial comment during the early days of the populist press?

4. What accounts for Horace Greeley becoming the most famous editor of the mid-19th century? Do you think the esteem in which he was held was fully merited?

5. From examples in the chapter (plus other examples if available) contrast the writing styles of Horace Greeley and William Cullen Bryant. What does the difference suggest concerning readers of their papers?

6. Why has Charles Dana remained better known than E.L. Godkin?

7. Based on material in this chapter and information from other sources, does it seem reasonable to hold the *New York Journal* and the *New York World* primarily responsible for the political atmosphere that allowed the Spanish American War to occur?

8. Why did most of the writing about social problems in the early 20th century appear in magazines rather than in the daily press?

9. What factors contributed to the trend toward editorial anonymity in the corporate newspaper era?

10. Why have recent decades produced no modern-day Horace Greeleys, Henry J. Raymonds, William Randolph Hearsts, Joseph Pulitzers or William Allen Whites?

The Editorial Page That Should, and Could, Be

The first step toward understanding the role that the American editorial page can play today is to understand the nature of the readership of the page. In general, readers today are better educated than readers of the past. They are probably also more sophisticated, although many may not be as interested in public issues as were the faithful followers of editorials in the more partisan papers of the past. Most of today's readers do not read editorials as consistently as readers did when they could subscribe to, and relish reading, a newspaper with which they agreed politically. In most communities today, readers have little or no choice of a daily paper; they take the one that is available or none at all. In fact, a growing percentage of families today does not subscribe to a daily paper. Those who do subscribe represent not the narrow range of the faithful, as in the past, but a diverse political, philosophic, economic and social range. Unlike newspaper readers of the past, most of today's subscribers are exposed to many other sources of information and opinion from other channels of information—television, radio, cable, magazines, Internet, satellite and fax—and from social, civic, labor and business organizations.

All these characteristics of contemporary readerships suggest major implications for editorial page editors and writers who want to inform and persuade their readers as effectively as possible. This chapter examines those implications and how editors deal with them in an age of a more diversified, more disinterested audience. My major point will be that there is still room for strong editorial leadership—for editorial crusades—but that the best chances for editorial writers to achieve credibility and to be persuasive lie in being informed, reasonable, articulate and sensitive to the feelings and opinions of others.

◼ A FEW BUGLE CALLS

"Today's editorial trumpet, when it sounds at all, too often sounds not so much like a trumpet as like a kazoo." That's the judgment of Robert Reid, former editorial writer, now associate professor at the University of Illinois. He sees a need especially for editorials "of an outrageous or even irresponsible" type. "We need loud, clamorous, jarring, persistent voices in our newspapers, hitting people hard enough in their prejudices to make them think and act in the public arena rather than in effect encouraging readers to slouch around feeling as if what they think doesn't matter or won't do any good," Reid wrote in an article titled "More Hell-Raising Editorials."[2]

A San Francisco Bugle

One of today's newspapers that has risen to that challenge is the *San Francisco Bay Guardian*. Editor and publisher Bruce B. Brugmann and his wife, Jean Dibble, founded the struggling weekly in 1966, in Brugmann's words, "to print the news, and raise hell, for just causes."[3] Since then, one of the newspaper's causes has been to survive and maintain an independent voice in a newspaper community dominated by the *San Francisco Chronicle* and the *San Francisco Examiner*.

For almost 30 years, according to Brugmann, "we were a lone voice in the wilderness" in a fight to bring to public attention what he called "the PG&E/Raker Act Scandal." In 1969 the *Bay Guardian* published its first investigative story. In Brugmann's words, it "laid out how for decades the Pacific Gas & Electric Co., the local private utility, had used its political influence to keep San Francisco from bringing its own cheap Hetch Hetchy public power to San Francisco residents in defiance of the federal Raker Act of 1913 and a 1940 U.S. Supreme Court decision." During the next three decades, according to Brugmann, "almost every reporter and editor at the *Bay Guardian* . . . [had] in one way or another been involved in the research and reporting of this story and its many ramifications." Finally, in 1993 and again in 1999, spurred by *Bay Guardian* reporting and editorials, San Francisco voters approved two open-records ordinances that made it possible for the public to obtain information on the power situation. In a nomination letter to the Pulitzer Prize Committee, Brugmann wrote that, as a result, "We demonstrated through an ongoing series of stories the clear advantages of public power: lower rates, more reliable service, local accountability through an elected board, independence from a private utility conglomerate that went bankrupt due to the fatal flaws in its own state deregulation (which we opposed vehemently then and now)."

Eventually a citizens committee, with the support of the *Bay Guardian*, collected signatures for two initiatives to form a Municipal Utility District (MUD), with an elected board mandated to municipalize PG&E. Shortly thereafter a newly elected board of City of San Francisco supervisors (a majority of the members endorsed by the *Bay Guardian*) placed the two initiatives on the ballot.

Two weeks before the election, in an editorial titled "Don't buy PG&E's lies," the *Bay Guardian* accused MUD opponents of making the "misleading claim" that one of the initiatives would cost the public $3 billion. "That's a world-class lie, wrong on just about every level," the editorial said. "For starters, the 'No on 1' folks came up with that staggering sum of money by combining the costs of buying out PG&E, AT&T, the local garbage company and Pacific Bell's local phone system." In theory the MUD would have that authority, the editorial noted, "but none of the MUD Board candidates is talking about doing anything beyond running an electric utility anytime in the near future." Furthermore, the editorial said, the initiative "doesn't involve buying out anything . . . [It] just creates a MUD."[4]

According to Brugmann, "The initiatives were under-funded and up against PG&E's multi-million dollar campaign onslaught, but they gained wide support and came within a whisker of winning an election marred with charges of fraud on many fronts." Brugmann remained optimistic. He told the Pulitzer committee that "The end of the PG&E/Raker Act scandal is now in sight and the city may soon be able to enjoy the fruits of its own cheap Hetch Hetchy public power after all these years."[5]

Four months after the election, the *Bay Guardian* described as "good news" that the city's chief electric-power expert had drafted a plan for future electricity use and development. The "bad news," however, was that the plan "barely addresses the critical issue: who will own and operate the system."[6]

Brugmann ended one of his bugle-call editorials, written during another, but ultimately unsuccessful campaign, with the charge: "On guard!" Bugle-call editorials don't always lead successful charges.

Southern Bugles

Between 1955 and 1965 six Southern newspaper editorial writers won Pulitzer Prizes for daring to speak out about civil rights. One of these was Buford Boone, publisher of the *Tuscaloosa* (Ala.) *News*. When the board of trustees refused to allow Autherine Lucy to be admitted to the University of Alabama in 1956, Boone, in a front-page editorial, criticized the board for having "knuckled under to the pressures and desires of a mob" and for making "an abject surrender to what is expedient rather than what is right." He concluded: "Yes, there's peace on the University campus this morning. But what a price has been paid for it!"[7]

Hazel Brannon Smith, editor-owner of the *Lexington* (Miss.) *Advertiser,* knew speaking out on civil rights was risky. She had written: "There was a time, almost a decade ago, when we Mississippians were free . . . we did have the habit of liberty. Newspaper editors were free to write editorially about anything in the world, giving our honest opinions, and there was no fear of economic reprisals or boycott. Today a newspaper editor thinks a long time before he writes anything that might be construed as controversial." That fear did not keep her from speaking out, among other occasions, about the bombing of the home of an African-American man who had tried to register to vote. "This kind of situation would never have come about in Holmes County if we had honestly discharged our duties and obligations as citizens in the past; if we had demanded that all citizens be accorded equal treatment and protection under the law. This we have not done."[8] She received the Pulitzer Prize in 1964.

A Personal Experience

In most instances in which a newspaper achieves an editorial goal, it is difficult, if not impossible, to determine precisely to what extent an editorial campaign contributed to the outcome. This was true for the hardest fought campaign waged by the *Columbian* of Vancouver, Wash., while I was on the paper. The Port of Portland, a local government agency, wanted to expand the runways and parking areas of the Portland International Airport by dumping a square mile of fill into the Columbia River. The river separates Portland from Vancouver as well as Oregon from Washington. The Portland newspapers and, at the beginning, the major public figures in Portland firmly supported the expansion. In Washington some citizens were concerned that altering the course of the river would have detrimental effects, especially on the Washington bank. But others feared that, if the airport were not expanded at that location, convenient to Vancouver, the Port would relocate it on the other side of Portland.

Two people whose homes sat on the Washington bank came to the newspaper with research they had done on the hydrological and legal aspects of changing the channel. They were trying to raise money to retain a prominent environmentalist as an attorney to press a court suit. They convinced me that they had a worthy cause. We supported them and questioned the wisdom of expanding into the river. During the next two to three years opponents of the expansion won not a single court decision. Fortunately for them, the Port had agreed to wait until the last legal hurdle had been cleared.

Our paper was able to make no discernible impact on opinion in Oregon, but in a succession of editorials over those years we made a strenuous effort to shore up support on our side of the river, while the opponents carried their battles through the courts and later to Congress. Delay proved the undoing of the project. A new projection of future usage of the airport scaled down the original estimates. The environmental movement began to gain strength about this time. Finally, a new mayor, Neil Goldschmidt, was elected in Portland. He began questioning the expansion. Soon the port abandoned its plan and came up with one that would fit on existing land. In this instance several factors came together to scuttle this project, but I am convinced that without the bugle-call editorials of the *Columbian,* calling on Washingtonians to stand their ground, the airport would have been built.

A number of picturesque images have been used to warn editorial writers against expecting too much from editorial campaigns. Bernard Kilgore, when he was publisher of the *Wall Street Journal,* said he thought it was all right for newspapers to regard themselves as thunderers and for editorial writers to picture themselves "with a bolt of lightning in each hand about to smash down on something." But he urged writers to be "very careful about demolishing a subject with one swoop, because good subjects for the editorial pages are very hard to come by."[9] Most topics, he warned, require analysis and comment over a period of time, not a single definitive pronouncement. Donald Tyerman, then editor of the *Economist* of London, reminded editorial writers at a meeting of the National Conference for Editorial Writers (NCEW) that they are neither Moses nor God. He warned against the Tablets of Stone theory—"that you can hand down the truth or, indeed, that you have it to hand down." Nor did he believe that editorial writers can effect a conversion such as occurred to Saul of Tarsus on the road to Damascus.[10]

At another NCEW meeting, Philip Geyelin of the *Washington Post* recalled that James Cain, who served with Walter Lippmann on the *New York World,* had argued that a newspaper ought to fight for its beliefs as hard as it could. He turned to music for an illustration, noting that a piano has eight octaves, a violin three, a cornet two, but a bugle has only four notes. "Now if what you've got to blow is a bugle there isn't much sense in camping yourself down in front of piano music," Cain said. To which Lippmann replied, "You may be right, but goddammit, I'm not going to spend my life writing bugle calls."[11] A bugle call may be appreciated by readers once in a while, and it may mobilize them in a worthy cause, but readers can quickly tire of answering bugle calls. Editorial writers may not have an eight-octave persuasive tool at their disposal, but they ought to be able to play more complex tunes than "Reveille" and "Charge!"

■ A MORE COMPLEX MELODY

Readers look to the editorial page for more than bugle calls. One newspaper survey found that the highest percentage of regular readers followed the page either to feel they were participating in current events or to strengthen their arguments on issues. Others read the editorial page to help make decisions on issues, to use in discussion with friends, to determine what is important, to keep up with the latest events, to agree with editorial stands or to help form opinions. These results suggest that readers use the editorial page more to gain information than to seek guidance in forming opinions.[12]

I am not one to urge editors slavishly to fashion their journalistic products to reflect readership surveys. Editors must still decide whether to give readers what they want or what the editors think they should have. A wise choice may be a compromise between the two, but if a choice must be made, editorial writers generally ought to come down on the side of facts and logic. The aim of the writer should be toward the mind, Lenoir Chambers advised editorial writers. (Chambers, while on the *Virginian-Pilot* of Norfolk, Va., was one of the six Southern Pulitzer Prize winners mentioned earlier.) Editorial writers had better aim for the mind, he said, "for everybody is better educated now, and the editorial writer has a harder job to stay out in front." If writers don't know what they are talking about, readers soon spot them for phonies.[13]

Columnist James J. Kilpatrick, formerly of the *Richmond News Leader*, has warned editorial writers: "Unless an editorial can add something to what appears in the news columns—something besides mere opinion—it has no business in the paper." He urged writers to use historical background, comparisons of parallel situations, fresh facts from other publications and research sources, interpretive analysis and corrections of misinformation.[14]

The *Rutland* (Vt.) *Herald* followed Kilpatrick's advice when, according to editor David Moats, a controversial court ruling relating to same-sex couples put the "statewide community of Vermont" into "a sort of perilous state." To help calm public reaction, interpretive editorials attempted to put the ruling in perspective and to correct misinformation. The 2000 state legislature faced the task of carrying out the state Supreme Court mandate that the state provide same-sex couples with the same benefits as heterosexual married couples. Many citizens not only opposed granting such benefits, they opposed on strong moral and religious grounds. Moats said he saw it as the role of newspaper to help "frame the whole question [of equal benefits] in a way that the state wouldn't end up tearing itself apart."[15]

When the first public hearings were held, legislators heard emotional and diametrically opposed views on whether gays and lesbians should have the right to marry. Following the hearings, a *Herald* editorial noted that legislators had to make up their minds and reminded them: "It is important, however, that our legislators are elected, not to represent a specific religious denomination or to impose a personal moral code. They are elected to represent all the Vermonters within their districts and to follow the secular code embodied in our state constitution and laws." The editorial reminded readers that "our secular democracy is broad enough to allow for the legitimacy and freedom of the diverse and opposing religious viewpoints that were on display Tuesday night." Reminding readers that the contentious issue could not be ignored, the editorial said that "it is clear that if the Legislature fails to act, the court will impose its own solution."[16] The editorial left it up to readers to imagine what the court might find necessary.

Three months later, the Legislature had approved a bill to establish civil unions for same-sex couples. By that time, the *Herald* had published 19 editorials on the issue. A theme through most of them was the need for people to respect the opinions of those with whom they disagreed and to recognize that some action had to be taken to satisfy the court. When the civil union idea was being considered, one editorial said: "Compromise on a matter of principle is harder if one believes one's opponents are absolutely wrong. But if one can accept the fact of honest disagreement, then compromise is more plausible."[17] When the civil union legislation was approved, the *Herald* recognized, "People on both sides of the issue have been troubled by things said on the other side." The editorial also said: "But the conduct of the Legislature is reason to take heart. Legislators on both sides of the issue worked from conviction and maintained a respectful atmosphere. . . . Let us hope that Vermonters of diverse views appreciate and respect the courage and leadership provided by the Vermont Legislature on this trying question."[18]

The 10 *Herald* editorials submitted to the Pulitzer Prize Committee won the Pulitzer Prize for editorial writing in 2001. (Two especially noteworthy editorials from this series appear in Chapter 12, "Subjects That Are Hard to Write About," under the topic of "Touchy Subjects.")

The Pulitzer committee also has recognized editorial writers who have not just written commendable editorials but have put in a prodigious amount of on-the-street work before sitting down to write. For more than a year Maria Henson of the *Lexington* (Ky.) *Herald-Leader* interviewed and wrote the stories of women who were victims of beatings. "In fear, Betty Ashby turned to the law," Henson wrote in her first editorial. "She went through all the steps. She appeared in court, signed statements, told her story to police. But nothing, it seemed, could keep Carl away."[19] The editorials were accompanied by pictures of some of the victims. Editors of the *Herald-Leader* reported that the series "led to dramatic improvements in Kentucky's efforts to shield women from violent men."

The 2002 Pulitzer Prize for editorial writing went to Alex Raksin and Bob Sipchen of the *Los Angeles Times*. They "researched for months the issue of chronically ill street people," spending "time on the streets, in shelters and in the courts, looking for answers." Their editorials were credited with "helping pass long-stalled legislation and raising awareness."[20]

■ A VARIETY OF TUNES

The diverse composition of today's editorial page audience presents another challenge to editorial page editors. When they write their own editorials, they must not only recognize that readers hold a variety of opinions, they must also create opportunities for those viewpoints to be presented. Because of time limits and the fleeting nature of their messages, most broadcast media cannot carry varied viewpoints in depth. That responsibility must fall to the print media. When you are the only newspaper in town, that responsibility falls on you.

Providing opportunities for and encouraging readers to write letters to the editor represents a start in this direction. But providing a forum is not enough. Some readers are less inclined to write than others, are less likely to write on one side of an issue than another, or are less likely to write on some subjects than on others. So the editor must seek to diversify opinion on the editorial page in other ways. Syndicated columns for 70 years or so have been a traditional source of some diversity. The columnists have their limitations, since most write on national and international news and have their favorite topics. Trying to find provocative non-regular writers requires time and effort, but these writers can bring varied and fresh views to the editorial page. The addition of an op-ed (opposite-editorial) page on an increasing number of papers has expanded opportunities for publishing material that can not be squeezed into a single page. (Some ideas that editors have come up with to provide a variety of tunes are discussed at greater length in Chapter 19, "Innovations in Design and Content.")

Opinion pieces in one newspaper can't be expected to replicate faithfully all viewpoints of a community's readers. But with a little help from friends—and adversaries—newspapers should be able to create opinion pages that make readers feel their views are being taken into account.

TODAY'S SONG WRITERS

So how do today's editorial writers see their role? A 1994 survey conducted by Ernest Hynds and Erika Archibald found that 62 percent of editorial writers saw "expressing a viewpoint or opinion" as the primary function of editorials, compared to 38 percent in 1977. Almost half (47 percent) cited "quality of argument" as an important factor in writing editorials, compared to 29 percent in 1977. Only 23 percent saw "taking a strong stand" as important, but that percentage exceeded the 5 percent who cited it in the earlier survey. Editorial writers in both surveys expressed strong support (79 percent in 1994, 73 percent in 1977) for presenting views opposed to those supported by the newspaper.[21]

The editorial writers generally expressed confidence that their editorials have influence, but the influence varied in terms of its effect on officials, elections, and social and moral issues:

	Much influence	Moderate Influence	Sum of the Two
Officials	38	49	87
Elections	23	53	76
Social issues	24	51	75
Moral issues	15	45	60

These figures ring true with me. It makes sense that editorial writers think they have their greatest impact on local officials, who follow the news more and are more interested in public affairs than most readers. Editorial writers tend to write about the same public affairs with which these officials are involved. Editorials may have more actual effect on the outcome of elections than might be apparent, because in many elections a 5 percent swing in the vote can make the difference. A study I made of California elections made clear that endorsements had more apparent effect on social ballot measures (schools, taxes, etc.) than moral issues (abortion, homosexual teachers, etc.).[22]

Some newspaper editors are not content these days simply to have editorials speak out on public issues. They want to play a more active role, involving the newspaper in the community and involving their readers (the community) in public affairs. The "movement" generally has been described as "civic journalism" or "public journalism." The *Savannah* (Ga.) *Morning News* won the 2002 James K. Batten Award for Excellence in Civic Journalism for "a dynamic, community-driven project that targets failing schools and triggered the creation of a civic group to raise venture capital for education innovations." The Pew Center for Civic Journalism also presented awards to other civic journalism practitioners. The *Everett Herald* was recognized for developing a clickable web-site map that attracted more than 1,200 people to register their opinions on redevelopment of the city's waterfront.[23] The Huntington, W.Va., *Herald-Dispatch*, together with West Virginia Public Television, created an Internet focus group of 18- to 34-year-old former West Virginians to determine why they had left the state.[24] The *Cincinnati Enquirer* was one of several local partners in a "Neighbor to Neighbor" initiative to generate discussion of racial issues.[25] The *Philadelphia Daily News* and WHYY-TV (PBS) sponsored a year-long effort, including town meetings, to improve local schools.[26] The Tacoma, Wash., *News Tribune* and two television stations polled citizens on how they thought the state's parole system should be overhauled.

Some civic journalism projects, and in fact civic journalism itself, have raised questions about the role of newspapers and newspaper editorial pages: Should they promote and conduct community project or merely report and comment? (For further discussion and other examples, see Chapter 9, "Relations with the Community," and Chapter 19, "Innovations in Design and Content.")

■ THE TUNE PLAYERS

Finally we come to editorial writers themselves, the players of the tunes. Because of the unique role that an editorial page plays in a community, it has become fashionable in editorial-writing circles to describe the page as the conscience of the community, the soul (or heart or personality) of the newspaper, the moral substructure of the paper. Editorial writers should hope their pages are all of these and more. But writers who set out to be the conscience/soul/heart of the community/paper risk committing one of the follies of editorial writing. At a time when philosopher-kings and prophets are rare and the credibility of institutions is low, the role of truth-seeker should be a humble one. Modern readers don't want truth through revelation; they want to feel they are discovering it for themselves. Writers who would lead must become servants of those readers.

The editorial writer is "uniquely equipped to stand at the corner of life and represent us all," somewhat like the person who hangs around in the piazza in the little towns in Italy, R.S. Baker, an assistant professor of humanities, once told Pacific Northwest editorial writers. Baker said he had often wondered how Italians, who read very few newspapers, could be so well informed. The mystery was solved when he observed the buzzing chatter, the exchange of information and gossip and the constant movement of people in the piazza, the public square. Over a period of days, you could spot the person who was the equivalent of the editorial writer. Baker described the person in this manner:

He is usually middle-aged with a face made grave by experience yet softened by flickers of humor. Most of the time his head is inclined in attentive listening while his eyes scan the square, alert and skeptical. But when he speaks he is listened to. He does not orate. He does not preach. He does not even adopt a tone of outraged innocence. Softly but clearly, he suggests how the matter appears to him. In his words there is a ring of wisdom based on his balancing of claims of past, present and future, the claims of the ideal and the actual, the desirable and the probable. If he lived here he would have your job—would, from his station in the piazza, keep one eye on the new-book shelf in the library and the other on City Hall, on the till.

Baker urged the writers to drop the pose of divine authority and accept simple humanity. "Do not aim to be Zeus the Thunderer (your 19th- and early 20th-century crusading editor) nor even Jove the All-Seeing (your cool, shrewd commentator on legislative/administrative matters). Rather, you should settle for being wily Odysseus, content to be—in all its terror and glory—a man among men, *primus inter pares.*"[27]

■ CONCLUSION

How does the editorial writer become the woman or the man in the piazza instead of a publisher's mouthpiece, an ivory-tower dweller, an impersonal penman or a judgment imposer? No secret magic will cause such a transformation. The chapters that follow are intended to offer suggestions for writers who may not have all the answers but, like the wise one in the piazza, want to be listened to when they speak.

■ QUESTIONS AND EXERCISES

1. Examine newspapers in your area for a period of several days. Do you get the impression from reading the editorial pages that the editors are trying to find a wide variety of opinions to present to their readers? In what forms do these opinions appear?

2. Examine the editorial pages of these papers for evidence of the personalities and individual opinions of editorial writers. Are the writers faceless persons, or do their names appear on the masthead or on bylined articles?

3. What seems to be the general tone of the editorials on these papers? Are the writers issuing bugle calls or something more subtle and complex? If a mixture, is the tone chosen for individual editorials appropriate?

4. Put in your own words what you think R.S. Baker meant by likening the editorial writer to the person in the piazza.

Anybody for Editorial Writing?

Here we are, the practitioners and champions of a profession which, we modestly like to think, assists the sun to rise and set—and we are doing very little, seemingly, either to seek out the young people with brains and judgment who we hope will be our successors or to interest them in the virtues and satisfactions of editorial writing.

—ROBERT H. ESTABROOK,
WASHINGTON POST [1]

Why would anyone want to become an editorial writer? What kinds of people make the best editorial writers? Where do they come from? These are some of the questions raised in this chapter, which is intended to give prospective editorial writers some idea of what it is like to be an editorial writer.

In the 1950s and early 1960s, when I was beginning my newspaper career, few young journalists gave much thought to becoming editorial writers, at least not until they had had their fill of walking a news beat. So I was surprised when, at age 28, I was asked by a friend and former professor if I would be interested in an editorial writing job he knew about in Des Moines, Iowa, on the *Register and Tribune*. Having left my native Nebraska and taken a job in the Pacific Northwest only three years before, I was not keen on returning to the Midwest. But the editor of the editorial page in Des Moines, Lauren Soth, had recently won the Pulitzer Prize for editorial writing, and I had enjoyed writing editorials on my college newspaper. So I applied for the job, got it and never looked back. Editorial writing became my new life.

My professor-friend said something else when he was trying to interest me in that editorial writing job. "Someday," he said, "you ought to have an editorial page of your own." I could not possibly have dreamed that five years later the publishers I had been working for in Washington state would hire me back as editorial page editor of their newspaper. I had my own editorial page at age 33.

◼ THE ATTRACTIONS OF EDITORIAL WRITING

What have I and other editorial writers found so attractive about working on an editorial page?

Editorial writing offers the chance to step back a pace, to take a broad view of the stream of news that rushes through the pages of a newspaper. Reporters, from time to time, have opportunities to write interpretive articles that attempt to put news into perspective, but only editorial writers spend their entire working days trying to understand what's happening in the world. To interpret the news, editorial writers must have enough time to do a quality job of researching and writing. Editorial writers, at least on some papers, can take half a day, if need be, to dig out information for an editorial that, when set in type, might be only five or six inches long. Editorial writing tends to appeal to people who take pleasure in careful writing. Of all the duties editorial page people may be pressed to perform, the one they are likely to enjoy the most is turning out the one or two editorials that must be written each day.

Another attraction of editorial writing is having a ready-made "soap box" from which you can explain and persuade. Readers, of course, don't always fall in line with the editorials they read in their local newspapers, but over a period of time an editorial page with credibility will influence the thinking and direction of the community. It is exciting and rewarding to be a part of the decision-making process of a community.

The job of editorial writer may carry more importance at the newspaper and in the community than it did a few years ago. Editorial writers may not get their names in print as often as star reporters, but the position tends to be one of the most prestigious on the paper. An increasing number of papers are providing opportunities for writers to become known to the public, partly through signed articles on the editorial page. While most editorial writers don't spend as much time out in public as reporters, they do, and must, get out and become acquainted with the community.

From a financial standpoint, editorial writing also has its advantages. Editorial writers generally are better paid than reporters and newsroom editors, and their job tenure is usually longer. A 1988 survey found that 72 percent of editorial writers thought they were paid "very well" or "well" compared to other staff members of their newspapers. The average salary was $38,500.[2] A follow-up survey in 1995 found that the average salary had increased to $55,191.[3]

The writers were not asked how satisfied they were with their salaries, but editorial writers seemed generally satisfied with the work they do. In 1988, 68 percent said they found their jobs "very satisfying" and an additional 29 percent said their jobs were "satisfying." The 1995 survey asked editorial writers to rate their job satisfaction on a scale of 1 to 5. The average was 3.7, with 92 percent selecting 3.0 or higher.[4]

Summing up the 1995 survey, David E. Klement, editorial page editor of the *Bradenton Herald* in Florida, concluded that "editorial writers clearly are an elite group in terms of education, prestige and pay."[5]

Editorial writing doesn't appeal to everyone who works for a newspaper. One survey found that only 30 percent of reporters and editors were interested in editorial writing.[6] Some of the uninterested saw too many restrictions and a lack of freedom of expression. Others saw the job as too removed from reality.

■ THE QUALIFICATIONS FOR EDITORIAL WRITING

Some of the news people who responded to the survey about their interest in editorial writing saw themselves as lacking the necessary scholarship or experience to be editorial writers. In fact 58 percent of the respondents thought the qualifications for a competent editorial writer were different from those for a competent news staff writer. In addition to scholarship and experience, editorial writers were perceived to be more in need of analytical and writing skills, sharper insights and a grasp of issues and trends.[7]

What qualities are required for editorial writers?

First, they need a wide variety of interests. Editorial writers on large staffs may have opportunities to specialize in subject matter, but those on most papers need to be able to write on almost any subject on almost any day. Even those who specialize need to understand how their topics fit into the broader world. Writers need to know about economics, politics, history, sociology, the arts and the sciences. In stressing the catholic interests of editorial writers, Warren H. Pierce of the *St. Petersburg* (Fla.) *Times* said that writers "should know more about all these subjects than any except a specialist in one of the fields, and enough of each so that even the specialist will not scoff" at their opinions.[8]

Second, editorial writers need to be good reporters. They must be able to dig out information and to recount accurately what they find. No editorial is stronger than the facts behind it. Previous experience as reporters can help editorial writers know where to go and with whom to talk when they need information.

One might think that, because editorial writers deal with opinion, they require less ability to be objective than do reporters. But the capacity to understand an issue or situation fully may be even more important for editorial writers than for reporters. In arguing for the need for objectivity, David Manning White, then a professor at Boston University, said. "To the editorial writer is given the power to exercise the most unrestrained use of language in the name of rhetoric and persuasion." For this reason, he said, editorial writers must check and double-check that what they write "conforms as closely as possible to objective, examinable truth."[9]

A third qualification is good writing. Editorial writers must write succinctly, since the editorial page is usually tighter for space than the news pages. Writers also need to be able to write in an interesting and convincing manner. Newspaper readers may have to read the news columns if they want to know about news, but they don't have to read the editorials, and they won't if editorials are dull or don't say anything.

Fourth, editorial writers need a quality that is sometimes called a sense of fairness or justice, sometimes called a spirit of the reformer, a commitment to principles, or integrity. The subjects they write about should be approached with a sense of purpose.

A fifth qualification is the desire to express an opinion. Hoke Norris of the *Chicago Sun-Times* saw reporters who became editorial writers as moving "from the sidewalk to the parade, from the press table to the speaker's table." As participants, Norris, said, editorial writers "must study, weigh, deliberate, contemplate, meditate, judge, discuss, talk over, think through and generally know all there is to know about any given subject, and . . . must be capable, at times, of completing the entire process in five minutes."[10]

Another desirable quality is the ability to reason cogently. Warren Pierce, a professor at the University of Oregon, had this ability in mind when he quoted the philosopher Arthur Schopenhauer as saying that geniuses share one characteristic: an ability to proceed from the particular to the general. Pierce thought that editorial writers need that ability, as well as the ability to do the reverse. Editorial writers must be able to go from one specific case of juvenile delinquency to the general causes of such delinquency, and "from one deep-freeze or white convertible Oldsmobile to a proposition of ethical conduct in public office." They should be equally able to give meaning to reciprocal trade agreements in terms of a clothes-pin factory in their community or of cotton or corn growers in their state.[11]

One view of an editorial writer's qualities was expressed by Irving Dilliard, editorial page editor of the St. Louis *Post-Dispatch,* who compiled an impressive list in an article titled "The Editor I Wish I Were." His principal points: Editorial writers should know their community, state, nation and world and read a great deal. They should be courteous, treating readers as individual human beings. They should be cooperative, working with associates to produce the best possible newspaper. They should be curious; perhaps they are not the first to learn everything in the community, but they at least should know more new things than anyone else. They should have imagination, seeing opportunities for improving the press in content, service and leadership. They should be persons of conscience and courage, with the ability to stand up to interest groups or a superior editor or publisher. They should have judgment, avoiding "the heavy artillery . . . if a spatter of birdshot will suffice." They should be able to criticize others, but also able to accept criticism. They must take care to avoid activities that might prove embarrassing or detrimental to editorial independence. Writers should be "sparing" in friendships because friendships outside their newspapers "may at any time force the hard choice between personal kindness to a friend and devotion to duty as an editor."[12]

Frederic S. Marquardt of the Phoenix *Arizona Republic* was so overwhelmed by Dilliard's description of the ideal editor that he asked: "Doesn't the guy ever have any fun?" The need to find out about so many places in the world "would give most newspaper auditors acute melancholia," Marquardt said. "I would need at least 72 hours [a day] to keep up with Dilliard, even if I didn't stop for a short beer now and then." Marquardt was especially critical of the admonition to be sparing in friendships. "Show me an editor who bends an elbow in a neighborhood tavern once in a while, or who occasionally sees if he can fill an inside straight, or who goes to a football game without the slightest intention of improving his mind, and I'll show you an editor who knows more about life than all the Ivory Tower boys," Marquardt said.[13]

■ WHO ARE THESE WRITERS AND EDITORS?

Who are these journalists who become editorial writers and editors? Surveys show that they tend to be male, white, Protestant, college-educated, married and middle-aged. From 1988 to 1995, the percentage of women on editorial page staffs increased from 16 to 29 percent, but they remained a clear minority.[14] In both surveys, 97 percent of respondents were white. In the 1995 survey, 49 percent were Protestants, 17 percent were Catholic, 8 percent were Jewish, 3 percent were Unitarian-Universalist and 22 percent had no religious affiliation. The percentage holding bachelor's degrees increased from 91 to 96 percent; those holding graduate degrees from 45 to 46 percent. In 1995, 83 percent of respondents were married and had an average of 1.7 children. The greatest shift came in political affiliation. In 1988, 53 percent of respondents identified themselves as Democrats, 30 percent as Republicans, 17 percent as neither (the only options listed on the survey). In 1995, 26 percent of respondents were Democrats, 15 percent Republican, 32 percent Independent and 16 percent said they had no political affiliation.[15]

More women are filling editorial leadership positions. They are increasingly being named as editorial page editors. By 2004, eight women will have served as president of the National Conference of Editorial Writers. Thirty-three men had filled that position by 1981, when Ann Merriman of the *Richmond* (Va.) *News-Leader* became the first woman president.

A survey of men and women on editorial pages concluded that "the hiring of women . . . does bring about a more diversified staff." Those polled suggested that women tend to "offer different expertise, somewhat different motivation, a possible different generational outlook and a different political orientation."[16] Women who were editorial page editors tended to work on smaller papers; women who were writers tended to work on larger papers. Women editors and writers tended to be younger and have less journalistic experience but more post-graduate education than male editors and writers did. They had lower salaries. Women were likely to regard themselves as specialists or experts in specific subject areas, notably science and health, "women's issues," education and minority issues.

As noted earlier, little progress has been made in bringing racial minorities onto the editorial page. That level is stuck at about 3 percent. Although noting that the National Conference of Editorial Writers (NCEW) had made efforts to recruit minority editorial writers and to schedule diversity sessions at its meetings, Rekha Basu, then of the *Des Moines* (Iowa) *Register*, expressed the opinion that the low representation of racial minorities at the conventions, and by extension in editorial boards, "is reflected in the missing perspectives on a whole gamut of issues—from rap music to the death penalty, from the presidential campaign to the L.A. riots, to international affairs."[17]

■ WHERE EDITORIAL WRITERS COME FROM

Because editorial writing requires so many skills and qualities, it is not surprising that editors and publishers despair when they face the task of finding an editorial writer. Any publisher or editor who has found the right person will say that such success is one of the most satisfying experiences in the field of newspapering. I know; I have experienced both despair and success.

It is infinitely more difficult to predict the potential ability of a would-be editorial writer than it is to decide whether a candidate will make a good reporter. Few guidelines exist for judging whether a former reporter, a college professor, a recent liberal arts graduate or an editorial writer from another newspaper will do the job a publisher or an editor has in mind. For one thing, most people who hire editorial writers, no doubt thinking of some of those qualities mentioned above, are not certain whether editorial writers are born or made. Some editorial writers seem to have what it takes; some seem not to. James H. Howard, a professor at the University of California, Los Angeles, thought that editorial writers probably had innate talent but that "those not blessed with the talent at birth" could be taught to improve their research, sharpen their writing and "present readable results of logical thinking."[18] Donald L. Breed of the *Freeport* (Ill.) *Journal Standard* said his experience on small newspapers showed that adequate editorial writers were usually found "only by accident."[19]

One dilemma an editor faces when looking for a new writer is whether to look in the newsroom for a person with no editorial page experience or to search outside for a person who has had editorial experience in another community. Most editors in a *Masthead* symposium said they looked first in their newsrooms but were not especially optimistic about finding exactly the right person.[20] An employer identified only as "an editor in the West" said he was discouraged by what happens to good reporters "who can pound out several thousand words of news copy a day" when they sit down in front of the editorial typewriter. "That clear, decent prose becomes stilted, 'literary' or arch. Why can't they relax?" One reporter who started on Monday ran out of things to say by Thursday. Another didn't work out because of lack of background. "I don't think he's read a book since he left college," the editor said.[21]

In a *Masthead* symposium on "The Nontraditional Editorialist," Lynnell Burkett of the *San Antonio* (Texas) *Express-News* noted that she had gone into editorial writing after earning two journalism degrees, editing a magazine, teaching journalism and advising a student newspaper and magazine. A single father on her staff who had written sports and covered Congress was "deeply concerned about issues affecting the disabled because of his son's disability." A working mother "brought particular passion to writing about lack of day care, child abuse and family violence." The staff also included two younger writers familiar with current popular culture and an African-American who had knowledge of "issues involving urban poverty, the civil rights movement and emerging African nations."[22]

Susan Nielsen reported that she had followed a more traditional path. Before becoming an editorial writer for the *Seattle Times*, she had been a reporter and an editor on a nearby weekly as well as an editorial writer on a mid-sized Washington newspaper, the *Columbian*, in Vancouver.[23]

I must acknowledge that, in seeking new editorial writers on the *Columbian* (years before Susan Nielsen joined the staff), we did no more planning than most papers. My first search represented a classic case of frustration. An ad in *Editor & Publisher* elicited more than 100 applications. Few came close to the person we thought we wanted. Some were "hacks," old-timers looking for an easy chair. Many were acquainted with neither editorial writing nor the territory. Almost in desperation, we allowed a *Columbian* reporter, who eagerly wanted the job, to try out for it. Here was the exact opposite of the reporter who has trouble moving from fact to opinion. After a few weeks of overexuberantly expressing her opinion, she settled down to become a fine, if still flamboyant, editorial writer. In the next search for a writer, we hired a person who had been an editorial writer, in fact the editor, on a small daily newspaper in California. He knew how to write editorials, and it didn't take him long to learn the territory.

My first editorial writing employer hired me when I knew very little about editorial writing and even less about Iowa, where the newspaper was located. But my return to the Vancouver paper represented an almost ideal set of circumstances. I had become acquainted with that community during three years of news reporting. I had had five years of editorial writing experience under a respected editorial page editor and excellent teacher. To make my situation even sweeter, I was brought back to Vancouver six months before the retiring editorial page editor was to leave the paper, enough time to get re-acquainted with the community and break in slowly. I recommend this combination of experiences, but these opportunities do not arise often.

■ CONCLUSION AND A WARNING

My comments and the surveys of editorial writers may suggest that editorial writers think highly of themselves. They think they practice the best of professions. The jobs they hold require all those "fantastic" qualities discussed above. Thus if they hold those jobs, editorial writers reason, they must be fantastic themselves.

Some of this self-esteem is merited. Some of the best-informed, most talented, incisive, conscientious people I know are editorial writers. In my experience, nothing can be more stimulating than bringing editorial writers together at an editorial staff meeting or a meeting of writers from several papers. But as praiseworthy as these wordsmiths generally are, perhaps a warning about too much self-congratulation is in order.

Editorial writers may be well-educated, draw good salaries and have their own offices, but they are still newspaper people. Newspaper people tend to be held in high esteem these days—higher than half a century ago certainly. But much of this esteem comes from the jobs they hold, not from their own individual qualities. Press critic Ben Bagdikian has warned that, with newspapers becoming "a respectable institution and editorial writers the most respected of all," newspaper people shouldn't forget where their journalistic predecessors came from. "Newspapers were born and raised in the bloody arena, kicking and gouging their newspaper competitors in the ring while the crowd screeched . . . ." Now most competitors have been "carried out on stretchers." The few that are left are not scrapping but giving their audiences pompous "lecture[s] on the Manly Art."[24]

Among middle-aged and older members of NCEW, perhaps the best-remembered call for humility came from Jonathan W. Daniels, editor of the Raleigh, N.C., *News and Observer,* who delivered an address titled "The Docility of the Dignified Press" to a 1965 NCEW convention. Speaking at an evening banquet at an exclusive country club on the outskirts of Milwaukee, Daniels told the writers that the editors and publishers who gathered for meetings of the Associated Press and the American Newspaper Publishers Association at the Waldorf-Astoria Hotel each spring were "indistinguishable from bankers." He quickly added: "You look pretty impressive yourselves." He reminded them that they were courted by senators, cabinet members and generals. "You really cannot blame the press for wanting a little dignity," he said. "Its members, as their social positions improved, naturally did not want to seem to be like Horace Greeley, who before he founded the famous *Tribune* was fired from one paper because its owner wanted 'only decent looking men in the office.'" Why shouldn't members of the press like their "pants pressed—sometimes striped?" He acknowledged that, "if [the press] didn't appear full-armored from the brow of Jove, it doesn't twist genealogy more than some other people do in suggesting that it is descended from the Bill of Rights." But he reminded his listeners that there were other ancestors. "There was the guitar player on the back of the patent medicine salesman's wagon. Also there was the ink-stained impertinent fellow who began long ago to put embarrassing reports on paper."

Now it had become more fashionable, he said, to look like Walter Lippmann, the distinguished columnist, than Heywood Broun, the disheveled-looking columnist of the 1920s and 1930s who had rankled publishers by trying to organize labor unions in their newsrooms. Perhaps it was at this point in Daniels' speech that one of the editorial writers suddenly rose from his table, lurched drunkenly toward the right side of the room, uttered a profane epithet at Daniels and staggered out, never to be seen at an NCEW meeting again.

Daniels bade him farewell and continued with his speech: "There is, of course, something disreputable about any business devoted to prying into matters," he said. "It is a nosey business. And it should remain so. Anybody who would never wish to hurt anybody's feelings, who never wishes to make anybody mad, should stay out of the newspaper business. The editor who deserves the respect of his community can be no respecter of persons in his community. He must be nosey and often a public scold."[25]

So when editors and publishers want to hire a new editorial writer, all they have to do is find a man or a woman who is a writer, a thinker, a scholar, an objective viewer, a critic, a scold and a person with humility. Is it any wonder that good editorial writers are hard to find—or any wonder that, once found, they think pretty highly of themselves?

■ QUESTIONS AND EXERCISES

1. What are the reasons for trying to find a new editorial writer in an editor's own newsroom?

2. What are the reasons for looking elsewhere?

3. How do you account for the slowness in opening editorial page positions to women and racial minorities?

4. Are there women editorial writers or members of racial minorities on editorial pages in your area? How long have they been editorial writers? What education and experience did they have when they became editorial writers?

5. What do you regard as the most important qualities of an editorial writer?

6. What aspect of editorial writing would appeal to you most? What would appeal to you least? Why?

7. If you wanted to land an editorial writing position on a major news paper within 10 years, what route would you attempt to follow?

8. On what newspapers with which you are acquainted could you feel philosophically comfortable writing editorials?

Preparation of an Editorial Writer

It is hard to imagine any discipline that would not benefit a journalist.

—RESPONSE TO A QUESTIONNAIRE CONCERNING COLLEGE CURRICULA[1]

Everybody has a sort of reading anxiety neurosis.

—ROBERT B. FRAZIER, EUGENE *(ORE.) REGISTER-GUARD* [2]

Preparing oneself to be an editorial writer is like preparing oneself for life. Everything the potential editorial writer thinks, learns or experiences is likely to become pertinent someday in the writing of some editorial. The same is true of journalists who are already editorial writers. Every word they read can provide an idea or information for an editorial. Compulsive readers who find themselves reading the sides of the breakfast cereal box may write editorials that day, or another day, about the dangers of the sugar content in children's breakfast foods or the lack of meaningful nutritional information. A casual conversation may provide an insight into Social Security or the minimum wage.

In this chapter a discussion of the unending education necessary for editorial writing is limited to five areas: undergraduate education, continuing education, firsthand experiences, reading and culture. A sixth area, professional experience, was discussed in the previous chapter.

■ UNDERGRADUATE EDUCATION

Bring an editor and an educator together—or even two editors or two educators—and you will have a debate on how best to prepare students for careers in journalism.

Journalism schools are a rather recent invention. Many editors before World War II saw little need for them. They hadn't gone to journalism school—perhaps not even to college. Reporting and editing, they knew from experience, could be learned on the job. But the world was becoming more complex, and readers were becoming more knowledgeable and sophisticated. To the GI Bill, which provided educational and other benefits for World War II veterans, must go much of the credit for sending more Americans to college than ever before. Students poured into journalism and every other field of study. Before many postwar classes had graduated, the competition for jobs made a college degree a necessary ticket for many positions.

Skills vs. Liberal Arts

With the legitimacy of journalism programs gradually becoming accepted, the debate turned to skills courses versus liberal arts. How many courses in journalism were necessary to prepare students to write a news story? How many courses in "academic" subjects were necessary to prepare students to know what they were writing about? Out of that debate came general acceptance of the 75:25 ratio set by the American Council on Education for Journalism, the national accrediting agency in journalism. In other words, 75 percent of graduation credits should be in liberal arts and related areas and not more than 25 percent in journalism. More recently this arbitrary rule has been relaxed, but it still remains a reasonable guideline for educators who want to ensure that prospective journalists get a broad liberal arts background.

Green Eyeshades vs. Chi-Squares

Next came arguments over which journalism courses should be offered and required. The protagonists in these arguments were sometimes referred to as the "green eyeshades" and the "chi-squares." Now you hear these disagreements discussed more in terms of "professional" versus "history and theory" courses.

The term "Green eyeshades" was a reference to the transparent green bills that copy editors used to wear to cut the glare of overhead lights. "Chi-square" is a mathematical procedure used in statistics to measure differences in sets of numbers. The green eyeshades feared that journalism schools were shifting from old-fashioned skills to theory and research. They wanted the schools to concentrate on reporting, news writing, feature writing, copy editing and editorial writing, plus courses in media law and history. They wanted attention paid to spelling, grammar, punctuation and style.

The chi-squares were interested in creating courses in communications theory, communications research, surveys of mass communications, media effects, and mass media and society. One of their goals was to make journalism and communication studies academically respectable among their research- and theory-oriented colleagues in other university departments. Coupled with their emphasis on history and theory has been a sharp trend toward valuing advanced degrees over professional experience in hiring new faculty members.

Members of the newspaper business and some educators have expressed concern. Hugh S. Fullerton, associate professor at the University of North Florida, in a letter to the newspaper division of the Association for Education in Journalism and Mass Communication (AEJMC), complained: "The 'academic' side has raised barriers against the professionals. I know many professionals who would be happy to teach if they received the respect that they have earned by many years' experience. But instead, we professionals are told again and again that we are unqualified because we don't have Ph.D.'s."[3]

Anticipating what concerned Fullerton, when I switched from newspapering to teaching I immediately enrolled in a Ph.D. program within commuting distance of the school at which I was teaching. Six years and an editorial writing textbook later, I was able to obtain a position at a university that regarded degrees, research and publications as important. Since then, these qualifications have become even more important at most four-year schools. The trend is not likely to be reversed.

Non-Professional Courses

Some critics argue that journalism programs have no place in higher education. "Indeed, a good case can be made for abolishing J-schools," Jake Highton, associate professor at the University of Nevada–Reno, has written.

"What journalism students need is an education—not a journalism education . . . . [Time] would be better spent having students take courses in literature, history, political science, fine arts and economics," with some "critical analysis of media performance."[4]

Most editors probably would not go so far as to advocate abolishing journalism programs but would agree with Otis Chandler, then publisher of the *Los Angeles Times*, when he complained that among job applicants "we're getting too many hopefuls who lack a background in economics, literature, philosophy, sociology and the natural sciences" and who "know little of government." He also deplored journalism students' inadequate exposure to ecology, energy, land-use planning and economics, as well as to the physical sciences, birth control and bureaucracies.[5] When NCEW (National Conference of Editorial Writers) members were asked to recommend areas of study, they suggested, in this order, U.S. history, composition, state and local government, introduction to sociology, principles of economics, critical writing, constitutional law, comparative economic systems, geography, history of political thought, political parties, history of modern Europe, economic history of the United States, public financing, urban and regional planning, and philosophy.[6]

Some educators have concluded that, because of the need to know about so many things, the journalism program should be a five-year one. Such a program might lead to a master's degree.[7] Other educators think that four years is enough to produce a working newspaper person, that he or she can grow on the job and later pick up additional education on the side or return for a master's degree, perhaps in another discipline.[8]

Because reporting and commenting on the news are becoming more specialized as the world becomes more complex, the student who comes to a newspaper with training in a particular field—economics, the arts, the health sciences or the criminal justice system, for example—can prove to be a valuable asset to a news or editorial staff, especially when a newspaper seeks to fill a beat or an editorial writing position that requires knowledge in that field.

Practical Experience

One method of impressing students with the need to learn basics—and to teach them at the same time—is through an internship on a newspaper or with another news operation. If interns have at least a couple of news writing and reporting courses, within a three-month internship they can acquire the ability to substitute on several of the regular beats, handle most stories that come into the newsroom and write a simple feature story. The internship experience helps when applying for a job after graduation. The prospective employer knows that the applicant has had some practical experience and that the internship supervisor can provide an evaluation of the applicant's work. Often a successful internship can lead to a job on the paper on which the student worked as an intern.

Another valuable experience is reporting and editing on a campus newspaper, especially if the work is supervised and criticized by faculty advisers or knowledgeable senior staff members.

■ CONTINUING EDUCATION

Editorial writers and would-be editorial writers should never stop trying to expand their educations. Science, mathematics, agriculture, medicine, politics, geography, education—all have vastly changed from the days in which many of today's editorial writers were in college.

Educational Fellowships

The most formal way for writers to recharge themselves intellectually and psychologically is through educational programs. "I cannot urge too strongly the desirability, for editorial writers particularly and working journalists generally, of a good dose of formal legal education," wrote an editorial writer who had taken a year's leave of absence to study law at Harvard University. "It sharpens the mind, provides valuable sources of information and advice on legal issues in the news, and generally enhances one's understanding of the legal process."[9] After completing a fellowship at Stanford University, an editorial writer said that the experience had given him the chance to think about "the big, tough questions that editorial writers seldom have time to dig into deeply." He added: "Think how rewarding it would be to spend nine months at a great university contemplating these concerns—without deadlines, spats with the boss, phone calls from ired readers; without mandatory term papers or exams; without significant restraints on tour freedom to explore and reflect."[10]

Probably the most prestigious fellowship is the Nieman Fellowship for Journalists at Harvard University, where the fellows are allowed to study any combination of courses that they choose. Information may be obtained at http://www.nieman.harvard.edu.

Editorial writers have been awarded $40,000 grants as part of the Eugene C. Pulliam Fellowship, offered through the Sigma Delta Chi (SDX) Foundation, an arm of the Society of Professional Journalists (SPJ). The fellowship is named after one of the founders of SDX (the original name of SPJ) and the owner of several newspapers in Cincinnati and Phoenix. A recipient has the opportunity to write a book or engage in investigative journalism. Or, as an announcement suggested, "just, maybe, you need some downtime to read, think and study in a manner impossible amidst daily pressures."[11] Inquiries can be made at http://www.spj.com.

A $35,000 grant has been awarded for research and reporting to professional writers, editors and photojournalists by the Alicia Patterson Foundation, 1730 Pennsylvania Ave., NW, Suite 850, Washington, DC 20006. Patterson was a founder and editor of *Newsday*.

The Knight Center for Specialized Journalism at the University of Maryland has offered fellowships for editorial writing seminars it sponsors on U.S. foreign policy. The Knight Center for Specialized Journalism is at 290 University College, University of Maryland, Building #345, College Park, MD 20742. The web site is http://www.knightcenter.umd.edu.

The *American Journalism Review* annually publishes a special section listing awards, fellowships and scholarships. From time to time *The Masthead,* the NCEW's periodical, publishes announcements of fellowships and other educational offerings.

Seminars

Among briefer programs, the best known is at the American Press Institute (API) in Reston, Va. For nearly five decades API has provided one- and two-week seminars in almost all aspects of newspaper work. An announcement for an editorial writing session said, "The week-long program will focus on new thinking, flexibility, experimentation, new technology, ethics and connecting with communities and a diverse readership."[12] The seminars are financed through tuition. For information, e-mail the American Press Institute (info@americanpressinstitute.org).

The Hechinger Institute on Education and the Media has offered weekend seminars in partnership with the NCEW. For journalists who are accepted, the institute covers the cost of lodging and several meals and a travel stipend. Information is available at http://www.tc.columbia.edu/hechinger.[13]

Editorial writers who feel the need for more education can also enroll in courses in nearby colleges. Evening courses in economics and public administration, for example, can help editorial writers write more knowledgeable editorials as well as provide intellectual challenges.

Teaching College Courses

One way to learn is to teach. Possibilities exist at several universities for editors and writers to return to campus as visiting editors or visiting professors. The School of Mass Communications at the University of South Florida offers an annual professorship in editorial and critical writing named in honor of James A. Clendinen, who served as NCEW president and editorial page editor of the *Tampa* (Fla.) *Tribune*. For details write: Chair, Clendinen Search Committee, School of Mass Communication, University of South Florida, CIS 1040, 4202 Fowler Ave., Tampa, FL 33670-7800. The pleasure I received as a visiting editor at the University of Montana had a lot to do with my decision a year or so later to accept a one-year teaching position at Washington State University.[14] That experience led me to 20 years of teaching journalism.

Editorial writers have helped introduce opinion writing to college students at several universities around the country. According to an account in *The Masthead*, the visiting writers offered "a lively afternoon session of discussion, debates and critiques."[15] At Columbia University, as part of a week-long seminar on journalism, seven editorial writers staged a mock editorial board meeting. One of the editorial writers reported: "We invited the students to jump in whenever they wanted and things quickly became lively."[16]

NCEW also has worked with the Freedom Forum First Amendment Center at Vanderbilt University in sponsoring a series of Minority Writers Seminars.[17] A *Masthead* article noted that several participants had become editorial writers.[18]

■ FIRSTHAND EXPERIENCES

The editorial writer who hopes to address a changing world must get out of the office. "There is no real substitute in journalism for the face-to-face confrontation," Terrence W. Honey of the *London* (Ontario) *Free Press* wrote in an article titled "Our Ivory Tower Syndrome Is Dead."[19] Unfortunately for some editorial writers it is not dead.

Local Level

Busy editorial writers are often tempted to write editorials on local topics on the basis of what has appeared in the news columns, interpreted in the light of past editorial policy, rather than attend meetings of city councils and local citizen bodies. Such meetings can become an every-evening job. Most of the time spent at them may seem boring and unproductive, so writers tend to put off going to local meetings until a hot issue comes along.

Attending only at crucial times is better than not attending at all. But most of the work of local government bodies is done in regular, humdrum meetings, out of the public eye. Editorial writers who want to know how a council or council member functions under normal circumstances should attend at least some of these dull assemblages. Editorial writers also can boost their credibility with members of local organizations and with anyone else who happens to be at these meetings.

More informative than public meetings are private ones, perhaps over lunch, with key persons. Editorial writers, or the editorial board, may find it advantageous to meet separately with members of opposing sides of issues. On other occasions inviting representatives from all sides to meet and discuss an issue may prove an effective way to gain information. To make certain that such conferences are not limited to times of crisis—and that lethargy does not win over good intentions—some editorial boards schedule a weekly meeting to which they invite one or more sources. Writers should meet, from time to time, with labor officials (as well as rank-and-file members), Chamber of Commerce leaders, other business groups and individuals, environmental groups, utility officials, energy-interest groups, consumer groups, education groups (professional and citizen), religious leaders, social activists, sports people, transportation people and even people from rival media.

It also is important for journalism students to become acquainted with people who are making, or trying to make, public policy. An editorial writing course offers an opportunity to bring speakers to class or to take students out into the community to learn first-hand what they are writing about.

State Level

Face-to-face confrontation can be more difficult at the state level. Unless a newspaper is located in a state capital, attending legislative sessions and committee hearings is difficult and time-consuming. Most provide little immediate information for editorials, since the legislative process is spread over an extended period of time. But much of what was said about local meetings applies here too. Writers need to get a feeling for the process at its usual slow pace to see how it works and how its practitioners function. Editorial writers need to show their faces and make their presence known, at least among their local legislators. Credibility with the legislators, as well as knowledge, is the goal.

It was easier to follow legislatures when they met for short sessions every two years. Now critical moments in the process are spread out, and opportunities for strategically directed editorials become more difficult to spot. Some of the difficulty can be alleviated if a newspaper assigns skilled reporters to the legislature to keep editorial writers informed about the timing of bills as well as to track down information for editorials.

Maintaining contact with the executive branch of state government is even more difficult from a distance. Decisions can come at any time and often without public notice. Probably the best approach to establishing contact is through people at the assistant level—governors' aides, assistant attorneys general, the elections supervisor in the secretary of state's office, a key assistant in the state planning office, a high-level career employee of the tax commission.

These second-level people are more likely to be expertly informed than their bosses and, even more important, are usually easier to get on the telephone.

Another way to keep abreast of state affairs is to watch for statewide conferences of such groups as county commissioners and city officials, as well as meetings on specific issues, such as taxation, education and legislative or judicial reform.

Students who attend universities in state capitals should find it easy to become acquainted with officials and issues by following the media and dropping in on legislative- and executive-branch meetings. I found that taking students to the capital (200 miles away) for even a few days helped awaken their interest in state government, particularly when the legislature was in session. It is easier to arrange these visits if the news and editorial people from the capital city newspaper help with the arrangements.

For quick Internet access to the status of bills in a state legislature, editorial writers can go to http://www.leg.state.xx.us (insert state abbreviation in place of xx).

National Level

In the past, for national issues, most editorial writers relied heavily on the news services, a few major newspapers and *Congressional Quarterly*. Now, through the Internet, they have instant access to almost every newspaper, wireservice, government office, interest group and research institution. (See Chapters 12, 13, 14 and 15 for a sample of Internet resources, classified by subject matter.)

The Internet, however, cannot supplant the need for personal contacts at the federal level—with the state's two senators, local House representatives and sources of information about matters of local or regional interest. E-mail and fax, however, have been added to the telephone as a means of getting information quickly from these sources.

Short visits to Washington, D.C., may seem even less productive for an editorial writer than trips to the state capital. But through periodic visits, a writer can begin to cultivate sources in the federal government, especially in departments that deal with issues pertinent to the writer's own region.

While teaching at Virginia Polytechnic Institute and State University, I took students on three-day travel seminars to Washington, D.C., to meet with people of various opinions—usually on international topics. These seminars were arranged with the help of the local YMCA and some of the campus ministries.

Useful Internet sites at the national level include:

Roll Call (covers Congress): http://www.rollcall.com

United States Senate: http://www.senate.gov

U.S. Census Bureau: http://www.census.gov

U.S. Supreme Court: http://www.supremecourtus.gov

White House Briefing Room:
   http://www.whitehouse.gov/WH/html/briefroom.html

For additional listings, see the "Legal Issues" section in Chapter 12, "Subjects That Are Hard to Write About," and Chapter 15, "Editorials on Elections."

International Level

NCEW members have taken advantage of State Department briefings on international issues. Jim Boyd of the Minneapolis, Minn., *Star Tribune*, reporting on one briefing, noted that in previous years "[t]here were grumblings from some that we weren't getting balanced views." His response: "[T]he United States has only one State Department and one foreign policy. We were being briefed on that. Challenge it, please, but don't insist on 'equal time' for the views of Heritage [Foundation], AEI [American Enterprise Institute] or Brookings [Institution]."[20]

NCEW members also have attended briefings at the United Nations. Following a two-day session, one participant reported the editorial writers "had virtually the entire United Nations hierarchy spread before it, from [U.N. General Secretary Kofi] Annan to a buffet of undersecretaries general."[21]

Since the mid-1970s NCEW has sponsored trips abroad, including trips to Eastern Europe, Cuba, China and Israel. Following the trip to Israel, Nancy Q. Keefe, retired editorial writer and columnist with the Gannett Newspapers in suburban Westchester County, N.Y., noted, "On our return from Gaza, the light in the distance was not the proverbial, hopeful light at the end of the tunnel, but an in-your-face searchlight from the Israelis that kept you from seeing where you were going but could make you a target for snipers on the hills."[22]

Useful Internet sites at the international level include:

The Embassy Web (links to U.S.-based embassies and consulates):
   http://www.embpage.org
The United Nations: http://www.un.org

For additional listings, see the "International Affairs" section of Chapter 12, "Subjects That Are Hard to Write About."

Professional Level

Associating with journalists with similar interests can help rejuvenate editorial writers' enthusiasm for their work and challenge them with ideas for doing a better job. One of the main purposes of NCEW is to improve the quality of editorial pages by bringing editorial writers together for sessions of mutual enlightenment and criticism. A valuable and consistent feature of NCEW's annual meeting has been the day- or half-day-long critique session in which participants study the editorial pages before arriving, then analyze, praise and criticize one another's pages. The NCEW meetings also give members a firsthand (though brief) look at other communities. The speakers are almost consistently good.

NCEW over the years has encouraged and sponsored shorter conferences in nearly every region of the country. Generally the organizers enlist the help of a state or regional newspaper or press association to provide financial and clerical support. Participants critique each other's pages. Sometimes an outside speaker provides another perspective on their editorial products.[23] NCEW also has partnered with the Society of Professional Journalists in sponsoring regional meetings. At one meeting the editorial writing component included a panel discussion and an all-day critique session. Dick Mial of the *La Crosse* (Wis.) *Tribune* said that format allowed NCEW "to raise its flag during the conference, and to offer any editorial writers an opportunity to participate in critiques."[24]

■ THE EDITORIAL SHELF

Robert B. Frazier of the *Eugene* (Ore.) *Register-Guard* once surveyed 100 editorial writers to determine their reading habits.[25] Later he wrote an article for *The Masthead* titled "The Editorial Elbow," in which he offered a "more-or-less compleat [*sic*] listing of reference works useful, day by day, to the editor, reporter and copyreader."[26] Frazier concluded that, although writers consistently thought they read too little, probably no other group in the country "read more or more catholically." Writers on smaller papers, with smaller editorial page staffs, he said, followed a more varied reading diet than writers on larger staffs.

Nonfiction was more popular than fiction. Only about 40 percent of respondents said that fiction accounted for a quarter or more of their reading. Half said they read essays, poetry or plays. About 10 percent read often in a foreign language. Some bought only two or three books a year, but one bought 200. Forty percent were regular patrons of libraries. Twenty-five percent said they read in bed. Two got up to read in the middle of the night. Three read early in the morning. Four admitted to being bathroom readers. One had read Gibbon and one Spinoza. Shakespeare appeared on several lists.

Columnist James J. Kilpatrick thinks that editorial writers do not read enough, and "it shows up with painful transparency in the superficiality, the shallowness, the gracelessness, of our editorial writer."[27] He advised writers to read the Bible and Shakespeare and to read heavily "in the older classics"—Thucydides, Plutarch, Homer, Aeschylus, Disraeli, Gibbon, De Qnincey, Spinoza, Voltaire—and then the more recent works of Thorstein Veblen, William James, John Dewey, Alfred North Whitehead and Peter Finley Dunne. To this assignment, Kilpatrick added a list of poets, from Alexander Pope to Edna St. Vincent Millay, and fiction writers, from Charles Dickens to O. Henry. Irving Dilliard of the *St. Louis Post-Dispatch* said an editorial writer should be "familiar with the monumental publishing projects of his time in biography, in history, in the social sciences, regional life, in the messages and papers of the great Americans—Franklin, Adams, Jefferson, Lincoln."[28]

Magazines and Newspapers

In moments when they are not reading the classics, where do, and should, editorial writers turn for help in writing their daily assignments? Editorial writers' answers to a survey question about how they became familiar with their newspapers' ideologies provided one insight. The editors of smaller news-papers tended to say they read their own newspapers. Editors on larger newspapers tended to read other newspapers.[29] Editorial writers should read state, regional and national newspapers, in print or on the Internet. They should read news and opinion magazines, in print or on the Internet.

A 1995 survey found that 45 percent of editorial writers regularly read *Newsweek* and 33 percent read *Time*. Readers of the *New York Times*, *The New Republic* and the *Wall Street Journal* ranged from 27 to 29 percent of respondents. Regional newspapers and *The Economist* were read by 22 percent. From 10 to 19 percent of respondents read each of the following: *U.S. News & World Report*, *The New Yorker*, *Washington Post*, *The Nation*, *National Review* and *The Atlantic*.[30]

Writers should seek out various points of view on public issues, if only to know what the opposition is saying. In examining how conservative voices commented on the war on terrorism, Nina J. Easton, writing in *American*

Journalism Review, looked at *National Review, The Weekly Standard* and the *Wall Street Journal.*[31] Among the "liberal-left" press Easton examined were *The Progressive, The Nation, The American Prospect* and *The New Republic.*[32] (Easton noted that *The New Republic* had begun to diverge from other liberal magazines in the 1980s. In a later issue of *AJR* a letter writer also commented that "*The New Republic* is not a 'liberal' magazine, certainly not in the sense of *The Nation* and *The Progressive.*")[33] Less political *Harper's* and *The Atlantic* traditionally have been popular with editorial writers. *Business Week* publishes easy-to-understand articles on business and economics as well-written editorials that discuss issues beyond a narrow business orientation. *Foreign Affairs* offers writing by recognized international experts. *The Economist* offers a British point of view, but includes a strong section on the United States. *Columbia Journalism Review, American Journalism Review* and *Editor & Publisher* are helpful in keeping up on media issues.

Other Periodical Resources

The following sources of information are generally available on a weekly basis:

> *Facts on File* is a weekly service that boils down the essential elements of the news into a ready-reference form. It is a good source for elusive facts. Telephone: 212-629-5634. Web site: http://www.factsonfile.com
>
> *The CQ Researcher* (formerly *Editorial Research Reports*) provides background material on a variety of current issues 48 times a year. Congressional Quarterly, 1255 22nd St., Suite 401, Washington, DC 20037. Telephone: 1-800-834-9020. Web site: http://www.cqpress.com
>
> The *National Journal,* published 50 times a year, provides weekly reports on current national issues and more in-depth reports on major topics. National Journal, 1501 M St., Suite 300, Washington, DC 20005. Telephone: 202-739-8400. Web site: http://www.nationaljournal.com

Published on a daily basis while Congress is in session is the *Congressional Record,* which can be obtained through your senator or representative in Congress. This publication provides a day-to-day account of what happens in Congress (and some things that don't happen but that legislators wish had happened). The *Record* also contains a large amount of reprinted material, including editorials. The daily volumes present a storage problem and far too much material for most editorial writers, but one way to use the *Record* is to glance through the index that arrives every 10 days or so. It does not take long to look up your state and district legislators to see what they have said or inserted into the *Record.* Current, and especially regional, topics also can be checked quickly, as can the names of editorial writers' newspapers and the cities in which the editorials are published. It is nice to know when you have been reprinted in the Record. You can request information by e-mail at: gpoaccess@gpo.gov.

Internet

The Internet, of course, potentially can provide an editorial writer with more information than any other source or combination of sources. The World Wide Web truly offers access to a world of information. The challenge is to find the desired information easily and quickly.

Basically there are two ways to get information efficiently. One is to use a general web directory (or search engine) that offers a multilevel system of organizing Internet subject matter.

Major search engines include:

Excite: http://www.excite.com

Galaxy: http://www.einet.net/galaxy.html

Google: http://www.google.com

Infoseek: http://www.infoseek.com

LookSmart: http://www.looksmart.com

Yahoo!: http://www.yahoo.com

Using various approaches, these sources provide you with lists of web sites that match the criteria that you have specified.

The other way to get information efficiently is to acquire a list of your own favorite sites, those that specifically meet your needs. Through this book I have suggested a number of sites (generally by subject matter). In compiling these lists, I have been aided by two (of many available) published Internet guides. One is *Internet for Dummies* ("Your road map to more than 900 of the best sites on the Web"), Foster City, Calif.: IDG Books Worldwide. The other is *Que's Official Internet Yellow Pages* ("With links to thousands of the best sites on the World Wide Web!"), Indianapolis, Ind: Que Corporation.

Falling somewhat between a directory and a web site is the Drudge Report, which provides "Controversial commentary, plus a directory [of] links to other news sources": http://www.drudgereport.com

For local and regional newspapers, there are:

InfiNet Newsstand: http://www.infi.net/newsstand.html

Newslink: http://www.newslink.org

Editor & Publisher: http://www.editorandpublisher.com

The National Conference of Editorial Writers has established a website that provides information about NCEW and about editorial writing and journalism in general. NCEW also offers an online "mailing list," in which messages by whoever chooses to speak up are shared among subscribers. Instructions for joining this mailing list can be found at NCEW's website, http://www.ncew.org. Some of the reference material that is available on the Internet is described in the following section.

Reference Works

Every editorial office and certainly every good-sized library should have a supply of reference materials, including a fairly recent encyclopedia, *Webster's Third International Dictionary* (or the *Second* if the writers are purists), foreign language dictionaries, a thesaurus, a quality atlas, a music dictionary or encyclopedia, a biographical dictionary (or *Current Biography)*, a geographical dictionary, a medical dictionary, a legal dictionary (or at least a media law dictionary), one or more annual almanacs, a book of quotations, *Who's Who in America*, probably *Who Was Who*, a regional *Who's Who*, the *Congressional Dictionary*, the *United States Government Manual*, the annual *Statistical Abstracts of the United States*, the *Official Postal Guide* (plus a book of zip codes), a state directory (usually referred to as the "Blue Book"), city directories going back as many years as possible, telephone books from assorted cities, the Bible and perhaps the works of Shakespeare.

Some major reference works are also available online, including:

Atlas of the World: http://cliffie.nosc.mil/~NATLAS/atlas

Bartlett's Familiar Quotations:
  http://www.cc.columbia.edu/acis/bartleby/bartlett

Dictionary.com (translates to and from English):
  http://www.dictionary.com/translate

Elements of Style: http://www.columbia.edu/arts/bartleby/strunk

Encarta Online (concise encyclopedia.): http://www.encarta.msn.com

Global Statistics: http://www.stats.demon.nl/g

Government Information:
  http://www.galaxy.einet.net/galaxy/Government.html

Internet Public Library: http://www.ipl.org

Merriam-Webster Online: http://www.m-w.com

Reference Tools: http://www.washington.edu/tools

Roget's Internet Thesaurus: http://www.thesaurus.com

The Library of Congress: http://www.loc.gov

Translating Dictionaries: http://www.dictionaries.travlang.com

U.S. Census Bureau: http://www.census.gov

U.S. Gazetteer: http://www.census.gov/cgi-bin/gazetteer

Vital Records Information (United States): http://www.vitalrec.com

Books on Language Usage

Here are a few books on language usage that may be helpful to editorial writers:

The Elements of Style, 4th ed.. William L. Strunk Jr. and E.B. White. (New York: Longman, 2000).

Working with Words: A Concise Handbook for Media Writers and Editors, 2nd ed. Brian S. Brooks and James L. Pinson. (New York: St. Martin's, 1993).

The New Fowler's Modern English Usage, 3rd ed. Edited by R.W. Burchfield. (Oxford: Clarendon, 1996).

The American Heritage Book of English Usage. (Boston: Houghton Mifflin, 1996).

REA's Handbook of English Grammar, Style and Writing. (Piscataway, N.J.: Research and Education Association, 1996).

The Chicago Manual of Style, 14th ed. (Chicago: University of Chicago Press, 1993).

The Careful Writer: A Modern Guide to English Usage. Theodore M. Bernstein. (New York: Atheneum, 1977).

Watch Your Language. Theodore M. Bernstein. (New York: Atheneum, 1976.) Out of print; look for it in used-book stores.

The Associated Press Stylebook and Briefing on Media Law. (Cambridge, Mass.: Perseus). Updated annually.

The New York Times Manual of Style and Usage. (New York: Three Rivers, 1999).

Word Court, Barbara Wallraff. (San Diego: Harvest, 2000)

The Heritage Book of English Usage. (Boston: Houghton Mifflin, 1996).

On Writing Well, 6th ed. William Zinsser. (New York: HarperCollins, 2001).

Words into Type, 3rd ed. (Upper Saddle River, N.J.: Prentice Hall, 1974).

The American Language, 4th ed., with Supplements 1 and 2. H.L. Mencken. (New York: Knopf, 1962).

Woe Is I: The Grammarphobe's Guide to Better English in Plain English. Patricia T. O'Connor. (New York: Putnam, 1996).

Here are some additional reference books for writers:

Howard Lauther's Complete Punctuation Thesaurus of the English Language. (Boston: Branden, 1991).

Random House Webster's Word Menu Dictionary Thesaurus Almanac. (New York: Random House, 1998).

The New York Times Almanac. (New York: Penguin). Updated annually.

Time Almanac. (New York: Information Please). Updated annually.

The World Almanic. (New York: World Almanac Books). Updated annually.

Geographica's World Reference. (San Diego: Laurel Glen, 2000).

The New Oxford American Dictionary. (Oxford: Oxford University Press, 2001).

The Oxford American Thesaurus. (New York: Oxford University Press, 1999).

Bartlett's Roget's Thesaurus. (Boston: Little Brown, 1996).

National Geographic Atlas of the World, 7th ed. (Washington: National Geographic, 2001).

■ CULTURE (POP AND OTHERWISE)

Editorial writers should know something about music and be comfortable at a symphony concert, whether the orchestra is playing Beethoven or some composer whose work features only drums, cymbals and whistles. They should be somewhat knowledgeable about art and be comfortable at an exhibit of Monet or a local artist. They should know something about various religions and the divisions among religions, even if they are not comfortable at services that are much different from their own, if they attend them.

Editorial writers may scoff at television as trivial and entertainment-oriented. But nearly every family has at least one television set, and one show may be watched by as many as 60 million Americans. If editorial writers want to know what their fellow citizens do and think about in their leisure hours, they had best watch the tube enough to know what's on. They should watch the network news broadcasts, the talk shows, CNN, a sampling of the cable channels and enough local broadcasts to know the news their readers are getting. They will never know when television is presenting quality programs unless they read *TV Guide* or the daily TV listings. Columns by television critics are worth following.

Much of radio is an intellectual wasteland. News is sketchy, except for all news stations. But writers should know what songs the younger generation and not-so-young generations are listening to. They may never write an editorial about any of the top-40 tunes or country music, but they almost certainly will write about the people who listen to this music. Writers ought to tune in from time to time to the call-in programs.

Public radio and public television offer more intellectual stimulation, with more extensive news coverage and programs on topics worthy of editorial comment. I would guess that many editorial writers listen to "All Things Considered," an hour and a half or more of news, comment and reports on a variety of topics aired on public radio; and that they watch the MacNeil NewsHour on public television.

Writers also need to keep abreast of the movies—not necessarily seeing every major show but making certain they are aware of what is being seen by their readers. And they should follow the newspaper comics. Most comics may be intended for entertainment, but they often provide insights into what is going on in the younger, older or middle generation. Some are works of art. Some carry political messages that are as forthright and controversial as any editorial on an editorial page. Editorial writers should look in on MTV.

■ A NOTE ON PLAGIARISM

This seems an appropriate point to issue a warning about relying too heavily, and carelessly, on material from other sources, since editorial writers rely on newspapers, magazines and the Internet for essential, easily accessible information. Most editorial writers have little time to do original research, especially on national and international issues. They rely on other sources for facts, interpretation and analysis, even for ideas about what to say about an issue. A column by Thomas L. Friedman of the *New York Times* on the Middle East, for example, might provide an editorial writer with enough current information to write an editorial on a Palestinian-Israeli clash, an idea for the approach that the editorial will take and maybe even a suggestion of a conclusion. In this case the writer probably should credit Friedman for information that seems unique to his column. After all, the value of information depends on the reliability of the source. If Friedman's exact words are used, of course, they should be placed in quotes and the source cited. If Friedman's words are paraphrased, the writer should take care: If words are not in quotation marks, it is important to use your own wording, not Friedman's, to make your point.

You might think that, with care, plagiarism would not be an issue. Yet in recent years several writers have been fired for using others' words without attribution. In addressing the issue in *American Journalism Review*, Lori Robertson wrote: "You're on deadline; you don't have time to do the research someone else has already done. . . . It used to be to plagiarize from another publication, you'd have to type the information in letter by letter[;] . . . now [you] cut and paste some words from a Web page you can call up in seconds."[34]

■ CONCLUSION

Perhaps more than anything else, editorial writers must come to editorial writing equipped with curiosity and a good memory. They must want to find out about everything that comes within touch or sight or hearing. Editorial writers who hope to address the human condition must know about that condition in all its aspects. The specific list of books or newspapers or television programs that writers tackle is not as important as the open, searching attitude good writers bring to whatever they approach. If they are restless, energetic and curious, enough material worth examining will come to their attention to keep them on a productive search for information, insight and truth that will last a lifetime.

If what writers find in their quest goes "in one ear and out the other," the time they have spent will have been wasted. Writers must assimilate and remember—or at least remember where they can find what they want. Shakespeare and the Bible may be worth reading and rereading, and so may a few other books. But demands on the time of editorial writers are too great, and life is too short, to have to spend time searching for information and ideas that they should have tucked away in their heads or for materials that they should have at their editorial elbows.

▌ QUESTIONS AND EXERCISES

1. What do you regard as the ideal undergraduate preparation for a potential editorial writer? For a journalist?

2. The American Council on Education for Journalism, the national accrediting agency for journalism schools, is reluctant to allow a school to give more than a minimum number of credit hours for internships because the council considers that most of the journalism credit hours should be earned under close supervision of faculty members. Do you think that this limitation is reasonable? Why or why not?

3. Among the periodicals you are acquainted with, which do you think would prove most beneficial to an editorial writer? Why?

4. What reference books and books on writing do you consider most appropriate for your own personal library?

5. What computerized data bases are available at your school?

Who Is This Victorian "We"?

A good deal of confusion exists among readers, and even among newspaper people, over the identity or identities behind the editorial "we." That confusion is reflected in a humorous piece that *The Masthead* reprinted from *Quill* magazine. It was written by Fred C. Hobson Jr., professor at the University of North Carolina. Here is a portion of it:

> It was not intended this way, but when I started to write we got so pronouly—er, profoundly confused—we changed my mind.
>
> Besides, when we sat down at my typewriter, I first-personally felt singular.
>
> Hopefully now, what I say, you see—in an editorial, why am I we? Enough poetics. Now for how I—er, we—got confused.
>
> We had an interview the other day. It went fine until we wondered if the person I was interviewing were plural too. If so, then I was we and he was they. But if I am we and he is they, then how the hell is *he*?
>
> And should was be were, if I be we? Or is be are, if she be they? . . . .
>
> After all this, I've decided to stick to the editorial I. You should too. After all, there is an old adage . . . we Southerners especially like. . . . You can't legislate plurality.[2]

This confusion did not exist in the days of the popular and populist press in the 19th Century. When the *New York Tribune* published an editorial in the mid-1800s, readers knew who wrote it, or thought they did. Subscribers read the *Tribune* to find out what Horace Greeley had to say, and, if someone else on his staff wrote it, everyone assumed that it expressed Greeley's point of view.

When the days of the great editors began to pass, following the Civil War, it became less clear who was writing the editorials and for whom the editorials spoke. As the era of corporate newspapers emerged, editorial writers retreated anonymously into their ivory towers and took to writing what a publisher or an editorial board asked them to write. When Greeley said "we," he meant "I." When these writers used "we," they may have meant the views of "the publisher, the editor, an editorial board, or even a member of the staff or a newspaper reader who has persuaded the board of the rightness of a certain position."[3] The purpose of this chapter is to discuss who the speakers of editorials are on American newspapers today and to examine competing arguments over whom editorials ought to speak for.

■ THE CASE FOR THE SIGNED EDITORIAL

If you asked casual newspaper readers whether editorials should be signed, probably a majority would say, "Yes. We want to know who wrote the editorial."

The most persistently heard objection to unsigned editorials, and the most frequently heard argument for signed editorials, is that editorials are generally the work of individuals and that, while they may reflect some broad newspaper policies, the thinking and the words that go into them are more important than any general philosophy. A flamboyant argument along these lines, in the form of an attack on "editorial transubstantiation," was made by Sam Reynolds of the *Missoulian* in Missoula, Mont. In Roman Catholic and Eastern Orthodox rites, bread and wine are transubstantiated (or converted) into the body and blood of Christ although their appearance is unchanged. "I view editorial transubstantiation with less awe," he wrote. "Editorial transubstantiation is the basis for editorial anonymity. It is not a miracle; it is nonsense." He argued that "flesh-and-blood human beings" write editorials, and usually it is only one of them who does so. How does the work of a human being become the product of an institution? "The answer must lie in faith, not fact," Reynolds said. Editorial transubstantiation "is merely a lie; a lie eloquently defended by its many priests, but in the end a complete lie."

When Reynolds switched from unsigned to signed editorials he found that he was no longer blamed for editorials that someone else had written and that the advertising staff no longer had to "fend off attacks from persons aroused by my editorials." He also found his editorials had more influence, and he felt that signing editorials was more honest than pretending that editorials represented an institution.[4]

The most elaborate case for signed editorials was a two-part series in *The Masthead* written by Professor Warren G. Bovee of Marquette University.[5] Bovee set out to debunk what he saw as seven myths about editorial anonymity.

The first myth was that newspapers traditionally have run unsigned editorials. Our look into the history of the editorial page in Chapter 1 has shown that anonymity is only about a century old.

The second myth was that editorials represent the views of the paper, not an individual. Bovee argued that, "until the time arrives when editorial positions are decided by the total personnel of a newspaper. . . . it is misleading to attribute those positions to 'The Paper' . . . ." While publishers might set broad guidelines, Bovee likened them to the lines that define "the ball field within which the editorial writers must still decide how to play the game." He said that "editorial writers say more than most publishers would ever think of saying."

The third myth, that editorials represent an editorial conference point of view, could be resolved by all members signing the editorial, he argued.

A fourth myth, that "anonymity is necessary to protect the writer from verbal and physical abuses," Bovee saw as the "real, secret reason" why readers think editors do not sign editorials. His comment was that writers ought to be as subject to "phone calls, crank letters, crosses burned on the lawn and stones thrown through picture windows" as readers whose signed letters also appear on editorial pages. (My own experience is that this fear of personal abuse figures minimally in editorial anonymity. Most editorial writers I know would appreciate more public recognition.)

A fifth myth is that, if an editorial is signed, it becomes only a personal article or column. But Bovee contended that signed pieces by William Randolph Hearst and Jenkin Lloyd Jones were regarded as editorials.

As to a sixth myth, that unsigned editorials carry more weight, Bovee argued that the impact depends more on what the editorial says than on who signs it.

To the seventh myth, that there are no good reasons for signing editorials, Bovee replied that signing might help overcome reader mistrust of newspapers, giving writers greater freedom to write. "If the occasion demands it," he said, "the signed piece can be as personal and informal as a love letter, or it can be as formal and impersonal as a doctoral dissertation."

Finally, Bovee argued, when a paper has a number of editorial writers, there are bound to be occasions on which the writers disagree with one another. By allowing each to offer his or her view with a byline, the paper would have a more interesting editorial page.

A case for using initials, at least sometimes, was offered by Robert Schmuhl, associate professor of American studies at the University of Notre Dame.[6] His interest in identifying writers grew out of his students' reports that they found editorials "bland and boring." One answer to "Why?" was: "It's as though there's no one behind what's being said."

"Initialing editorials provides an authorial recognition in an understated yet useful way," Schmuhl wrote. "The writer receives credit for composing the editorial, while the finished product appears in a manner quite distinct from a bylined column or even a signed editorial."

If there is a trend, it is away from signed editorials. The *Missoulian* no longer uses signed editorials. In 1996, the Vancouver, Wash., *Columbian* had begun attaching the name of the editorial writer to the end of an editorial, followed by "for the editorial board." On September 11, 2001, however, an editorial about the events of that day was not signed. *Columbian* editor Lou Brancaccio argued that "An individual's name should not be attached to what should be our collective voice on this enormous event." A few months later, the newspaper changed its policy. "A signed editorial puts far too much attention on the writer of the editorial," Brancaccio told readers, "and not enough attention on what it really is: the combined thoughts of a newspaper's editorial board."[7]

■ THE CASE FOR THE UNSIGNED EDITORIAL

Surveys that show that a large majority of editorials are published anonymously suggest that most newspapers' owners and publishers want their editorials to speak for someone or something other than an individual writer. One survey found that more than 70 percent of 178 editors and editorial writers said they never signed editorials. Sixteen percent said they signed them occasionally; 14 percent signed regularly. More signatures appeared in smaller than in larger papers.[8] My guess is that the percentage is lower than that now.

One reason advanced for unsigned editorials is that, even when written by a specific editorial writer, they reflect policy set by the paper's owner or the publisher. Robert U. Brown, editor and publisher of *Editor & Publisher,* asked:

"[W]hose name should be put on the editorial when the owner-publisher—whose prerogative cannot be questioned—says 'tomorrow we will endorse such-and-such candidate and I want a strong editorial endorsing him'?"[9]

William Randolph Hearst once reminded an editor on the *New York American* that the editorials that Hearst wrote "are written to outline policies of the paper to be pursued at every opportunity thereafter until rescinded. . . . Will you please so regard them and will you please keep a scrapbook of them, and let the scrapbook serve as a guide to editorial writers?"[10] He wanted to make it clear that the unsigned editorials reflected his opinions. Of course Hearst also wrote signed editorials, often printed on the front page.

For a time on the *Chicago Tribune*, both Robert McCormick and Joseph Medill Patterson served, in effect, as publishers. The cousins alternated control of the editorial page each month. For example, in 1914, as World War I approached, the conservative McCormick might editorialize in favor of a deep waterway to the Gulf of Mexico and military preparedness as a defense against becoming embroiled in wars outside the hemisphere. The next month, the more liberal Patterson might write about what McCormick biographer Richard Norton Smith described as "the alleged racial advantages enjoyed by German militarism and the need to redistribute American wealth and guard against the proliferation of unearned fortunes by enacting heavy inheritance taxes."[11] The unsigned editorials reflected the policies of the publishers, but readers must have been confused.

With the current trend toward group ownership, publisher domination of editorial pages may be waning. In a survey, three-quarters of editorial writers on group-owned newspapers reported that owners or publishers exerted little or no influence in determining editorial policy, although only a quarter of writers on family or independent newspapers said the same of the owners and publishers. The survey also revealed a widening gap between publishers' and editorial writers' political views.[12] In another survey, 85 percent of group editors reported that they never consulted with group headquarters before taking a controversial stand, while 71 percent of writers on independent papers said they consulted with owners.[13] A *Masthead* symposium found that people at 11 out of 12 group newspapers surveyed reported that editorial policies were set at the local level.[14]

There are exceptions. Shortly after CanWest Global Communications acquired 136 Canadian newspapers in 2001, the new owners announced that each week all 14 of its big-city newspapers would run the same national editorial, sent out from CanWest headquarters in Winnepeg. The announcement drew protests from Canadian journalists and from the National Conference of Editorial Writers (which has Canadian members). The NCEW said prescribed editorials were "likely to backfire with readers who are accustomed to editorials on national and international subjects that take account of the diversity of views in their communities."[15]

If an increasing number of editorials do not reflect policies of the owners, and perhaps not even those of the publishers, for whom do they speak?

The most common explanation for unsigned institutional editorials is that they express more than one person's opinion. *Editor & Publisher*'s Brown pointed out that in many cases an editorial is not the product of one writer's opinion "but the amalgam of thought pounded out in an editorial conference of several people." He wondered what purpose it would serve to attach to the editorial "the name of the technician (a skilled editorial writer, albeit) who was assigned to express in words the agreed-upon thought or policy?"[16]

The opinion might be a general one worked out over time among writers on a paper, or it might be worked out on a single issue during a morning editorial conference. In any case the writer would be expressing a combination of ideas. It might then make as much sense to put every staff member's name on the editorial as that of the actual writer.

Sometimes the actual writing of an editorial will end up being the work of more than one person. Most editorials must pass through an editor or a publisher before they go into print. Since the editor or the publisher has the final say, the end product may be slightly, or greatly, different from the original version. Whose name, or names, should go on in this case? The original writer might not want to be identified with the editorial after the editor or the publisher has made substantial changes.

Sometimes institutional editorials are explained as something more than the sum of the opinions of the members of the editorial page staff. "Editorials express the opinion of an institution, sometimes older than the writer," a Florida editor argued in response to a bill in the Florida Legislature that would have required editorial writers to sign their names.[17] "Editorial writers come and go. . . . But The Paper stays in the community for decades, through depression and prosperity," another editor wrote.[18]

Some defenders contend that unsigned editorials carry more weight with readers because they are not just the personal opinion of an individual. "A signed editorial carries about as much punch as a letter to the editor," Ann Merriman of the *Richmond* (Va.) *News Leader* wrote in arguing that signed editorials have no place under the masthead of a newspaper's editorial page, "even though it would be a good thing if every editorial were written as if it were to be signed."[19]

What about the one-person editorial page staff where it is fairly obvious who is writing the editorials? When Michael J. Birkner took over as editorial writer for the *Concord* (N.H.) *Monitor,* he wrote a bylined column introducing himself. He explained that he would become the "anonymous voice" that henceforth would appear every day in the upper-left-hand corner of the opinion page. "The anonymous voice representing the opinion of this newspaper is, of course, not truly anonymous," he wrote. "A fallible, flesh and blood person can be found behind the 600 or so words that fill the editorial space every day. . . . The editorial 'we,' in this case, is me."[20]

■ EDITORIAL BOARDS

On a number of newspapers, probably a growing number, the editorial "we" is an editorial board. In some cases it remains anonymous to readers, but in other cases the masthead on the editorial page identifies the names and positions of board members. The makeup of boards varies widely. In some instances the board is limited to members of the editorial page staff. Some boards include an editor with responsibility for both news and editorial departments, the publisher (or general manager) or representatives of other departments of the newspaper. In some instances not all staff members who write editorials are included on the board. Some newspapers have experimented with asking people outside the newspaper to serve on editorial boards. (See "Bringing the Community Aboard" in Chapter 19, "Innovations in Design and Content.")

The main purpose of an editorial board is to set general editorial policy. In addition, a board might determine editorial stands on major issues and decide on editorial endorsements. The power that boards exert over the day-to-day editorials varies greatly from paper to paper. Meetings may be formal or informal, regular or irregular.

Richard T. Cole, a professor of public relations, has suggested that the editorial board is a "great charade" or at least a "polite fiction" on most newspapers. Citing the two major dailies in Detroit, he wrote, "Neither has a formal editorial board, although I would venture to say I could introduce you to dozens of politicians, business, labor, association and public relations leaders who would say they have appeared before them. There are no voting members, no quorums, no amendments, no regular meetings, no public notice. Editorial chiefs assemble colleagues and staff to hear a case. My guess is that if an important person insists on meeting the editorial board, the meeting gets called an 'editorial board meeting,' and the innocent fiction lives on. Long live the editorial board."[21] My experience, however, is that editorial boards on most mid-sized to large newspapers operate much more formally and have more input into editorial policy-making than the boards Cole was talking about. (See "Sitting in on an Editorial Conference" in Chapter 8, "The Editorial Page Staff.")

Sometimes the first-person plural in an editorial can be confusing or amusing. Examples of both occurred in an editorial in the Eugene, Ore., *Register-Guard* about a local young woman who was among the first women admitted to Virginia Military Institute. The editorial began this way: "At 17, many of us would have told Beth Hogan: 'You can have it.'" Readers might wonder whether the newspaper has so many editorial writers that it can refer to "many of us." Of course, on second thought, most people will recognize that "us" means readers as well as editorial writers (or even people in general). Later, however, the editorial uses "we" to refer to the newspaper: "We hope she's also physically, mentally and emotionally tough." Then comes, to my mind at least, a humorous image: "We would no more attend VMI than we would bungee-jump off the U.S. Bank building in downtown Eugene."[22] Who is this "we" that declines to bungee jump? It's hard to imagine a *newspaper* jumping. It's also hard to imagine an entire editorial page staff jumping (maybe holding hands together as they go down?). More seriously, the reference suggests that more than one person wrote the editorial. Of course, an editorial may have been edited or modified by one or more persons before it reaches print, but most editorials are *written* by one person.

■ A COMPROMISE— BYLINED ARTICLES AND COLUMNS

Some of the fire may have been taken out of the debate over signed editorials by an increasing use of articles and columns bearing the names of editorial writers. Publishers have been able to give their writers public recognition and increased opportunities to express their individual views without giving up the principle of the institutionalized editorial. One survey of editorial writers found that almost all of them wrote signed articles, as contrasted with signed editorials, at least on occasion.[23] In another survey 30 percent of editorial writers said they were using a more personal writing style.[24]

The advantages most cited in the survey were that signed articles help make the editorial page more human, allow for more casual and informal writing and provide more space than editorials for background or firsthand accounts, especially about local matters. Less often mentioned was the function of the signed article as an expression of a writer's views that might be at variance with the paper's editorial policy. This function can provide an outlet for frustrated editorial writers, but it also can cause problems. Some publishers may be willing to allow writers to express contrary opinions; some publishers may not. Some publishers may be willing to allow writers to disagree on some issues but not on others.

Most publishers probably would have no objection to the balance between signed and unsigned pieces that we maintained on the *Columbian,* in Vancouver, Wash. In my later years there, when three of us were writing for the editorial page, I urged other writers to write bylined articles and on occasion to write pro-con articles, with each person signing one of the articles. We did not use those articles to express opinions directly opposed to the official editorial policy, but through the use of the byline we gained a greater feeling of editorial freedom for ourselves.

If most newspapers have been reluctant to give up the anonymous editorial "we," they have at least largely abandoned the "we" in personal columns and in obvious references to individuals. The change in philosophy on this point can be illustrated by the case of David V. Felts, who wrote a personal column for half a century for the Lindsay-Schaub newspapers. After his retirement Felts wrote an article for *The Masthead* in which he said: "I chose to use first-person plural 'we' in order to avoid the capital I, which seemed at the time . . . to suggest a vanity I did not care to confess, or an arrogance I would deny. So I rejected Teddy Roosevelt's 'I' and instead went along with Queen Victoria's 'We.'" However, Felts acknowledged, logical extension of the "editorial we" can be embarrassing and even ridiculous. He recalled that on one occasion a radio disc jockey, who was a friend of his, quoted from his column. Felts wrote: "I had written, so he read, 'When we stepped on the bathroom scales this morning. . . .' Then my friend observed: 'Oh, well, couples who weigh together, stay together.'" Felts then wrote: "Should I someday be assigned to one of those golden typewriters in the great city room in the sky to write celestial chit-chat, I will use the first person singular pronoun, even if only a modest, chastened lower-case i. Queen Victoria probably will not be amused, but Teddy Roosevelt surely will be 'dee-lighted.'"[25]

There is no historical evidence, or even a suggestion, that Horace Greeley could have done what Dave Felts did—look back years later and laugh at a ridiculous use of "we." Greeley's editorials abounded with "we's." In 1846, for example, Greeley was recalling the first election in which he had taken an interest, the presidential race of 1824: "We were but thirteen when this took place."[26]

■ PERSONAL EXPERIENCES

In my 12 years on the *Columbian,* we ran editorials that were not signed, presumably to indicate to readers that they represented the opinions of the newspaper, not just one person. But I would have counted myself as among those who did not consult with the owners in most cases. My co-publishers and I had spent considerable time, before they hired me, sounding out each others' views. When they decided we were compatible, they, in effect, handed me the editorial "we" to use as I wished (subject of course to cancellation at any time they thought we should go our separate ways). On occasion the publishers were not wholly pleased with what I had written, but for the most part they kept silent. At one point one of the publishers thought the paper should be taking a stronger stand in favor of legalizing marijuana, but he made no attempt to change the policy. On another occasion I found out (several months later) that this publisher had not been in sympathy with the paper's strident opposition to plans to expand Portland International Airport onto a square mile of fill in the Columbia River. But he had made no effort to soften or change our editorial stand.

You learn who the real "we" is during elections, especially presidential ones. In the 1972 election my publishers had their minds set on endorsing Richard Nixon for re-election, and neither the other editorial writer on the paper nor I could budge them from that decision. We argued for no endorsement, since we saw neither Nixon nor George McGovern as meriting our support. I wrote an editorial pointing out the weaknesses of both candidates, but the publishers wouldn't consider it. I suggested that it be published as a signed article elsewhere on the editorial page. The publishers said no; readers might be confused by conflicting viewpoints on the page. Neither the other writer nor I was required to write the Nixon editorial. A semi-retired former managing editor, who had written editorials over the years, accepted the assignment.

The only other disagreement over who "we" was in those 12 years also involved an election, this one for a local judgeship. The publishers had their candidate. Two other editorial writers and I preferred another candidate, although we would have settled for kind words for both. In this instance the publishers agreed to look at an editorial that said either candidate would be a good judge. What emerged in print, however, was an editorial, using many of the words I had written, that added praise for the publishers' choice and a firm conclusion backing their candidate. That was one occasion when it would have been impossible to have put one person's name on an editorial.

■ CONCLUSION

The pendulum that once swung so far from the personal journalism of Horace Greeley to the anonymity of the corporate newspaper has begun to swing back. A few newspapers publish signed or initialed editorials. Many more promote the identities of editorial writers by encouraging signed articles and columns and by listing their names on mastheads. Some writers are allowed to express opinions contrary to their newspapers' official policies.

Editorial writers are getting out of their offices and becoming better known in their communities. Editorial writers are also strengthening their positions on editorial boards. Editors on group newspapers think they have more independence from management in setting editorial policy than do editors on independent papers. On all papers, personal expertise provides the best opportunity for editorial writers to achieve stronger and more public voices. In an era of complex issues, writers who know what they are talking about stand a good chance of convincing not only their readers but also their editors and publishers. They stand a good chance of getting a piece of the editorial "we."

Whether editorials are signed or unsigned, newspapers perform a service to their readers—and bolster their own credibility—when they spell out exactly who determines editorial policy. Readers should have the right to know who is telling them what to think and what to do.

In even the most compatible relationships between editorial writers and publishers, writers are almost certain to find out from time to time that, as smart and knowledgeable as they think they are, they are not the final bosses.

If they have too many disagreements, they need to find other jobs or try some other lines of work.

I asked students in one of my editorial writing classes about the types of disagreement they thought they could tolerate with a publisher. Almost to a person, they said they would quit if asked to write an editorial contrary to their opinions on apartheid or abortion, but they generally would not quit because of disagreement over a president, a local judge or a school bond measure. "I don't think that editorials endorsing presidential candidates really make that much impact on the voters," one student said, but on abortion she would tell her publisher that, because of her "religious belief and moral attitudes, I could not write an editorial that supported taking away legalized abortion." She said she would ask "very nicely" to have someone else write it, and "take the consequences of my actions."[27]

■ QUESTIONS AND EXERCISES

1. Try to find a newspaper with signed or initialed editorials and read them for three or four days. Compare them in terms of tone and style with unsigned editorials on the same subjects published in other newspapers. Do you think that readers would respond differently to these editorials?

2. Look through a number of editorial and op-ed pages of papers in your area. Try to find bylined opinion articles by editorial staff members. Do these articles express opinions that differ from the papers' editorials? Analyze how a reader is likely to respond to specific editorials and opinion articles that express different views.

3. Select an editorial with which you disagree and write a signed opinion piece expressing your view that would be suitable to publish alongside the editorial.

4. Select several editorials that use the editorial "we" in referring to the newspaper's opinion. Does the "we" clearly convey the impression of a corporate opinion behind the editorial? Rewrite the sentences to make the same point without the use of "we."

5. Can you find a column in which the writer refers to himself or herself with the Victorian "we"? Could "I" have been used just as well?

6. Write a letter to an editorial writer on one of the papers in your area to ask about specific instances in which he or she and the editor or publisher might have disagreed on issues. How were the disagreements resolved? Did the writer end up producing an editorial he or she disagreed with? Was he or she allowed or encouraged to write a dissenting opinion? How often and on what kinds of issues has disagreement occurred?

7. Can you uncover, perhaps by reading *Editor & Publisher*, instances in which editorial writers have resigned or moved to noneditorial positions because of disagreement over editorial policy?

Relations with Publishers

Editorial-page editors and their publishers should fight. How else can a paper consistently come up with good editorials? "Good" in the sense of researched, definitive, you-can-tell-where-we-stand editorials. Arguing helps clarify positions and quickly knocks down ones that are poorly defended.

—MEG DOWNEY,
POUGHKEEPSIE (N.Y.) *JOURNAL* [1]

When they drew up the Bill of Rights in the late 1780s, the Founding Fathers did not have to worry about whether they intended freedom of the press to apply to publishers or to editors because most of the printers who produced periodicals, books, pamphlets and handbills were owner-editors. The authors of the First Amendment anticipated, in the words of Hugh B. Patterson Jr. of the *Arkansas Gazette,* "that the editor would most likely be the owner whose resources as well as reputation would be at stake; that newspapers would be vigorous critics and advocates on public questions; that newspapers would generally be locally owned and controlled; and that readers would have available from different publications a variety of views, sometimes directly competitive, from which to choose, whether the question was local, regional or national in scope."[2]

Today the editor and the owner (or publisher) most often are not the same person. With the demise of the owner-editor, the relationship between editor and publisher became what Bernard Kilgore called "a new kind of problem." Kilgore experienced the problem from both sides, as editor and then later publisher of the *Wall Street Journal.* "The question which somebody is likely to ask," Kilgore said, is "whether publishers are necessary."[3] In any other industry, he said, the job parallel to that of publisher would be clear: He or she would hire and fire. But in the newspaper business, "that's where we get into all the trouble. . . . A publisher just does not hire and fire editors because our business is not that kind of business." The difference is that the product a newspaper sells is "a completely intangible thing." Newspaper people should remind themselves that all the physical plant and machinery around the newspaper business provide only the package or container of the product, "just something to wrap up the ideas that editors have" and carry these ideas to the public. But the newspaper business has become "a great big manufacturing operation and great big selling operation," Kilgore said. Consequently, "the general management of a newspaper has more and more come to be regarded as a job for a manufacturer or a salesman, and the editorial function . . . has tended to become a secondary consideration."[4]

How prophetic those words proved to be! Kilgore's comments appeared in *The Masthead* in 1954. Foresighted though he was, even he would be amazed today at how the ownership and management of the newspaper industry has changed in a half century. Cities with two newspapers (let alone cities with more) have almost entirely become one-newspaper cities. Local ownership has become rare. The largest ownership groups continue to expand, seemingly without limit. Barriers to cross-media ownership in local communities are being breached. Newspaper and other media companies are being taken over by corporations concerned primarily with other business interests. Corporations are going public, selling stocks and bonds to investors who are primarily interested in the rate of return on their money. All these changes have foreboding implications for a local or locally owned newspaper.

LOCAL OWNERSHIP

The era of the local family newspaper may look rosier in retrospect than it actually was. Many publishers did not make enough profit to produce good newspapers. Some owner-publishers did not know what good journalism was, and some didn't care.

They could do what they wanted with their newspapers without worrying about satisfying a bigger boss somewhere else. The publisher-editor who runs the whole show "in theory . . . is the happiest of mortals, if he can keep his separate selves from warring with one another," Donald L. Breed, editor-publisher of the Freeport, Ill., *Journal-Standard*, wrote.[5] The second happiest may be the editorial page editor (or editorial writer) who works (and gets along well) with a local owner-publisher. Ideally, as it was in my case, the editorial page editor (or writer) would have been hired after extensive conversations that had assured both publisher and editorial writer that their views were sufficiently compatible to result in a congenial, trustful relationship. With the publisher's office only a couple of doors down the hall, the writer had amble opportunity to keep touch with the boss and get an immediate response to any questions about editorial policies.

Of course a close-by, hands-on publisher also can produce some unpleasant surprises from time to time. In a *Masthead* symposium titled "Problems from on high," Michael Zuzel (who later went to the *Columbian* in Vancouver, Wash.) described what he called his "earliest exposure to the ugly exercise of the publisher's prerogative": a spiked editorial that had been "mildly critical of a local group of business leaders who had been pushing for development of a suburban shopping mall."[6] Ed Williams of the *Charlotte* (N.C.) *Observer* described the "first disagreement I'd had with a publisher over a major endorsement" when the publisher insisted on endorsing for re-election a U.S. senator who had not been "in tune" with the paper's editorial positions. Considerable efforts to dissuade the publisher led to a nonendorsement. With tongue in cheek, Williams commented, "We compromised by not firing the publisher. And he didn't fire us."[7]

GROUP OWNERSHIP

Editorial writers who have been reasonably content working with publishers on locally owned papers have suddenly found themselves employed by out-of-town publishers from out-of-town groups who come with different editorial ideas.

Group ownership has come to most daily newspapers—and, in recent years, to weeklies as well. (In the third edition of this book, I cited five locally-owned family newspapers among the best newspapers with which I was personally acquainted: the *Free Lance–Star* in Fredericksburg, Va.; the *Riverside Press-Enterprise* in California; the *Register-Guard* in Eugene, Ore.; the *Columbian* in Vancouver, Wash., and the *Daily News* in Longview, Wash. Since then, two of the five, the *Press-Enterprise* and the *Daily News,* have been sold to groups.)

Publishers of most group newspapers these days are not home-grown. Often they are sent in for a few years, then transferred elsewhere. Another publisher from another community is brought in. Many group publishers are strictly business people.

A survey of newspaper editors, sponsored by the American Society of Newspaper Editors, found that editors who worked for a group thought they had better career opportunities and greater access to shared ideas, financial resources and outside experts, while editors on independent papers had larger newsroom budgets, closer involvement with their communities, less bureaucracy and "a tendency to be peculiar."[8]

This survey and an earlier one under the same sponsor suggest group ownership may offer some advantages for editors and editorial writers. The first survey found that, before taking a stand on a controversial issue, 85 percent of group editors said they did not consult with group headquarters, while only 27 percent of independent editors said they did not consult with their owners.[9] In the more recent survey, 39 percent of group editors said they had consulted the publishers (or group headquarters) six or more times during the preceding 12 months before taking a controversial stand, compared to 50 percent of independent editors.[10] These figures suggest that out-of-town ownership and publishers who are not oriented toward journalism values may provide opportunities for editorial writers on group newspapers to emerge less cautiously and more outspokenly from publishers' offices and editorial conference rooms.

A survey conducted by David Demers, however, suggested that it was not group ownership but the corporate form of the organization that accounted for the relative freedom to set editorial policy. In corporate newspapers, he concluded, the owners and top managers were "more insulated" because they generally came from out of town and stayed for relatively brief periods; their orientation was more to the corporation than to the community. He also suggested the decisions made by corporate editors tended to be "more heavily influenced by professional norms and values, which place a higher premium on truth and criticism than on local parochial interests."[11] Demers also found that corporate papers run more editorials and letters, carry more staff-written pieces and publish more editorials critical of mainstream groups.[12]

Somewhat similar results were found in a survey of editors of independent and group-owned newspapers, who were asked to identify what they saw as the principal editorial roles of their newspapers. Those who conducted the survey were surprised to find that differences were less between independent and group newspapers than among large, medium and small groups. Editors with the larger groups more often identified their newspaper's editorial role as "adversary," "global interpreter" and "critical watchdog." The surveyors interpreted the findings as suggesting that, as news organizations increase in size and prominence, their "editorial orientations" become increasingly activist. They concluded that this tendency could be good or bad depending on whether the larger organizations "choose to harness their structurally determined editorial activism to promote their own ends or to serve the public interest."[13]

If these studies are to be believed, there is some good news: Perhaps editorial pages, under group ownership, will become more aggressive and more critical. But it seems ironic that this supposed benefit has arisen because the new managers are more concerned about corporate issues than local affairs.

■ FINANCIAL EMPHASIS

An editorial page can be restricted as much by financial as editorial restraints. When a newspaper is locally owned, the publisher can determine the profit levels that seem proper and desirable. But with group newspapers, budgets and requirements for profit margins tend to be set at group headquarters. In addition, with groups and major newspapers going public and selling stock on the market, owners are becoming even more concerned about profits. If profits lag, the stock is likely to fall in value. If the newspaper ventures into an area of controversy in its news or editorial columns—and perhaps stakes its reputation in tackling a sensitive public issue—the paper's stock may skid in value. As early as 1970, Robert T. Pittman of the *St. Petersburg* (Fla.) *Times* perceived "a basic conflict" between an editor's responsibility to readers and the responsibility of an investor-owned newspaper to its stockholders: "What's good for Media General stock isn't necessarily what's good for the country."[14]

Defenders of groups contend that ownership of several papers allows groups to use their combined resources to stand up to the pressures of advertisers or other special interests. That may be true, if the owners are sufficiently dedicated to the newspaper business that they are willing to forgo some profits while the paper fights its battle. But if the publishers and groups must answer to stockholders who are interested in profit, not journalism, it may not be possible to remain so idealistic.

A 2001 study conducted at the University of Iowa found that that is exactly what is happening as newspaper owners become more concerned about stockholders than readers. According to the researchers, "Operating margins, which have historically been in the 10 to 15 percent range for newspapers, now range between 20 and 30 percent in the newspapers owned by the public companies."[15] To maintain this level of profit, the study found that the companies' short-range strategy was to cut news personnel, who "are often seen as not contributing to revenues or margins."[16] In accord with earlier studies, researchers found that the large size of corporations often resulted in "decentralized control over editorial content, but within the framework of very strict and increasingly aggressive financial controls that constrain choices about content . . . ."[17] The study also concluded that offering stock and other financial incentives to news and editorial personnel "over time may compromise the independence of news judgments from financial self-interest and the firm's strictly financial objectives." With increased emphasis on readers as advertising consumers rather than as news consumers, newspapers were found to be deliberately cutting back on circulation in lower-income inner cities and in outlying areas.[18] These practices raise the question of whether these newspapers will continue to serve as truly *community* newspapers or will orient themselves to only the most affluent and most convenient to reach.

"So what can editorial page editors do in the face of financial pressures, whatever the source, that affect their pages?" asked Gilbert Cranberg, a co-author of the 2001 study. In an article in *The Masthead*, he suggested they ask three questions:

- "Is pagination taking time from editing, research and writing?" (Pagination, or page makeup, was once done in separate composition departments. Now, it is often done by news and editorial staff.)
- "Is your paper shortchanging readers in the inner city?"
- "Do incentives support good journalism?"

"Editorial page editors are a nosy lot who do not hesitate to tell others how to run their businesses," Cranberg wrote. "They should be as willing to speak up in private to management in behalf of quality journalism as they are to sound off to readers on their pages."[19]

One of the first examples of what might happen when editorial and news decisions are driven by concern over stock prices occurred at the *Washington Post* in 1971. On June 15, publisher Katharine Graham had bought the first share of Washington Post Company stock at $24.75. When the stock was offered to the general public the same day, the price moved up to an encouraging $26. Two days later she had to decide whether the *Washington Post* would publish the Pentagon Papers, a 47-volume, top-secret study of how the United States had become increasingly involved in the Vietnam War. (The Papers had been leaked to the *New York Times* as well as the *Washington Post*.) Although the study did not relate directly to the Nixon administration, then in power, some of Graham's advisors feared that the federal government would try to shut down the newspaper if the papers were published. "The timing . . . could not have been worse," David Halberstam wrote in *The Powers That Be*. "In addition to everything else, there was one little clause in the legal agreement for the sale of the stock that said that the sale could be canceled if a catastrophic event struck the paper."[20] In her autobiography, *Personal History*, Graham said that she realized that "I would be risking the whole company on this decision. . . . Frightened and tense, I took a gulp and said, 'Go ahead, go ahead, go ahead. Let's go. Let's publish.'"[21] The first article appeared on June 18. The federal government immediately obtained court injunctions against the papers.

Fortunately, as matters turned out, she made a sound decision. The U.S. Supreme Court, by a vote of 6-3, removed injunctions issued against the two newspapers, allowing them to resume publication.

Unfortunately there are not many Katharine Grahams who are willing to run such risks. As the University of Iowa study found, not many publicly traded companies are willing to forego 20 to 30 percent profits for the sake of the editorial product.

■ THE PUBLISHER'S ROLE

Weighing on the publisher's mind almost as heavily as making a profit is maintaining "harmonious relations" among employees. Publishers like to run smooth operations and generally do not like to employ personalities that clash. Publishers dislike friction between news and advertising or between news and editorial operations. Publishers tend to subscribe to the philosophy expressed in *The Economics of the American Newspaper*, by Jon G. Udell, which suggests to news and editorial people that the entire newspaper staff is in this together and that no one can benefit without everyone helping. "So why doesn't everyone cooperate and forget differences of opinion and interest?"[22]

One threat to the why-can't-everyone-be-friends atmosphere is posed by the publisher's responsibility to negotiate with labor unions. Most editorial writers do not have to worry about conflicts with the publisher in contract negotiations, since most are excluded from newsroom organized labor groups. But publishers who are worried about strike threats or angered by what they see as an unfair tilt of federal or state labor relations laws may hold strong opinions about what editorial writers ought to say about organized labor. More than one newspaper has departed from its generally moderate-to-liberal social philosophy when the subject of labor has arisen.

Since publishers' first concerns are usually to function successfully in the economy, they are also likely to have firm views on business topics. "There is one special interest always present, and that is the pro-capitalist bias of a newspaper," publisher-editor Donald L. Breed wrote. "Privately owned and operated newspapers are expressions of newspaper enterprise, and they must make a profit to survive. . . . Therefore, it must be taken for granted that American newspapers will support the free enterprise system."[23] But the free enterprise system has been made substantially less free by government support and protection of business, direct and indirect government intervention in the economy and increasing control by huge corporations. Commenting intelligently on the economy these days requires a lot more information and sophistication than it used to. Publishers may be up-to-date on economic matters affecting their own businesses and fellow local merchants. They may also be familiar with property and income taxes, state and federal health and safety requirements, unemployment and workmen's compensation, and perhaps local zoning and building regulations. While experiences in these areas may provide publishers with some insights for editorial comment, they need to recognize that they have special interests in these matters.

If publishers have contributions to make in evaluating economic issues, they probably have fewer to make in other areas. It is not that publishers, given time and resources, are not smart enough to hold their own with editorial writers. But most publishers are likely to have neither the time nor the frame of mind for knowledgeable editorial writing. They are often hard-pressed to find time to read their own newspapers thoroughly. (One of my publishers, acknowledging this difficulty, asked that his staff forewarn him about any news or editorial items that were likely to bring him a phone call or personal comment.) Publishers simply do not have the time to be editorial writers. Therein lie the makings of both conflict and a good working relationship between publisher and writer.

If publishers try to act as editorial writers, they are likely to drive the editorial staff out the door, up the wall or into the closet. The result will be a weak, submissive staff that stands no chance of putting out a vigorous editorial page. On the other hand, if publishers allow themselves to be too busy to think about the editorial page or to discuss ideas and issues with the writers, conflict is likely to occur at some point. The publisher should exercise leadership continuously and cooperatively, rather than intermittently and imperiously. Almost as annoying as having publishers constantly breathing down the necks of editorial writers is having them descend suddenly and unpredictably into the editorial department.

Surveys of publishers and opinion-page editors found substantial publisher participation—but not necessarily control—in editorial policy-making. Sixty-two percent of the publishers said they attended editorial page conferences at least once or twice a week. Sixty-six percent said they express their views at these conferences most of the time. Forty-five percent said they discuss social, economic and political issues with executives once a day; another 33 percent once a week. Fifty-nine percent said they had the final decisions on editorials, but the same percentage said they were "not concerned" or "only a little concerned" that the writing of editorial page staff members may not be consistent with the newspaper's editorial stands.[24] As noted in Chapter 5, "Who Is This Victorian 'We'?" about three-quarters of editorial writers on group-owned newspapers reported that owners and publishers exerted little or no influence in determining the priority given to editorial topics.[25]

One of my publishers used to say that he expected disagreements to arise between us, although he expected me to convince him of my point of view most of the time, since I (presumably) knew more about the subject than he did. That usually proved to be the case, or at least he let me think so. The degree of freedom that individual editors achieve thus lies partly within their own control. As author Robinson Scott has said, editors owe whatever freedom they enjoy to "force of character. . . . knowledge and the strength of [their] convictions."[26]

GETTING ALONG WITH PUBLISHERS

Relationships between editors and publishers probably vary as widely as do the personalities of editors and publishers. The relationship depends partly on the rules that are set when a publisher hires an editor. Some publishers and editors are easy to get along with; some are not. Some personalities work better together in an editor-publisher relationship than others. Publishers and editors are almost certain to encounter some differences of opinion. (The survey of publishers and editors mentioned above found that the two groups gave measurably different opinions when asked a series of questions about liberal, conservative and pragmatic issues, but neither group was consistently more liberal or more conservative than the other.)[27]

Disagreeing with the Publisher

The first thing that editors need to recognize is that, even in the most congenial relations, an editor and a publisher are bound to disagree from time to time. "Editorial-page editors and their publishers should fight," in the opinion of Meg Downey, editorial page editor of the *Poughkeepsie* (N.Y.) *Journal*. "How else can a paper consistently come up with good editorials? 'Good' in the sense of researched, definitive, you-can-tell-where-we-stand editorials. Arguing helps clarify positions and quickly knocks down ones that are poorly defended."[28] David Holwerk of the *Lexington* (Ky.) *Herald-Leader* made the point more picturesquely: Conflicts are not inevitable, he said, "if either you or your publisher is a brain-dead cretin who doesn't give a fresh-frozen's rat's rump what your paper stands for."[29]

A survey of editorial page writers concluded, however, that communication channels with publishers are "fairly" open. "Not only do editors in all circulation categories indicate a high frequency of opinion exchange at [editorial] conferences with publishers, but they also stress that editors' opinions prevailed in these conferences very frequently."[30]

Of course no editorial page editor wants to be constantly battling with the publisher over policy, if for no other reason than that, when fights go all the way to the mat, the publisher almost always has the authority to win and usually does.

In a *Masthead* symposium on "problems from on high," Ed Williams of the *Charlotte Observer* offered six pieces of advice on preventing or avoiding disagreements with publishers:

1. "Get the controversial issues on the table before opinions harden," so that there is time to work disagreements.
2. "Put yourself in the publisher's shoes"; try to understand where the publisher is coming from.
3. "Remember, our job is to inform and persuade—readers, certainly, but also publishers."
4. When you disagree, "your job is to stand up for what you think, not to shut up and follow orders."
5. "When you lose an argument, don't sulk or whine"; recognize that publishers as well as readers "see the priorities differently."
6. "If you disagree on principle, you have a choice: Go along and live to argue another day, or resign. If the disagreement seems to be an anomaly, I'd say stick it out. If you think it reveals a fundamental difference over the newspaper's core values, I'd say resign."[31]

Choosing a Publisher

The first advice for editorial writers is to choose their papers and publishers carefully. Writers need to know enough about the personality of a prospective publisher to have a pretty good idea that they can get along despite disagreements. They need to know enough about the prospective newspaper's editorial policy so that they can, in most cases, feel comfortable writing editorials expressing that policy.

Throughout the country editorial writers looking for jobs may find some middle-of-the-road (apple pie and motherhood) newspapers on which writers of moderate convictions might be able to muddle through a lifetime of editorial writing. Kenneth McArdle of the Chicago *Daily News* may have had these papers in mind when he said, referring to publishers, "Generally speaking, it would be hard to be utterly out of synch with them unless you, yourself, were on the kooky side, because they tend to be rational people."[32] But at least some newspapers, to their credit, have stronger editorial convictions, and, fortunately, so do some editorial writers and would-be writers. Nevertheless, unless a writer's views fall within the middle 50 to 60 percent of the political spectrum, opportunities for signing on with a congenial editorial page are limited.

The task of finding a congenial editorial page may also be more difficult today than in earlier times because journalists don't seem to hop around the country from newspaper to newspaper as much as they once did. They get married, raise families, buy houses and try to find decent school systems in attractive communities. They put their roots into their communities and may develop as deep a concern for them as any publisher. Their concern for and knowledge of their communities, in fact, may go deeper than publishers' because of newspaper groups' practice of moving their publishers around.

Writers may feel they have bigger stakes in their communities than the representatives of ownership do. Such feelings are not likely to ease working relationships with publishers who have different ideas on editorial policy.

Speaking the Publisher's Language

Dialogue helps to keep editors and publishers from suddenly being surprised to learn that they hold differing opinions on important issues. If publishers and editors can talk about issues before they need to make decisions, chances of compromise improve greatly. Bernard Kilgore warned that misunderstandings between publishers and editors are sometimes caused by editors. He suggested that editors should "get into the business side of a newspaper and try to see what the thing is all about."[33] Editors who want a bigger slice of the corporate budget might stand a better chance of succeeding if they could convince the business side that they understood the problems of producing income and holding down costs. On occasion my publishers took several department heads out to solicit new subscriptions. (My principal memory of those occasions was of all the reasons that people had for not taking the paper.) For a greater understanding of the community as well as for purely pragmatic business reasons, editorial writers should keep abreast of circulation and advertising lineage figures. If they have a head for figures, so much the better. (In my experience, journalists and journalism students tend to shy away from anything that sounds like math.) If editorial writers can talk the publisher's and the circulation manager's languages they are more likely to project an image of having their feet on the ground—and stand a better chance of selling their editorial ideas.

Educating Publishers

One of the principal functions of editorial writers may be to educate their publishers. "If the editor is willing to educate everybody, including the world, and foreign countries, then it is also necessary for the publishers and the owners to be educated," Kilgore said.[34] But the writer must educate the publishers with what Hoke Norris of the Chicago *Sun-Times* called "a certain tact—even a tenderness." Norris described an editor friend who saw his function in "the care and feeding" of the publisher: "His publisher always believes that he originates the ideas and holds his own opinions. This is perhaps a harmless deception and it might even save a publisher, on occasion, from making a damn fool of himself."[35] A writer who is more educated and informed than the publisher must handle the boss with special care. Otherwise, the writer may run the risk of making the publisher feel resentful or intimidated rather than favorably impressed. As Frank Taylor of the *St. Louis* (Mo.) *Star-Times* put it, "More than one inferiority complex parades the precincts of publishers."[36]

Publishers might feel less intimidated if they availed themselves of opportunities to keep abreast of current events, took time to dig deeply into local issues or enrolled in a course at a local college. Houstoun Waring, publisher of the *Littleton* (Colo.) *Independent,* warned that it is "only partially effective to educate the reporter and the feature writer if the arteries of the man who calls the tune continue to harden. . . . Publishers may feel they are omniscient, but adult education programs are good for them, too."[37] He had in mind such formal programs as the Nieman Fellowship and other sabbatical opportunities, local press councils and discussions over breakfast with local sources. Nathaniel B. Blumberg, professor of journalism at the University of Montana, recalled press critic "A.J. Liebling's essentially accurate aphorism that without a school for publishers no school of journalism can have meaning."[38] The American Press Institute offers sessions for publishers, but establishing a service-oriented editorial policy for a community, if it is done at all, is likely to rank far down the line on the agenda after more business-related subjects.

Methods generally available to editors for educating publishers, however, are likely to be much less formal. Editors can send memos and background articles (although probably not books) across publisher's desks to help them understand issues before decisions are made, although busy publishers may not find time to read the material. Editors can invite publishers to public meetings, speeches, panel discussions and workshops where a variety of points of views are likely to be aired. Editors can invite publishers to lunch to exchange ideas about what their newspapers should be doing and saying, in a less formal atmosphere than the editorial conference.

Publishers who want a hand in editorial policy should accept as much responsibility as editorial writers to sit and plow through all the material necessary for making intelligent decisions. Publishers also need to understand that editorial writers do not appreciate being descended upon at the last minute, after all the hard work is done, to give an opinion, even if the opinion is a modest one.

To avoid unexpected, last-minute opinions or decision changes, editorial conference members should try to establish the habit of delaying decisions on important matters until all members have aired their opinions and the issue at hand has been fully discussed. Once a person—especially a publisher, who could lose face before employees—declares even a tentative position on an issue, moving off that position becomes difficult. An editorial page staff that anticipates disagreement with the publisher might find it advantageous to meet before the editorial conference to plan a strategy. If the writers anticipate that they will not be able to convince other conference members of their opinion, they might try to agree beforehand on a compromise that they would find acceptable.

Coping with the Publisher's Special Interests

Editorial writers need to be especially sensitive to editorial topics that touch on activities or causes with which the publisher is personally involved. In a survey of editorial page editors, 94 out of 101 reported that their publishers were active in community affairs. Only about a fourth of them (25), however, reported that the publishers' activities had "affected how editorials were written." Several editors said their publishers voluntarily excused themselves from participating in decisions concerning their activities. One editor said the publisher checked with the editorial board before joining boards of local organizations. Another editor said that the publisher would sometimes suggest editorials "but will ask us not to comment on activities he is involved in."[39] Many editors thought publisher involvement was good for the newspaper and for the community. "Those who advocate volunteer involvement and shirk it are guilty of the worst hypocrisy," said one editor. Still, the potential conflict of "boosterism" remained a major concern of the editors.

Phil Duff, executive editor of the Red Wing, Minn., *Republican Eagle*, argued in *The Masthead* that publisher involvement benefits the newspaper and the community, especially in a small community. "There's an inverse proportion at work," he wrote. "The smaller the newspaper and the smaller the town, the more extensively the publisher may legitimately involve himself in civic-political affairs."[40]

Editorial writers on the *Seattle Times* faced the situation of a publisher taking out an ad in the newspaper to state a position on a ballot proposition. Editorial page editor Mindy Cameron recounted that she had found the situation "awkward and confusing." To the *Times* editorial writers the issue was not the content of the ad, since both the ad and the editorials took the same position—against a proposal to end affirmative action programs for women in state and local government and in college and university admissions. One concern was that the editorial page had been established as the place to express the newspaper's opinions. Further, Cameron asked, "What did running ads to reiterate an editorial position (though with fewer words and lots more white space) say about the relative merits of the editorial page vs. paid advertising?" She said that the news reporters and editors, who were trying to maintain "doggedly balanced reporting," found the ad "even more difficult" than the editorial page staff did. Cameron reported: "I did not storm the publisher's office. We agreed to disagree." (Despite the efforts of the *Times*, the initiative was approved by 58 percent at the polls.)[41]

Staff members in Idaho Falls, Idaho, also found themselves in a difficult position when their publisher ran for governor. Editors said that they would treat him like any other candidate and that he would have no role in the newspaper's coverage during the election. But the acting publisher said he did not "like the notoriety" of a publisher running for governor and "wouldn't wish it on anyone." During the election campaign a local communications professor served as an ombudsman and periodically wrote a political-comment column.[42]

How should a writer respond to a special-interest request from a publisher? If the editorial idea is a good one and seems in the interest of the community, the writer should produce it—posthaste. If the request is obviously self-serving or out of character with the paper's policy or contrary to reason and common sense, the editorial writer has a problem. The best course is to dig into the subject, document arguments against writing the editorial and present them to the publisher boldly and positively. Confidence and facts are the best weapons. (I found myself in this spot when a publisher asked me to write an editorial on certain practices of labor unions that offended him. In addition to convincing him that the idea was not a good one, I faced the task of convincing him that I had not intentionally ignored him.) A writer stands a better chance of fending off undesirable requests by confronting the publisher and risking an argument than by ignoring the request. Publishers don't like to be ignored.

Writers who disagree with their publishers or editorial boards might seek to express their dissident opinions in a signed article or column on the editorial or op-ed page. But many publishers and some editors are reluctant to open this avenue for contrary opinions from staff members.

Taking on the Publishers

Several articles in *The Masthead* have suggested that editorial writers as a group "take on" their publishers. One of the first rallying cries came in 1970, from Curtis D. MacDougall, professor of journalism at Northwestern University. He quoted with approval a statement that had been made by one of the (unidentified) founders of the National Conference of Editorial Writers (NCEW) a couple of years earlier: "During our first two decades we have educated ourselves. Now let us devote our energies toward doing the same for our publishers."[43]

Over the years editorial writers have carried a lot of ideas back to publishers from NCEW conferences. At subsequent meetings, writers often report that suggestions that emerged from critique groups were accepted back home and that the editorial pages were better for them. That is one way of bringing the collective enlightenment of editorial writers to bear on publishers. But ideas are not always accepted. Editorial writers on some papers receive criticism for the same deficiencies year after year. When asked why they don't change, the answer is usually that the publisher (or editor) "wants it that way."

An editorial writer once issued a battle cry for the NCEW to wage a full-fledged offensive against publishers. In 1977 Sam Reynolds, then editorial page editor of the *Missoulian* in Missoula, Mont., wrote: "We must lay down standards of what is good in a publisher, and what is bad. We must, as an organization, sharply criticize shabby publisher performance." He called on NCEW to encourage good publisher practices and attack the bad.[44] Reynolds' call for NCEW to "blow the whistle" seemed to go unheeded.

Perhaps editorial writers did not know what they wanted to put into a code of ethics for publishers. A survey of editorial page editors at 101 newspapers found that 56 of their newspapers had ethics codes. In 34 instances the codes applied to the publisher, but only 17 mentioned the publisher's involvement in community activities.[45]

What might a code of ethics for publishers contain? For starters, NCEW members can look at their own Statement of Principles. That statement suggests that a code might emphasize the integrity of the editorial decision-making process—the need for previously agreed-upon procedures to be followed in setting editorial policy. It might contain something like the NCEW statement that the editorial writer "should never write anything that goes against his or her conscience." The Statement also emphasizes that "sound collective judgment can be achieved only through sound individual judgments," suggesting that editorial policy should evolve through discussion, not be imposed from the top. A code might also state that publishers (and editors, for that matter) should participate in editorial decision-making only when they have participated in the information and discussion phases of the process. And as the NCEW Statement does, a code might state that publishers (and editors, too) should refrain from participating in editorial decisions that involve conflicts of interest.

■ THE CASE FOR THE EDITOR

One survey of editorial page editors on 82 of the largest daily newspapers in the U.S. found that more than half (45) reported to a news-side editor, compared to 37 who reported directly to the publisher.[46] This pattern may be changing. In 2002, in an informal poll of editorial writers on NCEW's e-mail discussion group, 13 of 14 who responded said that they reported to the publisher. One said that editorial page staff reported to a higher-ranking editor.[47] Those in the 1989 survey who reported to the publisher tended to argue that their chain of command was better suited to maintaining a wall of separation between news and editorial departments. "If the editorial page is put in charge of an editor who is also in charge of news, that indicates a lack of concern for the opinion function," said one editorial page editor. "It makes it just another so-called function of the newspaper." But those who reported to an editor contended that their structure kept editorials from being tainted by the business side of the newspaper. "The drawback in reporting to the publisher is that in the final analysis the publisher is a businessman," said one respondent.[48]

Whether editorial page editors report to the publisher or an editor, a strong case can be made for the argument that, once editorial page editors get the job, they should be entrusted to carry out the newspaper's editorial policy. Hugh B. Patterson Jr., then publisher of the *Arkansas Gazette*, contended that editorial page editors should be allowed to set policy and that owners and publishers should support them completely. Just as career politicians are generally best suited to hold high public office, he said, so "career newspaper editors are best qualified to run newspaper editorial pages."[49]

Sevellon Brown III, then editor of the *Providence* (R.I.) *Journal-Bulletin*, saw three reasons why "the editor *ought* to be the one—and the only one—to make decisions on editorial policy." First, editors are "relatively uncluttered by other professional duties and responsibilities." Publishers, with all their other duties, can give only limited time and energy to the editorial page. Second, editors have the "closest, broadest touch with the news," one of the primary ingredients in editorial policy-making. Third, editors are best qualified because they are, or ought to be, "*relatively* disinterested, *relatively* uncommitted to any particular cause or faith or point of view."[50]

Yet, when it is necessary to make basic policy and settle disagreements—and in fact to hire the editorial page editor—someone must assume the final authority, and it is a rare newspaper where that final authority does not rest with the publisher, general manager or other representative of ownership. "Ownerships generally last longer than editorships," William H. Heath, then editor-emeritus of the *Haverhill* (Mass.) *Gazette*, once wrote. "Therefore, policy made by ownership is more stable. There is a rock-of-ages quality about a newspaper that is distinguished by editorial policy. This quality strengthens public confidence in the paper."[51]

■ CONCLUSION

Publishers do have the final say on most newspapers, but on many papers editors and editorial writers have more say than they did several years ago. Editorial writing is increasingly regarded as a career, not just a job that a newsperson from some other part of the paper has wandered into at a late stage in his or her working life. The job on many papers is beginning to lose its image as a mouthpiece for the bosses. Publishers are hiring editors and giving them increased editorial freedom. One reason for this new confidence is that editorial writers and editors are better prepared for their jobs. In recent years they have become better educated, more interested in their communities and more willing to speak up for what they know and believe. Knowledgeable, confident writers these days can expect to win a considerable amount of freedom from publishers, at least from those publishers who recognize the value of strong, enlightened editorial pages.

■ QUESTIONS AND EXERCISES

1. If you were a publisher, what role would you choose to play in regard to the editorial page? If you were an editorial page editor, what would you want the role of the publisher to be?

2. Should the role of publisher vary with the size of the newspaper? Should whether a paper is owned locally, by a distant owner or by a group make a difference in the role of the publisher?

3. Judging from the newspapers with which you are acquainted, what chances do you think you would have to sign on with a publisher with wholly compatible views on issues?

4. Among the group-owned newspapers with which you are familiar, have you detected any evidence of control of editorial policy by the group headquarters? Have you seen any evidence of similar editorial policies among newspapers of the same group?

5. What do you think are the most effective ways for an editorial writer to keep a publisher happy and to achieve a maximum sphere of freedom?

6. If editorial writers were "to take on the publishers," as suggested in *The Masthead* articles mentioned in this chapter, what steps might they take?

Relations with the Newsroom

Historically the relationship between the newsroom and the editorial page has been a one-way street. The newsroom produces the news. The editorial writers sit back in Olympian reflection, rearrange their dandruff into new patterns, and then write comments on or interpretations of that news.

—CLIFFORD E. CARPENTER, ROCHESTER (N.Y.) DEMOCRAT AND CHRONICLE [1]

American newspapers have grown out of an early tradition that made no effort to keep editorial views or comment out of the news sections. For the past hundred or more years, most newspaper owners have subscribed to a policy, more or less successfully, to keep editorials and news separate. Most provide separate editorial pages and tell readers that is where newspapers' opinions should go.

Sometimes, intentionally or unintentionally, editorial policies will influence how a news story is written or played in the paper. Sometimes, intentionally or unintentionally, the news side will influence the editorial side. Ideally, news will be written and played in as objective a manner as writers and editors are capable of achieving. Ideally, people on the news side will keep their opinions to themselves, not sharing them with editorial writers, sources or readers. To encourage this separation, most newspapers—certainly large and middle sized ones—have erected a journalistic barrier, if not a physical wall, between their news and editorial departments. In some extreme cases, an editorial writer in a newsroom is viewed as suspiciously as an advertising sales representative.

But times change. One change, as noted in the previous chapter, is that newspaper bosses have begun to subscribe to the philosophy that, because everyone on the paper is in the same business, everyone should understand and help everyone else. Another change is a growing realization, among news and editorial staff members, that they can help each other without threatening the integrity of either of their departments.

A survey of editorial page editors of 82 of the largest newspapers found that 69 (84 percent) saw the need for a wall between news and editorial, but nearly half of those (32) added that such a wall should not rule out communication between the two departments.[2] Reporters can be especially helpful to editorial writers, providing tips, insights, facts and contacts. Unfortunately, because of the tradition mentioned above, jealousy, antipathy or misunderstanding, much of that potential help never gets past the partition that separates the offices.

"In the eyes of some editorial writers," wrote Edward M. Miller of the *Oregonian* of Portland, "the news department is manned by fugitives from the world of intellect. The news department is notable for misjudging the news. It is concerned with trivialities at the expense of Things That Really Matter." To news people, the editorial page is staffed by "fugitives from the world of reality." Editorial writers "commune with God, and do that with considerable reluctance."[3]

Another source of news-editorial trouble is the resentment sometimes felt by news personnel who disagree with a paper's editorial policy, especially policy involving endorsement of candidates. Readers, they contend, assume that editorials speak for the entire journalistic side of the paper (or the entire paper), when in fact editorials represent the views of only a few policy makers. On occasion newsroom people have been known to purchase advertisements in their own paper to support policies or candidates different from those endorsed by the editorial page.

Sometimes relations between news and editorial people can be soured by an excessive amount of competition. Editorial writers may take delight in scooping the news department—finding a story and writing an editorial before the story appears in the news columns. Once in a while reporters may find sardonic pleasure in reporting a story that makes the editorial staff look as though it didn't know what it had been writing about. Repeated efforts on one side of the news-editorial partition to embarrass the other can be destructive to the morale of a newspaper staff and can harm the credibility of the paper. But a little friendly competition between news and editorial can help keep both departments on their toes. It may provide the only such competition in one-newspaper communities.

Problems of a different sort arise when a firm partition is not maintained between news and editorial content, when a publisher does not insist that editorial writers hold complete responsibility for policies expressed in the editorial columns and that news personnel have complete responsibility for the news columns. The editorial staff must not expect the news department to produce articles aimed at bolstering an editorial viewpoint, and the news staff must not allow its opinions to filter into news articles.

■ REPORTERS AS SOURCES

Reporters and editorial writers have tended to go their own ways. As noted in Chapter 3 ("Anyone for Editorial Writing?"), 70 percent of reporters and editors who were interviewed expressed no interest in editorial writing. Some saw too many restrictions. Others regarded the job as too "Ivory Tower" for them.[4] In many cases in which editorial comment is called for, editorial writers have no need to talk with reporters. They have their own sources, or the subject of the editorial may already have been fully explained in the news columns. But ignoring help available on the news side is a "recipe for disaster," in the words of one editorial page editor. "Your perspective can get limited without talking with the beat reporter[s]. . . . You can go off half-cocked if you don't talk to them."[5] Since a newspaper invariably has more reporters than editorial writers, the news people are likely to have more sources of information and spend more time in the community than editorial writers. They may have information, not yet ready for print, that might make a big difference in how editorial writers evaluate an issue.

Ellen Belcher, who spent time as a reporter after being an editorial writer, said she could personally attest to the value of checking with the newsroom. "In part because I saw how much information reporters knew that they couldn't fit into their stories, I . . . promised that . . . I'd redouble my effort to make sure that I talk to reporters before I write my editorials, asking them even more questions than I had previously."[6] Reporters, William J. Woods of the *Utica* (N.Y.) *Observer-Dispatch* pointed out, "are invaluable in keeping the egg of silly mistakes off the editor's chin."[7]

Editorial writers who want to tackle a subject in which they are not experts can ask a knowledgeable reporter to brief them on the subject. If a proposed zone change is coming before the city council, a reporter may be able to recount the history of the case, from the developer through the planning staff and zoning commission. The reporter may also be able to provide technical information on zoning procedures. The editorial writer might ask the reporter to clarify the issues involved—to recap the arguments of the developer, the protesting neighbors and the zoning commissioners.

■ REPORTERS IN THE OPINION PROCESS

"There's nothing wrong with editorial writers sitting down with news types to get their observations," one editorial page editor said. "You have to be careful, though, because if you carry it too far the reporters begin to articulate your policy, and that's not good."[8] In the zoning case, the editorial writer might ask the reporter for a personal opinion on the issue. The reporter might reply that, in comparison with other similar changes, this one does not seem out of line— or perhaps that the change does seem out of line. In seeking an opinion, the editorial writer should be wary. Reporters are responsible for maintaining the appearance of fairness in reporting the news as well as fairness in their writing. A city editor who is concerned about the credibility of reporters may not appreciate having reporters offer opinions to an editorial writer on subjects that they write about. A reporter's relations with a news source can be adversely affected if it becomes known that the reporter has voiced an opinion. To think public matters through to editorial conclusions is the job of the editorial writer, not the reporter.

Some editors—on both news and editorial sides—are receptive to encouraging reporters to express opinions, in print and personally. Desmond Stone of the *Rochester* (N.Y.) *Democrat and Chronicle* reported that inviting reporters to participate in editorial board meetings for a period of two weeks was one way that his paper and its sister paper, the *Times-Union,* tried to make news personnel feel more a part of the editorial decision-making.[9] Rufus Terral of the *St. Louis* (Mo.) *Post-Dispatch* suggested picking two promising writers in the newsroom to contribute editorials from time to time, so that they could fill in when members of the editorial staff were on vacation or ill and possibly become regular editorial page staff members when a replacement was needed.[10] Some papers ask reporters to write editorials or bylined opinions on a regular basis on particular subjects on which they are experts, but this practice runs the risk of weakening the wall between news and editorial sides.

In the survey of editorial page editors cited above, a few said they would be willing to undertake joint projects with the news department. "I'd like to be able to send out a reporter and an editorial writer for six weeks to cover a controversial issue and have the reporter write the news story and the editorial writer write the editorials," one said. "Now, when the news side does a big investigation, the editorial page gets left out until the stuff appears in the paper, and then we have to play catchup."[11]

It is understandable that an editorial page editor would like to have someone already available when an editorial writer is needed on a short or long-term basis. But, if an interchange on the NCEW (National Conference of Editorial Writers) e-mail discussion group is any indication, most editors are set against bringing reporters onto the editorial board as members or interim writers. Reporters, however, especially those have been covering government, schools and social issues, are logical sources for editorial writers when full-time openings occur.

In some instances reporters and editorial writers have teamed up for extended research into a subject of mutual interest. When the project was completed, the reporter wrote the news stories, and the editorial writer, equally informed, wrote the editorials. I see no serious problems with such cooperation if it is not overdone.

Some papers ask reporters to write interpretive pieces or bylined opinion pieces on subjects about which they are particularly informed. In an interpretive article, which has a proper place in the news columns, the writer is expected to bring perspective and employ analysis in presenting a fair account of the subject, but not to reveal his or her personal opinions or conclusions. If the writer's opinions become evident, the piece crosses the line into opinion, the province of the editorial page. The dividing line is not always clear, however.

When I was an editor with supervision over both news and editorial sides, I did not encourage reporters to express opinions in their news articles. I did, however, encourage them to write in-depth, analytical articles for use in either the daily news columns or the Sunday opinion section. My experience as both a reporter and an editorial writer convinced me that something happens inside writers when they write pieces that express opinions. As an editorial writer, I often ended up having much stronger opinions on a subject after I had written an editorial. Once a writer has thought through the arguments and embraced one of them, his or her attitude on an issue is likely never to be the same again.

■ EDITORIALS IN THE NEWS COLUMNS

Two ideas for introducing editorials into the news pages were considered in early issues of *The Masthead*. Neither idea has been given much credence by editors.

The first is the front-page editorial. William Randolph Hearst occasionally ran signed editorials on page one,[12] as did William Loeb of the *Manchester* (N.H.) *Union Leader* and *New Hampshire Sunday News*.[13] Such editorials have become rare in recent years, but occasionally an editor or publisher will run an editorial on page one to call attention to a statement considered to be especially important. Fred A. Stickel, president and publisher of the *Oregonian*, wrote a signed page-one editorial urging Oregonians to vote against a ballot measure that would have restricted the rights of homosexuals.[14] Nathaniel Blumberg, however, has argued that page-one editorials may confuse readers about what is news and what is opinion and may increase their "suspicions that the news coverage might not be impartial."[15]

Some papers summarize election endorsements in a front-page box, and some editorial page editors use front-page teasers to call attention to editorials on the editorial page. The criticisms directed at front-page editorials would seem to apply equally to these front-page teasers as well.

Another suggestion for bringing opinion into the news columns apparently originated in 1935 with historian Douglas Southall Freeman, then editor of the *Richmond* (Va.) *News Leader.* While going through old *News Leader* files in the early 1950s, James J. Kilpatrick found that Freeman had suggested to his publisher that the news needed interpreting when and where it was printed. The reader should not have to wait until the next day, "when his interest in it has been diminished or has been distracted by some new event." Freeman suggested that the editorial page be abolished and that interpretation and comment be appended at the end of news stories that merited opinion.[16]

Kilpatrick's resurrection of the proposal prompted the laboratory newspaper at the University of Michigan, the *Michigan Journalist,* to try Freeman's proposal. Students found that one advantage of tacking an editorial on the end of a news story was that the editorial did not require so much space; there was no need to rehash factual information. But the professor who worked with the students said he feared that readers would think that news sources had not been "given a square shake if the newspaper proceeds to bludgeon those views editorially in the same news column." He also feared that the instant editorial would encourage off-the-cuff reactions and discourage the double-checking, digging for more information and calm reflecting required for first-rate editorial comment.[17] Appending comment to news stories is an interesting idea, but one not likely to take root in U.S. newspapers, where the tradition of physical separation between news and opinion remains strong.

■ EDITORIALIZING ABOUT NEWS POLICIES

One approach to lowering the bar between news and editorial that seems justified is the use of editorial columns to explain news policies and practices—and editorial practices, for that matter. An editorial or a signed article on the editorial page can be a proper forum for telling readers why certain types of news and not others are covered in the news columns or why new features have been added and others dropped.

In the last couple of years in which I was on a newspaper, I regularly wrote a Sunday op-ed column, which I usually devoted to a journalistic issue. Some of the columns dealt with my own paper's policies and practices. Others concerned matters of more general interest, such as protecting the confidentiality of news sources, libel, invasion of privacy and the signing of editorials. Reader response seemed good. Subscribers wanted to know more about their newspaper, and the press in general.

Some newspapers assign a full or part-time person to respond to complaints of readers and to write about media matters. Their work usually is published on the editorial or op-ed page. When the remarks of these media critics have pertained to the newspaper industry in general, they have been given considerable freedom to draw conclusions. On some newspapers, however, when criticism comes too close to home, critics find they don't have as much freedom as they may have thought.[18] (See section on "Media Criticism" in Chapter 16, "Other Types of Writing.")

■ CONCLUSION

The newspaper that wants to maintain the credibility of its news and editorial columns must draw a line between the two and take every opportunity to remind readers of this line. But news and editorial are two parts of a package. It may be possible to produce an outstanding news product without a good editorial page. It is virtually impossible to produce an outstanding editorial page without the support of a good news product. Editorial writers need reporters more than reporters need editorial writers: They simply don't have enough arms and legs and eyes and noses to do their jobs all by themselves.

■ QUESTIONS AND EXERCISES

1. Why do you think that editorial writers have tended to ignore reporters and newsroom editors?

2. Do reporters, in your opinion, have a legitimate complaint when the editorial page expresses views with which they strongly disagree? What steps should be open to them?

3. Should news persons be allowed to purchase advertising space in the newspaper for which they work to express views contrary to those of management?

4. Should reporters be invited to write editorials on subjects with which they are familiar? Or to write signed opinion pieces for the editorial and op-ed pages?

5. Do reporters on papers in your area write editorials and/or signed articles for the editorial or oped pages? How far do they go in expressing their opinions?

6. Do you think that editorial writers should ask reporters for their opinions on issues that the reporters are covering?

7. Are there occasions when a page-one editorial can be justified? What about page-one election endorsements?

8. What do you think of the idea of tacking editorial comments to the ends of news stories?

The Editorial Page Staff

Many editorial pages in this country's newspapers are wretchedly understaffed.

—LAURENCE J. PAUL,
BUFFALO EVENING NEWS [1]

Mine, by damn, all mine.

—DON SHOEMAKER,
ASHEVILLE (N.C.) CITIZEN [2]

An editorial page staff, no matter how large or small, never seems quite the right size for all members. Ask editorial writers if they need more help in putting out the editorial page, and chances are they will answer "Yes." But ask a writer who puts out a page all by himself or herself or better yet one who used to put one out alone—and chances are you will get a lecture on the freedom, rewards and misery of doing the whole job by yourself.

Writers on one-person staffs know they are overworked and don't get enough time to write editorials. Writers on some two-person and three-person staffs, especially on larger papers, think they need more help. On some days, on papers with large staffs, a writer may wish that not so many colleagues were competing for space, promotion and community recognition. Some members of large staffs think back fondly to the days when they wrote all the editorials, handled the letters and still found time for a Chamber of Commerce luncheon. I did when the editorial staff on the *Columbian* grew from one to two, and then from two to three members.

Just as editorial-page people hold a variety of views about staff size, so do they have differences of opinion concerning how much freedom each member of the staff should have and how much members should collaborate through editorial conferences.

■ WHAT SIZE STAFF?

A 1979 survey of editorial writers ago found that the one-person staff was the most prevalent on U.S. daily newspapers (27 percent),[3] and a recent, informal poll on the National Conference of Editorial Writers (NCEW) e-mail discussion group suggests staff sizes haven't changed much. Of the 15 people who replied to a question, five reported having one writer. Weekday circulations of the five papers varied from 35,000 to 85,000. Four papers (circulations from 28,000 to 65,000) had two writers. Four (circulations from 66,000 to 230,000) had three writers. A paper with 608,000 weekday circulation had four writers, and one with 240,000 had six writers.

It seems there is no rule of thumb to apply to editorial staff sizes comparable to the often-cited guideline for news staff on small to middle-sized newspapers: one newsroom person for every thousand of circulation. It seems reasonable that more reporters would be required to cover more news sources, and produce more news stories, in a larger community. On the editorial page the staff, whatever the size, has the same number of column inches to fill each day, regardless of circulation or size of community. One difference, however, is that op-ed pages are more prevalent among larger newspapers. Another difference is that a larger paper may turn out seven sets of opinion pages a week instead of five or six.

Still, if one person can turn out an editorial page on an 85,000-circulation newspaper, why think about hiring anyone else? The obvious answer is "quality." The editorial page is supposed to be the reflective part of the newspaper. With rare exceptions, the person who handles the letters, selects the columns and cartoons, and lays out the page can't be expected to find much time for reflecting, let alone for researching editorials or getting out into the community.

Laurence J. Paul of the *Buffalo* (N.Y.) *Evening News* suggested that papers with circulations between 50,000 and 100,000 should have a minimum of two writers, papers with circulations between 100,000 and 150,000 should have at least three and papers with 150,000 to 200,000 should have at least four.[4] Larger papers could be expected to maintain larger editorial staffs because they have more resources, more advertising and more money to spend. Larger papers also tend to serve not just a local community but a region or an entire state. These papers thus have an opportunity—an obligation—to provide leadership in public affairs in the more diverse areas that they serve. They will not make full use of that opportunity unless they provide writers with the time and the incentive to do their own research and their own thinking on the issues.

◼ THE ONE-PERSON STAFF

Putting out a page by yourself has its advantages. You can write what you wish if you have a good relationship with your publisher. You don't have to worry about disagreements among staff members. You get full credit, or discredit, for whatever you do. Your readers know whom to praise or blame. You can go home at night and point to what you have accomplished.

"I should confess that I still recall with pleasure some of the aspects of those years when I wrote editorials for a semi-weekly and later a small daily newspaper without conferring with anybody in advance," recalled Wilbur Elston, then of the *Detroit News*. "I won't say those editorials could not have been improved. Obviously they could have been. But they were all mine. Whatever praise or criticism I heard from readers was especially pleasant to my ears." Unfortunately, Elston also recalled, most of the editorials "were, I fear, written off the top of my head."[5]

The one-person show is a tough one, and it's not for everyone. In the words of Don Shoemaker of the *Asheville* (N.C.) *Citizen,* it's like being "the keeper of the zoo." Shoemaker, who was the inspiration for the leading character in Jeff MacNelly's cartoon strip, "Shoe," saw the single editorial writer as "more put upon" than any other person in the field of newspapering. The writer had to please "crotchety and sour-bellied" printers, select and edit editorial page features that would complement the locally written editorials and satisfy the publisher—and know all about proofreading, page layout and makeup. The writer had to worry about "any novice journeyman who happens to be around the shop" fouling up the page. At the same time the one-person staff had to "keep a weather eye cocked for the passions and prejudices" of the community, the state and the region. "As any fool kin plainly see, the curator has an impossible, a thankless, a miserable job," Shoemaker wrote. But mostly the "fool" loves it. "I (ugh!) do," he concluded. "But there are moments."[6]

Michael Loftin was reminded of a scene from the movie *Raiders of the Lost Ark*. "Archeologist Indiana Jones, having captured an ancient artifact, is trying to escape from a giant rolling boulder chasing him through the tunnel. Think of the boulder as the looming daily deadline and the production of 800 to 900 words of (reasonably intelligent) commentary as the goal and you can understand why those of us in this situation were cheering for Mr. Jones."[7]

Turning out the letters, the columns, the cartoons and the page layout, while handling telephone calls and office visitors, can account for a good share of the working day. But, once you get into the swing of it, composing one thoughtful, researched editorial and another quick one every day turns out not to be impossible. Topics always abound. Karli Jo Hunt, of the *Home News* of New Brunswick, N.J., said that she has learned "to get through a five-day week writing seven days' editorials, . . . to read, read, read, clip, clip, clip, and pace my 'production' so that Thursdays and Fridays are only nine- or 10-hour sessions at the tube."[8]

Some editors—in fact, some editors who also double as publishers or managing editors—are able to produce two, three or four editorials a day and say something significant in each of them. They seem able to cover an unlimited range of topics. But my experience has been that single writers make the best use of talent and time if they concentrate on one major topic a day, a topic they know about.

■ DIVISION OF DUTIES

A one-person staff doesn't have to worry much about how to split up the duties of producing an editorial page. He or she does whatever needs to be done. But help, primarily with letters to the editor, might be available from a newsroom secretary, copy clerk or someone with clerical skills. That helper could check addresses of letters, enforce the newspaper's rules concerning letters to the editor and retype letters on video display terminals. The person might be encouraged to try writing headlines for letters. Assistance with letters is probably the greatest help that a one-person staff can get. Next best is with messages and phone calls.

As staffs increase in size, one person may be assigned the letters to the editors as a full- or part-time job, another the syndicated columns and the layout. Both may write editorials as they find time. One person may have responsibility for the weekend opinion section. The editorial page editor will probably edit the editorials of other staff members and meet with the public and newspaper management.

At one of the five newspapers mentioned earlier that have only one editorial writer, the editorial page writer-editor reported getting help from a copy editor and a columnist who worked on the Sunday section and wrote editorials when the editorial page editor was out of town. On the other four one-person staffs, the writer-editors seemed to be working alone. On two two-writer staffs, the writers were unassisted; on another, they got help one or two days a week from the copy desk. One two-writer paper had an editorial assistant to handle letters and proofreading. Another had a 20-hour-a-week letters editor. The pattern suggests that on one-writer and two-writer staffs the help that is most needed is in copyediting and handling letters.

As staffs increase in size, writers may have their own special subject areas. Specialization can produce a more knowledgeable editorial writer and thus more knowledgeable editorials. If an editorial is directed primarily toward experts in the subject, it may fully serve its purpose. But specialization has limitations. First, writers may become so engrossed in their specialties that the editorials they turn out are incomprehensible to the average reader. Second, when a paper's specialist on a subject is sick or on vacation, or has left the staff, an editor may find that no one else on the staff is capable of writing on that topic. Ideally, editorial writers should be able to write about many subjects in addition to their specialties.

■ EDITORIAL CONFERENCES

Editorial writers and editors divide sharply over the value—or lack of value—of regular editorial conferences. Proponents argue that they provide an opportunity to bring the thinking of several people to bear on topics, that give-and-take discussion can produce ideas that might otherwise not emerge. Discussion can also reveal that a topic needs more research or possibly ought to be dropped entirely as unworthy of comment. John G. McCullough of the *Philadelphia Evening Bulletin* said that when his staff skipped the morning editorial conference he and the other writers missed it. "When the free give-and-take of these conferences is missing, I feel it shows in [the resulting editorials]," he said. "They seem to have a structural narrowness reflecting the absence of other, counter, views."[9]

Some of the critics of conferences contend that this mixing contributes to bland editorials. Hugh B. Patterson Jr., of the Little Rock *Arkansas Gazette,* acknowledged that discussions could help clarify and sharpen arguments but could also result in "the lowest common denominator of mutual agreement."[10] Pat Murphy, of the Phoenix *Arizona Republic,* contended that his staff members did not need editorial conferences. "Our staff is made up of self-starters who spin out ideas and suggestions and hit the ground running every morning," he said. Instead of holding a conference, he made the rounds of staff members first thing in the morning to suggest ideas and listen to their proposals. "Fie on daily conferences," he said. "They're a waste of time."[11]

Between those extremes is the pattern established by the *Sun-Sentinel* in Fort Lauderdale, Fla. Editorial page editor Guy Kingsley, in a "Problem Solving" feature in *The Masthead,* reported that his editorial board meets three times a week. The main meeting, held on Monday, includes the publisher (when his schedule permits), the editor, two senior copy editors and a cartoonist as well as Kingsley and four editorial writers. On Wednesday and Friday, the board meets without the publisher and the editor. On Tuesday and Thursday, Kingsley said, he meets "individually with members of my staff" to "discuss their ideas with them." He said his approach is to lead the meetings, maybe bring up "an obvious topic," but "quickly get the other board members to put issues on the table they believe are important." Each board member can bring up a maximum of three topics. The four editorial writers take turns, from one meeting to next, getting first crack at putting forth their ideas. Kingsley said he tries to move the meetings swiftly. "I'm a firm believer that no souls are saved after an hour at church," he wrote, "and that nothing of substance comes out of an editorial board meeting that lasts more than 60 minutes."[12]

Daily editorial meetings were the policy when I was on the *Register and Tribune* in Des Moines, Iowa. The meetings were attended by up to 10 writers and editors (who contributed to both the morning *Register* and the evening *Tribune*). On the *Columbian* in Vancouver, Wash., we had a daily meeting of the three editorial staff members and a biweekly meeting of the editorial board, which consisted of the editorial staff members, the co-publishers and two or three representatives from other departments.

Sitting in on an Editorial Conference

In preparing for this edition, I asked to meet with the editorial board of the *Register-Guard* in Eugene, Ore. Editorial page editor Jackman Wilson told me that daily get-togethers generally are informal and amount mostly to touching base on what the writers are working on that day. On Monday mornings, however, Wilson, associate editors Henny Willis and Paul Neville, executive editor Jim Godbold and publisher Alton F. Baker III meet to talk about possible editorial topics for the week. At the Monday session I attended, Wilson, Willis and Neville each came armed with a yellow notepad that listed editorial topics that the writer had previously written about (and crossed off) and new ideas for the week. Each writer in turn offered his proposed topics. During the hour-long conference 10 or so topics were discussed. During the following three days, five of the topics received editorial comment.

The longest and most heated discussion was prompted by an article that had appeared in the paper that morning. The article called attention to possible conflicts of interest involving two county commissioners and the lawyer for a sand and gravel company that was asking for approval to open a new gravel pit. What set off the discussion was the news report that one of the commissioners had been fired by the company 30 years before. His employment by the company had previously become known, but Neville said that just the previous week the commissioner had insisted in a telephone conversation with him that he had not been fired and that a grievance the commissioner had filed at the time was directed toward a labor union, not against the company.

The news story had also recounted earlier reports that another commissioner had met privately with the head of the sand and gravel company and that the company's lawyer, who had headed the state Land Conservation and Development Commission the previous year, had contacted the commission in connection with the gravel pit application. After extended discussion, the board decided not to make an issue of the ex-employee-turned-commissioner. Instead, the board chose to admonish both commissioners and the lawyer in an editorial that put the conflicts involved in the case into broader context.

An editorial about the gravel pit application appeared at the top of the page on Wednesday morning, the day the commissioners were to hold another hearing on the case and possibly take a vote. A conflict-of-interest editorial appeared in the second position on the page. During the editorial board meeting one of the writers had speculated that running an editorial on the day of the hearing might look like an attempt to affect the voting. The comment drew a couple of chuckles and a smile or two. (After all, what's the purpose of an editorial, if not to have an effect?)

The lead editorial took a judicious approach, stressing that what was at stake was not "the future of Western civilization" but only whether the company had met the standards for new gravel pits established by the state. Almost as an aside, the editorial reiterated a position that an earlier editorial had taken: "Our evaluation is that Eugene Sand has met the state's requirements, and that its application should be approved." (That stand might have surprised readers, since over the years the *Register-Guard* had established a strong record on environmental issues, particularly those involving land use.)

On the next morning, Tuesday, two editorials on subjects discussed at the meeting appeared: a bold proposal for a new basketball arena for the University of Oregon and the death of Common Cause founder John Gardner. On Thursday an editorial appeared on a topic Willis had brought up: the state Democrats' decision to abandon the open primary election (which had allowed independents to participate). The editorial applauded the decision, arguing that the open primary had attracted few independent voters and that party members should select their party's candidates.

The Thursday page carried an editorial on a topic that had come up after the board meeting: President George W. Bush's proposals for dealing with global warming. The opening sentence gave an idea of the *Register-Guard*'s evaluation of the proposals: "If President Bush succeeds in selling his new global warming strategy to Congress and the American people, he'll have pulled off the biggest heist since a Dutch colonial governor named Peter Minuit bought Manhattan Island from the Indians in 1626 for beads, cloth and trinkets worth $24."[13]

Friday's and Sunday's pages each carried two editorials that had not been discussed at the conference. On Saturday a topic that had been talked about appeared: a proposed offer to turn the Oregon Institute of Technology into a private college. "A bad idea," said the editorial, "especially at a fire-sale price."[14] On Monday appeared the last topic that had been discussed the week before: a celebration of the American Red Cross moving into new offices, three months after the newly completed building had been vandalized and trashed.

During the seven days following the editorial conference, seven of the 14 editorials that appeared in print had been discussed at the conference—in my opinion a productive use of an hour of discussion. (The other seven were on topics that arose during the week.)

■ LONG-RANGE PLANNING

Editorial writers, even those who hold regular meetings, need to step back a pace or two from time to time. Gilbert Cranberg, while on the *Des Moines* (Iowa) *Register*, found that putting out the daily editorial pages kept his staff members so occupied that they had no chance to examine how they really operated or how the pages could be improved. Cranberg tried a 90-minute luncheon for the writers and found that the session produced ideas for improving use of syndicated features, increasing locally written material for the pages and instituting a sabbatical leave program.[15]

When I was on the *Columbian*, the three of us occasionally left the office early with a six-pack of beer, to talk about the broader issues, some details and the interaction among our personalities. The result was to clear the air in a way that could not have happened in a hurried morning meeting and to allow us to develop some ideas for improving the page that did not spring full-blown from the mind of any one participant.

A more elaborate get-together, a one-day retreat, was tried by the editorial page staff of the *News Journal* in Wilmington, Del. Two weeks' worth of newspapers had been sent to an outside editorial page editor. The first two hours were devoted to his critique, with staff members asking questions. Then, Editorial Page Editor John H. Taylor Jr. reported, "[W]e started on our principal concerns": page content, letters, editorial board agenda, community advisory board and page design. "What the retreat offered," he said, "was a chance to talk and argue without interruption, to come to an agreement all could live with." He counted it a success.[16]

■ THE EDITORIAL WRITER AT WORK

A "typical day" for editorial writers on most papers is a contradiction in terms. Writers who have contact with the outside world or with other members of the staff are not likely to have a *typical* day. It is hard, if not impossible, to plan a day and stick to a schedule. Nevertheless, editors of *The Masthead* asked several writers to describe how they spent their days.[17] If you could average the various schedules of the 25 or so respondents, the result might look something like this:

6 a.m. to 8 a.m.:	at home, read the morning newspaper(s) while drinking coffee and eating breakfast
8:30 a.m. to 9 a.m.:	peruse other newspapers and the news wires
9 a.m. to 9:30 a.m.:	attend editorial board meeting to discuss and pick topics for editorials
9:30 a.m. to noon:	conduct research and begin writing assigned editorial noon to 1 p.m.: lunch, perhaps with fellow staff members, perhaps with sources
1 p.m. to 2 p.m.:	complete editorial
2 p.m. to 4 p.m.:	work on another editorial, a long-range project; get out of the office for first-hand research, etc.
4 p.m. to 5 p.m.:	check page proofs, tend to correspondence, perhaps take some time to read

Now all this assumes that someone else is handling the letters, the syndicated columns and the cartoons (local and syndicated), as well as taking telephone calls and dealing with walk-ins. It also assumes that someone else is managing the budget, meeting with the editor or publisher and attending all the meetings and training sessions that modern managers want their employees to participate in. The schedule doesn't include time for long-range planning, election interviews or special projects outside the daily run of editorials. It does not include 7:30 to 10 p.m. for one or two nights a week, during which the conscientious editorial writer is likely to be attending a civic, political, cultural or social event. Nor does it include family or personal time for Little League or high school basketball games, school concerts, ballet lessons or choir practice.

A 1999 survey of 250 NCEW members found that, on average, each spent 3.2 hours researching and writing a typical editorial. They each wrote an average of 6.7 editorials a week. During the workday they averaged 2.8 hours on editing and layout tasks, 2.1 hours on administrative duties, 1.3 on reading periodicals, 1.1 on dealing with the public, 0.9 on attending meetings and 0.9 on planning. The average workweek added up to 49.15 hours.[18]

■ CONCLUSION

The staff size that editorial writers are likely to regard as ideal may depend on their own prior experience. To writers who have run a one-person show, a two-person staff may look like a luxury. To writers who have worked on a larger staff, two persons are likely to seem wholly inadequate. Although some attempts have been made to prescribe staff sizes for papers of varying circulation sizes, the circulation of a newspaper has little correlation with the work that needs to be done on an editorial page. The page must come out every day, whatever the circulation; columns and letters must be edited; a certain number of editorials must be written; visitors and callers must be dealt with; meetings, editorial conferences and research must be attended to.

All things being equal, a larger editorial page staff should be able to turn out a better product. If writers have an opportunity to spend time thinking about one or two areas of editorial writing, instead of having to render the judgments of Solomon on all issues, they should be better editorial writers. If they write only one editorial a day, they should be able to do a better job than if they have to write three. However, if they overspecialize, they may work themselves out of their jobs. Editorial writers must never stop being generalists.

■ QUESTIONS AND EXERCISES

1. Editorial page staffs on the average apparently have not been growing in size. What does this seem to say about the attitudes of publishers and other holders of the newspaper budget purse strings?
2. What are the advantages of a one-person editorial page staff? The disadvantages? Do you think the disadvantages outweigh the advantages?
3. Determine the number of editorial page persons on papers in your area. How do these staffs compare in size with the staff sizes mentioned in this chapter?
4. How are the editorial duties distributed among the staff members of these papers?
5. How do the editorial conferences—if any—work on these papers? Who attends? How often do they meet? How are assignments made? Does the editor, the publisher or the editorial board make the final decisions?

Relations with the Community

Some of the toughest decisions that editors and editorial writers face involve the degree to which they allow themselves to participate in or contribute to civic, business and political causes. Implicit in these decisions is the question: How can editorial writers be a part of a community without becoming biased, or appearing to be biased, through associations with groups with special interests? Closely related to this aspect of maintaining integrity and the appearance of integrity is the problem all journalists face: To what extent, if any, can you accept drinks, meals and trips from people with whom you deal without compromising yourself? These questions have provoked a lot of conscience-searching among editorial writers and have led several organizations in the newspaper business to conclude that consciences need help through codes and guidelines.

■ TO PARTICIPATE OR NOT TO PARTICIPATE

Those who defend participation in community affairs contend that editorial writers should recognize that they are part of their communities and should feel a responsibility to help make them better places in which to live. But others contend just as strongly that, if writers become involved, they compromise their credibility in commenting on community affairs.

The principal argument against joining organizations and participating in political and civic activities is that association with organizations and causes may lead to "conflicts of interest, real or apparent," in the wording of the Basic Statement of Principles of the National Conference of Editorial Writers.

If editorial writers were to subscribe wholeheartedly to either philosophy, decision-making would be easy. If they thought that working through organizations was as appropriate for them as molding opinions through their writing, they would say yes when asked to participate in a worthy cause. If they thought they should undertake no obligations, they would say no. Most editorial writers, however, seem to think that there are some occasions when they can or should become involved and some occasions when they cannot or should not.

Political Activities

Editorial writers increasingly agree they ought to avoid public partisan politics. A 1988 poll conducted by G. Cleveland Wilhoit and Dan G. Drew found that 89 percent of editorial writers said they agreed or strongly agreed that they should avoid partisan political organizations. Only 9 percent (down from 19 percent in 1979) reported that they had given money or bought tickets to help a party or a candidate. A similar percentage had urged individuals to vote for a party or candidate. Only 7 percent had attended meetings, rallies or dinners not required by their jobs.[3] Another survey found that the percentage of editorial writers who were affiliated with either Democratic or Republican party had decreased from 83 percent in 1989 to 41 percent in 1995.[4]

The 1988 survey showed that 46 percent of the newspapers prohibited political participation by employees and an additional 37 percent discouraged or strongly discouraged participation. These percentages marked a sharp increase over polls taken in 1971 and 1979, when 0 (!) percent and 29 percent of newspapers, respectively, prohibited participation.[5] The 1988 and 1995 surveys did not ask about participation policies, but they did show an increasing tendency of editorial writers (from 20 to 48 percent) to consider themselves politically independent.

Government Positions

Despite the apparent consensus against political participation, editorial writers and other newspaper staff members from time to time are invited, and tempted, to serve on boards or advisory bodies to government agencies, from the local to the national level. In the Wilhoit-Drew survey, 6 percent of the editorial writers said they had participated in governmental boards or agencies.

While he was on the *Richmond* (Va.) *News Leader,* James J. Kilpatrick accepted an appointment to a state commission that at first seemed innocuous but eventually came to embarrass him. He served on the state Commission on Constitutional Government, an agency organized to encourage states to defend their reserved powers under the federal government. He also was chairman of publications for the agency. When the commission came under attack in the Virginia General Assembly, Kilpatrick said he found himself trapped. "I could not defend the Commission's publications without appearing to be saying what a great guy am I." In the end, he said, he wrote a "lame piece" saying that the incident ought to have taught him a lesson about becoming involved with boards and commissions.[6]

Civic Organizations

A state commission is one thing. What should an editorial writer do when asked to serve on the board of the local library, the symphony orchestra, the community college or the art museum, or on a committee on race relations? In a 1988 survey 31 percent of editorial writers said they participated in nonprofit, nongovernmental organizations. In any of these organizations, public policy issues can arise. What, for example, should the library do, and what should an editorial writer say, about a proposal to restrict children's access to potentially pornographic Internet sites? What role should an editorial writer play during the orchestra's annual fundraiser? What conflict arises in writing an editorial responding to a reader's complaint about nude art displays at the art museum?

The answers to these questions are not easy. In addition, Laird B. Anderson, a journalism professor at American University, expressed concern that, in overreacting to disconnect themselves from public bodies, editorial writers and other journalists have become second-class citizens. "In following this road to second-class status so that we can be viewed as more ethical and credible, we have righteously denied ourselves equality with the citizens whose conscious- ness we want to reach," Anderson said. "Our offices have all too often become havens, a refuge to scurry back to after dipping a toe in the vast sea of public affairs, and then writing about what we've seen or learned. Many of us, I suspect, like this protection buffer. It uncomplicates our lives."[7]

Professional, Religious and Fraternal Groups

In the 1988 survey, 66 percent of the editorial writers said they participated in professional journalism societies and 46 percent in civic, religious, fraternal and veterans groups. These organizations might seem harmless. But what should editorial writers who write on social issues do when the church board on which they serve considers applying for federal funds for a faith-based program? Paul Greenberg, then editorial page editor of the *Pine Bluff* (Ark.) *Commercial*, reported a conflict that arose when he agreed to serve as president of his local temple. Within two months the temple became involved in a zoning controversy. Since then, he said, "I would say that serving spaghetti at a fund- raising dinner is the highest role to which the editorial writer ought to aspire."[8]

Charitable Causes

Only an editorial writer who is related to Scrooge would turn down all the requests that come daily from charitable organizations. The problem is where to draw the line—for ethical as well as financial reasons. In a *Masthead* sympo- sium, several editorial writers drew that line between what Lewis A. Leader of the *Monterey County* (Calif.) *Herald* called "joining a non-profit group and contributing to one."[9] Susan Hegger of the *St. Louis* (Mo.) *Post-Dispatch* said she thought it was generally "acceptable to contribute money to organizations whose purposes are endorsed by one's paper" but not organizations "whose platforms or principles run counter to one's editorial page."[10] Van Cavett of the Allentown, Pa., *Morning Call* reported that, because his paper "supported poli- tics advocated by Planned Parenthood," he and his wife Caroline saw no conflict when she was asked to serve on the local board of the organization. "We realized going in that financial contributions and participation of fund- raisers would be necessary," he said.[11]

Others took a harder line. Charles J. Dunsire of the *Seattle Post-Intelligencer* said he limited his contributions to the local United Way (a payroll deduction), his church and a non-profit hospital foundation. He admitted, however, that he contributed annually to his alma mater, the University of Washington, "because such contributions have become necessary to retain the privilege of buying season tickets to the games of one of the nation's most successful and popular football programs."[12]

Personal Friendships

Seemingly innocent friendships, through unforeseen consequences, can pose conflicts of interest. When David Boeyink went to Owensboro, Ky., as editorial page editor of the *Messenger-Inquirer*, he renewed a casual acquaintance he had made with a fellow student at Harvard Divinity School. The families became friends. They attended the same church. As a staff member of the Owensboro Chamber of Commerce, the friend "was a great source of insights into local political figures," Boeyink recalled, but then the friend was promoted to chief administrative officer. That caused "a few moments of concern, particularly on rare editorials involving the chamber," Boeyink write in an article in *The Masthead.* Then the friend decided to run for mayor and at the same time became executive director of a citizens committee on which Boeyink served. Boeyink resigned from the committee. The two stopped talking politics. The families saw each other less frequently. Before he was put to the test of dealing with a mayor as friend, Boeyink left town for a job elsewhere.[13]

■ TO ACCEPT OR NOT TO ACCEPT

Another potential conflict of interest concerns what to do about "freebies," the gifts, large and small, that people with views to push are only too willing to share with newspaper people. In recent years government and business, including the newspaper industry, have tended to become more sensitive to possible conflicts because of such gifts. Tighter codes have been written for public officials, and in many instances editorial writers have written in support of the tougher restrictions. If newspapers expect public officials to observe a higher standard, should not newspapers themselves observe an equally high standard?

In 1975, following the lead of other journalism organizations, the National Conference of Editorial Writers (NCEW) tightened its Statement of Principles. The conflict-of-interest portion of the original statement, adopted in 1949, had merely said: "The editorial writer should never be motivated by personal interest, nor use his influence to seek special favors for himself or others. He should hold himself above any possible taint of corruption, whatever its source." The revised conflict-of-interest portion now reads:

> The editorial writer should never use his or her influence to seek personal favors of any kind. Gifts of value, free travel and other favors that can compromise integrity, or appear to do so, should not be accepted.

> The writer should be constantly alert to conflicts of interest, real or apparent, including those that may arise from financial holdings, secondary employment, holding public office or involvement in political, civic or other organizations. Timely public disclosure can minimize suspicion.

> Editors should seek to hold syndicates to these standards.

> The writer, further to enhance editorial page credibility, also should encourage the institution he or she represents to avoid conflicts of interest, real or apparent.[14]

The Professional Standards Committee and the Executive Committee of NCEW had wanted more specific language on freebies: "Gifts, free travel and other things of value can compromise integrity. Nothing of more than token value should be accepted." A majority of NCEW members, however, preferred to rely on their own consciences, rather than on a strict rule, to tell them what was acceptable and what was not.

Free Trips

The wording in the statement regarding travel was softened partly because NCEW officers at that time were hoping to arrange a trip for members to the

People's Republic of China, and a trip partly paid for by the Chinese was seen as the only way to get there. Similar concerns were expressed by all six editorial writers who responded to invitations to participate in a *Masthead* symposium on junkets. Basically they argued that the benefits of subsidized trips abroad outweighed any dangers that might arise from possible conflicts of interest. H. Brandt Ayers of the *Anniston* (Ala.) *Star* said he never would have been able to travel to the then Soviet Union and meet leaders firsthand if the trip had not been subsidized. "What we wrote is a better standard for judging independence, intelligence and integrity than who paid for the trip," he said.[15] John Causten Currey of the *Daily Oklahoman* and *Oklahoma City Times* said that familiarization trips offered by the armed services provided the only way that editorial writers could see what the defense budgets bought. He said a paid trip to Israel as an official guest provided him a picture of the Middle East he could not have obtained as a private citizen.[16] Smith Hempstone, then a syndicated columnist, contended that any problems involved in accepting a subsidized trip could be overcome by letting readers know who paid for the trip.[17] Richard B. Laney of the *Deseret News,* Salt Lake City, wondered how free travel could be compromising to those who accepted it, since he suspected that invitations are extended only to those known, or thought to be, friendly. "The persuasion of those already persuaded may not be gutsy PR," he wrote, "but it's hardly an attack on editorial morality either."[18]

One of the earliest, and strongest, statements concerning the dangers of accepting free trips was made more than 20 years before NCEW tightened its code. In 1952 Robert Estabrook of the *Washington Post* wrote:

> At least a respectable argument can be made that the public interest is served in making available to newspaper readers more information about governmental programs, particularly programs abroad. The plain fact is that many newspapers, if left to their own resources, would neglect these areas and their readers would be the poorer for it. . . .
>
> If we expect to persuade our followers there is something wrong with unreported political funds or junkets by Congressmen at the taxpayers' expense, then we have an obligation, it seems to me, to pay our own way. We properly criticize "influence" with public officials, but I wonder if our readers, if they knew of the all-expense tours, would see much difference.[19]

Stricter codes, unless one stays home and makes no junkets, cost more money. In general, however, newspapers and the other media are more prosperous than they were when Estabrook wrote. If editors and publishers think their staff members should be sent off somewhere for a story, they should pay as much of their way as they possibly can. What they pay out in money they will regain in credibility with readers.

Gifts

When newspaper salaries were notoriously low, some reporters reasoned that free liquor and tickets to shows and games helped make up for the bucks they didn't get. Today salaries are up and gifts are down. Some newspapers have attempted to stop the flow of gifts, however inconsequential. "We no longer see cases of scotch arriving for the sports staff at Christmas," Catherine Ford, associate editor of the *Calgary* (Alberta) *Herald,* wrote in a *Masthead* symposium on ethics. "The shopping columnist does not furnish his house with presents from retailers; the fashion editor buys her own clothes. No newspaper with any sense of ethics at all accepts free trips, considerations from advertisers or free gifts to staff members. Only rarely will an editor approve of staff participation in media events offering prizes, or accept complimentary tickets for staff."[20]

Some editors contend that if writers can be bought for a bottle of whiskey or a lunch they have no integrity worth buying. Mark Clutter of the *Wichita* (Kan.) *Beacon* has asked why newspaper people should "be offended by gifts of whiskey, ham or similar items." Sometimes the gifts are a matter of "public relations routine"; sometimes they are "expressions of genuine friendship or admiration," he said. "Whatever the motive, it would be churlish to refuse. . . . No one can give payola to a man of integrity. To a man who has no integrity, practically everything is payola."[21] Jack Craemer of the *San Rafael* (Calif.) *Independent Journal,* however, said everyone on that paper sent everything back to donors, even though they "look upon us as goof-balls."[22]

■ ECONOMIC INTERESTS

Economic and business interests of publishers and other non-news, non-editorial executives, as well as their civic interests, can also make credible editorial writing more difficult for staff members and hurt the overall credibility of the newspaper. Nor can editorial writers themselves expect exemption from economic effects. The newspaper is a business; one of its owners' first concerns is to make a profit. One of the editorial writer's concerns is to make enough money and have a steady enough job to live securely and comfortably.

To a larger extent than many businesses, the profitability of a newspaper is tied to the growth and prosperity of its community. When a community grows, for a newspaper the result is likely to be more circulation and more advertising. The temptation to ally a newspaper with whatever brings growth and income to a community remains a fairly consistent one in most communities. This temptation may be a little easier to resist when all the financial and environmental costs of unplanned growth are faced squarely. Still, it's difficult not to get excited editorially when a major industry, especially a "clean" one, is looking at your town for a new plant.

Greensboro, N.C., faced that situation when local business leaders seemed about to convince the Carolina-Virginia Fashion Exhibitors to move from another North Carolina city to Greensboro. Local leaders hoped the new headquarters would provide a catalyst for lagging downtown renewal. The Greensboro *News & Record* gave the story major news coverage and editorials initially praised the coming of the facility. But then, as editorial page editor John Alexander noted, "the price tag for city tax contributions in support of the effort" kept changing. An editorial chided the campaign leaders for not keeping the community better informed and for not "lay[ing] out the facts as quickly as possible." Meanwhile, community business leaders, including the newspaper publisher, who enlisted the assistance of the newspaper's marketing staff, waged an all-out and eventually successful effort to bring in the organization. Alexander said that "the contrast in approaches" between the business and editorial sides of the newspaper became "a sore point with many business and government leaders." Alexander saw no perfect solution but concluded: "Whatever the newspaper's involvement as a corporate citizen, the editorial page must be free to state its opinions freely, consistent with its own philosophy—even if it means not backing a favored project, or raising questions about it."[23]

Closely related to the temptation to look favorably on growth is a tendency among editorial writers toward what might be called local or regional provincialism. Writers should take pride in their cities, their states and their regions. They should want to see their areas prosper and become attractive places in which to live. But it is hard sometimes for them to see beyond their own circulation areas—and such provincialism can become a vested interest. For example, a writer may condemn a proposed federal dam halfway across the country as a congressional boondoggle but praise a proposed local dam as an economic necessity. An editor in Southern California may look with longing toward what appears to be an excess of water flowing into San Francisco Bay, but an editor in Northern California is likely to argue that water in the north should stay there. One challenge for editorial writers is to lift their sights and those of their readers beyond the city limits and the near bank of the next river.

Another test of editorial independence can come when a major advertiser threatens to withhold advertising because of something that has appeared—or might appear—in the editorial or news columns. Does the publisher stand firm and let the advertiser pull out? What does a newspaper do when it learns that an advertiser has been caught in an unfair trade practice or sex discrimination? What happens when a local supermarket wants to build a new store or local business leaders want to build a football stadium in an area that the community had previously designated as noncommercial or protected wetland?

Taking a strong stand against business interests can be tough, especially if the financial well-being of the newspaper itself is at stake. In the long run, newspapers probably serve themselves best if they take a firm stand at the beginning of a confrontation. A publisher who refuses to back down to an advertiser's threats will let it be known to other potential threateners that the paper will stand firm against them as well. A paper that can take an editorial stand against its own immediate financial interests can gain public respect that may eventually help not only its credibility but its economic condition as well.

■ CIVIC OR PUBLIC JOURNALISM

When the previous edition of the book was being prepared, "civic journalism" or "public journalism" was a contentious topic. Newspaper editors had—and still have—different ideas about what it means. All agreed, however, that this type of journalism posed two questions: To what extent should a newspaper seek input from readers in setting its news and editorial agendas? To what extent should a newspaper become involved in community issues?

Civic journalism is no longer a radical idea, according to Jan Schaffer, executive director of the Pew Center for Civic Journalism, citing an overflow of applications for the center's seminars.[24] "This journalism," she said, "tries to treat people as players in a self-governing society, not just passive spectators."[25] According to Chris Peck, then editor of the Spokane, Wash., *Spokesman-Review*, which has engaged in civic journalism projects, "[C]ivic journalism arose from a concern over the growing disconnection between readers and newspapers and community life."[26]

The person generally recognized as the guru of "public journalism," Jay Rosen of New York University, has said that while traditional journalism seeks to "inform the public" and act as a "watchdog" over government, civic or public journalism "tries to strengthen the community's capacity to recognize itself, converse well and make choices."[27] Its purpose, according to Rosen, is "to encourage civic participation, improve public debates and enhance public life, without, of course, sacrificing the independence that a free press demands and deserves."[28]

But to William F. Woo of the *St. Louis* (Mo.) *Post-Dispatch,* talk about organizing communities sounded as though newspapers had declared "that they have become the electorate." Woo asked: "What if IBM or the Yellow Pages or Bill Gates were to [designate] themselves as the convener of the community?"[29]

The extent of disagreement among editors was illustrated during an exchange on the NCEW e-mail discussion list. After considerable discussion, the list moderator, Phineas Fiske of *Newsday,* said he thought a principal problem was that civic journalism had been ill-defined. "It seems to range from finding out what's on your community's mind, at one end, to directing your community to solutions for its problems, in the middle, to leading your community by the hand to those solutions, at the other end." He saw the first alternative as "unexceptionable" and the second as "problematic for the news-side but well within the ambit of the editorial page." He saw the third as "asking for trouble when pursued news-side (although that's where it tends to be pursued, I gather), and a little worrisome for an editorial page."[30]

In an attempt to determine their attitudes, more than 1,000 newspaper journalists were asked to judge the merits of four aspects of civic journalism. Of these respondents, 62 percent said they "strongly approved" of the first aspect listed, to "provide information on alternative solutions"; 60 percent said they strongly approved of the second, to "develop enterprise stories to focus attention on community problems"; 31 percent strongly approved of the third, to "poll the public to determine most pressing issues." Only 25 percent strongly approved of the fourth aspect, to "conduct town meetings to discover key issues." The survey suggested that two-thirds of the journalists drew the line between developing and providing information, on one hand, and inserting themselves directly into the public opinion process.[31]

A survey of NCEW members found that "some editorial writers [feel] that public journalism projects are encroaching on their turf." More than 75 percent of those surveyed saw "a natural relationship between public journalism and the opinion pages"; 60 percent saw public journalism as an area in which news and editorial staffs should cooperate. However, Camille Kraeplin, who conducted the survey, concluded that the answers implied "that support [among editorial writers] might be stronger for efforts that are overseen by the editorial staff." She also suggested, "Reporters concerned about maintaining their objectivity may feel less threatened by projects that involve the newsroom but are officially under editorial auspices."[32]

Descriptions and examples of what several newspapers have done with civic journalism appear in the section titled "Bringing the Community Aboard," in Chapter 19 ("Innovations in Design and Content").

■ PERSONAL EXPERIENCES

In the nearly two decades in which I worked on editorial pages, I tried to limit my civic activities to those that required little time and seemed to pose little risk of conflict with editorial policy. Looking back, I think I should have limited myself even more. I inherited a Rotary Club membership from my predecessor on the *Columbian,* faithfully attended luncheon meetings for nearly 12 years and never encountered any conflict of interest that I recognized. I was never asked to serve on the publicity committee. I never had an occasion to write an editorial either praising or criticizing the club or its activities. Membership benefited me, I thought, because it brought me into contact with leaders of the business community whom otherwise I might have found difficult to get to know. I allowed myself to think my membership benefitted the newspaper too. Instead of being an unknown person in an ivory tower, expressing opinions more liberal than most of those of the club's members, I was a fellow member whom they could poke fun at over typographical or other errors that appeared in the paper. I tried to avoid such activities as clerking at the club's rummage sale and selling tickets for its travel series.

An organization in which I was not so successful in avoiding conflict was Design for Clark County. It consisted of civic-minded citizens who wanted to ensure good government and a good environment for the community. The conflict began when I agreed to head one of four goals committees, the one on government. The committee proved to be the most active of the four, perhaps because goals can be expressed more specifically in government than in other areas of the community. Because of the attention the committee received and because the goals generally coincided with the *Columbian*'s editorial policies, some members of the community began to think that the newspaper and I were running Design. I later backed off sharply in my participation, but the association between the paper and the organization had been established so strongly in people's minds that it was several years before the effect of my initial involvement was forgotten. Design might have been more effective if it had been perceived as a voice more independent of the newspaper.

I also served for a short time on the board of the Washington Environmental Council, a private non-profit organization. No problems resulted as long as the council focused on general environmental policies, but when it began to talk about supporting and opposing candidates for the legislature, I got out fast. I found myself in a more difficult position, however, when I agreed to serve on the Washington State Planning Commission. It was not a real planning commission. I would not have served on an official state policy agency. It was a two-year ad hoc committee of citizens and officials charged with proposing a new state planning act. Mostly it held hearings on what other people thought the state should do. Eventually the staff, with some help from commission members, drew up a model act to submit to the legislature. The act didn't get very far—or I probably would have encountered greater conflict than I did. I thought I should not comment editorially on the proposal, although I did write an article for the op-ed page trying to explain the model act (with an editor's note pointing out my connection with the commission). Participation on the commission made for two interesting and informative years. If the act had been seriously considered for adoption, though, a conflict of interest would have prevented me from commenting editorially on it and probably would have hurt the credibility of anything the *Columbian* said, even if someone else had done the writing.

I felt less concern about the four years that I served on the Washington Commission for the Humanities, a private, non-profit organization that awarded money mostly to local groups to bring humanities scholars' ideas to bear on public issues. Some of the awards were controversial among the commission members, but I don't remember any that would have called for editorial comment in my newspaper. (This was before the National Endowment for the Arts and, to a lesser degree, the National Endowment for the Humanities, became matters of public controversy.) One reason I enjoyed the commission was that it gave me the chance to know and associate with the other members. It was a stimulating group, concerned with projects that generally were far enough away from my circulation area to present few chances for conflict. Besides, I told myself, an editorial writer needs to have some stimulating, continuing associations beyond those of family, religion and the Rotary Club. Editorial writers aren't supposed to be hermits.

▧ CONCLUSION

Probably few editorial writers, and newspaper people in general for that matter, are directly influenced by the gifts, travel and other favors they receive. The publicity over tougher codes has made many of them sensitive to the most blatant forms of handouts. They know that they are not being influenced by the ticket or the drink. Editorial writers may know that they have made every effort possible to report objectively on a free trip they have taken. But do their readers know? If they were told, would they believe it?

When conflict of interest is involved, appearance can be as important as reality in maintaining credibility.

▧ QUESTIONS AND EXERCISES

1. As an editorial writer, where would you draw the line on participation in political and civic affairs? Would the size of the community make a difference?

2. Does an editorial writer or editor have a responsibility to participate in the life of the community in addition to contributing through work on the paper? Again, might the answer depend on the size of the community?

3. Should an editorial writer feel freer to accept a civic task that is less likely than other tasks to affect the community in which the paper circulates? Does distance, in other words, make a difference?

4. Should an editorial writer feel freer to contribute to causes supported by the editorial policy of the newspaper than to other causes?

5. Should newspaper management people feel freer to participate in community affairs than news and editorial people do?

6. Should a newspaper establish a code that spells out what freebies, trips and other perquisites news and editorial people can accept? If so, where should the paper draw the line?

7. If a newspaper does not establish a code, how should it avoid conflict of interest or the appearance of conflict of interest?

8. How do you respond to the argument that, if journalists are not honest and trustworthy, no code will make them so?

9. If you were an editorial writer, what trips would you regard as acceptable?

10. Have you seen evidence in the columns of newspapers in your area that indicates the writers do or do not accept free trips? If they do, do they explain the circumstances to their readers?

11. Do the papers in your area have official codes concerning professional conduct? If so, what do they prescribe?

Section III

The How of the Editorial Page

CHAPTER TEN

Nine Steps to Editorial Writing

I would not suggest that writing editorials can be codified like a law book or that anyone can learn to write good editorials by learning a few rules. But . . . it would be possible, I submit, for editorial [writers] to advance their craft by giving a little more thought to . . . what would . . . not be rules but intelligent guides.

—VERMONT ROYSTER, WALL STREET JOURNAL [1]

No magic formulas exist for writing editorials. No two editorials are ever exactly alike. Editorial writers have their own styles. Newspapers have different editorial policies. Each day brings new topics for comment. Yet, in spite of all the many possible ways to approach writing editorials, the process is basically the same.

An experienced writer may be able to turn out a prize-winning editorial in an hour or so. A beginner may struggle all day. But each, consciously or subconsciously, proceeds through a succession of steps to produce the journalistic writing form that we call an editorial. The purpose of this chapter is to walk the editorial writer or would-be editorial writer through these steps, one by one. The steps can be defined in different ways, but for our purposes let us identify these nine:

1. Selecting a topic
2. Determining the purpose of the editorial
3. Determining the audience
4. Deciding on the tone of the editorial
5. Researching the topic
6. Determining the general format
7. Writing the beginning of the editorial
8. Writing the body of the editorial
9. Writing the conclusion

To provide an illustration, we will select a topic for an editorial and follow the writing of the editorial through the nine steps.

■ SELECTING A TOPIC

Selecting a topic usually involves deciding among a variety of subjects that might seem appropriate on any one day.

Editorial writers typically scan the morning newspaper, which usually carries international, national, regional, state and local stories that might be worthy of comment, plus off-beat stories that can provide topics for change-of-pace editorials.

On a several-person staff, where writers have their own specialties, some of these topics may automatically fall to certain writers. Selecting a topic may be more difficult on a small staff, especially a one-person staff. Writers with limited time for editorial writing are likely to select subjects that they know about or that they can research easily. When time runs short, it is often easier to write about a national or international issue than about a regional or local one, on which you are likely to have to do your own digging for information. Even where writers are few, they should try to select topics from day to day that will provide readers with a variety of subjects at different levels, from local to international.

Questions a writer might ask in deciding on a topic: Can I make a significant contribution to public understanding on this topic? Do I have information or insights that are not generally held among my readers? Is discussion of the topic timely: does it come at an appropriate time for public discussion? Some of these questions may overlap with our next steps, determining the purpose and the audience of the editorial, but they are part of the process of picking a topic.

For the example in this chapter, let us decide that from the topics available to write about today, we will select a controversial advertisement that was submitted to a number of college newspapers. In February 2001, Black History Month, David Horowitz, president of the Los Angeles–based Center for Popular Culture, attempted to place an ad in several college newspapers. It was titled "10 Reasons Why Reparations for Slavery Is a Bad Idea—and Racist Too." At least 18 newspapers refused to run the ad. Four papers apparently ran it without incident. At the University of Wisconsin–Madison, however, 150 protesters visited a campus newspaper that had run it.[2] At Brown University, the entire press run of the campus paper was stolen and trashed. At the University of California, Berkeley, when 40 students stormed the office of the *Daily Californian*, objecting to the ad, the staff pulled the remaining copies from newspaper racks. The editors ran a front-page apology—an in-depth editorial explaining the situation—and offered a full page for rebuttal.[3] The topic should be of interest to journalists, because editors constantly make decisions about what is appropriate or inappropriate to print and on occasion about what to do when a mistake has been made.

Picking editorial topics is, in itself, an important part of trying to persuade readers. Communication research shows that the mass media exert their strongest influence when they help set the agenda for public discussion. What the media choose to write and talk about is seen as having a more significant effect on the public than what the media say about the chosen topics.[4] Selecting also is the first step toward getting readers to read what you write. You should not pick topics solely to attract the most readers, but if you write about obscure, technical or dull topics, potential readers are certain to move on to other parts of the paper.

■ DETERMINING PURPOSE AND AUDIENCE

Determining the purpose and determining the audience of an editorial are related. The purpose of an editorial is to convince a certain audience to think or do something. The purpose may not be to persuade all of our readers. We may want to urge all readers to vote for a certain candidate for office, or we may want to direct our editorial primarily toward convincing readers who are not inclined to be favorable to this candidate. We may want to urge readers in general to turn out for a public hearing on a proposed freeway through the city, or we may want to convince members of the highway commission that the freeway is not a good idea.

We may have more than one audience in mind for an editorial. We may want both to convince the highway commission and to get people to turn out for a hearing. On occasion an editorial, addressed to readers in general, will contain sufficient technical information to speak to the experts as well. On other occasions an editorial will be directed specifically to the narrower group. In two-level editorials, writers should be careful not to become so involved in the fine points that they lose their general readers.

One type of two-level editorial is an "open letter" that is nominally addressed to one person, perhaps a public official. When John Ashcroft was sworn in as U.S. attorney general, the *Detroit Free Press* wrote an editorial directed toward Ashcroft titled "Dear John." The theme was expressed in this sentence: "Your new job will require you to rise above your history."

Most editorials are less specific in terms of intended audience or intended action. In many cases editorials, at least on state, national or international issues, will never be read by the people likely to make the decisions on those issues. In such instances, an editorial may urge some action, but the purpose is primarily to enlighten and convince local readers.

Such was the case involving another Oregon issue discussed in an editorial that appeared in the *St. Petersburg* (Fla.) *Times.* In an incident that got national attention, a prisoner's private confession to his priest was surreptitiously taped by local law enforcement authorities, who planned to use the confession in court. Since most readers probably would not be aware of a case from that far away, and because the circumstances were complex, the writer provided an extended explanation. The editorial ("The sanctity of the confessional") cited the position of the Catholic Archdiocese of Portland and civil rights groups in support of the claim that the tape should not be used and should be destroyed. (Eventually the courts ruled that the tape should not be admitted into evidence.)

The purpose of an editorial and the audience for it will depend partly on our understanding of how persuasion through editorials takes place. Half a century ago mass communications were thought to exert a strong, direct influence on audiences. The Bullet Theory (or Hypodermic Needle Theory) that was popular then suggested that information and opinion from the media flowed directly into the heads of recipients. Editorials, presumably, would be read and acted upon by readers. Then, in the 1940s, researchers began to find that audiences were not paying as much attention as had been thought and were not being persuaded to the degree anticipated.[5] To explain this apparent inattention, researchers came up with the Two-Step Flow Theory. It maintained that ideas tended to flow from the media to a select group of opinion leaders, who in turn passed ideas on to the general population. Thus, if only 20 percent of readers read editorials every day, this theory suggested, that was all right, since presumably those few were the opinion leaders. But that theory didn't last long either. Further research showed that information flow is much more complex. The population is not neatly divided into leaders and followers. Much information goes directly to users of the media, not through a middle level.[6] Reader surveys show that relatively large percentages of readers read editorials at least once in a while.[7]

Current theory suggests that it is upon this general audience that a newspaper's editorials have the most effect over a long period. The effect is produced not so much by specific editorials as by the day-to-day dripping of the editorial writer's ink on the stone of the public consciousness. It is the members of a community who decide elections, decide whether to stay or move to another city,

THE SANCTITY OF THE CONFESSIONAL

Of the recognized privileged communications, the confession of a penitent to a priest would seem the most sacred. The act of confession, ridding one's soul of the missteps in a life, is by its nature incriminating to the penitent. That is especially true when the confession is heard in a jail and, unbeknownst to priest and prisoner, is taped by officials.

That is what happened in Eugene, Ore., last month. A 20-year-old prisoner implicated in the deaths of three teens asked for a Catholic priest. But before the Rev. Tim Mockaitis met with Conan Wayne Hale, prison authorities arranged for the confession to be taped without the knowledge of either of the participants. A confession is sacred, and its confidentiality is protected by law. The tape should be destroyed. Prison officials should be disciplined in such a way that this will not happen again.

The district attorney in Lane County where this occurred, Doug Harcleroad, cites a portion of Oregon law that he says allowed the taping.

He acquired the tape through a court order and may decide to use it in the prosecution of Hale. His primary concern is to solve the triple homicide, an admirable sense of purpose if he were not trampling rights, laws and long-held customs in the process. Hale faces burglary and theft charges in the triple deaths.

The Catholic Archdiocese of Portland called for the tape to be destroyed, quoting to Harcleroad the portion of Oregon law that protects the confidentiality of what is said between priests and followers.

The American Civil Liberties Union also protested. The Catholic League for Religious and Civil Rights, an association of lay Catholics, called for a federal investigation of the incident.

All of this is an appropriate uproar over an egregious invasion of privacy and an assault on freedom of religion. No question, the tape should be destroyed.

St. Petersburg Times

or feel good or bad about their community. All these people are the editorial writer's principal audience, even when an editorial calls on a school board to fire a superintendent or criticizes a city manager for a mistake. Public officials are as likely to be motivated by an aroused public as by an editorial's eloquent logic.

In determining the purpose and audience for the "10 Reasons" editorial, we have two distinctly different possibilities. If we are writing for a college newspaper or for a paper in a college town, we might write the editorial primarily for a college-oriented audience. One purpose might be to explore and explain issues thoroughly. A different purpose might be to take a clear, strong stand on one side of the controversy, perhaps to admonish the editors who, in our opinion, made wrong editorial decisions. If we are writing for a more general audience, our purpose might be to describe and explain the issues involved as briefly as possible and then draw a conclusion that recognizes some merit on both sides. In this case let us assume we are writing for a general audience. Since most of our readers are not especially versed on this issue, our purpose will be to explain and weigh the issues before drawing a conclusion.

■ DECIDING THE TONE

At least as far back as Aristotle, writers have been concerned with how they can best persuade their audiences. Aristotle identified three avenues available to the persuader: the character of the persuader, the attitude of the hearer and the arguments themselves.[8] The more credible the persuader, the more likely it is that an audience will be persuaded. If an editorial page has attained credibility with its readers over the years, editorials on that page are likely to be viewed favorably. Aristotle thought the communicator needed good sense, good will and a good moral character—appropriate prescriptions for an editorial writer.[9] Concerning the attitude of the audience, Aristotle saw that "persuasion is effected through the audience when they are brought . . . into a state of emotion." For example, "pain or joy, or liking or hatred" can have an effect in changing attitudes. Concerning the third avenue, he saw that "persuasion is effected by the argument themselves."[10] Thus, at least from the time of Aristotle, persuaders have recognized that they have a choice: They can appeal to the emotions or to the rationality of their audiences.

When editorial writers select a tone for an editorial, they have many choices, ranging from deeply serious to satirical and humorous. As for the choice between an appeal primarily to emotion or one primarily to reason, some recent research suggests that emotion and reason may not necessarily be in opposition to each other and that simultaneous appeals to both may serve to reinforce persuasion.[11] For the purposes of most editorials, however, writers choose between an appeal based mainly on feelings, values and symbols and one based mainly on information, evidence and logic. Their decisions will depend on the subject matter and the occasion as well as their own preferences. On the day following the assassination of a prominent political figure, for example, a writer might use an emotional tone to express outrage and grief over the tragedy. The next day the writer might take a more rational approach to talk about what contributed to the killing and how to prevent such incidents in the future. An emotional approach might be appropriate to provide entertainment, to arouse readers to action, to chastise or to praise. A rational approach might be more appropriate to explain to readers something they don't know or to convince them of the correctness of the editorial writer's conclusions.

Emotion undoubtedly plays a smaller role in editorial writing today than several decades ago, when daily newspapers were numerous and subscribers could take the paper that came closest to expressing their own opinions. Readers relished reading emotional, partisan appeals, and, if opinions were not changed, they were at least reinforced. Today's editorial writers must appeal to readers with a much broader spectrum of opinions. A rousing editorial based mostly on bombast may please a small group of partisans but leave other readers unconvinced or repulsed. Today's readers are better educated than readers of a hundred years ago and people as a whole are better informed: they should be more able to recognize incorrect or incomplete information.

It may be more fun to dash off an editorial that attacks a person or policy without mercy, and perhaps without much thought. Such an editorial may draw the strongest, most immediate response from readers. But what value does the editorial have beyond giving a momentary emotional high to some readers and long-term pain to others? Henry M. Keezing of the *New Britain* (Conn.) *Herald* said that one of his prized possessions was a letter to the editor lauding a flamboyant editorial he had whipped up in a matter of minutes. The letter was highly complimentary but it "was written in pencil, in a scrawling longhand, on a piece of paper which a beer distributor gives to cafes and taverns for use for menus." Keezing had made a hit with someone in a tavern. But he said he would have much preferred to hear from a community leader, a legislator or a person of influence.[12]

Columnist James J. Kilpatrick, who writes with more indignation than most American newspaper writers, has described how the complexities of today's world have inhibited him from just sounding off. He noted that writing about something you know nothing about is easy; "when research fails, prejudice is there to prop you." But "what raises the sweat and paralyzes the fingers on the keys is to grapple with an issue in which the equities are divided," he said. "It is a maddening thing, but damned little in the editor's world is all white or all black; the editor's world is full of mugwump grays."[13]

The time has come to decide on the tone we will take in our editorial about the *Daily Californian* controversy. That should be an easy decision. On occasion it might be appropriate to write in an emotional manner on a First Amendment or racial topic. It might be desirable to raise a public outcry against trampling journalistic or religious freedoms, or against racially discriminatory policies or actions. If the editor had been fired or the newspaper shut down, we might sound off in loud protest. But this situation is more complicated. Given our general audience, the subject probably will require explanation of editorial and advertising practices as well as the First Amendment status of advertising. A rational, explanatory approach seems needed here.

■ RESEARCHING THE TOPIC

When we decide whether our editorial will be primarily emotional or rational in tone, we also determine the type of research we will have to do. If we can write the piece off the tops of our heads, we can skip research. If we are going to present only one point of view (about which we will say more when we discuss the next step) we can limit our research to the arguments on one side.

The amount of research conducted by writers depends to some extent on how much time they have and the availability of resource materials. Very few writers have the luxury of going to the public library, a law library, the city hall or the courthouse to dig out information for that day's editorial. In the past a telephone call—to an office across town or to the capital—might have provided a writer with the only opportunity to obtain information that was not immediately available in the newspaper office. Today, of course, writers have a vast array of information available, literally at their fingertips, on the Internet. At a minimum they are likely to have, easily at hand, a complete or recent version of the news account that prompted the editorial.

In this instance the available material includes four articles from the editorial pages of the *San Francisco Chronicle.* On March 15 the *Chronicle* ran an article by the editor of the *Daily Californian*, Daniel Hernandez, explaining and defending the actions of the newspaper staff.[14] Eleven days later came three articles. One, written by Horowitz, defended his right to run the ad and to raise the reparations issues.[15] A second article, by a Berkeley resident and member of the National Council for African-American Men, accused Horowitz of racism. He wrote that the ad's contention, that reparations already had been paid in the form of welfare, amounted to characterizing an entire race as living on welfare.[16] The third writer, an El Cerrito freelancer, accused Horowitz of running the ad just to make trouble and to promote himself.[17] The newspaper's actions thus drew criticism from two distinctly different points of view.

Critics on one side contended that the issue was racism and that the ad should not have been run in the first place. Critics on the other side saw the First Amendment as the issue, arguing that Horowitz had a right to place the ad, however controversial, as a matter of free speech.

▩ DETERMINING THE GENERAL FORMAT

Deciding whether to be basically emotional or rational in our editorial does not determine how the editorial will be written, especially if we decide on a rational tone. Communication researchers have devoted a lot of effort to trying to discover how arguments can be presented in the most persuasive manner. Among their concerns have been (1) one-sided versus two-sided arguments, (2) the ordering of arguments and (3) the degree to which opinions can be changed.

Research going back to World War II suggests that the one-sided versus two-sided decision partly depends on the audience being addressed. One-sided arguments were found to be more persuasive when the receivers of messages already agreed with the arguments, when receivers were of lower intelligence or less educated, when the receivers were not familiar with the issue being discussed and were not likely to be exposed to opposition arguments in the future, or when the topic was not controversial.[18] Two-sided presentations, which present opposing arguments, were more effective when the receivers were initially hostile to the persuader's view, highly educated, accustomed to hearing both sides of an argument or likely to hear the other side eventually.[19]

Researchers have come up with contradictory findings about the order of arguments. Both primacy (the favored argument first) and recency (the favored argument last) have been found to be persuasive. The primacy approach has the advantage of drawing an early favorable opinion from the audience, an opinion that may remain unchanged during the remainder of the presentation. The recency approach has the advantage of giving the last impression a better chance of being remembered. One line of reasoning suggests that, if you have arguments that your audience is likely to receive favorably, you should present them first to establish a favorable setting for less favorable arguments later. If you have a solution for a problem or a need, it may be better to present the problem or the need first, then suggest your solution.[20] Researchers agree that the weakest spot for an argument is in the middle of the message, so you might put arguments unfavorable to your position there.[21]

The third aspect of communication research involves the extent to which readers can be persuaded to change their opinions. It seems clear that readers' first inclinations are to seek and perceive information that reinforces their present viewpoints. Some studies suggest that reinforcing opinions is about all that can be expected of editorials. Readers, they point out, tend to ignore, disbelieve or reinterpret information that does not conform to their own beliefs. Still, some research shows that readers sometimes seek out information that is contrary to their beliefs and, within limits, are willing to modify their beliefs. A person presumably is able to feel comfortable with a different opinion if it is perceived to fall within a certain comfort zone. The closer the offered opinion is to the outer edge of that zone, the greater the change that will have to occur in the person's opinion. If the offered opinion is even barely outside the zone, however, it is likely to be perceived as more divergent than it actually is, and therefore unacceptable. The trick for the editorial writer is to know enough about the newspaper's readers to be able to push for a maximum amount of opinion change without going so far as to antagonize readers with demands for too much change.[22]

In selecting the format of the editorial, we might decide to present the arguments on only one side if we thought that side was clearly right and we stood a good chance of convincing readers with such a presentation. We might also take this approach if we felt we needed to make a very strong statement on the issue. In this case, however, the articles that we have at hand express two different points of view to be expressed and considered:

- that, because of the blatant racism expressed, the advertisement never should have been run in the first place
- that, whatever the content, publication of the ad was protected as free speech under the First Amendment

Making, examining and weighing these two points seems to call for a two-sided editorial. If we do a good job of presenting the arguments, readers may not know what we conclude until the end.

In teaching editorial writing classes, I have found it helpful, in explaining these and other formats, to analyze editorials using formulas that look like something that might come out of a chemistry course. SA_1A_2DC describes a two-sided editorial. S stands for the statement of the *situation* that prompted the editorial. A_1A_2 indicates the presentation of the *argument* on one side of the issue (A_1) followed by *argument* on the other side (A_2). D is *discussion*, following by the *conclusion* (C). SAC indicates a one-sided editorial with the conclusion at the end; CSAC, a one-sided editorial with the conclusion stated at the beginning. Not many editorials are written strictly according to these formulas, but they give the beginning editorial writer an idea of the options that are available.

■ WRITING THE BEGINNING

The beginning of an editorial may be the most important part. The first few words must prove sufficiently interesting to attract readers to the editorial. Although we have noted types of editorials that start by stating the conclusion, the most common beginning is a brief statement of the proposal, incident or situation that has prompted the editorial. It may be a simple restatement of information that has been reported in the news columns. This approach is especially appropriate for readers who have no previous knowledge of what the editorial writer is talking about. It also provides a way into the editorial without antagonizing readers who may hold views different from the editorial writer's.

Sometimes a writer needs to present an even broader approach than a statement of the facts of the situation. Starting with some background (designated B in our editorial-writing formula) might help readers understand how the immediate topic relates to more general information with which they may be familiar. Sometimes an effective way to get readers to modify their opinions is to begin with the statement of a generally accepted point of view. After readers have become comfortable with what the editorial writer is saying, the editorial can take what I call a "Yes, but" switch to try to convince readers that another point of view makes even more sense. This approach might be particularly effective in an editorial that seeks to debunk commonly held views or takes a stand that may surprise readers. This approach is not the same as building up an artificial argument to be knocked down. The opening argument needs to be credible. "Yes, but" might be useful when a newspaper wants to change or modify an earlier editorial stance on an issue. A "yes, but" editorial can be readable and persuasive, especially if the writer sneaks up on the reader and presents the counterargument unexpectedly.

An editorial sometimes can be started with a question (Q). This question can serve to focus the point of an editorial immediately and tell readers that they can expect to find the answer by reading the editorial. A question that arouses curiosity can be effective in attracting readers. But, if a question simply asks, "What should be done about such-and-such?" and the reader answers, "I don't care" or "I don't know," the editorial writer has lost a reader. A meatier question might suggest alternatives: "Should River City continue with the city manager form of government or return to a system with elected commissions?"

If we wanted to write an editorial taking a firm stand and presenting only one side, our first sentence quite likely would make our stand clear to readers. If we thought the editors should have stood their ground and defended publication of the ad as an expression of free speech, we might write: "The editors of the *Daily Californian* have a lot to learn about the First Amendment." If we thought they were wrong in running the ad and right in apologizing, we might write: "Let's hope the editors of the *Daily Californian* have learned a hard First Amendment lesson." If we thought they were wrong in running the ad and wrong in apologizing so abjectly, we might write: "The editors of the *Daily Californian* have a lot to learn about running a newspaper."

Because we want to consider both points of view in this editorial, we could begin with a statement of the situation (S) such as this: "The editors of a student newspaper at the University of California, Berkeley, have apologized for running an ad that protesters have described as racist." But how dull! First, it's not much, if any, different from a news lead. Even more important, it doesn't frame the issues we want to talk about: What is the right thing for a newspaper staff to do when confronted with an ad with questionable or inappropriate content? A more interesting opener: "Editors of a student newspaper at the University of California, Berkeley, are being attacked from both front and rear for publishing, and then apologizing for, an ad that some critics say was racist." This lead briefly describes the situation and also sets the framework for our two-sided presentation. It provides no hint of what our conclusion is likely to be.

■ WRITING THE BODY OF THE EDITORIAL

The steps we have discussed thus far, starting with picking a topic, have covered a number of pages and involved quite a lot of explanations. Except possibly for research, most of the steps could have been taken quickly. Not more than a few seconds may be required for an experienced editorial writer to select a topic, decide on the purpose and the proper audience, determine the tone and select the general approach. Much of the process takes place without conscious reflection. After writing editorials for a few years, editorial writers get a feeling for the right way, for them, to write an editorial. With the beginning determined, at least tentatively, and all the other steps behind them, they are ready to write the body of the editorial—the explanations, the arguments and the analysis. Here is where they either will or will not convince their readers. Here is where they win or lose in the battle to persuade.

If we decide to use the opening sentence that appears near the end of the last section, we will need to compose an editorial based on the SBA_1A_2DC

To Publish or Not to Publish
To Apologize or Not to Apologize

Editors of a student newspaper at the University of California, Berkeley, are being attacked from both front and rear for publishing, and then apologizing for, an ad that some critics say was racist.

The *Daily Californian* at the University of California, Berkeley, recently accepted an advertisement that contended that African-Americans do not deserve reparations for the long years during which their ancestors were enslaved because they already have been receiving their due through welfare support. Before the newspaper was fully distributed across campus, 40 protesters stormed the *Daily Cal* office protesting that the ad was racist, that it characterized African-Americans as a race as welfare recipients. Staff members immediately withdrew the remaining copies from newsstands. The following day the editor wrote a front page editorial apologizing for running the ad.

Some journalists have criticized the paper for accepting the ad, which they contended was racist and inflammatory. To suggest that African-Americans had been compensated for their years of slavery by welfare payments, they say, was both demeaning and unfair, since they are a minority among Americans who depend on welfare to make ends meet.

Other journalists have criticized the paper's staff members for not standing their ground and insisting on their right, as a business, to accept or reject ads from whomever they wish. They contend that, if the contents of the ad were inflammable or inaccurate,

even potentially libelous, the editors, if they had known their media law, could have cited *New York Times v. Sullivan.* In that case the Supreme Court declined to find as libel an ad run in the *Times.*

If the paper had rejected the ad, probably nothing more would have been heard, since the sponsor of the ad, David Horowitz, president of the Los Angeles–based Center for Popular Culture, raised no apparent objection when 18 college papers turned it down. He did make an issue of the *Daily Cal's* rejection and subsequent apology. Once the paper had accepted the ad, published it and distributed it to newsstands, a free-speech question could arise. Barring the potentiality of libel or violence, editors open themselves to censorship charges when they "trash" their own newspapers in mid-distribution.

The newspaper staff could properly have accepted or rejected the ad. Once the paper accepted the ad, except for extenuating circumstances, it should have let the ad run. Once the ad was published, staff members should have held to the courage of their First Amendment convictions to stand up to the protesters, and tell them to write letters to the editor or take out their own ads.

If, later, the editors concluded that the contents of the ad were racist, unfair, misleading or inaccurate, they could have written an editorial saying so. Journalists and the other critics should have focused on the merits of the issues raised by the ad, not on the decisions of the newspaper staff.

model (situation, background, argument on one side, argument on the other side, discussion, conclusion). The opening is followed by an explanation of what the controversy is about. Then we will present the argument that the staff should have rejected the ad on the ground that it was excessively blatant in its depiction of African-Americans. Then we will turn to the argument that the ad merited being run on free speech grounds and that the staff should have stuck to its original decision to run it.

In the discussion section we will point out that, if the paper had rejected the ad, probably no more would have been heard. Horowitz himself noted that 18 papers had turned it down without any apparent objection from him. Once the paper had accepted the ad, published it and distributed it to newsstands, however, a free-speech question arises. If the ad was not libelous or likely to provoke violence, by "trashing" it in mid-distribution the editors opened themselves to charges of censorship. As for libel, they would have been on safe grounds. It is often forgotten that in *New York Times v. Sullivan*, the Supreme Court decision that assured the right to criticize public officials, an ad, not a news story, was at issue. As a business, a newspaper generally can accept or reject ads from whomever it wishes.

■ WRITING THE CONCLUSION

Well-written beginnings help attract readers. Well-written endings help convince readers. Possible conclusions for an editorial are as infinite in number and variety as the manner in which the editorial is written. Conclusions vary according to the purposes of the editorial, but a conclusion should express what the writer intends the editorial to accomplish.

The editorial will conclude that the newspaper staff could properly have accepted or rejected the ad, but that once a newspaper accepts an ad, barring extenuating circumstances, it should let it run. In this case staff members should have had the courage of their First Amendment convictions to stand up to the protesters and tell them to write letters to the editor or take out their own ads. If the editors had later concluded that the ad was racist, unfair, misleading or inaccurate, they could have written an editorial saying so. Public discussion should have focused on the issues raised by the ad, not on the decisions of the newspaper staff.

Editorial conclusions vary according to the degree of firmness intended by the writer. I have found it helpful, in acquainting would-be editorial writers with possible varieties of conclusions, to think of them as coming in six general forms. Within each form are variations that primarily reflect degrees of firmness. In order of descending firmness, the six categories are urge, approve, disapprove, conclude righteously, take consolation and come down softly. The categories, ranked in that order, are explained below. The examples within each category are also ranked in descending order of firmness. (I go on at some length about these conclusions, partly to call attention to the wide variety of subject matter covered in editorials.)

Urging

The most specific and direct conclusion is one that urges readers, a government official or a private party to do something. An editorial may urge voters to support or oppose a candidate or ballot proposition. It may urge the president or Congress to compromise on tax cut proposals or welfare reform. It may urge a city council to lower the speed limit on a street or fire the city manager. It may urge readers in general to support something, such as a chemical weapons freeze.

1. *Do*—write or vote or give (to the United Way, for example). This conclusion urges readers to perform a specific action. The *Register-Guard* of Eugene, Ore., said that it was "imperative" that theater, opera, ballet and other arts organizations spend more—not less—to provide Americans access to the arts.

2. *Must*—intended to leave no doubt in the reader's mind about what the editorial writer wants to have done. Referring to criticism of the Vatican's actions during the Holocaust, the *Star Tribune* of Minneapolis, Minn., said the Vatican "must invite scrutiny of its entire past." The *San Diego* (Calif.) *Union-Tribune* concluded that a local airport "must find a way to reduce interference with other airports."

3. *Ought*—less forceful than "must" but still a firm stand. The *Boston Globe* said, "For the sake of children throughout the North [of Ireland] who are not yet confirmed in their prejudices, the IRA ought to give up some of its guns." Referring to proposals to give young people more freedom, the *Omaha World-Herald* said, "Someone ought to take a closer look at whether this makes sense."

4. *Should*—slightly less emphatic than "must" and "ought," but used much more frequently. "As long as utility companies are virtual monopolies," said the *Grand Rapids* (Mich.) *Press,* "they should go out of their way to accommodate customers' needs." The *Detroit Free Press* said, "Private agencies that serve specific ethnic and cultural groups should have programs, or at least counselors, to deal with the problem." The conclusion of our editorial included a "should" statement: "Journalists and the other critics should have focused on the merits of the issues raised by the ad, not on the decisions of the newspaper staff." ("Should" can have two meanings. The manner in which "should" was used in the preceding examples implies obligation, necessity or duty. The other use implies expectation or anticipation of an occurrence. The *Boston Globe* said that a "sentencing reform bill should go a long way toward repairing the flawed system of sentencing convicted criminals in Massachusetts.")

5. *Needs to*—a little less forceful than "ought" and "should." The *Detroit Free Press* said that dialogue concerning a proposed highway project "needs to resume."

6. *We urge*—appropriate when urging voters or public officials to take specific actions. The *News-Times* of Danbury, Conn., said: "We call on New Medford citizens to turn out in good numbers [for a forthcoming town meeting]." Some newspapers try to avoid, or even forbid, the use of "we" in editorials. Usually the point can be made without "we." (See Chapter 5—"Who Is This Victorian 'We'?"—for further discussion of the editorial "we.")

7. *Hope*—"We hope" tempers a recommendation by suggesting that it is only the newspaper's opinion. The *Camden* (N.H.) *Herald* said: "We hope [area students] will take this opportunity to achieve the same success in citizenship [as in academics, music and sports]." The *Denver Post* said: "We sincerely hope the [Schwinn] company finds a 'white knight' to turn it around and preserve the brand name . . . ." (Although you will find "hopefully" in the conclusions of some editorials, it is not an acceptable substitute for "we hope." "Hopefully" is an adverb and, as such, modifies a verb or an adjective.)

Approving

Sometimes no specific action is expected on a public or private matter. Perhaps some action already has been taken that deserves praise, such as a contribution an individual has made to the community or a decision made by a government body. Sometimes an editorial writer may want to commend a proposal without going immediately to the next step to urge its approval. The following, in descending order of enthusiasm, are variations of positive editorial endings:

1. *Badly need*—The *Daily News* of Newport News, Va., concerning plans of a local affairs network to televise coverage of the Virginia General Assembly, said, "Such coverage is badly needed."

2. *Critical*—The *Daily News-Record* of Harrisonburg, Va., said that "scrutiny and oversight of all governmental functions, of which higher education is one, is critical to achieving the kind of accountability taxpayers expect, and deserve."

3. *High praise*—The *Missoulian* of Missoula, Mont., noting a favorable state financial picture, said: "It doesn't get any better than that." The *Daily Camera* in Boulder, Colo., said that if a patients' rights bill passed, "Americans with health insurance will have reason to applaud."

4. *Makes sense*—The *Denver Post* said the ruling on a certain immigration law "makes sense in a country of immigrants."

5. *Good*—*Newsday* of Long Island, N.Y., saw a decision involving power plants as "a triple win: good politics, good sense and good for the environment as well."

6. *Promising*—The *Litchfield County Times* in New Medford, Conn., saw a commission's commitment "to its watchdog role" as "a promising sign."

7. *A step*—According to the *Burlington* (Vt.) *Free Press,* the Department of Forests, Parks and Recreation "is taking a step toward the kind of accountability it owes all Vermonters."

8. *Balance*—The *Detroit Free Press* said a decision by the National Park Service "has struck a fair balance with accessibility and protection." The *Bulletin* in Bend, Ore., described a project as an "excellent balance with economic and environmental concerns."

9. *Interesting*—About a proposal involving ferries, the *Times Colonist* in Victoria, B.C., said: "Interesting idea. Worth looking at."

10. *Depends*—Concerning alternatives for a landfill, the *Akron Beacon Journal* said: "Whether they are worth pursuing depends on the cost to the larger community."

Disapproving

The types of editorials that end in disapproval are similar to those that end in approval, except that the editorial writer decides to come down on the negative side. Disapproving editorials seem not to be as abundant as approving. Here, in descending order, are examples of negative endings:

1. *Condemn*—The Cleveland, Ohio, *Plain Dealer* said that scientists who were risking human lives in experimenting with cloning "deserve to be condemned and shunned." Condemnation certainly was implied in the *Boston Globe*'s reference to "Governor Swift's Draconian sentencing bill."

2. *Bad*—"[A]n incredibly bad idea" was the description that the *Register-Guard* gave to a tax proposal that "would result in a 2003–05 budget earthquake that makes this year's difficulties look like a mild tremor."

3. *No sense*—The *Hartford* (Conn.) *Courant* said that "U.S. indifference to the Caribbean's struggle against AIDS would make no sense at all."

4. *Not worth the risk*—The *Portsmouth* (Ohio) *Daily Times* described "further oil explorations in Big Cypress as well as off Florida's coast [as] not worth the risk."

5. *Shouldn't*—The Scottsbluff (Neb.) *Star-Herald* said that "Missile defense of the United States shouldn't be scrapped because other nations are pitching a fit."

6. *Serious question*—The *Omaha World-Herald* saw proposals to clone pets as "open to serious question."

7. *Less . . . than*—The *Boston Globe* saw tax breaks for the "wealthiest Americans" as "less an economic political program than a political gift wrapped in patriotism."

Concluding Righteously

One of the ministers in Vancouver, Wash., used to call me "the village preacher." Being a preacher himself, he must have intended this epithet as a compliment. I accepted it as such, since I thought I was upholding the moral standards of the community. The adjectival form of "preacher," when applied to an editorial, is not particularly complimentary; readers may resent "preachy" editorials. Still, one purpose of an editorial page is to serve as a community conscience, and one duty of editorial writers is to protect and promote the public good, as they perceive it. So, if editorials take on a high moral tone from time to time, perhaps no one should complain about a little preaching. Here are a few examples of concluding righteously.

1. *The public's rights*—a favorite touchstone for editorial writers making a case against government secrets or private interests. Writers find particularly gratifying the invocation of rights involving the First Amendment and freedom of information. Newspapers can perform a worthwhile function speaking up for these rights, though it is easy for such editorial statements to become clichés. The public gets tired of being preached to about rights, especially when they seem to benefit editors and reporters more than readers. In Montana, the Bureau of Land Management released the names of persons and companies that had "nominated" (proposed) various federal lands for coal leasing but refused to reveal who had nominated what lands. Concluded the *Missoulian:* "The public has a right to know who wants to glom onto what public coal. It has a right to have coal development carefully controlled." In this instance, the paper was contending that the public should know the names, but some who opposed publication might have argued that the *Missoulian* wanted the names for the purpose of publishing an interesting news story.

2. *Preservation of liberties*—another strongly righteous conclusion. In an editorial titled "Freedom's Protector," the now-defunct Los Angeles *Herald Examiner* noted "the never-ending assault on liberty itself by powers that protect themselves—or seek to—by forbidding public criticism of their actions." The editorial saw "the best protector of existing human liberty as a free press, whose importance cannot be overstated," then concluded: "Preservation of these liberties is critical to the health and even the survival of any true democracy. Keep that in mind the next time another judge tries to interfere with full press coverage of a public trial."

Taking Consolation

When events don't go exactly the way an editorial writer wishes, an alternative to disapproving is taking some consolation that the outcome isn't all bad. Here are three of these endings:

1. *Yes, but . . .* — a conclusion that may acknowledge that something untoward has occurred but insist that things aren't so bad as they may seem. When Montana voters turned down an initiative that would have restricted nuclear power plant development in the state, the *Missoulian* concluded: "Industry beat Initiative 71. That means people do not want a ban. But that does not mean the people want nuclear power development."

2. *But at least . . .* —a conclusion that suggests some, but not enough, progress has been made. The *Florida Times-Union* noted that a plan for removing land mines in Bosnia was "painfully slow . . . . but at least it is progress."

3. *Not without faults, but . . .* —a way for editorial writers to indicate that something is less than desirable. The *Danville* (Va.) *Register and Bee* described a health care plan as "not without its faults, but at least it opens the debate on [the] issue."

Coming Down Softly

As any reader of the editorial page knows, not every editorial reaches a firm or clear conclusion. In fact, many editorials purposely remain inconclusive. (Others, unfortunately, arrive at no conclusion in spite of the writer's efforts to do so.) Writers might use inconclusive endings when they want to interpret what is happening or bring their readers information and insights that have not appeared in the news columns. Writers also may resort to this form if they can envision no solution to a problem. Editorial writers, after all, don't have to know all the answers. Here are some examples in decreasing order of firmness.

1. *Could*—used to indicate uncertainty or a suggestion. Uncertainty: The Portland *Oregonian* said that, unless certain steps were taken, "Portland's high-flying vision of itself as an international city could be permanently damaged." Suggestion: The *San Francisco Chronicle* said then-President Clinton "could demonstrate that his loyalty to the welfare of America's economy is important to him as his political future by firing [Commerce Secretary Ron] Brown before his administration is stained even more . . . ." The conclusion of our editorial included a "could" statement: "If, later, the editors concluded that the contents of the ad were racist, unfair, misleading or inaccurate, they could have written an editorial saying so."

2. *Might*—used to indicate an uncertain conclusion. Concerning a proposal that the Canadian prime minister visit South Africa, the *Calgary Herald* concluded: "A formal visit . . . might be in order, but only if he can be sure it would help, not hinder."

3. *But . . .* —suggests that the writer is not fully convinced one side is wholly right. A writer on the *Cleveland Plain Dealer* was not convinced by a study that showed redlining (a bank loan process that makes it harder for African-Americans to obtain financing to purchase homes) was not a

A WORD ABOUT LIBEL

By W. Wat Hopkins
Virginia Polytechnic Institute and State University

The notion that a person could be punished for expressing an opinion is obnoxious to most Americans. Deeply rooted in the heritage of a free press is the concept that newspapers have a duty to comment upon matters of public concern. That concept has been endorsed by the U.S. Supreme Court, but in a roundabout way.

The court's grant of protection for expressions of opinion is one of the murkiest areas of libel law. Indeed, in the case in which the court made it clear that opinion is constitutionally protected, the court specifically said that opinion *is not* constitutionally protected.

The oddly worded opinion was written by Chief Justice William Rehnquist in a case called *Milkovich v. Lorain Journal* (1990). The case began when a sports columnist criticized a finding of a state high school athletics panel that cleared a wrestling coach from wrongdoing in a brawl that occurred during a match. The columnist opined that the coach beat the charge with "the big lie." The columnist claimed he was expressing an opinion, but the court found that calling someone a liar was not an opinion, but a statement of fact. Indeed, Justice Rehnquist wrote that opinions, as a category of speech, are not protected by the First Amendment. He added, however, that the court, in a previous case, had held that for a libel case to be maintained, the plaintiff in the case must be able to prove that the objectionable statement is false (*Philadelphia Newspapers v. Hepps*, 1986). Without proof of falsity, therefore, there is no liability.

In effect, then, because a statement of pure opinion cannot be proved to be true or false, it cannot be the basis of a libel suit. "The mayor is incompetent," therefore, cannot be the basis of a libel action, because one cannot prove that the mayor is or is not competent. "The mayor is a crook," however, is not a statement of opinion; it is a statement of fact, and, even if the statement appears in an editorial, it may be the basis of a libel action. Nor is the statement protected if it is prefaced by the words "we believe" or "in our opinion." The heart of the statement is still that the mayor is a crook—a statement that can be proved to be true or false.

problem in Ohio. "Continued scrutiny is warranted," the editorial said. "But this study is worth noting."

4. *No easy solution*—when no answer seems to be a good one. For example, when sheriff's deputies were searching students attending concerts at the University of Montana, the *Montana Kaimin,* the student newspaper, said "people should be safe from injury [from thrown bottles and cans], but they also have the right to be safe from a random search without a warrant." The editorial concluded: "There is no easy resolution to the problem. UM students and officials should attempt to devise an equitable way to ensure safe concerts."

5. *No solution*—when an editorial writer has no solution at all to offer. Lamenting previous studies aimed at eliminating duplication in the Montana college system, the *Helena* (Mont.) *Independent Record* concluded: "We thus hesitate to advocate another study. Nor do we offer any solutions. Meanwhile—uneasy rests the head wearing the crown."

6. *No issue*—the final step toward softness. These are for editorials that don't even attempt to present an issue. Noting changes in fashions in

slang, for example, the *Montana Standard* of Butte said that things used to be "cool" and "neat" but now were "weird," and that "type" was being attached to a word to create an adjective: "Many newspapers today use a photo-printing process that yields something called 'cold type,' to distinguish it from the actual 'hot metal type' of days gone by. So far, we haven't heard anybody refer to cold-type type, but it's bound to happen. We've got no particular reason for discussing these things. We just did it to be weird."

■ CONCLUSION

Experienced editorial writers do not consciously follow the nine steps to editorial writing that we have taken in this chapter. (In fact, it is arbitrary even to suggest that editorial writing involves nine steps.) But, consciously or subconsciously, writers need to give thought, before they begin writing, to the purpose of an editorial, the audience for which it is intended and the approach that is likely to be most effective with that audience. Sometimes writers can dash off a high-quality editorial without looking for additional information, but trying to find all you can about a subject (given your time constraints) usually pays off. Experienced editorial writers may not give much conscious thought to the organization of their editorials or to the formulas suggested in this chapter. But I have found that beginning writers find the models of one-sided and two-sided editorials helpful in presenting their arguments. I also have found that they appreciate being introduced to various ways to start an editorial and the myriad ways to conclude it. After a few weeks, they no longer need to be reminded of the nine steps, the formulas for editorials or the classifications for endings. They have internalized the process of editorial writing.

■ QUESTIONS AND EXERCISES

1. Find editorials on the same subject that are written in at least three different formats. How are the facts (background information, etc.) handled differently by the writers? What seem to be the writers' assumptions concerning the pre-existing attitudes and prior knowledge of their readers? In what ways are these assumptions different? The same?

2. Find editorials on the same subject that are different in tone. How would you describe the tone of each? Would the approach of any tend to antagonize readers? Cause readers to identify with the writer? Put readers to sleep?

3. Pick a topic and write two editorials using distinctly different formats, for example, SA_1A_2DC and CSAC. Which do you think would be more convincing to most readers in this instance?

4. Select an editorial on a topic that interests you. Then rewrite it in an entirely different tone. Use any of the formats you like. Which editorial is likely to convince more readers?

5. Find several examples of each of the six major types of editorial conclusions. Can you find endings that would fall into categories other than these six?

6. Without substantially changing the editorial, rewrite a coming-down-softly ending to create a conclusion expressing firm approval or disapproval. Do the reverse with an editorial that has a firm conclusion.

7. Select an editorial that is directed toward a single audience and rewrite it as a two-level editorial (addressing a dual audience). For example, pick an editorial that seems directed primarily toward a city council and rewrite it so that general readers will understand how the issue being discussed will affect them and what they ought to do about it.

Ten Steps to Better Writing

Now that we have taken a look at the basic steps in writing an editorial, let us turn our attention to some of the finer points of turning out an editorial that is convincing, terse and well written. We will concentrate on the following ten areas:

1. The right amount of fact
2. Logical conclusions
3. Consistent point of view
4. Clear referents and antecedents
5. Sentences of appropriate length
6. Economy of words
7. Correct grammar
8. Absence of clichés and jargon
9. Proper use of individual words
10. Colorful writing

As one example of how editorials can be improved, I will use the editorial that was written to illustrate the steps described in the previous chapter ("To Publish or Not to Publish").

■ THE RIGHT AMOUNT OF FACT

Editorials should contain only those facts that are necessary for the purposes for which the editorials were written. "Facts are precious things, and to be thoroughly enjoyed must be tasted sparingly and drooled over leisurely," Vermont Royster of the *Wall Street Journal* advised editorial writers.[2] Usually the detail required in an editorial is less than that needed in a news story on the same topic. In many cases editorial readers will have read the news reports and will not need a repetition of all the facts before finding out what the editorial writer has to add. Still, editorial writers cannot assume that all readers have seen or remember the original story. So a compromise between a brief reference and a full factual account must be worked out. Editorial writers must rely on their judgment, but should try for brevity. Space in editorial columns is far more limited than in news columns.

TO PUBLISH OR NOT TO PUBLISH
To Apologize or Not to Apologize
(Revised Version)

Editors of a student newspaper at the University of California, Berkeley, are being attacked from both front and rear for publishing, and then apologizing for, an ad that some critics say was racist.

The *Daily Californian* at the University of California, Berkeley, recently accepted an advertisement that contended that African-Americans do not deserve reparations for the long years during which their ancestors were enslaved. The ad claimed they already have been receiving their due through welfare support. Before the newspaper was fully distributed across campus, 40 demonstrators stormed the *Daily Cal* office protesting that the ad characterized African-Americans as a race of welfare recipients. Staff members immediately withdrew the remaining copies from newsstands. The following day the editor wrote a front page editorial apologizing for running the ad.

Some journalists have criticized the paper for accepting the ad, which they contended was racist and inflammatory. To suggest that African-Americans had been compensated for their years of slavery by welfare payments, they say, was both demeaning and unfair. African-Americans are only a minority among Americans who depend on welfare to make ends meet.

Other journalists have criticized the paper's staff members for not standing their ground and insisting on their right, as a business, to accept or reject ads as they wish. They contend that, if the contents of the ad were inflammable, inaccurate or potentially libelous, the editors, if they had known their media law, could have cited *New York Times v. Sullivan*. In that case the Supreme Court ruled that a political ad run in the *Times* was not libelous.

If the paper had rejected the ad, probably nothing more would have been heard. The sponsor of the ad, David Horowitz, president of the Los Angeles–based Center for Popular Culture, did not object when 18 college papers turned it down. He did make an issue of the *Daily Cal's* rejection and subsequent apology. Once the paper had accepted the ad, published it and distributed it to newsstands, removing and destroying the remaining copies raises a question about the advertiser's right of free speech. Barring the potentiality of libel or violence, editors opened themselves to censorship charges when they "trashed" their own newspapers in mid-distribution.

The newspaper staff could properly have accepted or rejected the ad. Once the paper accepted the ad, except for extenuating circumstances, it should have let the ad run. Once the ad was published, staff members should have held to the courage of their First Amendment convictions to stand up to the protesters and tell them to write letters to the editor or take out their own ads.

If, later, the editors had concluded that the contents of the ad were racist, unfair, misleading or inaccurate, they could have written an editorial saying so. Journalists and the other critics then could have focused on the merits of the issues raised by the ad, not on the decisions of the newspaper staff.

The "To Publish or Not to Publish" editorial is of moderate length (482 words). It does not seem overburdened with unnecessary information. Paragraph two provides the background. Some readers might have wanted to know more specifically what was said in the ad that provoked the charge of racism—but the issue raised in the editorial was how the ad was perceived by people on the two sides, not the actual content of the ad. Additional material would have lengthened the editorial, perhaps discouraging readers.

■ LOGICAL CONCLUSIONS

It is not always easy to judge whether an editorial presents logical arguments that lead to an appropriate conclusion. To a large extent, whether the arguments work depends on the point of view of the person who is judging.

The editorial in the previous chapter was written as an SBA_1A_2DC editorial. (See that chapter for a discussion of this formula.) The editorial consists of a statement of the situation, background, the argument on the first side, the argument on the second side, discussion and conclusion. The third paragraph presents the argument advanced by those who thought the ad was racist and should have been rejected. The fourth paragraph argues that, whatever the message of the ad, the student editors should have held their ground and defended publication of the ad.

In the discussion section (paragraph five), the editorial considers what might have happened if the ad had been rejected, as well as the free-speech implications of "trashing" the remaining papers. In paragraph six, the editorial first draws conclusions based on the previous paragraph: that either accepting or rejecting the ad would have been proper and that, if the ad ran, the editors should not have aborted distribution of the paper. The final paragraph tries to bring a broader issue into perspective: the issues raised by the ad.

■ CONSISTENT POINT OF VIEW

The editorial writer should use a consistent point of view in an editorial: the first-person ("we"), second-person ("you") or third-person ("he," "she," "they").

Some papers discourage or forbid the use of "we" in editorials. Other papers regard it as appropriate. In any case, care should be taken to use "we" infrequently. If you use "we" to refer to the paper, do so consistently; don't switch back and forth between "we" and the name of the paper.

On occasion writers find it appropriate, especially when writing on informal topics, to address editorial readers in the second-person "you." Once adopted, this form of address should be maintained throughout the editorial. Use of "you," of course, can be overdone. Writers must be careful not to switch suddenly to a "you" point of view in the middle or at the end of an editorial.

I detect no switching of persons in the "To Publish or Not to Publish" editorial. It is written in the third person throughout. Switching to the second person is not common in editorials, although there is an implied second person (you) in a sentence such as: "For more information, call so-and-so." A preferable third-person alternative: "More information may be obtained by calling so-and-so." Wordier, but it keeps the persons straight.

■ CLEAR REFERENTS AND ANTECEDENTS

To avoid repeating words in a boring fashion, writers sometimes use pronouns to take the place of nouns. To avoid repeating phrases and sentences, even whole paragraphs, they use "that" or "that idea" or "that concept" or "that development." Sometimes readers become confused by this shorthand. Professor R. Thomas Berner of Penn State referred to pronouns as "those unemotional, ambiguous, spineless parasites we use to refer to other parts of speech somewhere else in the same sentence, or, on occasion, in another sentence in the same paragraph, or, the worst of all possible contortions, in another paragraph." Berner cited the following sentence as an example of what he was talking about: "The city collects only swill from the university, and because of it, it has determined that the rate was higher than it should have been."[3] The only unambiguous "it" in the sentence is the last one, referring to the rate. But to what do the first two refer? According to the rules of grammar, a pronoun should refer to the nearest preceding logical referent—both of them should refer to university. But the first "it" apparently stands for the whole idea that only swill comes from the university, and who knows whether the second "it" means the university or the city?

The "To Publish or Not to Publish" editorial presents no problems in this area. The editorial refers either to editors in plural or to the staff. That approach avoids the problem of using a singular pronoun when referring to a person when the sex is not known. (In this case the editor was a male.)

■ SENTENCES OF APPROPRIATE LENGTH

You might expect to find that sentences in editorials would tend to be longer and harder to understand than those in news stories. Yet at least two studies made 20 years apart have shown that readers have found editorials easier to understand than news stories. Professor Galen R. Rarick, who did one of the studies, speculated that the apparent anomaly occurred partly because most editorial writers have been in the writing business longer than most reporters have. Another reason, he suggested, was that news writers may be better at reporting and investigating than at writing. Editorial writers also have a longer time to rewrite and polish their work than most reporters do, and so should produce better writing.[4]

The earlier study was based on *The Art of Readable Writing,* by Rudolph Flesch. This book and a subsequent Flesch book, *How to Test Readability,* attracted considerable attention in the late 1940s and 1950s.[5] Because longer sentences were considered harder to read than short ones and longer words more abstract than short ones, Flesch came up with a "readability" scale based on average sentence length and average word length (number of syllables). Writing was measured on a scale from "very easy" to "very difficult." Although Flesch himself warned against taking the scale too seriously, the response to his books was such that Francis P. Locke of the *Dayton* (Ohio) *Daily News* felt moved to write an article for *The Masthead* titled "Too Much Flesch on the Bones?" "We have cultivated a cult of leanness," he wrote. "The adjective is packed off to a semantic Siberia. The mood piece, if tolerated at all, must be astringent and aseptic."[6] Simplification can be overdone. Still, writers should remember that readers, even of the editorial page, are usually in a hurry and are not likely to labor over the heavy prose that an E.L. Godkin or a Charles Dana gave readers in the late 19th century. A good rule is to keep the writing simpler than you are at first inclined, because most readers are still likely to perceive it as more difficult than you intended.

So how does "To Publish or Not to Publish" rate on the Flesch scale? With an average sentence length of 27 words and 185 syllables in 100 words, the editorial rates as "difficult." "To Publish or Not to Publish," as originally written, does have some rather long sentences: 43 words in the second paragraph, 38 in the third, 43 in the fifth and 39 in the sixth paragraph. An effort to improve the editorial resulted in breaking up the first three of the long sentences. The result was that the average sentence length was reduced to 23 words, a length that falls in the "fairly difficult" range on the Flesch scale. The average number of syllables remained the same.

The Flesch scale should be regarded as only one indication, and a rather arbitrary one, of writing quality. Using easily understood words and sentences can provide a start toward comprehensible writing, but good writing requires more than keeping words and sentences short.

■ ECONOMY OF WORDS

Long or confused sentences are a tip-off to wordiness. But wordiness also can show up in words and phrases that are parts of short sentences. Here are examples of long sentences, wordiness or unclear wording in the "To Publish or Not to Publish" editorial as well as suggested revisions. (See "To Publish or Not to Publish II.")

Original

The *Daily Californian* at the University of California, Berkeley, recently accepted an advertisement that contended that African-Americans do not deserve reparations for the long years during which their ancestors were enslaved because they already have been receiving their due through welfare support.

Revised

The *Daily Californian* at the University of California, Berkeley, recently accepted an advertisement that contended that African-Americans do not deserve reparations for the long years during which their ancestors were enslaved. The ad claimed they already have been receiving their due through welfare support.
Comment: One long sentence is broken into two.

Original

. . . 40 protesters stormed the *Daily Cal* office protesting that the ad was racist, that it characterized African-Americans as a race of welfare recipients.

Revised

. . . 40 demonstrators stormed the *Daily Cal* office protesting that the ad characterized African-Americans as a race of welfare recipients.
Comment: Avoid repetition of "protesters" and "protesting"; eliminate "racist" as redundant.

Original

To suggest that African-Americans had been compensated for their years of slavery by welfare payments, they say, was both demeaning and unfair, since they are a minority among Americans who depend on welfare to make ends meet.

Revised

To suggest that African-Americans had been compensated for their years of slavery by welfare payments, they say, was both demeaning and unfair. African-Americans are only a minority among Americans who depend on welfare to make ends meet.
Comment: Make two sentences; insert "only" for emphasis.

Original

. . . their right, as a business, to accept or reject ads from whomever they wish.

Revised

. . . their right, as a business, to accept or reject ads as they wish.
Comment: Avoid the awkward "whomever."

Original

They contend that, if the contents of the ad were inflammable or inaccurate, even potentially libelous, the editors . . . .

Revised

They contend that, if the contents of the ad were inflammable, inaccurate or potentially libelous, the editors . . . .
Comment: Simplify wording.

Original

. . . the Supreme Court declined to find as libelous an ad run in the *Times*.

Revised

. . . the Supreme Court ruled that a political ad in the *Times* was not libelous.
Comment: Simplify and clarify wording ("political ad").

Original

If the paper had rejected the ad, probably nothing more would have been heard, since the sponsor of the ad . . . raised no apparent objection when 18 college papers turned it down.

Revised

If the paper had rejected the ad, probably nothing more would have been heard. The sponsor of the ad . . . did not object when 18 college papers turned it down.
Comment: Make two sentences; simplify wording.

Original

Once the paper had accepted the ad, published it and distributed it to the newsstands, a free-speech question could arise.

Revised

Once the paper had accepted the ad, published it and distributed it to the newsstands, removing and destroying the remaining copies raises a question about the advertiser's right of free speech.
Comment: Make the free speech question clear.

Original

. . . editors open themselves to censorship charges when they "trash" their own newspapers in mid-distribution.

Revised

. . . editors opened themselves to censorship charges when they "trashed" their own newspapers in mid-distribution.
Comment: Past tense verbs are more specific; they focus on this case.

Original

If, later, the editors concluded that the contents of the ad . . . .

Revised

If, later, the editors had concluded that the contents of the ad . . . .
Comment: "Had" makes clear that they had not concluded this.

Original

Journalists and other critics should have focused on the issues raised by the ad, not on the decisions of the newspaper staff.

Revised

Journalists and other critics then could have focused on the issues raised by the ad, not on the decisions of the newspaper staff.
Comment: "Could" is parallel wording to "could" in previous sentence ("could have written"); "then" helps clarify the point.

◼ CORRECT GRAMMAR

A person who attains the august position of editorial writer should automatically use correct grammar. Agreement of subject and predicate can be tricky, however, when the two are separated by a prepositional phrase. For example, an editorial written by a student had this sentence: "The response to the letters from women were mostly from men." "Response," of course, is the subject and requires a singular verb.

Agreement of nouns and pronouns is another problem. In the "To Publish or Not to Publish" editorial a careless writer might mistakenly have used a plural pronoun to refer to the newspaper staff. "Staff," of course, is singular even though it consists of several people. A problem for anyone who writes in the English language is what to do when you wish to use a pronoun to refer to a person whose sex is not known. The language does not have a neuter, singular, personal pronoun. Constructions such as "he/she" and "s/he" are awkward and should never be used in editorial writing; "he or she" ("she or he") should also be avoided if at all possible. Alternating "he" and "she" is confusing. Using "she" to refer to a person of unknown sex is as biased as using "he." The most acceptable solution is to use the plural form: editors . . . they, etc.

Everyone and anyone (both singular) can be troublesome. For example, one student editorial had this sentence: " . . . everyone is the master of their own body." One solution: "People have control over their own bodies."

I am chagrined by how often comma splices occur in student editorials. The previous example, in fact, was part of a sentence with a comma splice: "Whether someone wants to pose is not really the issue, after all everyone is the master of their own body." A period, of course, is needed after "issue."

I saw no grammar problems in "To Publish or Not to Publish."

Today's word-processing programs usually offer a grammar check that the writer can run—or that automatically calls attention to possible errors as the words being entered into the computer. Such programs can catch punctuation errors and incomplete sentences, as well as disagreements between subject and predicate and between nouns and pronouns. They can catch dumb mistakes—but they can never become the means to good writing.

◼ ABSENCE OF CLICHÉS AND JARGON

Clichés and jargon, in a sense, are at opposite ends of the spectrum in terms of comprehensibility by the general reader. Clichés tend to be used in everyday conversation by the sophisticated and the unsophisticated, the educated and the not-so-educated. Jargon is a special set of words used by a specific group of people. Everyone understands clichés; only the ingroup fully understands jargon. The editorial writer must resist the easy temptation to use jargon, because many readers will not easily understand what the words mean. They must avoid clichés because good writers need to make clear that they are thinking their own thoughts, not echoing someone else's. Clichés may be appropriate on occasion if they truly are appropriate and no better way can be found to make a point. Some of these expressions have been around for a long time, and they do "ring bells" with readers, but in most cases a little more thought can produce a more exact phrase than the cliché. Instead of "ring bells," I could have said "are easily understood by readers."

Problems with jargon tend to increase with the specialization of editorial writers. When writers associate with educators, lawyers, doctors, sociologists, government bureaucrats, politicians or farmers, they pick up their language and tend to forget that many words full of meaning to these people are either incomprehensible or lacking in meaning to many readers. Writers must constantly be on guard against such words sneaking into their writing.

"To Publish or Not to Publish" seems clear of clichés and jargon. Student editorials over the years have produced these examples of clichés:

> . . . left a bad taste in students' mouths.
>
> We do not throw away a whole bushel because of a few bad apples.
>
> One bad apple spoils opportunities for others . . . .
>
> People are still smoking up a storm. . . . a step in the right direction.
>
> . . . protect what all Americans hold dear.
>
> . . . pawns on a global chess board.
>
> . . . time that the administration . . . got off their collective backs. [Note also the disagreement between noun and pronoun.]

From a short stack of editorials written by professional editorial writers, I came across these clichés:

> It'll soon be time to fish or cut bait. Montanans can breathe a sigh of relief . . . .
>
> Inflation has reared its ugly head.
>
> Time marches on.
>
> The country went absolutely bananas . . . .
>
> That's a real can of worms.
>
> . . . time to stir the pot again.
>
> . . . the computer . . . coughed up the latest . . . report.
>
> A natural tendency to "let George do it."
>
> Into the breach leapt the Jaycees.

Some of the overworked words and phrases that I have come across over the years include:

alarming trend	on closer examination
amazing	only time will tell
basic	problem
broadly speaking	program
factor	remains to be seen
gratifying	responsible observers
incredible	the economy
in fact	thoughtful people
in order ("A new examination is in order.")	to be deplored
	underlying ("underlying causes")
in terms of	unquestionable
major ("major event")	would seem
obvious	

■ PROPER USE OF INDIVIDUAL WORDS

After all of these potential writing traps have been checked, we also need to check for weak or inappropriate words. One quick check could determine whether the writer uses unnecessary adverbs. Here are the adverbs that appear in "To Publish or Not to Publish":

> "before the newspaper was *fully* distributed . . . ."; probably necessary to make clear that some readers had seen copies.
>
> "Staff members *immediately* withdrew the remaining copies . . . ."; needed to make clear their urgent action.
>
> " . . . are *only* a minority . . . ."; important for emphasis.
>
> " . . . staff could *properly* have accepted . . . ."; absolutely necessary to get the writer's point across.

The editorial thus appears to be clear of unnecessary adverbs.

The words "think," "feel" and "believe" create problems for writers of news stories and editorials. In most instances writers should use "think" when they recount the thoughts and ideas of their sources. "Feel" should be reserved for statements concerning feelings and emotions. "Believe" implies a faith or conviction about something. One student writer said that "they felt that Tech needed exposure." "Thought" was the proper word. The same writer said: "They believe that students attend college in order to receive the best education possible. . . ." In this case, "believe" seems fine, since that is their conviction.

Here, from student editorials, are some examples of using not quite the right word:

Student Wording	Improved Wording
The university could start to *aid* in this problem.	The university could start to *solve* this problem.
The university is poorly *represented* when its athletes commit crimes.	The university has a poor *reputation* for handling crimes committed by athletes.
The coaches should suspend players *whom* they feel have an ill effect on	The coaches should suspend players *who* they feel have an ill effect on . . . .
The football team thinks *they* are above the rules that the *remainder of* the *campus* must follow.	The football team thinks *it* is above the rules that the *rest of* the *student body* must follow.
It would not be *fair* to say that all students at Tech study livestock on a farm.	It would not be *accurate* to say that all students at Tech study livestock on a farm.
In fact, the animal science department *represents* a small portion	In fact, the animal science department *accounts for (makes up)* a small portion . . . .
If the situation were turned on them	*If* the tables were turned on them . . . [but this is a cliché], *or:* *If* they found themselves in a similar situation . . . .
Some people *forget* to realize	Some people *fail* to realize . . . .
The problem has become more *evident then* just getting different types *of* people onto the same campus.	The problem has become more *complicated than* just getting different types *of* people on the same campus.

Why are *their* no resources	Why are *there* no resources . . . .
The university should go *out of there* way to accommodate them.	The university should go *out of its* way [but, if the plural were proper, it would be *their*].

The last three examples contain what might be called a "spell check" error (then-than and there-their). No doubt most writing instructors will agree that students' spelling improved remarkably with the introduction of the "spell check" function, but most spelling checkers cannot tell students whether they should use *then* or *than; there* or *their; accept* or *except; it's* or *its; rein, reign* or *rain*—or, for that matter, *for* or *four.*

In attempting to get away from dull, plain words, students sometimes get carried away. Slick footpaths, one student wrote, "could easily spawn broken bones and twisted ankles, not to mention plenty of embarrassing moments and soiled clothes." As a Pacific Northwest person, I got a lot of enjoyment imagining all the things that salmon could spawn as they worked their way up the Columbia River. Another student, although technically correct, also provoked a mistaken vision in my mind on first reading: "Asphalt is much easier to plow over than gravel," she wrote. Missing the "over," I could see snowplows plowing asphalt into huge piles (which, unlike snow, would never melt).

Avoiding Biased Words and Phases

Editorial writers—all writers in fact—need to be especially sensitive to words and phrases that reflect or imply bias toward one sex or the other; toward members of a race, religion or nationality; or toward persons of a certain age, physical condition or lifestyle.

Words containing "man" often introduce gender bias. Here are several possibilities for alternatives:

Biased	**Alternative**
man-made	manufactured
man-hours	hours
layman's terms	lay terms
man-on-the-street interviews	on-the-street interviews
manhole cover	utility cover
policemen	police officer
fireman	firefighter
founding fathers of journalism	pioneers of journalism
Founding Fathers of the nation	Founders of the nation
foreman	supervisor
workman's compensation	worker's compensation

Sensitivity is needed in referring to race and ethnic groups, especially because references that were acceptable to members of a race in one decade may be unacceptable in another decade, or may be acceptable to some members and not others. During the last century "colored," "Negro," "black" and "African-American" have each, in succession, become the name that seemed most generally—but not universally—preferred by people of that race. "Native American" has become a preferred name, supplanting the generally accepted "Indian" of earlier years. Several high schools and colleges have been asked to change the names of their athletic teams from Indians, Chiefs and Braves. These names, along with Bears, Lions, Huskies, Ducks and Cougars, suggested that Native Americans were akin to wild animals or team mascots. Some teams changed their names. Some didn't. Some defenders of the original names said those names should be considered compliments.

A few years ago, some people raised objections to the Washington professional football team's name, "Redskins." Assigned to write an editorial on that topic, one student wrote that those who objected "perceive 'Redskins' to be a relic of white frontiersmen who judged the various tribes they encountered to be wild, uncivilized and violent . . . ." But another student wrote that those who defended the use of "Redskins" "say that they, indeed, are honoring Native Americans, and, if they didn't have the utmost respect for the group, they wouldn't waste their beloved team's moniker on the Indian."

After the September 11, 2001, attacks on the Twin Towers and the Pentagon, a resolution was adopted at the national convention of the Society of Professional Journalists that (quoting an article in the society's publication, *Quill*) urged SPJ members and other journalists to "take steps against racial profiling in their coverage of the war on terrorism." They were urged to use informative, not inflammatory, language, to portray Muslims and Americans of Middle Eastern origin "in the richness of their diverse experiences" and to seek "a variety of voices and perspectives" to help their audiences "understand the complexities" of events.[7]

The American Society of Newspaper Editors has distributed a card that contains a guide to "acceptable" and "unacceptable" terms to use in writing about the disabled. A person who is "handicapped" ("acceptable") is not necessarily "crippled" or "deformed" ("unacceptable"). A person "uses" a wheelchair, not "is confined to a wheelchair." A person "resides in" and is not "confined to" a nursing home.[8]

■ COLORFUL LANGUAGE

The use of picturesque images not only adds color to an editorial, it can also help clarify the point being made. Metaphors and similes are two figures of speech that can help color and clarify. Metaphors, which occur much more often in editorials, refer to something in terms of something else. The *Star Tribune* of Minneapolis, Minn., for example, imagined a struggling economy headed into a stiff wind: "The result is both exhilarating and troubling as the economy now lowers its shoulder to the wind."

A more elaborate metaphor was in an editorial in the *Register-Guard* of Eugene, Ore. Noting that "conservative legislators might feel they were "being painted into a corner" by the governor's balanced budget, the editorial said, "If they look beyond the current biennium, however, lawmakers will find that they are the ones holding the paintbrush."

Robert Landauer of the Portland *Oregonian* employed the image of covering a corpse in talking about the failure of the Enron corporation to follow its own statement of values in carrying out accounting, stock buying and selling practices that provided misleading or wrong information to stockholders, stockbrokers, employees and other corporations: "[P]lease, place a sheet over the corpses of the 'obligation to communicate' and to 'treat others as we would like to be treated ourselves' that are trumpeted as 'Our Values.'"

On another occasion, Landauer brought together two images in discussing the plight of at-risk families: "These are people we used to send into lifeboats first. Now we conscript them and push them into front-line battle trenches first."

The *Denver Post* united two fictional characters in talking about a Greek *taverna* that the city was about to tear down to build something else: "However noble the project, the city looks like Zorba the Grinch to us."

In the business world, the *Detroit Free Press* described the economy of the auto industry as "starting to sputter" (like an old car) and the *Akron Beacon Journal* referred to the enormous "power in Washington" of the electricity (power) industry.

In the educational world, the *Times Herald-Record* of Middleton, N.Y., referred to students who insisted on having Coke machines in their schools as "sugar hounds."

With Boise State University about to play its first football game in the Western Athletic Conference, the *Idaho Statesman* said, "for fans, the move into the big time really kicks off today."

The Minneapolis, Minn., *Star Tribune,* noting that just as parents need to "teach their children . . . to keep their sticky fingers out of the church collection plate," the Minnesota Park and Recreation Board should learn a similar lesson in "a dispute with churches that take turns using the Lake Harriet bandshell for Sunday services."

The *Boston Globe* likened "these first days of August" to "the start of the last act of a terrific play. There's definitely more to come—the best, really, given the tomato and sweet corn harvests."

The Massillon, Ohio, *Independent* described arguments as coming "from outer space."

The Cleveland *Plain Dealer* saw President George W. Bush "negotiating a slippery slope" on stem-cell research.

Using references some readers might not recognize, the *Boston Globe* said that a sentencing bill was "Draconian," and the *Register-Guard* said that Springfield "has been noodling" in trying to revitalize its downtown. Draco was a harsh law maker in Athens during the 7th century B.C. To "noodle" is to improvise on an instrument in an idle and haphazard fashion. These are appropriate references, if not universally recognized.

This section contains only a few suggestions that might improve your writing. Additional words of advice on how to avoid bias in writing can be found in a book by Judy E. Pickens, *Writing Without Bias: A Guidebook for Nondiscriminatory Communication.*[9] Several books on writing in general were suggested in Chapter 4, "Preparations of an Editorial Writer."

■ CONCLUSION

Simply following all of these steps, and those described in the preceding chapter, will not guarantee a good editorial. Thought, imagination and lively writing, none of which can be reduced to a simple how-to formula, are even more essential than the format of the editorial or the correctness of the words. No matter how technically correct or skillfully organized, an editorial is not likely to be effective unless it also carries hard-to-define qualities that attract and persuade readers.

James J. Kilpatrick has described the goal of the editorial writer "to be, in 300 words or less, temperate, calm, dignified, forceful, direct, catchy, provocative, stimulating, reasoned, logical, literate, factual, opinionated, conclusive, informative, interesting and persuasive. And put a live head on it."[10]

That's all it takes to write an editorial.

▪ QUESTIONS AND EXERCISES

1. Find an editorial with what you regard as an overabundance of factual information. Rewrite the piece using only those facts that are necessary to make the subject understandable.

2. Apply a heavy editing pencil to an editorial to remove unnecessary words and phrases.

3. Try to find an editorial in which the arguments and evidence presented do not support the conclusion. Can the editorial be rewritten, with the information that is contained in it, to bring the conclusion into line with the supporting material?

4. Count and average the number of syllables for every hundred words and the number of words per sentence in the editorials of several news papers. How do the editorials compare in terms of word and sentence length? Are the editorials with longer words and sentences more difficult to understand? If not, why not?

5. In examining these same newspapers, do you find a general trend in individual papers toward long sentences and long words or short sentences and short words, or do editorials vary within the papers?

6. Find an editorial in which the simplified style of the writing seems condescending to readers. Can you rewrite the editorial to overcome this problem?

7. Scan a handful of editorials for clichés. Which—if any—can you justify? How could you eliminate the remainder?

8. Rewrite an editorial that relies excessively on government or other types of jargon. Translate the offending language into understandable English.

9. Examine several editorials for euphemisms and for more difficult words and phrases than are necessary to convey meaning.

10. Find improper and ambiguous uses of "it" and "that" as referents. Rewrite to clarify the meaning.

11. Find several sentences that begin with a form of "there is" and rewrite them in a clearer and more direct manner.

12

Subjects That Are Hard to Write About

Is it necessary or desirable to fill the editorial columns with pieces on government and politics to the virtual exclusion of all else . . . ?

—CREED BLACK,
NASHVILLE TENNESSEAN[1]

Any survey of American editorial writers would reveal that government is the favorite topic of editorial writers. This discovery shouldn't be surprising, since the news business seems concerned primarily with public affairs and much of public affairs involves government. Writers also may follow the same tendency as a matter of least resistance, since their own interests are likely to be in this direction. Nonpolitical subjects may not get written about, or taken seriously, for at least three other reasons. First, writers may regard some subject areas as too difficult to write about— at least in the time available to them. Second, they may regard a subject as so easy to write about that they dash off an editorial devoting little time or thought. Third, they may regard a nongovernment topic as not sufficiently serious to warrant taking time from the "great issues of the day." This chapter will look at the first of these categories: subjects that are tough to write about. Chapter 13 will look at subjects that are deceptively easy. Chapter 14 will discuss subjects that editorial writers often ignore.

Any subject can be hard to write about if you don't know what you are writing about. Over the years, I have found that, because of the fear of not knowing enough about the topic, writers have tended to shy away from seven subject areas: economics, legal issues, international affairs, culture, medicine and health, religion and sports.

▪ ECONOMICS

For the writer who wants to write more than clichés, the editorial on economics is one of the hardest to write. Of all the topics I assigned my students, economics is the one they resist most. Those who have taken introductory economics courses seem bewildered by theories, laws and graphs. Those who have not taken these courses are filled with horror at the thought of writing about what has been called "the dismal science." Part of the reluctance of both groups stems from their impressions that editorials on economics are boring and filled with numbers. If they have read editorials on the subject, they probably think of them as dealing with taxes (too high), government spending (too much), unemployment (too high) or inflation (too rapid). Or they think that editorials on economics deal with the theories of John Maynard Keynes, Milton Friedman or Arthur Laffer. None of this seems to have much to do with daily life.

But economics does relate to how readers live. A shortfall in electric power can boost prices to consumers and cause brownouts. It can force industries to cut back production and lay off workers. As a result, editorial writers have found themselves having to write about the merits of deregulating electric power. Because of the mercurial nature of supply and demand for oil products, writers face the task of explaining sharp increases and equally sharp decreases in the prices that motorists pay at the gas pump and deciding whether opening up the Alaskan oil fields is a good idea. As everyone now knows, a large share of the reading public is affected by the ups and downs of the stock market and the rise and fall of interest rates.

So how does an editorial writer produce an editorial on an economic topic that does not simply say that a cutback in the capital gains taxes is or is not a good idea or that extended unemployment benefits should or should not be extended to workers who are out of jobs? I offer two suggestions. First, write in a manner that readers can easily understand. Second, know whom to call on for reliable information and insights on the topic you are writing about.

Writing Simply and Clearly

Some of the best advice on writing about economics has come from Lauren K. Soth, who as editorial page editor of the *Des Moines Register* and later as a syndicated columnist, frequently wrote on economics. Economics editorials, according to Soth, should explain and interpret, not merely spout official newspaper policy. They should discuss "what is happening here and now" and concentrate on how current economic phenomena actually affect people's well-being. They should avoid the temptation to "pontificate on every little economic event in terms of . . . grand ideologies." Soth emphasized that organization of the subject matter is extremely important, that the writer needs to proceed in a manner that seems logical to readers—from the known to the unknown, spelling out each major step of reasoning from the beginning to the conclusion. Each editorial should concentrate on one central idea and drive it home, avoiding getting involved in side issues.

While Soth did not contend that economics can be made simple and entertaining, he believed that the writer can, and should, arouse interest by talking in terms of what people are interested in—people. "Instead of saying, `Wheat acreage increased to 10 percent,' why not say, 'Farmers planted 10 percent more acres of wheat'?" Without oversimplifying complex issues, the writer can make them understandable. For instance, instead of stringing facts and figures together in prose comparisons, data can be organized in tables and rounded off for easier comprehension.[2]

Editorials on economic issues need to take a hard look at facts and not try to spare speaking bluntly. An editorial in the *Des Moines Register* did just that. "Get over it, Iowa, and move ahead" told urban and rural Iowans to stop fighting each other and to join forces to build a more prosperous state. "Urban Iowans should support small-town life in Iowa, for that is our heritage and in many respects our best feature," the editorial said. "Rural Iowa should become cheerleaders for urban growth, for that is the pathway to growth in all of Iowa."

A *Greensboro* (N.C.) *News & Record* editorial ("Yet another big box for West Wendover") criticized a proposal to build another big-box store in an "already

GET OVER IT, IOWA, AND MOVE ON

Iowans must adjust their thinking in accord with what they already know to be the truth: The 160-acre farm isn't coming back.

By Register Editorial Board

"We cannot afford to be two Iowas," Gov. Tom Vilsack said last week. "We are, and we must be, one Iowa." It was perhaps the most passionately delivered line in his Condition of the State address, and the one most roundly applauded in the House chamber.

Well, that's a start. If the highest officials of this state can talk openly about how progress in Iowa is held back by internal division, there might be hope for overcoming it.

The existence of two Iowas—rural and urban—whose people do not recognize their common interests is the single biggest constant in Iowa politics. Sometimes it's just below the surface. Sometimes it flares into raw emotion, as it has recently. Hard times bring out bad feelings.

Evidence that something is holding Iowa back is all around us. Almost every state in the region is growing faster than Iowa—some more than twice as fast. Other states in the region have been losing farm population for decades, just like Iowa. The difference is that growth in the urban centers of our neighbors has more than offset the loss in farm population.

Not so in Iowa. Overall population has been stagnant for two decades because the growth in our cities has been insufficient to mask the population decline in rural Iowa.

Why?

Is it because a "growth in all 99 counties" approach to economic development has meant not enough growth in any of them?

Is it because Iowa is so intent on maintaining a healthy agricultural economy that it neglects other opportunities? Or because the expense of maintaining widely dispersed rural schools and roads and too many local governments crowds out spending for other improvements?

Is it because the political division between rural and urban essentially produces a standoff in which neither can advance?

It is easy to see why urban-rural resentments have flared recently. From a rural perspective, it appears urban Iowa is getting all the good stuff. Rural Iowa sees its young people leave, its main streets boarded up, its community fabric tattered. No wonder a plan to close county clerks' offices or a campaign to change distribution of road money causes consternation.

From an urban perspective, there is frustration in seeing taxes flow out of the cities to subsidize rural schools and roads. That spending might spur more growth if it were invested where growth is more likely to occur—in the urban centers.

There is frustration when rural (and some urban) lawmakers think it is a hilarious joke to kill any legislation that is perceived as benefiting Des Moines. There is frustration when some farming practices pollute Iowa's lakes and streams, making it a less attractive place to live. There is frustration when enhancements such as bike trails and national designation for the Loess Hills are blocked by rural interests that see land-ownership rights as superseding all others.

Only if attitudes change can such conflicting interests be reconciled.

Urban Iowans need to accept that lightly populated parts of the state need more schools, roads and local government than their taxes alone can support. Taxes paid by urban Iowans should continue, within reason, to subsidize the small-town way of life.

Rural Iowans should be willing to accept reasonable consolidation of schools and local governments, not only to save money but to actually improve education and services.

continued

---

concluded

Urban and rural Iowans alike must accept, as a consequence, that this cannot be a low-tax state. If Iowans want to maintain rural roads and schools and all the other public spending that assures a high quality of life, we have to be willing to pay for them.

All Iowans must adjust their thinking in accord with what they already know to be the truth: The 160-acre farm isn't coming back. The fortunes of small towns will never again lie in selling retail goods to farm families. They will lie in fostering local enterprises and in allying themselves with regional growth centers. Small towns will start growing again when Iowa's big towns start growing more robustly.

Urban Iowans should support small-town life in Iowa, for that is our heritage and in many respects our best feature. Rural Iowa should become cheerleaders for urban growth, for that is the pathway to growth for all of Iowa.

A breakthrough may have occurred in 2000 when the Legislature adopted the Vision Iowa Program. For the first time, the state provided grants to assist in building major projects intended to make Iowa's urban centers more attractive. At the same time, the Legislature enacted a less noticed program of grants for community improvements in small towns.

It was urban-rural together. Let's do more—much more—of that sort of thing.

Des Moines Register

---

nerve-rending snarl of shopping centers, car dealerships and big-box stores." "Lack of planning and political will in the past," the editorial said, "have made West Wendover a place where you grit your teeth and grip the steering wheel, if you go there at all."

One approach to writing about an economic issue is to focus on an example—a specific company, agency or individual. "Part of the challenge for us is to . . . try to think about the issues that mean something to people's lives" said Bruce Little, an economics writer for a Canadian paper, Toronto's *Globe and Mail*.[3] The *Bulletin* of Bend, Ore., took that approach in an editorial titled "Where there's a sale, an appeal will follow." The editorial cited the layoff of 80 people by Ochoco Lumber as an example of the problems that local lumber mills faced in trying to survive. The *Bulletin* saw, as the larger problem, the Endangered Species Act and other laws "used as economic clubs to close down mills, throw people out of work and allow combustible material to accumulate on public lands."

The opening sentence of a Salt Lake City *Deseret News* editorial ("Utah's heavy tax burden"), noting that Utahns had "the highest tax burden per household among seven Western states," no doubt caught readers' attention, but offered no hint of where the editorial might be headed. It took the writer about a third of the way through the editorial to offer "the best solution": tuition tax credits for private schools.

Reliable Sources

"Get your experts lined up in advance" when writing about economic issues, was the advice offered by panelists at a convention of the National Conference of Editorial Writers. "Develop your own Council of Economic Advisers," suggested

YET ANOTHER BIG BOX FOR WEST WENDOVER

The last thing Wendover Avenue needs is another place to shop. Be that as it may, the already nerve-rending snarl of shopping centers, car dealerships and big-box stores will get another big box anyway.

The architects of arguably the city's biggest planning disaster decided to make a bad situation worse by voting unanimously Tuesday night to rezone the site of the closed Guilford Mills Greenberg plant so that a new membership warehouse, similar to Sam's, can occupy the spot. The council's rationale seems to be that something has to go there and that another mega-store is the lesser evil.

A membership warehouse, they reasoned, is preferable to the variety of smaller tenants that might occupy the site if the zoning remained as it is, though we have yet to witness an office park, car wash or convenience store that attracts enough traffic to stall commuters and invite accidents.

Arguing for the rezoning, lawyer Henry Isaacson also pointed to a shopping center in northwest Greensboro, Lawndale Crossing, as an example of the type of unobtrusive success the new Wendover tenant would pose.

True, like the Guilford Mills land, Lawndale Crossing is an "in-fill" project that took an abandoned industrial site (the old Sears warehouse) and remade it into retail. But Lawndale does not handle nearly the volume of traffic that daily chokes West Wendover. And Lawndale Crossing provides shopping in an area not already overwhelmed by retail stores.

To be fair, this was a tough dilemma. Council member Sandy Carmany, in whose district this land is located, said she adamantly opposed the rezoning until she considered the rock-and-hard-place options. Better a big box, she reasoned, than piecemeal commercial development that could be more chaotic. Further, city transportation officials note that the effects of the rezoning on traffic could be accommodated by street improvements that include a median and an additional turn lane.

Yet, the glut of retail on the busy thoroughfare continues unabated, while some communities in east Greensboro are desperate for more convenient places to shop.

Realistically, Wendover, which is at once a visionary achievement (an effective east-west connector) and a case study in shortsightedness (a maze of willy-nilly commercial clutter), may be too far gone to save. Any chance for reasonable, creative development approaches there was surrendered years ago. A lack of planning and political will in the past have made West Wendover a place where you grit your teeth and grip the steering wheel tightly, if you go there at all.

If nothing else, maybe West Wendover will serve as a monument to what happens when development is driven by zoning rather than planning.

News & Record

Matt Miller, senior writer for *U.S. News & World Report* and a former adviser to the U.S. Office of Management and Budget. "When you find [academics who talk] sensibly, treasure them," Miller said. "They're quite helpful when journalists pay attention, sometimes because they have an ax to grind or the interests of their institutions to advance, but often just because they're educators at heart, and I often think of economics writing for newspapers as an education job." Bruce Little of the Toronto *Globe and Mail* suggested also finding sources among people at think tanks or central banks as well as the Brookings Institution, the Center for Budget and Policy Priorities and the American Enterprise Institute. He also recommended checking the annual *Statistical Abstract of the United States.*[4]

UTAH'S HEAVY TAX BURDEN

Many conclusions could be drawn from the Tax Commission study released last week showing Utahns with the highest tax burden per household among seven Western states.

One is that local governments, from mosquito abatement districts to city councils, need to stop operating in a vacuum. Each has projects that would add just a tiny bit to the tax burden, but together they add to a considerable amount. Another is that the state may not be as fiscally conservative as its Republican face may lead people to believe.

But those are simplistic. Each, while valid, misses the larger point. The tax burden is high because the state has an enormous number of children to educate. While large families ultimately are of great advantage to society, the lesson is that Utah cannot afford to continue looking at its education problems the same way it has for generations. In other words, the state cannot simply continue to tax people more and more to meet the growing needs for school teachers, salaries, books supplies.

The best solution is to give private schools an incentive to relieve some of this burden. The time has come for lawmakers to approve a tuition-tax-credit program, which would grant partial tax credits to people who pay private-school tuition.

Legislators came close to doing this last year, spurred in part by anger over a one-day teacher strike that came despite a healthy increase in education spending. Even though the effort fizzled, it ought to be clear that financial pressures are bound head to friction between public schools and lawmakers again and again. Meanwhile, those schools now face the great challenge of a growing non-English-speaking population, which is bound to further strain existing resources.

By some estimates, the state will need $1.5 billion more to fund its education needs over the next 10 years. Add that to the Tax Commission figures that show the average Utah household now pays 8.3 percent of personal income in taxes, which is higher even than California, which pays an average of 7.8 percent per household.

Utah does not have a strong private-school tradition. Only about 3 percent of the state's school-age population attends a private school. Even with a tax credit that figure is likely to rise no higher than the national average of 13 percent, but even that would relieve enough pressure on the public schools to save taxpayers hundreds of millions of dollars.

The Tax Commission's study represents the flip side to the state's education problem. Teachers' unions like to emphasize the side that says schools need more money, even as they bash lawmakers for failing to give them what they want. The flip side, of course, is that Utahns already pay an enormous share of their personal income for education.

There are but a few possible solutions to the problem. The state could raise the tax burden even higher. It could increase the higher of students per classroom, stop buying books and supplies or put students in double sessions. Or it could relieve some of the pressure by giving a few students the chance to afford a private alternative.

Frankly, the choice ought to be obvious.

Deseret News

Economics Web Resources

ABCNews.com: Business (click business link on home page):
   http://www.abc.com

All Business Network (links to online publications): http://www.all-bus.com

Better Business Bureau (business and consumer alerts): http://www.bbb.org

BigBook (quick information on virtually any U.S. company):
   http://www.bigbook.com

Bloomsberg News (top business stories):
   http://www.bloomberg.com/welcome.html

Business Wire (latest international press releases):http://www.businesswire.com

CompaniesOnline (100,000 public and private companies):
   http://www.companiesonline.com

Forbes Digital Tool (technology, investing, media, politics from
   Forbes publications): http://www.forbes.com

LEXIS-NEXIS Communication Center (legal, news, business information
   retrieval, storage and management service): http://www.lexis-nexis.com

■ LEGAL ISSUES

Discussion of a legal issue can become so involved that readers may stop
trying to understand what an editorial writer is talking about. Writers need to
keep in mind that most readers know little about legal matters, so legal terms
should never be used when plain English will do. If a legal term is used, it
should be defined in the simplest language possible. Writers should keep a
pocket law dictionary handy. Simplifying complex and technical legal
matters, however, may distort information or mislead readers, so care must be
taken to include enough of the complexities to persuade those knowledgeable of the subject.

In "Heat-sensing justice," in words that readers could easily understand, a
Eugene, Ore., *Register-Guard* writer used the first sentence to summarize, praise
and put into context a U.S. Supreme Court ruling. The decision had
"reaffirmed Americans' fundamental right to privacy in their homes" while as
the same time "new law enforcement technologies make breaching their
privacy frighteningly easy." The 5-4 "crazyquilt" liberal-conservative alignment
of the justices offered the writer an opportunity to personalize a complex issue,
noting that two conservatives had team up with "more liberal" justices and that
the "liberal's liberal" had written the dissenting opinion.

The writer attempted to enliven a serious editorial with sentences and
expressions as these:

"Chalk one up for the Fourth Amendment and its ban on unreasonable
   searches and seizures."

"Yes, that's right, Scalia."

"Such a go-figure split on the court . . . ."

"This strange concoction of conservative and liberal justices . . . ."

" . . . ranging from heating a Hot Pocket in the microwave to
   sexual intimacy . . . ."

" . . . they must keep their thermal imagers and other Dick Tracy devices
   switched to the off position."

The question of whether cameras should be allowed in courtrooms is a
perennial, and favorite, subject for editorial writers. Since both legal and
journalistic issues are at stake, writers need to be careful that they are not
perceived as being primarily concerned with the rights of the press as

HEAT-SENSING JUSTICE
Court bars high-tech searches without warrant

In a ruling this week that involved a Lane County drug case, the U.S. Supreme Court reaffirmed Americans' fundamental right to privacy in their homes, even in an era when new law enforcement technologies make breaching that privacy frighteningly easy.

The justices ruled 5-4 that police use of thermal imaging devices, which can detect heat patterns radiating through walls, amounts to an unconstitutional invasion of privacy unless police have first obtained a judge's permission by showing evidence of a crime.

Chalk one up for the Fourth Amendment and its ban on unreasonable searches and seizures. As Justice Antonin Scalia wrote for the court, at the "very core" of the amendment "stands the right of a man to retreat into his own home and there be free from governmental intrusion."

Yes, that's right, Scalia. It was the most conservative member of the court who weighed in on behalf of a majority that made a crazyquilt of the normal conservative-liberal alignment of the justices. Joining him was another conservative, Justice Clarence Thomas, as well as three of the court's more liberal members: Justices David Souter, Ruth Bader Ginsburg and Stephen Breyer.

In a dissenting opinion, Justice John Paul Stevens, a liberal's liberal, said that because thermal imaging devices detect heat radiating "off the walls," they are "simply gathering information in the public domain" and was joined by three members of the court's conservative bloc: Chief Justice William Rehnquist and Justices Sandra Day O'Connor and Anthony Kennedy.

Such a go-figure split on the court is enough to send a veteran courtwatcher to bed with a raging fever—a fever that just might be picked up by a thermal imaging device like the one an Oregon National Guard sergeant pointed at Danny Lee Kyllo's home in Florence at 3:30 a.m.. on Jan. 16, 1992.

The imager, which gathers infrared radiation just as a camera gathers visible light, detected unusual amounts of heat coming from the garage roof and a side wall. It also revealed that Kyllo's triplex residence was giving off significantly more heat than the adjoining units.

Using that information, along with an informant's tip and Kyllo's suspiciously high electrical bills, federal agents secured a warrant. When they searched Kyllo's home, they found more than 100 marijuana plants and the high-intensity grow lights that gave off the tell-tale heat.

Kyllo pleaded guilty to a drug charge but reserved the right to appeal on the search issue. The San Francisco–based 9th U.S. Circuit Court of Appeals ultimately upheld the plea, concluding that law enforcement officials didn't violate the constitutional bar against unreasonable searches.

In this week's ruling, the Supreme Court held that the information police gathered with the thermal device cannot be used against Kyllo. The court sent the case back to lower courts to determine whether police had enough other basis to support the search warrant that was eventually served on Kyllo.

The court's ruling provides much-needed limits on how police should apply increasingly powerful high-tech surveillance equipment, including devices that may yet be developed, that enable them to peep inside private homes.

This strange concoction of conservative and liberal justices correctly perceived that private homes need to be protected not only from physical intrusion by police but from advancing technologies that allow police to monitor human activity inside. In the majority opinion, Scalia noted that directional microphones, monitoring satellites miles in the sky, and radar scanners that can look through walls already exist or are being developed to aid police in crime detection.

Thermal imaging already has the potential to reveal private activities in the home, ranging from heating a Hot Pocket in the microwave to sexual intimacy. Future improvements in technology will dramatically increase police capabilities—and citizens' need for Fourth Amendment protection.

continued

The court has made it clear that if law enforcement officials want to do a high-tech scan of a private residence, they must first prove in court that there is, in the precise words of the Constitution, "probable cause" to believe that criminal activity has occurred on the premises. If they lack the information needed to obtain a warrant, they must keep their thermal imagers and other Dick Tracy devices switched to the off position.

Register-Guard

OPEN UTAH COURTROOMS TO TV NEWS CAMERAS
We need statewide debate on benefits of TV cameras in state courtrooms

Judge Clint Judkins stepped on state law when he allowed a television news camera to tape a preliminary hearing for Cody Nielsen, the suspect in one of the most notorious murder cases to come out of Cache County in years.

Nielsen is charged with the abduction and murder, in particularly gruesome manner, of a 16-year-old Hyrum girl—one of the many children treasured and nurtured throughout the small communities that Cache encompasses. Trisha Autry was a town's sister and friend—and now a symbol for the vulnerability and willfulness of 16-year-old girls. Her death has deeply touched the county and beyond.

So perhaps the error was not so much Judge Judkins', but a state code that hasn't kept up with the times, and technology. Today, all but two states allow some form of camera in their courtrooms. In Utah, for instance, still photographs can be taken, with the judge's approval. You'll see these newspaper photographs of high-profile cases, like the recent Tom Green polygamy trial. Local news photographers work an a "pool" basis—that is, each newspaper takes turns sending a photographer, who then shares his or her work with all media outlets. You'll even see these still photos on TV news reports.

This has worked well in the past. But technology and news consumers' expectations have changed. It's past time to allow a statewide experiment with video cameras in the courtroom, similar to a three-year experiment that in the early 1990s permitted TV cameras in some trial and appellate courts.

For years, the primary argument against TV cameras in court has been twofold: Some fear that a "media circus" may result, others that the extra exposure might harm an individual's right to a fair and impartial trial.

Well, controversial court cases are already media circuses. The exposure exists. And it's not all the product of media maneuverings: People want to know. And, in many cases, they have a right to know. The U.S. Supreme Court, long a closed bastion, conceded this fact when it released, for the first time ever, audio recordings of deliberations on the presidential election outcome.

The need in Cache County and throughout Utah is no less apparent.

That's not saying that we should let chaos reign. Strict rules are applied to still photographers: Their number is limited; they're restricted to a specific area and they're not allowed to disrupt the proceedings. The same conditions should be applied to video cameras. By all reports in the Nielsen hearing, the judge set straightforward rules; and no one in the room was apparently bothered.

One last point: TV stations should be required to share their footage with all media, including [print] media, in a timely manner—as newspapers do now.

As this type of legislation proceeds through the Senate—the U.S. House has already OK'd a bill that allows cameras into federal court rooms but gives unilateral veto power to any named party—perhaps our state lawmakers. should take their own look at what's truly an issue for our times: meaningful access to the courts.

Standard-Examiner

opposed to the rights of the public. The *Standard-Examiner* in Ogden, Utah, in "Open Utah courtrooms to TV news cameras," responded in what might have seemed an unexpected manner to a judge's allowing television cameras to tape a preliminary hearing for a suspect charged with murder. While expressing its support for allowing cameras in the courts, the editorial said the judge nevertheless was in "error" for "[stepping] on state law." In Utah, the editorial pointed out, still photos can be taken with the judge's permission, but not video. Addressing arguments against video, the editorial argued that "controversial court cases are already media circuses" and pleas for coverage are "not all the product of media maneuverings." More importantly: "People want to know. And, in many cases, they have a right to know." Lawmakers, the editorial concluded, should take a look at "meandering access to the courts."

Legal Issues Web Resources

ACLU Freedom Network (what's happening in Congress and the courts): http://www.aclu.org

American Bar Association: http://www.abanet.org

Death Penalty Information Center: http://www.deathpenaltyinfo.org

Federal Bureau of Investigation: http://www.fbi.gov

FindLaw.com (information that is law-related; some at a fee): http://www.findlaw.com

Internet Legal Resource Guide (4,000 Web sites related to law): http://www.ilrg.com

Justice Information Center: http://www.allaw.com

LEXIS-NEXIS Communication Center (legal, news, business information retrieval, storage and management service): http://www.lexis-nexis.com

National Association of Attorneys General: http://www.naag.org

National Crime Prevention Council (information about its programs and upcoming public service announcements): http://www.ncpc.org

National District Attorneys Association: http://www.ndaa.org

National Institute of Justice (research and development arm of Department of Justice): http://www.ojp.usdoj.gov/nij

National Law Journal: http://www.nlj.com

United States Commission on Civil Rights: http://www.usccr.gov

United States Supreme Court: http://www.supremecourtus.gov

■ INTERNATIONAL AFFAIRS

International subjects may be both the hardest and the easiest topics to write about. They are easy in the sense that, when you write about a faraway country, you will not have the mayor, governor or next-door neighbor calling to say you don't have your facts straight, as they might on a local topic. Writers used to say the safest editorial was a hard-hitting one about Afghanistan. That led to the term "Afghanistanism" to describe editorials on topics that no one knows or cares about. What more needs to be said to make the point that, in a global community, there is no place on earth that is *not* a fit subject for an editorial?

No doubt editorials on international topics are among the least read editorials in the United States. When I asked students in my editorial writing class to rank the editorials in the newspapers they were assigned to read, international editorials always came in last. For many people the little international news that they get mostly comes from the 6 o'clock or 11 o'clock television news, where a news item might get 15 seconds and a fleeting news clip. The next morning's newspaper may devote eight or 10 inches to a major story and two or three inches to eight or 10 other items, most of which deal with flooding, fires, sinking ferries and political coups.

Fortunately, beginning with the Iranian hostage situation in 1979, CNN came into its own as a source of information from abroad, especially in times of crisis. The major networks responded with evening news journals that have continued in one form or another. Readers and viewers have responded when events have affected their lives or the lives of other Americans: during the Iranian hostage crisis, the war against Iraq ("Desert Storm"), the destruction of the World Trade Center Towers, and the subsequent war against terrorists in Afghanistan and around the world.

When events such as these arise, often unexpectedly, they capture the public's attention. Readers are eager to find out what thoughtful commentators have to say. In most cases, the writer's task is to find an angle or information that will make readers care about what's happening in other countries. One obvious approach is to write editorials that explain how events abroad are affecting, or can affect, labor, business or political affairs in this country. "Make them look local," suggests Stein B. Haughlid of *Dagens Naeringsliv* in Oslo, Norway. "When it is a theme like ex-Yugoslavia or Somalia, where American troops are sent in, personification or localizing should not be too difficult. The same goes for the embargo of Iraqi oil that might affect the price of oil all over the world, including the local gas station, the owner's profits and hence the contribution to the church and local tax revenue."[5] Readers can be attracted to international editorials that make people in other countries seem like real people, not just groups or numbers. There is no reason that an editorial about starving Afghan refugees or AIDS victims in Africa can't be accompanied by a wire service photograph.

Joe Geshwiler of the *Atlanta* (Ga.) *Constitution* noted that a place like Peoria, Ill., the headquarters for Caterpillar Tractor, "which does business all around the globe," is "home to a multitude of international business specialists with high standards about the quality of their informational sources." He suggested, as sources for international editorials, "a local university with overseas connections, or a service or religious organization with projects overseas, or far-sighted businessmen, or an ethnic community in your midst." The "trick," he said, "is to identify the connection" to the local community.[6]

Editorial writers on small staffs should not be expected to provide new insights on tribal wars in a Central African country, but, if they follow the news, read a few national newspapers and magazines, peruse the Internet and check out local sources, they should be able to provide intelligent comment on issues relevant to their readers.

The Horn of Africa is one of those far-off places that readers are not likely to care much about, or even know where it is located. When writers on the *Star Tribune* in Minneapolis, Minn., undertook to write about famine in that region ("Famine"), they personalized their approach by working a familiar political figure from a neighboring state, George McGovern, into the editorial, even using his name to begin the editorial. Before the editorial made clear what McGovern

FAMINE
It looms, again, over Horn of Africa

George McGovern wasn't a presence at the Democratic National Convention in Los Angeles. He has bigger fish to fry in Rome, where he is the permanent U.S. representative to the U.N. Food and Agricultural Organization (FAO). McGovern is focused on feeding the world's hungry, and he's doing a bang-up job. But he could use help—lots of it. In the Horn of Africa alone this summer, 20 million people face severe hunger, malnutrition, even starvation. Many more tons of food and millions of dollars will be needed to avert disaster in Kenya, Eritrea, Ethiopia, Sudan, Somalia and Uganda.

It's easy to join McGovern in his anti-hunger effort: Almost every relief agency—from Save the Children to the Mennonite Central Committee—is collecting money to help. Contact the agency of your choice and make a donation. And you needn't be a liberal Democrat to join the McGovern anti-hunger brigade. Bob Dole, for example, is a prominent member.

Dole joined McGovern on Capitol Hill recently to promote a brilliant McGovern idea: a $300 million pilot program to provide free school lunches for hungry children worldwide. To blanket the globe, the program would cost $3 billion annually, with the U.S. share estimated at $750 million. Much of the U.S. donation would come in the form of excess grain and other farm products, boosting the market for American farmers.

President Clinton immediately signed on when McGovern broached the idea last February. The president announced the program at the recent G8 meeting on Okinawa. It is to be administered by the FAO's World Food Program. Secretary of Agriculture Dan Glickman announced recently in Nairobi that Kenya will be the first country enrolled in the pilot.

Kenya needs the help. Drought and crop failures there have killed much of the livestock in some regions and left an estimated 3.5 million hungry people at risk of starvation. Widespread malnutrition is already evident among children.

In Ethiopia, an estimated to million people also confront severe hunger and the specter of starvation. In Sudan, the vulnerable number 2.5 million; in Somalia, 1.2 million; Uganda, 750,000; and Eritrea, 550,000.

In several cases, the hunger has been made worse by warfare or civil disorder. But in every case, the primary problem has been a sustained drought. In Ethiopia, the failure of three successive crops has pushed food stores almost to the level of 1984, when the world witnessed mass starvation there.

The Horn of Africa faces the worst food shortage in the world, but it is by no means the only one. Some experts have begun to express fear of long-term food shortages because of changing weather patterns linked to global warming. It may prove out that this year's wildfire season in the western United States is linked to the same causes as the drought in Ethiopia and Kenya, as some have speculated.

Regardless of the cause, the world needs to fashion a community response. Bad as the fires are in Montana, they are not anywhere near as deadly as the drought in East Africa. And if global integration means anything at all, it must mean global humanitarian integration. The First World, so drenched in wealth and privilege, must respond to the emergency of East Africa in a manner that demonstrates as much concern for the lives at risk as for the emerging markets those countries may become. Just ask George McGovern.

Star Tribune

had to do with the Horn of Africa, it explained why he hadn't been "a presence at the Democratic National Convention in Los Angeles." He was in Rome, doing

BELFAST FLASHPOINT

It is unconscionable that small children and their parents would be harassed on their way to school in the Ardoyne section of North Belfast. The people manning the gauntlet are Protestant unionists, who are experiencing the slow erosion of their control over Northern Ireland. Their anger, and the resentment of thousands of less militant Protestants, need to be channeled through the political process established by the Good Friday peace agreement.

That agreement is under threat because the Irish Republican Army has yet to make a convincing disarmament gesture. The IRA may not be behind the Catholic reaction to the Ardoyne protest, although it surely has many members and sympathizers in the area. It cannot avoid taking responsibility if the peace process finally breaks down.

Over the past 30 years, as North Belfast has become a flashpoint of sectarian violence, the area has experienced a slow draining of the Protestant population. Protestants complain of continual harassment and are now cruelly taking out their anger on the schoolchildren.

Throughout Northern Ireland, Protestants feel powerlessness in place of the old authoritarian certitudes that encouraged them to suppress the aspirations of Catholic nationalists. The IRA and its political wing, Sinn Fein, exude far more confidence, anticipating increases in the Catholic population that will probably be confirmed when census figures are released in 2003. In North Belfast, the changes are already obvious. "Ten years ago, we [Catholics] had 40 percent of the votes. Now we have 48 percent," said city councilor Martin Morgan in the Toronto *Globe and Mail.*

The Ardoyne protests grew violent on Wednesday, but by late in the week the Protestants had backed down, and, instead of small bombs, they greeted the Catholics with the blasts of whistles, many of them played by Protestant schoolgirls. Youngsters on either side should not be exposed to hateful protests, and it would be best if Catholics took the back way to school, giving their foes a meaningless victory.

The peace process has already produced a great decrease in violence throughout the province, but the North Belfast troubles could be the forerunner of trouble elsewhere unless the government established by the Good Friday agreement is allowed to function without the fits and starts of the last three years. The IRA has kept its part of the bargain to stop fighting, but it must do more to meet the continuing Protestant condition that it give graphic evidence of its peaceful intentions.

Catholics and Protestants outside the Holy Cross School cannot let go of their old hatreds. For the sake of the children throughout the North who are not yet confirmed in their prejudices, the IRA ought to give up some of its guns.

Boston Globe

"a bang-up job" as U.S. representative to the U.N. Food and Agricultural Organization in its efforts to fight worldwide hunger. "But he could use your help—lots of it," the editorial told readers, then explained what they could do. After mentioning another familiar name, Bob Dole, the editorial went into the details of the extent of hunger and what was being done to fight it. At the end, the writer, for good measure, again dropped in George McGovern's name.

The *Boston Globe* attempted to humanize an editorial ("Belfast Flashpoint") about violence in Northern Ireland with opening references to "small children and their parents . . . harassed on their way to school" and "people manning the gauntlet. . . ." Next, the editorial discussed how the Good Friday peace agreement has broken down and "Protestants feel powerlessness in place of the old authoritarian certitudes that encouraged them to suppress the aspirations of Catholic nationalists." At the end of the editorial the writer returned to the children: "For the sake of the children throughout the North who are not yet confirmed in their prejudices, the IRA ought to give up some of its guns."

International Affairs Web Resources

American Foreign Service Association (educational programs, reference materials, speakers, conferences): http://www.afsa.org

Amnesty International: http://www.amnesty.org

Asian American Resources (Asian-American Web sites):
    http://www.mit.edu/afs/athena.mit.edu/user/i/r/irie/www/aar.html

LatinoWeb (information on Latino culture): http://www.latinoweb.com

NATO: North American Treaty Organization: http://www.nato.int

The Electronic Embassy (links to Washington, D.C., embassies):
    http://www.embassy.org

The Embassy Web (links to U.S.-based embassies and consulates):
    http://www.embpage.org

The United Nations:
    http://www.un.org

U.S. Agency for International Development:
    http://www.usaid.gov

■ ARTS AND CULTURE

Surveys show that newspaper readership of news about the arts ranks low compared to most other features. Few daily newspapers have good arts and music coverage, even though the surveys have encouraged papers to expand and beef up their "life style" sections. As for opinion pages, according to a former editorial writer turned art-center director, Aubrey Bowie, "Editorial writers seem to turn their attention to the arts only when something very good or very bad grabs the headline and catches their eye, [and] in either case, they are forced to shoot from the hip without the day-to-day research that they do routinely on other community issues."[7]

According to Bowie, funding of the arts should get as much attention as the funding of more traditional public programs. He noted, however, that changes in federal tax laws have reduced the tax advantages for contributions to non-profit organizations and that government support for the arts has been decreasing, partly because of tight budgets and partly because of objections to the propriety of some of the programs and artworks that have received government funding.

The Minneapolis, Minn., *Star Tribune* addressed the problem of funding in two editorials published on the same day. The first editorial, "The care and feeding of culture" (not reprinted here), noted that "Once upon a time, Minnesota's elite families, corporations and foundations could instruct arts organizations to line up single file and wait their time for a new concert hall or museum." But no longer. The editorial suggested that those who had benefited economically ask themselves a tough question: "Is it wise to pass all of your wealth on to your children?" The editorial urged the affluent to invest their money in the arts.[8]

AS ESSENTIAL AS ANY OTHER SUSTENANCE

When politicians—or friends, neighbors and commentators, for that matter— talk about funding for the arts, a widespread assumption always seems to underlie the debate. It is that the arts are a luxury—varyingly enjoyable, provocative, boring, revelatory or amusing, but a luxury in any case. Yet a remarkable transformation has occurred over the past few weeks; the horrific acts of terrorism visited on New York and Washington have resulted in a collective—if unacknowledged and temporary—realization that the assumption is profoundly false.

In the months ahead, as diverse arts organizations reach out for support, Minnesotans should not forget this for-now-shared insight.

Luxury connotes several intertwined elements: It is something costly that offers comfort and satisfaction—and is, as Webster's New World puts it, "usually something considered unnecessary to life and health."

Americans' search for comprehension, expression and consolation these past weeks have taken them—individually and collectively—into the interpretive worlds of music and poetry, of photography and dance. They've poured their hearts and minds into the writing of poems and essays. They've shipped their work off to friends on the Internet, to newspapers, to strangers. People want—no, they *need*—to express themselves, whatever form that expression takes.

They need, too, to experience the art of others. In city concert halls, on town greens and in front of the living room TV, Americans have gathered to hear sounds and words—from Bach to Barber, from spirituals to "The Star Spangled Banner"— interpreted by artists as strikingly different as Willie Nelson and Denyce Graves.

Whether expressing or receiving, whether listening to Nelson in a benefit concert or Graves at the National Cathedral, people of all walks of life have turned to the arts. For some, Samuel Barber's "Adagio for Strings" will forever be associated with photographs of a devastated lower Manhattan after a news program so effectively coupled them. Others will remember the comfort and resolve they found in the Bible's Book of Psalms—the source not only of the 23rd Psalm but of the line of resolve from a spiritual that Oprah Winfrey employed as a cadence at the Yankee Stadium memorial service: "We shall not be moved."

Like any human expression, works of art can not only uplift but outrage. They can inspire or insult, gird or fracture. They can be tasteless or elegant, banal or exquisite. But let our collective and individual experience of music, of poetry, of all manner of arts in these days be remembered for its power— and, yes, its necessity.

Star Tribune

The second editorial, "As essential as any other sustenance," was prompted by "the horrific arts of terrorism visited on New York and Washington" on September 11, 2001. The editorial noted how, in the wake of the disaster, people had "poured out their hearts and minds" through music, poetry, photography, dance and other forms of expression as they "[searched] for comprehension, expression and consolation."

To call attention to the need to support the arts, the Eugene, Ore., *Register-Guard* has run a series of editorials accompanied by a logo with these words: "The Arts in Our Community—part of an occasional series." One editorial in the series ("Energize Oregon arts—Now's the time for Legislature to act," not reprinted here) urged support for creation of "a Trust for Cultural Development that would energize the arts throughout

---

STEM CELLS
Bush's compromise will move the debate along, but won't satisfy the absolutists on either side

Negotiating a slippery slope is hard, but not impossible. In addressing the nation Thursday night on federal funding for stem-cell research, President George W. Bush took a half-step—and erected a fence.

Some of this promising research, he said, may be done with federal funds. But because human embryos are destroyed in the process of extracting the stem cells, he will limit federal support to research done with stem cells already harvested from embryos freely donated by the couples to whom they belonged. Created in a petri dish, stored in a freezer, those embryos would have been destroyed in any case. To ignore their research and medical utility would be a total waste.

To staunch critics of stem-cell research, even Bush's half-step is a moral misstep and a political betrayal. If life begins at conception, then each embryo is a human life not to be destroyed for even the noblest of reasons. Adults, too, have stem cells, as do placentas, both useful and obtainable without taking life. Using embryos created for reproductive purposes is unethical enough; using embryos created for therapeutic purposes, which is now possible, transforms a life into a "bag of parts." In the presidential campaign, candidate Bush agreed with that perspective.

To staunch champions of stem-cell research, Bush's half-step is an undue delay of revolutionary treatment for the unquestionably living, particularly those with degenerative diseases. The "lines" of stem cells grown from those already harvested are privately owned and inadequate for the thorough research required. Bush's policy may not forestall possible benefits, but his funding constraint will stall them.

Critics of every stripe complain that Bush is just groping for the middle ground. But that's where most Americans sit, and most support stem-cell research likely to thwart diseases they know all too well. But it may be just as true that he found in discussions with opponents and proponents alike a complexity that he—and most of us—didn't expect.

Bush's is not the last word. The courts or Congress may well lift his funding constraints, and privately funded projects remain unaffected. But Bush has led us on to this slope with a warning implicit in his limited federal imprimatur and not to be ignored: Step carefully.

Plain Dealer

Oregon." Oregon voters subsequently approved two ballot propositions, one creating a trust that contributors could support with tax-free donations, the other providing funds for the trust from sale of surplus state property.[9]

Arts and Culture Web Resources

American Society of Composers, Authors and Publishers:
   http://www.ascap.com

Artcyclopedia (art information by artist, movement, medium, subject or nationality; links to museums and other sites):
   http://www.artcyclopedia.com

Current Theatre (theater reviews from the *New York Times*):
   http://www.nytimes.com/library/theater

Metropolitan Museum of Art, New York: http://www.metmuseum.org

Museum of Modern Art, New York: http://www.moma.org

Music Critic (reviews of music, movies, etc.): http://www.music-critic.com

National Music Federation (newsletter, press releases, links to music sites): http://www.nmc.org

National Endowment for the Arts: http://www.arts.endow.gov

Performing Arts Online (links to performers and composers; current theater shows): http://www.performingarts.net

The Smithsonian Institution: http://www.si.edu

Theatre Link (links to theater-related resources): http://theatre-link.com

World Wide Arts Resources (directory of arts resources on the Web): http://www.wwar.com

■ MEDICINE AND HEALTH

The health sciences represent another area in which editorial writers may feel ignorant. "Few issues more readily trip the typical editorialist into silence, drivel or pompous balderdash," D. Michael Heywood of the Vancouver, Wash., *Columbian* wrote in a *Masthead* symposium on health care. "Anything deeper than a turf battle between ambulance companies involves chopping through layers of increasing complexity. Burrowing through a vein of valuable explanation or suggestion for public action can seem as daunting as attempting heart surgery with kitchen cutlery."[10]

Writers need to display knowledge of their topics as well as understanding and sympathy for those who hold different opinions on abortion, AIDS, euthanasia, artificial insemination, life-preserving treatment, organ transplants, cloning, stem-cell research and holistic medicine. A Cleveland *Plain Dealer* editorial writer attempted to do exactly that in an editorial titled "Stem cells" that commented on the President Bush's "half-step" compromise on the highly controversial issue of federal funding for stem-cell research. After explaining the policy, the editorial devoted a paragraph to expressing the views of "staunch critics" of stem-cell research, then a paragraph to the views of "staunch champions," followed by a paragraph on the "middle ground . . . where most Americans sit." The conclusion is a cautious one: "Step carefully."

Taking a different approach, the *Daily Camera* of Boulder, Colo., expressed one point of view in its support for a patients' bill of rights. First, the editorial ("Minor surgery") made clear to readers what the proposed bill did not do: It didn't help 43 million Americans without health insurance, and it didn't increase the quality of care patients receive in medical offices, let alone provide "universal access to quality care." But the bill did provide for "certain types of care" and did allow patients to have their cases reviewed by independent medical experts and subsequently by the courts. Even though the bill was not in final form, readers should have gained a general understanding of what the legislation was intended to do.

Medicine and Health Web Resources

AMA Health Insight (general health issues): http://www.ama-assn.org/ama/pub/category/3457.html

DrugInfoNet (information and links healthcare and pharmaceutical Web sites): http://www.druginfonet.com

Healthtouch (updates on health, diseases, wellness; guide to organizations and government agencies): http://www.healthtouch.com

MINOR SURGERY
A patients' bill of rights? Well, it's a start

What's wrong with a "patients' bill of rights"? Nothing—unless Congress, the president and the people mistake it for the last word in health-care reform.

The bill now heading for approval in the U.S. Senate isn't much more than the first word in reform, although you'd never know that from some of the rhetoric surrounding it. Here are some of the fundamental health-care issues the bill doesn't address:

It doesn't reach the 43 million Americans with no health insurance at all.

It doesn't help the 15 million others who buy bare-bones coverage at high rates because they don't receive coverage through an employer.

It doesn't address in any significant way the quality of care patients receive when they walk into a medical office.

In short, it doesn't address what should be the long-term objective of national health policy—universal access to quality care. No bill with that ambitious goal would receive more than a cursory look in today's Washington. Ever since the early '90s, when the Clinton administration's elaborate and doomed health-care plan drew jeers across the country, national politicians have approached health care only in modest, carefully calculated steps.

The patients' bill of rights certainly fits that description. It appeals to a formidable constituency—the millions of reasonably well-off Americans who already have health insurance—and pins a marketable label on a useful refinement in the law.

Democrats and Republicans are still arguing over the specifics, but every version of the bill would give anxious consumers a new set of tools to fight back against the big companies that provide their health insurance. Right now, many of those plans enjoy unwarranted immunity from lawsuits when they refuse to pay for health care that patients consider medically necessary.

The bills in Congress would remove that exemption and provide for some form of mandatory external review. Patients would have to take their case to independent medical experts, and from there to court. Critics of the concept worry that it will generate a flood of litigation, but the experience of states with external review suggests that it may decrease the number of lawsuits.

The bills also guarantee patients access to certain kinds of care—emergency rooms, clinical trials, specialists and pharmaceutical drugs. Democrats and Republicans are struggling toward agreement on other details, such as where patients can sue (federal or state court?) and how much they could receive. The Senate cleared one major hurdle on Wednesday, with a bipartisan agreement to shield most employers from lawsuits.

Once the bill clears the Senate, the House of Representatives will have its say—and so will President Bush, who threatens periodically to veto the bill if it doesn't emerge in a form he can support. Down the road, though, even the president will want to share in the credit for what has become a popular concept. The odds are good that he'll sign some version of a "patients' bill of rights" with appropriate bipartisan fanfare.

If he does, Americans with health insurance will reason to applaud. And the 43 million uninsured? They'll have to wait until another day.

Daily Camera

National Safety Council: http://www.nsc.org
OSHA (Occupational Safety and HealthAdministration):
   http://www.osha.gov

■ RELIGION

Newspapers traditionally have not covered or commented on religion, except for the most mundane stories about church activities and the public controversies that spring up within and between religious groups. Reporters and editors don't want to get bogged down in what Susan Willey, who had been a religion writer on the *St. Petersburg* (Fla.) *Times,* described as "the complexity and diversity within religion." Reporters also have the problem of determining appropriate sources. Writing in *Quill,* Willey said that a journalist who is not very knowledgeable about religious matters finds it "much easier to fall back on traditional journalistic news criteria and cover religion on the basis of conflict and aberration." They are much more comfortable dealing with facts than with opinions and beliefs, she said. "They lean toward the concrete rather than the abstract."[11] Within journalism, and in fact within American society, there also long has been a belief that one's religion is a private matter and therefore not a proper topic for public discussion. Most Americans, for example, are embarrassed by public preaching in the streets.

Despite their inclinations toward reticence, journalists have been increasingly forced in recent years to report and comment on moral and religious issues. Issues with public policy implications literally run the gamut from birth to death: At what point does the fertilized embryo become a person? When, if ever, is abortion justified? When, if ever, should euthanasia or physician-assisted suicide be allowed? Between birth and death are such issues as prayer in the schools, subsidized private-school tuition, use of public schools by religious groups and the Boy Scout requirement that members profess faith in God.

Religious and religion-related groups that traditionally have not been politically active have not only become active but also politically astute at wielding influence. (A few years ago that last sentence would have referred to "church groups." Now writers talk about the activities of churches, mosques, temples, synagogues and religious cults, as well as religious groups that are not connected with a specific denomination—the Christian Coalition, for example.)

The issues arising among these groups are not limited by national boundaries. Following the terrorist attacks on September 11, 2001, most Americans quickly found out how little they knew about the Muslim religion, the Koran and the six million or so fellow Americans who considered themselves to be members of that faith.

The Boy Scout issue arose when an Oregon judge ruled that, as long as the organization excluded boys on the basis of religion, it had no right to recruit members in schools during school time. In an editorial titled "Atheist makes her point," the Portland *Oregonian* reminded readers that they should be as tolerant about "other people's irreligions" as they were toward "other people's religions."

An issue that may not appear to be religious to some may seem so to others. Take the Kennewick Man, for example. In 1996 skeletal remains were found along the Columbia River in the vicinity of Kennewick, Wash. Scientists wanted to examine the bones to determine whether, as some thought, they had Caucasoid features, which would suggest European origins. Pacific Northwest tribal leaders, however, wanted to take possession for burial according to their religious practices. Three years later, with the issue still tied up in the courts, an editorial ("Ancient remains need scientific inquiry") in the Bend, Ore., *Bulletin* said it was time for the Interior Department and the federal courts to "stop dragging their feet" and let the scientists check the DNA and then let "the proper religious group . . . take over."

ATHEIST MAKES HER POINT

The Boy Scouts cannot have it both ways: Exclude some boys and yet make a pitch to every boy during school

Americans have become increasingly tolerant of other people's religions over the last few decades, but what about other people's irreligion?

In that department, we may still have a ways to go. A recent court ruling in favor of a Portland atheist, though, should provide a nudge in the right direction. True, many Portlanders will be dismayed by the ruling, which went against a rightfully beloved community organization, the Boy Scouts.

But the Scouts, Portland Public Schools, State Superintendent Stan Bunn—and we, too, we must admit—were wrong about this one. Atheist Nancy Powell has insisted for years that the Scouts should not be allowed to use schools during school hours to recruit new members.

She's right, and with 20-20 hindsight, we can see she's been right all along.

Her reason? The Scouts require boys to believe in God. Officially and on paper at least, if not always in practice in every troop, the Scouts exclude boys like her son, Remington, who are avowed athiests.

In some ways, it may seem a small point she's made, while what could be sacrificed by this court decision is something very important to the community—the exposure of more boys to Scouting. We'd expand the number of Scouts, if we could, and do nothing to contract their numbers.

The Scouts have argued that they need what amounts to a competitive advantage over other youth organizations, the ability to recruit boys during the school day. But an after-school fair, where many community organizations are represented, would attract boys without violating the separation of church and state.

And it would have this advantage, too: Parents could attend and decide which activities they wanted to steer their children toward. Given the explosion of diversity in our society, this is wise. Parental supervision adds a double-check that makes sense whenever children are being recruited for any activity, however worthy.

Interestingly, the Girl Scouts made the reference to God in their own promise optional in 1993, out of recognition of the range of religious belief in the United States. "Flexibility in expressing the promise can empower girls to more closely examine their beliefs," Girl Scout materials say.

But then again, the Girl Scouts' goal is to reach "every girl everywhere."

The Boy Scouts might want to emulate that approach. It would certainly cut down on recruitment problems.

To be sure, the Boy Scouts have the right to exclude. They just don't have the right to have it both ways—to exclude boys based on their religion, and still give their pitch to all boys during school time at a public school.

Now a judge has backed Powell up. The schools must change their policy, and it's time for the rest of us to rethink our positions, as well.

Could a Boy Scout today get away with not believing, or simply not caring very much about religion? Absolutely. A boy who went along, who mouthed the right words during the Scout promise and at other appropriate moments, could fudge the entire issue.

But no boy should have to do that. That is why we must concede, if a bit reluctantly, that Powell and this court decision are both correct in principle.

It is up to the school, now to ensure that after-school fairs or forums are put in place, so that Boy Scouts and other worthwhile organizations continue to have every opportunity to reach boys.

Oregonian

ANCIENT REMAINS NEED SCIENTIFIC INQUIRY
The act gives Indian groups control of any human remains found to predate documented European settlement.

Dead men don't lie; although some aren't given the chance. Such is the case with the Kennewick Man whose remains were found along the Columbia River in 1996.

At issue are control over the skeletal remains and the right to give them an appropriate burial. Caucasoid features have led some groups to believe Kennewick Man might have been European. This theory motivated the Asatru Folk Assembly, a California group that practices a religion based on their ancestors' ancient Northern European traditions, to file suit in U.S. federal court requesting a DNA test be performed on the remains to determine accurately exactly who descended from the Kennewick Man. If he was European, the Asatru want control over his remains.

However, Northwest tribal leaders have also made a bid for control based on the Native American Graves Protection and Repatriation Act of 1990. Essentially, the act gives Indian groups control of any human remains found to predate documented European settlement. When initial testing indicated the remains are 9,000 years old, Northwest Indians argued the Kennewick Man be placed under their control. Given control, they will not allow any DNA tests to be performed because the resulting desecration of the remains would offend their religious sensibilities.

Pulling at the remains from a third direction are eight noted anthropologists who wish to have DNA tests performed on the remains because of the important scientific information the results could provide. From wherever the Kennewick Man originated, simply knowing this location would help fill out our picture of North America's earliest settlers.

Caught between the three parties is the U.S. Interior Department which currently has control over the remains. The original dating of the remains has been called into question and the department is conducting tests to better determine their age. The department steadfastly refuses to allow DNA tests, though.

The struggle points to a critical flaw in the Graves Protection Act. Remains found to be older than documented European settlement are given to Native Americans. A DNA test, were it to reveal a European, or even Asian, connection, would provide the necessary documentation of early settlement, but Native Americans are not inclined to give permission for the test because of their religious convictions. The end result is a block placed by Northwest Indians on tests despite the fact that were the tests conducted, it might well invalidate the right of the Indians to block them.

President Clinton has backed the Indians in this matter thus far. There is little doubt Indian leaders are genuinely concerned about preserving their religious integrity and the sanctity of one of their ancestors. It is interesting to consider, though, that if the Kennewick Man were found not to be an Indian ancestor, his presence in the Northwest so early would call into serious question Native American claims to land and resources based on having been the first to settle North America.

The fate of the Kennewick Man should not be determined based on religious beliefs or questionable legislative acts. At the heart of the debate is the unanswered question of just who the Kennewick Man was. The only way to answer this question is to proceed with scientific inquiry. Given the potentially staggering implications of DNA tests, the eight anthropologists should be permitted to go forward with their plans. It is time for the Interior Department and the federal courts to stop dragging their feet in this matter. Science can finally put the Kennewick Man to rest. The proper religious group can then take over.

Bulletin

BOISE STATE STARTS ON ROAD TOWARD BIG-TIME SPORTS

Boise State University joined the WAC July 1, but for fans, the move into the big time really kicks off today.

When BSU takes on South Carolina tonight, it begins a new era for the school's athletic programs.

The rivals are new and so are the challenges. We wish the university luck on both fronts.

University officials say it will take money— a lot more of it—to compete in the Western Athletic Conference.

BSU's current-year athletic budget of $10.3 million makes it one of the poorer members of the WAC. That figure doesn't come close to the richest program in the WAC, Fresno State, which puts $17 million into athletics.

Is bigger better? In some ways, it is; in some ways, maybe not.

While BSU heads to South Carolina, Fresno State's football team hosts Oregon State this weekend. That's a coup for Fresno State—a home game against the team ranked No. 1 in the Sports Illustrated preseason football preview. And Fresno State can bank on a handsome share of the revenue from Sunday's game.

Fresno State's budget also allows the university to afford head basketball coach Jerry Tarkanian. Tark the Shark is known, in no particular order, for his sideline towel chewing; his 1990 national championship at UNLV; and the off-the-court problems of his players.

The big time brings bonuses and costs. It brings bigger-name programs and national TV interest. But it can bring a win-at-all-costs attitude that should never play in Boise.

BSU athletic officials need to keep that in mind.

They are hoping to pay to compete by getting more bucks from the fans. They hope better competition will mean increased ticket sales. They hope it will translate into other support; BSU athletic director Gene Bleymaier is hoping to draw at least 1,000 new members into the 3,000-member Bronco Athletic Association.

But ticket sales and booster support rise and fall with win-loss records. And we're not misreading Boise when we say winning in the WAC is not an end that justifies all means.

That's the challenge ahead for BSU.

And even though the South Carolina game isn't a WAC game, it represents the step up for BSU.

At a recent luncheon sponsored by the Boise Metro Chamber of Commerce's Leadership Boise program, BSU football coach Dan Hawkins was asked point-blank about opening the season with a road matchup against South Carolina and its coaching legend, Lou Holtz.

Hawkins, who talks about his profession with the intensity of a linebacker, admitted he was given the option of backing out of the South Carolina game and taking on Eastern Washington, which plays in the Big Sky Conference BSU abandoned in 1996.

He said he decided to keep South Carolina on the schedule, since it represents the direction BSU wants to go.

The road to the big time begins on the road tonight, more than 2,000 miles from the blue turf.

Good luck, Broncos.

Idaho Statesman

Religion Web Resources

Academic Info: Religion (directory of Web sites devoted to world religions):
     http://www.academicinfo.net/religinindex.html

Al-Muslim (information about Islamic religion): http://www.al-muslim.org

BBC World Service—Religions of the World:
     http://www.bbc.co.uk/worldservice/people/features/_world_religions

PUT SCHWINN BACK ON A ROLL

For generations of American youngsters—especially millions of baby boomers—few gifts could equal the thrill that came from receiving a Schwinn bicycle.

Now, for the second time in less than a decade, the famous marque once again is in financial peril.

Schwinn, founded in Chicago in 1895 but headquartered in Boulder since 1997, for decades produced the peculiarly American balloon-tired bikes that were much heavier than lightweight European models but as indestructible as a Sherman tank.

The genre reached its zenith with the Black Phantom, which sported a sleek curvilinear frame, aerodynamic "tank" and sporty red, black and chrome finish.

But lightweight imports, once called "English bikes" by American GIs serving in Britain during World War II, soon made inroads in the American market, followed by an invasion of even lighter foreignmade 10-speed "racers" in the bicycle boom of the early '70s.

Schwinn offered American-made versions but took production overseas to Taiwan to stay competitive.

Still, the best-known American brand filed for Chapter 11 bankruptcy in 1992, then was rescued by two investment groups in 1994.

Along the way, Schwinn acquired GT, a California manufacturer of mountain bikes—which Schwinn once had dismissed as a passing fad—and was sold to Questor Partners Fund in 1997.

The company branched out into the fitness equipment market, but Questor announced in April it's getting out of both businesses.

Now, the company says, its sales are slower than expected and it's in arrears to several suppliers.

Questor wants to sell off Schwinn, GT and Schwinn Fitness, either together or separately.

We sincerely hope the company finds a "white knight" to turn it around and preserve the brand name so fondly regarded by so many Americans whose first foray on two wheels came aboard one of Schwinn's bulletproof bikes.

Denver Post

Catholic Online (Roman Catholic information service):
   http://www.catholic.org
Christianity Online (current events, politics; links to other magazines):
   http://www.christianitytoday.com
Mining Co. Guide to Judaism (guide to Jewish Internet resources):
   http://www.judaism.about.com
Religion News Service (daily newsletter): http://www.religionnews.com
   Various Theories of Origins (evolution versus creation science):
   http://www.religioustolerance.org/evolutio.htm
Webocracy Web Guides—Religion and Philosophy (links to major religions):
   http://www.webocracy.com/Websaurus/Web_Guides/_Religion_Philosophy

■ SPORTS AND RECREATION

The sports world seems more and more regarded as an appropriate subject for editorial comment. One reason is that sports pages have broadened their

LET STATES REGULATE AMUSEMENT PARKS

Stricter regulation of permanent amusement parks to prevent death and injury is, of course, a good idea. The most recent proposal for achieving that, however, is not.

U.S. Rep. Edward Markey, D-Mass., recently proposed the National Amusement Park Safety Act that would give the federal Consumer Product Safety Commission jurisdiction over all amusement park rides. Markey's proposal was part of a House Commerce subcommittee session looking into whether federal regulation should be reinstituted.

"In 1981, Congress concluded that permanent amusement park rides were not consumer products and thus did not require federal regulation," Newsday reported. "Since then, rides have become bigger and faster, and regulation of them has been left up to a sometimes haphazard system of state enforcement."

Portable rides, such as those at carnivals, are regulated nationwide but regulation of the fixed operations—Disneyland, Great America, Marine World and the like—is left to the states. Markey's proposal comes about after hearing horrific reports of death and injury throughout the country. His concern is well taken. Between 1994 and 1998, the Consumer Product Safety Commission estimated, there were 4,500 injuries at fixed amusement parks that required hospitalization, double the number for portable rides.

The president and chief executive officer of the International Association of Amusement Parks and Attractions, a trade association of some 1,500 permanent parks, told the Commerce subcommittee those figures are distorted because attendance at fixed parks has significantly increased in recent years. In fact, John Graff said, amusement park rides are among the safest forms of entertainment.

Bay Area residents were shocked and saddened in 1997 by the death of Quimby Ghilotti, 18, in the collapse of a tall slide at Waterworld in Concord. A handful of incidents within the span of a week last summer, including the death of Sunnyvale 12-year-old Joshua Smurphat at Paramount's Great America in Santa Clara, reinforced concern about the safety of amusement park rides.

Thankfully, lessons learned from Ghilotti's death and other fatal accidents included the need for new, tougher safety

coverage far beyond the mere reporting of the outcome and description of events. At the high school level, local citizens argue whether athletes need to maintain passing grades in all subjects. College issues involve minimal scholastic standards, illegal payments to athletes, the professionalization of college athletics and imbalance in women's and men's sports. At the professional level are arguments over "instant replay," players' salaries, foreign ownership of golf courses and baseball teams, and exclusion of countries from the Olympic Games. Many times, of course, sports editorials praise teams and individuals for outstanding performances or offer condolences over losses. Expressing pride in the hometown team is an appropriate editorial function, but sports editorials, like other editorials on the page, serve readers best when they seek to enlighten or evaluate.

The *Idaho Statesman* in Boise cheered for the hometown team in an editorial marking promotion of Boise State University to a "big time" athletic conference ("Boise State starts on road toward big-time sports"). After hailing the season as a "new era for the school's athletic programs," the editorial concluded: "Good luck, Broncos." But the editorial was not all bravado. "The big time brings bonuses and costs," the writer said, citing the dangers of a "win-at-all costs attitude," adding:

regulations at California's permanent parks. Last year's problems helped Assemblyman Tom Torlakson, D-Antioch, push through legislation that does just that. Admittedly, passage of the bill was achieved only after two years of study, hearings and compromise.

We believe passage of tougher regulations on a national level could be even more time consuming, and a lot more complicated. Additionally, federal regulation, through the Consumer Product Safety Commission, would bypass the unique knowledge of its operations each state individually brings to its permanent parks. Federal regulation would require creation of a whole new division of the Consumer Product Safety Commission that not only would be costly but potentially far less efficient than local control.

It is in the best interests of the states, especially the big ones in tourism and amusement park entertainment—Florida, California and Texas—to make sure the rides are safe. The park operators whose attractions benefit the states to the tune of hundreds of millions of dollars surely place the very highest priority on safety—not only out of regard for their

fellow citizens but because failure to do so would subject them to high-digit litigation and would be bad for business.

We cannot see how turning over those responsibilities to a federal bureaucracy would be an improvement. Let's first see how new state laws passed in the wake of last year's rash of well-publicized injuries and deaths work.

A system with federal inspectors scattered about the country, running from the remote reaches of the Idaho panhandle to the Oklahoma prairie to the shores of Maine when it's not necessary would be a waste of time and money.

They would have to constantly familiarize themselves with facts and circumstances that locals already know. They would have to thoroughly accommodate all the vagaries of climate—from scorching summers to hard-freeze winters to toxic air and corrosive fog—vital to engineering safety.

Most importantly, they would need to know the park operators, their competence, history and trustworthiness. States can do that. Let's give them that chance.

Oakland Tribune

"And we're not misreading Boise when we say winning in the WAC [Western Athletic Conference] is not an end that justifies all means."

"Sports" editorials these days are not limited to what takes place on the playing field. A *Denver Post* editorial ("Put Schwinn back on a roll") expressed concern over the possible demise of the Schwinn bicycle, noting that since the company began production in 1885 Schwinn probably has accounted for more physical exertion for American teenagers than any contact sport. The writer hoped that a "white knight" could be found to "preserve the brand name so fondly regarded by so many Americans whose first foray on two wheels came aboard one of Schwinn's bulletproof bikes."

Unregulated amusement park rides—another popular recreation pastime—attracted the attention of the *Oakland* (Calif.) *Tribune*. Citing the dangers of death and injuries, an editorial ("Let states regular amusement parks") suggested that states should be given the opportunity to pass laws regulating amusement park rides before proposed federal legislation was considered.

In an editorial raising the question of what is or is not a sport, a Minneapolis, Minn., *Star Tribune* editorial (not reprinted here) criticized a proposal to legalize "shooting preserves" as an unethical attempt to make "killing confined animals . . . look like sport." The editorial said: "Humane consideration demands that the slaughter of animals be conducted in a way that reduces their suffering to the barest minimum. Shooting (in a confined space) cannot be made consistent with that principle."[12]

Sports and Recreation Web Resources

Aquatic Network (information about issues, events, and studies of the aquatic world): http://www.aquanet.com

Baseball Links (links to baseball resources): http://www.baseball-links.com

CBS SportsLine: http://www.sportsline.com

CNNSI (CNN plus *Sports Illustrated*): http://www.cnnsi.com

The Earth Times (environmental issues): http://www.earthtimes.org

EnviroLink (information clearinghouse on the environment): http://www.envirolink.org

ESPN.com: http://www.espn.com

Fox Sports Online: http://www.foxsports.com

National Wildlife Federation: http://www.nwf.org/nwf

Selectsurf (links to extreme sports sites): http://www.selectsurf.com/sports/extreme

USA Basketball (news releases, links): http://www.usabasketball.com

■ TOUCHY TOPICS

Editorials can be hard to write when writers know that what they say will offend a few or many of their readers.

An example is "Bigotry 101," published in the *Siuslaw News* in Florence, Ore. The editorial took a strong stand against a state ballot proposition that was intended to prohibit "public school instruction encouraging, promoting, sanctioning homosexual, bisexual behaviors." One indication of the controversial, sensitive atmosphere in which the editorial was written is that the proposition received 49 percent of the votes cast on the November 2001 election. An indication of how the editorial was regarded by Oregon journalists: The writer, Robert Serra, won a first-place award among nonweekly newspapers in a statewide contest sponsored by the Society of Professional Journalists. Serra minced no words. He called the sponsoring group "misguided and ill-intended," accused it of attempting "to denigrate a class of Oregon citizens by casting them as evil spore" and described the proposal as "a wicked, mean-spirited attempt to isolate and intimidate a segment of our society that the OCA [Oregon Citizens Alliance] and its backers seem to fear out of ignorance, prejudice or bias." (One reader responded, "How and why one should get an award [a complimentary one anyway] for advocating a life style condemning young school children to aids [*sic*], suffering and early death is beyond me!")[13]

On the other side of the continent, the *Rutland* (Vt.) *Herald* won the Pulitzer Prize for a courageous stand in a series of editorials that supported the legalization of same-sex civil unions in Vermont. The issue arose when the Vermont Supreme Court decided that same-sex couples deserved the

---

BIGOTRY 101

By Robert Serra

The Oregon Citizens Alliance is coming out to a school near you. That is, if Lon Mabon and his ultra-conservative OCA backers can curry voter favor for their upcoming course in Bigotry 101.

The latest offering by this misguided and ill-intended group cloaks itself in the dark, dark school colors of hatred and bias. Measure 9, if passed in the November general election, would prohibit Oregon's public schools from "encouraging, promoting or sanctioning homosexual or bisexual behaviors." It would require sanctions for schools that in any way violate its intent, and would include the loss of all or part of state funding.

This is not the first time the OCA has attempted to denigrate a class of Oregon citizens by casting them as evil spore. In the early 1990s, the group crafted alarming measures to deny civil-rights protections for homosexuals. The measures were rejected by Oregon voters.

Lon Mabon would have us believe that homosexual activist teachers and administrators hold gay pride parades in school cafeterias, and that a school district's board of directors, administrators and teachers encourage and promote any type of sexual lifestyle.

In reality, this measure is a solution in search of a problem. The Oregon Department of Education has received no complaints against teachers promoting homosexuality in Oregon schools.

As the so-called "Student Protection Act," the measure is not intended to help or protect anyone, other than perhaps the perpetuation of Lon Mabon's job. Measure 9 is a wicked, mean-spirited attempt to isolate and intimidate a segment of our society that the OCA and its backers seem to fear out of ignorance, prejudice or bias.

The measure, if successful, would paint the ugly face of bigotry on our fair state, and it would lead to a dangerous and destructive atmosphere for law-abiding groups from which we may feel set apart.

We must realize that, as a society entering the third millennium, we must work beyond primitive urges to brand those who are "different" as "dangerous" or "evil." Most people are good, and that includes people of all virtuous persuasions, not just ours.

If the goal of education is to help all of our students, passage of this measure would severely compromise our achievements. If the goal of a tolerant society is to respect all people of good will, their individual characteristics notwithstanding, passage of this measure would severely retard our advancement.

Let's reject this Measure 9 with the loud thud of a big strong school-house door shutting tight on a dejected Lon Mabon and his OCA.

Siuslaw News

---

same basic rights as heterosexual couples. From December 1999 to April 2000, the *Herald* published 19 editorials on the subject. (For a more complete account, see the section titled "A more complex melody" in Chapter 2, "The Editorial Page That Should, and Could, Be.") According to David Moats, who wrote the editorials, the ruling put the "statewide community of Vermont" into "a sort of perilous state." He said that he "had the sense that it was important to frame the whole question in a way that the state wouldn't end up tearing itself apart."[14] In April 2000, the legislature finally passed and the governor signed a bill legalizing same-sex civil unions.

Of the 10 editorials that the *Herald* submitted for the Pulitzer competition, two were especially noteworthy efforts to help frame the challenge facing

A Charitable View

The House Judiciary Committee heard moving testimony last week from one of the lawyers who brought the suit that led to the Supreme Court's decision requiring the state to provide equal benefits to gay and lesbian couples.

The lawyer, Susan Murray, described the pain of people who must listen to frequent and repeated public denunciations of their morality and character. "It's really painful to hear people say, 'You're immoral. You're an abomination,'" Murray said.

Gay and lesbian Vermonters have heard a full range of denunciation in the past several weeks. It is something they have heard all their lives, beginning with common school yard taunts and culminating in the passionate condemnations heard at the two public hearings inside the State House.

Murray used the words of Episcopal Bishop Mary Adelia McLeod in saying, "Gays and lesbians are the only group that are still politically correct to kick."

Sometimes, the attacks on gays are plainly mean-spirited and oblivious to the pain they cause. In some cases an unholy mix of anger and fear suffuse the language of those who condemn gays and lesbians as immoral. These attacks are the equivalent of the fire hoses and police dogs that were turned on civil rights workers in the South in an earlier day. They are a reminder that seeking justice exacts a price.

But opposition to same-sex marriage or domestic partnerships comes in many shadings, and it is useful to distinguish those who hate from those whose opposition has other origins.

Bishop Kenneth Angell has prompted resentment in asserting the Roman Catholic opposition to same-sex marriage. It's helpful, however, to realize that the Catholic position arises, not from bigotry, but from a specific teaching about sexuality, a teaching that a lot of people have difficulty with, including millions of Catholics.

It is the Catholic teaching that sex is a gift meant for the purposes of procreation and that sex indulged in for other reasons is a misuse of that gift. Thus, sex outside of marriage is not condoned. Even sex within marriage when the possibility of procreation has been blocked by birth control is not condoned. Gay sex, in this view, does not fall into the category of permissible sex.

It is possible to disagree with this view while still recognizing it to be a legitimate doctrine of a major religion aimed at providing guidance in the chaotic realm of human sexuality. It may offer some comfort to supporters of same-sex marriage to see through to the humanity of the opposition and to recognize the reasons for opposition are not always founded in bigotry.

At the same time, opponents of same-sex marriage have an obligation to see through to the humanity of a vulnerable minority. Anyone tempted to condemn homosexuality as other than normal ought to consider that it is quite normal that within our population 5 to 10 percent—the number is not important—happen to be gay or lesbian. For each of us, it is normal to be who we are, whether we are heterosexual or homosexual. It has always been that way, and the sooner we recognize it the better.

There are among us already those eager to sharpen the swords of conflict on the issue of same-sex marriage.

But the people of Vermont are in this together. Opponents and supporters of the Supreme Court's ruling are part of the same community, and as the discussion moves forward it is important to cultivate a charitable view of those on the other side. That way, however the issue is resolved, Vermont will be a better place in the end.

Rutland Herald

LISTENING TO VERMONT

One of the most commonly heard complaints about House actions on civil unions is that House members have not listened to the people.

The House, responding to a Supreme Court ruling, has passed a bill allowing for civil unions for same-sex couples. The Senate will take up a similar bill soon. The charge that House members did not listen to the people arises in part from town meeting votes in which people in some towns expressed their disapproval of same-sex marriage or civil unions.

The assumption is that, unless legislators heed the perceived will of the majority, they have not listened. To the contrary, however, House members and senators have done an extraordinary amount of listening. The outpouring of sentiment on all sides has been voluminous, and an awareness that civil unions are unpopular has certainly not been lost on members of the Legislature.

In considering the actions of their legislators, however, private citizens might ask themselves how they make up their own minds on important public questions. How many of us would be proud of admitting that, in determining what is right or wrong, we allow our minds to be made up by our neighbors? Doesn't the individual citizen form his convictions on the basis of his own values and his assessment of the public good? How could any of us say we have convictions at all if we were to let the majority of our neighbors determine what our convictions are?

A legislator has a greater responsibility than an individual citizen in making decisions on public issues. The legislator has to take into consideration the views of the public and to balance public opinion with his or her own reading of the public good. But to ask our legislators to surrender their judgment in order to reflect the shifting shape of public opinion is to ask them to leave at home the very qualities for which we elect them to office: their intelligence, judgment, sensitivity, and courage.

Members of the Legislature have listened to the public, and what they have heard is complex. As they listened, they heard, among other things, that it is fair and decent to treat all Vermonters with compassion and not to exclude same-sex couples from the benefits that attach to marriage. The House wouldn't have passed the bill it passed if members hadn't been listening to Vermonters who said these things. Nor would they have passed the bill they passed if they had checked their judgment at the door and allowed themselves to be swayed by the majoritarian winds.

There is a segment of the population that will never accept civil unions for same-sex couples. One of the fundamental divides on the issue has to do with people's understanding of homosexuality. Some people believe homosexuality is a choice and that those who choose it are immoral. The actions of the Supreme Court and the House are premised on another view: that sexual orientation is a condition, like left- or right-handedness and that sexual orientation is no justification for condemning a segment of society to pariah's status.

Some people will never be reconciled to that view. But the moral condemnation of homosexuality has not prevailed. Rather, a Legislature that has listened to the many voices of Vermont is moving toward a conclusion that humanity is diverse and that fair treatment for all should be the goal.

Supporters of civil unions have shown exemplary courage in heeding the call of conscience, but it is not fair to say that they have a corner on conscience. Conscience is active on both sides of the question.

As the Senate nears a vote on civil unions, senators have the job of hearing what Vermonters say and then putting the question to test of their convictions. That is all anyone could ask.

Rutland Herald

Vermonters. The first, which came after "moving testimony" on the proposed legislation, was titled "A charitable view." It was a plea for both sides "to see through the humanity of the opposition" and "to distinguish those who hate from those whose opposition has other origins." The editorial concluded, "As the discussion moves forward it is important to cultivate a charitable view of those on the other side. That way, however the issue is resolved, Vermont will be a better place in the end."

The other editorial ("Listening to Vermont") appeared when it seemed certain that the legislation would pass a bill even though more Vermonters probably opposed than supported same-sex civil unions and when legislators were being charged with not listening to the people. The editorial judged that "Members of the Legislature [had] listened to the people" but they also had "heard that it is fair and decent to treat all Vermonters with compassion . . . ." Furthermore, the editorial said, a legislator "has a greater responsibility than an individual citizen in making decisions on public issues" and must balance the views of the public "with his or her own reading of the public good."

CONCLUSION

Editorials on the subjects discussed in this chapter are not hard to write if you do enough homework to know what you are writing about and if you write in a manner that enables readers to understand what you are writing about.

QUESTIONS AND EXERCISES

1. Find an editorial on an economic topic. Compare the writing and approach to the suggestions offered in this chapter. Does the editorial follow these suggestions, especially concerning the use of figures and the personalizing of the writer's points? If not, how could it be improved?

2. Analyze an editorial that talks about taxes, property taxes if possible. Is it easy to understand? Could it be simplified? Should more points be spelled out?

3. Find an editorial that relies excessively on legal terms. Rewrite it using more common language.

4. Can you find an editorial that formerly would have been labeled an "Afghanistanism"? Does the editorial seem to have absolutely nothing to do with the interests of the readers most likely to read the editorial? Could the subject have been made more pertinent to readers?

5. Find an editorial on an international topic that stands a good chance of catching the reader's attention—one that is not on a current hot topic. What is it about the editorial that makes it readable?

6. Compare several editorials on cultural subjects. Which seem to have been written simply to get promoters of causes off the backs of the editorial writers? Which are most likely to attract readers? Could the run-of-the-mill editorials have been made more interesting or pertinent?

CHAPTER THIRTEEN

Subjects That Are Deceptively Easy

If you don't like people, you're called a misanthrope. And if you detest holidays, you're called an editorial writer. [If you decide not to run an editorial on Columbus Day], stand by for irate calls and letters from what seems like every Italian American for miles around.

—JAMES E. CASTO,
HERALD-DISPATCH, HUNTINGTON,
W.VA.[1]

Several standard types of editorials have acquired the reputation among editorial writers as being easy to write. They usually can be dashed off, without much thought. Of course they usually are worth no more than the effort that went into producing them. A score or so of editorial writers had fun on the Internet exchanging tongue-in-cheek messages identifying some of these clichéd editorials. Here are some of them with their shorthand designations:

DBI—a "dull but important" editorial

C&D—condemn and deplore

DFS—deserves further study

Q&E—quick and easy

EI—evil incarnate (somebody we hate does something stupid)

LJ—lapse of judgment (somebody we like does something stupid)

US2—an issue so big that everyone is writing about it, so we'll weigh in, too

In this chapter I look at four categories of deceptively easy-to-write editorials: obituaries, the local pride piece, the favorite subject (or "easy shot") and the "duty" piece. In each of these categories, the writer often is tempted to dash off, perhaps cynically, a standard piece that just gets by.

■ OBITUARIES

De mortuis nil nisi bonum is not a good rule for writing editorials about persons who have died. Speaking nothing but good of the dead may be fine for funeral orations, but telling readers only some of the facts has no more place in an obituary editorial than it has in any other kind of editorial. Relating the full story is relatively easy when you write about a national, or even state, figure. Information is often readily available and indisputable. The family of the deceased is not likely to see the editorial, at least not immediately after publication, so the writer can feel free to tell the good and the not-so-good. But when the person is a local figure, inhibitions take hold. The temptation is to stick with the favorable facts and throw in a dash of

ROY DRACHMAN HELPED SHAPE TODAY'S TUCSON

Roy Drachman was the father of modern Tucson.

Mayor Bob Walkup said, upon learning of Drachman's death at age 95 yesterday, that the businessman's "fingerprints are all over Tucson."

Drachman's legacy is indeed broad and deep.

■ Tucson Medical Center was built after Drachman and his associates raised $250,000 to convert an old sanitarium into a nonprofit community hospital.

■ Raytheon Corp., the community's largest private employer, is here only because in the 1950s, Drachman quickly assembled thousands of acres of land at the behest of the company's predecessor, Hughes Aircraft Co.

■ The University of Arizona would look far different and would not be as strong without the millions of dollars Drachman donated to the College of Medicine, to athletics and to other areas. And from 1987 to 1992, Drachman co-chaired a private fund-raising drive to collect $100 million for UA. The drive raised $190 million.

■ The Tucson Open professional golf tournament, which raises money for youth sports, was started by Drachman and his friends who loved golf.

BASEBALL AND TCC AMONG HIS LEGACIES

There were many other accomplishments. Drachman was largely responsible for bringing spring training baseball to Tucson, for the building of the Tucson Convention Center and for passage of numerous bond proposals that helped local government and schools grow.

There are many local nonprofit organizations that survived and thrived because of Drachman's generosity.

"she'll be missed." This is no time to add to the family's bereavement, the reasoning goes. Yet undeserved praise is no praise at all, since those likely to care the most about what is written will know that the words are hollow.

The trick to writing an obituary editorial is to catch some detail—words, behavior, description—that makes the person seem unique and human, something that distinguishes him or her from everyone else, something for which the person can be remembered. You don't always have to write about a widely known person. Fitting subjects might be a person who had taught a long time in the local schools, someone who had been quietly helpful to neighbors and friends, a mail deliverer, someone who had clerked in the same store for many years, a person who had sold newspapers on the same corner ever since anyone could remember.

One task in writing a complimentary editorial is to explain why the deceased is being praised, especially in the case of an elderly person whose praiseworthy deeds may have been forgotten or never known by most readers. When the man described as "the father of modern Tucson" died at age 95, a *Tucson* (Ariz.) *Citizen* editorial ("Roy Drachman helped shape today's Tucson") spelled out what Roy Drachman had done for the community, including contributions that went back to the 1950s. "He came along at precisely the right time to shape this young city and to nurture it as it grew during the past century," the editorial said. Looking ahead, the writer added: "The community now has a substantial challenge: to grow the next generation of leaders to assume the mantle left by Drachman."

But his legacy is far deeper. Using experience in community activism, business, education and sports, Drachman took the lead in shaping what Tucson is today.

He remained to his last breath an unbridled booster of his hometown and someone deeply concerned about and involved in community issues.

As a developer of commercial property, especially shopping centers, Drachman literally directed the growth of Tucson. There were some who disagreed with his development moves, but virtually all respected him as a gentleman.

PIONEER BECAME AN HISTORIAN

Drachman was a member of a pioneer Tucson family. He was born in Tucson six years before Arizona became a state and went to work at the age of 10, hawking The Tucson Citizen on downtown streets. From those roots, he became a 20th century pioneer in Tucson's development.

In recent years, Drachman became a historian, working to ensure that the early years of his beloved city were forever preserved.

He wrote his memories, published as columns in the Citizen, during the past few years. Those memories, including details about Tucson's development during much of the 20th century, were later published in a book, "From Cowtown to Desert Metropolis: Ninety Years of Arizona Memories."

If any one man can laid claim to the title of "Mr. Tucson," it is Roy Drachman. He came along at precisely the right time to shape this young city and to nurture it as it grew during the past century.

The community now has a substantial challenge: to grow the next generation of leaders to assume the mantle left by Drachman.

For all of that and much more, Tucson will miss Royers Phillip Drachman.

Tucson Citizen

Most Fresno readers probably never heard of Frank M. Johnson Jr., but when he died the *Fresno* (Calif.) *Bee* took the occasion in "A hero, not a celebrity" to recount the role Johnson played in bringing "equal justice and equal treatment under the law" during his four decades as a federal judge. Readers were reminded that it was Johnson who struck down the Montgomery, Ala., bus segregation ordinance in 1955 when Rosa Parks refused to take a seat in the back of the bus.

When Maureen Reagan died, the *Independent* in Massillon, Ohio, gave credit to a person who had her own life and her own causes, but who had been overshadowed by her father. One point made in the editorial ("She'll be missed") was that the Republican Party "has a long way to go to persuade people that it welcomes the Maureen Reagans of America as much as it does the Ronnies."

Perhaps the toughest job is writing an obituary about a young person who has died. A writer on the Eugene, Ore., *Register-Guard* faced that task in commenting on the death of the second child of a prominent family to die from a mysterious ailment ("Kirsten"). The life and death of Kirsten Frohnmayer had been widely reported in the local media. Her father, David Frohnmayer, president of the University of Oregon, had been state attorney general. Her uncle, John Frohnmayer, attained national attention in the 1980s as the controversial head of the National Endowment for the Arts. The editorial writer chose to focus primarily on the bright spots, pointing out that, in her 24 years, Kirsten had exhibited an "immense capacity for life." The writer was reminded of one of

---

A HERO, NOT A CELEBRITY
Frank M. Johnson Jr. brought justice to the South.

The media that devoted hundreds of hours and acres of print to the airplane crash that killed John F. Kennedy Jr. barely noted the death last weekend of Judge Frank M. Johnson Jr.

Only a hundred people attended the burial Tuesday in his hometown of Haleyville in northern Alabama—a far cry from the crowds that lingered outside the New York City church where the young Kennedy was eulogized. But when our grandchildren read the history of the second half of this century, they will find much more to learn about Johnson.

In his four decades on the federal bench, as a district court judge in Alabama and as an appeals court justice, Johnson did as much as any other single person to reshape his beloved home state, and the South, to the Constitution's ideals of equal justice and equal treatment under the law.

Every schoolchild rightly learns the name of Rosa Parks, the African-American seamstress who refused to move to the back of the bus, as Jim Crow laws required, on a December day in 1955 in Montgomery, Ala. Few may know that it was Judge Johnson who, in his first major decision as a newly appointed federal judge, struck down the city's bus segregation ordinance as a violation of the equal-protection clause of the 14th Amendment.

In the years that followed, he swung the sturdy club of the 14th Amendment time and again against the racial injustices of Alabama life. He forced open the door for the registration of African-American voters, smashed Alabama's poll tax, ended the exclusion of African-Americans from Alabama juries and outlawed the discrimination that kept African-Americans out of the Alabama State Police.

His insistence on applying the law of equal protection made him an outcast among some in Alabama. He was a target of death threats and cross burnings. His old law school classmate, Gov. George Wallace, called Johnson an "integratin', carpet-baggin', scalawaggin', baldfaced liar."

But Martin Luther King Jr. called him a judge who had "given true meaning to the word 'justice.'" Standing with the Constitution as his tool and his guiding star, Johnson prevailed over ignorance, hatred and fear, and helped the South to prevail, too. He was no celebrity, just a true American hero.

Fresno Bee

---

the best-known obituary editorials ever to appear in American newspapers: William Allen White's tribute to his 16-year-old daughter, Mary. The editorial ends with the concluding remarks Kirsten had given her high school graduating class six years previously: "Good night and good luck."

■ LOCAL PRIDE

Second cousin to the obituary editorial is the local pride editorial, which comments on the activities of local people, local teams or local organizations. As with obituaries, there are ways to make these editorials more than sheer puffery. Sometimes, for example, an editorial may boost the spirits of some person or organization after a disappointment. Sometimes residents of a community need to take a realistic look at how they appear to others. Is the community as friendly as its promoters say it is? Does it have residential areas that those concerned with its image do not talk about much? Are residents going elsewhere to shop because they can't find what they want in local stores?

SHE'LL BE MISSED

No father could have asked for a better champion than Maureen Reagan.

She defended Ronald Reagan's honor, fought for causes he believed in, took up causes he could not. When Alzheimer's Disease silenced the former president, she became its most effective national spokeswoman.

When Eureka College asked, she happily joined the board of his alma mater. She also did not hesitate to speak up when she disagreed with him.

Many parents have suffered the same experience, but rarely in such a public venue as that in which presidents and First Daughters engage.

Maureen Reagan supported the Equal Rights Amendment; her father did not. She favored abortion rights; he opposed them. At one point, her outspokenness prompted the

> *She defended Ronald Reagan's honor, fought for causes he believed in, took up causes he could not.*

president's advisers to try to silence her. Reagan the president silenced them instead. She was entitled to have a mind and speak it, he said.

" . . . when she believed in a cause, she was not afraid to fight hard for it," Nancy Reagan said Wednesday of her stepdaughter, after the fight had gone out.

Maureen Reagan died at 60 of skin cancer that reached the brain. Her absence will be felt in many circles—in her family, of course, but also at Eureka College; in women's organizations that benefited from her support; among Alzheimer's victims and advocates; and in the Republican Party, which has a long way to go to persuade people that it welcomes the Maureen Reagans of America as much as it does the Ronnies.

Independent

Are building and development restrictions keeping out all but a select, privileged class of citizens?

Editorial writers cannot be expected to be able to view their communities completely objectively. After all, if these writers didn't think their communities were pretty decent places, why would they be living there? Writers should take pride in their communities and should work hard to make them better places. But without true understanding of the limitations as well as the advantages of their areas, writers cannot help their communities deal with problems and successes.

Pointing with pride sometimes involves not just extolling local virtues but also making self-congratulatory comparisons with other communities. The *San Jose* (Calif.), *Mercury-News* responded with such an editorial ("Sorry, Boston") to a prediction from the president of Harvard University that Boston would eclipse San Jose as the center of technology. Acknowledging some of Boston's assets, the editorial itemized three reasons why "the honor . . . should remain Silicon Valley's."

Sometimes editorial writers, intent on improving their hometowns, can point out the good things other communities are doing that deserve a look. After attending a convention of the National Conference of Editorial Writers (NCEW), a *Providence* (R.I.) *Journal* writer said: "Providence has a lot to learn from Seattle. In Seattle, motor vehicles and pedestrians have reached a truce." Referencing the Seattle experience, the editorial offered

KIRSTEN

In her graduation speech at South Eugene High School six years ago this month, Kirsten Frohnmayer said: "My family jokes that by having this serious health problem, we provide an important community service. We remind people that things in their own lives may not be as bad as they seem."

That was no joke. Following the joys and sorrows of the Frohnmayer family has been a community activity here for more than two decades. Their lives are at least more instructive than soap operas. Kirsten's own story, her cheerfully determined battle against a mysterious disease with a strange name and a lethal record, has been particularly gripping.

But not all stories have happy endings. This one is particularly sad because all of us were rooting so hard, hoping against hope. The community genuinely grieves with the Frohnmayers, as in some degree does the whole state.

At 24, mentally and spiritually Kirsten had done more living than many people twice her age. She had an immense capacity for life. Partly because of her disease, she had a keen appreciation for each day's possibilities.

Her positive outlook calls to mind the obituary editorial famed Kansas editor William Allen White wrote 76 years ago after his own 16-year-old daughter was killed in a freak riding accident: "Her humor was a continual bubble of joy. . . . No angel was Mary White, but an easy girl to live with, for she never nursed a grouch five minutes in her life."

> *At 24, mentally and spiritually Kirsten had done more living than many people twice her age. She had an immense capacity for life.*

On the list of personal tragedies to which humankind is vulnerable, the death of a child must rank at the top. It does not matter whether the child is struck by a limb while riding her horse or is worn down over many years and finally defeated by a vicious disease; the loss is tremendously hard to bear.

Hearts go out to David and Lynn Frohnmayer and to Kirsten's three remaining siblings. But we know, too, that they will manage, because they are blessed with intelligence and strength of spirit—and because they understand the wisdom of what Kirsten told her classmates at the close of her remarks in 1991:

"A final thought I'd like to share with you tonight is my belief that sometimes we should live for the day. Too often life consists of anticipation of the future or regrets about the past. But we can't change the past, and we don't know what the future will hold. So, at least some of the time, we should concentrate on the present. Whatever path you've chosen, whether you're talking about college, a job, volunteer work, or family, you're talking about life and life must be fun. Find the fun in life, for as Ferris Bueller said on his day off, 'life moves pretty fast, and if you don't stop and look around once in a while, you are going to miss it.'

"So . . . I hope that you will remember to appreciate and protect what you have, be optimistic and constructive in the face of adversity, and stop to smell the roses. Good night and good luck."

Register-Guard

suggestions, including an educational campaign aimed at pedestrians and drivers. Noting that efforts had been successful in other cities, the editorial expressed confidence in Providence: "It should be fairly easy to do it here in little old Providence."[2]

SORRY, BOSTON

In the '80s, Silicon Valley vaulted past the Boston area to become the center of technology and hasn't looked back. Route 128 minicomputer companies like Digital, Data General and Wang Computing crumbled amid the tectonics of the computer industry. Boston became an urbane outpost of ingenuity, a place where companies like Cisco Systems set up regional hubs.

But new phases of innovation, led by biotechnology, are emerging fast, creating new opportunities and, with Silicon Valley reeling from a dot-com hangover, potential competition. One Boston luminary, the new president of Harvard University, has gone as far as to predict that the epicenter of technology will again shift, this time to his backyard.

"I am convinced that the next Silicon Valley . . . will happen in the biomedical area," Lawrence Summers said in a speech late last year. "And it will happen where the most knowledge resides and where the best systems for its application exist. I believe that can be, should be, and will be here in the Boston area."

Harvard has an eminent medical school (not that Stanford doesn't, too). Boston's hospitals are among the nation's top. From the Charles River to beyond the Wellesley Hills, high tech is happening.

But Summers, who's made headlines lately for questioning grade inflation at Harvard, may himself be a victim of inflated confidence. As long as he invited a comparison, we'll try not to be smug. Consider:

- The biotech sector's still a baby, but already Boston has catching up to do. As of last October, the Bay Area has, by far, the nation's largest concentration of bioscience, according to a report last month by Joint Venture: Silicon Valley Network. The Valley has 76 public companies, with 26,500 employees and revenues of $5.9 billion, compared with No. 2 New England, with 48 companies, 24,600 employees and $3 billion in revenue.

- The convergence of high tech and biotech will drive the bioscience revolution. It will be built not only on medical discoveries but also on bioengineering research at Stanford, UCSF and Berkeley, massive computing power supplied by firms like Oracle, Sun and Intel, and venture capitalists' money. These partnerships will feed off each other. Boston lacks such an intense concentration.

- Silicon Valley's entrepreneurial climate still gives it a distinct edge over the historically secretive, risk-averse climate of Boston–Route 128 that author Anna Lee Saxenian found in her study "Regional Advantage." In a preface to her 1995 edition, Saxenian wrote, "As a native of the Boston area, I may wish that the Route 128 region turns itself around quickly; as a scholar, I know that it is likely to take decades to overcome the management practices, culture and institutions that have hindered the region in the past."

Beantown isn't likely to overtake Silicon Valley as the world's high-tech and bioscience leader.

In an e-mail last week, Saxenian, a regional planning professor at UC–Berkeley, said the transformation has indeed begun. The demise of companies like Digital and Data General "freed up lots of engineering and managerial talent that essentially reorganized into smaller, more focused companies and now looks more like Silicon Valley.

"I see no reason to expect the new biotech firms to make the mistakes of the minicomputer companies. But I also don't see any evidence that Boston will become the leading biotech center."

That honor, she confirmed, should remain Silicon Valley's.

San Jose Mercury News

REGION MAKING PROGRESS

Although it is only about one-third complete, the year 2001 has already been momentous for Rockford and the Rock River Valley.

As the weather warms into a beautiful northern Illinois spring, a string of positive developments have collectively improved the region's outlook, in spite of a slowing economy.

From the Rockford schools being released from federal court control, to high-level discussions on the Greater Rockford Airport, to a regional vision project to coordinated transportation planning, there is much to be enthused about.

These developments and others are part and parcel of the Register Star's Editorial Agenda for 2001, which was rolled out over four Sundays (Jan. 28–Feb. 18). Today we'll give the first quarterly progress report on the agenda: What has happened and what needs to happen to make the Rock River valley a better place to live, work and raise families.

Just a few of the 2001 highlights include:

■ A federal appeals court ruled that the Rockford School District will be granted unitary status at the end of June 2002, giving local control of education.

A three-judge panel said Rockford has desegregated its schools. The ruling came only weeks after voters passed a school tax referendum, with 62 percent in favor, and three new school board members were elected.

■ Rockford got a new mayor in Doug Scott, who defeated two strong opponents following a spirited campaign. New village presidents also took office in Machesney Park, Rockton and Pecatonica.

■ The Rock River Valley Visioning Project was formed, bringing together leaders from Winnebago, Boone, Ogle and Stephenson counties to study common issues and look for solutions to the region's biggest needs. At the same time, the Rockford Area Council of 100 has commissioned a study of the Interstate 90 corridor to create a blueprint for economic development.

These steps and others are driving the key elements of the Register Star's Editorial Agenda for 2001. Much work remains, but it's a strong start.

Rockford Register Star

The *Rockford* (Ill.) *Register Star* took pride not only in its community's achievements but also in its own progress toward the newspaper's Editorial Agenda for 2001 ("Region making progress"). The agenda for making "the Rock River Valley a better place to live, work and raise families" had been published in the paper over four Sundays in January and February 2001. The four articles, which covered education and training, regional planning, positive identity and the next generation of leaders, remained available to readers throughout the year on the *Register Star* web site.

■ FAVORITE SUBJECT

Editorial writers cannot be expected to produce fresh wisdom on every topic, every day. Reiterating a message is one solution to the lack of more inspiring topics. Since most readers don't read the editorial page every day, remaking a point is not likely to seem repetitive. Another, and less defensible, solution is writing on a

THE ASSEMBLY GAME

Veteran observers dread the return of the General Assembly, which at times seems like a forced march through the Gobi Desert with a garrulous drunk. Those wishing to make the time go by faster might want to play The Assembly Game. The rules are similar to those of The Car Game children play on long trips (one point for a blue car, two for a red, three for a white . . .). Players collect points for following the legislature's progress and spotting the following perennials.

■ A bill is referred to as "leveling the playing field": **1 point.**

■ A bill is referred to as a "slippery slope" or as letting "the camel's nose under the tent": **1 point.**

■ A speaker at a public hearing urges legislators not to "balance the budget on the backs of" his or her favorite special interest: **1 point.**

■ Lawyers get into a contest with another profession—bankers, doctors, real estate agents—over an arcane bill that is of immense interest to the two groups but of approximately zero interest to everyone else: **1 point.**

■ A parental-notification rider is attached to a bill having nothing to do with health care, such as one regarding speed limits on county roads: **2 points.**

■ Lieutenant Governor Don Beyer rules a parental-notification rider non-germane: **2 points.**

■ Something is named an official animal, vegetable, or mineral of the Commonwealth: **2 points.**

■ State colleges and universities complain they are under-funded: **2 points.**

■ Someone gets hurt in the General Assembly's annual basketball game: **3 points.**

■ Roscoe Drummond is spotted on the Capitol grounds: **3 points.**

■ A legislator is photographed (a) asleep, (b) checking his watch, or (c) looking really, really bored: **3 points.**

■ A senior legislator is photographed with his arm around a junior legislator in what looks like camaraderie but what is really a bit of strong-arming: **3 points.**

■ A legislator brings in a ridiculous prop, such as a Civil War–era sword or a large foam "We're No. 1" hand, to buttress a ridiculous argument: **4 points.**

■ Delegate George Grayson trashes Secretary of Natural Resources Becky Norton Dunlop or rakes one of her employees over the coals: **4 points.**

■ Governor Allen is accused of being a "credit-card Governor": **4 points.**

■ Allen blasts Democrats as (a) monarchical elitists, (b) tax-and-spend liberals, (c) pattering nabobs of negativism, or (d) pinheaded cowards who are afraid to come on out and fight like men: **5 points.**

First player to reach 100 points wins.

Richmond Times-Dispatch

subject on which the writer has to do little or no research or new thinking. Sometimes the subject is a favorite target. I call this type of editorial "an easy shot."

An example of an easy shot that some editorial writers take every year is the editorial that appears on the day that average taxpayers have stopped "working for the government" and started earning money to keep for themselves. Every year some tax association notifies newspapers of this date and usually points out that it falls one or two or three days later this year than last year. The first

---

A LEGISLATIVE GOOSE?

Thank goodness the General Assembly still has time to deal with important matters. Apparently, it will not allow such trivial concerns as budgets and taxes to prevent it from designating an official state reptile. It is moving to bestow that honor on the timber rattlesnake.

Why the legislature favors a poisonous snake over the harmless blacksnake that helps mankind by killing rats and other pests is a mystery. Perhaps there is a subterranean message in the legislators' preference for a reptile that spews venom. When they return next year, will they designate the black widow Virginia's official spider?

The General Assembly seems to designate an official something or other at every session. One of the most interesting examples is the state dog—the foxhound. When that designation was made a number of years ago, two different donors presented the state with portraits of foxhounds to hang on the walls of the Capitol. One portrait was of a champion foxhound named White Ella. The other was of a composite hound. But while the State Art Commission approved both portraits, no Governor has ever had the courage to put up either one.

Because of the Assembly's interest in designating official flora and fauna, many people will wonder why it never has adopted an official mascot. Good idea. May we suggest the goose—as in "silly as a . . . ?"

Richmond Times-Dispatch

---

time that editorial appeared it had merit; the idea is clever as a piece of propaganda. Since then, the editorial has become a cliché.

Another perennial piece is the one that criticizes the salaries paid state legislators or members of Congress. This editorial is usually accompanied by an attack on the legislative body for not doing its job and for letting personal interests and pleasures interfere with the public's business. The editorial writer often adds something to this effect: "It is no wonder the voters have lost faith in government." No doubt some legislative bodies deserve criticism for the sneaky ways in which they slip benefits for themselves into legislation and for the seemingly petty politicking that frustrates the legislative process. But an editorial written to condemn a specific misdeed should stick to the particular subject and avoid generalizing about all the wicked ways of government officials. One strange thing about this tendency of editorial writers to pick on legislative bodies is that when it comes time for endorsement of candidates all past sins seem forgotten. Congress is bad, it seems, but our own local member is good enough to merit another term.

The editorial writers on the *Richmond Times-Dispatch* seem to take special delight in needling state legislators. When Virginia lawmakers showed up for the 1997 legislative session, they were greeted with an editorial titled "The Assembly Game" that began: "Veteran observers dread the return of the General Assembly, which at times seems like a forced march through the Gobi Desert with a garrulous drunk." The editorial proposed a game like "The Car Game" children play on long auto trips.

The *Times-Dispatch* poked fun at legislators' naming fad on another occasion ("A Legislative Goose?"), concluding with this paragraph: "Because of the Assembly's interest in designating official flora and fauna, many people will wonder why it never has adopted an official mascot. Good idea. May we suggest the goose-as in 'silly as a. . . . ?'"

■ THE "DUTY" PIECE

"For tomorrow's page we're going to need an editorial on _____ . Who's going to write it?" Fill that blank with "Thanksgiving," "the Fourth of July," "the annual United Way campaign," "the state high school basketball championship" or "a highway safety campaign," and you will understand what is meant by a "duty" piece. It is an editorial that you think you ought to run to mark an occasion or boost a good cause, but it is almost impossible to think of anything more to say than you did the last time you wrote on the subject.

A few days before Earth Day 1997 an editorial writer asked other members of the NCEW e-mail discussion group whether they had any ideas for an editorial commemorating that day. Barbara Drake of the Peoria, Ill., *Journal Star* suggested calling attention to "extraordinary things" being done by a Scout group, a class or a school. Maura Casey of the *Day* of New London, Conn., also had schools in her sights, but from a different point of view. She said that schools have now so indoctrinated students that they now "lecture their parents [un]mercifully if they try to do anything as innocent as toss out a piece of tinfoil without putting it in the recycling bin first." Even less enthusiastically, Mike Heywood of the *Columbian* of Vancouver, Wash., wrote that Earth Day "ought to be skipped unless you already have a ripping idea so compelling that you cannot type fast enough to get it on the screen or page."[3]

At least two points should be made on behalf of editorials that support worthy causes. The first is that, while an endorsement of an annual fund drive may be repetitious to the veteran editorial writer, whatever is said is usually appreciated by the promoters. If an editorial doesn't actually raise any more money, it at least serves to legitimize the cause. Second, an editorial writer can regard a duty editorial as a challenge to say something creative or imaginative on an old topic.

If a newspaper does publish editorials endorsing causes, it should know what it is backing. Lauren K. Soth of the *Des Moines* (Iowa) *Register* said that when readers see an editorial supporting a drive for contributions, they ought to be able to assume that the editors have studied the cause and found it to have merit.[4]

Richard B. Childs for the *Flint* (Mich.) *Journal* said his first rule for handling "the drudgery aspects" of "duty" pieces was "to evade." If you are lucky, someone else on the staff will get the job. But if you can't evade, he advised, "relax and enjoy it." Childs said he actually had begun to look forward to Abraham Lincoln's birthday: Each year he tried to find something new to say. He had written about Lincoln's concept of the Constitution, his role as a politician, his faith in people and democracy, his literary abilities, his defense against black writers who sought to picture him a racist and his continuing image as a national hero despite changing national moods.[5]

One Christmas the *Fort Worth* (Texas) *Star-Telegram* ran a "wish list" discussing what the editorial writers would "ask Santa" for at each level of government: city, county, state and nation.[6] The *Richmond* (Va.) *News Leader* filled its editorial columns with Christmas poems, carols and stories, the right side of the page with a Christmas sampler of Thomas Nast drawings.[7] For the Fourth of July, the *Hartford* (Conn.) *Courant,* "the oldest daily newspaper in continuous publication," has dug back in its files of 200 or more years and reprinted contemporaneous accounts of the Revolutionary War.[8] The *Miami Herald* has

WE STILL DECLARE

Anyone with a basic knowledge of American history knows about the Declaration of Independence, that document in which the representatives of 13 colonies declared their freedom from the king of England.

It was an incredibly bold statement for its time and remains today a ringing proclamation of the American ideal—an enduring set of principles to which, it must be said, America has not always measured up.

That's why it's worth reading by Americans today. Most people are familiar with its best known section—in the second paragraph, about our rights to "life, liberty and the pursuit of happiness."

But there's so much more that's worth reflecting upon and renewing in the American spirit—there is anger, pride, defiance and a list of grievances and system failures that compelled this ultimate act of disloyalty to the crown. The old ways were not working in the new world. It was time for new ways.

The brave authors and signers of the declaration could not possibly have foreseen

Declaration of Independence should continue to inspire

what America would become, but they resolved to create a framework for enormous possibilities in the new land—if the people were resolved to seize them.

Starting this month, Americans will have a chance to read one of the 22 remaining first copies of the Declaration of Independence. A foundation set up by television producer Norman Lear bought one for $8 million and is taking it on the road for a never-ending tour to remind us of the big idea that begat this amazing nation 225 years ago. The tour schedule is tentative, with Michigan listed as a stop in 2002 or later.

"I hope it will spark what is maybe a latent desire in people to become active citizens," Lear said. "Parents should take their children to see it. Children should take their parents."

The Declaration of Independence. Coming soon to a location near you. Maybe the most important writing an American will ever read.

Detroit Free Press

reprinted the Bill of Rights and the Preamble to the Declaration of Independence.[9]

On July 4, 2001, the *Detroit Free Press* printed a reproduction of the Declaration of Independence with an editorial ("We Still Declare") praising the "brave authors and signers" and pointing out that one of the remaining 22 first copies would be "put on the road for a never-ending tour to remind us of the big idea that begat this amazing nation 225 years ago."

Modifying the last words of the Declaration to reflect a well-known Midwest jingle, the *Omaha* (Neb.) *World-Herald* titled a July 4th editorial "Our Lives, Our Fortunes, Our Corn." The editorial took a serious, cautionary look at the prospects for a good corn crop that year. "Knee-high by the Fourth of July" was supposed to be a prescription for an adequate corn crop—before hybrid corn came along. Unfortunately, as the editorial pointed out, "In some parts of the Corn Belt, the plants are only ankle-high." Noting that the eventual crop "depends on those small green plants, swaying in the July breeze under a Midwest sun," the editorial concluded: "Few works of fiction rival the drama of mankind's annual struggle to wrest sustenance from the soil against all the natural and man-made perils."

OUR LIVES, OUR FORTUNES, OUR CORN

It's the Fourth of July. But what of the corn? Most years, it's supposed to be knee-high by today. In fields with modern hybrids and good growing conditions, it's often a good deal taller than that by Independence Day.

This year, growing corn has been a struggle in some places. In parts of the Corn Belt, the plants are only ankle-high. Some growers would consider themselves fortunate indeed if they could stroll through the fields and feel the tickle of a corn leaf on their kneecaps.

Making the struggle more difficult is the fact that last year's record-breaking harvest of 10.1 billion bushels prevented the price from going as high as growers had hoped to receive. Some of them reacted by making plans to plant less in 1995. Altogether, they told the government that they would reduce by 5 percent the acreage they put in corn this year.

That was in March. Then came the unusually harsh planting season, with fields too wet to plant and soil too cold to promote germination. Corn went in late or sometimes not at all. By last week, when the government updated its forecasts, corn plantings were down 9 percent.

The best that could be hoped for, forecasters said, was a 23 percent reduction in this year's harvest.

Out came the electronic spreadsheets and pocket calculators in commodities houses and farm kitchens. Market analysts said the smaller crop could mean higher prices for growers, perhaps in the range of $3.10 a bushel. That would be about a 15 percent increase over what farmers were getting for 1994 corn last week. Growers tried to determine how much the price would have to rise to offset the effects of too much cold and too much moisture.

In the livestock industry, feeders contemplated higher feeding costs and considered cutting back. Demand for replacement calves sagged. Meat industry analysts speculated that a smaller corn crop would mean higher beef and pork costs at the supermarket.

Much depends on those small green plants, swaying in the July breeze under a Midlands sun. Much, indeed, depends on agriculture. Few works of fiction rival the drama of mankind's annual struggle to wrest sustenance from the soil against all the natural and man-made perils. This year, the story shows the potential to be especially thrilling.

Omaha World-Herald

Martin Luther King Day would seem to an occasion for "duty" editorials. A check of 51 major newspapers on the Internet on January 18, 2002, found MLK Day editorials in 25 papers. Most of the editorials followed one of two themes: that expressed in the title of an editorial in the *Kansas City* (Mo.) *Star*, "Area residents should work to fulfill King's dream" (not reprinted here) or in the title of the *Roanoke* (Va.) *Times*, "King Day: A celebration for all people" (not reprinted here). The *Charlotte* (N.C.) *Observer*, however, observed that not everyone was celebrating. An editorial ("King fought for all Americans, not just blacks") recounted a "dust-up" in a North Carolina county over designating the holiday.

The duty editorial often is intended to praise some local deserving cause or person. The *Times Colonist* in Victoria, B.C., Canada, ran an editorial ("Candy cane memories") paying tribute to John and Marilyn Bale and their neighbors for, year after year, transforming "the 1200 block of Saanich's Tattersall Drive into Candy Cane Lane, a fantasyland of light and decoration." The editorial expressed thanks and paid tribute to the people of Candy Cane Lane for exemplifying the "essence of Santa Claus" in the community.

KING FOUGHT FOR ALL AMERICANS, NOT JUST BLACKS

Holiday that honors him remains mired in the politics of race

By Fannie Flono

On Monday, as millions here and elsewhere celebrate Martin Luther King's birthday, some will bemoan anew the "black" holiday.

More than 30 years after individual states—New York, Maine and Rhode Island being the firsts—began commemorating the life of the most famous civil rights advocate the United States has ever spawned, the holiday remains mired in this country's politics of race.

That was underscored in these parts last August when a dust-up ensued in Albemarle over designating a local Martin Luther King holiday. Stanly County had considered for a decade recognizing King by closing government offices and giving employees the day off. But when commissioners decided to do so last fall, they proposed honoring King and Confederate hero Gen. Robert E. Lee on the same day in a joint King-Lee Day.

Commissioner Michael Coble gave their reasoning: "We were trying to look out for everyone in the county, not just one group, not one race, but everyone."

In the end, the commissioners acknowledged the absurdity of their plan and agreed to recognize the two on different days, with government offices closing and employees getting a day off for both. The closings create no additional costs for the county.

Coble's rationale, though, gets to the crux of continuing debate about the Martin Luther King holiday. For many people, far too many people, the celebration remains a celebration for "one group, one race." But the reason to celebrate Martin Luther King's birthday, to remember the man, the message and the movement he led, is precisely because he would not limit his aspirations to one group, or one race. And he fought valiantly to keep this country from doing so as well.

It is no accident or preacher rhetoric that sparked the enduring words of his most famous speech in 1963: "I still have a dream, a dream deeply rooted in the American dream—one day this nation will rise up and live out its creed: We hold these truths to be self-evident, that all men are created equal."

In closing he added: "And when this happens we will be able to speed up that day when all God's children, black men and

---

CANDY CANE MEMORIES

Every Christmas for the past three decades, John and Marilyn Bate and their neighbours have transformed the 1200 block of Saanich's Tattersall Drive into Candy Cane Lane, a fantasyland of light and decoration. Growing year by year, it has become a local tradition, with adults who thrilled to the sight as youngsters now bringing their own children to share in the magic.

Alas, when they switched on the lights last night, it marked the last season for Candy Cane Lane. Putting it together is a huge job, requiring time, energy, money and a tolerance for thousands of strangers whose fascination with the displays sometimes bring their cars uncomfortably close to the rose bushes. Residents feel the time has come to pull the plug. Perfectly understandable.

We would like to thank the people of Candy Cane Lane for the joy they have brought to ourselves and our children, and for the ready answer we can now give to those children when they ask, inevitably, whether Santa is real. The essence of Santa can be found in goodness, selflessness and the spirit of giving, we can say. If you believe in those things, then you believe in Santa. And if you want to see evidence that Santa is real, look no farther than Candy Cane Lane.

Times Colonist

white men, Jews and gentiles, Protestants and Catholics, will be able to join hands and sing, in the words of the old Negro spiritual, 'Free at last! Free at last! Thank God Almighty, we're free at last!'"

King's historical significance has been dimmed and overshadowed both by time and events. Too many young people, and some older ones as well, know him only in broad caricature—with his weaknesses as a man and his family's determinedness to milk money from every existing part of his legacy most prominent.

But the Civil Rights Movement was a seminal event in this country's history. Like the American Revolution and the Civil War, the Civil Rights Movement helped define who we are as Americans. Not black Americans, but Americans. The fight King led for justice and equality was and remains America's fight.

Despite the death, violence and lasting images of police training dogs on adults and fire hoses on children, the Civil Rights Movement was one of our finest hours. Through it, as King prophesied in his speech, we continued the push to live out the high ideals embodied in our Declaration of Independence.

Though he credited rightfully a whole host of people for their roles in the turning points of the Civil Rights Movement, there is no mistaking the impact of the man on the important moments of his time.

The Voting Rights Act, the changes in public transportation and public accommodations, the very dismantling of segregation nationwide benefited from his leadership. For that work, in 1964 King became the youngest man in history—he was 35 at the time—to receive the Nobel Peace Prize.

Toward the end of his life, King focused his attention on the problems of unequal distribution of wealth and economic parity, now a concern around the world among people of all races.

Martin Luther King's birthday became a federal holiday in 1986, the first new holiday since Memorial Day became one in 1948.

Though King remains controversial in the minds of some, his ideas have gained credence over time. His crusade for justice and equality was and is an American crusade. And it remains a worthy one. Martin Luther King's birthday is the perfect day for all Americans to remember that.

Charlotte Observer

"Duty" Piece Web Resources

American Memory (multimedia museum of tradition, history and lore):
  http://www.rs6.loc.gov/amhome.html
Biography: http://www.biography.com
The Fourth of July: http://wilstar.com/holidays/july4.htm
The History Channel: http://www.historychannel.com
History Net: http://www.TheHistoryNet.com
Holidays: http://www.holidays.net or http://wilstar.com/holidays
HyperHistory:
  http://www.hyperhistory.com/online_n2/History_n2/a.html
Library of Congress: http://www.marvel.loc.gov
Martin Luther King Jr. Day: http://www.holidays.net/mlk
National Archives and Records Administration: http://www.nara.gov
Smithsonian Institution: http://www.si.edu

■ CONCLUSION

The purpose of this chapter is to suggest that writers, using some imagination and flair, can tackle seemingly dull or clichéd subjects and turn out editorials that are interesting and informative.

■ QUESTIONS AND EXERCISES

1. Find an obituary editorial that is mostly factual and another that goes beyond the facts. What is the difference in the effect of the editorials? What makes the difference?
2. Examine an editorial that expresses pride in the community or some aspect of community life. Is the editorial sheer puffery, or has the writer made an effort to put the event in perspective?
3. Clip some "easy shot" editorials. What makes them fall into this category? What could save them from this category?
4. Find several "duty" editorials. Would you have published them? If not, what could you have written on the same subjects that you would have felt comfortable writing? What angles could the writers have taken that they missed?

Subjects That Are Neglected

Like many journalists with a non-science degree . . . , I previously thought of science as dry and boring. In working with scientists, however, I have learned that science lies at the heart of many of our most important news stories: AIDS, Star Wars, the Challenger disaster, Chernobyl and many others.

—DAVID JARMUL,
NATIONAL ACADEMY SERVICE[1]

Editorial writers often neglect subjects that are difficult to write about, don't often make the front pages or seem not to involve major public policy issues. As the quotation on the left suggests, however, many difficult subjects can be become pertinent to readers—if writers inform themselves on the subject and write in a way that speaks to those readers. This chapter deals with several kinds of editorials that are frequently neglected: editorials on science, natural resources, the media and lives of people, humor and satire.

■ SCIENCE

Science is not a popular or easy subject for editorials. A survey of five of the nation's largest newspapers found that less than 4 percent of all editorials dealt directly with science or technology.[2] That percentage no doubt is higher now, with widespread public discussion of anthrax, DNA, cloning, stem-cell research and possible life on Mars. The survey found that editorial writers were "most likely to discuss science, technology and health care in the context of some broader issue, such as the economy or a political dispute." That doesn't seem surprising, as editorials generally are expected to discuss public issues.

One reason that science gets little play in editorial columns may be that writers don't feel qualified to comment on scientific matters. Another may be that science supposedly involves facts, so what's left to debate in an editorial? The first reason may have a lot of validity, but the second does not. Scientific findings, after all, are only the first step toward formulating public policy. The developers of the atomic bomb were not the same people who had the responsibility to decide how, and whether, it was to be dropped on Hiroshima.

Editorial writers had no trouble identifying the public policy and moral issues when they commented in 2001 on a team of scientists' announcement of a plan to clone 200 humans. Leaving no doubt about its position on the matter, the *Plain Dealer* of Cleveland, Ohio, began an editorial ("Risking disaster") by noting that "the best minds involved in science" were calling these scientists "crackpots." Acknowledging that the project was technically feasible, the editorial said that the "moral, ethical,

RISKING DISASTER
With moral, ethical and scientific questions pending, this is no time to press ahead with human cloning

The best minds involved in the science of human reproduction are calling Panos Zavos, Severino Antinori and Brigitte Boisselier crackpots.

When the three told a conference at the National Academy of Sciences on Tuesday that they plan to begin cloning 200 humans just three months from now, they were ridiculed and condemned by their most eminent colleagues.

But they were not dismissed, because there is no doubt that the technology and the know-how exist to begin cloning humans. What is lacking, though, is the scientific ability to finish the job.

Leaving aside for just a moment the almost incomprehensibly thorny moral and ethical issues that attend the concept of cloning people, the massive problem of technical ignorance ought to be enough to stop a scientist from proceeding.

But as their testimony made clear, no problem—whether moral, ethical, technical or legal—appears insurmountable to Zavos, Antinori, Boisselier and their collaborators.

Nor will such considerations deter those desperate or self-seeking enough to make their cells and their wombs available to the rogues.

The rule with animals created through cloning is deformity and death, either before birth or shortly after. Even the "successes" that appear outwardly normal, like Dolly the sheep, suffer from imperfections including an anatomical age advanced far beyond the chronological age.

If the experimenters carry out their plan for 200 clones in the near future, perhaps 20 will survive to see the delivery room. And in what condition will they be? No one can know, and the strong impression is that the researchers don't particularly care.

The clones will be merely the counters in a lottery played with human lives against incredibly long odds. Some might be lucky. The vast majority certainly will not be.

The assurances from Zavos and company that they are acting in the best interests of both science and humanity ring hollow.

To hear them say that they will not allow a deformed baby to be born is chilling: Oh, this one is defective—a failure. Better get rid of it.

"If the process is not successful, we will discontinue our efforts," Zavos said Tuesday.

But he is taking upon himself the task of defining success. If one clone out of his first 200 lives a year, or even a month, is that not a measure of success? Might that not be a reason to try 200 more?

True pioneers may show their bravery by risking their own lives. These scientific outlaws prefer to risk the lives of others. They deserve to be condemned and shunned.

Plain Dealer

technical [and] legal" questions were so fundamental that the decision on whether to proceed should not be left to a small group of "scientific outlaws."

The *Independent* of Massillon, Ohio, took a more evenhanded approach ("Not worth the risks"). It recognized that one of the scientists was "well credentialed" and that some scientists were saying "that it was about time for the cloning adventure to begin." But, citing the risks of "producing dead baby after dead baby after dead baby until there is one that is living, but is possibly deformed," the *Independent* reached a similar conclusion: "It is just a handful of people who want to move ahead at this moment, but they could cause a great deal of damage before they are through."

NOT WORTH THE RISKS

Two doctors and a biochemist testified on behalf of human cloning in Washington this week, and if it seemed to you their arguments were from outer space, you might want to know that at least one of them believes that is where the human race came from.

Brigitte Boisselier, the biochemist, is the director of Clonaid, a Bahamas company owned by a religious group known as the Raelians Movement. Adherents, it seems, believe that scientists from elsewhere in the universe created human beings. Now, the creed goes, it's the turn of scientists on this planet to use the same techniques of genetic manipulation—namely, cloning—to give humans eternal life.

While Boisselier is well-credentialed—she holds doctorates from French and American universities—it seems reasonable to wonder whether it is her religion and other factors more than science that give her so little pause about cloning dangers. At the conference at the National Academy of Sciences, she made it clear she did not think a long wait would be necessary. The problem is that most cloned animals die soon after they are born and that many of those that do survive for very long are freakishly abnormal. You

To undertake human cloning— certainly now and perhaps ever— would be a horror.

are reassured on the Clonaid Web site that if you come knocking, you will only pay if the baby survives. The amount will be as little as $200,000.

Others saying at the conference that it was about time for the cloning adventure to begin were Panos Zavos, an American physician, and Severino Antinori, an Italian physician best known for in vitro fertilization treatments that have enabled women in their 50s to have babies—and even a woman who was 62. The Roman Catholic Church has been sharply critical of the practice, but he has backed up not an inch. According to him, the Vatican is a "criminal enterprise."

To undertake human cloning—certainly now and perhaps ever—would be a horror. How can anyone in good conscience take the risk of producing dead baby after dead baby after dead baby until there is one that is living but is possibly deformed?

As interested as it legitimately is in genetic research, mainstream science wants nothing to do with this. It is just a handful of people who want to move ahead at the moment, but they could cause a great deal of damage before they are through.

Independent

Scientific effects are not limited to human beings. The *Omaha* (Neb.) *World-Herald*, in an editorial titled "When Fido goes unmourned," commented on businesses that "take a DNA sample from [a] pet to presumably be used at a time when cloning technology is sufficiently refined to make it pay." The conclusion: "Even when it concerns pets, much less people, the psychological healthfulness of such delusion is open to question."

Science Web Resources

American Museum of Natural History:
http://www.amnh.org
AstroInfo (recent astronomical events):
http://www.astroinfo.org/english.php

WHEN FIDO GOES UNMOURNED

Some people simply have more money than substance in their lives.

That conclusion may easily be drawn from a report that hundreds of wealthy people are figuratively lining up to fork over large sums of money in the hope that the science of cloning will eventually produce a carbon copy of a beloved pet. At least three businesses exist that will gladly accept the money and take a DNA sample from the pet to presumably be used at a time when cloning technology is sufficiently refined to make it pay.

Think of it. If such a thing were possible, Roy Rogers wouldn't have had to take his beloved Trigger to a taxidermist to have his body, and the memories, preserved. Roy could have just called the rendering truck, had the carcass hauled away and then selected a replacement from the Trigger clone corral.

Old Yeller would never have to be cried over. Lassie would live forever. Whenever one shell wore out, her owners could just order a copy.

Of course all that is pure fantasy. A genetic copy is a separate being, not a rein-carnation. Every living thing is a product not only of its heredity but also its environment. A cloned Fido—even assuming one could be produced without some hidden and horrible genetic mis-wiring—might very well develop different behavior patterns based on formative influences alone. Concerns about those hidden and horrible anomalies intensified last week with a report from Britain identifying persistent and profound abnormalities in cloning experiments involving mice.

But it isn't persistence against the likeli-hood of failure that makes the pet story fasci-nating, or even the cynicism of the exploiters. It's the matter of what all this might say—if, indeed, anything—about our evolving cultural values.

Anthromorphism—the attributing of human characteristics to an animal—seems to be more widespread. The animal rights movement has done its part, with some of the wackier city councils around the country passing ordinances forbidding the owner-ship of animals and decreeing that pets are "companions," not "possessions." Eating meat, in some circles, has been likened to the abridgement of human rights.

(Some of these same people want grizzly bears to be reintroduced in areas where people live; how that meshes with the right of people not to be eaten by animals, we don't know.)

A similar distortion of perspective is suggested when a person will pay $100,000 in the hope of someday getting Fido back. Loving a pet is a wonderful thing, but a dog is still just a dog. We don't make a practice in these columns of lecturing rich people about how they should spend their money. We don't want to give aid and comfort to the various income-redistribution plans and other neo-Marxist notions that crop up so often in modern political debate. But doesn't it seem immoral to spend $100,000 in the hope of cloning a pet in a world in which human suffering is far from vanquished?

In addition to moral, it also seems spiritu-ally empty. Suppose Fido is hit by a truck. A new clone of Fido is promptly procured. The new Fido becomes Fido; the old Fido is not mourned. The way some people seem to approach these issues, the dead pet (or child), having been replaced, can be forgotten. Closure, in an ultimate and perverted sense of the term, is achieved.

But death is a part of life. To deny it is hubris. To seek the reincarnation through cloning of a dead loved one, or thing, is self-delusion. Even when it concerns pets, much less people, the psychological healthfulness of such delusion is open to serious question.

Omaha World-Herald

TRAIL OF MISTAKES

The felled trees have been cleared at the popular Phenn Basin conservation area in Fayston. But Vermonters still need an accounting from the state officials who ordered this trail damage.

Yes, the work was a misguided attempt to prevent mountain bikers from using the route and causing erosion, but if ever a cure were worse than the disease, this is it.

Vermont Forests and Parks Commissioner Conrad Motyka can help restore confidence in his department by speeding up his promised internal review of what appears to be a botched and out-of-proportion action by government.

By now the story is familiar. Though there were no signs warning mountain bikers off what is technically an old logging road, some conservationists worried the bikes were causing erosion. After the Vermont Land Trust alerted the state to this possibility, the Division of Forests paid $8,000 to a contractor who cut trees and dug trenches to block the route.

The result: a forest that looked as though a tornado had hit. Outcry predictably followed and the state has since attempted to clean up the mess at additional taxpayer expense.

The public deserves to know why the state slipped here in its role as land steward. The

> *The public still has no explanation why the state ransacked a forest in a purported effort to prevent trail damage.*

controversy does not stop there, though. It raises broad questions about public access to lands conserved partially with public money.

Balancing recreation with the need to protect fragile natural areas and important animal habitats is not easy. In some areas, activities like mountain biking are, indeed, too intrusive. In others, an overly restrictive approach is unfair. Many Vermonters who support conservation enjoy outdoor recreation that brings them close to the land. Barricading them without justification hurts the conservation movement—and that hurts Vermont.

The fulcrum of any lasting balance on access is public dialogue. In the case of Phenn Basin, that dialogue never began. It was supposed to occur five years ago when the parcel was conserved and put under state management. Only now in the wake of the trailwork debacle has Motyka ordered the first public meeting to draft a management plan for the parcel—Oct. 25 at the Fayston Town Hall.

This meeting is years overdue. But in scheduling the meeting, the Department of Forests, Parks and Recreation is taking a step toward the kind of accountability it owes all Vermonters.

Burlington Free Press

Science Daily: http://www.sciencedaily.com/index/htm
Science News Online: http://www.sciencenews.org
Scientific American: http://www.sciam.com
The Astronomy Page: http://www.teresa.pmbc.com/astronomy.html

◼ NATURAL RESOURCES

When daily editorial writing assignments are being made, it is easy to skip over or put aside environment and natural resources issues. It's not that

OIL'S SPOILS
Open Alaska refuge to drilling? No way

Eleven years ago this week, the Exxon Valdez ran aground in Prince William Sound and transformed an environmental wonderland into a huge, deadly oil puddle.

If the catastrophe had any upside, it was that it killed then-President Bush's proposal to open the Arctic National Wildlife Refuge to oil drilling. Yet today, with the high spiral of pump prices as an excuse, congressional Republicans are again pushing to turn the sensitive, wildlife-rich refuge into an industrial oil field.

You'd think they'd learn. Time and again voters of every political stripe, from conservative to liberal, have voiced support for environmental protection. According to the prestigious, nonpartisan Zogby Poll, nearly half of Republican primary voters in this election season consider themselves to be environmentalists, and 93 percent say protecting the environment is important in deciding who they'll vote for. It's no coincidence that, after gaining control of Congress in 1994, Republicans lost seats just two years later after attempting to scrap the Clean Water Act, the Clean Air Act, the Safe Drinking Water Act, the Endangered Species Act—and again attempting to open the Alaska refuge to drilling.

The real motive this time has nothing to do with high gasoline prices and everything to do with money—lots of it. Alaska's congressional delegation is spearheading the drive to turn the drillers loose on the refuge, because every barrel of Alaska oil sold means more money for Alaskans. And more money for the politicians, too: According to the Center for Responsive Politics, the oil industry has contributed $56 million to politicians in the past decade.

All that money talks, but so do the facts: The Arctic National Wildlife Refuge is the last protected area on Alaska's north slope. It is home to polar and grizzly bears, caribou and musk oxen, wolves and foxes, and millions of migratory birds. Although it covers some 19 million acres, only 1.5 million acres of that comprises the oil-rich coastal plain. And that 1.5 million acres represents a mere 5 percent of the north coast; the other 95 percent is already open for oil exploration and drilling.

For evidence of what happens when industry mixes it up with a sensitive environment, we need only look to the Oregon coast, where oyster growers say fuel oil that leaked from the grounded New Carissa has destroyed half of their oyster beds, or to Washington's Dungeness Bay, where high levels of fecal bacteria have resulted in the first-ever closure of commercial shellfish beds this spring.

America needs to reduce its reliance on foreign oil. It can do that by banning the export of Alaska oil, by raising automobile fuel economy and by developing alternative energy sources. It cannot do it by delaying the inevitable and gutting another irreplaceable natural treasure.

Columbian

editorial writers and editors don't recognize that there are plenty of these issues. It's just that these issues don't often capture front-page headlines—unless a governmental body proposes loosening pollution regulations or environmental activists set up camp in the forest treetops. Without a specific news angle, it is often hard to frame these issues in a manner that is timely and easy for readers to understand. Yet nothing could be more important than what goes on in the physical world around us.

SNOWMOBILES DON'T BELONG IN YELLOWSTONE

President Bush should pay attention to the wise counsel of the National Park Service and resist those who advise him to roll back limits on snowmobiles in the nation's oldest park, Yellowstone.

Limits on snowmobiles in the park were set to take effect in two years, but industry lobbyists have persuaded the Bush administration to reconsider. While a decision has not yet been made, many fear that snowmobiles will be permitted back into the park during a 12-week winter season.

Yellowstone was a marvelous choice for the nation's first national park. Its mix of natural wonders, wildlife and sheer beauty have delighted generations of Americans who have traveled there.

In winter, snow cloaks the park in even greater splendor. For visitors and the animals that live there, it is a time of solitude and peace.

That is, solitude until the quiet is disturbed by the buzz and roar of two-cycle snowmobile motors and the clouds of exhaust.

Last winter, when snowfalls were much lighter than normal, 83,548 people rode snowmobiles into the park. The irresponsible among them disrupt not only the quiet but also wildlife herds when they are most vulnerable.

Public resources such as national parks must be shared by all who wish to use them. When the method of use of one group destroys the ability of others, then restrictions must be put in place.

A ban on use of snowmobiles in Yellowstone is in the national interest, and that of the park's wildlife and natural wonders.

Daily Times-Call

In an editorial in the *Burlington* (Vt.) *Free Press*, the issue was "public access to lands conserved partially with public money," but that broad description did not appear until the sixth paragraph. The first part of the editorial ("Trail of mistakes") focused on a specific example of how these lands had been mishandled: "The felled trees have been cleared at the popular Phenn Basin conservation area in Fayston." The editorial noted that the Vermont Forests and Park Department had finally begun to hold public meetings to draft management plans for these areas.

The *Columbian* in Vancouver, Wash., used the eleventh anniversary of the Exxon Valdez oil spill as a peg to write about congressional Republicans' renewed efforts to open the Arctic National Wildlife Refuge to oil drilling. The editorial ("Oil's Spoils") did not appear to be prompted by a specific public action or news story. It noted that "the catastrophe had . . . killed then-President [George H.W.] Bush's proposal" to open the refuge. "The real motive this time," it said, was "money—lots of it . . . for Alaskans [and] . . . for politicians, too." As alternatives, the editorial suggested banning Alaska oil exports, requiring greater automobile fuel economy and developing alternative energy sources.

Editorials in the *Daily Times-Call* of Longmont, Colo., and the *Detroit Free Press* were prompted by a report that the George W. Bush administration would soon roll back a Clinton administration proposal to limit snowmobiles in Yellowstone Park. On June 29, 2001, the Longmont paper carried an editorial titled "Snowmobiles don't belong in Yellowstone." The editorial noted that the previous year 83,548 people had ridden snowmobiles in the park and that "[t]he irresponsible among them disrupt not only the quiet but also wildlife herds when they are most vulnerable." On July 2 the *Free Press* used the expected Yellowstone development to call attention to other pending threats: "snow machines in the Alaska's Denali National Park for the first time since the park's creation in 1917" and "motorized intrusions at Pictured Rocks," a national lakeshore on the Great Lakes. In all those locations, the editorial said, "natural wonder should trump motorized access."

Natural Resources Web Resources

Agriculture Online (news, links): http://www.agriculture.com

Earth Online (site of Foundation EARTH Environment, Agriculture, Research and Technology): http://www.earthonline.org

Economic Research Service (agriculture, food, natural resources, rural America.): http://www.ers.usda.gov

Envirolink (up-to-date environmental resources): http://www.envirolink.netforexchange.com

Environmental Education Resources (endangered flora and fauna): http://www.eelink.net

Environmental Issues (stories, essays, book reviews): http://www.gopher.well.com/11/Environment

Friends of the Earth International: http://www.foei.org

International Wildlife Coalition: http://www.iwc.org

National Agricultural Library (research, education, applied agriculture): http://www.nalusda.gov

National Audubon Society: http://www.audubon.org

National Oceanic and Atmospheric Administration: http://www.noaa.gov

National Recreation and Park Association: http://www.activeparks.org

National Wildlife Federation: http://www.nwf.org

The Nature Conservancy: http://www.nature.org

U.S. Fish and Wildlife Service: http://www.fws.gov

U.S. Environmental Protection Agency: http://www.epa.gov

USDA (U.S. Department of Agriculture (programs, news releases, current events, legislation): http://www.usda.gov

◼ MEDIA ISSUES

Newspapers traditionally have been reluctant to talk about their media competitors: "If you don't criticize me, I won't criticize you." This reluctance has been changing, probably partly because national and regional journalism reviews have not hesitated to award "darts and laurels" (*Columbia Journalism Review*'s designations) to local newspapers and television stations as well as to the national media. Another reason editorial writers may shy away from media issues is that they don't want to appear self-serving. How does a writer comment on the Newspaper Preservation Act, proposals to ease cross-media ownership restrictions or the subpoena of a reporter's notes without arousing suspicions of only looking out for the newspaper's interests? The answer is "very

WELCOME CHANGE

The Utah Alcoholic Beverage Control Commission's initial reaction to a federal appeals court ruling July 24 that found the state's ban on wine and liquor ads "irrational" was disconcerting, but the powerful agency wisely has decided to revisit its rules to bring them into conformity with the court's decision.

After the 10th Circuit Court of Appeals ruling, the ABC chairman declared the state law still in effect. U.S. District Judge David Sam followed up with an order that the ABC quit enforcing the state's alcohol ad ban, a nudge that was sufficient to cause the agency to think twice about the quixotic posturing it initially appeared to be taking in the matter.

The case through which these rulings have come remains to be tried, but given the fact that the Utah laws are restraining what the appeals court ruling suggests is a constitutionally protected activity, namely advertising a legal commodity, the interim court rulings were necessary.

Restraining a constitutionally protected activity trumps whatever damage theoretically is possible if wine and spirits are advertised like beer and other commodities.

The appeals court was correct in spotting an inconsistency in the state's alcohol advertising ban. The state allows the advertising of light beer, but forbids the advertising of wine and spirits. This is tantamount to saying wine and spirits are worse than beer, though all are alcoholic beverages. This is not only "irrational," as the appeals court noted, but arbitrary and capricious, too.

All this is suggested in the appeals court's ruling, which goes so far as to suggest the Utah law is not likely to survive adjudication. Therefore, Judge Sam's amplification of the appeals court ruling was proper.

Utah's ABC deserves recognition for overcoming its initial reluctance and realizing the need to change its advertising rules to ensure they conform with the federal court's rulings.

Salt Lake Tribune

---

judiciously." First, the writer needs to make these interests clear to readers. If the newspaper stands to benefit, it should say so. Second, the writer needs to make clear where the public's interest lies. First Amendment guarantees were written primarily to assure the public's right to know, not to guarantee success and profits for the media.

Most newspapers attempt to establish, and respect, a line between news-editorial and advertising. The principal concern is that advertisers and the advertising side of the newspaper may try to influence (or appear to influence) what is published in the news and editorial columns. The appearance of conflict can arise when editorial writers comment on regulations relating to advertising. Often the regulations concern the advertising of alcohol. A *Salt Lake* (Utah) *Tribune* editorial ("Welcome change") expressed approval of an appeals court ruling that the state's ban on wine and liquor ads was "irrational" because the state allowed advertising of light beer. Some readers may have wondered whether the newspaper might be one of the beneficiaries of relaxed restrictions on liquor advertising. Might the prospect of additional advertising have affected the paper's stand? No doubt the editorial writer would have answered with a strong "No!" Editorial page staffs generally insist on their commitment to the separation between advertising and news-editorial. Some suspicion might have been allayed, however, if the editorial had acknowledged—at least in passing— that some of that advertising might end up in newspapers.

The Missoula, Mont., *Missoulian* might also have been affected by a city attorney's efforts "to force a student journalist to turn over video footage she shot during last summer's mayhem accompanying the Hells Angels' visit." If the efforts had succeeded, *Missoulian* reporters at some time might have been pressured to turn over their notes. The editorial ("City's pursuit of tapes is wrong") might well have pointed that out. Emphasizing, properly, "that citizens are entitled to a free flow of information," the editorial said that taking the footage "would interfere in the news media's ability to fulfill the duties America's founding fathers assigned to us." The public angle was reiterated at the conclusion of the editorial: "The general assumption, reflected in the Bill of Rights and the Montana Constitution's Declaration of Rights, is that you, as a citizen, are the one who should decide what information is useful."

These days, of course, issues regarding the free flow of information are not restricted to traditional mass media. The Internet has introduced new and difficult challenges. An *Oregonian* editorial ("Protecting anti-abortion speech") tackled an especially tough one—a federal court case in which (in the words of the editorial) "the operators of a rabidly anti-abortion Web site" had been sued by doctors who had been listed and pictured on "wanted" posters on the web site. Names of doctors who had been killed or maimed had been x'd out. The district court held that the messages "merely encouraged," but did not actually provoke, terrorism and thus were protected by the First Amendment. The *Oregonian*'s editorial was written after the Ninth Court of Appeals had reversed the ruling and sent the case back to the lower court.

Media Issues Web Resources

American Journalism Review. http://www.ajr.org

American Society of Newspaper Editors: http://www.asne.org

The Association for Practical and Professional Ethics (links to professional ethicists at academic institutions):
http://php.indiana.edu/~appe/home.html

Columbia Journalism Review: http://www.cjr.org

Editor & Publisher. http://www.editor&publisher.com

Fairness and Accuracy in Reporting (FAIR):
http://www.fair.org

The Freedom Forum:
http://www.freedomforum.org

Foundation for American Communication (independent, nonprofit institution providing education for journalists):
http://www.facsnet.org

Investigative Reporters and Editors (IRE): http://www.ire.org

The Journalist's Toolbox (ethics-related links):
http://www.geocities.com/mike_reilly_2000/newswriting/ethics.html

Media News:
http://www.poynter.org/medianews

National Conference of Editorial Writers:
http://www.ncew.org

The Obscure Store ("dark counterpart" to *Media News*):
http://www.obscurestore.com

CITY'S PURSUIT OF TAPES IS WRONG

A Missoula city attorney Wednesday asked a judge to force a student journalist to turn over video footage she shot during last summer's mayhem accompanying the Hells Angels' visit. As we've pointed out before, the city doesn't have a leg to stand on in this case. The Montana Media Confidentiality Act clearly shields Linda Tracy from having to provide authorities tapes or any other material from her news gathering. Beyond that statute loom the U.S. and Montana constitutions with explicit free-press guarantees that the city of Missoula would tear to shreds.

The news media aren't government agents. In fact, we're supposed to be government watchdogs. Allowing police free access to notes, tapes or other information we gather would interfere in the news media's ability to fulfill the duties America's founding fathers assigned to us. Citizens would have good reason to fear speaking to reporters if they knew everything they said could wind up in a police file.

The speciousness of the city's case is most obvious in its contention that Tracy doesn't qualify as a journalist. This despite the fact that her peers and profession recognize her as a journalist. She even produced a short documentary televised last summer. The only reason city officials know she has video footage is that they saw her report. They didn't much like her documentary. It didn't paint a flattering portrait of police as they engaged citizens on the mean, hot streets of Missoula last summer. The city wants her unedited video footage in hopes that somewhere on the cutting-room floor are snippets that will help the city prosecute people arrested in clashes with police and perhaps help the city defend itself against lawsuits.

SUMMARY: Missoula's on the wrong side of state law, Bill of Rights and Montana Constitution in its pursuit of young journalist's video footage.

Weakest of all the city's arguments is the notion that only reporting judged by the government to be "objective" qualifies as journalism protected by the Media Confidentiality Act. This is preposterous on its face.

Objectivity is a goal and convention of mainstream newspapers, certain television and radio news shows and a few magazines. Objectivity is a fuzzy standard that, no matter how you define it, is difficult to achieve. It's harder than it seems. Trust us on this. One thing's certain, however, and that's that the First Amendment's guarantee of freedom of the press is not conditioned on impartiality or objectivity. In fact, it's unlikely the framers of the Constitution had any exposure to objective news reporting. It wasn't much practiced in their day.

The whole idea behind state and federal press freedoms is the notion that citizens are entitled to a free flow of information and, in fact, that democracy depends on it. Nothing in our constitutions suggests citizens must be content with information spoon-fed to them by the mainstream press or some elite media recognized by the government as objective. The quality and fairness of journalism varies greatly from one purveyor to the next. Sometimes the best of us are guilty of poor journalism, and occasionally some of the most irresponsible news organizations unearth something important or useful. The general assumption, reflected in the Bill of Rights and the Montana Constitution's Declaration of Rights, is that you, as a citizen, are the one who should decide what information is useful.

Missoulian

PROTECTING ANTI-ABORTION SPEECH

The Ninth U.S. Court of Appeals works hard to clarify the line between free speech and threats of violence

It's easy to talk about free speech when the topic revolves around what Kipling might have called a penny fight. But the Ninth U.S. Circuit Court of Appeals had a real fight on its hands when it handled the appeal of a lawsuit originating in Portland over the Internet's Nuremberg Files, a now-defunct anti-abortion site.

To its credit, the court sorted through a difficult thicket of issues and came to a wise decision Wednesday. It overturned a 1999 verdict by a Portland federal court jury that ordered the operators of a rabidly anti-abortion Web site to pay $109 million in damages to the people they threatened.

There is little doubt that the operators of the Web site went about their business with the worst intentions. They listed the names and addresses of doctors who performed abortions. Their writings singled out such doctors. They made up Old-West-style "Wanted" posters. When snipers and bombers struck, the website operators x'd out the victims who were killed and listed those who were maimed in gray type, in an ominous warning to others on the list. It was awful stuff.

They advocated despicable, violent acts against Americans who were exercising their constitutionally protected right to perform abortions. If these fringe characters had done even a portion of the things they advocated, they should have been tracked down and thrown in jail for a good, long time.

But their writings, as Judge Alex Kozinski wrote for the three-member Ninth Circuit panel, "merely encouraged" terrorism and were thus protected by the First Amendment to the Constitution in the same way that admiring views of Palestinian car bombers are, and should be, protected.

All that appeared on the anti-abortion Web sites was at the outer fringe of speech that must be protected in a free society. No bright line separates something like the Nuremberg Files from the kind of thuggery that they could easily engender. Even explicitness—and the message of the Nuremberg Files came as close to being explicit as anyone with a normal sense of self-preservation could want—is hard to define outside of a direct threat.

In interpreting the federal law allowing access to abortion clinics, the U.S. Supreme Court tried, in 1995, to define unprotected speech using context and reasonableness as standards. Federal judge Robert Jones tried to follow it in the Portland case, but as Wednesday's decision shows, that's no easy task. That decision may have been marginally useful in defining the line between protected rhetoric and direct threats of violence, but it will remain blurry.

And, of course, none of this is any comfort to the people on the hit lists of anti-abortion terror, or their spouses and families—who were sometimes also singled out by the advocates of violence. The threat represented here is real and federal authorities recognized it back before the Nuremberg Files disappeared from the Internet. One of the signals that the Bush Justice Department should send explicitly as a result of this case is that it will spare no effort to protect potential victims of anti-abortion violence—and will hunt down and prosecute anyone who turns the worst of the rhetoric into violence.

In the meantime, it's important to remember that squelching the kind of speech represented in this case doesn't change the minds of the speakers or make them less dangerous—it just limits the rights of everyone else.

Oregonian

The Poynter Institute for Media Studies (seminars, articles, links to
    resources): http://www.poynter.org/classes/ethics.htm

Reporters Without Borders (code of ethics, guidelines):
    http://www.rsf.fr/uk/home/html

Society of Professional Journalists (SPJ Ethics Committee contact; links):
    http://www.spj.org/spj_ethics.asp

■ LIVES OF PEOPLE

Editorial writers tend to forget that most readers are more interested in their
own lives than they are in public affairs. Except for letters to the editor, they are
not likely to find anything on most editorial pages that speaks to them about
their daily lives. The editorial that may have received more favorable response
than any other I have written was one I hastily typed for use after a Labor Day
weekend. My second daughter was to enter kindergarten the following
Tuesday. The result was "To a barefoot girl," written in the form of a letter to
her. At a session of NCEW (the National Conference of Editorial Writers) later
that year, other editorial writers questioned whether it was an editorial, since it
was written in the first person and did not comment on an issue. But readers
of the *Columbian,* especially parents of small children, didn't care whether it
met the requirement of an editorial. One woman, several years later, told me
she still carried a copy of it in her purse.

The life of Jacqueline Kennedy (Onassis) probably will continue to
interest a good many people for a good long time. Recognizing that, directors of the John F. Kennedy Library decided to display a collection of the
clothes that Mrs. Kennedy wore during her years at the White House. The
exhibit opened four days after the September 11, 2001, attacks on the World
Trade Center and the Pentagon. Noting that the crowd was "mostly women
over age 40," a *Boston Globe* editorial ("Style and substance") quoted one
woman: "Events pushed me to come, to check back with people who had
handled catastrophe." Said another woman: "I'm remembering how she
pulled the country together."

■ HUMOR AND SATIRE

When press critic Ben H. Bagdikian critiqued the pages of editorial writers
attending an NCEW convention, he found few examples of humor and the
humor that he found was not very good. "Funny" people are hard to find, he
said. "Perhaps it isn't a funny world."[3] When columnist Andy Rooney was asked
about humor writing in a *Masthead* symposium, he concluded that "[g]enerally
speaking . . . editorial pages, like the Bible, are better off without humor." He
said he had found that "[a]lmost every time someone sets out, deliberately, to
write something funny, the effort falls flat."[4]

Other participants in the symposium were not so pessimistic. "[B]adly executed
humor can decapitate an argument faster than a guillotine," but "humor can
smooth the way to making [a] point," Nordahl Flakstad of the *Leader-Post* of
Regina, Sask., Canada, wrote. "After all, some of the most persuasive writing—
running back to Jonathan Swift and earlier—has used a light touch to make a
sometimes heavy point." But Flakstad thought it was a wrong use of limited space
to "drop a funny piece into editorial pages merely for entertainment and comic

TO A BAREFOOT GIRL

Letter to a daughter who went to school for the first time today.

By the time I get home from work tonight, you will have experienced your first day of kindergarten. You'll be bubbling over with stories about the excitement of school—that is, if you aren't already worn out answering questions from your mother, your big sister and the girls next door.

If I know you, you weren't even a little bit scared today. An article in the paper the other evening said parents should expect their five-year-olds to be a little scared the first day, scared of spending two or three hours away from home in a new place. But that's nothing new to you. You've been gone from home longer than that this summer—without telling your mother where you were going. She was the one who was scared.

If your teacher let you paint or color today, I hope she kept a close eye on you. You can do a good job of staying within the lines when you want to. But your mother tells me that every time she turns her back there's a new mark on the living room carpet or your pillow case. How your teacher is going to keep track of you and 29 other children is beyond me. I wish her luck.

I also wish her luck in getting you to stay on your rug when it's rest time. If she has to stand over you the way your mother and I have to when it's nap time at home, 29 other children are going to be up and around and doing whatever they want to.

I hope you came home wearing your shoes, or at least carrying them. You are a big school girl now, and it's time to start learning to keep track of your shoes. It's all right sometimes to take them off, but you've got to stop forgetting where you left them. The tennis shoes you lost this summer didn't cost too much, but those big saddle shoes we bought you for school cost a lot of dollars, a whole lot more than the six cents you charged me yesterday for lemonade. Maybe it would help if you wrote your name on the inside of your shoes.

I hope you're not going to be disappointed with kindergarten. You have been looking forward to school ever since you knew where your big sister went to school. You always thought she was so smart. She could read and write and do numbers. I've heard you tell people that as soon as you went to school you'd be able to read and write and do numbers, too. It will take you quite a while to learn enough so that you can read a book, or the funny papers, or this letter. Kindergartners these days don't get much chance to learn to read. Maybe it's just as well. Maybe kindergarten should be a time only for enjoying your new friends, playing games and painting pictures.

The most important thing about school is being able to enjoy it. A lot of big boys and girls are scared of school—boys and girls who are bigger than your sister. Most of them aren't doing very well in school either. They aren't learning what they should be. Maybe they started out being scared from the first day. But maybe what happened was that somewhere along the line they forgot that school ought to be fun. Maybe they had some cranky teachers. Or maybe their parents put too much pressure on them.

I'm not sure you know what I'm talking about by this time. But I guess what I'm saying is that I hope that, even though you are now a big school girl, you will still be that smiling, laughing little kid who has a mind of her own and who is interested in more important things than keeping track of a pair of shoes. We can always buy another pair of shoes or clean the pillow case. But it's not so easy to repair the damage if you let the big people in the world who have forgotten how to smile and laugh keep you from smiling and laughing.

I hope you have fun in school—even if you come home barefoot.

Columbian

STYLE AND SUBSTANCE

Jacqueline Kennedy was much more than her clothes, and the collection of outfits from her White House wardrobe on display at the John F. Kennedy Library is much more than a fashion show.

The exhibit, which opened Sept. 15 and runs through February, is both a time capsule for a political era and balm for the tumultuous present, reconnecting Americans with the person whose grace and dignity piloted the country through what many people remember as their first encounter with national grief.

"Events pushed me to come, to check back with people who had handled catastrophe," says Dorothy Rogers of Dedham, at the exhibit Wednesday. The crowd is mostly women over age 40, and many say they have never been to the library even though they live near Boston. Some say they've come to remember or to feel patriotic, while others say they are trying to forget.

Rogers stands in front of a glass case containing a black and white checked wool suit that Mrs. Kennedy wore during the presidential campaign. The accompanying photo shows the former first lady looking girlish and windblown, but like all the pictures and film clips that put the 70 dresses and suits into exquisite context, this one seems infused with sadness, for the viewer has seen the future. There is no mention of the assassination, except briefly at the exit door, but it is on everyone's mind.

"We all know where we were when it happened," says Priscilla Peavey of Bangor, Maine, standing in the room with the inaugural gowns. "I was in Montreal, and someone said, 'They killed your president.'"

Further on in the exhibit, the weighty, plain, long black dress and mantilla that Mrs. Kennedy wore for her visit with Pope John in 1962 seem to foreshadow a state funeral.

"I'm remembering how she pulled the country together," says Barbara Romano of Hanover. "How she handled this and helped us handle it."

The dresses are simple, dazzling in their straight lines, basic colors, and timeless style. Many of the outfits could easily be worn now and not look dated or ridiculous the way so much haute couture looks today. Clothes often wear people now, and trendsetters are exhibitionists.

Jacqueline Kennedy's quiet firmness of purpose, character, and intellect are woven into each ensemble and are her legacy. She never slipped into another persona after leaving the White House, never wrote the confessional, never spoke publicly about what she considered private.

She remains the quintessential class act— the woman who carried the Camelot crown and its burdens as gracefully as she wore a tipped-back pillbox hat.

Boston Globe

relief."[5] Columnist Rick Horowitz saw an "occasional light touch" as the best way to get readers to the page and keep them there. "Being funny doesn't mean you aren't being serious," he said; "it's simply a different way of making points."[6]

Horowitz warned would-be satirical writers that, "[i]f you write satire for a living, you run the risk that somebody just won't get it." He said that one time, when he was attempting to question how Bill Clinton had managed to avoid the Selective Service, he imagined "a news-conference grilling of a certain George Washington" about chopping down a cherry tree. From Portland, Ore., came a letter from a reader who said he "had a hard time believing that a Jew would write this sort of innuendo about America's first president. . . . There is no predicting the level to which you, and your colleagues, will stoop to further the Jewish agenda of division and disloyalty."[7]

When the University of Oregon cracked down on the university's "most ardent football fan," the *Bulletin* in Bend couldn't resist exercising what the

HOW TO PLAY FOOTBALL IN EUGENE

For several years, 40-year-old Scott Spaan has been the University of Oregon's most ardent football fan. To every game, he brings a miniature version of the opposing team's mascot tied to a length of rope. Until this month, Spawn has celebrated every Oregon score by whacking the critter du jour against a stadium bench once for each point the Ducks put on the board.

That has come to an end, however. Spawn's ritual, you see, appalled a number of people in the stands, who expressed—quite loudly— their belief that a football game is no place for such violence. Consequently, Spawn was recently summoned to a meeting with the university's athletic director, Bill Moos, who convinced him to tone down his act. Now, instead of smashing an opposing team's mascot, Spawn will hoist it above his head in an up-with-people manner.

Since that fateful meeting, some unchari-table observers have called the university's treatment of Spawn silly. We disagree. We think it's wonderful—so wonderful, in fact, that we believe what happens on the field should change in like manner. To that end, we have come up with a number of football rules folks in Eugene ought to appreciate:

1) No tackling. It hurts, and it sends the message that violence is OK. Instead, participants will doff their helmets and pads and play two-hand touch.

2) The football will henceforth be constructed of woven fronds volun-tarily shed by organically grown palm trees. Leather comes from murdered cows; rubber comes from maimed trees; and plastic is based on oil, which is gathered by punching holes in Mother Earth.

3) The makeup of the team shall reflect the diversity of the student body. Players will be chosen not only according to class, race and sex, but also according to height, weight, sexual preference and physical ability. Same goes for the cheerleaders.

4) Coaches will no longer be permitted to swear or criticize, harsh words being detrimental to players' self-esteem. Instead, all comments will be positive.

5) The sport's terminology will be purged of all language that suggests war or violence. Thus, "bomb" and "blitz" will be known, respectively, as "ambitious pass" and "communal surprise." The term "red shirt" will also be changed to "mauve shirt."

6) The quarterback, halfback and fullback will be renamed in more egalitarian fashion.

7) Finally, to preserve the tradition of the scholar-athlete, all players will be required to carry at least a 3.0 grade point average.

On second thought, scratch number seven. No need to get carried away.

* * *

Coming this spring: the Eugene Baseball Rules, in which we will deal with such poten-tially offensive terms as "pinch hitter" and "bottom of the inning."

Bulletin

editor called "bittersweet humor" in speculating on where such treatment might lead: An editorial ("How to play football in Eugene") suggested seven rules "folks in Eugene ought to appreciate."

Writers at the *Keene* (N.H.) *Sentinel* poked fun at the direction in which tele-vision news seemed to be headed, in a short piece titled "Way it is." They also

---

WAY IT IS

Notice television news? Evolving, changing. Tight competition, ratings going down. Desperation. Seeking a sense of excitement. Everything breathless. New kind of poetry? Just a jumble?

Happening everywhere. Fox doing it most, Janet Reno, shark attacks, Condit. New kind of shorthand. CBS, MSNBC, ABC. NBC too. CNN White House correspondent.

Speaking normally: Brokaw, Rather, Jennings.

Speaking strangely: many reporters. One doing it, others soon following, becoming the new fashion, everything running together. Leaving out subjects. Sometimes even verbs.

Watching at home, having some trouble. Seeing people, fires, floods, graphics. Cars going by, stocks falling, demonstrators demonstrating, people in motion, talking for seven seconds. All headlines, no stories. Pretty much understanding what. Not getting where, who, especially why. Frustrating.

Language evolving throughout history, nothing surprising. Trying to follow. Be up to date. May be the wave of the future. But happening too fast, no time to adjust. People not talking like this in the street. Only on TV. Bits and pieces, not tied together. Viewers getting the picture, missing the point. Everything much shorter.

The way it is.

Keene Sentinel

---

responded humorously to what a Japanese prime minister had to say in an even shorter editorial ("A dry brow").

One risk in writing humorously is that readers might take what you write seriously—and not get the point. That risk is even greater with satire. The *Oregonian* of course didn't really mean what the words said in an editorial titled "An Ivy League jail." The editorial satirized the unsuccessful efforts of a person, wanted on an arrest warrant, to turn herself in to a county sheriff's office.

In a *Masthead* symposium on satire, Mark L. Genrich of the *Phoenix* (Ariz.) *Gazette* said that, as a person who hates fruitcake, he sometimes writes editorials calling for its abolition. In one editorial he suggested that the state police "establish roadblocks at Christmas time to intercept the transportation of the distasteful stuff." Violators would be "punished by forcing them to eat, on the spot, the fruitcakes they were caught transporting across state lines." Some readers thought he was serious and wrote long letters describing the wonderful taste of fruitcakes. Others accused him of harming the fruitcake industry. On another occasion he wrote an editorial opposing the extension

---

A DRY BROW

We thought about publishing an editorial today concerning Japanese Prime Minister Kiichi Miyazawa's outrageous remark that Americans "lack a work ethic . . . to live by the sweat of their brow." But we decided to knock off early and watch a little TV.

Keene Sentinel

AN IVY LEAGUE JAIL
Turning yourself in at the Washington County Jail? Bring a résumé, bad references and some wanted posters

Sometime when the rest of us weren't looking, the Washington County jail apparently upped its entrance requirements. Murder suspects—the top of the class, in jail terms—are no longer guaranteed admission there.

Waltz in and announce you're surrendering yourself on an arrest warrant, as dancer Jessica Rydman did last week, and nobody will even ask you the next logical question;

"For what charge, ma'am?"

Even if your face seems vaguely familiar—possibly because your photograph has been splashed across the state for days, linked to a story about the killing of a Portland banking executive—nobody will look you up in the computer. Nobody will even interview you.

And don't think, either, that you can get yourself into jail by handing over some evidence in a paper bag—say, a gun. That stuff doesn't faze Washington County's jail deputies. They'll just politely see to it that you get your gun back, before they send you on your merry way.

As luck would have it, Rydman did manage to turn herself in elsewhere—someplace not quite so selective. But to get arrested, she had to show a degree of perseverance more commonly associated with the pursuit of suspects—not their surrender.

"We screwed up big-time," Washington County Sheriff Jim Spinden admitted Wednesday. "We should know better. It's basic Cop 101."

Move over, "World's Dumbest Criminals." It's not the first time this year that Washington County jail deputies have auditioned for their own spinoff show. Earlier, Spinden had to fire a deputy who allowed a convicted rapist to escape after a court appearance.

Spinden's candor—and the mirth generated by re-tellings of this latest fiasco—shouldn't obscure the enormity of this bureaucratic bungle. The first jail deputy who talked to Rydman did one thing right—he asked his boss, a recently promoted sergeant, what to do. That's where the process broke down.

The sergeant was hot off a telephone call in which she had been haggling with the Multnomah County Jail about another case. After leaning that Rydman's warrant was out of Multnomah County, too, "she thought, 'OK, Multnomah County, take care of your own mess here,'" Sheriff Spinden told The Oregonian's Holly Danks.

Now that's outrageous—for a superior officer to allow her irritation over a territorial tug-of-war between the two jails to overshadow common sense, and public safety. That isn't one bit funny.

Oregonian

---

of daylight-saving time, "pointing out that the time change means more hours of sunlight in the afternoon, drying crops and grasslands," leading to the need for farmers and suburbanites to use more water to keep fields and lawns green. Dutifully a number of readers wrote to "explain carefully and patiently that the sun is not controlled by earthly clocks."[8] Satire had gone awry with these readers.

Joseph Plummer of the *Pittsburgh Post-Gazette* said he saw the opportunity for "an occasional alliance between the generally understood mission of the editorial page as a vehicle for biting criticism and the intent of sarcasm, which is to deride and taunt," but he wouldn't use it often, "because sarcasm is truly a blunt instrument." He suggested that sarcasm could be appropriate in "criticizing the egregious misbehavior on the part of a public official" but "unsuitable when some point of public policy is being weighed in an editorial."[9]

CONCLUSION

Editorial-page readers deserve a break from the traditional topics of government, politics and world-shaking events. Instead of writing only about breaking-news stories, editorial writers can take a broader look at other things their readers are interested in—science and natural resources, for example. Instead of writing only about "serious" subjects, they can try their hand from time to time at writing something personal or humorous.

QUESTIONS AND EXERCISES

1. Find an editorial dealing with science. Did the writer achieve a balance between oversimplifying and writing beyond the comprehension of most readers? Is the topic discussed in terms that are relevant to readers? Did the writer do more than rehash what had appeared in the news columns?

2. Find an editorial dealing with natural resources. Ask the same questions about it.

3. Find a humorous or satirical editorial. Is the humor or satire likely to be misunderstood? Is the use of humor or satire appropriate in this editorial?

4. Find several editorials dealing with everyday life. Do the writers succeed in making the commonplace seem interesting? Might the space have been better used for comment on some public issue?

Editorials on Elections

Some editorial writers, some scholars and some lay readers think editorial endorsements have little impact on elections. Other writers, scholars and readers worry that endorsements carry too much weight with voters, that newspapers control elections. Among the writers who think they have influence, some worry about making mistakes in making endorsements through lack of information about or prejudice toward a candidate.

The endorsement process is a difficult and time-consuming process, if done right. It involves conducting research into the candidates' backgrounds and political stands, conducting interviews, perhaps attending candidates' meetings and then sitting down to figure out whom to endorse. In a local election with several positions on the ballot, or an election that involves statewide and legislative district candidates, scores of candidates may have to be researched and interviewed. Before an election is over, because of this burden, editorial writers may begin to wonder whether newspapers ought to be in the business of endorsing candidates at all. They may wonder even more if they find themselves disagreeing with their editors or publishers about whom to endorse.

The hell that editorial writers feel that they go through during endorsement season may be one reason why some newspapers—although still a minority—forbear from endorsing candidates in some or all races.

■ WHY ENDORSE?

Most newspapers endorse candidates for public office, but more and more newspaper people, as well as readers, are questioning whether endorsements play a legitimate role in today's changing political world. Some critics contend that endorsements play an unfair role, giving newspapers undeserved power to influence elections. Others contend that endorsements play virtually no role at all in influencing voters.

In any case, the percentage of newspapers that endorse seems to be declining. An editorial in *Editor & Publisher* noted that 30 percent of newspapers polled in the 1996 election cited a "no-endorsement" policy. It said that "This steady trend away from presidential endorsements has been noticeable since 1940 when only 13.4 percent of the newspapers remained neutral."[3]

Endorsing is not an all-or-nothing matter. Some papers make recommendations for offices from president to local judge and school board members. Some endorse in state and local elections; others only in national and state elections. Some newspapers consider it especially important to endorse in local elections. Others avoid endorsing local candidates, either for fear of antagonizing readers or for fear of unduly influencing the vote.

The Case against Endorsements

Among readers, probably the most frequently heard argument against endorsing is that a paper has no right to use its position of influence to impose its views on the voters. A reader accused the editor-owner of the *Daily News* of Longview, Wash., of inflicting on the community "a slanted and one-sided opinion or recommendation" that "could affect the lives of many people." The letter writer feared that people would "take that recommendation as an easy way out for the solution of their undecided vote." The writer thought that if the editor-owner wanted to express his views, he should take out a political advertisement and label it as such, just like anyone else.[4] A letter writer charged the Eugene, Ore., *Register-Guard* with "meddling into the political affairs of the people of Lane County, dictating to Republicans and Democrats alike." The selection of candidates "belongs to the people. . . . It's their vote," the writer said.[5]

A similar view was expressed by an editor-publisher, Dick Timmons of the *Daily News* of Rhinelander, Wis. "Who are newspapers to tell our readers how to think or how to vote?" he wrote in a letter to *Editor & Publisher.* "[S]top playing God, editors," he wrote. "Readers don't give a hoot whom you vote for."[6]

Another argument against endorsing is that readers might think that, if a paper supports a candidate in its editorial columns, it will be biased in that candidate's favor in the news columns. A study of newspapers in Chicago and Louisville, Ky., during the 1984 presidential campaign found some evidence that endorsements did affect how readers perceived the news coverage of a newspaper. Reagan supporters tended to think the papers that endorsed Mondale favored Mondale in their news coverage; Mondale supporters tended to think the single paper that endorsed Reagan favored Reagan in its news coverage. (An analysis of the news columns of the major paper in each city found that, indeed, each newspaper gave slightly better coverage to the candidate it endorsed.).[7]

Some critics contend that endorsements give endorsees an unfair advantage. In 2001, Peter Kohler, vice president of editorial services for Cablevision Systems Corp. in Bethpage, N.Y., said, "I think many editorial writers who are calling for campaign finance reform that curbs political advertising haven't really examined the question of whether editorial endorsements constitute another form of 'unfair' speech. If you buy the argument that advocacy advertising has to be regulated by government, then why shouldn't editorial endorsements in print be treated the same way?"[8]

One argument, sometimes offered by editorial writers themselves, is that endorsing is a waste of time, effort and space. In a discussion in the NCEW (National Conference of Editorial Writers) e-mail discussion group, Thomas J. Lucente Jr., of the *Lima* (Ohio) *News*, said: "Newspaper endorsements carry little weight, certainly less weight than endorsements by special-interest groups.

As editorial writers we can better serve the readers by discussing the issues of the race rather than what the candidate tells us in a formal interview."[9]

The Case for Endorsements

The principal argument in favor of endorsements is that taking a stand on an issue or candidate in an election is no different from taking a stand on any other public issue. In the same e-mail discussion, Jackman Wilson of the Eugene, Ore., *Register-Guard* said that discussing issues and not making endorsements was like discussing issues involved in a trial but declining to editorialize on the verdict.[10] James G. Lakely of the Fredericksburg (Va.) *Free Lance–Star* said, "[I]f an editorial board cares enough to write about the issues involved, it should take the next logical step and name the candidates who would best advance those positions."[11] An editorial in the *Register-Guard* noted the paper's practice of commenting on public matters throughout the year and contended that for the paper "to comment on issues between elections and then to duck the tough choices would be irresponsible."[12] In a *Masthead* symposium on endorsements Dave Kushma of the Memphis, Tenn., *Commercial Appeal* said that since the *raison d'etre* of his newspaper was that "Editorial pages routinely express opinions on issues of public policy . . . . Why would we refrain from sharing with our readers our independent judgment of the men and women who would make that policy and spend our tax dollars?" He said that it was not a "question of telling readers whom to vote for" as it was "giving them some additional information, and, we hope, something to think about."[13]

Defenders of endorsements contend that the newspaper is unique in most communities, in that no other institution, aside from government and political parties, devotes as much attention to political affairs. "The end result [of not endorsing] leaves the major political campaign largely up to hucksters writing the pitches for print and broadcast political advertising, which isn't known for its fairness, and to the talk show hosts who demonstrate no restraint about their political leanings," said an editorial in *Editor & Publisher*.[14] Aside from professional politicians, political reporters and editorial writers probably know more about the qualifications of candidates and the merits of ballot propositions than anyone else does. They have the added advantage of being less partisan and hence more able to evaluate candidates and issues with some measure of detachment. The editorial columns of a newspaper are among the few places in a community where the pros and cons of issues can be discussed at length and in a logical, factual manner. Why should editorial writers not participate in this forum?

To the contention that endorsements have little or no effect, Jackman Wilson of the *Register-Guard* replied: "Endorsements can be influential, particularly when they reach an unexpected conclusion or when they deal with an obscure race, but usually they have little effect. So what? The same can be said of our editorials on national, and even state, affairs, but we keep on writing them anyway."[15] Michael Smith of the Spartanburg, S.C., *Herald Journal* contended that "[w]eight is not a legitimate criterion," then added: "I write to stimulate thought and discussion. . . . I write [an endorsement] because, believe it or not, some readers actually care about what we think and will call to ask why we've not editorialized on a particular issue."[16]

Primary Elections

Primary elections raise a different question concerning endorsements. In the NCEW e-mail discussion, John H. Taylor Jr. of the Wilmington, Del., *News Journal* said that his newspaper did not endorse in primaries "because our primaries are closed, and, besides, I consider nominations the party's business."[17] Mike Smith said the *Herald-Journal* did not participate in the primaries "[b]ecause the newspaper does not align itself with any party." It "allow[s] the members of that particular party to choose the party's nominees."[18]

In response, Jeffrey M. Brody of the Bremerton, Wash., *Sun* said: "[I]n my opinion, newspapers that refuse to endorse in the primary are abrogating their duty to educate voters and inform the public of issues in the election that are important to their communities. If a paper is silent during the primary process, it may lose its ability to endorse the best candidate."[19]

Evaluating Candidates

Of course the argument that endorsements serve a valid function is good only to the extent that writers of endorsements make certain they are as informed as possible before they share their knowledge and evaluations with readers. Aside from keeping generally informed about government and politics, writers have invited candidates to their newspapers for in-depth interviews and/or asked them to respond to questionnaires. Responses to the questionnaires might provide information for subsequent interviews or publication in the newspaper.

In a *Masthead* article titled "Assessing the candidates," Ronald D. Clark of the *St. Paul* (Minn.) *Pioneer Press* urged writers who faced the task of evaluating candidates to examine three broad categories of information:

> *Objective indicators*: education, job history, civic activities, acquaintance with issues, well-defined positions on issues, supporters, financial contributors, "threshold test of competence."
>
> *Political and interpersonal skills*: "likely to seek common ground or hold fast to a point of view," pleasing personality, relates well to people, effective at fostering teamwork, held office before, independent thinker, enjoys working with people, "political knowledge and resources to be elected."
>
> *Subjective indicators*: motivated by public service or ego, mature or unstable views on issues, trustworthy, honest, "a philosophy that guides decisions."[20]

Interviewing can become a tedious, even horrid, task if an editorial staff faces the necessity to talk to candidates for a long list of positions. In an NCEW online exchange, Kay Semion reported that writers on the *Tallahassee Democrat* interviewed 100 candidates and wrote 35 editorials during the 1996 election.[21] Phineas Fiske of the Long Island, N.Y., *Newsday* said his staff conducted 72 interviews in 37 races, but sometimes only two editorial board members were present. Lynnell Burkett reported that the *San Antonio Express-News* hit on the idea of interviewing all candidates for a particular position at the same time. Robert White said the *Cincinnati Post* helped smooth the interviewing of 50 candidates by sending them questionnaires ahead of time.[22]

Writing in *The Masthead*, Ed Williams reported that the editorial staff of the *Charlotte* (N.C.) *Observer* had followed a three-point plan to avoid "editorial masochism":

- Interview only the candidates "we need to interview."
- Assign an editorial writer to research specific races and make recommendations to the editorial board
- Attend and/or sponsor candidate forums[23]

Richard Mial of the *La Crosse* (Wis.) *Tribune* has pointed out that contacts with candidates can have another advantage: "Particularly for smaller dailies, the endorsement process is a time when the candidates for governor and U.S. senator pay attention to us, and that gives us the opportunity to be better connected with state and federal politics." But the smaller papers have a downside as well. Describing local endorsements as "personal affairs," Mial recalled that, the day after making an endorsement in a "contentious local judicial race," the first person he ran into was the candidate who was not endorsed. "Another time," he said, "a candidate's wife called to grill me about why we had not endorsed her husband for district attorney."[24]

Personal Note

In the years in which I was engaged in writing editorials, the papers on which I worked consistently endorsed candidates and ballot propositions. I was not unsympathetic to the concerns of those who contended that the *Columbian* was trying to impose its candidates on the community. After all, over the years a large majority of the candidates that the paper endorsed were elected. Some critics argued that since the *Columbian* was the sole source of political reporting in the community, the editors should keep their editorial preferences to themselves. But my publishers and I thought that, precisely because we were the only consistent source of political information, we had a responsibility to dig into the backgrounds of candidates, present the arguments for and against propositions and tell our readers what we found and what we had concluded.

■ WHAT EFFECTS?

Whether endorsement editorials do in fact influence voters has been a matter of speculation and argument for a long time, especially since Democrat Franklin D. Roosevelt began winning elections in spite of overwhelming opposition from the editorial writers on predominantly Republican newspapers. By 1952, journalism historian Frank Luther Mott, in an article titled "Has the Press Lost Its Punch?" concluded: "There seems to be no correlation, positive or negative, between support of a majority of newspapers during a campaign and victory in a presidential canvass."[25] Following the 1952 election, Professor Nathaniel B. Blumberg noted that "in the 37 presidential campaigns preceding the 1952 election, the winner had the editorial support of a majority of newspapers 18 times and did not have it 19 times."[26] In the 13 presidential elections between 1952 and 2000 the press accumulated a better record, with a majority of newspapers supporting the winning candidate in 10 elections, for an improved record of 28 wins and 22 losses.

Of course, this tallying proves nothing. Except for Lyndon Johnson in 1964 and Bill Clinton in 1992, the majority of newspapers have endorsed Republicans in every election since the Civil War. The record says more about the politics of the newspapers than it does about their power to influence elections. The presidential race is only one of thousands of contests that regularly take place in the country—and the presidential vote may be the one least influenced by editorial endorsements, or endorsements of any kind. Voters have many other sources of information in presidential races.

In spite of the popularity of television, surveys suggest, presidential elections aside, that the public still tends to look to the print media for information and guidance on public matters, especially on state and local ballot propositions and candidates.[27] "Our philosophy is that we don't change many minds endorsing the president," Frank Partsch of the *Omaha World-Herald* said in an NCEW online exchange; "that's more tradition and self-definition. But we can make a difference in a school board race. And that can be important."[28]

Supporting the idea that local endorsements have greater impact were studies of the 1996 presidential election and a 1999 mayoral election in Philadelphia. The studies found that "no more than 29 percent of registered voters knew whom a newspaper endorsed" for president, while 41 percent of registered Democrats knew whom their paper endorsed in the mayoral election.[29]

Fred Fedler has concluded that endorsements are most effective when the election is local or nonpartisan, when candidates are not well known, when the ballot is long and complicated and when voters receive "conflicting information or have conflicting loyalties."[30]

Studies that I conducted in California suggested that endorsements have more effect:

- On ballot propositions than on candidate races.
- In primary than in general elections.
- On government issues (taxes, schools, constitutional amendments) than on emotional issues (death penalty, abortion, gun control, homosexual teachers).[31]

In addition, I found that smaller newspapers seemed to have more influence than larger ones and independent newspapers more than group newspapers.[32] In all of these cases, effects appeared to be modest (from 1 to 5 percent), and hard to measure and prove. Of course, in a close election, a few percentage points can make the difference.

Editorial-writing literature includes several examples of the apparent influence of editorials. During one election, 47 percent of voters leaving the polls in Orlando, Fla., said they had considered the local newspaper's endorsements "very" or "somewhat" helpful; about half of those (23 percent) went a step farther and said the endorsements actually had helped them decide how to vote.[33] A study of the campaigns of congressional candidates found that newspaper endorsement editorials were "the strongest predictor of percent of vote for . . . non-incumbent[s]"— but that incumbents were much more successful in obtaining endorsements.[34]

■ WHOSE VIEWS?

If an editorial should ever represent more than the views of the specific person who wrote it, that time should be during elections. But whether the editorial should be the voice of the owner (publisher), editor or a consensus of staff members is an issue being fought out in newspapers across the country. In most instances the publisher has the power to win in any dispute. But each year an increasing number of newspapers seem to allow staff members to influence, if not decide, endorsements.

Some evidence of this trend was found in a survey of publishers following the 1996 presidential election. Forty-seven percent of publishers said they had voted for Republican Robert Dole, but only 39 percent of their newspapers endorsed Dole. *Houston* (Texas) *Chronicle* publisher Dick Johnson thought that the results reflected a decline in family-owned newspapers. Because newspapers had "become an institution, rather than part of one family's breakfast table," he speculated that endorsements had become more of a shared responsibility between the publisher and the editorial page staff.[35]

Publishers probably still exercise their final editorial prerogative more strongly and more often on endorsements than on any other editorial page decision. One survey found that, while 46 percent of publishers played an active role in determining editorial positions on major political issues, 81 percent exercised a strong voice in endorsements.[36]

John J. Zakarian, then of the *St. Louis* (Mo.) *Post-Dispatch,* described what he called "the publishers' four-year itch" and the "editorial writers' agony." For 47 months many papers carry moderate-to-liberal editorial policies but "on the 48th month of reckoning turn conservative." He described presidential elections as "sacred cows of the highest order."[37] Byron St. Dizier, professor at the University of Alabama at Birmingham, found evidence of this 48th-month turnaround in a study of newspapers in the 1984 presidential election. Newspapers that supported Democrat Walter Mondale showed "unswerving loyalty" in support of Democratic positions on issues. Among newspapers that supported Republican Ronald Reagan, however, more than half opposed his position on six out of nine key issues. "The findings may help to explain why some endorsement editorials fail to mention issues when endorsing a candidate," St. Dizier wrote. "In the case of most of the newspapers supporting Reagan, any discussion of the campaign's issues would make the paper's editorial page appear inconsistent at best."[38]

As might be expected, the 57-to-33 percent ratio of Reagan and Mondale endorsements by the newspapers in the survey (10 percent did not endorse anyone) did not coincide with the opinions of the editors of those papers. The editors supported Mondale over Reagan 55 to 43 percent. Of the Mondale backers, 43 percent said they wrote editorials for newspapers that endorsed Reagan. (They did not say that they themselves wrote the Reagan endorsements.) Only one Reagan supporter worked on a paper that backed Mondale.

Supposed differences between publisher and editorial page staff became a campaign issue when the Minneapolis, Minn., *Star Tribune* endorsed Democrat Gov. Rudy Perpich for re-election in 1990. A columnist on a rival newspaper had claimed that the editorial staff had preferred write-in candidate Arne Carlson eight to two. Robert J. White, the editorial page editor, explained that among the editorial page staff members as a whole (including the copy editor, artists and op-ed editor) the preference was for Carlson, but among the *writers* the split was even, with White and his deputy favoring Perpich. White said he recommended the Perpich endorsement to the publisher, and the publisher accepted it.[39] (Carlson won.)

This case, while not typical, helps make the point that it is not always easy to explain how endorsement decisions get made and who is ultimately responsible for them. Douglas J. Rooks of the Augusta, Maine, *Kennebec Journal* reported that his readers were confused and "felt betrayed by an endorsement they saw as arbitrary and undemocratic." The editorial board had narrowly voted to endorse former Gov. Joseph Brennan, but the board chairman, who had not attended the board meeting, "acting on previous instructions from the publisher," announced that the newspaper would endorse his opponent, John McKernan. Rooks reported that the story about the endorsement "was quickly out on the street and was a prominent issue in the waning days of the campaign."[40] (McKernan won by about 2 percent.)

Another variation on publisher-editorial staff disagreement was described by Mindy Cameron of the *Seattle Times*. Organizers who called themselves pro-family and religious had obtained enough signatures to place on the ballot an initiative to repeal a city ordinance that extended the same sick and bereavement leave benefits to domestic partners that were provided to married persons. Cameron reported that "Much of the support for Initiative 35 smacked of gay-bashing, though proponents consistently denied it was an anti-gay measure." According to Cameron, even though several editorial staff members "were outspoken in their opposition," and "others felt less strongly or had mixed views," the publisher "had made up his mind" to support the measure. He was concerned about the cost of the same-sex benefits and the image Seattle might get for embracing alternative lifestyles, but he also encouraged staff members to write signed columns expressing a different viewpoint. A day after the paper's pro-initiative editorial appeared, one staff member wrote a sharp dissent. On the Sunday before the election, below a summary of endorsements, Cameron wrote a column explaining what had happened during the endorsement process, including the staff's efforts to dissuade the publisher. She concluded: "I'm voting 'no' on the initiative, I hope you will, too."[41] (The initiative—endorsed by the *Times*—lost by 16 percent of the vote.)

One question raised in recent studies concerns the role of newspaper groups in making endorsements. Most studies have looked only at presidential endorsements and, not surprisingly, found a good deal of homogeneity among endorsements, since most newspapers, group-owned or independent, endorse Republicans for president. But some studies have found differences among groups. Cecilie Gaziano, president of Research Solutions, Inc., of Minneapolis, divided the groups into three categories: consistently homogeneous in their endorsements, somewhat homogeneous and consistently heterogeneous. The homogeneous groups tended to be regional in nature. Papers in this category tended to be smaller, evening papers with no competition, and Republican. The heterogeneous groups tended to be more national in scope, and to be larger, morning papers with more competition. She speculated that in future elections "The growth of large, heterogeneous groups may reinforce tendencies [of voters] to vote Democratic."[42]

Noting that the largest groups own a wide variety of types of newspapers, John C. Busterna and Kathleen A. Hansen of the University of Minnesota suggested, "It may be that region of the country, circulation size, metro vs. rural, or some other local characteristics have more influence on endorsement decisions than chain ownership per se." They also suggested that group endorsement patterns may result, not from directives from the group, but through other, more subtle, forces: "The socialization of newspapers and newspaper executives, the pressure to conform to professional and industry norms, the need to meet superiors' expectations within the organization, and the desire to please powerful sources outside the organization are recognized as forces that may affect media content." They concluded that "chain ownership may play no role, or only a minor one, in affecting the content performance of daily newspapers . . . ."[43]

One study, concerned with the group homogeneity of Gannett newspapers, examined their stands on three national issues (none of them endorsements).

It found a higher uniformity of editorial positions on all three issues among Gannett papers than among other papers included in the study. The authors of the study concluded that "a homogenizing effect on editorial position and policy results from chain ownership" but that "the outstanding question . . . concerns the process through which such uniformity results." The authors expressed the concern that "Any tendency on the part of large newspaper chains to orchestrate editorial opinion on national issues would seem to represent one of the most serious threats posed by chain ownership to freedom of information in a democratic society."[44]

WHAT APPROACH?

Writers generally employ one of two basic approaches to endorsement writing. A form that goes back to the early days of the Republic involves making the strongest possible case for your chosen candidate and either ignoring or criticizing the opposition. The second approach presents the good and bad points of all candidates and then, on the basis of the points made, concludes that one of the candidates is the best. On occasion an editorial will conclude that one candidate is not significantly better than the others.

The endorsement that evaluates all the candidates is similar to the SBA_1A_2DC editorial described in Chapter 10, "Nine Steps to Editorial Writing." We noted that this type of editorial offers a chance to persuade the reader who may have started out disagreeing with the conclusion, in this case the endorsement. It also is appropriate for races in which readers have received little information from other sources. The editorial that basically presents the case for only one candidate, as an SAC editorial might, might be appropriate if the arguments are overwhelming for a candidate, if voters have previously been fully informed on the issues or if the editorial writer is mainly concerned with encouraging readers who already agree with the endorsement position.

To illustrate such endorsements, I have selected samples of editorials written during the 2001 state elections in Virginia and New Jersey. In Virginia, candidates for governor were Democrat Mark Warner and Republican Mark Earley. Candidates for attorney general were Democrat Donald McEachin and Republican Jerry W. Kilgore. In New Jersey, candidates for governor were Democrat James McGreevey, Republican Bert Schundler and Independent William Schluter.

Our Candidate Only

In its pure form, the one-candidate-only endorsement is found less often in U.S. newspapers today than it was in the past. Most papers are not as partisan as they once were. Editors recognize that readers who do not agree wholly with an editorial are likely to resent having an endorsement that presents only one side.

Whether a decision is made to talk about only the endorsed candidate may depend on the newspaper's endorsement policies as well as the nature of a specific race. In 2001 the Fredericksburg, Va., *Free Lance–Star* ran an editorial ("and for attorney general") that devoted all but two sentences to the candidate it supported for attorney general. Of the opponent, it said that as a personal-injury lawyer his "counterterrorism background is a little thin."

AND FOR ATTORNEY GENERAL

No brainer is probably too flip a way to put it, but in fact there isn't an easier call in the 2001 Virginia General Election than Jerry Kilgore for attorney general. Mr. Kilgore, of Southwest Virginia, worked as assistant U.S. attorney for the Western District of Virginia during the late Reagan and Bush I years, as assistant commonwealth's attorney for Scott County after that, and then as Gov. George Allen's secretary of public safety. Those credentials should serve him, and Virginians, well in the post-Sept. 11 world.

Owing to its proximity to Washington, Virginia is perforce a major governmental player in the war on terror. The air attack on the Pentagon took place in Arlington. Suspects in the atrocities obtained driver's licenses here. State law-enforcement agencies will be going all-out to find the guilty and prevent future attacks. This is no time to trust to beginner's luck in the A.G.'s office, which supervises more than 330 prosecutors and staff and argues to uphold convictions in the appellate courts.

It is no time, either, for Richmond Del. Donald McEachin, Mr. Kilgore's opponent, whose counterterrorism background is a little thin: He's a personal-injury lawyer.

It isn't just Mr. Kilgore's prosecutorial seasoning that recommends him to the post, however. He understands that 2+2=4, and favors delaying the phaseout of the car tax if going full speed ahead would mean skimping on public safety. Though no disarmer, he is willing to abide Virginia's reasonable gun-control laws, such as the one-a-month maximum handgun purchase. His program to combat domestic abuse deserves serious legislative consideration.

A victory by Mr. Kilgore on Election Day, if current polls are to be believed, would give not only political balance to the top state offices but geographical balance, too. Frontrunning Democrats Mark Warner (governor) and Tim Kaine (lieutenant governor) are from Northern and Central Virginia respectively. Mr. Kilgore would make sure the Appalachians weren't shut out of the action in Richmond.

Young (40), personable, energetic, smart, and experienced, Jerry Kilgore would be a great candidate for attorney general in any year. In 2001, he's the only realistic one.

Free Lance–Star

Predominantly Our Candidate

The *Press of Atlantic City* ran a mostly-our-candidate editorial in "New Jersey governor." Bret Schundler's Democratic opponent was not mentioned by name until the ninth paragraph of a 13-paragraph editorial. The three paragraphs devoted to him were entirely critical.

Even though an editorial ("Jerry Kilgore for attorney general") in the Norfolk *Virginian Pilot* began by saying either of the two candidates for attorney general is "likely would prove capable in the office," Republican Kilgore received twice the space devoted to Democrat McEachin. Two of three paragraphs about McEachin were negative.

More about the Other Candidate

Even though labeled "For governor, Mark Warner," the *Roanoke* (Va.) *Times* endorsement editorial devoted more space to Earley (and current Gov. Jim Gilmore) than to Warner. The second and third paragraphs referred to the "bungling incumbent" and "Gilmore's unhappy legacy." A paragraph later

NEW JERSEY GOVERNOR
Elect Schundler

On Sept. 11, the world changed. So, too, did what we expect from our political leaders.

Candidates' opinions about parkway tolls are now far less important than whether the candidates possess the leadership qualities needed in these troubled and uncertain times.

Republican candidate Bret Schundler has those qualities—thoughtfulness, intelligence, courage and commitment to principles. He takes a creative approach to problem-solving, which he demonstrated as mayor of Jersey City. And he is independent from the entrenched interests that so often stifle creativity in government.

For those reasons, The Press endorses Bret Schundler for governor. We believe he is the best man for the job, even if we disagree with him on many issues.

Like his Democratic opponent, Schundler seems blind to the rapidly deteriorating fiscal condition of the state and the probability that the situation will get worse before it gets better. We hope Schundler is pragmatic and flexible enough, in the face of fiscal realities, to at least defer some of his more ill-advised and costly promises—such as having taxpayers bear the cost of eliminating parkway tolls.

But any proposal Schundler has made still needs to clear the state Legislature. That's a powerful bulwark against initiatives that are either unpopular or unwise.

What Schundler brings to New Jersey politics is a refreshing idealism and intellectual courage.

He is pro-business but hardly unsympathetic to the poor—nor is he likely to ignore New Jersey's crumbling cities, which too many Republicans in this state have long neglected. In fact, Schundler seems most passionate when he speaks about better education for poor children and revitalizing the state's urban areas.

Democrat James McGreevey is a smart, competent politician. He, too, has made expensive promises without saying where the money will come from.

His overall lack of specificity during the campaign has been troubling. He has failed to offer any real vision of where the state should be going. He seems to be sitting on his lead in the polls, trying not to say anything wrong. Pragmatic? Perhaps. But hardly a profile in courage.

To a far greater degree than Schundler—who has gotten only tepid support from many Republicans—McGreevey is a product of the political system in New Jersey. That's not necessarily bad, just limiting.

Schundler appears to be an intellectually driven and principled leader. We suspect McGreevey's term in office would be that of a politically cautious, competent caretaker.

These are different times. They demand a different style of government. We think Schundler would be an exceptional leader for exceptional times. He deserves your vote.

Press of Atlantic City

criticized Earley for "foolishly vow[ing] no new taxes under any conditions." Warner was described as "a successful telecommunications businessman" who was familiar with Southwest Virginia issues and seen as "offer[ing] the better hope for progress." It seems clear that the previous administration (of the same political party) was the major issue for the *Roanoke Times*.

Edge to Our Candidate

In its editorial "Edge to McGreevey," the Trenton, N.J., *Times* took a thorough look at not only the two major candidates but also the independent

JERRY KILGORE FOR ATTORNEY GENERAL

Either of the two candidates for Virginia attorney general likely would prove capable in the office. Both Jerry W. Kilgore, the Republican, and A. Donald McEachin, the Democrat, are attorneys. Both have been around politics for several years. And both have a grasp of how state government works: Kilgore was secretary of public safety under Gov. George Allen, and McEachin is a state delegate.

Voters in Virginia, meanwhile, know that candidates for state attorney general often view the position as a steppingstone, sort of a "way station" for higher office. The winner can be expected to later run for governor or Congress— and that's not necessarily a bad thing. So, while the attorney general is primarily an administrator and legal arbiter, his political viewpoints draw obvious scrutiny.

However, the job should be used to promote the law, not politics.

On balance, we believe that Jerry Kilgore would make the better attorney general. We have some concerns, not the least of which is whether Kilgore would use the office to promote a highly partisan, conservative agenda.

Kilgore, 40, has taken some stands with which we agree. He wants state government to be more open and accessible. He has called for ethics reform, and he wants lawmakers to specify how they use their $15,000 annual allowance in office expenses.

For safety and security, he wants trained police officers assigned in every school, which would require 1,500 more officers statewide. It's unclear what the cost would be to implement the program. We also wonder whether officers are truly needed, for example, at the elementary school level, and whether their presence justifies the cost of the proposed program.

Kilgore would seek to clear the backlog at the state's DNA lab, which also could be costly but is necessary.

His administrative experience could be valuable. As secretary of public safety, he ran a $1 billion budget and supervised 17,000 employees.

We oppose Kilgore's support for the death penalty. The Earl Washington case, among others, has shown the flaws in the criminal justice system. And in Virginia, the quality of legal representation for poor defendants is still worrisome.

Kilgore's opponent, McEachin, has exhibited an independent streak that defies stereotypes and is refreshing. He has represented everyday people in his law firm, and he seems to have a grasp of basic concerns of individuals. He is neither cookie-cutter liberal nor doctrinaire conservative.

McEachin, also 40, was first elected to the House of Delegates in 1995. He represents the Richmond area. He supports the death penalty but also favors a moratorium until a legislative study commission finishes a review of capital punishment. He supports DNA testing in all felony cases, but McEachin also wants those records expunged if a suspect is found not guilty or the case is dismissed.

However, his campaign has been hard to define in some respects. Take McEachin's stand on guns. He says he supports gun rights, gun safety, Virginia's one-gun-a-month law and a ban on guns in bars. Yet, he seems to have distanced himself from gun control statements he made during the Democratic Party campaign.

Considering experience, administrative skills and agendas, Kilgore would be the better choice for attorney general.

Virginian-Pilot

candidate who stood no chance. After comparing Schundler and McGreevey on administrative abilities, state finance, education, the parkway and development, the editorial concluded that future "prospects would be slightly better

---

FOR GOVERNOR, MARK WARNER

In this year's battle of the Marks, businessman Warner appears likelier than former Attorney General Earley to succeed in restoring reality-based management to the office.

A signal blessing of this year's gubernatorial election is that the bungling incumbent is not a candidate. Under the Virginia constitution's one-term-and-out provision for governors, Jim Gilmore cannot run for re-election.

But Gilmore's unhappy legacy will linger. The next governor must work to remedy deficiencies—underfunded K-12 and higher education, a woefully inadequate transportation system, an archaic structure of local government, tax inequities, slipshod fiscal planning, executive-legislative gridlock—that arose or got worse, sometimes precipitously, under Gilmore's maladroit administration. An uncertain economy, after years of national prosperity, will make the struggle no easier.

In undertaking the hard task, Democrat Mark Warner presents the clearly preferable candidate.

Although both he and Republican Mark Earley have been too timid in their responses to the state's declining condition, Warner at least has avoided some of the policy straitjackets in which Earley has bound himself.

Earley's pledge not to allow Northern Virginians to decide for themselves whether to impose an additional regional sales tax for desperately needed local roads there is emblematic. It would make the difficult task of restoring common-sense government to Virginia all the harder. He has foolishly vowed no new taxes under any conditions. Warner, though not calling for new taxes, has wisely declined to make such blind commitments.

That reflects a seriousness of purpose, which in turn may reflect Warner's background as a successful telecommunications businessman. It also may explain why a number of prominent Virginia Republicans, including at least two GOP members of the General Assembly, are publicly supporting the Democrat.

Warner is from Northern Virginia, Earley from Tidewater, but Warner is more familiar to Southwest Virginians. His interest in the region, including health-care and venture-capital projects, predates not only this campaign but also his 1996 race against U.S. Sen. John Warner.

Earley is a decent man and able politician. As a state senator, he championed mental health services; as attorney general, he performed creditably. But he shows little sign of recognizing the existence of the Gilmore hole in which the state finds itself, let alone of knowing how to lead Virginia out of it.

Warner, more open-eyed and more open-minded, offers the greater hope for progress.

Roanoke Times

---

under Mr. McGreevey, if he can rise to the occasion. Of the two, we believe he's the better choice."

Timing of Endorsements

With elections held on a specific date, usually a Tuesday, newspapers traditionally have scheduled endorsements so that the last to be published appears a few days before Election Day. A summary of endorsements may appear in the Sunday edition, perhaps again on Monday and, in the case of morning papers, even on Tuesday. In some states, editorial page editors are extending the endorsement period and making endorsements earlier, and will probably

EDGE TO MCGREEVEY

Of the three most prominent candidates for governor of New Jersey, the best is the one with no chance to win.

State Sen. William Schluter of Pennington is a Republican running as an independent. Independence has been the story of his political life. His fellow Republicans in the Legislature treat him as a pariah, and were happy to see him redistricted out of the Senate, because he single-mindedly pursues the reform of things they (and the Democrats, as well) prefer to see left alone: the corrupt campaign finance system, the easy standards of ethics in public service, the undue influence of lobbyists, the way the two dominant political parties elbow third parties and independents out of the election process, the abuse of the confirmation procedure that's called "senatorial courtesy." He's in the pocket of no political bosses, no powerful special-interest groups, no ideological movement. He's Jesse Ventura without the attitude—and with a ready-made knowledge of how government works.

Of all the candidates, only Bill Schluter is campaigning as if he understands how heavy a burden the state's reliance on the property tax to fund government imposes on individuals, businesses, cities, suburbs and public schools and how it frustrates attempts to achieve smart growth and curb sprawl. Only Sen. Schluter is saying that the state needs more than politically palatable palliatives like NJ Saver and homestead rebates and assessment freezes for senior citizens. Only he is making the point, which history confirms, that the lawmakers at the State House are incapable of taking the bold political steps necessary to fix the tax system. Only he proposes a plausible alternative: a tax-reform convention of elected delegates from all over the state that would draft a unified package of statutes and constitutional amendments that the public then would vote up or down.

Running a lonely, largely symbolic campaign, Sen. Schluter has been unable to raise the threshold amount in contributions needed to qualify for matching public funds and a spot in the televised gubernatorial debates. Accordingly, he has had little success projecting his candidacy and his issues to a statewide audience. That's New Jersey's loss, and it means the senator almost certainly won't be a factor in the Nov. 6 voting between the two major party candidates, Democrat James McGreevey and Republican Bret Schundler.

* * *

The principal strength of those two candidates is the solid administrative experience they bring to the table. Mr. Schundler was a three-term mayor of Jersey City, and Mr. McGreevey is the mayor of Woodbridge. Both have been hands-on executives. If elected governor, it's certain that neither would manifest the kind of baffling indifference to detail that characterized former Gov. Christie Whitman's administration and allowed the colossal fiasco of privatized auto inspections to unfold on her watch.

In other respects, however, Mr. McGreevey and Mr. Schundler are very different from each other. Mr. McGreevey is cautious, at times almost programmed, a dealer in campaign generalities, a creature of the Democratic Party whose candidacy is unanimously backed by the party and its customary supporters among the special interest groups. Mr. Schundler is a loose cannon, a fount of policy ideas that don't hold up on close inspection, a Republican who defied his party's establishment to win the nomination and still hasn't been endorsed by its titular leader, acting Gov. Donald DiFrancesco. He's a conservative who receives campaign money from right-wing contributors across the nation while he strives to convince New Jersey's great moderate middle that his hard-line positions against abortion and gun control don't really matter.

* * *

Neither man has dealt in a realistic way with the harsh fact of life that will greet the next administration: a state revenue stream that's falling far short of original estimates. Experts believe the sinking economy will confront the new governor with a hole of up to $1.5 billion in the current budget. They warn that he'll face an even grimmer prospect for his own first (FY 2003) budget because of a host of expenditures now in the pipeline that have no committed sources of revenue.

Mr. McGreevey's basic response to questions about the budget has been to repeat the mantra that state government must "live within its means." The specific ideas he volunteers for doing so add up to small change, e.g. capping NJ Saver for filers earning over $200,000 and merging the state's three toll-road authorities to save administrative costs.

His strong point—until last week, that is—had been his refusal to take a no-tax-increase pledge, as Mr. Schundler had challenged him to do with taunts that he was a clone of Jim Florio, the tax-hiking last Democratic governor. Mr. McGreevey had called the idea of such a pledge "irresponsible" in the midst of a national crisis. It was the right position; no candidate with confidence in himself and in the voters should tie his own hands in such a way, especially at a time of profound uncertainty about what the next day and the next year will bring.

Then, in Thursday night's debate, even though he was sitting on a 12-point lead in the polls, Mr. McGreevey caved in. "We are not going to raise taxes," he said. ". . . I'm committed not to raising taxes."

His retreat was startling—and deeply disappointing.

Mr. Schundler, for his part, not only has repeatedly taken the vow of tax chastity; he has promised to implement untested and/or unnecessary programs that would slash state revenues still further.

For example, the keystone of Mr. Schundler's education plan is a set of tax credits for parents who send their children to private schools or educate them at home, and for contributors to private-school scholarship funds. The candidate believes these incentives will enable 84,000 children to leave the public school system, saving the state $480 million in per-pupil aid, which towns could use to lower property taxes.

However, the nonpartisan Office of Legislative Services, with no political axe to grind, estimates that only 18,000 students would transfer, resulting in a net loss in state revenues of $199 million and no significant operating savings for local public schools.

Then there's Mr. Schundler's free-the-Parkway scheme. The Garden State Parkway pays for itself through tolls, with no state tax money involved. The problem is that tolls are collected at a series of lane-straddling plazas that create traffic jams and hazards. This problem could be solved by extending and improving the E-ZPass system. Mr. Schundler, however, wants to throw out both the baby and the bathwater. He has promised to tear down the toll booths in nine months and dump onto the taxpayers the costs of retiring the road's outstanding $622 million debt, funding its needed capital improvements, and covering the annual $116 million tab for maintaining and policing the highway. Mr. Schundler—who has demanded that all other state borrowing plans be put to referendum—has said nothing about submitting his Parkway scheme idea to the voters, a step some bonding experts believe would be required.

Here again, however, Mr. McGreevey has allowed Mr. Schundler and his campaign tactics to intimidate him into taking an unwise position. On freeing the Parkway, Mr. McGreevey says "me too"— except that he'll do it in seven years, not at once.

Mr. Schundler says he can cover the cost of removing Parkway tolls, and reduce state taxes to boot, through unspecified savings in the budget. He'd also like to get rid of the state's $8.6 billion borrowing program for public-school construction, although it's unclear how he'd do it, inasmuch as a large chunk of the program has been mandated by the state Supreme Court.

* * *

On the key issue of growth management, Mr. McGreevey's positions are preferable to Mr. Schundler's. He supports strengthening the State Development and Redevelopment Plan to steer new construction into areas with existing infrastructure. He favors state legal assistance for towns that need it to

continued

concluded

defend zoning that conforms to the State Plan. Mr. Schundler disagrees with all those positions. Mr. Schundler blames sprawl, in large part, on the state Supreme Court's Mount Laurel decision that requires suburban towns to provide affordable housing, and would work to repeal that decision; Mr. McGreevey advocates change without repealing Mount Laurel, and correctly sees the causes of sprawl as far-reaching and complicated.

* * *

A vote for Bill Schluter would be a vote for the best candidate. Unfortunately, it wouldn't affect the outcome of the race. One of two other men, Bret Schundler or James McGreevey, is going to win.

Mr. Schundler, as governor, would be fascinating to watch: a smart, charismatic, stubborn, often wrongheaded chief executive waging a four-year running battle with the Legislature's Democrats and Republicans alike. In the process, however, the prospects for mitigating the state's chronic problems—budgetary, educational, environmental—would be small.

Those prospects would be slightly better under Mr. McGreevey, if he can rise to the occasion. Of the two, we believe he's the better choice.   *Times*

continue to do so in the future. The reasons are three-fold: (1) As was evident in the 2000 election, more and more voters are casting absentee ballots. (2) States (notably Arizona) are experimenting with balloting by computer. (3) One state (Oregon) has converted completely to vote-by-mail. In all three cases voters make their decisions and cast their ballots up to three weeks before Election Day. A survey of Oregon editors found that most were attempting to run the complete slate of endorsements by the time the mail ballots reached voters (about three weeks before Election Day). Then they faced the necessity of reprinting (or at least summarizing) the endorsements during the following weeks, right up to Election Day. The result was that they found themselves making the first endorsements before most voters were interested and devoting a lot more space to endorsements in their editorial columns (at a cost of squeezing out commentary on other topics).

Summaries at appropriate times, and especially right before Election Day, of course cannot provide a full explanation of the newspaper's endorsements. Published at appropriate times, however, especially right before Election Day, summaries can provide readers with a handy reminder of the newspaper's recommendations. Mike Oakland of the Olympia, Wash., *Olympian*, noting that his paper publishes an endorsement wrap-up about a week before the election, reported that "The poll watchers tell us that a lot of people bring the wrap-up in with them when they vote."[45] That provides at least some testimony to the role endorsements can play in the political process.

Election Web Resources

Following are some Internet resources on election campaign issues:

Campaign and Elections: http://www.camelect.com

Campaign Finance Reform: http://www.brookings.org/GS/CF/CF_HP.HTM

The Christian Coalition: http://www.cc.org

CQ's Campaigns and Elections: http://www.campaignonline.com

Elections: http://www.multied.com/elections

Electronic Policy Network (spin-off sites): http://www.epn.org

Mojo Wire (Online *Mother Jones* magazine): http://www.mojones.com

The National Journal: http://www.nationaljournal.com

National Political Index: http://www.visi.com/juan/congress

OnPolitics.com:
>   http://www.washingtonpost.com/wp-srv/politics/talk/talk.htm

Politics1.com: http://www.politics1.com

Public Affairs Web: http://www.publicaffairsweb.com

Roll Call (covers Congress): http://www.rollcall.com

United States Senate: http://www.senate.gov

White House Briefing Room:
>   http://www.whitehouse.gov/WH/html/briefroom.html

The following web sites provide information on particular political parties:

The American Party:
>   http://www.visi.com/~contra_m/cm/features/_cm04_american.html

Communist Party USA: http://www.hartford-hwp.com/cp-usa

The Constitution Party: http://www.constitution.net

Constitution Party: http://www.ustaxpayers.org

Democratic Socialists of America: http://www.dsausa.org

Fusion Party: http://www.members.tripod.com/~fusionparty

Green Party USA:
>   http://utopia.knoware.n1/users/oterhaar/greens_america/usa.htm

Labor Party: http://www.igc.apc.org/lpa

Libertarian Party: http://www.ip.org/ip.html

Natural Law Party: http://www.natural-law.org

New Party: http://www.igc.apc.org/newparty

Republican National Committee: http://www.rnc.org

Socialist Party USA: http://www.sp-usa.org

■ CONCLUSION

Following an election, editors are likely to find themselves in situations as untenable as they had before the election. If most candidates they have endorsed win, the editors and their newspapers are accused of controlling the election and influencing the election of the candidates of their choice. If more than a few of the endorsed candidates lose, the newspapers are perceived to have lost credibility.

I have often had voters say to me on election night that the newspaper was, or was not, right in its predictions. Somehow these voters seem to think that a newspaper is calling a horse race—waiting to tie its endorsement to winners.

Election time also can be hazardous for editorial writers. The heightened emotion of a political campaign, plus the black-and-white nature of endorsement decisions, can produce crises and magnify differences of opinion between writers and publishers that might be reconcilable at other times. Perhaps these periodic crises serve a purpose in forcing publishers and writers to re-evaluate whether they still see eye to eye on major issues. Perhaps such crises keep writers from being lulled into writing whatever they know will get by their publishers and not infringe too deeply on their consciences. But in these tense situations both publishers and writers can overreact and later regret that they acted precipitously.

Credibility is the only thing a newspaper has to offer in its editorial endorsements. If a staff thinks it can fairly and knowledgeably endorse one candidate over another, it should be able to do so in a credible manner. If, on the other hand, the staff does not know enough about the candidates, or does not see one candidate as better than another, or lacks the fortitude to risk the wrath of unhappy readers, it should not endorse. A major task of the editorial page is to comment knowledgeably on public issues, whether you prefer to call that urging voters or merely informing them. An editorial page staff that sits out an election loses out on a big part of the political process.

■ QUESTIONS AND EXERCISES

1. What do you think should be the role of the editorial page in an election? Should a newspaper endorse candidates?
2. How do you evaluate the argument that endorsements exert undue and undesirable influence on voters?
3. How do you evaluate the argument that the credibility of the news columns is jeopardized when newspapers endorse candidates?
4. Do you think a presidential nominee has legitimate grounds for complaint when newspaper endorsements are lined up four or five to one against him? Why or why not?
5. Could you work on an editorial page that had "publishers' four-year itch"—a congenial editorial policy for almost four years and then for a month or two a policy with which you did not agree?
6. Ask editors of newspapers in your area or state how editorial endorsements are determined on their papers. Who is involved in the decision-making? Who has the last say if there is disagreement?
7. Ask editors to evaluate the comparative impact they think their editorials have on ballot issues vs. candidate races and on local vs. state and national races.
8. Have any papers in your area allowed dissenting editorial staff members to disagree in print with the papers' endorsements? If so, how were the dissents presented? How did the paper explain the presence of more than one opinion? Did publication of the dissent draw comment from readers in the letters column?
9. Find two or more editorials from different newspapers on the same ballot issue or candidate race. Compare their approaches. What type of reader is most likely to be influenced by each approach? For the particular race or issue involved, which editorial do you regard as more appropriate or more likely to influence readers? Why?
10. Write an endorsement editorial that equitably compares two candidates and avoids making a choice between the two until the conclusion. Then rewrite the editorial to make clear from the beginning your choice of candidate. Which was easier to write? Which types of voters are likely to be influenced by each of them?

Other Types of Opinion Writing

Newspaper editorials are not the only type of opinion writing that journalists are likely to have the opportunity to write. In this chapter we will look at:

Signed articles

Local columns

Reviews

Broadcast editorials

■ SIGNED ARTICLES

Editorial writers today have more opportunities than ever before to write signed interpretive and opinion pieces. One reason is that more newspapers are providing additional space—a partial or full page—for opinion articles and artwork. The added page typically is referred to as the op-ed page (the page opposite the editorial page). Another reason is that publishers seem more willing to allow staff writers to put their names on articles that are not intended to be the voice of the newspaper. These articles range from interpretation to analysis to opinion to media criticism.

Personal Opinion

The point made in a personal opinion column may or may not differ from the newspaper's institutional editorial position. The personal column, unlike an anonymous editorial, is likely to be written in first person singular and written in a more personal, informal manner. It may be written, in whole or in part, in a narrative manner. A powerful example of such writing is a column by Myriam Marquez of the *Orlando* (Fla.) *Sentinel* ("Make no mistake: Evil child-abusers should die"). Marquez describes at length the incident that provoked her column, then explains how it affected her.

When parents of teenagers raised objections to a Harry Potter book and a Madonna music video, Mary Pilon took advantage of her position as a member of the Eugene, Ore., *Register-Guard's* 20Below News Team to write a column headlined "Censorship stunts teens' intellectual growth." (The "20Below" section gives space to high

MAKE NO MISTAKE: EVIL CHILD-ABUSERS SHOULD DIE

By Myriam Marquez

The father turned on the oven to 500 degrees and waited. What was going through his mind?

One minute, two, three. Fifteen minutes passed until it was sufficiently hot to suit his purpose.

Then he put on oven mitts, pulled out the oven rack and set it on the floor.

Cold, calculating, evil, the man picked up his 14-month-old baby, who had been stripped of any clothing, and dropped her on the 500-degree rack as if she were a piece of meat to be seared for a meal.

He then cast her aside, propped up the rack by a wall and proceeded to press the baby's back onto the still hot rack, over and over again.

Finally, the man wrapped wet towels around the baby, put some ointment on

> *"I'm queasy about the death penalty because we know that in a few instances innocent people have been fried by Old Sparky. But right now I would like to see this man fry."*

the child's back and waited for her 19-year-old mother, who was at a job interview. After the mother picked up the baby and her older brother Monday, the man took off to a watering-hole for a few stiff ones.

The mother, who doesn't live with the monster, discovered the welts and rushed to the hospital. The baby spent the night crying in a hospital intensive-care unit.

Jerry Gray, 23, admitted to police in a tape-recorded statement Wednesday that he burned his baby girl. Of course, Gray doesn't consider himself cold, calculating, or evil. But how else to describe what he has done?

This was not an incident that involved someone snapping and immediately shaking a baby, a common abuse that can lead to internal bleeding and death.

school team members each Monday for news, feature and opinion pieces that they have written.) Mary wrote that teenagers also have First Amendment rights and ought to be given the opportunity to learn from making mistakes.

Interpretation and Analysis

Frequently much longer than editorials, interpretive or analytical articles may reveal the writers' viewpoints, but their primary purpose is to provide readers with information and insights and, perhaps, to raise questions. In "Church, state should serve different masters," Donald C. Lyons of the Fort Lauderdale, Fla., *Sun-Sentinel* describes Al Gore's and George W. Bush's positions on "faith-based initiatives" for government funding of private social service programs. He identifies some of the problems posed by such funding and offers his opinion that he's "not sure the church as substitute [for government] is the answer."

Media Criticism

In media criticism, the microscope is turned around to examine the job that the newspaper and other media are doing. For an extended discussion of media criticism, see "Media Critics (Reader Advocates, Ombudsmen)" in Chapter 19,

This was not about angrily spanking a child so hard that she falls against the floor and cracks her head open.

Such acts are committed in the heat of the moment. They're wrong, but one at least can understand the immediacy of the rage.

But to turn an oven on, wait a quarter of an hour until it's crackling hot and commit such horror on a defenseless child is beyond comprehension.

I long ago stopped reading newspaper articles (or watching television news) about abused children, because I get too emotional and angry. I feel like grabbing a gun and shooting the abuser dead—or, better, taking a branding iron and putting it—well, this is a family newspaper.

I get frustrated, too, with a child-protection system that puts so much focus on parental rights that children sometimes are returned to parents who aren't fit to raise pigs.

I get sick over public outrage about abused puppies and kitties and boat-scarred manatees—not because I don't like animals but because there seems to be passive public acceptance that child abuse, like cow manure, just happens.

Orange County detective John Moch said Gray told him his daughter "got under his skin and aggravated him to the point that he snapped." The little girl's painful screams in the hospital were enough to make the veteran cop break down and sob before the television cameras as he tried to give a detailed account of what happened.

I'm queasy about the death penalty because we know that in a few instances innocent people have been fried by Old Sparky. But right now I would like to see this man fry. God forgive me.

For evil bullies who abuse children in cold and calculating ways, who tear up little bodies with burns and cuts and bruises, there's no more fitting punishment than death.

Would that be a deterrent for other sicko, evil child-abusers?

Gray faces the possibility of 10 years' imprisonment for each of 30 counts of abuse, but 300 years would be too kind. At the very least, he should be held in a cell with red, hot bars, heated to 500 degrees. He should be tied to those bars and left there to rot.

Orlando Sentinel

"Innovations in Design and Content." As an example, see "Analyses lead readers to subject, don't tell them what to think" by Dan Hortsch of the *Oregonian*.

◼ LOCAL COLUMNS

Topics for local columns come in all descriptions—from silly to serious, from pop culture to politics, from purely personal to profound. When the Portland *Oregonian* published a full-page ad to publicize its columns, it ran pictures of eight men and four women with a line of type that said: "Keep up with everything that's happening from every possible direction." "What interests you?" the ad asked. "Sports? Politics? People? How about money or pop culture? Our columnists cover just about every topic imaginable. That's why it takes so many of them."

Variety of Columnists and Columns

To give some idea of the variety of topics local columnists write about, during one week *Oregonian* columnist Steve Duin wrote about people losing jobs when a local race track changed hands and the way people in Washington, D.C., were responding to the anthrax scare ("too many in Washington are lunging forward instead of stepping back").[3] Another *Oregonian* columnist, Margie Boule, wrote

CENSORSHIP STUNTS TEENS' INTELLECTUAL GROWTH

By Mary Pilon

What do Harry Potter, Madonna and an eighth-grade teacher at Jefferson Middle School have in common? All have been challenged by parents in one way or another.

Parents contend that "Harry Potter and the Sorcerer's Stone" deals with issues of abandonment and endorsed witchcraft. Parents are aghast at Madonna's "Like a Prayer" music video. Recently, a parent complained that a Jefferson teacher made inappropriate comments about slavery.

Where do parents draw the line between morals and mayhem? Who determines what is inappropriate for young people?

Every aspect of teen life has been censored: books (sometimes the same ones assigned by their teachers), television, video games, music, and now more recently, the Internet. Parents are worried about a generation of heathens, raised by rap, trashed with TV, and broken by books ("inappropriate" ones, that is).

Youths "protected" by censorship become incapable of appreciating the difference between independence of thought and dependence on society to tell them what's "right" and what's not.

What kind of future is one full of drones spoon-fed on 18 years of "Sesame Street"?

(Oh, that's raised controversy, too. Mississippi parents objected to the multicultural cast.)

If "Huckleberry Finn," "To Kill a Mockingbird" and "A Wrinkle in Time" are not appropriate reading materials, then what is? Of course, these things could seem inappropriate if teens have never discussed sex, drugs, violence or the darker side of history before.

It's natural for parents to want the best for their children, and it's wonderful that parents are involved in aspects of their budding adolescents' lives. But is shielding somebody from all of society a healthy thing to do?

Censorship brings in stereotypes, too. Not everyone who is pro-censorship is a "right-wing, uptight prude" and not everyone who is anti-censorship is a "liberal, immoral hippie."

I know where I stand on the issue. I'm not a "careless earth muffin"—just a teen who cares about what I'm exposed to. It's ironic that in the battle to be protective and politically correct, people call each other names.

Can people be so politically correct that they're functionally incorrect?

If teens are old enough to be charged as adult criminals, shouldn't they be allowed to choose what they want to read or see or hear?

Most likely, it's not the music/book/Internet site/TV show that make kids shoot classmates,

about a man who flew from New Jersey to claim the recently discovered body of a brother who had disappeared on Mount Adams in 1980, urban-myth e-mails that were circulating after the destruction of the World Trade Center Towers and the tough time local nonprofit groups (such as the Portland Youth Philharmonic) were having in paying increased rental costs to use public school facilities.[4]

It's unlikely that a newspaper not published in a major metropolitan area can afford or find space for a dozen local columnists. But my perusal of medium-sized and even small newspapers suggests that more and more newspapers are hiring their own column writers, and not just to write about food and sports.

The Eugene, Ore., *Register-Guard,* a mid-sized paper, has two general columnists. It is an indication of the attention that columnists receive that, on one day in the letters column, each columnist was the subject of a letter in which a reader took issue with a column. Karen McCowan had researched the owners of properties along a proposed parkway and found they were members of a commit suicide or get pregnant. It's the lack of discussion around these issues.

Instead of protesting the issues of sex and isolation in Judy Blume's books, parents could use the books as a springboard for discussion. The American Library Association reports 6,364 book challenges in the past decade. It would be interesting to know how many teens objected to books compared to their parents.

Last week, a parent of a middle-schooler complained about a teacher who referred to herself as a "slavemaster" and her student as her "slave" while teaching her students about the Civil War. The teacher publicly apologized and will be evaluated to see if she will lose her job.

Although referring to students as "slaves" is not acceptable, the teacher recognized her actions and took responsibility.

It's easy to blow things out of proportion when somebody gets offended. Racism should not be taken lightly, but what's too easily overlooked is the 23 years of dedicated teaching.

For every parent who complains of moral garbage, there must be a teen-ager who looks at something "indecent" and interprets it differently. Some teens are renewing beliefs in abstinence after seeing Britney Spears' music videos on MTV. A young attorney might be inspired by Atticus Finch in "To Kill a Mockingbird." Does banning something cause more harm, or good?

I don't believe that teens should start hitting up porno sites, dressing like the skankiest music artist or watching 20 hours of TV a day. But teens should have the right to choose what they want to be exposed to.

Sometimes I wonder what would happen if books and Internet sites were given ratings; such as is done with video games, TV shows and movies. Then, teens and their parents could monitor what they're exposed to. Who knows? Maybe, ratings could even inspire independent thinking (gasp!).

Learning from mistakes is important. But the mistakes don't necessarily have to be our own. How many teens read "Go Ask Alice" (the anonymous and brutally honest diary of a drug addict) and then go buy heroin so they can be just like the depressed and tormented Alice? These are issues that can't be solved by taking a book off a shelf, boycotting a TV show or tuning out a song.

The bottom line is that people have individual rights. Those rights were guaranteed by America's founders in the U.S. Constitution (I'm sure that in the 1700s, people wanted to ban that, too). But these are individual rights, not the right to determine what is acceptable for an entire culture.

If something is offensive, don't read, watch, listen or visit it. It's simple.

No one can make parents embrace Harry Potter, Madonna or even a teacher. But parents don't have the right to censor them for the rest of us.   *Register-Guard*

---

group pushing a ballot proposition that favored the parkway. The letter writer pointed out that these property owners weren't the only ones who had an interest in the parkway.[5] Another writer accused columnist Bob Welch of simplicity in choosing between "pacifism and military force" when he said he was "bothered by a chorus of cries from letter writers who don't seem to have taken Sept. 11 personally enough."[6]

In 1998–99 *The Masthead* ran a six-part series titled "Trailblazers" in which the editors introduced "women and people of color [who] have been bringing new and welcome perspectives to editorial pages and broadcast studios." All the "trailblazers" were or had been columnists on local newspapers. At least three have been syndicated. Columns written by two of the six (Myriam Marquez and Donald C. Lyons) were reproduced earlier in this section as examples, respectively, of a personal column and an interpretive column. One of the others, Joe Rodriquez, an editorial writer/columnist with the *San Jose Mercury News*,

CHURCH, STATE SHOULD SERVE DIFFERENT MASTERS

By Donald C. Lyons

Thank God Martin wasn't hamstrung by a government "faith-based initiative." Imagine what might have been if the young Baptist minister not-yet civil rights leader had to risk public funding that paid for a popular community program operating out of his church by participating in the Montgomery bus boycott.

Rosa Parks might still be at the back of the bus. King was fortunate. He never had to worry about his church's 501(c)3 tax status, government auditors, grant contracts, site visits, and year-end reports. Ministers today aren't so lucky.

Many churches now have separate nonprofit agencies that accept government funding and private contributions to operate an array of social service programs.

If the two presidential frontrunners have their way, the church's government agency role will only increase.

Vice President Al Gore and Texas Governor George W. Bush are pushing for a new partnership between church and state as part of their campaigns in the 2000 presidential race. The pair's proposals resonate with faith and values. What better litmus test is there than using the vast resources of government to strengthen the good works of the church?

It may work for the candidates, but this latest wave of campaign promises called "faith-based initiatives" contain potential pitfalls for two very important institutions—the church and the state.

Gore the Democrat wants to "scale up" the role of faith-based organizations, extend the 1996 welfare reform law to enlist more churches in the fight to move people from welfare to work, and wants corporations to give and match more contributions to faith-based organizations.

Bush the Republican wants to transform the role of government to the point where it first turns to faith-based organizations, charities, and community groups to help people in need. He'd create a White House "Office of Faith-Based Action" and spend $8 billion to expand the role of faith-based charities

provides an example of a local column with a local angle. In "City hall's spending policies leave 10-year-old boy holding his nose," Rodriguez contrasts conditions in a neglected neighborhood center with those in "one of San Jose's most desirable neighborhoods" and questions the city's spending priorities.

Characteristics of a Local Column

The variety of the columns and columnists mentioned in the previous section should suggest that it is not easy to characterize local column writing. It covers a wide gamut. Still, some devices are common:

First person—Columnists frequently use "I" in their columns, sometimes to express what they think, sometimes to describe a personal experience.

Narrative form—A favorite approach is to describe events in a chronological order, telling a story to make a point.

Opening example—A columnist may capture readers by starting with a dramatic, startling or heartwarming example of the point the columnist wants to make.

Direct quotes—Quotations tend to enliven a column and make the people involved seem more real.

and other community groups in delivering social services.

Churches and other faith-based organizations could benefit from tax breaks intended to spur greater contributions from businesses and individuals.

But anyone who believes in good government and the even higher calling of the church should be leery about any government initiatives that blur the important roles of church and state.

The two should serve different masters. Religious institutions remind individuals that they are accountable to a far greater power, more important than government regulations, international law, societal mores, and life itself. Relying on public funding can make religious institutions dependent on the government, a new form of welfare and regulation that churches don't need. Faith-based initiatives can also undermine the church's advocacy role. A minister may have a hard time calling for meaningful change if his convictions to a higher calling are questioned by an influential politician or an impersonal bureaucrat who holds a hefty government grant over the

church. Government is primarily responsible for administering needed services to its citizens. Clearly, the state has its problems, but I'm not sure the church as substitute is the answer.

Government agencies have been buffeted, and ultimately diminished, by changing public attitudes. A government job used to mean a prestigious career of public service. Now there's little prestige in being a bureaucrat, and the public testimonies linking a gig in government with the ideal of public service are few and far between.

The demonization of government has to stop. Pouring more public money into a religious organization in hopes it will do a better job than its public counterpart strains credibility.

Attracting men and women who truly believe in the principles of accountability, faith, love, and service from faith-based organizations into government service will have a far greater impact on society.

More importantly, it should restore a bit of badly needed faith in both the church and state.

Sun-Sentinel

Dialogue—Columnists sometimes use an "I said"—"he said" or a "he said"—"she said" format.

Local angle—Local columnists write about local affairs and local people, and may also use the local angle to comment on national and international issues.

Not an editorial—Columns generally are not written in the more formal manner of an editorial. With some exceptions, columnists do not engage in the amount of research expected of editorial writers. The opinions may not reflect the editorial policies of the newspaper.

News columns—Personal columns often run on the news pages in the left- or right-hand column of page one of the local section. Even though the columns may run alongside the news, any faithful reader knows that there is no shortage of attitude or opinion, or spice, in a good local column.

Personality—Over time a skilled columnist's personality will emerge. Some readers will respond favorably, others unfavorably, to what is said and how it is said. The worst thing that can happen to a columnist is to be boring.

Unpredictability—Of course columnists have their own favorite topics and axes to grind, but one mark of a successful column is that readers are constantly surprised by what's being written about and how it's being written.

ANALYSES LEAD READERS TO SUBJECT, DON'T TELL THEM WHAT TO THINK

By Dan Hortsch, The Public Editor

The strike by nurses at Oregon Health & Science University reached a tentative settlement last week. A ratification vote was scheduled for today.

In last Sunday's Business section, Joe Rojas-Burke, one of three reporters who has covered the strike closely, examined how the strike might be ended. The body of the story detailed a half-dozen potential resolutions to key issues.

That discussion was built on a foundation of weeks of detailed reporting on the issues and the individuals on both sides of the strike. It was straightforward enough that it might have been considered a good background story, but it also reflected the reporter's accumulated understanding of the issues.

As a result, the piece carried a red "analysis" label to signal to readers that the article was something more than straight news coverage.

All well and good.

Except: The lead paragraphs of the piece appeared to go beyond analysis. In fact, they appeared to be the writer's opinion.

The article began, "Enough with the nurses' strike." It went on to say "enough" with nurses on picket lines instead of at bedsides; "enough" with huge outlays by the medical center to fight the strike. The fourth paragraph read, "This has got to stop."

Such an assertion is appropriate on the editorial page as an opinion or in a signed column. However, it reaches beyond the concept of "analysis."

Andre Meunier, the assistant business editor who worked with Rojas-Burke on the story, said the intent of the opening paragraphs was not to utter the reporter's opinion.

Rather, he said, he and Rojas-Burke wanted to reflect "the sentiment we were picking up from both sides" as an introduction to the specifics of the piece.

That intention was not clear.

Just what is an analysis in newspaper journalism? Editors at The Oregonian describe it in different words, but they arrive at much the same place.

Sandy Rowe, editor of The Oregonian, said it is "interpretation and explanation of the significance of facts, events or situations." Bob Caldwell, editor of the editorial page, called it "a story about what something means."

Bruce Hammond, Politics Team editor, said an analysis "allows us to shine different lights on a subject at the same time." That is, to see a situation from various perspectives.

In another recent example from this newspaper, John Harvey, senior editor in charge of the National/International Team, selected an analysis piece following President Bush's State of the Union address to run in Jan. 30 editions.

It appeared on Page One along with a news story describing the address. The text of the address appeared on an inside page. That is how The Oregonian typically uses analyses: to supplement, not substitute for, news coverage.

The analysis looked at Bush's dual challenge: to "prevail as a wartime leader and resurrect the economy." Harvey said that particular piece was as much straight news reporting as it was analysis.

Readers might wonder why editors publish analyses on news pages. The answer lies in using the knowledge of reporters who cover a beat and know an issue or situation inside and out.

Rojas-Burke, along with reporters Don Colbum and Wendy Lawton, have been eating and sleeping strike issues. Political writers and other reporters who delve deeply into given topics, often for months at a time, build up a similar knowledge and perspective.

Such reporters can offer a wide-angle perspective.

The trick, not an easy one, is to stick within the boundaries of educated discussion and interpretation, while not lapsing into personal opinion.

In the end, of course, readers think for themselves. A good analytical piece might help them do that. *Oregonian*

CITY HALL'S SPENDING POLICIES LEAVE 10-YEAR-OLD BOY HOLDING HIS NOSE

After much nose-holding, the parks and recreation department wangled more cleaning money from the city council.

By Joe Rodriguez

At the tender age of 10, Jacob Ramos already has a sharp eye for the hypocrisies of our city's spending priorities.

One day not long ago, he was sitting with about 30 other children in an after-school program at the Olinder Neighborhood Center in central San Jose. By then, the children had noticed a few rotten things about the city-run center, the worst being the old and smelly restrooms.

After-school director Eva Chavez was giving Jacob and the other children a self-esteem pep talk, which are all the rage these days in public education.

"You children are all special," Chavez said to them. "Don't ever forget that."

Afterward, Jacob approached her.

"Mrs. Chavez?" he asked. "If we're so special, how come the bathrooms are so bad?"

Chavez didn't know how to respond.

"I felt so contradictory," she said. "I didn't have an answer."

I visited Jacob and the center this week. Jacob was right. The boys and girls restrooms, which are shared daily with adults, simply stink. The tired, old fans cannot filter out the smell. The toilet seats are broken. The corroded faucets have turned green, the molding around the sinks is black.

Outside, Jacob played on an old jungle gym and socked a tetherball posted on the cracked concrete play-ground. The drinking fountains were stopped up.

Jacob told me another story. He and his younger brother Gabriel recently visited a public park across the city in Willow Glen, one of the San Jose's most desirable neighborhoods.

"Everything was nice and new," Jacob said. "When we came back here to play, Gabriel started crying. He didn't like our playground anymore."

OK, so I'm giving you heart-tugging anecdotes that get the public riled up. City Hall's always a big, fat target. I plead guilty to making an emotional argument, but not with apology, because Jacob's observations underscore the broad consequences of San Jose's spending priorities.

For 20 years, City Hall lavished attention and money—about $1 billion—on big, flashy, prestige-building projects downtown in hopes of attracting business, arts, and industry to the city. Some projects succeeded, others failed, but the downtown was saved.

To be fair, most of that "redevelopment" money was restricted to blighted areas, such as downtown. And the city spent some on run-down neighborhood business districts. But overall, I think City Hall became obsessed with big-ticket projects, and gave neighborhood services second-class priority.

Until last year, the restrooms at most city neighborhood centers and parks were cleaned only twice a week. You can imagine the consequences. After much nose-holding, the parks and recreation department wangled more cleaning money from the city council.

I'm told Olinder's restrooms are cleaned four times a week. Better, but nothing to cheer about. The restrooms at City Hall are cleaned each day.

More to the point, things should never have deteriorated so badly. You can only do so much to clean up old restrooms. Olinder's facilities desperately need a major overhaul, but it's not a priority.

What is a top priority is a brand-new, $255 million City Hall building downtown. Hmm. I wonder if its restrooms will have marble sinks and brass faucets?

Some will argue that second-class status in booming San Jose is better than second-class

continued

---

concluded

in declining Detroit. But as Tip O'Neill once said of politics, all inequality is local.

With the fresh eyes of youth, Jacob Ramos and his classmates see the inequalities in front of them every day, and no amount of self-esteem pep talks can hide the reality from them.

San Jose Mercury News

■ REVIEWS

Reviews can range from A to Z, from art exhibitions to the opening of a new zoo. Books, television, films, theater, dance, music and art are most commonly reviewed in newspapers. Writers associated with the editorial page are most likely to be called upon to write book reviews.

The reviewer's task is not much different from the editorial writer's. All the advice about opinion writing offered in Chapters 10 and 11 applies to review writing. Reviewers have two responsibilities: to briefly describe to their readers the subject of their review and then to comment on the subject. Beyond that, writers are relatively free to organize their reviews as they wish.

The purpose of a review is not just to pronounce a production "good" or "bad," but to describe, explain and evaluate. Laura Reina, in an article in *Editor &Publisher,* asked why the "blurbs" for movies in newspaper ads rarely cited newspaper reviewers. Most come from television and other sources. Her explanation was that it is difficult, and unfair, to reduce to a few words "a review that took a lot of time to write" and that broadcast critics seem less critical and more ambitious to get a name.[7]

In writing reviews, a writer should keep in mind both the background and sophistication of the reading audience as well as the level of professionalism of the artists, authors or performers being reviewed. Reviews are likely to be more elaborate and scholarly in the weekly book section of the *New York Times* than on the book page of the *Roanoke Times*. Similarly, amateur performances should not be expected to meet the standards of professional productions.

If the subject matter itself is likely to catch the reader's eye, the reviewer might begin with a description of what the play is about. Martin F. Kohn of the *Detroit Free Press* did that in writing about a play titled "The Glow of Reflected Light":

> Slavery was a horror, but in 1832, when Stepsu Aakhu's "The Glow of Reflected Light" takes place, freedom wasn't much of an improvement for many black Americans.[8]

An alternative is to start with a provocative comment or evaluation. Christine Dolen of the *Miami Herald* left no doubt about how she evaluated a play by Neil Simon:

> Walk into the downstairs theater at Actors' Playhouse to see Neil Simon's "Proposals" and before the play begins, you'll discover the best part about it: M.P. Amico's set.[9]

In most instances, before proceeding more than a sentence or two, reviewers should provide a very brief description of what they are reviewing. After they get an idea of what the review is about, readers want to know what the reviewer thought of the subject of the review. They may even scan the review for a quick indication of the reviewer's evaluation. Here are some examples of how reviewers found ways to praise a production:

> From the opening statement by the clarinets, dark-toned and seamless, to the triumphant finale with plenty of bite in the brass, this was music-making as impressive as anything [the Seattle Orchestra had done all year].[10]

> "The 1940s Radio Hour" is one of the most successful shows of this sort. The songs are well chosen, and the dramatic framework by Walton Jones is genuinely appealing.[11]

Here are some examples of how reviewers found critical things to say:

> "The Guys," like the healing process it dramatizes, is still a work in progress.[12]

> You can't blame director David Ariso or the actors for the deficiencies of "Proposals." They may have wanted to construct a Rolls Royce, but Simon has given them the parts of a scooter.[13]

> . . . to an American audience, this two-hour-long, disconnected ramble about people and events from a time in history that means little to the rebel country is boring business.[14]

Most reviews contain a mix of praise and criticism. Here are examples of where the mix occurs within one or a few sentences:

> The Mesa choreography isn't as polished as the film's—then, again, it took Hollywood director Stanley Donan nearly two weeks to shoot the movie dance.[15]

> *The Adventures of Stanley Tomorrow* is a sweet little play about fathers and sons that takes a while to get into, but delivers a wallop at the end.[16]

A word of advice for reviewers: Don't pretend to know more than you do. Until you become more knowledgeable and sophisticated, stick primarily to sketching the plot, identifying the principals and making comments that are likely to interest general readers. Even as your expertise grows, don't forget these readers.

To be persuasive, reviews should appear to be fair and logical. Scathing reviews, like flamboyant editorials, may be fun to read, but emotion is less likely to be convincing than statements of fact and careful evaluations. In warning reviewers against "heavily negative reviews," William L. Rivers wrote, ". . . whatever the value of a book, be aware that the author has suffered the agonies of the creative process that you could not possibly know about. Think of the author as an individual who, in the middle of writing, may spend 'endless' periods scratching deep grooves on the table before him or her, waiting for the right words to present themselves."[17]

Film and Theater

Tim Bywater and Thomas Sobchack have described the reviews that appear in most newspapers as "journalistic reviews."[18] The reviewer generally is writing about a single film (or play or other cultural event) for readers, most of whom have not seen the production. Usually reviewers are "working journalists writing on a deadline, with no special qualifications except [in the case of film] consistent film viewing of weekly releases."[19] The purpose of such reviews is to give

BECOMING AMERICAN
'Immigrant' a celebration of humanity

By John Moore, Denver Post Theater Critic

Monday, January 28, 2002 —The Denver Center Theatre Company's heroic world premiere of "The Immigrant" is a journey as emotionally moving for the audience as its lead character's move from Belarus to Texas.

Somehow this sentimental, old-fashioned musical that tells a simple turn-of-the century story of friendship and assimilation turns out to be a more powerful and meaningful exposition on the roots of racism and our common American humanity than the incendiary manipulation of those subjects on the stage right next door.

"The Immigrant," a sweeping adaptation of Mark Harelik's acclaimed 1985 play about his grandparents' immigration to America in 1909, is a buoyant, heartbreaking achievement that renders the infantile "Spinning Into Butter" at the Ricketson inconsequential.

Randal Myler's remarkable production is a 10-minute tightening and an occasionally insipid lyric from perfection, but its simple goodness resonates much longer than its 2-hour-45-minute running time.

The story centers on young Haskell Harelik (Adam Heller), who comes to Hamilton, Texas, in 1909 and is taken in by Milton and Ima, an older couple (Walter Charles and Cass Morgan) whose humanity

quashes their own prejudices. Haskell sends for his wife, Leah (Jacqueline Antaramian), and the sweeping story takes us through 1942 while addressing issues of assimilation, religion and friendship.

This is Haskell's story, but it is all of our stories. Harelik's banana-peddling grandfather in Texas could have been my potato-peddling Irish grandfather in Oklahoma. It could have been about Cubans in Florida or Asians in California. Everyone came from somewhere. "The Immigrant" speaks to what it means to become an American, and how we are treated by those whose only real claim to superiority comes from having gotten here first.

The story has just four characters, but Myler's production brings five to life. The fifth is Texas itself, which is made into a living, undulating entity in a masterful collaboration between set designer Ralph Funicello and lighting designer Don Darnutzer. The stage floor's wheatgrass-lined, rolling prairie blends into a painted horizon inspired by "Road to Ambrose," a portrait of the unspoiled Texas landscape by Carl Rice Embry. Darnutzer uses simple lighting techniques that breathe life into this beautiful painting, complete with

general readers some idea of whether they will want to spend their time and money on what is being reviewed. If the performance is past, a review can help readers decide whether to attend future productions of the group or theater.

Readers want to know, first, what the film or play is about. They want to know whether it is a mystery, comedy or musical. They expect a brief description of the plot (without giving away surprises, of course). They want to know who the producers, the directors and the performers are.

Only after they have some idea of whether they are interested in the performance do they concern themselves with the reviewer's opinion (even if that opinion appears early in the review).

The last statement is not intended to suggest all comment should be reserved for the end of the review. As Irving Wardle has noted, "Reviewers soon learn to write to length, knowing that if they overwrite, it is their opinions that rolling clouds, soft night scenes and picturesque sunrises and sunsets.

The quality of the cast cannot be overstated. The endearing Cass Morgan is as warm as a freshly baked loaf of bread. Milton is an imperfect hero, a banker who risks his own safety to do right by this curious stranger. In the older couple's hearts, the immigrants take the place of their own lost son.

DCTC newcomer Adam Heller is such an earnest and enthusiastic Haskell he'll draw comparisons to a young Tevya from "Fiddler on the Roof." He's really more a middle-aged Motel ("Miracle of Miracles"). Heller sells Harelik to the audience as effectively as his character sells the virtues of bananas to the people of Hamilton.

Antaramian is a sensational actress with the doleful voice of an angel in mourning. When Leah arrives, she communicates sweetness, regret and fear before opening her mouth. She brings with her an unborn child and important cultural issues, such as how she is to raise a Jewish child in a town that has none. How do you adapt to a new world without throwing away your essence?

All four voices are majestic, but Antaramian can sing you into your sweetest memory.

One of "The Immigrant's" strengths is its mature portrayal of friendship. Haskell and Milton overcome age, language, race, religion and economic barriers to become father and son. Leah misses her mother in Minsk as deeply as Ima misses her son, and over time each fills the void in the other. The play's inherent sadness is in showing us our capacity to hurt most not those we hate but those we love the most.

The debate over the production will center on whether the musical improves or detracts from the play that in 1991 was the most-produced in America, and the answer will depend on personal taste. Music inherently softens moments of dramatic spoken power, but also mines emotional terrain to much greater depths. It's doubtful the original extracted as many hankies as the musical.

The light, complicated score by Steven Alper and Sarah Knapp blends easily into the action and accentuates the most powerful moments, such as the signature song "The Stars (God Is in the Dark)." Antaramian's songs are appropriately Eastern European folk in nature ("I Don't Want This") while Ima's are more Southern spiritual ("Take the Comforting Hand of Jesus"), all masterfully played by Kimberly Grigsby's four-person, string-based orchestra.

When the musical ended, I could have used a few more seconds before the lights went up. You'd have to be rootless and ruthless not to give in to it.

Denver Post

will be cut, while all the plottery will be left intact." His advice: "merging the usually segregated categories of fact and comment; a procedure not always appreciated by sub-editors into whose hands the copy . . . falls at dead of night."[20] When the editor begins whacking, for space or other reasons, according to Wardle, the first to go is "colour," then opinion, finally plot. The solution (and a more interesting one, from the reader's point of view) is to include "colour" and comment as the plot is described.[21]

In reviewing a performance of the musical play, "Becoming American," John Moore of the *Denver Post* wove commentary, evaluation and description through the first half of the review. The reader learns that this is a "sentimental, old-fashioned musical," "a sweeping adaptation" and "a remarkable production." In the second half the reviewer went into more detail about the music and the performances of the characters.

Commentary is not just a matter of scoring from 1 to 10 (although movies commonly are rated with stars). The reviewer should strive to project a personality and write in an interesting, witty manner. (Note the deeply personal comment in the last line of Moore's review.) One reason for writing in an individualistic, distinctive manner, of course, is to attract readers in the first place. It is just as important for the regular reviewer to establish a reputation, even for liking certain types of productions and disliking others. When readers become accustomed to a reviewer, they have some idea of whether they will like a production based on whether they usually agree or disagree with that reviewer's evaluations.

Concerts

Reviews of concerts serve a somewhat different purpose. Reviews of single performances are primarily evaluative, not prescriptive. Readers who were present are interested in comparing their impressions with the reviewer's. Those who were not there may be either glad or sad they did something else that evening. Both sets of readers, however, benefit if a reviewer's comments help them decide whether to attend future performances of the same group.

In reviewing the performance of a 24-year-old Atlanta singer whom readers probably had not heard about ("That ol' John Mayer ain't what he's going to be"), Ralph Berrier Jr. of the *Roanoke* (Va.) *Times* used his first paragraph to liken John Mayer to Jakob Dylan, Dave Matthews, Jimi Hendricks and Stevie Ray. The review wasn't entirely laudatory, using phrases such as "passable modern rock," "although well-intentioned . . . red flags," "a style that's been done absolutely to death," "breezy melodies." Yet the reviewer also said Mayer was "is already a fine wordsmith with a clever, mature lyric sheet," with "the stage presence of a 20-year veteran" and good prospects for the future. The reviewer obviously was telling his readers that this was a young man to watch.

Reviewers may run the greatest risk of getting in over their heads in covering musical events. They need to know about the music and the composer, but also (at least with familiar music) how passages and instruments should sound. Unfamiliar works may be even harder to interpret. Immediately before performances, however, some conductors provide brief explanations to audience members (and reviewers) who come early.

Books

Readers expect book reviewers to comment on the subject matter of the book, the organization, the comparative emphasis given to parts of the book, the quality of the writing, the qualifications of the author, and the adequacy and reliability of the contents. Reviewers should try to explain what the author intended to accomplish with the book and evaluate how well the author accomplished this purpose.

In "Shifting from dollars to sense," Carl Sessions Stepp, writing in *American Journalism Review*, used the image of a video game monster in an attempt to attract readers to a review of "an expensive, scholarly book published by a university press . . . [that] may not get a lot of attention." Sessions writes that the basic point of the book, in the authors' words, is that "news has become secondary, even incidental, to markets and revenues and margins and advertisers and consumer preferences." He summarizes six reasons that these practices "have taken root so deeply," then briefly mentions four suggestions for making changes at the "structural level." By highlighting the problems and the

THAT OL' JOHN MAYER AIN'T WHAT HE'S GOING TO BE
The 24-year-old Atlanta singer played to
a sold-out crowd of about 400 at Roanoke College.

By Ralph Berrier Jr.

It's no wonder John Mayer's generating such a buzz among young music fans and graying rock critics. He looks a little like Jakob Dylan, he sounds a lot like Dave Matthews and he slings guitar solos like he's conjured the spirit of Jimi as channeled through Stevie Ray.

Those strengths were evident when the 24-year-old Atlanta performer played to a sold-out crowd of about 400, mostly college-aged fans Saturday at Roanoke College's Alumni Gym.

Mayer's two-hour show drew heavily upon his major-label release "Room for Squares," and it followed an hour of passable modern rock of openers The Clarks from Pittsburgh.

The biggest among many crowd favorites were "Why Georgia," "No Such Thing" and "3x5." His humor was evident during "83," a song devoted to childhood nostalgia (which is quite a concept for someone who's 24) and littered with verses from Cyndi Lauper's "Girls Just Want To Have Fun," Matthew Wilder's "Break My Stride" and Kool and the Gang's "Joanna." His acoustic take on the Police's "Message in a Bottle" was as good as the version Sting played at the Roanoke Civic Center last year.

The Dave Matthews comparisons, although well-intentioned, raise bright-red flags. Mayer's singing and playing talents are irrefutable, but his songwriting is just as obviously derivative of Matthews-esque groove rock, a style that's been done absolutely to death.

Also, rather than being built upon classic, shout-it-out-loud hooks that stay with you in your sleep, most of his songs rely upon breezy melodies washing over occasional Elvis Costello-ish chord and key changes. He's already a fine wordsmith with a clever, mature lyric sheet longer than any artist this side of Eminem.

If there's a single attribute that loosens him from comparisons that shackle him, it's his attitude. He has the stage presence of a 20-year veteran. Mayer talks almost nonstop between songs, telling stories from his brief college career when he was the guy at the party with his guitar and all anybody wanted to hear him play was Pearl Jam.

If he produces the songs that match his estimable talents, he won't be playing college gyms much longer.

Roanoke Times

proposed solutions, the reviewer attempted to make the main points of the book accessible to the non-expert reader.

■ BROADCAST EDITORIALS

Should broadcast station owners feel the same responsibility that newspaper publishers feel to provide for exchanges of opinion on issues of the day?

A strong "yes" was the answer by Boyd A. Levet, then of KGW-TV, Portland, and the last president of the National Broadcast Editorial Association, even as his organization was preparing to disband because of a decline in broadcast editorial writing across the country. "Opinion is part of the full venue of journalism," Levet wrote in *The Editorialist*. "I know of no newspaper that earned community respect without opinion. Clearly stations diminish their journalistic influence if they do not air opinion."[22]

SHIFTING FROM DOLLARS TO SENSE
Taking Stock: Journalism and the Publicly Traded News Company
By Gilbert Cranberg, Randall Bezanson and John Soloski
Iowa State University Press, 212 pages; $49.95

By Carl Sessions Stepp

Have you ever played one of those bedeviling video games where you're trapped in a dangerous chamber, monsters closing in, and you're saved only after discovering a magic sword hidden somewhere that in retrospect seems fiendishly obvious?

"Taking Stock" may remind you of those games. Its authors, looking in obvious but relatively unexplored territory, identify several potential swords that could help reform today's corporatized news media.

Cranberg, Bezanson and Soloski are scholars with strong connections to journalism, and they are devotees of public-service news. Here, they choose to take on big journalism on its own terms—as business. By carefully examining the structures and inner workings of 17 publicly traded newspaper companies, they pinpoint key levers that might be used to induce change.

In the rush of media criticism being generated these days, it isn't easy to be original. But this approach is fresh and elegantly simple. Using documents, interviews and data, much of it in the public domain, the authors compile detailed financial and organizational information about the companies: how their stock is distributed, how their boards are composed and compensated, how their executives are rewarded, how their business strategies are promulgated.

Then, playing off this base of evidence, they offer pragmatic suggestions for rescuing public-service journalism through reforms at the corporate level.

This is an expensive, scholarly book published by a university press. It may not get a lot of attention, and who knows if its suggestions will actually work? But it deserves widespread consideration.

To begin, it is direct in defining the problem. Investor ownership is "indifferent to news or, more disturbingly, its quality," the authors write, turning papers into vehicles "controlled for financial performance, not news quality."

"News is no longer the focus of the newspaper. . . . Instead, news has become secondary, even incidental, to markets and revenues and margins and advertisers and consumer preferences."

These changes, the authors argue, are "compromising the newspaper's continued role as a fiercely independent source of information and opinion. . . . in a free, democratic, capitalist society."

Specifically, they are triggering reductions in news staffs, breakdowns in the wall between news and business, and compromises in the independence of news judgment. More and more, the goal becomes providing desirable audiences to advertisers rather than providing vital information to readers.

These developments have been well documented elsewhere, but "Taking Stock" provides a new layer of specifics, helping explain why they have taken root so deeply:

Broadcast editorials "show that the station is directly involved in the community—sufficiently involved to be willing to share management's opinions about community issues and events," G. Donald Gale, then of KSL-TV in Salt Lake City, wrote in a *Masthead* article titled "The Need for Broadcast Editorials."[23]

"The editorial is the most mature form of journalism," Daniel W. Toohey wrote, referring specifically to public broadcasting. "Without the right to

■ The boards of newspaper companies often lack journalistic sensibilities. "Of the 131 outside directors on the boards of the 17 companies, only 17 (13 percent) have had experience on the editorial side of a news organization."

■ Board members benefit from financial performance rather than improvements in quality.

■ Compensation of newspaper managers, including news executives, is tied to financial growth "Nearly three-fourths of the editors weinterviewed receive stock options."

■ Institutional investors such as banks and mutual funds are disproportionately influential. "For 14 of the 17 companies, institutional investors owned a majority of the publicly traded stock."

■ Changes in SEC rules allow "Institutional investors to speak among themselves, to join forces (informally) and present a united front" to newspaper managers.

■ Big investors and the stock analysts who serve them have easy access and influence. "I can get a meeting with s e n i o r management . . . any time I want," one analyst told the authors.

The authors are not naïve revolutionaries ("News is a business" is the book's first sentence), and they do credit several companies, notably McClatchy, Dow Jones, the Washington Post and the New York Times, for developing organizational structures that help insulate them from the worst market pressures.

But in general they show a systemic shift of power toward the business mindset and away from the culture of news.

We have two choices, the authors say: Accept this shift, or "seek change at the structural level." They select option two, and they issue, among others, the following suggestions:

Newspaper boards should have at least one independent journalist. Compensation for board members and news executives should be based on circulation and journalistic quality, not market performance. Laws should be changed to explicitly authorize directors to consider good journalism and community service in making business decisions. And federal authorities should revise regulations that give institutional investors "access to corporate information not generally available to the public" and undue influence on policy.

Without much fanfare, the authors also float an inflammatory suggestion: that the problem may require government intervention.

That they are prepared to crack open this can suggests how deeply passions are running. It was fear of government that prompted the media to move toward greater social responsibility after World War II, and maybe that fear is in the air again.

Overall, "Taking Stock" represents good research and constructive thinking. While the authors are mostly silent on how to enact their recommendations, the logic of their approach is persuasive. Whether or not they have found the magic sword, their ideas could give reformers a fighting chance.

American Journalism Review

editorialize, public broadcasting will be relegated to permanent adolescence."[24] He could have said the same about private broadcasting, although public stations have been more reluctant to editorialize than private stations.

In spite of these admonitions, broadcast editorials have been in decline. A 1978 survey found that 61 percent of television stations editorialized. A survey in 1994 found that only 33 percent did.[25] A 1999 survey found only 18 percent.[26] As further evidence, in 1982, the National Broadcast Editorial Association (NBEA) had 188 members. The number had declined to 65 in 1991, when the NBEA disbanded and surviving members were urged to join the National Conference of Editorial Writers (NCEW).[27] The 2001 *NCEW Membership Directory* listed only nine members associated with the broadcast industry.

The international broadcast journal *Electronic Media* has run editorials urging "the vanishing TV editorial and urged stations, especially those owned by groups, to demonstrate their new, but real interest in the community by taking the bold approach of trying to lead, through editorials."[28] But according to Neil Heinen of WISC-TV in Madison, Wis., "appeals to show leadership seem to be falling on deaf ears—or at least deaf pocketbooks—despite widespread acknowledgment that local news and information is a local station's chief franchise."[29]

The 1999 survey found that about one-third of the stations that did not run editorials reported that they were philosophically opposed to editorializing. Lack of financial resources also was frequently cited.[30] Another reason for few broadcast editorials was suggested by Tom Bryson of WJRT-TV in Flint, Mich.: "[T]he majority of managers who run television stations today may be less inclined to write editorials because they come largely from fields outsider the news environment, namely sales."[31]

The 1999 survey found some positive signs, however. One cable system had begun to editorialize (presumably Cablevision, the only cable system with NCEW members). One television owner (Raycom) had instructed its stations to editorialize.[32]

The networks have beaten a retreat from editorial comment. With the death of Eric Sevareid (CBS), the retirement of John Chancellor (NBC) and the stepping down of Bill Moyers (PBS), network editorials have disappeared.[33] One reason cited by a producer who worked with Sevareid was that it is a rare person who has the stature to do the job.[34] At both network and local levels, commentary has been squeezed out because of time limitations. With only 22 (or fewer) minutes available on a nightly news broadcast, news directors resist setting aside a minute or two for a talking head.[35]

The demise of the Fairness Doctrine has been cited as another reason for the decline in broadcast editorializing. In 1941 the Federal Communications Commission (FCC) ruled in the "Mayflower Decision" that a station should not be an advocate (state an opinion). In 1949 the FCC changed its mind but admonished stations to provide a reasonable opportunity for airing all sides of controversial issues. That was the beginning of what became known as the Fairness Doctrine. As part of their public service requirement, stations were expected to provide a balanced presentation of views (including their own) over the course of their broadcast schedule. In 1987 the FCC dropped the Fairness Doctrine. Consequently, "[a]s the regulatory touch grew lighter, and as stations look for ways to cut cost, cutting editorials was a way to save money," Nicholas DeLuca of KCBS-AM of San Francisco told *Quill* magazine.[36]

One of the strongest statements supporting broadcast editorializing came from Frank Stanton, one-time president of CBS: "Any station manager worth his salt will learn the law, hire the people, sacrifice the time, explore the issues, risk corporate or governmental intervention and welcome adverse public opinion to have said on his station what he thinks needs to—and ought—be said. And if he does not care enough, perhaps because he is afraid of losing sponsors, offending public opinion, or creating problems with stockholders, then he does not deserve the job."[37]

Broadcast vs. Print

Journalists who write in broadcast style are admonished to

- Keep it "short and simple."
- Write in a conversational style. Make points quickly and clearly. Use short, easily comprehended words.

The result of this type of writing, in the view of a surveyed group of newspaper editorial writers, is likely to be a broadcast editorial that is superficial, oversimplified and lacking in guts. But the broadcast editorial writers who were surveyed expressed a different view. They contended that brief editorials were not necessarily superficial, and that broadcast, especially television, offers a more personal, dynamic approach to opinion than the print media do.[38]

One television writer contended that, because television writers face strict time limitations and must make every section count, broadcast editorials are "just the opposite" of superficial. Television writers "must condense the issue and get more meaning in less time."[39] Television also tends to emphasize personality over content. Television audiences often pay more attention to the inflections, apparel, facial features and personality of the messenger than they do to the message.[40] Another characteristic of broadcast is that listeners can't reread a paragraph they failed to understand or return to a vaguely-heard editorial at a more convenient time. (With some effort, however, they may be able to find the editorial reproduced on the station's web site.)

Robert S. McCord, who has written editorials for both television and newspapers, said he was surprised to find that writing 200 words for television was a lot harder than writing 800 words for an op-ed column.[41] "As I have always done, I tried to vary sentence structure and length," he said. "But it doesn't work on television. You have to use simple sentences and be very direct and crystal clear." He found that he had to try for only one or two main points. He also learned that certain topics are too complex or too dull to lend themselves to editorializing on television. McCord said that another surprise was the amount of recognition and reaction he received from the public. "I've never experienced anything like it despite all the years I've been dishing out opinion in Little Rock," he said. "I can't go anywhere without being recognized and stopped by people I have never met."

Broadcast and print editorials differ most sharply in the manner in which they are presented. A television editorial is likely to include film footage and be delivered by an identifiable person. Even though the opinion expressed may be that of an editorial board, one person (often the station's general manager) makes the presentation. I don't know whether such presentations are more or less persuasive with viewers than anonymous print editorials, but probably the range of persuasive effects differs more within each type than between types. As is the case with print editorials, some broadcast editorials are far more effective than others.

Preparing the Broadcast Editorial

Until the time of actual writing, the editorial preparation process for broadcast is basically the same as for a newspaper. As with newspaper editorials, the broadcast editorial presumably represents the views of the management. Similarly, whether the editorial is specifically the opinion of the owner, the general manager, the news director, the editorial director or an individual editorial writer, it must be written by one person, though perhaps edited by others.

The person assigned to write a broadcast editorial should go through the same nine steps of editorial writing described in Chapter 10, "Nine Steps to Editorial Writing": selecting a topic, determining the purpose of the editorial, determining the audience, deciding on the tone of the editorial, researching the topic, determining the general format, writing the beginning of the editorial, writing the body of the editorial and writing the conclusion.

In selecting a topic and determining the audience, broadcast editorial writers probably are more limited than newspaper writers. Newspapers usually publish more than one editorial each day. A reader who is not attracted to one editorial may be attracted to another. Even if none of the editorials appears interesting, the reader can quickly move to other parts of the editorial or another part of the paper without "wasting" more than a few seconds between items of interest. Broadcast viewers and listeners have no such choices, unless they switch channels, which of course no editorial writer wants them to do. Listeners don't enjoy sitting through dull one-minute editorials on topics in which they are not interested. So the first task of the broadcast editorial writer is to pick a topic likely to appeal to the vast majority of listeners.

Broadcast writers also have a more limited range of options for the tone of editorials. Long expository pieces are clearly out. Editorials that require extensive or complex arguments are difficult to present over the air, at least in the framework of a typical news broadcast. Thoughts presented in a subtle or ironic manner may be misinterpreted or missed completely.

Broadcast writers, like print writers, have a choice of starting their editorials by stating their conclusions or reaching conclusions after arguments have been presented. Broadcast writers, like newspaper writers, may sometimes find it more appropriate to present opposing arguments or arguments on only one side. Of course, the time limitations of broadcast preclude the presentation of more than a few arguments, whether on one side or more than one.

Writing the Broadcast Editorial

Here are a few general rules for writing broadcast editorials:

- Writers should remember that they are writing for the ear, not the eye. A broadcast editorial should rate as "easy to read" on the Flesch readability scale mentioned in Chapter 11.
- A broadcast editorial must be brief, clear and interesting. A length of 150 to 250 words is typical.
- Sentences should be short and presented in a straightforward manner. Subjects and verbs should be close together.
- The writing should be free from hard-to-pronounce or easily misunderstood words.
- Strings of modifying words should be avoided. Instead of saying "Virginia Tech Communications Studies Professor Valerie Speer," say: "Valerie Speer, professor of communication studies at Virginia Tech." The latter uses more words but gives listeners a much better chance to comprehend the four separate ideas (name, position, department, university).
- Contractions, such as "The mayor's embarrassed by this," may sound more natural than "The mayor is embarrassed by this."
  Incomplete sentences may be used effectively. Some may start with a

conjunction, and even without a subject. Following the statement about the mayor, for instance, may be: "And should be."
- Verbs also may be dropped: "Good news on the economy today."
- "That" and "which" often are dropped if the meaning is clear without them.

Broadcast news writing places a lot of emphasis on "today," to make listeners think they are getting the latest information. Use of the present tense also helps to give listeners the feeling that they are hearing the news as it happens. Editorial writers should keep these listeners in mind, but they should not feel that they have to strain for the "today" angle.

In broadcast writing, it is even more important for writers to outline what they intend to say, to make certain that points are made clearly and in the appropriate order. Broadcast writers may find it helpful to clarify what they mean to say if they apply the designations suggested in Chapter 10: S (statement), A_1 (argument on one side), A_2 (argument on the other side), D (discussion) and C (conclusion).

To provide an example of how broadcast editorial writing differs from newspaper editorial writing, the editorial written in Chapter 10 and revised in Chapter 11 ("To Publish or Not to Publish") has been rewritten in broadcast style by G. Donald Gale, president of Words, Words, Words, Inc., and former editorial writer for KSL-TV, Salt Lake City. Gale said he made four basic changes:

1. *Fewer words.* Broadcasters have very limited time periods to present their arguments.
2. *Fewer secondary ideas.* We must focus on a single concept if we hope to communicate.
3. *Stronger opening.* The first sentence must not only grab the listener but state the case.
4. *Shorter sentences.* Broadcasters must breathe now and then.

There are several significant differences between the original editorial, written for print, and the revised broadcast version. The revised editorial contains 506 words; Gale's broadcast editorial 254. Sentences in the newspaper editorial average 23 words; sentences in the broadcast editorial 16 words. Listeners know from the title ("Student mistakes mock First Amendment") and the opening sentence of the broadcast editorial that the writer thinks the ad should not have been run. Readers did not know, for sure, until the end of the newspaper editorial.

An illustration of the relative brevity of broadcast editorials is provided by editorials written in commemoration of Martin Luther King Jr. Day. The editorial that appeared in the *Charlotte* (N.C.) *Observer* ("King fought for all Americans, not just for blacks") and that is reprinted in Chapter 13 has approximately 850 words. The editorial ("Melting pot or not?"), carried on Cablevision 12 Long Island, is 200 words.

This editorial also offers a good example of McCord's advice to keep it simple and make only one or two points. From the series of reports carried by the news side, writer Peter Kohler chose to focus on one aspect of racial segregation: "[T]he population in most of Long Island's 200 communities is 90 percent white; most blacks reside in just 25 communities." He cited only three numbers, and those numbers (200, 90, 25) could be easily grasped by listeners.

STUDENT MISTAKES MOCK FIRST AMENDMENT

STUDENT EDITORS AT THE UNIVERSITY OF CALIFORNIA-BERKELEY PUBLISHED AN ADVERTISEMENT THEY SHOULD HAVE REJECTED. THEY MADE MATTERS WORSE BY COLLECTING AND DESTROYING NEWSSTAND COPIES OF THEIR OWN NEWSPAPER.

THE AD IN QUESTION WAS CLEARLY RACIST AND OFFENSIVE. IT FALSELY STEREOTYPED AFRICAN-AMERICANS AS WELFARE RECIPIENTS. STUDENT EDITORS AT THE *DAILY CALIFORNIAN* SHOULD HAVE REJECTED THE AD, AS DID EDITORS AT OTHER STUDENT NEWSPAPERS AROUND THE COUNTRY. INSTEAD, THE *CALIFORNIAN* CHOSE TO PRINT THE AD CREATED BY A CALIFORNIA-BASED SPECIAL INTEREST GROUP.

BUT WHEN STUDENTS MARCHED ON THE NEWSPAPER OFFICE IN PROTEST, STAFF MEMBERS RUSHED TO RETRIEVE NEWSPAPERS ALREADY PRINTED AND DISTRIBUTED. THAT ONLY COMPOUNDED THE ERROR, SINCE THE BUYER HAD A CONTRACT TO HAVE ITS MESSAGE DISTRIBUTED. THE EVENT WAS SIMILAR TO ARRANGING FOR A GUEST SPEAKER AND THEN DRAGGING THE SPEAKER OFF THE PLATFORM PART WAY THROUGH HIS OR HER SPEECH. NEWSPAPERS HAVE THE FREEDOM TO REJECT ADVERTISING THEY DEEM INAPPROPRIATE. (BROADCASTERS ARE SOMETIMES DENIED THAT FREEDOM.) ISSUE GROUPS HAVE THE *FREEDOM* TO SEEK PUBLICATION OF THEIR IDEAS, NO MATTER HOW OFFENSIVE THEY MIGHT BE. HOWEVER, ONCE AN IDEA IS CIRCULATED IN PRINT, NO ONE HAS THE FREEDOM TO INTERFERE WITH ITS DISTRIBUTION—NOT THE GOVERNMENT, NOT PROTESTERS, NOT EVEN THOSE WHO PUT IT INTO PRINT.

TO THINK OTHERWISE IS TO VIOLATE THE PRINCIPLES OF THE FIRST AMENDMENT.

THE FOLLOWING DAY—TO THEIR CREDIT—EDITORS PUBLISHED A FRONT-PAGE EDITORIAL OF APOLOGY. BUT SUCH WISDOM SHOULD HAVE BEEN EXERCISED BEFORE THE FACT (OR FACTS), NOT AFTER THE VIOLATION OF A VALUED PRINCIPLE.

MELTING POT OR NOT

PRESENTED BY PETER KOHLER

YOU HAVE TO WONDER HOW THE REV. MARTIN LUTHER KING JR. WOULD REGARD RACE RELATIONS TODAY IN LIGHT OF THE DREAMS HE SPOKE OF SO MOVINGLY.

THAT QUESTION WAS RAISED BY NEWS 12 LONG ISLAND THIS WEEK IN A SERIES OF REPORTS, "MELTING POT OR NOT."

THE REPORTS FOCUSED ON RACIAL SEPARATION ON LONG ISLAND: THE POPULATION IN MOST OF LONG ISLAND'S 290 COMMUNITIES IS 90 PERCENT WHITE; MOST BLACKS RESIDE IN JUST 25 COMMUNITIES.

MUCH OF THIS RACIAL SEPARATION RESULTS FROM VOLUNTARY CHOICES PEOPLE MAKE ABOUT WHERE TO LIVE. SEGREGATION, AS ENFORCED THROUGH JIM CROW LAWS IN THE SOUTH, WAS ABOLISHED BY CONGRESS AND THE COURTS BACK IN THE 1960S.

WHATEVER THE CAUSE, SCHOOLS SEEM TO SUFFER THE MOST FROM RACIAL SEPARATION. BECAUSE SCHOOLS ARE SUPPORTED BY LOCAL PROPERTY TAXES, POORER MINORITY COMMUNITIES, LIKE ROOSEVELT AND WYANDANCH, STRUGGLE TO SUPPORT POORLY PERFORMING SCHOOLS. WEALTHIER WHITE COMMUNITIES CAN SPEND FAR MORE ON EXCELLENT SCHOOLS.

OF COURSE, GREAT PROGRESS HAS BEEN MADE IN RACE RELATIONS, LARGELY TO THE COURAGEOUS EFFORTS OF KING AND CIVIL RIGHTS LEADERS FORTY YEARS AGO. BUT INEQUALITY IN OUR PUBLIC SCHOOLS—A CENTRAL ISSUE IN THE CIVIL RIGHTS REVOLUTION—IS, SADLY, VERY MUCH WITH US ON LONG ISLAND.

CABLEVISION CHANNEL 12 LONG ISLAND

Also notice the familiar direct address (the second-person "you") in the first sentence and the first-person words in the last sentence: "our" schools and "very much with us."

Broadcast editorials need not be limited to words and talking heads. Neil Heinen provided a dramatic example on WISC-TV in Madison, Wis. On the same day during a heat wave, firemen were called out to fight a fire and a

IT'S NOT THE HEAT, IT'S THE STUPIDITY

BY NEIL HEINEN

A COUPLE OF CONTRASTING IMAGES, AS WE CONSIDER THE DEATH
OF MINNESOTA VIKINGS FOOTBALL PLAYER KOREY STRINGER.

(VIDEO OF MONDAY'S FIRE)

  THIS IS NECESSARY FOR PUBLIC SAFETY.

(VIDEO OF FOOTBALL PRACTICE)

  THIS IS UNNECESSARY.

(VIDEO OF MONDAY'S FIRE)

  THIS WE CAN UNDERSTAND AND APPRECIATE.

(VIDEO OF FOOTBALL PRACTICE)

  THIS DEFIES LOGIC.

(VIDEO OF MONDAY'S FIRE)

  THIS IS HEROIC.

(VIDEO OF FOOTBALL PRACTICE)

  THIS IS A GAME.

(VIDEO OF MONDAY'S FIRE)

  THIS DEMANDS RISK.

(VIDEO OF FOOTBALL PRACTICE)

THIS SHOULD NEVER RESULT IN DEATH FROM HEAT STROKE.

THE DEATH OF A YOUNG MAN IS A SAD, TRAGIC EVENT. BUT IT
WASN'T THE HEAT. IT WAS THE STUPIDITY.

WISC-TV

Minnesota Vikings football player died of heat stroke during a practice session. Alternating bits of video coverage of the fire and football practice, the editorial ("It's not the heat, it's the stupidity") must have had a dramatic impact on viewers.

A broadcast editorial on an emotional issue can draw strong responses from viewers. Editorial writer Chuck Stokes of WXYZ-TV in Detroit experienced that when commenting on the September 11, 2001, attacks on the World Trade Center and the Pentagon. In an editorial titled "Victims," Stokes first acknowledged the innocent victims on the hijacked planes, at the World Trade Center and at the Pentagon. Then, pointing out that in Detroit "our Arab and Chaldean community is being harassed and threatened because of this horrible attack," he told his listeners that "Americans who direct their anger at any of these groups of people are as wrong as the terrorists who attacked America." A few days later, in an editorial titled "Voter mail—discrimination," Stokes reported: "Our editorial urging people not to discriminate against Americans of Arab dissent stirred up a lot of reactions." Some who responded agreed with the editorial; some

VICTIMS

BY CHUCK STOKES

THE INCREDIBLE ATTACK ON AMERICA HAS MANY VICTIMS:

THERE WERE THE INNOCENT PASSENGERS ON THE HIJACKED PLANES; THE INNOCENT PEOPLE INSIDE AND OUTSIDE OF NEW YORK'S WORLD TRADE CENTER; AND THE INNOCENT PEOPLE AT WASHINGTON'S PENTAGON. AND THERE ARE OTHERS.

HERE IN DETROIT, OUR ARAB AND CHALDEAN COMMUNITY IS BEING HARASSED AND THREATENED BECAUSE OF THIS HORRIBLE ATTACK. AN ATTACK THEY DO NOT SUPPORT!

LET US NOT DISCRIMINATE AGAINST AMERICAN CITIZENS WHO IMMIGRATED TO THE U.S. FROM ANOTHER COUNTRY; PEOPLE FROM OTHER LANDS WHO ARE TEMPORARILY LIVING, WORKING, OR STUDYING IN AMERICA; NOR AMERICAN BORN CITIZENS WHO HAPPEN TO LOOK LIKE PEOPLE FROM ANOTHER COUNTRY.

AMERICANS WHO DIRECT THEIR ANGER AT ANY OF THESE GROUPS OF PEOPLE ARE AS WRONG AS THE TERRORISTS WHO ATTACKED AMERICA. DETROIT IS ONE OF THE MOST ETHNICALLY DIVERSE CITIES IN THE UNITED STATES. LET THAT BE OUR STRENGTH . . . NOT OUR WEAKNESS.

WXYZ-TV

VIEWER MAIL—DISCRIMINATION

BY CHUCK STOKES

THE SEPTEMBER 11TH ATTACK STIRRED UP A LOT OF EMOTIONS.
OUR EDITORIAL URGING PEOPLE NOT TO DISCRIMINATE AGAINST
AMERICANS OF ARAB DISSENT STIRRED UP A LOT OF REACTIONS.

CHRISTINE EZEKIEL OF DETROIT WRITES: "CERTAINLY, THIS IS
NOT A TIME TO BEHAVE IN AN UNCIVILIZED MANNER TOWARD
ANYONE. THERE'S NEVER SUCH A TIME."

THERE WERE DISSENTERS SUCH AS OUR NEXT TWO LETTER WRITERS:

"IT HAS ALREADY BEEN PROVEN THAT THESE TERRORISTS LIVE AND
WORK (AMONG US). WHY WOULDN'T WE LOOK AT THIS GROUP OF
PEOPLE WITH CAUTION?" LINDA A.

". . . LEST THEY START DRESSING LIKE US AND SPEAKING LIKE
US THEY WILL BE PICKED ON. THEY SAY THEY'RE AMERICANS BUT
THEN WHY DON'T THEY SHOW IT." J.R. UNZICKER.

CLAIRE WOLF OF WIXOM SENT US THIS MESSAGE: "THANK YOU FOR
THE EDITORIAL. IT IS SO IMPORTANT FOR ALL AMERICANS TO
STICK TOGETHER AND REMEMBER THAT OTHER THAN NATIVE
AMERICANS, WE ALL HAVE FOREIGN HERITAGE."

ANOTHER VIEWER WRITES: "INSTEAD OF AMERICANS STOOPING TO
THE LEVELS OF THE TERRORISTS, WE NEED TO STAND NEXT TO OUR
NEIGHBORS WITH LOVE AND SUPPORT." LYNN SIARKOWSKI.

EVEN THOUGH WE DON'T HAVE TIME TO READ THEIR LETTERS ON
AIR, WE WOULD ALSO LIKE TO THANK THESE VIEWERS FOR
SUPPORTING OUR POSITION:

TERRI POMFRET
DENNIS ERTZBISCHOFF
GERALD BARTKOWIAK—TAYLOR, MICHIGAN
TIM PRYOR—WINDSOR

THANKS FOR ALL OF YOUR LETTERS!

WXYZ-TV

disagreed sharply with his urging viewers not to "discriminate against American citizens who immigrated to the U.S. from another country."

The issue of how to treat people from other countries also concerned Mark Lowery of Cablevision New York when the City University of New York decided to double the tuition of undocumented immigrants. To personalize the issue, the editorial ("CUNY tuition hike") said a Jamaican student who had received a diploma from a Bronx high school would have to pay "34 hundred dollars" (note the broadcast wording), twice what fellow classmates would have paid in tuition. Note the short sentences: "Should CUNY treat him differently?" "In the past, the answer has been no." "The proposed change is not going over well." "They're right." "Ironically, even CUNY supports the bill." Only two numbers are cited.

CUNY TUITION HIKE

PRESENTED BY MARK LOWERY

HOW SHOULD THE CITY UNIVERSITY OF NEW YORK TREAT UNDOCUMENTED IMMIGRANTS? TAKE, FOR EXAMPLE, A JAMAICAN STUDENT—WHO WAS BROUGHT HERE BY HIS FAMILY, ENROLLED IN A BRONX HIGH SCHOOL—LET'S SAY JANE ADDAMS—AND EARNED A DIPLOMA. SHOULD CUNY TREAT HIM DIFFERENTLY?

IN THE PAST, THE ANSWER HAS BEEN NO. CUNY CHARGED THE CITY'S UNDOCUMENTED IMMIGRANTS IN-STATE TUITION RATES. BUT THE UNIVERSITY REEXAMINED THAT POLICY FOLLOWING 9/11, AND DECIDED THAT IT DIDN'T COMPLY WITH FEDERAL LAW. CUNY NOW PLANS TO CHARGE IMMIGRANTS WHO ARE LIVING IN THE CITY UNLAWFULLY OUT-OF-STATE RATES.

IN OTHER WORDS, THAT JAMAICAN STUDENT, IN SOME CASES, WOULD PAY TWICE AS MUCH TUITION AS SOME OF HIS HIGH SCHOOL CLASSMATES. HE WOULD BE TREATED JUST LIKE SOMEONE HERE ON A STUDENT VISA.

THAT PROPOSED CHANGE IS NOT GOING OVER WELL. SEVERAL STUDENTS AND PROFESSORS RECENTLY WENT ON A THREE-DAY HUNGER STRIKE, AND THE PUERTO RICAN LEGAL DEFENSE FUND HAS FILED SUIT AGAINST THE UNIVERSITY. THEY SAY THE NEW POLICY IS AN OVERREACTION, AND THAT CHARGING UNDOCUMENTED IMMIGRANTS OUT-OF-STATE RATES WILL KEEP MANY FROM GETTING A HIGHER EDUCATION.

THEY'RE RIGHT. UNDER THE NEW PLAN, THE COST OF ATTENDING
ONE OF CUNY'S FOUR-YEAR COLLEGES WOULD MORE THAN DOUBLE
FOR UNDOCUMENTED IMMIGRANTS, FROM 16 HUNDRED DOLLARS A
SEMESTER TO 34 HUNDRED DOLLARS.

THE TUITION CHANGE IS ON HOLD PENDING COURT ACTION.
MEANWHILE, A MORE REASONABLE APPROACH IS BEING PUSHED BY
STATE ASSEMBLYMAN PETER RIVERA OF THE BRONX. HE INTRODUCED
A BILL THAT WOULD ALLOW ALL IMMIGRANTS THAT GRADUATE FROM
A NY HIGH SCHOOL TO PAY IN-STATE TUITION AT CUNY.
IRONICALLY, EVEN CUNY SUPPORTS THE BILL.

CABLEVISION NEW YORK

Higher-education finance also was the subject of an editorial carried by
WISC-TV in Madison, Wis. State legislators had proposed limiting the power of
the Board of Regents to raise top administrators' salaries and raise tuition. The
editorial ("UW—Does governing mean support?") asked, in effect: If the legislature tightens controls on finances, will it assume the responsibility for paying
the bills? Notice the use of the editorial "we." This is a relatively short editorial,
but three long sentences account for the bulk of it. The first sentence begins
with a dependent clause, usually a difficult construction for broadcast.

UW—DOES GOVERNING MEAN SUPPORT?

BEFORE STATE LEGISLATORS WORK UP TOO MUCH RIGHTEOUS
INDIGNATION THIS WEEK IN SUPPORT OF PROPOSALS TO LIMIT
THE BOARD OF REGENTS' POWER TO RAISES SALARIES FOR TOP
ADMINISTRATORS AND TO RAISE TUITION, WE ASK IF THAT
MICRO-MANAGING IS REALLY THE DIRECTION THE LEGISLATURE
WANTS TO GO. OR WE SHOULD SAY RETURN TO. AND IF SO, WILL
THERE BE A CORRESPONDING INCREASE IN STATE AID TO THE U-W?

THE TREND OVER THE LAST DECADE OR MORE IS FOR THE STATE TO
OFFSET ITS DWINDLING TAX DOLLAR SUPPORT FOR THE U-W SYSTEM
BY GRANTING THE SYSTEM, AND IN PARTICULAR THE U-W CAMPUS,
MORE AUTONOMY IN GOVERNING ITSELF. THE RESULT HAS BEEN A
UNIVERSITY THAT HAS BECOME A NATIONAL LEADER AT SECURING
OUTSIDE REVENUE INCLUDING ALUMNI SUPPORT, BE IT FOR
RESEARCH, FACULTY, OR BUILDING CONSTRUCTION.

THERE'S A TRADE OFF HERE, FINANCIAL AND PHILOSOPHICAL, AND
IN MANY WAYS THEY'RE CONNECTED. WHO GOVERNS THE U-W? AND
WHO PAYS TO SUPPORT IT?

WISC-TV

The issue of concealed weapons on campus prompted an editorial at
KSL-TV in Salt Lake City, Utah. The state attorney general had said that the
University of Utah's ban on firearms was illegal. The editorial ("Guns and the
university") gave little credence to the possibility that the legislature would
"acquiesce to our reasoned view, or to overwhelming public opinion" and
change the law. Going to the court was seen as the better course. Notice the
use of present-tense verbs: "the attorney general says," "University President
Berne Machen says," "lawmakers say," "[i]t's what polls say."

GUNS AND THE UNIVERSITY

AMERICA HAS A PRACTICAL SYSTEM FOR SETTLING LEGAL
DISPUTES. GO TO COURT, PRESENT ARGUMENTS WITH CIVILITY,
THEN LET A JUDGE OR JURY DECIDE WHO'S RIGHT.

AS THINGS STAND NOW, THAT'S PRECISELY WHAT NEEDS TO HAPPEN
WITH THE UNIVERSITY OF UTAH AND THE UTAH LEGISLATURE IN
THEIR CONFLICT OVER CONCEALED WEAPONS.

FOR MORE THAN 24 YEARS, THE UNIVERSITY HAS BANNED MOST
FIREARMS ON CAMPUS. THE POLICY DIDN'T CHANGE A FEW YEARS
AGO WHEN THE LEGISLATURE PASSED A LIBERAL CONCEALED-CARRY
LAW. NOW, THE ATTORNEY GENERAL SAYS THE UNIVERSITY'S BAN
IS ILLEGAL.

UNIVERSITY PRESIDENT BERNIE MACHEN SAYS THE PRESENCE
OF WEAPONS IN THE CLASSROOM STIFLES EDUCATION AND
SHORT-CIRCUITS ACADEMIC FREEDOM. LAWMAKERS SAY IT DOESN'T
MATTER. THE LAW THEY PASSED GIVES THEM THE AUTHORITY TO
DECIDE, NOT THE UNIVERSITY.

THE STAGE, APPROPRIATELY, IS SET FOR SOME COURTROOM DRAMA.

BY THE WAY, WE THINK THERE'S A BETTER WAY TO RESOLVE THE
DISPUTE AND SAVE THE TAXPAYERS SOME HEFTY LEGAL BILLS. THE

LEGISLATURE COULD MODIFY THE LAW TO ALLOW SCHOOLS TO BAN
CONCEALED WEAPONS. IT'S WHAT POLLS SAY THE PUBLIC WANTS.
IT IS WHAT KSL SUPPORTS. BUT, DON'T EXPECT LAWMAKERS, ON
THIS HOT-BUTTON ISSUE, TO ACQUIESCE TO OUR REASONED VIEW,
OR TO OVERWHELMING PUBLIC OPINION.

A RESOLUTION THROUGH LITIGATION, AS SUGGESTED BY PRESIDENT
MACHEN, AT THIS POINT, SEEMS THE BEST WAY TO DEAL WITH THE
DISPUTE.

KSL-TV

■ CONCLUSION

By no means is the anonymous newspaper editorial the only outlet for opinion. In daily or weekly newspapers, new opportunities are opening in reviewing literary and cultural productions, partly because newspapers are seeking ways to provide more information for consumers. New opportunities also lie on the growing number of op-ed pages, which are open to bylined pieces that range from interpretation to media criticism to personal opinion. More and more publishers and editors are relaxing the old rule that editorial writers should remain anonymous.

Until a few years ago, broadcast editorial writing seemed to have a bright future. Then editorial writing jobs began shrinking. Budgets got tight. Broadcast people have always been nervous about having to provide equal time for opinions expressed by themselves and others. But why should broadcast stations allow newspapers to hold a monopoly on opinion in a local community? If owners of broadcast stations were to recommit themselves to offering opinions to their listeners and viewers, radio and television could provide not only jobs for opinion writers but also leadership for their communities.

■ QUESTIONS AND EXERCISES

1. Find a newspaper editorial on a topic that interests you. Rewrite it in broadcast style. Read it aloud to see if any of the wording is awkward or difficult to enunciate clearly. Rewrite to clear up these spots.
2. Keep your ear open for editorials during radio and television news broadcasts. Write to the station manager to ask for a copy. When it arrives, read it aloud. Are there any awkward or difficult spots? How does the editorial approach the subject? Is it analytical or outspoken, one-sided or two-sided? Is the conclusion at the beginning or the end? Would listeners be convinced?
3. Pick a topic, conduct the necessary research and write an analytical article that would be appropriate for an op-ed page. Then write an editorial based on the article that could run the same day.

4. Write an op-ed piece based on an experience that you have had. Try to make it appeal to as broad an audience as possible.

5. If you can find a media criticism column in one of the newspapers that you read, write the media critic. Ask about the newspaper's policies relating to media criticism and the responsibilities of the media critic.

6. If you spot something that you think merits attention in a newspaper that has a media criticism column, write or call the media critic about it.

7. Select a recent book on a media or current events topic. Write a book review that might be suitable to a book section of a newspaper or an op-ed page. Before writing it, you might read several reviews in newspapers that have strong book departments.

8. Watch for a cultural event that interests you: an art exhibit, a play, a concert, a musical or movie. Write a review for the arts and entertainment section of the paper. Again, it is a good idea to read several reviews before you start writing, and in fact before you attend the event.

CHAPTER SEVENTEEN

Letters to the Editor

When a letters section is well done, you'll see people poring over it at coffee shops and at lunch counters. That's because letters reflect the diversity within a community—young, old, witty, down-to-earth, eccentric, demurring, optimistic, liberal. In fact, letters are often the first reason people turn to the editorial pages, and treating them as a valuable resource can help us build a loyal readership of our pages.

—KAY SEMION, *NEWS JOURNAL*, DAYTON BEACH, FLA.[1]

Letters to the editor are about the only part of the editorial page that comes free. But in terms of time, effort and headaches, a good letters column is probably the most expensive part. It's quicker and easier for an editorial writer to knock out a couple of paragraphs of prose than to prepare a letter of equal length for print.

"Letters give life to an editorial page," Barry Bingham Sr. of the Louisville, Ky., *Courier-Journal* said. "They also come near to beating the life out of the fellow who has to handle them. Many are illiterate. Others are long, rambling and inchoate. Still others are so abusive in tone that they recall the Turkish proverb, 'Letters written after dinner are read in Hell.' Some of the ones that come to us must be written in the fine frenzy of after-dinner dyspepsia." Then he added: "Letters are worth every bit of trouble they cause, however."[2]

■ WHY LETTERS?

Editorial page editors put up with—and encourage—letters for one reason: Letters help give readers a better feeling about the newspaper. Letters give readers, as citizens, one of the few chances they have to speak their minds in public. Letters also help create interest in the editorial page and increase readership. Surveys, in fact, show that letters are among the most-read parts of the paper.

Looking from the reader's point of view, one inveterate letter writer who had had 46 letters published in one year said that after his first letter was printed, "It dawned on me that my opinion not only had validity but also interested others. Let's be honest: It stoked my ego, too." What concerned him, he said, was "how often I see poor logic, lack of complete comprehension of the subject matter and emotion-based work by columnists, op-ed contributors and other letter writers. And, sometimes I just disagree with their conclusions." Addressing his remarks to editors of letters, he said: "It's not that I have a moral obligation to straighten out the world or even my home of Englewood, Fla. But it's fun. And [no doubt said with tongue in cheek] invariably I'm right—just like you are."[3]

Letters give readers a chance to talk about what they want to talk about, which is especially important in a one-newspaper town with no built-in voice of opposition. Readers are not stuck with the editor's agenda; they have their own agendas.

■ BUILDING A LETTERS COLUMN

Scholarly studies and reports from editors indicate that readers are increasingly turning to letters columns to express their opinions. A 1995 survey by Suraj Kapoor found that 80 percent of the newspapers reported an increase in letters received over the past 10 years. Seventy-five percent reported an increase in the amount of space devoted to letters.[4] In a 2001 *Masthead* symposium, a 40,000-circulation paper, the Bremerton, Wash., *Sun,* reported receiving on average 12 letters a day, while the *Denver Post* reported 50 a day and the Minneapolis, Minn., *Star-Tribune* about 70.[5]

Some newspapers have begun reporting to their readers the numbers of letters received and published each week. In mid-March 2001 the Eugene, Ore., *Register-Guard* reported that 62 letters were printed from among the 143 received during the week,[6] while the Portland *Oregonian* printed 75 of 606.[7] Both papers reported the numbers of letters received on the most popular topics. The *Reno* (Nev.) *Gazette-Journal,* under the heading of *Hot*TOPICS, provides a weekly count of topics that generate the most letters.

In a *Masthead* symposium, Keith Carter of the *Desert Sun* in Palm Springs, Calif., offered nine suggestions for building a stronger letters column:[8]

- Localize.
- Print as many letters as possible.
- Encourage debates.
- Set up rules and follow them.
- Identify letter writers.
- Run letters quickly.
- Verify, verify, verify.
- Stay flexible.
- Stimulate interest.

It is clear what Carter had in mind in offering most of these suggestions. The "localize" advice was directed toward urging strong editorials on local topics as a means to stimulate letters. The "stay flexible" advice was intended for editors who seem more concerned with enforcing rigid rules than with printing good (but perhaps excessively long) letters. Probably for as long as there have been letters to newspapers, editors have been concerned with two of Carter's points: stimulating more letters and setting rules for deciding which ones to print. These two areas are discussed at length in the following sections.

■ STIMULATING INTEREST

In seeking ways to stimulate more and better letters, editors have experimented with ways of displaying letters, methods for speeding the delivery of letters and ideas for encouraging readers to write.

Display of Letters

Displaying letters prominently and attractively is one way editors can indicate to readers that the newspaper takes letters seriously. Letters typically are placed on the right side of the editorial page, beneath the editorial cartoon. When Professor Robert Bohle of Virginia Commonwealth University examined a series of editorial pages, he found no fault with this placement, but said that editors underplayed individual letters. Headlines tended to be small, consisting of one line with few words ("terse and enigmatic," he called them). He preferred two lines to let the reader know what the letter was about.[9]

Bohle applauded papers that worked illustrations or political cartoons into their letter columns. (He might have added photographs.) He urged editors to place the how-to-submit-a-letter box at the top of the column. He suggested that a letter could be made more understandable by placing a summary of the article or editorial that prompted it at the top of the letter.

"Choosing which letters to publish and how to use them makes the difference between a lively letters section and one that is routine," Sue O'Brien of the *Denver Post* suggested in a 2001 symposium. The *Post* gives top priority to "people who have grievances with the paper, particularly editorials." Next are "the best-written letters, with the goal of having a healthy variety of topics each day." When many letters come in on the same subject, the *Post* sometimes groups them together: "The first one or two set the scene and then others are edited, usually to a couple of paragraphs, to represent the range of opinions."[10]

In a sample of 50 newspapers, I found a wide variety of ways in which editors display letters. The *Dallas Morning News* added prominence to a letter by setting lines two columns wide, placing the letter at the top of the letters column, then putting a box around the letter and adding artwork. The *Denver Post* boxed multiple letters on the same topic, with a subject label at the top of the box. The *Hartford* (Conn.) *Courant* used a similar display at the bottom of the page. The *Portsmouth* (N.H.) *Herald* ran letters down the left-hand column. The Idaho Falls *Post Register* devoted two columns on the left side of the page for letters. The *Daily News* in New York set the first letter two columns wide in slightly larger type than the other letters. The *Reno* (Nev.) *Gazette-Journal* ran a one-column photo of firefighters adjacent to a letter praising their work in putting out forest fires. Instead of the traditional one-column headline, the Cleveland, Ohio, *Plain Dealer* placed two- and three-column heads on letters. On a "Community Voices" (op-ed) page the Portland *Oregonian* devoted the lower two-thirds of the page to letters with a page-wide "Letters to the Editor" heading. The *Daily News* in New York used two-part headlines: a one-line kicker stated the topic of the letter ("Fluoride," for example); a two-line subhead summarized the letter ("Take toxic material/out of our water"). The *Maine Sunday Tribune* ran, in larger type, a pullout quote from a letter, calling attention to the letter and breaking up the gray space.

I found that newspapers use a wide variety of labels for letters: "Point of View," "Letters in the Editor's Mailbox," "Letters: What You Think," "Letters to the Editor," "Reader Reaction," "Your Views," "Voice of the People," "The Public Forum," "The Mailbox," "Our Readers' Views," "My Nickel's Worth," "Open Forum," "Point of View," "Letters to The Day," "Letters from Readers," "Potpourri," "Voice of the Reader," "The Public Pulse" and, most popular of all, simply "Letters."

Transmission of Letters

Editors have been trying for years to speed up their receipt of letters to the editor. Now an array of electronic devices improve on the mail. Once only a few newspapers were experimenting with letters delivered via fax or e-mail, but when I checked the letter policies of a sample of 20 newspapers recently, I found that 17 specifically stated that they accepted letters by mail, e-mail and fax. Only one mentioned mail only; one mentioned mail and fax; one mentioned mail, e-mail and voice mail.

Three of the 17 papers used artwork to call attention to the three methods of delivery. The *Deseret News* of Salt Lake City, Utah, used a large @ sign for e-mail, a picture of a phone for fax and a picture of a mail box for mail. The *Akron (Ohio) Beacon Journal* used a picture of a mouse and a portion of a keyboard for e-mail, a section of a stamp for mail and a section of a fax machine for fax. The Boise *Idaho Statesman* used pictures of the corner of a keyboard for e-mail and portions of several envelopes for mail. All had the effect of drawing readers' attention to the several ways they could get their messages to the newspaper. The sample suggests that e-mail and fax generally are much more widely used than voice mail (the hardest to edit into a publishable form).

Encouraging Writers

Editors have tried a wide variety of methods to encourage readers to write letters. As an "interactive step," the *Denver Post* "set up an automatic e-mail response to e-mail letters" that included "the rules for publication (200-word limit, need name, address and telephone number for verification, etc.)"[11] On Saturdays, the Baltimore, Md., *Sun* publishes responses (sometimes enough to fill a whole page) to a question it asked the week before. On Sundays the *Sun* encourages more letters through three zoned editions "that carry letters specific to the areas covered." Editors reported that every time they increased space for letters, the number of letters "increased dramatically."[12]

The Harrisburg, Pa., *Patriot-News* acknowledges all letters. To writers whose letters have been rejected, editors send "an information form that includes all the criteria for not publishing: no poetry, no letters to other people; no complaints about business, no commentary on matters currently in adjudication, no personal attacks or name-calling."[13]

The letters editor of the Minneapolis, Minn., *Star-Tribune*, in dealing with readers whose letters have been rejected, tries to use empathy: "I try to remember that I had a letter published when I was in the 10th grade (over parity in girls' and boys' sports). I think about how I felt, how I went to school the next day, and the history teacher and everybody was talking about the letter."[14]

The *Bay City* (Mich.) *Times* attributed an increase in volume of letters to loosening "restrictive" letter-writing policies: "The letters had been too heavily edited, and too many rules excluded letters from being published."[15]

To make the letters column more appealing, quite a few newspapers use artwork, even for shorter letters.[16]

The editorial staff of the *Seattle* (Wash.) *Times* selects a favorite letter each month, then features "the writer with a mug shot and a short explanation of who the writer is and what motivated the letter." At the end of the year all of those who were featured are invited to a special dinner honoring them.[17] The Baltimore *Sun* held an evening reception for about 100 of its "most prolific and effective" letter writers. The result: "Response was outstanding, and the writers really felt appreciated." A few newspapers denote exceptional letters with a star (or some other identifier) beside the name of the letter writer. The *Omaha* (Neb.) *World-Herald* puts the writer's name at the top of the letter ("From Pat Jones, Bellevue"). A Canadian newspaper, the St. Johns, N.B., *Telegraph-Journal* prominently displays a "Letter of the Day" on the editorial page. The *Boston Globe* sometimes prominently displays a letter, setting it two columns wide with artwork and with dotted rules above and below it.

The Portland *Oregonian* uses its web site to encourage and display contributions to its "In My Opinion" op-ed feature. Limited in the number of full-length articles it can publish, the *Oregonian* generally runs eight or so synopses of other, longer letters about once a week. Readers can see these letters in complete form by going to the newspaper's web page.

The *Hartford* (Conn.) *Courant* sought ways to make its opinion pages more appealing to women when a study showed that two-thirds of the letters were written by men. When women readers were asked why they wrote so few letters, the biggest response was that they were too busy, that they had no time left over to write. A second reason was fear that they might be harassed by threatening letters or phone calls. *Courant* editors also found that some women "assumed that letters from men would get preference, or that a woman's opinion would not be taken seriously. Some said "they were raised to think their opinions don't count as much as do men's".[18] After the results of the study were published, letters from women temporarily picked up, then fell back to the earlier one-third. (Readership surveys show, however, that "the *Courant*'s editorial pages are read by as many women as men.")[19]

■ SETTING UP THE RULES

How readers view a newspaper's letters column and respond to it can depend on how the editors of that newspaper handle the letters they receive. Both the quality of the column and readers' perceptions of it can be affected by the policies of the paper. By no means do editors agree on how best to run the letters column. Policies generally concern seven areas: use of names and addresses, verification of names, subject matter, length and frequency, editing letters, editor's notes and political letters.

Names and Addresses

Whether publication of writers' names and addresses should be required has been discussed and argued since the establishment of letters columns. A sample of the editorial pages of 60 newspapers indicates that policies vary little these days. Every letter that was printed carried at least one person's name. Only two newspapers (the *Missoulian* in Missoula, Mont., and the *New Hampshire Sunday News* in Manchester, N.H.) published the writer's street address. The *Oregonian* published the name of the letter writer's city. For writers who lived in Portland, it indicated a section of the city (Southeast Portland, for example). The other papers named only the writer's city, town or township.

Many newspapers follow writer's names with identifications such as "Suffolk University, Juvenile Justice Center," "Executive Director, Family Services of Boston," "President, Yankee Peddler and Pawn," "Chairman, 2001 Fund for the Arts," "Presidio Committee, Sierra Club," "Urban Development Consultant," "retired biology teacher" and "dog owner, trainer and groomer."

The Eugene, Ore., *Register-Guard* identified one writer as a "seventh-grader at Agnes Stewart Middle School." The *Reno* (Nev.) *Gazette-Journal* noted that one writer was age 13.

Verifying Names

Editors these days spend more time verifying the authenticity of letters than they did in the past. They seem less inclined to presume the good will of letter writers. They also have become more wary of the legal dangers posed by letters. One survey found editors about equally divided between those who verified the authors of all letters and those who verified only when their suspicions were aroused. Most relied for verification on the telephone; a third on the mail.[20]

Among the 60 newspapers that I sampled, only nine specifically stated that letters were subject to verification. A typical statement: "Include your name, address and daytime phone for verification." Two newspapers also asked for occupation. One paper warned readers: "Writers who sign letters with false names will be permanently barred from publication."

Experienced letters editors tend to develop a sixth sense for the fake letter. "How to sort them out?" Dale A. Davenport of the Harrisburg, Pa., *Patriot-News* asked in a 2001 letter symposium. "Usually these letters are critical of a particular person or institution. Or they're from writers who have a personal ax to grind."[21]

Once in a while an editor will be burned. The *Cleveland* (Ohio) *Press* once printed a seemingly harmless letter about a streetcar accident. After the first edition appeared on the street, a woman called to say that the professed family name signed to the letter was "an obscene Hungarian word" too nasty to repeat.[22]

James J. Kilpatrick told how a Mr. Stuart Little of New York seduced space from the *Richmond* (Va.) *News Leader* with a request for help in finding authentic stories about old crows. His hobby was old crows, he said, the older the better. Many people responded to his requests, including one who sent a package "containing a bottle of an old-time beverage." Another volunteered to send "an elderly female relative by marriage." Kilpatrick reported: "Smiling fondly at the quirks of the amateur ornithologist, we published Mr. Little's letter." Then came a second letter. "But we are not running any more of Mr. Little's crow: We are eating it," Kilpatrick told readers. "For right in the second sentence and in the fourth paragraph was another reference to that 'Kentucky beverage,' and down in the last sentence was still a third mention of this estimable product, and the whole business had about it the faint but unmistakable aroma of the gag, the gimmick, the phonus bolonus." Little turned out to work for a public relations firm that had the account for Old Crow bourbon whiskey. Fifty newspapers had apparently run the first letter.[23]

Subject Matter

Once you decide that a letter is legitimate, you must determine whether the subject matter is appropriate. Most newspapers have rules, published or unpublished, concerning what they will run. Most will not publish a letter unless it pertains to an issue of some public interest, although most do not specifically say so on their editorial pages. The Provo, Utah, *Daily Herald* informs readers that it "encourages community discussion in a responsible manner." The Middletown, N.Y., *Times Herald-Record* states that letters "should contain constructive comment on issues of general interest." The Longmont, Colo., *Daily Times-Call* gives "timely topics" preference. The *Repository* of

Canton, Ohio, states that "letters of accusation may be referred to our news reporters for possible investigation as stories."

Letters editors face a dilemma when dealing with letters that relate to religion. Some newspapers once tried to keep religious issues entirely out of their letters columns. Some allowed religion-related letters if they were tied to a public issue. Most tried to avoid blatant religious pitches and arguments based on religious writings (Christian, Moslem, Jewish or any other). As recently as 1994, Glenn Sheller of the *York* (Pa.) *Dispatch* wrote: "We don't want to see letters and columns of diverse viewpoint, style and wit driven out by mailbags full of the familiar type in which every sentence ends with a scripture citation and whose 'argument' consists of nothing more than an appeal to supernatural authority."[24]

Now, however, editors are finding it more difficult to draw a line against the use of religious citations and religion-based arguments when the public is debating abortion, the death penalty, creationism, use of embryos in research, aid to parochial schools, prayer in the schools, posting the Ten Commandments in public places and the rights of gays. It may be impossible to draw a line now that religious differences, or at least religious perceptions, underlie many important and flammable issues. Letters columns, and editorial pages for that matter, may be among those things that will never be the same after September 11, 2001. Religious beliefs and opinions, as well as scriptural citations, have become part of public discourse. No longer can editors try to insulate their pages from them.

Many newspapers try to avoid thank-you letters, especially those thanking individuals. Some weed out publicity seekers who try to get their names in print by praising editorials lavishly. Some are tough on politicians who try to find excuses for getting their names in the letters column.

Many editors will not publish letters from outside their general circulation areas unless they address a local issue or something that appeared in the paper. Among 60 sample papers, two had stated policies: The Minneapolis, Minn., *Star Tribune* requires that "all submissions be exclusive to Minnesota."[25] The Canton, Ohio, *Repository* will generally print letters only "within our circulation area."[26]

Most readers of letters columns must realize that newspapers do not run poetry in their letters columns. I found no poetry on 60 editorial pages that I sampled, but the editors of only three newspapers (the Longmont, Colo., *Daily Times-Call*, the *Repository* and the *Star Tribune*) thought it necessary to state that they do not accept poetry. "Print a bit of amateur verse and the next day's mail brings a deluge because everyone is a poet at heart if not in pen," M. Carl Andrews of the *Roanoke* (Va.) *World-News* warned.[27]

Editors need to be on the lookout for inspired letter-writing campaigns. Sometimes they can tell that several letters have been written on the same typewriter or printer, or have the same wording. Editors also can be trapped by massive mailings from school letter-writing assignments.

Editors sometimes have to decide to call a halt to the discussion of some issue when it has gone on so long that nothing new is being said.

Editors are not in agreement on what to do with letters that seemingly fall beyond the range of rationality. Carol Suplee of the Willingboro, N.J., *Burlington County Times* recounted that she had a letter writer who was "blatantly inaccurate and unnecessarily inflammatory when he relate[d] his version of history," especially concerning Jews. Sometimes she would write to him explaining her reasons for not running a letter. Other times she would run a letter, when she "felt that exposition of his amazing bigotry might serve the community well," but she usually heard objections from local Jewish organizations.[28] Often there is no clear course to follow. The reputation of a letters column can withstand the publication of a goofy letter from time to time but not publication on a regular basis.

While on the *Columbian,* I was blessed with a persistent letter writer who could start writing on almost any subject but within a couple of handwritten pages would wend her way to talking about sublimating sex as a means of delaying marriage, births and population crisis. She would write several times a week for awhile, then not write for several months. She had been writing to the paper for several years when I took over the editorial page. She was still writing 12 years later when I left. One of her letters consisted of 125 six-by-nine-inch pages. I sometimes could use the first few paragraphs before she headed off into sublimation.

Length and Frequency

Most papers have policies on length of letters. I found in a sample of 51 newspapers that 31 specified or suggested length limits, which varied from 150 to 400 words. Eight set a limit of 250 words; 21 specified 250 or 300 words; two allowed more than 300 words. Twenty-five editors who discussed length on an NCEW (National Conference of Editorial Writers) e-mail discussion tended to be more restrictive. Thirteen said letters had to have fewer than 250 words; 10 specified no more than 250 or 300; two no more than 300.

Newspapers use various ways to prescribe word limits. The *Burlington* (Vt.) *Free Press* suggested: "Most topics can be addressed in 200 words or less." The *Bangor* (Maine) *Daily News* advised readers: "Letters of more than 300 words stand less chance of publication." The Missoula, Mont., *Missoulian* said: "Letters should be about 300 words or fewer." The Elmira, N.Y., *Star-Gazette* stated: "Letters of more than 250 words may either be condensed or returned to the writer." The Longmont, Colo., *Daily Times-Call* warned: "Letters longer than 300 words will be shortened." Concerning longer letters, the Massillon, Ohio, *Independent* said: "Letters longer than 350 words will not be used," while the *Portsmouth* (Ohio) *Daily Times* warned: "Letters longer than 250 words will be discarded."

Some newspapers have other, less restrictive, outlets for readers. The *Oakland* (Calif.) *Tribune* and the Hayward, Calif., *Daily Review* will allow up to 550 words for a reader comment called "My Word." The *San Francisco Chronicle* will accept up to 650 words for its "Open Forum," the Wilmington, Del., *News-Journal* 600 to 700 words for "Delaware Voice" and the Minneapolis, Minn., *Star-Tribune* up to 700 words for "Counterpoints."

Only eight of the 51 newspapers specify a minimum time limit between letters by the same writer. Six require at least 30 days between letters; one, three weeks; one, 60 days. Some editors will acknowledge that they have an informal rule (say, 30 days) but prefer to maintain flexibility if a frequent writer has an appropriate comment or merits a chance to reply to another writer.

Editing of Letters

Editors disagree on what is desirable or permissible in editing letters. Some edit lightly, some heavily. Most would probably agree that many letters can be made more effective through the efforts of a skilled editor.

Kapoor found that 96 percent of the papers in the 1992 survey reserved the right to edit in some form. About 66 percent edited to shorten letters; about 62 percent for grammar; about 26 percent for libel or taste.[29] Not surprisingly, larger newspapers tended to shorten letters more often than small papers did.

Among the 51 papers I examined, 15 specifically say they edit for length, 7 for clarity, 5 for libel (legal), 4 for grammar, 4 for taste, 3 for style, 2 for accuracy, 1 for spelling and 1 for punctuation. Most of the papers publish a general statement, such as: "Letters are subject to editing" or "This newspaper reserves the right to edit letters."

The task facing any editor, of course, is to preserve and clarify the meaning of the original letter. As the editing processes listed above suggest, few newspapers attempt to check for accuracy. Most letters columns could carry the label: "Reader, beware!"

Editor's Notes

Editor's notes at the end of letters used to be more prevalent than they now are. Clever or self-righteous editor's notes may have been fun to write in the past. As Charles Towne of the *Hartford* (Conn.) *Courant* recalled, "Some editors . . . publish caustic rebuttals out of a feeling of superiority, of being so far above such savage assaults as to be immune."[30] Editors today generally use their letters columns to promote exchanges of opinion among readers, not to attack them. If writers have the feeling that the editor is going to have the last word, they are likely to stop writing.

If a letter is clearly wrong in its facts but judged important enough to run, perhaps a note is justified. A note also might be called for when a reader raises a question about something that the newspaper has or has not done. A note can provide a chance for editors to explain. Responding to statements of an opinion or interpretation, however, is best left to other letter writers. After all, the purpose of a letters column is to establish a forum among readers.

I found only two editor's notes in checking the 51 newspapers. One simply identified the letter writer as the director of a medical center. (Most newspapers provide that identification without labeling it "editor's note.") The only true editor's note, in the *Providence* (R.I.) *Journal,* was used to clarify a point made in an editorial (that the "editorial referred to litter on Gano Street exit, not the street)." That note seemed appropriate.

Political Letters

Policies vary widely about what to do with letters relating to elections. Practices run all the way from treating political letters (including candidate endorsements) like other letters to telling writers who want to speak for a candidate to buy an ad.

In a *Masthead* symposium on "The Politics of Letters," Wally Hoffman of the *Salt Lake Tribune* said his paper treated campaign letters like other letters. A signature might be withheld, however, in a "case in which the writer's job might be jeopardized by disclosure of his or her identity."[31]

At the other extreme, Phil Fretz said the *Amarillo* (Texas) *Globe-News* had no trouble with endorsement letters, since it had a policy against running them. "If you run endorsement letters," he said, "you are a masochist. You open yourself to the charge that you didn't run somebody's letter because you endorsed his opponent."[32] On the other hand, if you endorse a candidate and don't give readers a chance to respond, you will almost certainly be accused of being unfair.

To head off last-minute accusations that can't be properly addressed, most newspapers set a deadline for election letters several days before Election Day.

◼ LIBEL IN LETTERS

Marc Franklin, a law professor at Stanford University with expertise in First Amendment issues, has argued that "editors should be protected against libel suits for published letters so long as the letters are authentic and the writers are correctly identified." Letters already serve as a sort of community bulletin board; in Franklin's view, exempting them from the threat of libel suits would make them even more so. Such a bulletin board would "provide access to the media and the community for many who have no other opportunity to get their thoughts before the public," Franklin has written. This access is especially important "as more newspapers become local monopolies." He estimated that about one out of eight letters that are rejected by editors is discarded because of concerns over libel.[33]

For now, however, courts treat letters no differently from the way they treat any other published material in a libel suit. "A long line of case law has held that the author of a libel bears the ultimate responsibility for it, and that everyone who takes part in publication of a libel may be held responsible for it," Professor Steve Pasternack of New Mexico State University warned editors in an article in *The Masthead*. Pasternack noted that a survey had indicated that editors were allowing the use of harsher language in letters columns than elsewhere in their newspapers. He attributed this laxity to the editors' misinformation or lack of knowledge of libel law, and to a reluctance to consult attorneys.[34]

◼ THE LETTERS EDITOR

The job of handling letters is not one for the novice—or for an impatient, careless or uncaring editor. Cliff Carpenter of the *Rochester* (N.Y.) *Democrat and Chronicle* saw some newspapers handling letters lovingly, others handling them ineptly, casually, and with fear or disdain. "Some pages handle letters as if they were ashamed of them," he said. "And by handling them that way, they get only mediocrity to use as letters—and a vicious circle is created."[35] A person who handled letters on the *Kansas City* (Mo.) *Star* was said to have done it "with a certain amount of tender loving care, a bit of prayer and some tearing of hair." Handling letters can take about as much time as an editor can find to work on them, if a paper receives a strong flow of mail.

The letters editor needs a thick skin—literally, at times. Palmer Hoyt of the *Denver Post* told of one letter that began: "Dear Palmer Hoyt: We want you to know that we are going to boil you in oil." A week later Hoyt got a letter that said: "Dear Palmer Hoyt: We want you to know that we are not going to boil you in oil after all. We got bigger turkeys than you to boil."[36] A woman brought to the office of the *Burlington* (Vt.) *Free Press* a three-page letter, typewritten, single-spaced, with a pen name. Franklin Smith tried to explain that the letter was too long for publication and pen names were not permitted. "Finally, after a long, long pause, she looked at me," Smith said, "and said plaintively, 'You don't like me, do you?'"[37]

Letters editors, faceless as they may be to the public, can build special relationships with readers. M. Carl Andrews of the *Roanoke* (Va.) *World-News* said that some of his best friends were regular letter writers who had never met him. Three of his most delightful contributors over the years, he said, had been "dear old ladies who always found something good to say about people or things." He reported that two of them had died. One had requested that he be one of her pallbearers.[38]

CONCLUSION

A good letters column can be a lot of work for an editor. Deciding what letters to print and what should be done to get them ready for print requires skill and judgment. Dealing with letter writers requires tact. Editing letters requires sensitivity, a sense of fairness and a heavy editing pencil. But efforts put into the letters column are usually worthwhile in terms of the readability and credibility of the editorial page. Letters bring readers to the page. They also help readers believe they have a voice in their newspaper. Perhaps the clearest sign of a good editorial page is a good letters column, especially one in which readers respond to the editorials, columns and other letters that appear on the page. Such a page is truly a community forum.

QUESTIONS AND EXERCISES

1. Examine the letters columns of the newspapers in your area to determine their policies on the use of names and addresses, condensation and frequency of publication. Are these policies spelled out for readers?

2. Compare the letters columns of these papers for quantity and quality of letters published. Which papers seem to have the best letters columns? Is there evidence available to explain the success of these columns?

3. Examine the letters specifically for references to previously published editorials or letters. Such references often indicate that the letters column is providing a lively community forum.

4. Can you find letters that sound as though they were produced by a letters mill that sends the same letter to many newspapers?

5. Can you find political letters that sound as though they were produced by a letters "sweatshop," letters that support a cause and sound as though they came from the same source?

6. Do the editor's notes seem fully justified in the columns you have examined? Do you think an editor might have been wiser not to have written one or more of the notes? Why?

7. Do any of the papers request letters on specific topics, perhaps in a weekly roundup or in answer to a question? If so, what kind of responses do the papers get?

8. Write a letter to one of the papers. See if any effort is made to verify your name and address. If it is printed, see what changes are made. If you think the changes altered the meaning of the letter, call and inform the editorial page editor. If it was not published, call to ask why.

Columns and Cartoons

Most newspapers devote more space and less attention to syndicated columns and cartoons than to any other element on the editorial page. These features are relatively inexpensive, undemanding of editorial attention and extremely useful for plugging editorial holes of any size and number. Some editors have streamlined their editing to the point that every day they slap a regular liberal columnist in one position on the page, a regular conservative columnist in another spot and maybe an interpretive columnist in a third spot. A cartoon by the same artist sits atop the page every day.

This is not the way to produce an editorial page that attracts readers seeking insights into issues that confront them, their communities, their states, their countries and the world. Fortunately, today's editorial page editors can choose among an abundance of columnists, many of whom are relatively new. Internet delivery of columns makes it relatively easy to check each day's batch and select and edit articles. A selection of one or more cartoons, also available on the Internet, helps enliven the page and, if picked properly, can add punch to other elements on the page. Pagination software makes it easy to vary the page design from day to day.

Even editors on one-person staffs are likely these days to have Internet access to columns and cartoons. They may not have a lot of time for fine editing and they may need to stick with two or three standard layouts, but they can surely spend enough time to select from among a variety of columns and cartoons.

It's hard to blame time-pressed editors who choose the shortcut of using the same page design and the same columns and cartoons every day, but what they gain in time they lose in the spontaneity of their pages. How enthusiastic will readers be if they can expect no surprises when they turn to the editorial or op-ed page?

In this chapter we will talk about the role of columns and cartoons on opinion pages, how editors decide which ones to use and how they handle syndicated materials.

■ DEVELOPMENT OF COLUMN WRITING

Signed political columns go back at least to the 1880s. Charles McClatchy, whose father James had worked for Horace Greeley on the *New York Tribune* and founded the *Sacramento Bee,* began a political column upon his father's death in 1883. From 1883 to 1897, he called the column "Notes," then, until 1936, "Private Thinks."[3] Heywood Broun began writing a political column in 1911,[4] first for the *New York Tribune,* then the *New York World* and eventually for syndication, until his death in 1931.[5] Arthur Brisbane began writing a signed front-page political column for William Randolph Hearst's newspapers in 1917 and continued writing it until his death in 1936.[6]

Political columnists began to flourish in the early 1920s. David Lawrence, who had accompanied President Woodrow Wilson to the peace talks in Europe after World War I, began writing a syndicated column in 1919.[7] Walter Lippmann, who had been writing for the *New York World,* on its demise became a syndicated *New York Herald-Tribune* columnist. Lippmann continued writing until 1971, Lawrence until 1973.[8]

Political columnists became popular in the early 1930s. One reason cited for their rise is that, with the coming of the New Deal, editorial page editors were eager to publish interpretive writers who, because of their inside sources, would be able to tell readers what was going on in Washington, D.C. At least some editorial page editors realized that they were unaware of what was going on in the federal government and out of touch with new trends in policy. The syndicated columnists moved in, Robert H. Estabrook of the *Washington Post* said, because newspapers were not doing a "good enough job providing background and interpretation in their news columns . . . and not doing a good enough job of providing informed comment in their editorial columns."[9] Readers wanted to know what was going on, and the columnists fulfilled this function.

Many early columnists, more in sympathy with the New Deal than most editors, provided contrasting opinions to the editorials with which they shared pages. Noting that most newspapers were editorially against President Franklin D. Roosevelt, Mark Ethridge of *Newsday* on Long Island, N.Y., wrote: "Rather than rouse the natives, or maybe to silence their protests, publishers thought it the better part of wisdom to let the columnists fight it out on their editorial pages."[10] The columnists who appeared about that time included Raymond Clapper, Tom Stokes, Drew Pearson, the Alsop brothers, Robert Allen, Marquis Childs, Dorothy Thompson and Frank Kent.

Although not among the earliest columnists, David Lawrence followed a career that typified what Ethridge called "both the rise—and . . . fall—of the columnists." Lawrence had been a favorite of Woodrow Wilson and Bernard Baruch, a prominent financier and presidential advisor. "He had the ears and confidence of the mighty, besides the energy to dig," Ethridge recalled. Columnist Walter Lippmann had also been a confidant of Woodrow Wilson and in fact was to pride himself on his close ties with public leaders through more than half a century of editorial and column writing. Robert Allen and Drew Pearson, with their "Washington Merry-Go-Round," provided readers with inside stories. Westbrook Pegler, sometimes published on the editorial page, became known for "reporting" demeaning things about public figures.

Columnist Ed Yoder has recalled that at the end of World War II Lippmann was still "the philosopher journalist of Jovian perspective," Arthur Krock was "only slightly less Olympian in tenor and tone" and Joseph Alsop, teamed with his brother Stewart, was calling himself a reporter "even when he was most opinionated." "Just below" (Yoder's description) were figures like Pearson, "who specialized in gossip," and Lawrence, "who specialized in indignation."[11]

The birth of syndicated column writing generally coincided with the coming of the New Deal. It is not surprising, therefore, that during the first years most columnists wrote from Washington, D.C., and were concerned with—and for the most part supportive of—New Deal initiatives. In the late 1960s most favorite columnists tended to be "liberal": among them, Walter Lippmann, Joseph Kraft, James Reston, Tom Braden and Frank Mankiewicz. The humorous, satirical columnists were Art Buchwald and Art Hoppe of the *San Francisco Chronicle*. For 35 years, in Buchwald's columns (as described in *Columbia Journalism Review*) "[e]very governmental and cultural idiocy was highlighted and held up to good-natured ridicule."[12] Aside from Dave Barry, who is not as political as Buchwald and Hoppe, those two humorists have no like today that I know of.

When I was looking for conservative columnists for the *Columbian* in 1965, editorial page editors generally had a choice of James J. Kilpatrick (who wrote a spritely column), William F. Buckley Jr. (who wrote an erudite column), Arthur Krock (never an easy read) and Richard Wilson (a dull read).

It was not until 1978, in what the *Columbia Journalism Review* called "The Rise of the Conservative Voice," that William Safire and George Will—readable as well as conservative—began appearing on editorial pages, enlisted by liberal-leaning newspapers. The *New York Times* hired Safire after he had worked for three Republican politicians: Dwight Eisenhower, John Lindsay and Jacob Javits. The *Washington Post* signed up George Will, who had been associated with Buckley.[13]

In 1989 Clarence Page became the first African-American to be syndicated nationally, by the conservative *Chicago Tribune*.

Eventually the popularity of the early columnists declined. The David Lawrence columns I edited for the *Des Moines* (Iowa) *Tribune* in the early 1960s were mostly a rehash of the daily news with a little conservative interpretation thrown in. Joseph Alsop was stuck on assuring readers that the war was being won in Vietnam. The news from Washington was reported well in the news columns, and the syndicated columnists did not have much more inside information than most reporters. The editorial policies of newspapers had also become more moderate. Editorial writers were more informed about and sympathetic toward what was going on in Washington. Readers also were more informed about the federal government and not satisfied with what Ethridge called the "pontificating. . . . griping, . . . off-the-cuff reflections" that came from the traditional columnists.[14]

■ COLUMNISTS TODAY

The best columnists today serve as more than opinion and information pipelines for public officials and offer more than knee-jerk reactions to the day's news. William Safire, certainly one of today's most admired columnists, has written this about the responsibilities of his profession: "Veteran reporters and creaking commentators have a single goal in writing about great events: advance the story. Unearth facts that policy makers do not know, do not want to know or do not want the public to know they know."[15] One hopes that readers appreciate good, even clever, writing, and it is to be expected that they will find themselves agreeing more with some columnists than others. But when they start reading a column, they want to find out something they don't know or haven't thought about, perhaps even on a subject they know little about. Columnist Ed Yoder has said that "the column is at best a chance to watch a mind and style at work, through time, on the topics of the day."[16]

Plenty of syndicated columnists are available to editors. In 1996, the *Editor & Publisher Syndicate Directory* listed 283 entries under "Political Commentary." The 2001 *Editor & Publisher Syndicate Directory* listed 273. (Of course both lists included more than just *editorial page* columnists.) In 1999 *Editor & Publisher* reported that 15 syndicated editorial columnists were being sold to 250 or more newspapers.[17]

In looking at editorial pages for the second, third and fourth editions of this book, I found little difference in the frequency with which editors used syndicated columns. In 1990–1992 I found that newspapers carried an average of 1.3 columns on each editorial page or editorial/op-ed page combination. In 1994–1997 the number was 1.6; in 2000–2001 it was 1.5.

For each edition I also counted occurrence of individual columnists. The chart below shows the most popular in the three sets of newspapers, in order of the number of papers in which I found them:

1990-92	1994-early 97	2000-2001
William Raspberry	Ellen Goodman	David Broder
James J. Kilpatrick	George F. Will	Ellen Goodman
Mike Royko	Mike Royko	George F. Will
George F. Will	David Broder	Maureen Dowd
Cal Thomas	William Raspberry	William Raspberry
David Broder	Cal Thomas	E.J. Dionne
Ellen Goodman	William Safire	Richard Cohen
Anthony Lewis	Molly Ivins	Mona Sharon
Richard Cohen	Joan Beck	*tied:*
		Thomas Sowell
		Debra Saunders
		Robert J. Samuelson
		Robert Reno
		Cal Thomas

This ranking, of course, reflects the newspapers that I came across. *Editor & Publisher* reported that Cal Thomas, with 540 papers, and George F. Will, with 400-plus, both conservative columnists, were the most widely syndicated columnists in 2001. Ellen Goodman was reported as being the most widely distributed liberal columnist, with "20 or 30" fewer newspapers than Will.[18]

I was impressed with the number of new names that appeared in the mid-nineties. Of the 87 columnists in the most recent survey, only 35 remained from the mid-1990s and only 26 from the early 1990s. But I also was impressed by the consistent ratings of the most popular columnists. Six of the nine most popular on the early 1990s list appeared high on the mid-1990s list, and five of the eight still living (Mike Royko had died) appeared high on the list in the early 2000s. The most recent additions to the list of leading columnists are Maureen Dowd, E.J. Dionne, Mona Sharon, Thomas Sowell, Debra Saunders, Robert J. Samuelson and Robert Reno.

The number of women columnists jumped sharply from the early to mid-nineties, both in numbers (from 10 to 28) and percentage (from 15 to 27 percent). The number remained unchanged in the early 2000s, but the percentage increased from 27 to 32 percent. More women are making the most-used list. Goodman, the only woman in the early 1990s, was joined by Molly Ivins and Joan Beck in the mid-1990s and by Dowd, Sharon and Saunders in the early 2000s.

(Back in the early days of column writing, Anne O'Hare McCormick of the *New York Times* and Dorothy Thompson of the *New York Herald Tribune* wrote columns on international affairs. Georgie Anne Geyer has been reporting and commenting on foreign matters since I have been editing editorial pages. Eleanor Roosevelt wrote a newspaper column, "My Day," beginning during her husband's presidency. Dorothy Thompson wrote a regular column, principally for the *Ladies Home Journal.* For a time Hillary Rodham Clinton wrote a syndicated column.)

Among African-Americans, William Raspberry has consistently ranked among the most popular. Clarence Page's column also continues to be syndicated.

The columnist who has persisted as long as any columnist today is David Broder, whom Kilpatrick described 20 years ago as "the most honest" writer in Washington. Broder probably is still the most respected. Kilpatrick continues to write an occasional column on matters before the U.S. Supreme Court as well as a weekly column on good (and bad) writing.

Current columnists represent a range of political ideology. *Editor & Publisher* reported in 2002 that, among the eight largest syndicates, conservative columnists outnumbered liberals "roughly 35 to 30"—plus "several dozen moderate or hard-to-categorize writers." "Conservative columnists are a bit more popular," said the director of one of the syndicates. He suggested that one reason was the influence of "conservative publishers" on smaller papers, which substantially outnumber larger papers.[19]

One positive sign of increasing diversity is evidence that more columnists are venturing beyond politics. One columnist in the *E&P* syndicate listing was identified as dealing with culture and society, another with ethics and religion, several with business, others with the First Amendment. One reason for Ellen Goodman's popularity is that she deals with public issues in a more personal style than the pundits who write standard political columns from Washington.

Humor columnists seem on the decline. I came across five in the early 1990s (Mike Royko, Art Buchwald, Mark Russell, Dave Barry and Andy Rooney). In the mid-1990s, I found only Art Buchwald and Art Hoppe. In the 2000–2001 survey I found a few Buchwald columns and a single Dave Barry piece. (Barry, who comments on current but not necessarily political topics, usually appears in other parts of the newspaper.) Royko and Hoppe have died.

■ SETTING POLICIES FOR COLUMNS

Editing syndicated columns involves more than placing them in predetermined positions on the editorial page. Editors must decide on the columns that they want to buy and on those that they want to run on any given day. They must make decisions about how extensively they will edit the columns and about how they will identify the columnists that appear on their pages.

Selecting Columnists

So how do editors decide which types of columnists to buy?

They basically have three alternatives of political stripes. When readers had a choice of newspapers in their community, it was not unusual for editors to subscribe to columnists that reinforced their own political views, but this practice is rare today. At the other extreme some editors think that, in one-newspaper communities, they should lean toward columnists that express views different from the editorial policies of their paper. Some editors make a special effort to run opposing views on the op-ed page (although "op-ed" refers to page opposite the editorial page, not opposite views). The third alternative is to try to balance differing viewpoints, perhaps with roughly equal numbers of "liberal" and "conservative" columnists. In one survey, 60 percent of editors who responded sought to balance columnists. Only 12 percent said they selected columnists with views similar to the newspaper's while 27 percent said they picked columnists for their ability to draw readers, regardless of their views.[20]

Using Columnists

Figures cited earlier indicate that, on average, newspapers run between one and two syndicated columns a day or about 10 a week. Columnists typically write three columns a week. If a newspaper subscribes to six columnists, it probably throws away eight columns a week. If it subscribes to more, as many papers do, an even higher percentage ends in the computer dump. Even though papers pay their regular columnists, whether they are run or not, syndicated columnists tend to think that, to build a following among readers, they should be run consistently and regularly. Readers like to know, they contend, that a certain columnist will run, for example, on Monday, Wednesday and Friday.

The sample of newspapers that I looked at suggests most editors no longer buy this argument. Most editors subscribe to more columns than they can use. They clearly think that their readers are more interested in what is said than in who said it.

Availability of Columnists

One problem facing newspapers, especially smaller papers that are geographically near larger papers, is how to get all the popular columnists (and cartoons). The metropolitan papers like to buy the most popular syndicated features on an exclusive basis, and who can blame them? Many are fighting to preserve their circulation and advertising in the face of competition from suburban newspapers. The suburban newspapers think it is unfair for the big, rich papers to tie up the best stuff.

A partial victory for the non-metros came in 1975, when, in response to threatened action by the Justice Department, the *Boston Globe* gave up its rights to the exclusive use of syndicated materials in Maine, Vermont, New Hampshire and eastern Massachusetts. But the problem persists. The *Daily Journal-American* in Bellevue, Wash., a paper published across Lake Washington from two Seattle dailies, had trouble obtaining syndicated materials when it went to a daily schedule.[21] When I worked for the *Columbian* in Vancouver, Wash., across the Columbia River from two Portland dailies, we had the same problem, particularly when we wanted to add a Sunday edition with a comic section.

The problem remains. In 1996, in a case involving the *Daily Herald,* a suburban Chicago paper, the U.S. District Court of Appeals held that territorial exclusivity fosters rather than hampers competition. The judges' opinion noted that the suburban newspaper "has never tried to outbid the *Tribune* or *Sun Times.*" The response from the *Herald* attorney was: "Once the *Tribune* or *Sun-Times* gets it, as long as they continue to pay for it . . . syndicates aren't going to give it to anyone else."[22] My response would have been: How can a small newspaper be expected to outbid a metropolitan daily, or two metropolitan dailies? Still, a lot of columnists are available, and, if forced to dig beneath the top layer of the favorites, who knows what new, fresh, innovative columnists are waiting to be discovered?

Identifying Columnists

It is important for a newspaper to make it clear that syndicated columnists are not staff writers or local people. Most newspapers I have looked at recently were doing a more consistent job than in the past of placing the names of syndicates at the top or bottom of columns. Some editors prefer to identify an author as, for example, "*Washington Post* writer." An increasing number of editors are providing readers with the e-mail addresses of their own writers as well as of syndicated columnists.

Conflicts of Interest

Another issue regarding columnists is possible conflict of interest. The issue first arose during the Watergate hearings in 1973 when Jeb Stuart Magruder, former deputy director of the Committee to Re-elect the President (CRP), told an investigating committee that one of the cash distributions he had made was $20,000 to a writer named Victor Lasky. An editor's inquiry to the North American Newspaper Alliance (NANA), for which Lasky wrote, brought the reply that Lasky had received the money for speeches he had written for Martha Mitchell, a neighbor of Lasky's and the wife of the attorney general.[23] The National Conference of Editorial Writers (NCEW) filed charges with the National News Council, alleging that Lasky had engaged in a conflict of interest and that NANA had failed to accept responsibility to inform its clients of the conflict of interest. The council upheld NCEW's complaint.[24]

A 1980 report found that all major syndicates had at least announced that they would require writers to "[avoid] undisclosed conflicts of interest in their subject area."[25] Twenty years after the News Council ruling, however, when Gilbert Cranberg of the *Des Moines Register* took another look at the practices of the syndicates, he saw "*deja vu* all over again." The syndicates, at least a good share of them, had slipped back into their old ways of ignoring responses and rebuttals. "Some syndicates need to be reminded that editors are more than just business customers, and the services more than simply go-betweens and conduits," Cranberg wrote in reporting on his findings.[26]

Then, in 1996, when columnist George Will reminded his readers that his wife Mari Maseng was a ranking staff member of presidential candidate Robert Dole, the whole issue of conflict of interest and disclosure was reopened. A month later Maseng left the Dole campaign. Editors who participated in a symposium in *The Masthead* on what was billed as "The George Will/Mari Maseng Affair" generally agreed that Will should give up his column or refrain from commenting on the presidential race. They were still uncomfortable over the continuing potential for conflict. Cranberg said that a one-time disclosure was not sufficient, that Will's syndicate should "append a standing reference to the Will-Maseng connection to every Will column that bears even tangentially on Dole."[27]

■ LOCAL COLUMNISTS

More newspapers seem to carry columns by staff members. The most opinion-oriented columns generally appear on the editorial or op-ed page and may be written by an editorial writer or editor. Columns by other staff writers are likely to run elsewhere—a sports column in the sports section, a business column in the business section, a column on local affairs in the local section. Local columnists usually look for the local angle in picking what they write about. (For a more extensive look at local columnists, see the "Local Columnist" section in Chapter 16, "Other Types of Opinion Writing.")

■ THE ROLE OF THE CARTOONIST

Roy Paul Nelson, retired University of Oregon journalism professor and part-time cartoonist, described the role of the cartoonist in these words: "The job of an editorial cartoonist, I found, was to take something complicated and simplify it. The cartoonist has no kinship with, say, the sociologist, whose job is to do the opposite."[28]

Today's editorial page editors and cartoonists partly, but only partly, see eye to eye on the role of the editorial cartoonist. Cartoonists, more than editors, tend to think of cartoonists as artists. They also tend to think they should be given more editorial freedom than editors generally would like them to have.

A 1984 survey of cartoonists and editors found that both groups rated "critic" as the first role of the cartoonist.[29] "I believe the fundamental role of an editorial cartoonist is to kick fannies—to convey one's opinion forcefully, graphically and unapologetically," said one cartoonist.

The editors' second most mentioned choice (third among cartoonists) was "opinion leader." One cartoonist who thought "opinion leader" was an inappropriate role wrote: "Editorial cartoons do not persuade. They affirm a reader's perhaps hazy stance on a subject by making concrete and graphic their positions. Readers say 'Aha! That's what I mean.'"

Among cartoonists the second choice (fourth for editors) was "artist." "Too many editors are poor judges of what is good cartoon art," one cartoonist wrote.

Who's in Charge?

Surveys have found that editors and cartoonists have somewhat different ideas about who is best qualified to judge cartoons and who should have the final word on cartoons. In a 1984 survey the largest groups of editors and cartoonists (56 percent in both instances) agreed editors and cartoonists should confer in deciding on cartoons. The remainder had different ideas, with 43 percent of the cartoonists saying cartoonists should make the decision and 35 percent of editors saying the editors should.[30] In a 1995 survey about 38 percent of editors thought they were better than cartoonists at predicting reactions to cartoons. Only about 8 percent of cartoonists agreed. Forty-eight percent of cartoonists thought that editors did not understand the function of editorial cartoons. Only 6 percent of editors agreed.[31]

Cartoonists and editors don't necessarily agree politically. In the 1984 survey cartoonists tended to be more liberal than their newspapers, but most thought cartoonists should conform to the editorial policies of their papers.

"Editorial cartoons reflect opinions of the paper and the skill of the cartoonist, and, if not, cartoons don't belong in the paper," one cartoonist wrote. "If he doesn't see things in the same way the publisher does, the cartoonist should look for another publisher," another cartoonist said.[32] But in the 1995 survey only 24 percent of cartoonists and 32 percent of editors said cartoons should reflect the editorial policy of the newspaper. If a cartoon conflicted with the newspaper's policy, 62 percent of cartoonists and 49 percent of editors still would run it on the editorial page. Seventeen percent of cartoonists and 15 percent of editors would run it on the op-ed page. Only 3 percent of cartoonists and 13 percent of editors would not run the cartoon.[33]

So perhaps some cartoonists are being given more opportunities to express views that differ from the newspaper's official editorial policy. The degree of freedom no doubt varies from newspaper to newspaper and from cartoonist to cartoonist. A cartoonist in the 1984 survey pointed out, "An Oliphant, for instance, should never be restricted," but to reach that status, a cartoonist had to be "good, well-versed and responsible enough to tell good slams from cheap shots."

Following the September 11, 2001, terrorist attacks, Steve Benson of the *Arizona Republic*, a Pulitzer Prize winner, drew several anti-war cartoons that did not agree with the newspaper's own editorial stands. The cartoons drew protests from readers and a comment by the paper's reader advocate that Benson "has veered way off the political mainstream." The cartoons were run as Benson's cartoons regularly are run—marked "opinion" and not run on the editorial page.[34]

A cartoonist's position can't be allowed to become "too revered," Mindy Cameron of the *Seattle Times* said during an NCEW convention panel on editor-cartoonist relationships. Editors, she said, must make their responsibilities clear to cartoonists, discuss what kinds of cartoons are expected and insist on keeping a dialogue between editor and cartoonist.[35] The cartoonists on the panel said trust was the most important part of their relations with editors. After years of drawing cartoons on the *Austin* (Texas) *American-Statesman*, Ben Sargent said his editors "trust me not to do something too *outre*, [and] I trust them to back me up."[36]

In a *Masthead* symposium on "Getting along with Your Cartoonist," Thomas Gebhardt, associate editor of the *Cincinnati* (Ohio) *Enquirer*, said that, when

Jim Borgman first started as a cartoonist, he drew what was expected of him. But, according to Borgman, as his skill matured and his reputation increased, Borgman began drawing cartoons that reflected his, and not necessarily the paper's, view.[37] "A decade ago it became clear to me that I could only do my best work only if granted that freedom," Borgman wrote for the symposium.[38] Not many cartoonists have this honey of a deal.

Perhaps a more typical relationship existed at the *Lincoln* (Neb.) *Journal.* Editorial Page Editor Dick Herman reported that cartoonist Paul Fell usually offered three or four rough drafts early in the morning. "We confer. We parlay. Sometimes I bounce Satanic counterproposals at him," Herman said. "But increasingly, his own commentary stands. It becomes a finished product by noon or early afternoon."[39]

■ SETTING POLICIES FOR CARTOONS

Editors face two policy questions when they select cartoons for the editorial page: Should cartoons, especially those at the top of the editorial page, reflect only the editorial policies of the newspaper? In buying syndicated cartoons, should editors seek a broad or a narrow array of opinions?

To Support Editorials?

Some newspapers (the *Seattle Post-Intelligencer,* for example) have a policy that encourages editorial writers and cartoonists to focus on the same subject for a particular day's editorial page. Some studies have indicated that cartoons are more persuasive if they are published in conjunction with editorials expressing the same point of view. On other newspapers that have their own cartoonists, the cartoonists and the editorial writers may have differing agendas, and only by chance hit on the same subject.

On papers that depend on syndicated cartoons, editors must rely on whatever comes in the mail that day. Saving unused—and even used—cartoons can provide a backlog from which to draw when a cartoon is needed to go with an editorial or column. Most cartoons, however, quickly become dated.

A Variety of Opinions?

A more serious question is whether editorials and cartoons on the same page should express the same editorial philosophy. One line of thought among editors is that any cartoon at the top of an editorial page should conform to, or at least not conflict with, the policies of the paper. According to this reasoning, a cartoon at the top of the page will have the most impact if it reflects the paper's position. Some publishers and editors think readers will be confused about the paper's policy if they see a conflict between editorials and the lead cartoon. Other publishers and editors consider cartoons as they do political columns, as intended to present a variety of opinions.

Most editors who subscribe to syndicated cartoons probably take a middle ground. First, they are not likely to subscribe to cartoons that are completely out of sync with their papers' policies. Second, unless editors subscribe to a large number of cartoons, they must take on a daily basis what they are sent by the syndicates. Contemporary layouts of editorial pages have encouraged editors to publish more cartoons. When cartoons are used to illustrate columns or articles, the reader may be less likely to ask, or care, whether they reflect the paper's policies.

In deciding which cartoonists to subscribe to, the editor must decide whether to limit the selection to those that generally agree with the newspaper's policies, to choose from a wide political range, or to seek the best cartoonists. My perusal of editorial pages suggests that very few newspapers subscribe strictly to cartoons of one political stripe. Editors may place their favorite cartoonist or cartoonists in the lead spot on the page, but most allow for the display of other cartoons. Just as editors are likely to want to provide readers with a variety of columnists, they are likely to want a variety of cartoonists.

■ CARTOONISTS OF THE PAST

When *Masthead* editors asked *Detroit News* cartoonist Draper Hill to take a look at the development of political cartoons in America, he started with Benjamin Franklin.[40] In 1847 Franklin provided an illustration for the pamphlet *Plain Truth* that, in Hill's view, was "clearly the invention of a wordsmith rather than a draftsman." Both editors and cartoonists are still divided over whether form or content is more important for cartoons, and whether satire or whimsy is more appropriate.

Hill credits Thomas Nast with initiating the "rough-and-tumble era" of the late 19th century, which "petered out with the death of Homer Davenport (1912) and the taming of Art Young." After cartoonists had been exhorted to "bash" the Huns during World War I, the 1920s began an era of "Good Taste." "Information, education and the nurture of consensus" replaced ridicule and satire, Hill wrote. By the end of World War II, and for another decade, cartoonists tended to take a "high-minded, generally predictable, over-labeled, under-caricatured tack . . . more bark than bite."

In 1946 the dominant cartoonists were Daniel Fitzpatrick of the *St. Louis* (Mo.) *Post-Dispatch,* J.M. "Ding" Darling of the *Des Moines* (Iowa) *Register,* and, later, the *New York Herald Tribune,* Vaughan Shoemaker of the *Chicago Daily News,* Herbert L. Block of the *Washington Post* and Bill Mauldin of the *St. Louis* (Mo.) *Post-Dispatch* and, later, the *Chicago Sun-Times.* Nearly all cartoons appeared in a vertical format (that is, they were narrower than they were high).

Then, using the same format, but with more bite and fewer words, came the first wave of younger cartoonists, whom Hill identified as Paul Conrad, Ed Valtman, Hugh Haynie, Jules Fieffer, Bill Mauldin (who had retired and returned) and Bill Sanders.

The second wave was mostly Australian Pat Oliphant, who introduced the horizontal format and a more detailed, more artistic style that did not necessarily rely on humor.

The third wave was led by Jeff MacNelly, who also drew in the horizontal, more artistic style, but used more humor. Hill noted that when MacNelly won his first Pulitzer Prize, in 1972 at the age of 24, Oliphant referred to the cartoonists who had adopted the horizontal style as "those bastards." "Before long the epithet 'clone' achieved a certain popularity," Hill said, and as the MacNelly style became popular, the epithet became "clone of a clone."

In spite of these disparaging labels, Hill concluded that Oliphant's and MacNelly's styles (which he called the phenomenon of "Oliphany" or "MacStyle") "energized committed, aware, talented, college-educated types in unprecedented numbers and propelled them into the profession" of editorial cartooning during the years between the Vietnam War and Watergate. This new generation, Hill said, was younger and more diverse and had "at least as much editorial freedom as they [knew] what to do with."

The author of a book on political cartoons, Professor John Fischer of the University of Minnesota–Duluth, has described 1969 to 1985 as the "golden age" of editorial cartooning. A number of artists did "spectacular" work lampooning Presidents Nixon and Carter, he said, and "futile but heroic" work during the Reagan administration.[41]

■ CARTOONISTS OF TODAY

Some observers of the editorial cartoon scene have perceived a decline in editorial cartooning—both in numbers and in prestige. Newspaper editorial cartoonists have been declining in number, no doubt about that. A decline in prestige is less clear. A 1995 study estimated that about 120 cartoonists were working on daily newspapers, compared to 170 in 1980.[42] Signe Wilkinson, then president of the American Association of Editorial Cartoonists, said that cartoonists were among those being affected as newspapers folded or made staff cutbacks.[43] In 1996 *Editor & Publisher* reported that five previously employed cartoonists no longer had a base paper.[44] In 1998 participants at an American Press Institute (API) symposium on "The State of Political Cartooning" noted that more and more cartoonists were finding themselves without a newspaper as a base (and major source of salary).[45]

Some cartoonists have worked their way up through a "farm system," being employed part-time or working freelance for weeklies and smaller dailies. One freelancer reported that sometimes editors allowed him to comment on a local subject of his choice but other times they had their own ideas. He said he didn't make a lot of money, but he got to see his work in print and the newspapers got localized editorials at relatively low cost.[46]

Those who remain on the job report feeling under pressure to produce only "bland, gag-oriented cartoons rather than hard-hitting ones."[47] Similar views were expressed by syndicated cartoonists Pat Oliphant and Steve Benson at the 1998 API symposium. Oliphant said he thought "that over the last eight or ten years the whole landscape has changed and that controversial cartoons are not as welcome as they used to be."[48] Steve Benson of the Phoenix *Arizona Republic* said he saw cartoonists as being subject to "more control and less freedom."[49]

Fischer, after looking back at what he called the "golden age" of editorial cartooning, expressed the opinion that many editorial cartoonists did not enjoy the respect and prominence of their predecessors because of competition with the Internet, television, radio and other media.[50] The keynote speaker at the API symposium, Stephen Hess, senior fellow at The Brookings Institution, expressed a more optimistic opinion concerning the Internet. He saw the wealth of cartoon material on the Internet as a sign that "young people are going to have an opportunity to be seen, despite the fact that newspapers, their major vehicle now, are contracting."[51]

Hess offered the symposium cartoonists another reason for optimism: that "over time you've moved [from politics] into everything—economics, religion, social activities of all sorts—and you now have glorious opportunities to get away from strictly political issues and to say something important—and with a bite—about other issues as well." Hess added: "[T]he one person who absolutely continues to amaze me in this way is [Garry] Trudeau in 'Doonesbury.'"[52]

1990-92	1994-1997	2000-2001
"Doonesbury"	"Doonesbury"	"Doonesbury"
Jeff MacNelly	Don Wright	Mike Luckovich
Patrick Oliphant	*tied:*	Patrick Oliphant
Don Wright	*Jim Borgman*	"Mallard Fillmore"
Jim Borgman	*Jeff MacNelly*	*tied:*
"Berry's World"	"Mallard Fillmore"	*Don Wright*
"Dunigan's People"	*Mike Luckovich*	*Dick Wright*
Dick Wright	*tied:*	*Jim Borgman*
Henry Payne	*Patrick Oliphant*	*tied:*
Bill Day	*Tom Toles*	*Tom Toles*
Mike Luckovich	"Berry's World"	*Jeff Danziger*
David Horsey	Jeff Stahler	*Robert Ariail*
Steve Benson	Steve Benson	*tied:*
	Chip Bok	*Jeff Stahler*
	Ed Gamble	*Mike Peters*
	Mike Peters	*Gary Markstein*
	Jimmie Margulies	*John Branch*

In an unscientific look at the cartoonists most popular with editors today, I examined the same stack of editorial and op-ed pages that I used in tallying columnists. I found 117 cartoons by 41 cartoonists, on 90 sets of editorial and editorial/op-ed pages for an average of 1.3 cartoons per set—about the same frequency of cartoons I had found five and ten years earlier. The most popular cartoonists have not changed much either. The chart above shows the cartoons and cartoonists I found most often, in order of their apparent popularity.

Rankings of the most frequently appearing cartoonists remain fairly consistent from one list to the next. Of the 13 cartoonists on the early 1990s list, eight appear among the 15 on the mid-1990s list and six on the 2000–2001 list. Of the 15 on the second list, nine appear on the third. One newcomer to the second list (tied for third) was "Mallard Fillmore," which some newspapers run side-by-side with "Doonesbury," providing a liberal-conservative balance on the editorial or op-ed page.

No woman cartoonist showed up in the first study. Ann C. Telnaes and Signe Wilkinson appeared in the second study; only Wilkinson in the most recent study.

"Comment" cartoons are not limited to the editorial page. "Doonesbury" and "Mallard Fillmore" probably are run more often in other sections of the newspaper. "Boondocks," with an African-American theme, speaks out strongly on current events. (In response to reader complaints, the Eugene, Ore., *Register-Guard* moved both "Mallard Fillmore" and "Boondocks" to the classified advertising section.)

Actually "the funnies" have a long history of what Mark McGuire of the *Albany* (N.Y.) *Times Union* has called "serious political commentary."[53] Harold Gray, creator of "Little Orphan Annie" (begun in 1924), was criticized for "his [conservative] political views and his alleged propagandizing."[54] Al Capp, who started "L'il Abner" in 1934, became known for his "right wing politics."[55] Walt Kelly's "Pogo," begun in 1943, offered social comment from the liberal side, as "Doonesbury" has done since 1970.[56]

■ THE POWER OF THE CARTOON

Today's cartoonists can pack a wallop when, with a sketch and a few words, they cut through to an issue that an editorial writer might take 500 words to explain. However one might have regarded the George W. Bush administration's ill-fated Office of Strategic Influence, the potential power of political cartoons was made clear in a *New York Times* news story that paraphrased Defense Secretary Donald Rumsfeld as saying that "commentaries and editorial cartoons about the office's proposed activities made it impossible for it to do its job." The *Times* article said that the office was intended "to provide news items, possibly even false ones, to unwitting foreign journalists to influence public opinion abroad."[57] In Chapter 1 ("The Editorial Page That Used to Be") we noted that *Harper's Weekly* cartoonist Thomas Nast, together with the *New York Times*, helped bring down William M. "Boss" Tweed. Tweed was quoted as saying, "I don't give a straw for your newspaper articles—my constituents don't know how to read. But they can't help seeing them damn pictures."[58]

The effectiveness of an editorial cartoon depends on many factors: the artistic ability of the artist, the clarity of the message, the political atmosphere at the time of publication and the receptivity of the audience—all subtle and difficult to predict or measure.

Cartoonists use a variety of techniques to help make their audiences understand what they are trying to say. One technique involves a familiar image that might seem to have no relation to the message of the cartoon. Jimmy Margulies of the *Bergen* (N.J.) *County Record* used that technique at a time when the NCAA basketball tournament playoffs were being announced. Pointing to a playoff chart, a husband tells his wife, "March madness." Filling all the slots—four games on the left, two in the middle and the championship game on the right—were identical entries: "Palestinian Terrorism vs. Israeli Retaliation." Another technique uses fictional or real characters that readers are expected to recognize. Two examples—one by Margulies, the other by Gary Brookins of the *Richmond* (Va.) *Times-Dispatch*—drew on the movie industry. When it was revealed that the Immigration and Naturalization Service had been routinely approving visas of international students, Brookins drew Laurel and Hardy figures rubberstamping INS visas as they passed them from a nearly empty in-basket to an overflowing out-basket. When the motion picture Oscars were awarded, Margulies showed Oscar statues labeled "Halle Berry" and "Denzel Washington." The cartoon was labeled "Guess Who's Coming to Winner," a reference to the movie "Guess Who's Coming to Dinner," in which the guest was an African-American.

YOUR OWN CARTOONIST?

Surveys show that about 10 percent of daily newspapers have a regular editorial cartoon. Editors who can't afford a full-time cartoonist are sometimes tempted to turn to free-lance artists or artists on their own staffs. Some successes have resulted. Jim Borgman had done only one cartoon a week for his college paper and wasn't particularly interested in public affairs when he went to work for the *Cincinnati* (Ohio) *Enquirer.*[59] Paul Fell was teaching art in a small college when he started sending an occasional cartoon to the *Lincoln* (Neb.) *Journal.*[60] (When Fell later was laid off by the *Journal* he turned to fax and radio. He faxed his daily cartoons to 200 local citizens, then went on the air to take calls from his subscribers.)[61] In looking through a group of Nebraska newspapers, I found a Fell cartoon in the *Kearney Hub,* suggesting he had found additional outlets for his work.

The *Gainesville* (Fla.) *Sun* found a free-lance cartoonist through a cartoon-drawing contest. Unable to afford a full-time cartoonist, the paper invited readers to draw cartoons on current issues. About 40 responded. The best of the submissions were published in a special Sunday "Issues" section. From the contestants, a *Sun* editor reported, came "the next best thing to an on-staff cartoonist, a talented and prolific free-lancer."[62] The *Arlington* (Mass.) *Advocate* acquired the part-time cartooning talents of a person whose regular job was engraving portraits on tombstones.[63]

Skilled local artists can bring life and controversy to a page, especially when commenting on local topics. But they must be more than artists or clever gag writers. When asked for ideas on how to get editorial cartoons from a good artist who didn't follow the news, A. Rosen of the Albany, N.Y., *Knickerbocker News,* then president of the National Cartoonist Society, advised: "Give up on that person; you'll never make him or her an editorial cartoonist. Instead, seek out a young person who may not draw well but who is interested in public affairs. Hire that person."[64]

CONCLUSION

Rosen's point was that the message is more important than the medium. Editors should not run syndicated columnists and cartoonists only because it is the standard thing to do, because these features spruce up the page or because they bring wandering eyes to the page. They should use these syndicated features—and their own local columnists and cartoonists—to present ideas to their readers. They should try to make their readers think—not just entertain them or present them with writers and artists who express opinions and ideas that readers already have. An editorial page should be a place where readers find some familiar faces and names, but also unfamiliar ways of looking at the local community, the state, the nation and the world.

QUESTIONS AND EXERCISES

1. Keep track of the syndicated columns in the newspapers of your area to determine whether they tend to run columnists that agree with their own editorial policies, that disagree or that express a variety of opinions.

2. Do these papers run a few columnists consistently or a variety of columnists infrequently? If they run a few, do these columns have something new and different to say each day? If they run a variety, do columns appear often enough to build regular followings among readers?

3. How would you judge the overall quality of the columnists published by the various newspapers you have studied? Do some of the papers seem to spend a lot of money on columnists and others only a little?

4. Do any of the newspapers label the columnists they carry, or attempt to describe the columnists' political positions? If so, are the labels accurate and appropriate?

5. Can you find letters to the editor concerning columns that have been distributed by the syndicates?

6. Which cartoonists seem to be most popular?

7. Do any of the newspapers have their own political cartoonists? Where do they appear on the editorial page? Does the local cartoon always agree with the editorial policies of the paper?

8. Ask editorial page editors in your area whether they have had trouble purchasing a column or cartoon because of territorial exclusivity.

9. While you have the editors' attention, ask them how often they receive letters from syndicates in response to columns and whether they always publish those letters.

10. If you still have the editors' attention, ask about their policies on trimming columns.

CHAPTER NINETEEN

Innovations in Design and Content

*Too often page patterns never vary.
While this provides the reader with
a familiar page, it often is boring,
especially if editorials are not noteworthy.*
—RALPH I. TURNER,
MARSHALL UNIVERSITY [1]

When editorial page editors sit down to plan the following day's editorial page, and the op-ed page if there is one, they must select editorials, letters, columns, cartoons and other materials. They must also decide on the layout that will best accommodate those features. Some editors, by their own choice or someone else's, are stuck with editorial pages that look the same every day and contain the same mix of features. But the trend among daily newspapers seems clearly to be in the direction of varying the editorial page, from one day to the next, in appearance and content. Varied page makeup can help attract readers; varied content can provide pleasant and rewarding surprises for readers. The purpose of this chapter is to trace efforts to transform the editorial page and the op-ed page from among the most stodgy-looking pages into spritely, stimulating pages.

■ THE "GRAY" TRADITION

For most of the 175 years of the American editorial page's history, editors attempted to gain distinction for their pages through gray respectability. When Professor Robert Bohle of Virginia Commonwealth University was asked to look back over 40 years of newspaper design in 1986, he found that editorial pages had changed the least.[2] The guru of newspaper typography, Edmund C. Arnold, agreed. "The page is still locked into a static page pattern," Arnold said. "It's more interesting than it was 40 years ago, but it's still static."[3]

Except for William Randolph Hearst, who jazzed up his editorial pages 50 years before nearly everyone else, most editors continued through World War II to make up their pages much as their 19th-century predecessors had.

Although the editorial page began to emerge as a separate page, or as a portion of a page, during the first decades of the 19th century, the page was hard to distinguish from other pages. All the type, news and editorial, was set one column in width. News and editorials ran from the bottom of one column to the top of the next column and sometimes from the bottom of one to the top of the next.

Aside from content, about the only distinguishing mark of an editorial, evident as early as 1835 in the *New York Sun,* was slightly larger type with lines spaced (leaded) a little farther apart. The only headlines were three or four words in italics of the same size and on the same line as the body type. (The *Sun* for August 11, 1835, is displayed in Figure 1, page 305.) The *Sun* page measured 11 by 16.5 inches, about the size of the modern-day tabloid, but the type was considerably smaller than the type used in newspapers today.

The height of type is measured in points, with 72 points to the inch. The height is measured from the top of the tallest letter to the bottom of the letter that drops farthest below the base line—for example, from the top of an M to the bottom of a p.

This is 6-point type.

This is 7-point type.

This is 9.5-point type.

Most news columns today are set in 9.5 or 10-point type, and editorials in 12-point or larger type. The text you are reading now is 10.5-point type.

The *Sun*'s page is set in 6-point type, with 2-point spacing between lines in the first two columns and 1-point spacing in the other two columns. Words totaled approximately 3,950.

A typical editorial page of Henry Raymond's *New York Times* in 1859 was about 60 percent editorial (set in 7-point type with 2 points spacing) and 40 percent news (set in 6.5-point type with no spacing). The 16-by-23 inch page contained approximately 6,900 words.

As mentioned, William Randolph Hearst was the exception to the long gray tradition. The October 27, 1933, editorial page of his *New York American* (Figure 2, page 306), also 16 by 23 inches, contained approximately 2,900 words.

A more typical example of the gray era was the January 20, 1953, *Washington Post* (Figure 3, page 307). Also 16 by 23, it had approximately 5,400 words. Editorials were set in 10-point type, the remainder of the page in 9-point type.

In comparison, the editorial page of a recent issue of the Minneapolis, Minn., *Star Tribune* (Figure 4, page 308) contained about 1,900 text words. Part of the difference is accounted for by today's narrower pages—12.5 inches as compared to 16 inches wide. (The length is 22 inches). The printed area of the *Star Tribune,* about 72 percent the size of the 1953 *Post* page, contains 35 percent of the number of words on the *Post* page. Artwork accounts for 25 percent of the page. (When the *Star Tribune* page carries no artwork in the editorial columns and no cartoon in the lower right corner, text words number about 2,400, 44 percent of the words on the *Post* page, and artwork makes up 14 percent of the page.) Artwork, larger type and larger, well-spaced headlines help make today's editorial pages more attractive, but also cut down on the space available for written opinion.

Editors were shocked when Hearst and Arthur Brisbane began to set editorials in larger type and wider columns, to run the editorials across several columns (perhaps the original horizontal makeup) and to introduce huge illustrations to the page. Hearst's clouded reputation may even have delayed the brightening of American editorial pages, since "respectable" editors did not want their pages to look like his.

Figure 1 **New York Sun**

THE NEW YORK SUN.

TUESDAY MORNING, AUGUST 11, 1835.

Distress in Ireland.—Accounts from Ireland, received by the Sheffield, represent many districts of Ireland as suffering great distress from famine. In one parish, consisting of thirty-four families, in the county of Galway, only three possessed provisions for a week. In another, comprising 322 families, only 37 were provisioned till harvest; and, should they extend relief to their famishing neighbors, the whole stock would not hold out a week. "From an authentic source, we have discovered that upwards of 6,000 persons in the barony of Erris, county Mayo, alone, have, on an average, but five days' provision on hand; and in that number there are 106 persons who can command but half a hundred of potatoes amongst them, and 300 without any, whose sole dependence is on chance shell-fish and sea weed, a sample of which we have seen."

Foreigners, and Foreign Influence.—It cannot have escaped the notice of even the most casual observer of what is passing about him in the moral and political world, that within a very short time past, the patriotism of certain of the presses of this city has become most suddenly and most afflictingly sensitive to the appalling dangers which they affect to have discovered overshadowing the liberties and institutions of our republic, by reason of the great influx of emigrants from foreign countries, and the overwhelming influence they are pretended, by these newly fledged patriots, to possess over the judgments and opinions of our native citizens, and the character and destinies of our government. We should do violence to our own imperfect discretion, and to the judgment which our observation of the progress and fruits of the alleged monstrous evil has compelled us to make upon the subject, were we to pretend that we have not ample testimony on every side of us, that the laws of our country, in the premises, do not stand in need of revision and restriction, and that they have entailed upon the country a train of troubles and evils which she could happily dispense with.

But it is not our object now to speak particularly of those evils, or their prospective consequences. Our more immediate purpose, at this time, has been incited by the very recent, and it would seem, almost miraculous discovery, by the presses above referred to, of the stupendous mischiefs against which they are now incessantly harping, and the tremendous and all-devouring force with which this Saul-like conviction has come over them. And, what is most remarkable of all, those very presses which are amongst the loudest in stirring up the bile of native against adopted citizens, are themselves either entirely controlled, or essentially managed by persons coming within the range of their own animadversions, and [illegible]

The Courier & Enquirer, for instance, one of the fiercest journals in the city in denunciations of foreigners and foreign influence, numbers among its stipendiary caterers no less than *three* to whom America was a stranger, except by reputation, till within a very few years past; and one of those, the notorious Hoskins, has the supreme control of its course and contents, not excepting even a supervision of the mad ebullitions of Webb himself, who seldom knows, for weeks together, what his paper contains, till it arrives to him at some distant place.

The Evening Star, too, which, under the management of the "King of the Jews"—the dead-American Noah, pretends to a sensibility to foreign encroachment which seems at times half frantic, is indebted for full four-fifths of its editorial matter to the pens of a couple of English scribblers—one of whom sits in the shadow of his principal's huge frame, and bespatters alike the venom of his master's disappointment upon American freemen, and his own spite and petty malice upon his own fellow emigrants, much of which perchance, is engendered by the fact that most of them left home with less sullied reputations than he did himself.

Indeed, almost every large paper in the city which has taken sides with the two above named in this sudden crusade of extermination against foreigners, is in a greater or less degree under the management of men who owe to other hemispheres their birth, breeding, principles, and education; and it is the greatest scandal they can utter against American character, that there is in its composition so great a share of gullibility and sycophancy that *themselves* have obtained the control of so large a portion of the mightiest engine of the land, the public press, and wield it with impunity against our purest patriots and most sacred interests and institutions. More hereafter.

Coroner's office, No. 118 *Wooster street.*—On Saturday evening the Coroner was called on to view the body of Martha Ann Finn, aged 23, born in Massachusetts, who was living as a prostitute at the house of Sallome Blanchard, over Ridgeway's grocery at the corner of Little Water and Anthony streets. It appeared in evidence before the jury, that the deceased was on Friday night in a state of gross intoxication, and that between the hours of 11 and 12 that night, fell out of the second story window of the house upon the side-walk, by which fall her skull was so badly fractured that she died in consequence on Saturday afternoon about half past 5 o'clock. Verdict of the jury: death by falling from the second story window while in a state of intoxication and fracturing her scull.

March of the Drama.—"Who saw the sun to-day?" exclaimed a votary of the sock and buskin, as he passed Park Row a few days since. "Here it is, sir," replied a sprightly little vender of a well-known and interesting penny diurnal, at the same time advancing towards the stage-stricken gentleman. "Begone, fellow—thou troublest me," returned the hero; "do you not readily perceive that I am spouting the immortal!" "Immortal d—l," reiterated the urchin; "you are spouting three-centers!"

Caution.—It has been the practice, for some time, for a great mass of well-grown boys, from 14 to 19 years of age, principally the sons and apprentices of respectable mechanics, to assemble, between 7 and 8 o'clock every night, and to continue, frequently, almost all night, at and about engine house No. 40, in Mulberry street, between Grand and Broome, and to insult and annoy the neighbors and persons passing by, as also to indulge in noise, and riotous and disorderly conduct. The other evening, they broke the windows of Mr. Bogardus, a gentleman residing hard by the place of their assemblage, and enveloped his hired servant girl in a cloud of flour they procured and threw over her. As these boys are known to the police officers, it will be well for them to desist, in future, from their riotous and disorderly assemblages and conduct, unless they wish to be honored with imprisonment, as it is the intention of the officers and some of the neighbors united, to arrest and punish them with the utmost severity, if they continue to indulge in their infamous practices any longer.

Troubles in Baltimore.—Passengers from Baltimore, who arrived here yesterday, state that they were witnesses to a serious riot which took place in that city on Saturday night and Sunday morning.—The mob attacked the houses of Reverdy Johnson and John Glenn, esquires, formerly directors of the bank of Maryland, and caused great destruction in the house of the latter. The citizens flew to arms, and *rumor* says eighteen lives were lost—a great many more were severely wounded;—among the latter Mr. Findlay, Mr. Cheeves, and Mr. Adams. As the passengers left early in the morning, they are not able to state minute particulars.

The Philadelphia papers of yesterday contain corresponding statements, brought by the Baltimore steamboats, and there is strong and lamentable probability that the above account is not exaggerated.

A Small Deluge.—The immense water tank of the gas works on Eighteenth street, which held 30,000 gallons, burst on Saturday last, when nearly full of water, and deluged the premises. At the time of the occurrence, one of the workmen was on a ladder looking into the tank, and another was standing near it on the floor; they were both swept to a corner of the yard as much as sixty feet distant. A horse and cart, the latter loaded with bricks, were lifted from the ground, and the cart turned bottom side up. Poor Dobbin looked perfectly astonished, and snorted loud his wonderment; but fortunately he was more scared than hurt.

A rumpus at Lynn, Mass.—Thompson, the abolitionist, held forth at Lynn on Thursday evening last. There was a large assembly (mostly females, as usual) in the house, and a still larger one, of men, without. There was a continual hallooing and noise, [illegible] and presently the ringing of the bell at the other end of the Common, created much confusion and affright for a few moments—some persons fainted. After the alarm had subsided in some degree, the cry of fire was again heard, but the audience kept their seats. The crowd and noise outside increasing, Mr. T. closed his harangue. The whole congregation then rose and sung the doxology, and the meeting was closed by prayer. The mob exasperated by the expressions of defiance used by Mr. T. in his discourse, closed round the steps and doors of the house, so as effectually to prevent the egress of the audience. Presently there was a rush at the doors by the mob, who threatened Mr. T., but by the prompt exertions of those within, the doors were closed. Rotten eggs were thrown and a missile came near hitting Mr. T.'s head.

The Wave at Boston.—A few days since we copied from the Boston Transcript a paragraph giving some account of a second race between Capt. Stevens's Wave, and the Sylph of Boston, in which the latter beat the former on rough water. Captain Forbes, of the Sylph has contradicted that assertion, in the Transcript, and states that his boat was fairly beaten both times. He however talks of further experiments.

Mortality among Children.—The deaths among the children in Baltimore have been very distressing. The weekly bills of mortality present more than three children to one adult.

Mrs. Hayes' Syrup.—The numerous instances which have within a few weeks past come to our knowledge, in which afflicting and apparently inveterate cases of dysentary and cholera morbus have been effectually relieved and ultimately cured, by the use of Mrs. Hayes' Syrup, induce us again unsolicitedly to call the attention of our readers to her advertisement on our last last page. A perfect conviction that we are but doing our duty to the community, in this age of quackery and humbug, alone induces us to press this invaluable preparation upon the attention of our readers and the public, to whom we recommend it as being, in our estimation and in the estimation of hundreds of others, who, like ourselves, have experienced its salutary effects, decidedly the most efficient and innocent remedy for complaints incident to the present season, of which we have any knowledge.

A Case of Conscience.—A mate of an East Indiaman, named Dennis Carter, aged 38 years, put an end to his life in London, on the first July, under the following extraordinary circumstances:—Since the return of the deceased from his last voyage, he addicted himself to drinking. Meeting with a Bible, he was struck with his bad conduct, and in it wrote the words as follows: "I promise from this day never to drink grog or blaspheme in the name of the Almighty.—Dennis Carter." In a very short time his passion for liquor overcame his resolution, and he got intoxicated; the next morning he was sadly grieved at having broken his vow, and the circumstances preying on his mind, in the evening he cut his throat.

The London Courier says the talked of marriage of the Queen of Portugal with the Duke de Nemours is now wholly given up on account of the known aversion of England to such a match.

The Office of the Sun has been removed to the corner of Nassau and Spruce streets, opposite the City Hall.

Trieste, June 18.—*Shocking Calamity.*—We have received the following melancholy intelligence from Malta:—An Austrian merchantman, which had taken in a cargo of cotton and gum at Alexandria, had already arrived off Malta, on its voyage to Leghorn, when three of the crew died of the plague, on which the remainder of the sailors were seized with such alarm that they unanimously declared that they would not continue their voyage in that ship. The captain, therefore, went into Malta, landed his crew, and took another that was not so fearful, with which he proceeded on his voyage to Leghorn. But they had not gone far when some men were seized with the plague and died. The captain adopted the usual precautions, such as fumigation, &c. and already entertained hopes of arresting the disorder, when fire broke out on board, and destroyed the ship and cargo; the captain escaped. It is not stated whether the whole or part of the crew had arrived at Malta.

From Jamaica.—By the arrival of the ship John W. Cater, Capt. Moncrieffe, we are put in possession of Kingston (Jam.) papers to the 17th July.

Previous to the sailing of the Comus, which arrived at Kingston, Jam., on the 15th, from the Caymanas, the island was perfectly quiet. Commander Hamilton brings the intelligence of the wreck of the American ship Atlantic, Bailey, belonging to New York.—She went on shore on the east point of the Grand Cayman on the morning of the 23d June—the master, crew, passengers, and the whole of the ship's stores and cargo were saved, and sold with the hull by auction to the inhabitants of the island. She was out fifty-two days from Havre de Grace, bound to New Orleans. The master has freighted a small schooner belonging to the island to convey himself, crew and passengers to New Orleans.

A proclamation has been issued calling on the house of assembly to meet and proceed to business on the 4th of August. [Commercial.

Ship Launch and Dreadful Accident.—On Thursday an immense crowd assembled on the banks of the Dry Dock, Lincoln, to witness the launch of a schooner. Upwards of 100 persons were on board the vessel, which had scarcely entered the water when she turned completely over, and all the persons on board, among whom were several women and children were precipitated into the water and against the banks of the dock. By the praise-worthy exertions of the spectators most of the drowning persons were rescued in a few minutes, and numbers escaped by swimming. The bodies of two children, quite dead have been dragged on shore, and other persons are still missing. [Lincoln Gaz.

More Walloping.—Finnell, of the Lexington Observer, and Vanderslice, of the Georgetown Sentinel, had a battle in Georgetown, on Sunday week. Out of respect to the day, they left their pistols at home and fought with fists; Vanderslice, who was the assailant, is said to have come of second best. We are no friend of Mr. Justice Lynch, but he would certainly do a good thing for these ruffian editors of Kentucky, by rendering them *hors du combat* for a time.

[illegible] Green, the editor of the Boydstown, Va. Expositor, was attacked a few days since in Warrenton, N. C. by two individuals, named Bragg, one of whom he had assailed in his newspaper. A bloody combat ensued. Green was beaten to the ground with a heavy bludgeon, but rising, he drew a dirk, cut the upper lip of one of his assailants nearly off, stabbed him also in the arm, and buried the weapon in the throat of the other, who is expected to die. A Mr. Somerville, who interfered to keep the peace, was severely wounded by the explosion of a pistol. At the termination of the fight, Green invited two others of the Bragg family to come on, and take a hand, if they felt disposed! Our civilization goes backward like a crab.

Mutiny.—In September last, the crew of the Halcyon, whale ship from New London, mutinied while she was prosecuting her voyage in the Indian Ocean, in consequence of which the captain was obliged to put into Port Louis, in the Isle of France, where he delivered up the mutineers, twenty-one in number, to the custody of the American consul. There they remained in prison sixty three days, during which one of them died, and the American consul sent the remaining twenty to England in the British ship Bencoolen. The American consul at London sent home ten of them, whose names are annexed, by the Toronto which arrived here two or three days back, and on Saturday they were brought to the police office, and temporarily committed to bridewell until they can be handed over to the authorities of the United States. Their names are Isaac Wood, Jason Goodrich, David Kenny, Erastus P. Cartwright, Isaac Delon, Henry Joseph Dower, Patrick M'Keever, and Patrick Cosgrane. [Jour. of Com.

The body of a man, named William Moody, a carpenter by trade, was found dead in the street by the city watch on Wednesday night last. There were no marks of violence on it—and the verdict of the coroner's jury, called by Justice H. T. Cox, was, that the deceased came to his death by intemperance. The deceased was supposed to have been a citizen of Portland, Maine, from his having in his pocket book a letter from his wife, addressed to him from that place. [Mobile Register.

Flood and Loss of Life.—We learn by letter from Mercer, Pa. that on the night of the 12th ult. the rain fell to the depth of fourteen inches in the neighborhood of the country north and west of the Broken Straw Creek, in Warren county, producing an unprecedented rise in the smaller streams, and swelling the Alleghany to a degree heretofore unknown for the season of the year. A number of mill dams were swept away, and the bridges of Broken Straw from its mouth to Sprigh Creek, a distance of thirty or forty miles, were entirely destroyed. Above, the flood was equally destructive. The Mercer Luminary states that at Linzora an accident of a most distressing nature occurred. On Sugarrun, in this township, a mill-dam was constructed, part of which ran some distance across the flat; and on this flat, below the dam, the owner had erected his dwelling-house. On the night of the storm he discovered that the water was rising very fast, and opened the flood gate: but finding this did not afford a sufficient outlet, he went a short distance to procure help. On returning, he found, to his utter consternation and distress, that his dam had broken, and swept away his house and its contents with his wife and two children! He arrived in time to hear their screams, but could afford them no relief. The bodies were found on the evening of the ensuing day, some distance below.

Philadelphia Inquirer.

The Cincinnati Whig, of the 30th, states six victims of cholera in Green township, Hamilton county, in that state.

Jackson Mahon, indicted in Baldwin, Superior Court, for the murder of Martin Smith, on the 4th inst., has been found guilty.

[Reported for the Sun.]

Police Office—Yesterday.

MORNING RETURNS.

Lawrence Clark, for intemperance and rioting in the street, was fined $1 and costs and committed.

Archibald Madden, for rioting and assaulting Elizabeth Leacroft; was committed.

Mars Kneas, of No. 9 King street, a young insolent piece of flesh and blood, who because of his name being *Mars*, conceived himself, no doubt, to be the very God of war; was brought up charged with abusing his father Michael Kneas, and the family, he being an inmate of the same house. As his father was not present to prosecute the complaint, he deported himself with the utmost insolence and haughtiness before the magistrate, endeavored to throw the entire blame upon his father, and proved by his own language that if he was not put in prison for abusing his father, he deserved to be for his impudence in the office; but was necessarily discharged.

Susan Sarles, Anthony Dow, a boy from Long Island, and Michael Hogan out of the alms-house, were brought up for lodging in the watch-house habitually; and discharged, the latter to return to the alms house.

Mary Byrnes, a sick vagrant, was sent to the Penitentiary for 3 months.

Frederick Steneck, a German, in a state of inebriate exhilaration, got his ideas raised so high, that he attacked Charlotte Johnson, a well dressed colored woman, of 93 Christie street, in the street, in a most indecent and ruffianly manner; struck her twice in the face, and on her resisting, tore her silk dress almost off her, seized her bonnet and reduced it to a wreck, and was pursuing her with other acts of violence, when he was arrested and brought in. For all of which he was committed to prison.

William Brown was brought in by James Ward, keeper of the Washington Hotel, who found him up stairs in bed in one of the rooms, under suspicious circumstances, and who, when attempting to be ejected, made a stout resistance, for which he received a black eye, was lodged in the watch-house, and in the morning committed.

Hugh McClean and Owen McClean, committed for riotous and disorderly conduct.

Francis Sheridan came in himself, in a state of supposed derangement, but in the morning was deemed sane enough to be discharged.

Juvenile Thieves.—Yesterday, George Burns, who keeps an old iron and junk shop at No. 127 Washington street, discovered three boys named Phillip King, John King, and Peter Coen, enter his premises and steal about 40 pounds of scrap iron, which they placed in a cart, and were conveying away to sell, when he pursued, overtook and arrested one of them, the first named, whom he brought to the police office, the other two escaping. These boys appeared to be not more than from 12 to 13 years old, and Mr. Burns stated, that during the last week, he had had stolen from him, by these and other boys, above 200 pounds of scrap iron, part of which had been taken and sold at the junk shop of his neighbor, Michael Klone, in Carlisle street. The young thief was committed to prison for examination.

Thefts.—The cabin of the brig Cyrus, of Portland, Maine, lying at the foot of Duane street, was entered on Saturday night, and robbed of a frock coat, pantaloons, and three vests. A white merino shawl was stolen from No. 14 Spring street, and a dark green overcoat from No. 4 Forsyth street; and from No. 34 Cedar street, five thick and thin coats, and two pairs of pantaloons.

On Saturday, Mrs. Margaret Navarra, widow, of No. 40 Avenue D, was robbed of a small black silk purse, containing $103 in bills and silver, which was stolen out of a small basket in her possession, and carried away.

Robbing a Sweetheart.—Yesterday about 6 o'clock, a girl of the town named Sarah Rocket, of 57 Orange street, met a young Englishman, named John Johnsoe, in Chatham street, and charged him with robbing her of $7, and a purse worth 50 cents, for which he was committed.

Land Operations.—We learn that a company of gentlemen from this city have recently purchased the principal part of the land at Elizabethtown point, N. J., including the privileges of the ferry, and intend laying it out in streets and lots; and encouraging the speedy settlement of the place as a new city. For manufactures there are great facilities; there is an excellent back country, and by the way of Amboy vessels of large burthen can come up to the dock.—The Sommerville rail road, already chartered, will terminate at this point. [Commercial.

Shocking Affair.—On Friday afternoon a man by the name of Reuben Amadon, Jr. of Sandlake, was in the act of going with his team, on the lands of one of his neighbors, by the name of William Briggs, when he was forbidden by the latter. Some altercation ensued. Amadon threw down his whip, seized a club, and struck Briggs a violent blow on the head, which killed him instantly. Amadon is committed to jail to await his trial. [Troy Whig.

Gen. William Brady, and Henry Bridly, Esq., died of cholera at Murfreesborough on the 23d, after a few hours' illness.

Two criminals escaped form the gaol at Haddam, Middlesex co., by sawing off the grates of their windows. A reward of $60 has been offered for their apprehension.

Cholera.—There has been no case of cholera at Nashville since the 24th.

The Fire Fly locomotive performed a trip from Ballston to Schenectady, N. Y. and back again, last week, in one hour and three minutes. Distance *thirty-one miles!*

Tunnel under our Harbour.—A few days since we gave notice of the commencement of a new entrance to our harbour, we have now to notice that arrangements are being made for the construction of a tunnel under it at the foot of Main street. Such a work when completed will do credit to those engaged in it and be useful to our citizens, there being now a large tract of land in a business part of the city lying almost entirely useless on account of the difficulty of access to it. The work it is thought can be accomplished with a double track, for from $30,000 to $40,000, leaving 12 feet of water on the arch. [Buffalo Trans.

A volume, written and compiled by two of the crew of Captain Ross's late Arctic expedition, has appeared in London; it brings charges of an unparalleled nature against the captain, and gives all the credit to commander Ross; the captain is declared to have monopolized all the trade with the Esquimaux, selling them the presents sent by government, and retaining the proceeds for their own use, &c. They state that the Esquimaux make sledges of salmon sewed in skins, having cross pieces of deer's bones, and in time of scarcity eat their sledges! It is stated in Ross's Narrative that one sledge was seen made of ice.

Practical Knowledge.—A young girl was presented to James I. as an English prodigy, because she was deeply learned. The person who introduced her boasted of her proficiency in ancient languages. "I can assure your Majesty," said he, "that she can both speak and write Latin, Greek and Hebrew."—"These are rare attainments for a damsel," said James, "pray tell me, can she spin?"

Figure 2 New York American

Jesus Christ, who hath abolished death, and hath brought life and immortality to light through the gospel. —II Timothy, I. 10.

Recognition of Soviet Russia Will Aid World Peace and International Justice

Jobs for Millions

Keep the Air Clean!

Your November Ballot

A Library in Miniature

Thwarting Romance by Law? By Winifred Black

The example of the Hearst style in Figure 2, above, uses a banner headline the width of the page for the lead editorial. Above the headline is a scriptural quotation. Columns are separated by white space and wavy lines, unlike on most editorial pages of that day, where columns traditionally were run close together with a thin rule between them. The *American* page is made even more dramatic by a large cartoon.

Figure 3 Washington Post

The Washington Post

FOURTH EDITION

AN INDEPENDENT NEWSPAPER — TUESDAY, JANUARY 20, 1953 — PAGE 14

Inauguration Day

This is a great day for the American system of government, and a thrilling day for all good citizens of this Republic. Dwight D. Eisenhower will take the oath of office as President of the United States...

Loyalty And Liberty

Conserving Resources

Symbol Of Tradition

The Law And Wilson

Thanks To Neely

"The President Of The United States"

HERBLOCK

Letters To The Editor

Eisenhower Maps Middle Road Course

By Marquis Childs

The Washington Post

Figure 4   Star Tribune

Commentary

A forum for opinions, reactions, dialogue and disagreement

Diagnosing the mammogram

Studies ponder thousands, but women decide one by one

By Ellen Goodman
Boston Globe

BOSTON — Some years ago, I was inducted into a special club. I hadn't applied for membership. I didn't want to join. I won admission the old-fashioned way: I inherited it.

After both my mother and my aunt were diagnosed with breast cancer, I automatically became a member of the High Risk Group. Today, I am happy to say that both these eightysomething women are alive and well, thank you very much. But my family membership entitles me to more than a casual interest in the disease that will afflict one in eight American women.

Every year, with a slight sense of foreboding and a bit of black humor, I go for what my friend and fellow club member calls "the breast sandwich." I leave — so far — feeling as if I've won a reprieve, a stay of execution.

I've made this pilgrimage religiously because like many in my peer group and my club, I've believed that early detection is the key to a cure.

We've been told that picking up cancer on a mammogram, before it's big enough to feel, improves the odds of survival by 30 percent.

Of course, that means mammograms often make no difference. Some cancers grow so slowly that the women would never die from them. Others grow so aggressively that the women don't have a chance. Still, 30 percent is nothing to sneeze at.

Now I sit in the clubhouse and stare at a study that says mammograms don't save lives. More than a year ago, two Danish researchers reviewed seven huge studies on mammography and cast doubt on their value. This fall, they returned in full force to the British journal Lancet, saying again that "there is no reliable evidence that it reduces mortality."

Theirs is by no means the final answer. Different scientists looking over the same data respond like the legendary blind men studying the elephant. Some researchers strongly disagree with the Danish conclusions. There are enough other factors — from the age of the patient to the effectiveness of new treatments — to make any study of mammograms subject to, well, more study.

But it is safe to say that the Danes have shaken the common wisdom and common confidence in the connection between mammograms and cures. Or maybe, on the other hand, they've just shaken a false sense of security.

Fran Visco, the tough-minded president of the National Breast Cancer Coalition, says, "We are finally beginning to question long-held assumptions about how to detect cancer earlier and what happens when we do. In this country, cancer has been reduced to a pink ribbon and a mammogram. Is [the] mammogram the key to saving lives? It's not un-American to ask that question."

The mammogram is the most popular, most promoted form of "early detection." Yet by the time cancer can be seen, it has been growing for seven to 10 years. Maybe, as breast doctor Susan Love suggests, our focus on screening has "made it sound like you just do your mammograms, your self-exams, and everything will be OK."

In fact, we learned a couple of years ago that monthly self-exams do not save lives. Now we are wondering if we've overestimated the value of mammograms.

What we really need, Love says, is the equivalent of the Pap smear for cervical cancer, a test that "gets to the cells that are just thinking about becoming cancer."

For now, the take-home message for a woman over 50 or a woman in the high-risk society is not likely to change. As Love says, "I have doubts about mammography, but I get my mammogram because it's the best tool we have for diagnosis and screening. It probably changes the odds for some women, but not all. I think this woman should get a mammogram but fight like hell for something better."

As for women under 50? Screening this age group has been controversial for years. Statistically, we would have to screen 2,000 40-year-old women for 10 years and do 600 biopsies to prevent one death. Is that good public policy? If not, explain it to the woman who feels her life was saved. Or to the politician who votes against insurance coverage.

Each year 233,000 women are diagnosed with breast cancer. Progress comes with dueling studies and evolving treatments. We read research done on thousands and make hard decisions one by one.

Kay Dickersin, a Brown Medical School professor and breast cancer survivor, says, "We have to become more comfortable with uncertainty. There aren't just yes-or-no answers. It's not a failure of medicine. It's where we are."

As for those who wish for more cure and less confusion, all I can say is . . . join the club.

Star Tribune Illustration by Eddie Thomas

Civil rights panel is past expiration date

By George F. Will
Washington Post

WASHINGTON, D.C. — Some whales have vestigial legs because their prehistoric ancestors were land mammals. The U.S. Commission on Civil Rights is a vestigial leg on whale-like Washington. The commission has no serious function, other than to illustrate how far things have evolved. Its head is a black woman, Mary Frances Berry, who, like many antebellum plantation owners and today's civil rights lobby, believes that blacks cannot cope with life in predominantly white America, that they are comprehensively victimized and must be perpetual wards of paternalistic government.

Berry, 63, was appointed chairwoman of the commission in 1993 by President Bill Clinton. She has been on the commission since President Jimmy Carter appointed her in 1980, perhaps to get her out of his Education Department, where she said we should not criticize Communist China's education policies for requiring students to "develop what they call socialist consciousness and culture." In 1982 she lamented that "a massive barrage of propaganda" by America's media caused blacks to misunderstand the Soviet Union's virtues, including "safeguards for minorities," "equality of opportunity" and "equal provision of social services to its citizens." She says that in the 1960s, the era of landmark civil rights legisla-

Mary Frances Berry

tion, blacks faced a "threat of genocide" that was "roughly comparable" to what Jews faced in Nazi Germany.

The Commission on Civil Rights has a $9 million budget but no enforcement powers. It is a megaphone, a hectoring institution. Berry was designed by nature for it. And notwithstanding her old enthusiasms for Communist countries, she strongly believes in private property. At least, she believes the commission is her private property. Hence the current fracas.

The eight-person commission has recently been split 5-3 in favor of Berry's worldview. However, a commission member died in 1998, and Clinton nominated Victoria Wilson to complete the member's six-year term, which expired Nov. 29. President Bush has nominated a black Cleveland lawyer, Peter Kirsanow, to replace Wilson.

But Kirsanow, former chairman of the Center for New Black Leadership, rejects the plantation paternalism of today's civil rights lobby (see paragraph one, above). So Berry insists that even though Wilson's certificate of service stipulates a November expiration date, Clinton really intended to appoint her to a six-year term. Berry, resembling George Wallace blocking the schoolhouse door, says U.S. marshals will be required to force Kirsanow onto the commission.

Berry also resembles another apostle of lawlessness in the name of civil rights — Clinton. He breezily conceded that when Bill Lann Lee served two years as "acting" — unconfirmed by the Senate — assistant attorney general for civil rights, this was not done "in an entirely constitutional way."

Al Gonzales, the White House counsel, speaks of seeking an "accommodation" with Berry. Gonzales is new in town and unfamiliar with Berry's well-earned reputation for unpleasantness, which would cause blushes below deck in a troopship.

The Department of Justice says Wilson's seat on the commission is vacant, and is going to court against Berry, whom the liberal Washington Monthly listed in 1987 as one of five people no Democratic president should hire: "Her bitter single-mindedness makes her not just unpleasant but incapable of guiding policy on difficult and controversial issues." In 1997 the General Accounting Office called Berry's commission "an agency in disarray, with limited awareness of how its resources are used," unable to "provide key cost information" and insisting that significant records documenting commission decisionmaking were "lost, misplaced or nonexistent." Berry's defense was that there was "nothing illegal." The ramshackle commission was created in 1957, the year U.S. soldiers enforced the integration of Little Rock's Central High School over Gov. Orval Faubus' objections. Then America actually had a severe civil rights problem. Today the civil rights lobby — speaking of prehistoric vestiges — continues to discuss blacks' problems in the anachronistic vocabulary of the civil rights movement. But the problems are mostly matters of social class. Consider: How much would the life chances of blacks in urban slums or rural poverty be improved if by the wave of a magic wand their skins were made white? Not much.

Last June, Berry's racism-is-everywhere-and-explains-everything monomania resulted in a 200-page commission tantrum that, mixing dubious anecdotes with preposterous statistical models, purported to prove widespread "disenfranchisement" of Florida's black voters in 2000. But President Bush still did not resign. America is hell.

When Berry goes to heaven (for her, the Soviet Union with China's educational system), her remains should be treated — she should like this — as Lenin's have been: preserved under glass as a reminder of the exotic fauna that once roamed through American politics.

Samples of great rhetoric from the past

Anne Boleyn: Last request to bear alone 'the burden of your grace's displeasure'

Editor's note: After failing to produce a male heir, Anne Boleyn (ca. 1507-1536), the second wife of England's King Henry VIII, was convicted on charges of adultery, incest and plotting the murder of the king, and beheaded at the Tower of London. Although the authenticity of the following letter is in doubt, it is eloquent in its protestations of innocence and is considered characteristic of Anne's bluntness toward the king. The daughter of Anne and Henry survived to rule as Elizabeth I.

Your grace's displeasure and my imprisonment are things so strange to me, that what to write, or what to excuse, I am altogether ignorant. Whereas you send to me (willing me to confess a truth and so obtain your favor), by such a one, whom you know to be mine ancient professed enemy, I no sooner received this message by him, than I rightly conceived your meaning; and if, as you say, confessing a truth indeed may procure my safety, I shall with all willingness and duty, perform your duty. But let not your grace ever imagine that your poor wife will be brought to acknowledge a fault, where not so much as a thought ever proceeded.

And to speak a truth, never a prince had wife more loyal in all duty, and in all true affection, than you have ever found in Anne Bulen — with which name and place I could willingly have contented myself, if God and your grace's pleasure had been so pleased. Neither did I at any time so far forget myself in my exaltation or received queenship, but that I always looked for such alteration as I now find; for the ground of my preferment being on no surer foundation than your grace's fancy, the least alteration was fit and sufficient (I knew) to draw that fancy to some other subject.

You have chosen me from low estate to be your queen and companion, far beyond my desert or desire; if, then, you found me worthy of such honor, good your grace, let not any light fancy or bad counsel of my enemies withdraw your princely favor from me; neither let that stain — that unworthy stain — of a disloyal heart towards your good grace ever cast so foul a blot on me, and on the infant princess your daughter.

Try me, good king, but let me have a lawful trial, and let not my sworn enemies sit as my accusers and as my judges; yea, let me receive an open trial, for my truth shall

Arguments through the ages

fear no open shame. Then you shall see either my innocency cleared, your suspicions and conscience satisfied, the ignominy and slander of the world stopped, or my guilt openly declared. So that, whatever God and you may determine of, your grace may be freed from an open censure; and my offense being so lawfully proved, your grace may be at liberty, both before God and man, not only to execute worthy punishment on me as an unfaithful wife but to follow your affection already settled on that party for whose sake I am now as I am, whose name I could some while since have pointed unto — your grace being not ignorant of my suspicions therein.

But if you have already determined of me, and that not only my death, but an infamous slander must bring . . . your desired happiness, then I desire of God that he will pardon your great sin herein, and likewise my enemies, the instruments thereof, and that he will not call you to a strict account for your unprincely and cruel usage of me at his general judgment-seat, where both you and myself must shortly appear; and in whose just judgment, I doubt not (whatsoever the world may think of me), mine innocency shall be openly known and sufficiently cleared.

My last and only request shall be that myself only bear the burden of your grace's displeasure, and that it may not touch the innocent souls of those poor gentlemen, whom, as I understand, are likewise in strait imprisonment for my sake. If ever I have found favor in your sight — if ever the name of Anne Bulen have been pleasing in your ears — then let me obtain this request; and so I will leave to trouble your grace any further, with mine earnest prayer to the Trinity to have your grace in his good keeping, and to direct you in all your actions. From my doleful prison in the Tower, the 6th May.

— Anne Boleyn, 1536. Letter to King Henry VIII.

A 1936 textbook warned editorial page editors:

> In these days, when the average newspaper reader has less time for reading
> than formerly—when he does more glimpsing than reading, and confines most
> of that glimpsing to the headlines and leading news stories or entertaining
> features—he seems to care little or nothing for newspaper editorials. If his
> attention is to be captured and held by the editorial page, that page must be
> unusually attractive physically. It must be even more inviting looking than the
> general-news pages, and even easier to read.[4]

But editors generally ignored this advice. Traditional editorial page makeup in
the 1940s, 1950s and 1960s was usually built around a vertical (higher than it
was wide) three-column cartoon at the top of the page. The newspaper's own
editorials were assigned to one or two columns to the left of the cartoon.
Columns and letters filled the remainder of the page. The *Washington Post* of
January 20, 1953 (Figure 3, page 000), reflected that makeup arrangement,
although the use of white space between the columns represented a step away
from tradition. In 1986, Bohle found that many newspapers still were using this
design.

▪ BOLDER, MORE FLEXIBLE

Partly spurred by editorial page critique sessions at the annual meetings of the
National Conference of Editorial Writers (NCEW) and by the needling of
designers such as Arnold, editors in the 1960s and 1970s began experimenting
with more flexible layouts. Wider columns and "cold type"—which could be
pasted anywhere and at any angle on a page—opened new possibilities that not
even the most skilled printer could have managed with unwieldy hunks of
metal type. Contributing to the flexibility was the introduction of a few
cartoons that were wider than they were high.

This combination led to pages that had wider columns, sometimes too wide
for easy reading. A rule of thumb suggests that for optimum newspaper
reading, lines should contain the equivalent of about one and a half lower-case
alphabets, or about 39 characters.[5] The December 19, 2001, editorial page
(Figure 5, page 310) and the December 17, 2001, op-ed page (Figure 6, page
311) from the Minneapolis *Star Tribune* present a rather bold example of a
design with wider columns. In this case the maximum line in letters and editorial columns is about 40 characters.

A recent survey of editorial page editors found that "virtually all of the
nation's larger daily newspapers, and many others, have improved the appearance of their editorial pages in recent decades by using larger body type and
wider columns for editorials, adopting easier-to-read type faces and making
greater use of white space." According to Ernest C. Hynds, who conducted the
survey, the most common change in the 1990s was "increased use of graphics"
(60 percent). Of the editors who participated, 54 percent said one change was
that they "occasionally used cartoons, other elements." The third most
common change was "increased use of drawings" (51 percent). Hynds' survey
of editors showed that more than half thought improvements in editorial page
design increased readership.[6]

Figure 5 Star Tribune

PAGE A24 • STAR TRIBUNE ★ WEDNESDAY, DECEMBER 19 • 2001

Editorials, labeled "Our Perspective," represent the institutional voice of the Star Tribune. They are prepared by the Editorial Department, which is independent of the newsroom.

StarTribune· Editorial

J. Keith Moyer, Publisher
News: Tim J. McGuire, Editor Pam Fine, Managing Editor
Editorial: Susan Albright, Editor, Editorial Pages
Jim Boyd, Deputy Editor, Editorial Pages

opinion@startribune.com

Our perspective

Richfield

A classic '50s suburb reborn

Geography conspires against Richfield, a place not aptly named.

Wealthy suburbs with big malls and big tax bases (Bloomington and Edina) dominate its southern and western flanks. The airport, with its notorious jet roar, lies just to the east, making Richfield a poor appendage of Minneapolis but without the city's stock of stately, pre-1945 houses.

Surely by now, a dowdy, postwar community with all of these disadvantages should be heading straight into the tank. But Richfield stubbornly refuses to play the role of declining older suburb. With an uncommon spirit and an aggressive approach to renewing itself, it has defied the odds and emerged as an example for others to admire.

Since 1991, Richfield has devoted $89 million of public money to infrastructure improvements and private development subsidies. The financial risk and political flak have been considerable. But the public ante has leveraged $348.3 million in private investment. Anyone with a car and an ounce of curiosity can see the evidence just by driving down Richfield's streets.

A decade ago, the city was at a tipping point. The population was declining, aging and becoming poorer. State Sen. Myron Orfield's scary maps (published in his widely acclaimed 1997 book "Metropolitics") showed clearly Richfield's plight.

"We were sliding into obsolescence and disinvestment," said Development Director John Stark. "This was becoming just a drive-through town."

But now Richfield's residential streets are as tidy as in their "Leave It to Beaver" heyday. Since 1991, city programs have helped 110 homeowners modernize and expand their modest bungalows, setting the tone for hundreds of other private renovation projects. The city also has replaced the thousand homes lost over the years to airport and freeway expansion with new townhouses and apartments, many of them going up near a new town center at 66th St. and Lyndale Av. S. Meanwhile, tired strip malls are being renovated, replaced or converted to a mixed format of housing over shops. A strip of land along Cedar Avenue will be converted to airport-compatible commercial development and the *big project*, Best Buy Company's corporate headquarters, is rising rapidly.

Three basic strategies are being pursued. One is to expand the city's office and commercial profile and, thus, its tax base. A second is to protect classic 1950s neighborhoods from commercial encroachment even if it means erecting heavily landscaped barriers, like those along 77th Street. The third is to blend new housing, shopping and transit into higher-density urban villages.

The result is an increasingly vibrant yet comfy suburb that offers a central location at affordable prices. The average Richfield bungalow still sells for under $150,000 — with no need to endure long, exhausting commutes. Richfield proves that a town can be successful without being affluent.

Surrounded by busy freeways and overhead jetliners, Richfield was dealt a poor hand. It responded the only way it could, by becoming more urban. Yes, there's nostalgia for the sleepy old Richfield, where kids rode their Schwinns to the Dairy Queen and lived down the block from Grandma. But if you look a little harder, you can still see those same possibilities. Maybe there's more traffic. Maybe the families don't quite look the same. Maybe the taxpayers grumble more loudly. But Richfield has been busy gathering lemons and making lemonade.

City of Richfield

A new mix of offices and housing at Lyndale Av. and 77th St. S.

Jean Harris

A fine example of public service

Though she worked in some of the highest levels of the national government, Jean Harris never forgot her humble roots as a black female from the racially segregated South. Nor did she forget that government *serves* the people; that part of its purpose is to help those in need. That history set her on the path of an exemplary career of public service that served Minnesota well for two decades.

Harris died last Friday of cancer at age 70. She had been the mayor of Eden Prairie since 1995 and was the first African-American woman elected to run a Twin Cities suburb. She is survived by her husband, Leslie Ellis, and three daughters.

By the time she came to Minnesota from her native Virginia, she had racially integrated the Medical College of Virginia, first as a student, then as a professor. She went on to assist five U.S. presidents, beginning as chief of the department that carried out the Medicaid and welfare programs under President Lyndon Johnson. An internist by profession, she later served as a consultant to the Department of Health, Education and Welfare, the U.S. Agency for International Development and to Congress. She also directed a national foundation that provided health care access to poor, inner-city residents.

With that impressive résumé, she was lured to the Midwest by Control Data to become the company's vice president for state government affairs. Later, she established the Ramsey Foundation and became a Republican candidate for lieutenant governor. The last years of her career were spent first as a member of the Eden Prairie City Council, then mayor of the fast-growing suburb.

Recalling her handling of controversial issues in the community, a Harris colleague called her "grace under pressure." When angry residents packed council meetings to express their opinions on the Hwy. 212 tollway proposal or the Flying Cloud landfill expansion, Harris led the contentious sessions graciously. Even if the meetings ran for many hours, the mayor wanted everyone to have a chance to speak. To her way of thinking, compromise and collaboration — not confrontation — were the best ways to get things done.

Jean Harris will be remembered for breaking through glass ceilings, crossing color lines and for accumulating a lot of "firsts" before her various titles. She'll also be known for having been a first-rate, classy and committed public servant.

STAR TRIBUNE SACK
ARMS RACE
ABM TREATY

Letters from readers

Clearly life partners

Why did the Star Tribune choose to print an ignorant, insulting column (Counterpoint, Dec. 15) from a person who first claims her ailing parents were her "domestic partners," then states that service dogs could also be considered "domestic partners," then implies that domestic partner health benefits are contrary to God's plans? Shame on the opinion staff.

I am a lesbian who has been in a committed relationship for 15 years. During five of those years, I provided care for my disabled father. Unlike Anne Collopy, I found it easy to distinguish between my life partner and my dad. I helped him apply for government benefits through the VA and Medicare. And no, I don't expect to be able to add my dog to my health insurance policy.

My life partner is not my parent and certainly not my dog. My partner is actively involved in her church, where they don't believe that "God's plan" is to exclude lesbians and gay men from society. Shame on Collopy for her hateful comments.

— ***Michelle Olson, Minneapolis.***

Trashy commercials

News flash: It's not just the Vikings games or ads for other NFL games, contrary to the premise of your Dec. 18 Variety article.

Two years ago I settled down with my daughter in front of the TV just after Thanksgiving to watch "Rudolph the Red-nosed Reindeer" at 7 p.m. Just prior to the start of the show, the local station ran a slew of ads, trumpeting their prime-time lineup. I hit the mute button too late to avoid hearing about how a major character in a "drama" was going to choose the sex of her child by having an abortion.

Charming holiday fare, don't you think? I complained to the television station but of course never got a reply.

— ***Barbara Wojcik, White Bear Lake.***

Lack of due process

The Court of Appeals decision last month questioning Richfield's tax increment financing district for the Best Buy Project is based on the inadequacy of the city's inspections and other actions. It exposes the Richfield Housing and Redevelopment Authority and Richfield residents to a significant financial liability. Whether you agree or disagree with the decision, the city's transgressions pale when compared with the state's actions in crafting the law upon which the court ruled.

Consider this: The bill passed in 2000 in the midst of the proposed Best Buy construction, had no Senate bill, had no Senate authors, provided for no Senate notice of any hearings, was given no Senate public hearings, provided no opportunity for anyone to be heard in the Senate, and when the bill was introduced on March 13, 2000, the House of Representatives' research staff described the bill as follows:

"This bill makes a number of minor procedural and clarifying changes in the tax increment financing law."

This total lack of due process always creates the perfect atmosphere for lobbyists and individual legislators to work their magic and "lo and behold" a bill becomes law attached to some unrelated statute.

Whether or not this happened in this case, the statute upon which the court relied would appear to be invalid as not passing the barest essentials of constitutionality.

How long will we have to appeal to our highest courts to stop this manner of creating the laws by which we must live?

— ***Ernest A. Lindstrom, Richfield; former House majority leader.***

Confronting terrorism

Thank you for publishing Herb Chilstrom's Dec. 16 Commentary article, "New York, Dresden and Wounded Knee." In his writing, Chilstrom has adeptly helped us to see a wider view of the madness and extremism that struck our nation on Sept. 11, and has wisely led us to focus on what we, as individuals, as religious institutions and as a nation, can do to help avert similar tragedies.

— ***Sandra L. Andersen, Minnetonka.***

Lobbying for school levies

A Dec. 15 letter writer is delusional if he thinks the last two decades of rhetoric from the right is what has caused the problems with our school systems. He ascribes to me that I think "all taxes are bad" and "government is the enemy." Neither of those is true.

We need to be taxed to provide for government services, including schools. However, when schools ask for my tax money in a referendum, they have the responsibility to fully explain, in lay terms, what it is that they need the money for. They also need to provide cost tradeoffs and options, not just scare tactics about laying off teachers if the referendum fails. If they cannot do that to my satisfaction, then it is incumbent upon me to vote "no" on that referendum.

— ***Jerry Bich, Wayzata.***

A school failure

We are two team teachers at Sanford Middle School in Minneapolis. Sanford was our governor's alma mater. Although we were not at Sanford at the time of his attendance, we recognize that no matter how hard we work, there are kids who occasionally fall through the cracks. We as teachers are willing to stand up and admit the failures of his education.

— ***John Heegard, Hopkins, and Brad Thompson, Minneapolis.***

Enron writ large

A Dec. 3 letter writer wondered if President Bush, with his plans for privatizing Social Security, was paying attention to the Enron Corporation's mismanagement of its employees' 401(k) accounts. Evidently, this incident teaches us that privatization is a very bad idea (or a "risky scheme" if you're a demagogue).

A request for this writer and those of like mind: Would you please take me by the hand to that bank, that vault, that drawer, wherein the federal government has been diligently depositing my Social Security taxes for the last 28 years? That is, show me the money in my government-run retirement account. Anyone who's been paying attention knows that the "company" in this case (the federal government) has been spending the savings of "employees" (the taxpayers) from day one.

The Enron debacle is notable because it is an exception in the realm of private retirement accounts. The Social Security system, on the other hand, exemplifies fiduciary recklessness and is the rule in the realm of government-run retirement accounts. Social Security is Enron writ very, very large.

— ***Dean Heuer, Greenfield.***

They weren't paid

A Dec. 16 letter supporting Mary Jo Copeland's plan to institutionalize children as young as age 4 refers to a panel of opponents as "hired experts." That is not true.

All of us on the panel donated our time and expertise. Because, unlike the other panelists, I had to travel a long distance, orphanage opponents agreed to reimburse my travel costs, which totaled $482. Neither I nor my organization received any fee or other compensation. I made the trip because of my strong, long-standing conviction that orphanages harm children.

— ***Richard Wexler, executive director, National Coalition for Child Protection Reform, Alexandria, Va.***

Discovering family history

Bouquets, laurels and Merry Christmas to Larry Oakes for his series, "Footprints of Family: A Scandinavian Adventure." He writes beautifully of such delicate and sensitive "matters of the heart." A book must be here somewhere.

— ***Vaughn L. Winter, Adrian, Minn.***

Yes, yes... I am obese, but I consider it being patriotic. It's all about consumption.

Cartoon by Peter Kohlsaat

Figure 6 **Oakland Tribune**

The Oakland Tribune

P. Scott McKibben, President and Publisher

Nancy Conway, Vice President, Executive Editor
Mario Dianda, Editor
Charles Jackson, Editor at Large
Michael Lynch, Executive Vice President, Advertising/Marketing
Dennis Miller, Senior Vice President/Production
Tom Tuttle, ANG Editorial Page Director
Patrick Brown, Executive Vice President, Administration
Jim Dove, Senior Vice President/Circulation
Robert Jendusa, Senior Vice President/Human Resources

OPINION

CONGRESS shall make no laws respecting an establishment of religion, or prohibiting the free exercise thereof; or abridging the freedom of speech, or of the press, or of the right of the people peaceably to assemble, and to petition the Government for a redress of grievances.

FIRST AMENDMENT TO THE CONSTITUTION OF THE UNITED STATES, RATIFIED DEC. 15, 1791

SATURDAY June 17, 2000 ANG *NEWS*PAPERS LOCAL 7

Let states regulate amusement parks

OUR OPINION

STRICTER regulation of permanent amusement parks to prevent death and injury is, of course, a good idea. The most recent proposal for achieving that, however, is not.

U.S. Rep. Edward Markey, D-Mass., recently proposed the National Amusement Park Safety Act that would give the federal Consumer Product Safety Commission jurisdiction over all amusement park rides. Markey's proposal was part of a House Commerce subcommittee session looking into whether federal regulation should be reinstituted.

"In 1981, Congress concluded that permanent amusement park rides were not consumer products and thus did not require federal regulation," Newsday reported. "Since then, rides have become bigger and faster, and regulation of them has been left up to a sometimes haphazard system of state enforcement."

Portable rides, such as those at carnivals, are regulated nationwide but regulation of the fixed operations — Disneyland, Great America, Marine World and the like — is left to the states. Markey's proposal comes about after hearing horrific reports of death and injury throughout the country. His concern is well taken. Between 1994 and 1998, the Consumer Product Safety Commission estimated, there were 4,500 injuries at fixed amusement parks that required hospitalization, double the number for portable rides.

The president and chief executive officer of the International Association of Amusement Parks and Attractions, a trade association of some 1,500 permanent parks, told the Commerce subcommittee those figures are distorted because attendance at fixed parks has significantly increased in recent years. In fact, John Graff said, amusement park rides are among the safest forms of entertainment.

Bay Area residents were shocked and saddened in 1997 by the death of Quimby Ghilotti, 18, in the collapse of a tall slide at Waterworld in Concord. A handful of incidents within the span of a week last summer, including the death of Sunnyvale 12-year-old Joshua Smurphat at Paramount's Great America in Santa Clara, reinforced concern about the safety of amusement park rides.

Thankfully, lessons learned from Ghilotti's death and other fatal accidents included the need for new, tougher safety regulations at California's permanent parks. Last year's problems helped Assemblyman Tom Torlakson, D-Antioch, push through legislation that does just that. Admittedly, passage of the bill was achieved only after two years of study, hearings and compromise.

We believe passage of tougher regulations on a national level could be even more time consuming, and a lot more complicated. Additionally, federal regulation, through the Consumer Product Safety Commission, would bypass the unique knowledge of its operations each state individually brings to its permanent parks. Federal regulation would require creation of a whole new division of the Consumer Product Safety Commission that not only would be costly but potentially far less efficient than local control.

It is in the best interests of the states, especially the big ones in tourism and amusement park entertainment — Florida, California and Texas — to make sure the rides are safe. The park operators whose attractions benefit the states to the tune of hundreds of millions of dollars surely place the very highest priority on safety — not only out of regard for their fellow citizens but because failure to do so would subject them to high-digit litigation and would be bad for business.

We cannot see how turning over those responsibilities to a federal bureaucracy would be an improvement. Let's first see how new state laws passed in the wake of last year's rash of well-publicized injuries and deaths work.

A system with federal inspectors scattered about the country, running from the remote reaches of the Idaho panhandle to the Oklahoma prairie to the shores of Maine when it's not necessary would be a waste of time and money.

They would have to constantly familiarize themselves with facts and circumstances that locals already know. They would have to thoroughly accommodate all the vagaries of climate — from scorching summers to hard-freeze winters to toxic air and corrosive fog — vital to engineering safety.

Most importantly, they would need to know the park operators, their competence, history and trustworthiness. States can do that. Let's give them that chance.

Dismal anniversary in Kosovo

HOLGER JENSEN

NATO and the United Nations are marking the first anniversary of their presence in Kosovo with little to celebrate.

Everyone concedes that majority Albanians in what is still, technically, a Serbian province — though in reality an international protectorate — are persecuting minority Serbs as savagely as they were once persecuted themselves. In other words, the protectorate protects no one.

The Cato Institute, a private think tank, blames President Clinton's "inept diplomacy and strategic miscalculation" for this "conspicuous failure."

Cato analyst Christopher Layne and Benjamin Schwarz, a correspondent for Atlantic Monthly, point out that the original intent of NATO's air war was to prevent a humanitarian disaster, but it "triggered the very debacle it was said to be preventing.

"Not until NATO began its bombing did (Serbia's) objective in Kosovo change from counterinsurgency to a deliberate campaign to expel the province's ethnic Albanians."

Saved by the bombing, "the war's only beneficiary has been the Kosovo Liberation Army, currently engaged in a brutal ethnic cleansing campaign against Serbs and other non-Albanians."

Yet Clinton's "nation-building adventure," say the authors, continues to be "premised on the notion that rival Balkan factions will settle into a society shaped by the values of democracy, diversity, and tolerance."

Though this is clearly not the case, the administration's "doctrine of virtuous power" allows it to console itself that it "did the right thing."

"Even granting that doubtful premise," say Layne and Schwarz, "this is not enough to exonerate policymakers from their responsibility for the situation the United States confronts today."

The situation, according to a report issued by U.N. Secretary-General Kofi Annan, is "a sharp upsurge of vicious attacks on Kosovo Serbs has undermined Serb confidence in the future. These attacks appear to be part of an orchestrated campaign. Understanding and tolerance remain scarce and reconciliation is far from a reality."

Annan complained that "the international community did not intervene in Kosovo to make it a haven for revenge and crime," but that is precisely what it has become. Besides targeting Serbs, the KLA has also splintered into rival factions battling for control of drug smuggling and protection rackets.

Although the guerrilla army was formally disbanded and turned into a "Kosovo Protection Corps," no one is under any illusions that the KLA still exists and is the real power behind both Kosovo's political establishment and its criminal enterprises. Members of the Protection Corps joke openly that its Albanian initials, TMK, stand for "Tomorrow's Masters of Kosovo."

But masters of what? At least 24 high-ranking former KLA guerrillas have been killed in Mafia-style turf wars over the past year. Former KLA commander Hacim Thaci blames "a few black sheep" among his former comrades-in-arms, but one of them is his own brother, recently caught accepting bribes from a Canadian construction company.

Kosovo averages a murder a day, causing the U.N. High Commissioner for Refugees to call the international mission there a "glaring failure."

UNHCR's annual review, issued jointly with the Organization for Security and Cooperation in Europe, lists almost the same number of violent crimes against Serbs, even though they constitute only 5 percent of the population, as against Albanians — 180 against Serbs and 215 against Albanians between February and May.

"We knew the hatred ran deep but we did not believe that the refugees and victims that UNHCR had helped in exile would soon become the oppressors," said spokesman Ron Redmond. "That means also employing many of the same disgusting tactics that were used against them."

So where do we go from here?

The top U.N. official in Kosovo, Bernard Kouchner, says it "could take a generation" to promote reconciliation between Serbs and Albanians. But Washington doesn't have that kind of patience.

Although the Senate recently killed a bill that would have required congressional approval to keep our troops there beyond next year, pressure is growing to bring them home.

Holger Jensen writes for the Denver Rocky Mountain News. E-mail: www.denver-rmn.com

Choosing a veep candidate

THOMAS OLIPHANT

AT least for the moment, Veepstakes 2000 has not degenerated into the traditional name and state game to which no adult with a life should pay any attention. Instead, it's a high-concept game for both George W. Bush and Al Gore.

At the risk of contradicting myself, consider these illustrative Republicans: Elizabeth Dole, John Danforth and Pete Domenici. And consider these illustrative Democrats: Robert Rubin, Jim Hunt, Dianne Feinstein and George Mitchell.

What they all have in common is either that they have never been elected politicians or that the presidency is not realistically on their horizons no matter what happens to Gore or Bush in November.

And yet they are part of the gradually evolving vice presidential picture this year.

Virtue, as ever in politics, is necessity's handmaiden, but the Bush and Gore search efforts are giving us more meaningful questions to ponder than whether Gov. Tom Ridge can really deliver Pennsylvania or whether Sen. Bob Graham puts Florida in realistic play.

Bush and Gore are thinking outside the box for good reasons. The most obvious one is that a nontraditional option offers the possibility of reflected stature and accomplishment if not necessarily glory. Each candidate could use some shoring up for the campaign ahead, and in at least one area (a female), each campaign could use the excitement and motivation that comes from breaking an out-of-date mold.

There's also a less obvious reason. Choosing from outside the typical talent pools helps avoid the inevitable consequence of a veep selection — the anointing of the most likely successor to the presidential nominee.

In addition, choosing someone who brings adjectives like distinguished, respected, or experienced to the campaign sends a message that the nominee is interested in actually governing the country should he be elected.

The guy with the July convention (Bush) will pick first, and the sifting process being run for him by former defense secretary Dick Cheney is a bit further along than the effort on Gore's behalf by former secretary of state (and Bill Clinton's '92 chief veep picker) Warren Christopher.

The order of selection is important because of the most obvious nontraditional option for a Republican — the party's first female. From what I can gather, Elizabeth Dole is in the middle of it. No one is better prepared for the job by experience or ability to work bipartisanly with Congress.

The fact that the choice of such a solid female would shake up the universe is the reason Christopher has to have an equivalent option for Gore. Sen. Dianne Feinstein may be on the California ballot this fall, but the need to consider matching a Bush selection requires that she be available.

But that's just for openers. Danforth, a minister as well, walked away from the Senate from Missouri early in the Clinton years, and his appointment to run the investigation of Waco is testimony to his bipartisan standing. Domenici, though somewhat more partisan, has stature from his long years as ranking member or chairman of the Senate Budget Committee.

Switching parties, Robert Rubin ranks with the best as an economic policy maker and manager. George Mitchell, like Domenici a more partisan figure from his Senate days, is stature itself, and his diplomatic achievements in Northern Ireland are the stuff of legend. And from North Carolina, Jim Hunt is arguably the most respected governor in the country and an education policy master in his twilight months.

History reminds us that veeps rarely matter to a campaign's result. Doing no harm remains the nominee's most important task.

In a close election, caution is understandable, but fresh thinking could change this equation without downside risk.

Dole, Rubin, Feinstein, Hunt and possibly Danforth could really shake the campaign up, which is why this speculation is anything but idle.

Thomas Oliphant writes for the Boston Globe.

LETTERS TO THE EDITOR

Open plugs pose a threat

HOW MANY more fire plugs will be opened after you printed that front page picture (June 14) of those children frolicking as if they were at a Water World attraction?

With the heat comes an increased danger of fire, and open plugs are a threat to the safety of our firefighters and community. I hope your photographer had the good sense to report the open hydrant.

Jeff Grande
Oakland

Support community center

THE ALAMEDA Multi-Cultural Community Center deserves support from the citizens of Alameda. The AMCCC is important in creating a place of cultural and intergenerational activities that is the cornerstone of the vision for downtown Alameda.

The League of Women Voters of Alameda encourages the informed and active participation of citizens in government and influences public policy through education. The League appreciates partnering with the AMCCC in disseminating voter education materials, primarily in West Alameda. We have also participated in voter registration activities at the Multi-Cultural festival, and will continue to participate in the festival this year at the College of Alameda.

The League is committed to the values of diversity, inclusiveness and the power of collective decision-making for the common good. Consistent with our commitment, the AMCCC plays an important role in improving the quality of civic engagement in our community.

It provides a venue for town meetings and helps publicize important hearings, including Get-Out-the-Vote campaigns, studies on affordable housing practices, a library needs assessment, dialogues on racism or immigration, the potential to train human services providers in how the legislative process works and much more.

The League understands the importance of grass-roots democracy and its role for our Island City as we move toward a vision of cultural competence and diversity. Cultural competence is the ability to interact appropriately with people of different cultures while minimizing culture shock, that is, the experience of being disoriented by the customs, beliefs and habits of others.

The League of Women Voters of Alameda supports the work of the Alameda Multi-Cultural Community Center in helping us educate voters.

Lena L. Tam
President
League of Women Voters of Alameda

Getting in touch with the editor

We invite readers to share their views. Letters must be 250 words or less and include your name, home address and daytime phone number.

Please limit My Word articles to 550 words or less. All letters are subject to verification, and to editing for legal aspects, brevity and clarity.

Write: Letters to the Editor, The Oakland Tribune, 401 13th St., Oakland 94612. Call 208-6409 or fax 208-6477. E-mail: triblet@angnewspapers.com

■ TODAY'S PAGES

In redesigning its pages, said Susan Albright, the editorial page editor, the *Star Tribune* set out to "create a brighter, cleaner and more dynamic look, as well as to highlight our institutional views as expressed in editorials."[7] Initially designers experimented boldly with using reverse type (white on black) for labels such as "Our Perspective," "Letters from Readers" and "Other Points of View," but the effect was judged to be too harsh. The labels were kept but in the traditional black type. Editorials were given more emphasis with black 36-point sans serif Franklin type for one-, two- or three-word main headlines, with a 24-point serif Walbaum italic secondary headline. (The distinctive characteristic of a serif typeface is a smaller line used to finish off a main stroke of a letter. The type you are reading now is serif. The section headlines are sans serif.) Newsroom design director Anders Ramberg used the word "elegant" to describe the Franklin-Walbaum combination. In his opinion the two type faces complemented each other.[8] To me the page projects a feeling of respectability, dignity and thoughtfulness, and it has an inviting appearance.

Is there a trend toward bolder makeup of editorial pages? Several newspapers now run editorials most of the way across the top of the page. I found several, including in the *Oakland* (Calif.) *Tribune* (Figure 6, page 311). In the *Billings* (Mont.) *Gazette* example (Figure 7, page 313) an editorial occupies four columns in the upper left corner of the page. In the Missoula, Mont., *Missoulian* (Figure 8, page 314) the editorial occupies three and a half columns in the upper right corner. The *Billings Gazette* and *Missoulian* editorials both wrap around editorial cartoons on the same subject.

Another example of an editorial displayed at the top of the page appeared in the *Daily Times-Call* (Figure 9, page 315) of Longmont, Colo. The editorial occupies the middle three columns of a five-column page. A cartoon, on another topic, appears below the editorial.

An example of an editorial set in a single, relatively wide column appeared in the Canadian *Telegraph-Journal* (Figure 10, page 316) of Saint John, N.B. The lines in the 3.75-inch-wide column averaged 60 characters, verging on the maximum for easy reading. Offsetting the long lines are an insert summarizing the editorial and a "Your View" coupon at the end of the editorial, inviting readers to fax their opinions on the topic. On the original newspaper page, the two "View" words were set in red, the big "D" in orange, the background of "We believe" in yellow and the photo of Julian Walker in full color.

Resources for Newspaper Design

Bowles, Dorothy, and Diane L. Borden, *Creative Editing for Print Media*, 2nd ed. (Belmont, Calif.: Wadsworth, 1997).

Garcia, Mario R., *Contemporary Newspaper Design*, 3rd ed. (Englewood Cliffs, N.J.: Prentice-Hall, 1993).

Harrower, Tim, *The Newspaper Designer's Handbook with CD-ROM*, 5th ed. (Boston: McGraw-Hill, 2002).

Moen, Daryl R., *Newspaper Layout and Design: A Team Approach*, 4th ed. (Ames: Iowa State University Press, 2000).

Figure 7 **Billings Gazette**

Billings Gazette

4A
Tuesday, April 30, 2002

OPINION

The Source

Publisher
Michael Gulledge

Editor
Steve Prosinski

Opinion Page Editor
Pat Bellinghausen

Contact us via e-mail
speakup@billingsgazette.com

Gazette opinion

Put priority on drug prevention

Alcohol is the drug of choice for our youth.

■ Thirty-four percent of Billings high school students surveyed last year reported binge drinking within 30 days of the survey. Binge drinking is having five or more drinks on one occasion.

■ Forty-seven percent of the Billings students surveyed said they'd had some amount of alcohol to drink within the month.

Marijuana, meth

The same Youth Risk Behavior Survey also gauged marijuana and methamphetamine use:

■ Twenty-four percent of Billings students said they'd used marijuana within a month of the survey.

■ Nine percent of Billings students surveyed said they had used methamphetamine sometime in their lives.

Fewer high school students reported smoking tobacco than reported drinking or using marijuana: 16 percent smoked and only 2 percent said they'd used smokeless tobacco within the month before the survey.

What accounts for the prevalence of illegal substance use among our youth?

Another survey, called the Prevention Needs Assessment sheds some light: A majority of our Billings students perceive that drugs are readily available. They believe their parents' attitudes favor drug use.

Fifty percent of 10th graders and 60 percent of 12th graders gave answers that indicated their parents favor drug use.

Billings youth also are at risk for drug abuse because 45 percent of the eighth-graders and 50 percent of the 10th graders have friends who use drugs. By 12th grade, 54 percent of students saw "rewards for antisocial behavior," also a risk factor for substance abuse.

Changing behaviors

What can we do to lower the risks?

First we must change adult attitudes. Adults must send clear messages that drug use, including underage drinking and tobacco use are unacceptable.

We must instill a sense of responsibility and accountability in our children. We must offer kids opportunities to be involved in the community in positive ways. We must reward good behavior. We must strengthen families.

The most cost-effective prevention is targeting our children and youth. Most adult drug addicts started using substances illegally as children or young teens. That's where a community must start its war against drugs.

Community action

The Billings/Yellowstone County Drug Prevention Planning Committee will meet from 2:30 to 4:30 p.m. Wednesday in Billings Clinic conference rooms 2-3 on the lower level of the clinic across the street from Deaconess Hospital. All interested community members are invited. The meeting is sponsored by Celebrate Billings community partnership.

Correction: Monday's editorial inadvertently stated that most methamphetamine users start by smoking the drug. Kathy Woodward of the Methamphetamine Treatment Project points out that the typical abuse progression is snorting the drug, then smoking, and finally, injecting.

Voice of the reader

Thanks for supporting Roberts CPR training

On behalf of the Roberts Community Foundation, I thank St. Vincent Healthcare for generous donation of time and resources to teach CPR in Roberts. Through these efforts, 54 students in Roberts High School, seven members of the Roberts teaching staff as well as 36 members of the community have been certified in CPR — a total of 97 persons! What an incredible bonus for Roberts!

Thanks to Brenda Potts, Roz Kelly, Gayla Janskovitch and the instructors of the St. Vincent Community Outreach Program; to Randy Durr, superintendent of Roberts School, for his cooperation in setting up this program and to the Roberts School for the use of facilities. The support and enthusiasm I encountered in setting these classes up was heart warming.

These generous CPR supporter have set up a fund to facilitate future CPR training for Roberts High School students: Montana Heart Institute; Stillwater Mining Company; BFI Waste Systems; the Children's Clinic; Orthopedic Surgeons, PC; Dr. Ronald Smith, DDS; Dr. James Wiggins, Pediatric Cardiology, and Dr. Ben Marchello & Oncology Associates.

It is a pleasure for the Roberts Community Foundation to have facilitated another of its mission statement goals to enhance the safety of the citizens in our rural community. Maybe we will have helped make a difference in someone's life!

Elta B. Ayre, RNCC
Roberts Community Foundation Chair
Roberts

U.N. should be target of war on terrorism

From the violations of national sovereignty and human decency in the Congo in 1961 through Korea and Vietnam (where the U.N. directed both sides of the conflict) to the war in Iraq which we were not allowed to finish, the record of the United Nations is terror and turmoil.

If President George Bush is serious about punishing governments which support terrorists, that would-be world government on American soil should be his first target. The United Nations has given a world-wide podium to Yasser Arafat, the terrorist come illegally to power, replaced the United States on the vital Human Rights Commission with a terrorist state and cost us $30 billion.

Even after the debacles in Korea (a stalemate) and Vietnam (a humiliating defeat) the U.N. also ran Desert Storm. In fact, President George Herbert Walker Bush proclaimed gleefully that the United Nations was now becoming what it was always intended to be, the framework for world government. The farcical peace was also dictated by the U.N. —an unenforceable no-fly zone and on-ground inspections at sites chosen by Saddam Hussein. No inspections have been allowed since 1998.

What a dilemma for both the former president and his son!

Surely by now, Bush, the elder, must see the continual, calculated betrayals of the United Nations for what they are. George W. Bush, a loyal son, cannot tell the world that his father made a monumental mistake by not deposing Hussein. He can only correct that error with a new, costly war. To win his war, and the peace the world so desperately needs, he must, somehow, escape the "help" of the United Nations.

Lola Perrins
Big Timber

Amend voter district plan for South Billings

On Wednesday, a commission will make a decision which we must live with for the next 10 years. They will select a plan determining how Billings residents elect legislators. Unfortunately they have shown a preference for Plan 300. That plan carves up downtown Billings neighborhoods into long, inappropriate strips. Then it slices the city's South Side into four odd-shaped fragments.

Naturally, residents are insulted and disturbed by Plan 300. Often, redistricting disputes are just partisan arguments. That is not the case here. Members of the Green party, Democrats and Republicans have spoken out against the damage which Plan 300 does. This failure to fairly represent citizens in the heart of Billings has united us.

Plan 300 is seriously flawed and would be illegal. Twenty thousand Billings residents will have their voices diminished, and votes diluted. Randomly dividing neighborhoods essentially guarantees many residents will have a legislator who does not represent them. Tearing apart our city's South Side also virtually assures low voter turnout will be driven even lower. The law requires "compact" districts. Yet Plan 300 creates districts that are several miles long while only a few blocks wide. Will the commissioners waste scarce taxpayer dollars trying to defend this, the indefensible?

There is a sensible solution. Plan 300 can be corrected. I submitted an amendment which will do this. It reconnects divided neighborhoods and recognizes our cultural communities. This amendment removes the flaws and brings Plan 300 back into compliance with the law.

We ask the commissioners to do what is right. Adopt this Billings amendment! Their votes will send a loud message across Montana. Are we citizens who have a right to fair representation? Or are we just pawns to be pushed around in a political game ? We await their answer.

Weldon J. Birdwell
Candidate, HD 13
Billings

Drivers impaired with .08 blood alcohol

In his April 25 letter to the editor, Donald Brocopp makes the absurd assertion that drivers with a blood alcohol content (BAC) of .08 - .1 are merely social drinkers. Explain that to the seven Montana families who experienced the death a family member in 1998 due to impaired drivers with a BAC of .08-.09 and the additional 200 people who were injured by these impaired drivers (source — Public Services Research Institute, Landover, Md.).

The .08 BAC level has consistently demonstrated significant impairment in a driver's ability to operate a motor vehicle safely.

Editorials running in Montana newspapers this month have quoted Montana Corrections Department Director Bill Slaughter as stating that some of the most dangerous drivers on the road are those who are marginally intoxicated and filled with a false sense of invincibility about their reflexes.

The Public Services Research Institute supports that lowering Montana's BAC limit to .08 will reduce alcohol-related fatalities by 8 percent. When compared with the rest of our country, Montana lags behind the nation in drunken driving laws. Our relatively lax DUI laws send a message of indifference regarding drinking and driving. Tougher laws will send a stronger message and will go far toward changing a culture that accepts alcohol-related tragedies as an acceptable norm.

Multiple DUI offenders are a big problem in Montana. Montanans United, Saving Lives (MUSL), a statewide coalition, has proposed strengthening enforcement and introducing policy aimed at the prevention of alcohol and drug tragedies.

It's not just about enforcement. It's about changing the culture which encourages over-consumption of alcohol and tolerates drinking, driving and the resulting carnage in Montana.

Betsy J. Webb, Project Manager
Bozeman Underage Drinking Reduction Project

Letter policy

Letters to the editor must contain the signature of the author, the writer's street address and work and home phone numbers. Maximum length is 300 words. The Gazette reserves the right to edit letters. Writers may have a letter printed no more often than once in every 30 days.

Mail letters to: Gazette Voice of the Reader, PO Box 36300, Billings, Mont., 59107 or fax to (406) 657-1208.

Signed editorial columns and letters do not necessarily reflect the viewpoint of the Billings Gazette.

David Broder

Cash-strapped schools get little federal help

WASHINGTON — Last week, Oregon newspapers carried an Associated Press report that more than 4,600 taxpayers had voluntarily donated almost $700,000 of their tax refunds from the state to a newly created fund for support of public schools.

It was a small percentage of the $240 million automatically rebated when revenue for the 1999-2001 biennium exceeded estimates. But with the economic slowdown now causing a budget crunch in Oregon, as in more than 40 other states, these taxpayers recognized that education is in jeopardy. A recent special session found the Legislature cutting the schools budget by $112 million.

What is happening in Oregon is happening across the country. The National Conference of State Legislatures reported last week that in the current fiscal year, 17 states faced reductions in their budgets for elementary and secondary schools, and 29 faced cuts for colleges.

Reality gap

The gap between this reality and the Washington rhetoric about raising standards in schools while assuring that "no child is left behind" is alarmingly large.

In just the last few days, parents and students in state after state have heard disturbing news about the schools. The Massachusetts House of Representatives received a committee-approved budget which would cut school spending 10 percent across the board, reducing state aid to local districts by $320 million.

At the other end of the educational spectrum, the administration of freshman New Jersey Gov. Jim McGreevey has petitioned for relief from the court order requiring the state to put extra funds into the 30 poorest school districts. These districts — urban areas with low property-tax bases — were supposed to get $83 million extra in state funds to help them repair buildings, hire teachers and improve instruction. Instead, like every other district, they will be level-funded next year.

States in a jam

No governors or legislators want to damage the schools their constituents use. But the requirement to balance budgets in a time of slumping revenues has left them little choice. While Washington goes blithely on its way, cutting taxes, running up deficits and borrowing from Social Security, the states are in a jam.

What is happening to elementary and secondary schools is minor compared to the hit on higher education. In the face of rising enrollments, Pennsylvania is cutting its higher ed budget by almost 5 percent. Penn State students, who were hit with an 8 percent tuition increase this year, will face another tuition boost and a fee increase of up to $600 when they come back to school.

They are better off than University of Washington students, where the budget calls for a 16 percent tuition increase. And in education-conscious Iowa, the presidents of the three largest state universities said in a joint statement that the Legislature's cuts "will unquestionably compromise the quality of our educational programs." State funding, which once paid 77 percent of the bills, now pays 60 percent, and most of the falloff has been made up by raising tuition.

Top priority

The irony is that even as all this is happening, a poll released last week reaffirms the importance of education to most voters. The Public Education Network and Education Week newspaper reported that when it comes to balancing state budgets, voters overwhelmingly say that schools are the top priority. Education leads the No. 2 choice, health care, by a 3-1 margin. Law enforcement, welfare, services for seniors, transportation and economic development lag far behind.

But that is not what the budgets reflect. Medicaid payments are the fastest growing state expenditures and those costs leave little room for education or other programs.

Washington is not helping much. The federal government is still falling far short on its promise to pay 40 percent of the bills for special education students, whose needs are a crippling cost for local school districts.

After boosting education spending by healthy double-digit percentages in the last year of the Clinton administration and the first year of the Bush administration, this year's federal budget calls for only a 2.8 percent increase.

With the feds preferring tax cuts to education aid, and the states cutting back because of their budget squeeze, America is in serious danger of backsliding on the promise to improve its schools.

David Broder writes for the Washington Post.

Mallard Fillmore By Bruce Tinsley

Doonesbury By Garry Trudeau

Figure 8 **Missoulian**

EDITORIAL DESK 523-5241

MISSOULIAN
A4
THURSDAY, MARCH 8, 2001

Opinion

EDITORIAL POLICY

The Missoulian strives to present ideas from a diverse array of writers. Missoulian editorials express the views of the newspaper's editorial board. Signed commentary, columns, letters and editorial cartoons represent the independent views of the authors.

EDITORIAL BOARD

Pardon me, but Bush was no Clinton

It was more Democrat bashing than the poor Washington Post could tolerate. For weeks, they had dutifully reported the sordid details Bill Clinton's pardon bazaar, but then it all became too much. And so in late February, on the front page of the Style section (the paper's beating heart), reporter Michael Powell let fly with this attempt at perspective:

"A lame-duck president grants a slew of controversial pardons, eleventh-hour Get Out of Jail Free cards for the politically well-connected. His pardon list includes: A former Cabinet official who could have been in a position to implicate the president himself in federal crimes. An assistant secretary of state who withheld information from Congress and a CIA official who lied to it. ... Outrage billows. Editorials thunder. ... The president in question was George H. W. Bush."

MONA CHAREN

James Carville couldn't have said it better. Ladies and gentlemen, the familiar "everybody does it" defense makes its debut in Pardongate.

But there was a world of difference between what Bush and Clinton did, and this casual equation of the two men really ought not to slide past without protest.

The wording is sly: "Get Out of Jail Free for the politically well-connected." It makes it sound as if Bush were simply giving special favors to those with suspicious access to the powerful. But that is not what happened at all.

In fact, the people who had been indicted in the Iran-Contra affair were high-ranking government officials who had done nothing for personal gain, nor did they betray their country or in any other way bring obloquy upon themselves. Former Defense Secretary Casper Weinberger, former Assistant Secretary of State Elliott Abrams and former CIA official Clair George, among others, were caught up in a policy dispute.

During the 1980s, the Congress was on again/off again about aiding the Contras. Most members of the Democratic caucus (and the Democrats ran the place then) were firmly opposed to Contra aid. But a minority of the Democrats did sometimes vote yes on aid. There were any number of votes on assistance to the Contras, and endless permutations of the so-called Boland Amendment, which forbade the administration from forwarding (it varied) lethal or nonlethal assistance to them. But Congress kept reversing itself.

The public was much more disappointed that Reagan had traded arms for hostages in the Middle East (breaking a promise never to negotiate with terrorists) than with the Contra angle that so outraged the Democrats and the press. But the independent counsel (which everybody now agrees is a bad idea) had all the time and money in the world to come up with crimes. And so he indicted Abrams, George and Weinberger, among others, for withholding information from Congress – which is not right but was not considered, until Lawrence Walsh pored over the code, to be the kind of thing that should land you in jail.

And the notion that Weinberger was "in a position to implicate the president himself in federal crimes" is sheer twaddle. It's bad policy to trade arms for hostages, but it is not a federal crime. As for the scheme to divert funds from these sales to the Contras – well, it was legal on Wednesday but not on Thursday, depending upon the mood of Congress. Consider the context: It was a decision to keep alive a bunch of rebels fighting a truly monstrous regime (our sworn enemy) while Congress dithered. The Reagan administration should not have done it because the Congress has the authority to dither. But to suggest that this goal was in any way comparable to the Rich or other pardons sold by Bill Clinton is ridiculous.

Bush announced his pardons on Christmas Eve, not Jan. 20. He had cleared them with Speaker of the House Tom Foley and Chairman of the Armed Services Committee Les Aspin. He did it because he believed, correctly, that they were honorable public servants victimized by the tendency of Democrats to believe that disagreeing with them is criminal. But it was nothing like the self-interested, contemptible actions of his successor.

Mona Charen is a syndicated columnist. You can write to her via her syndicate's Web site, www.creators.com.

MISSOULIAN EDITORIAL

Two heartbeats away from trouble

SUMMARY: In addition to the pulse of the nation, the president needs to keep close tabs on the pulse of two indispensable Republicans.

If we were president, we'd start paying more attention to health. Specifically, to the health of two pivotal players in Washington, D.C.

The first is Vice President Dick Cheney. He's certainly not one to lie down on the job. He's had one heart attack and two surgical procedures to open clogged arteries since his election in November, yet he continues performing a crucial role in the White House.

But if you want to talk work ethic, take a look at Strom Thurmond, the Republican senator from South Carolina. He's 98 and still serving as the Senate's president pro-tem. For how long, though? You might wonder.

The resiliency and commitment of these two men, Cheney and Thurmond, may have a lot to do with George W. Bush's success as president.

Cheney, by many accounts, serves as the nation's de facto prime minister. His experience and intellect complement the president's personal and political skills. Cheney is widely reported to be among the most involved vice presidents in history. He's the administration's point man on matters of budget, national security and energy. He's heading the administration's comprehensive review of the military. He's usually at the president's side whenever a foreign dignitary is in the room. Cheney is Bush's closest adviser.

As president of the evenly divided Senate, Cheney, formerly a highly regarded senator from Wyoming, also has the deciding vote in any tie election. He's also the administration's key liaison with Congress. His role in the Senate is far from ceremonial.

Cheney's had four heart attacks over the years. His first at age 37 (he's now 60). If his poor health interferes with his work, or ultimately forces him to step down, it would create a vacuum in leadership. Nominating and confirming a successor to Cheney would be relatively easy; replacing him would not.

Over in the Senate, Thurmond is not just the oldest person to serve. He also happens to be the 50th Republican. Serious illness or death – neither altogether unlikely at 98 – would almost certainly shift the balance of power in the Senate. Were Thurmond to resign or die, his replacement would be appointed by South Carolina Gov. Jim Hodges. He's a Democrat. Replace Thurmond, and the Democrats would have a 51-49 majority, ending the awkward power-sharing arrangement now in place.

Thurmond, in recent weeks, began cutting back his Senate duties. He also was hospitalized briefly for "fatigue" last month.

The loss of Cheney from the administration would be a blow to Bush and his ability to advance his agenda. But it would be a survivable blow. Without Thurmond, however, the Republicans would lose their tenuous control of Congress. That would effectively shackle the GOP. Democrats, at least, would be in a position to demand significant concessions from Bush and the Republicans in Congress.

Say you're sorry

GOP owes us a big apology for this deregulation morass

By BOB HEFFNER

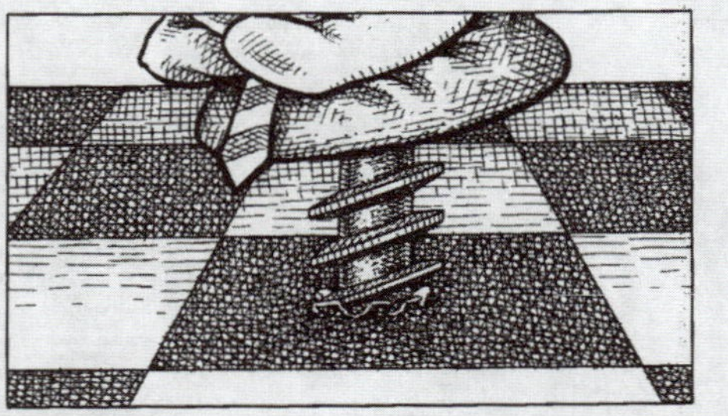

In a recent commentary on electricity deregulation (Missoulian, Feb. 25), state Senate Majority Leader Fred Thomas, R-Stevensville, assures us how hard he and his cohorts are working to "help salvage Montana's economy, provide jobs and economic development and protect residential consumers from high electricity prices." Isn't this a little like the Unabomber seeking to curry public favor on the claim that he was willing to help clear away the debris and bury the bodies?

Thomas sponsored, and an overwhelming partisan majority of his colleagues passed, deregulatory legislation which has done more, in less time, to destroy major Montana industries than the combined acts of the massed army of all environmentalists since the beginning of time. The low-priced and reliable power that they've discarded was one of the few major advantages Montana once had as an industrial location.

Now, in a series of articles penned over the last five weeks under the names of Fred Thomas, Senate President Tom Beck and House Speaker Dan McGee, the Republican leadership is trying to claim (a) the crisis caused by deregulation would have happened anyway; (b) their deregulation scheme protects us from yet worse consequences; and (c) even if deregulation caused our problems, it was still the right thing to do. This campaign is, to my knowledge, the most blatant example of self-serving sophistry in recent Montana political history.

It appears backers of deregulation have elevated an elementary, economics 101 conception of free markets to the status of religious principle. They follow such precepts because they must, one seems to say, no matter what the consequences in the real world, and no matter what the damage to the people who elected them.

Their main arguments collapse on the briefest review. They point to supply shortages and price increases in the Northwest and California as evidence that problems would have occurred anyway, and could have been worse. In fact, regional market conditions would have precisely nothing to do with electrical rates or availability in a regulated Montana market that produced, as we do, and controlled, as we once did, a power supply more than twice what we can use. No believable growth rate in Montana would lead to shortages over the next 30 years, even if we developed not a megawatt of additional power in that time. Arguments that blame supply, rather than deregulation itself, are not just weak – they are false.

The consequences of deregulation appear largely irreversible. Of course, many smart and decent people will pitch in to figure out how to soften, delay and otherwise partly mitigate the impacts. When the boat is sinking, we all have to bail, and we will. But that does not save the guys who pulled the bilge plug from owing the rest of us an apology and, above all, an explanation.

The cause of their error, is, after all, something of a mystery. Keep in mind that they had no problem to fix. In 1997, when the leadership embarked on this radical and irreversible path, Montana controlled the sixth lowest power prices in the country, and a supply more than twice the demand.

Fred Thomas may have offered us a clue, at least. Incredibly, in view of the damage already visited on the rest of us, and with the worst yet to come, he declares that "what we did in 1997 is right." What could he mean by that? (If a public policy action of such ill consequences is "right," one naturally wonders what could possibly be "wrong.")

The justification surfaces in a previous paragraph from the same Feb. 25 guest column in the Missoulian: "We relied, and still do, on free markets rather than government to establish fair prices for consumers." In other words, it appears that he and his colleagues have elevated an elementary, economics 101 conception of free markets to the status of religious principle. They follow such precepts because they must, he seems to say, no matter what the consequences in the real world, and no matter what the damage to the people who elected them.

In fact, free markets are an elaborate theoretical construct, understood with difficulty by experts, and apparently not at all by the Montana Legislature.

The Republican leadership has attached itself to a few simple-minded notions: for example, that unregulated markets are always better, and that industry should always get whatever it asks for. If such a primitive substitute for economics was responsible for getting us into this mess, we deserve to hear it confessed – so that we may all, hereafter, view such crude notions with the suspicion and skepticism they so profoundly merit.

But was blind ideology the root cause? After all, not one of our low-energy-cost neighbor states, despite their Republican majorities, leapt with Montana into the deregulatory pit. Or was ideology just an enabling factor, rendering our leadership easy stooges for the forces that stood to benefit? Is the story waiting to be told one of untoward influence by Montana Power Co., which led the lobbying charge, pocketed hundreds of millions from selling assets inflated in value by deregulation, then deposited its head lobbyist in rear-guard position as (it almost defies belief) the chief of staff to Governor Judy Martz?

Whatever the explanation, the people of Montana deserve to hear it. We deserve and must demand to hear it in plain terms, from the responsible parties – preceded by the admission of wrongdoing and the apology which the current legislative leadership now so clearly owes. Fred Thomas, Tom Beck and Dan McGee: This, rather than a propaganda campaign, is how your rehabilitation can begin.

Bob Heffner of Missoula was head of Montana's Business Development Division in Gov. Stan Stephens' administration.

Figure 9 **Daily Times-Call**

Friday, June 29, 2001

Kim Humphreys,
Editorial Page Editor
(303) 776-2244 Ext. 221

DAILY TIMES-CALL

OPINION

Page A4

To Build A Better World, Start In Your Own Community

Open Forum

U.S. schools sell moral authority to high bidder

For quite some time, I've been disturbed with the product government schools produce, but haven't been able to put my finger on the problem. Two events reported in the Times-Call in the past weeks give a glimpse into a truly frightening system and crystallized the source of my unease.

The first event is the decision to install metal detectors at Skyline. The second is the syndicated column a couple of weeks ago about schools renting out classrooms of children to corporations for market research. For me, those two stories came together with a bang! Government schools have lost moral authority and have been taken over by a cynical gang who regard children as little more than a cash crop.

Does this sound too extreme? The teachers' union, administration and school board rush to tell us how much they care about our children, how dedicated they are, how hard they work. Surely, you say, these fine folks who are our friends and neighbors can be trusted with our children. I no longer think so. There's an old Hebrew saying, "Show me your actions and I will tell you what you believe."

The highest responsibility of one generation is the rearing of its children. The core of education is instilling proper moral, ethical and spiritual beliefs. Surely the family, the church and other societal structures play a big part in this, but schools have more focused time with our children than any other single institution. So if the schools fail to educate our children within a civilizing framework, they drag everything else down.

A symptom of the schools' failure to civilize is that Americans are beginning to live in fear of our own children. Responsibility for this recent phenomenon can be laid directly to schools' active hostility toward all that is traditionally regarded as moral and decent. Metal detectors shout that government schools have discarded that moral authority. Rather than insist on right behavior, they are content simply to erect walls, hoping to keep mayhem to an acceptable level.

This observation is reinforced by the commentary about government schools renting out classrooms full of children for market research. The column explains that the schools are "under funded," and so turn to the corporate sector for more money. Unfortunately, they've gotten so greedy that the Senate has introduced a bill saying they must get parental permission before they sell off our children's educational time.

Longmont's decision on Skyline steps right into the fashion of selling out education for profit. A security company came along and offered its product "free" in exchange for endorsements. (Does anyone doubt that there will be consulting and speaking fees available to the administration once the test is "successful"?) The school board did a little hand wringing for public consumption and then jumped at the offer. And so there is another spike in the ideal that we should teach our children to live in peace with one another.

If you regard children as a cash crop, this whole thing makes a certain macabre sense. The highest priority is not civilizing the young but maximizing the profit. To do that, the administration must not get so greedy that parents object, and the environment must be safe enough that there are no incidents attracting TV cameras.

The sweet words from government schools tell one story; their actions tell a very different one. Believe their actions.

JON BEHRENS
Longmont

Forefathers know best

As the Fourth of July comes upon us, I urge the people of America to take time and remember why we celebrate this holiday. During those picnics, family gatherings, camping trips and fireworks, take a moment to say thanks; to all the soldiers who fought and died for our independence and freedom, to the leaders in government for facing the challenges to keep our country free, to the teachers, pastors and parents who pass on lessons of history to our children, and to the children who will face even greater challenges for our future.

Remember our forefathers did this by the grace of God (one nation under God) and living by His word. Today we seem to think we can do it without Him. Our forefathers would be ashamed to know how often we change the things they fought and prayed so hard for.

So on the Fourth, remember to display your flag proudly, and thank God for His word to guide us and allow history to continue in ways we can honor.

JUDY A. HAYES
Longmont

Editorial

Snowmobiles don't belong in Yellowstone

President Bush should pay attention to the wise counsel of the National Park Service and resist those who advise him to roll back limits on snowmobiles in the nation's oldest park, Yellowstone.

Limits on snowmobiles in the park were set to take effect in two years, but industry lobbyists have persuaded the Bush administration to reconsider. While a decision has not yet been made, many fear that snowmobiles will be permitted back into the park during a 12-week winter season.

Yellowstone was a marvelous choice for the nation's first national park. Its mix of natural wonders, wildlife and sheer beauty have delighted generations of Americans who have traveled there.

In winter, snow cloaks the park in even greater splendor. For visitors and the animals that live there, it is a time of solitude and peace.

That is, solitude until the quiet is disturbed by the buzz and roar of two-cycle snowmobile motors and the clouds of exhaust.

Last winter, when snowfalls were much lighter than normal, 83,548 people rode snowmobiles into the park. The irresponsible among them disrupt not only the quiet but also wildlife herds when they are most vulnerable.

Public resources such as national parks must be shared by all who wish to use them. When the method of use of one group destroys the ability of others, then restrictions must be put in place.

A ban on use of snowmobiles in Yellowstone is in the national interest, and that of the park's wildlife and natural wonders.

22 million and counting

AIDS: One deadly enemy we know how to defeat

WASHINGTON — If you were fighting typhoid, or if your family were in danger of meningitis, would you insist that the international banks forgive your nation's debt? If you were taking a trip to areas where malaria was endemic, would you deliberately journey to the jungle and not bother to take anti-malaria pills? If a friend were in grave danger of heart trouble, would you advise him to stay overweight, drink too much alcohol and smoke two packs a day — and then hold serious meetings about who should pay for his hospital care once his heart gave out?

As odd as it seems, those recommendations might well have been made, given the spirit of this week's U.N. special session on AIDS in New York. Yes, many activists, albeit on the anti-West fringes, did insist that, to treat the disease, the national debts of poor nations should be "forgiven." But the other two syndromes are more serious.

The cruel, wasteful AIDS virus is not like cancer, not like the plague, not like diabetes, for we KNOW what causes HIV transmission. The virus is passed through unprotected sexual intercourse, unclean needles and contaminated blood transfusions. Thus, we know how to prevent it.

Yet despite all the words spoken at the U.N., including some weak ones about "prevention" and occasional use of that troublesome word "condom," pathetically little was said about how to stop this pandemic.

Where was the prophetic voice this tragedy cries out for? Where was the true leader for this age, who would step forward and explain the obvious facts to a world that is, apparently, eternally embarrassed about sexual matters? Where was the activist message that would proclaim:

Let every government wage all-out campaigns to teach men to use birth control and to give women the right to demand it. Let us have billboards showing how condoms can save your life. Let us educate children in schools about responsible sexuality and respect for their fellow man and woman. Let us get as many pharmaceutical drugs to as many infected people as possible (of course!), but above all, let us stop a disease that has already claimed 22 million, and protect the 100 million that are expected to be infected by 2005.

Far from being immoral, as some would say, such a campaign could be the medical and reproductive concomitant of civil rights and human rights, and could serve as a rallying point for restoring spirit and hope in these afflicted and demoralized countries.

To be fair, there were voices of reason. One was Andrew Natsios, head of the U.S. Agency for International Development, who gamely argued for prevention, making a plea for wider distribution of condoms.

Meanwhile, some Muslim spokesman argued against giving explicit aid to homosexuals and to prostitutes, as though their "immorality" erased their common humanity with us. The conference raised a good deal of money and nudged some consciences, but there was no great message of transforming the world by realistically defeating this disease.

Nor did the White House exactly distinguish itself. One wonders how President Bush, if he cared about the AIDs fight, could possibly have spent the most crucial day of the conference, Wednesday, meeting with Thabo Mbeki? The controversial South African president, under attack for his bizarre theories about AIDS and his refusal to treat it widely, had pointedly missed the New York meeting to explain his "theories" to the president. Did the White House not understand the message it was sending?

But then, we have to realize that in May the White House put up for the crucial post of head of the Bureau of Population, Refugees and Migration at the State Department the man who represented the Vatican in its diplomatic mission at the U.N. The nominee, John M. Klink, holds both Irish and American citizenship and has always argued the Vatican's anti-abortion, anti-birth-control stance, including the Vatican's opposition to the U.N.'s providing emergency contraceptive pills to women who had been raped in the Balkans wars.

But there is one hopeful note: Not only do we know how to stop AIDS, but we also know how nations can do it. Uganda in Central Africa slashed its infection rates in half in the late 1980s, from 14 percent to 8 percent, by launching a broad-based multisectoral campaign that actually required all government officials to talk about preventing the spread of HIV — indeed, in every public speech. Even the military was engaged in the fight, according to an excellent new paper on "HIV/AIDS as a Security Issue" by the International Crisis Group.

Also in the late 1980s, Thailand in Southeast Asia checked the epidemic and prevented its serious spread into the general population by promoting condom use, expanding treatment, and directing new budgetary and personnel resources into a highly visible national campaign, led by the prime minister. And Senegal in Western Africa stopped the epidemic in its tracks, beginning in 1986, in part by enlisting even Muslim religious leaders, NGOs and the civil society in an education campaign.

And this very same week, Rotarians meeting in San Antonio decided to cooperate worldwide on balanced programs to eradicate AIDS, including treatment and "universal access to prevent unintended pregnancies," indicating that such private community groups may be another solution.

Still, there was no great call this week to credit and to replicate these courageous, farsighted examples. Most leaders prefer to act after the fact rather than anticipate problems and prevent them. AIDS is hardly an enemy that we should choose to live with when it is one that so clearly can be defeated.

Write to Georgie Anne Geyer in care of Universal Press Syndicate, 4520 Main St., Kansas City, Mo. 64111.

Declaration is worth its parchment

NEW YORK — This has not been a great year for Thomas Jefferson. Not only is David McCullough's splendid new biography of Jefferson's great rival, John Adams, the No. 1 best seller in the country, but the Virginian's most celebrated recent biographer, Joseph Ellis, is entangled in a dismaying web of lies about his own life. Then there is the digging up of DNA stories about the man and his slaves.

But the man from Monticello, who will prevail in the next turning of the historical wheel — cycles of historical favor are as predictable as the seasons — did write the best Declaration of Independence that we'll ever read. Professor Ellis, who will have better years, too, may have messed up his own life by lying about his military service for reasons best known to God, but his work remains insightful and valuable to anyone who cares about America and its "independency." The word was often used that way on our birthday, July 4, 1776.

> It was one thing for a philosopher to write such things. It was another for Jefferson ... to endorse them and try to raise an army to win them.

The first two lines of Ellis' 1996 study, "American Sphinx: The Character of Thomas Jefferson," tell us why, though John Adams was an admirable man and an exemplar of integrity, Jefferson is more important to us: "If Jefferson was wrong, America is wrong. If America is right, Jefferson was right."

Those sentences are from an 1874 biography of Jefferson by James Parton, the David McCullough of his day. And, after rereading Mr. Jefferson's declaration, corrected some by Mr. Adams and Benjamin Franklin, I would agree with that.

The Declaration was approved by a unanimous vote of a congress of 13 British colonies in North America in the Pennsylvania Statehouse (now Independence Hall) on July 4 and finally signed by all of them by Aug. 2. It was, at least to the British crown, not worth the parchment it was written on — and it took 13 years of war to make it official.

The rebellion followed a pattern we are all familiar with today: Local grievances were largely ignored in the capital of the colonizers, who then sent troops to disperse and suppress rebel leaders, but the rebels inevitably won a long war because they had no place else to go, and the people and government back in London grew weary of the expense and the endless, inconclusive battling. But back then such things had never happened before.

Most of the Declaration of Independence is, in fact, a list of subject grievances against the British crown: "He has dissolved Representative Houses repeatedly ... He has made Judges dependent on his Will alone ... He has kept among us, in times of peace, Standing Armies without the consent of our legislatures ... He has excited domestic insurrections amongst us, and has endeavoured to bring on the inhabitants of our frontiers, the merciless Indian Savages, whose known rule of warfare is an undistinguished destruction of all ages, sexes and conditions."

But the best stuff, the harnessing of ideas to action, was at the beginning, and Jefferson deserves the credit for it:

"We hold these Truths to be self-evident, that all Men are created equal, that they are endowed by their Creator with certain unalienable Rights, that among these are Life, Liberty and the pursuit of Happiness — That to secure these Rights, Governments are instituted among Men, deriving their just Powers from the Consent of the Governed."

Uh-oh! Those words, basically lifted from the works of the great 17th-century British philosopher John Locke, are interpreted in many ways today. But in 1776 they were a direct challenge to the "divine right" of kings. "All men are created equal" was not about uplift and the rights or worth of slaves or the poor. Those words meant that the king of England was no better than anyone else.

That represented a fundamental challenge to the established order — and not only in England and North America. It was one thing for a philosopher to write such things. It was another for Jefferson (and Adams and the rest) to endorse them and try to raise an army to win them. The world would never be the same.

And that is what we celebrate. The world is a better place now. Jefferson was right, and so are we. God Bless America.

350 Terry St., Longmont Colo. 80501
Telephone 303-776-2244
Classified 303-776-7440
Fax 303-678-8615

DAILY TIMES-CALL
Longmont and the St. Vrain Valley, Colorado

Edward Lehman, Publisher
Dean G. Lehman, Editor & President
Lauren R. Lehman, Vice President
Richard B. Simmons, Vice President/Finance
Michael A. Gugliotto, Vice President & General Manager
Curt Anderson, Managing Editor
Dale L. Carr, Vice President/Production
Kathy Pias, Circulation Director
Penny Dille, Advertising Director
Connie Coffield, Director of Promotion, Community Service and Newspapers in Education

Office hours: 8 a.m. – 5 p.m. Weekdays
Classified Saturday — 8 a.m. to noon
Circulation Monday – Friday 5 a.m. – 5 p.m. Saturday and Sunday 5 a.m. – noon

Letters welcome

The Daily Times-Call encourages its readers to share their views. Short letters, about one typewritten, double-spaced page, on timely topics get preference. We will print as many letters as space allows. Letters must be signed. We don't publish anonymous letters, poetry, letters signed with a pseudonym or letters addressed to a third party. For verification, please include your address and daytime telephone number. (We do not publish them.) Letters longer than 300 words will be shortened.

Send to:

Open Forum, P.O. Box 299, Longmont, CO 80502;
e-mail: opinion@times-call.com.

Figure 10 **Telegraph-Journal**

OPINION PAGE EDITOR: HOWIE TRAINOR
TELEPHONE: (506) 648-2133
E-MAIL: *trainor.howie@nbpub.com*

OPINION

TELEGRAPH-JOURNAL ▪ **SECTION B**
THURSDAY, SEPTEMBER 28, 2000

PUBLISHER
Victor Mlodecki
ASSISTANT PUBLISHER/EDITOR IN CHIEF
Howie Trainor
MANAGING EDITOR
Peter Haggert

OUR VIEW

A future for Extra-Mural

Documents compiled by the Premier's Health Quality Council and revealed this week seem to confirm what many New Brunswickers surely suspected: that the Extra-Mural Hospital program is no longer generating the benefits it once did. But this does not mean the program should be cut. Just the opposite – a re-thought and revived Extra-Mural service may be the most valuable remedy in the province's medicine chest.

Professionals working in Extra-Mural care paint a gloomy picture of a service that no longer meets the needs of patients or the goal of economy. This is a far cry from what the Extra-Mural program was intended to be.

We believe:
The province should rethink its delivery of Extra-Mural health care

Founded as a separate budgetary and administrative entity in 1981, the Extra-Mural Hospital deployed a combination of outpatient clinics, day surgery units, nurses and therapists to treat patients in their communities and homes. It was a striking success, and physicians from other countries came to N.B. to study it.

The program still has value – much of the palliative care N.B. offers is dependent on Extra-Mural services – but it is no longer the jewel it once was. In 1996, Extra-Mural responsibilities were brought under the regional health corporations as a cost-saving measure. The consensus seems to be that this decision has had myriad unexpected effects on service, few of them positive.

Ironically, Extra-Mural could be revived as a cost-saving measure. As the pressure to find effective, cost-efficient alternatives for community care grows, so does the impetus to rethink how these services are delivered.

In 1999, the province's Health Services Review Committee recommended renewing support for community care, Extra-Mural services and home care. Subsequently, the Lord government vaulted to power on a platform that included promises to provide a similarly decentralized, regional model for health care.

Last Month, Dr. Gordon Ferguson, the father of the Extra-Mural program, called on the province to renew and expand its commitment to Extra-Mural care. The Premier's Health Quality Council and Health and Wellness Minister Dr. Dennis Furlong should consider his proposals carefully.

New Brunswick proved that extensive Extra-Mural care could work in the first place. Now, it is to time to investigate whether it can be made to work better.

YOUR VIEW

How could the province use Extra-Mural services to improve the delivery of health care?

NAME **PHONE**

COMMUNITY

Fax your view to: 506-633-6758

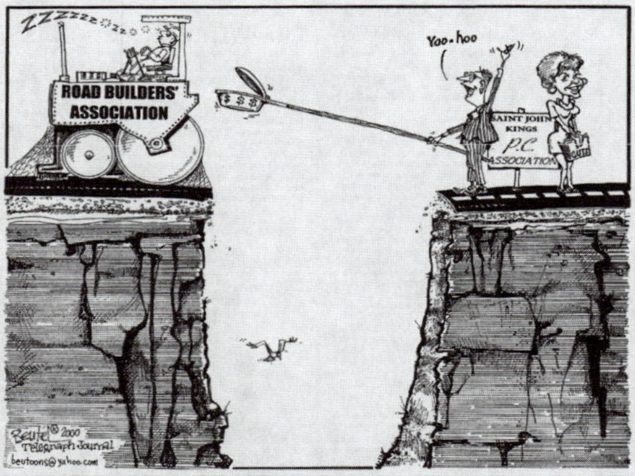

What's wrong with assimilation?

LETTER OF THE DAY

Columnist Rosella Melanson recently pointed out that Acadians are losing too many young to assimilation into the Anglo-American culture. Some linguists will explain this by referring to the steady decline of the use of the French language at the international level and by laying most of the blame of today's assimilation on globalism. All the while the English language has flourished.

This kind of assimilation is older than that. It goes back to the establishment of the Academie Francaise, in France, in the middle of the 17th century. Call it what you may: a governing body, a watchdog, a language police, this Adademie has forced the French language into a straightjacket that has stifled its development.

Deprived of any scope for flexibility, the Academie has made sure that the French language would remain static, that is, as dead as the Latin language. To achieve this, sets of complicated rules were issued and every generation of writers had to abide by a grammar textbook growing in thickness.

Take a look at today's Bible of the French language, usually known as *Bon Usage*. Its 1980 edition contains no less than 1,519 pages; its 1986 edition, exactly 1,768 pages – enough to deter any youngster from learning French. I'm a published author, and for the last 69 years I've been trying to master *Le Bon Usage* to little avail. Read my latest novel *La Tracadienne* , and you'll see what I mean.

Who can blame youngsters for switching to English at a rate of nine per cent? It's because there is no such thing as an English grammar, or a Spanish grammar, or an Italian grammar to frighten pupils away. "There are some rules for relating English spelling and pronunciation, but I usually make my own," as Winston Churchill said. Mind you, the assimilation rate could be a lot higher.

Why is assimilation a loss, as if our youngsters had been killed in some imaginary war in our imagined land? Those youngsters are a plus. What's wrong with being English-speaking Acadians? What's wrong with Louisiana? A strapped Napoleon sold it to the USA for 50 bucks, but apart from that it's OK. What about the McLaughlins, the Cools, the Couglans, the Melansons and scores of others who became assimilated into the Acadian culture? Are they dead now, or are they the only smart ones who flew over the fence?

To fend off assimilation, the high priests have come up with a drastic solution: stay clear from anything English and take action, like turning soup cans on the shelves at grocery stores to show the French labels or getting into a fuss when the clerk doesn't speak English. No wonder Ms. Melanson had to close her column with conflicting statements.

"New Brunswick is a bilingual province," she states, but goes on to explain that Acadian groups like teachers, seniors, etc., have separated from the provincial groups. In that case, N.B. is a province with a dual personality and not necessarily a bilingual province. We have two linguistic groups now, living side by side, and whenever there is a meeting attended by people from both groups, translation is required, not only to accommodate the English speaking, but the Acadians as well. So we are not bilingual after all. Flashing stop signs with STOP/ARRET have nothing to do with being bilingual.

What we have in N.B. is a duality, which is nothing less than separation, or maybe just an imaginary separation. "Still, Acadians are not separatists," says the Moncton columnist. Yet the author seems to have observed in our society all the ingredients needed to separate one community from another.

Fortunately, Ms. Melanson's column closes on a consoling thought: "Acadie will never be a Bosnia." Let's hope so, and let us not forget that banner- and flag-waving and nationalism based on race or religion, mixed with intolerance, have led to conflicts even larger than Bosnia.

LOUIS HACHEY
Moncton

WRITE US!

Telegraph-Journal,
P.O. Box 2350,
Saint John, N.B. E2L 3V8
Fax: **(506) 633-6758**
Or e-mail us at:
tjletters@nbpub.com

Letters must bear the writer's name, address and a daytime telephone number. We reserve the right to edit letters for length, libel, taste or non-verifiable information.

The Telegraph-Journal is a member of the Atlantic Press Council, which helps to maintain high standards and to consider public complaints about press conduct. Phone 1-800-363-2800, or e-mail kjtsims@super city.ns.ca

What Burnt Church dispute needs is a talking circle

JULIAN WALKER

AN HONOURABLE CALLING

If you hold the eagle feather, you will speak from the heart.

This is what we were told and what we found out for ourselves at an extraordinary aboriginal circle discussion a few days ago in Saint John.

It happened during Coastal Zone Canada 2000, a conference, which brought together players in the coastal zone from around the world. These coastal waters and the communities that depend on them are greatly at risk because of the huge demands on the fish and other living resources, as well as the hard resources such as minerals and oil.

The dispute over lobster fishing in Miramichi Bay in the vicinity of such communities as Burnt Church, Neguac and Baie Ste. Anne, is a good example of the battle over coastal resources.

As time goes on, and we see the value to our survival of the planet's vital resources, the coastal zone, still teeming in food and riches, will become even more important to us.

For now, there is a lack of understanding. But, of the some 100 people who took part in the conference circle discussion, no one could have come away with a diminished appreciation of the great problems that have resulted in confrontation, violence and hatred in Burnt Church.

A "circle" is just that, an open circle of people seated so that no one is left outside. In this case, the facilitator allowed discussion to go from one side of the circle to the other for a time, as people exchanged information about Burnt Church. There were many employees of the Department of Fisheries and Oceans (DFO) in the room. They participated, but not as official spokespersons.

The discussion then entered a new phase, as an eagle feather was passed in turn around the perimeter of the circle, and everyone had his/her chance to speak in turn. The aboriginal viewpoint was well represented, as there were aboriginal conference delegates from all over the world at the conference.

Canadians may have been surprised at the degree of solidarity felt with the Burnt Church native community. The right to fish was expressed as a matter of "sovereignty" on the part of an aboriginal First Nation.

There could be no talks about sharing the resource until this sovereignty was recognized.

The aboriginal delegates spoke with emotion as they held the eagle feather, and all in the room were aware of the importance of the feather and the need to speak truthfully, and from the heart.

Some of us argued that the example of the cod, and its near disappearance, made sovereignty a poor starting point in relation to conservation in the coastal zone. Was there not a need to go to the negotiating table with an appreciation of the vulnerability of the resource and a willingness to work out a way to share it, within the boundaries of good science and sustainability?

Of course, the argument has gone much further since this discussion was held. The federal government has strongly asserted it role as the only policing power and the defender of the stocks. That is right for the moment; the government had no choice.

But, as a long-term strategy, the DFO approach is fraught with difficulty.

There are simply not enough guns and boats to achieve, peace on our waters, and this applies to many more communities than simply the native communities.

There will always need to be an enforcer. Agreed. But letting the light in on the science pertaining to the stocks, would do a lot of good.

As one EPA official from the United States argued in the talking circle, transparency would contribute greatly to the process, if it were offered before there is a crisis on the water. The scientific information should be put out in a comprehensible, useable form, so that it is not a dark mystery, but part of everyone's decision-making.

The department of Fisheries and Oceans has within its ranks the desire to understand the social forces giving rise to the many problems of the coastal zone.

Yet for some at DFO, the temptation to turn to the familiar policeman's role is instinctive and, in many cases, a first rather than a last resort.

It's time to sit down with the different groups and start down that road, already favoured by many at DFO, to get closer to the community.

A wider facilitation/negotiation process is needed allowing all the players to at least understand the needs and problems of the others claiming a piece of the resource. We have passed the stage of relying only on one-on-one negotiation with the Big Guy.

Education is key to the process. We can't all be sovereign in the coastal zone, whether it is the traditional commercial fishermen or the natives. Governments have to get the word out, sit down with people, explain and explain again.

For their part, the native strategy, with some dramatic court cases like Marshall, appears sometimes to have put all their eggs in the "treaty rights" basket.

Given their unfortunate history at the hands of the white man, that may be understandable. But we all do have neighbours in this world, and it is not wise to act as if neighbours don't matter.

All sides in the Burnt Church dispute have rights. But if there is an escalating competition to exercise those rights, the different parties could end up with no fish and be, literally, dead right.

In the way of the talking circle, the great thinkers and talkers will ultimately bring more to bear on these problems than the aggressors from all sides.

Julian Walker is a public policy consultant based in Fredericton. His column appears every Thursday. He can be reached at jhwalker@nbnet.nb.ca.

Innovative Features

Editorials, columns, cartoons and letters—plus a Bible verse or short prayer and a "back when" column—have traditionally made up the American editorial page. Most of the religious and reminiscence features have disappeared by now, but I found "Bible Thought" and "Through the Century" on the editorial page of the Canton, Ohio, *Repository* and "Today in History" in the *Portsmouth* (Ohio) *Daily Times.* The *Rutland* (Vt.) *Herald* sometimes carries a box headlined "How to contact legislators: addresses, phones, fax."

In traditional days, except for letters to the editor, those who wrote and drew for the editorial page essentially talked to one another, mostly about politics and government. It was a page that belonged to the professionals. But as editors began to search for ways to enliven their pages and keep their readers, they came up with a variety of ideas for attracting more diverse views and more people to the page.

The innovations generally fall into four broad categories—those that:

- encourage reader participation
- seek a greater diversity of ideas
- simplify the editorial message
- experiment with alternatives to standard editorial pages

To some extent these innovations have been made possible through the addition of more editorial space, notably the op-ed (opposite-editorial) page, which will be discussed later in this chapter.

■ ENCOURAGING READER PARTICIPATION

Questions for Readers

Some papers pose a question of the week to help readers feel they have a say. The *Milwaukee* (Wis.) *Journal* and the *Philadelphia Evening Bulletin* were among the first to try this feature. One newspaper using this feature today, the *Telegraph-Journal* in Saint John, N.B., runs a feature titled "Your View." In one issue readers were asked to respond to the question: "Was the province right to divide Canada Games development among many communities?" To make it easy to respond, the editorial page contained a form that readers could fill in and fax to the newspaper.[9] The *Idaho Statesman* in Boise calls its question feature "What Do YOU Think?" One example posed multiple questions: "State agencies have until Sept. 24 to come up with their plans for meeting Gov. Dirk Kempthorne's $35.4 million holdback in state spending. How would you make the cuts? What would you fight for? What's expendable? What's untouchable?"[10] Readers were asked to mail in their responses.

The *Atlanta* (Ga.) *Journal-Constitution* used its web site to pose a question for readers. Beside an editorial on a cheating scandal at Georgia Tech appeared this question: "Have you ever cheated on a test in school?" Respondents were given the option of clicking on "Many times," "Once, but I felt really guilty and never did it again," "A few times" and "Never." Added to the innovative nature of the feature was a tabulation of how many people had already responded (a total of 320, with 35 percent, 6 percent, 20 percent and 39 percent, respectively, choosing the four options).[11]

The Cleveland, Ohio, *Plain Dealer* from time to time posts a "Question of the Moment," then publishes on the editorial page "a compilation of our favorite responses." One question was: "Should Election Day be a national holiday?" Seven published responses were generally in favor of making it a holiday. Three were firmly against.[12]

Reader Action

The *Billings* (Mont.) *Gazette* on occasion provides for reader to take specific actions. To participate in nominating candidates for an annual Heroes Award, readers could contact either of the two sponsors: They could respond to the newspaper online or make a telephone request for a form from the Red Cross. In another editorial, readers were told how to learn more about the Women's Foundation of Montana.[13]

Reader Rebuttal

Years ago editors used to relish attaching a stinging editor's note to a letter, setting the letter writer straight. So stung, the writer, and perhaps other potential writers, learned the hard way that the editor had the last word.

The *Roanoke* (Va.) *Times* tried an ingenious way to remove the sting of the editor's reply, but eventually gave it up as too time-consuming. "Talking It Over" involved a three-part conversation: (1) a letter to the editor that the editors wanted to highlight, (2) a reply by the newspaper, (3) a final reply by the letter writer. "Good idea, but the practicalities doomed it" was the judgment of editorial page editor Tommy Denton.[14]

Letters to the Editors

For the innovative ideas editors have found for encouraging and handling letters, see Chapter 17, "Letters to the Editor."

Reader Cartoons

Some newspapers encourage readers to submit their own cartoons. The Spokane, Wash., *Spokesman-Review* invites "painting, collage, computer art, drawing or artwork in any other style," especially cartoons concerning Inland Northwest issues. Accepted artists receive no money but are eligible for the paper's "Golden Pen" award. The cartoons are labeled "Your View."[15] (See Figure 11, page 326.)

■ ENCOURAGING DIVERSITY OF OPINION

Newspapers of all sizes are experimenting with ways to interact with readers to bring more diversity to their opinion pages. To get an idea of what was being tried, the Pew Center for Civic Journalism, with the support of the Associated Press Managing Editors Association and the National Conference of Editorial Writers, surveyed editors of all U.S. daily newspapers with circulations of 20,000 or more. Most frequently mentioned were "op-ed community forum pages" (74 percent) followed closely by "e-mail/voice-mail/web tip pages" (72 percent). Next came "reader articles" (45 percent) and "published reader feedback—not letters to the editor" (44 percent). Then came inviting readers to visit news-planning meetings (38 percent) and "reader advisory boards" (36 percent). Less frequently mentioned were "web chat groups" (20), "community publishing" (15) and "ombudsman/reader advocate" (13).[16]

A Question for Specific Respondents

To obtain a variety of opinions, some newspapers request responses from individuals who are knowledgeable about a specific topic. In a feature titled "What others think," the *Press Journal* of Vero Beach, Fla., asked four people associated with the public schools what they considered to be the most important part of the local schools.[17] In a "Question of the Week" the Portland *Maine Sunday Telegram* asked members of the state's congressional delegation whether they supported statehood for the District of Columbia. The senators, both Republicans, were opposed. The representatives, both Democrats, were undecided.[18]

Guest Columns and Articles

Articles written by outsiders come in many forms. One of the first successful attempts to bring nonjournalists to the editorial page was a column called "In My Opinion," begun by the *Milwaukee* (Wis.) *Journal* in 1970. An early participant was Milwaukee's mayor, one of the *Journal*'s severest critics.[19]

Many newspapers specifically invite knowledgeable or opinionated persons to share their views in such columns. The Nampa *Idaho Press-Tribune* uses a "Guest Opinion" label for this purpose. One issue carried a piece by a senior scholar at The Freedom Forum First Amendment Center, who was concerned about a student who was barred from reading a story from *The Beginner's Bible* in public-school class.[20]

The Portland *Maine Sunday Telegram* invites readers to submit "pieces of good writing" to be published on the editorial page under the headline "Maine Magazine." One person wrote a nostalgic article titled "September guilds a garden's waning glory." [21]

Newsday of Long Island, N.Y., invites college and high school students to send entries to "Fresh Voices," a "weekly column where you can submit nonfiction essays on topics ranging from local affairs to foreign affairs." Maximum is 400 words. In one issue students wrote about the bad condition of soccer fields in the area, the smaller basketball used by the Women's National Basketball Association and busy summers that give teens no relief. [22]

The Boise *Idaho Statesman* reserves "Reader's View" for longer articles. In one 700-word piece a writer complained about threats to the ecosystem from cattle trampling stream banks.[23]

Boards of Contributors (Advisory Boards)

A board of contributors is a more formal arrangement for obtaining local input. The *Post Register* of Idaho Falls, Idaho, uses a Readers' Advisory Board, described as "a cross-section of people from eastern Idaho who advise on this page, respond to editorials and offer a balanced voice." Appearing under the heading "Talk Back," one contributor argued that decisions establishing roadless areas should be made on a case-by-case basis.[24]

In 1997 Richard Hughes of the Salem, Ore., *Statesman Journal* reported in an NCEW e-mail discussion that his paper had appointed community members to serve several months at a time on the editorial board, with full rights to contribute and vote on editorial stands. When I contacted him several years later, he reported that community members were still participating and, in fact, the current representative was a high school senior. "Naturally, most day-to-day editorials don't go to the full board," Hughes said during the exchange, but on major issues "we have a highly democratic board with the big decisions made by straight vote." He said the board had some community members who "got upset when their views didn't prevail" and others "who wanted to argue . . . instead of debating issues." Hughes said he found the community members both "helpful" and "a big pain," but "worth it."[25]

The Wilmington, Del., *News Journal* has a 12-member Community Advisory Board. Three are chosen every six months to serve two years, on the "basis of their ability to write occasional guest columns, their particular skills and community interests." As ex officio members, they are invited to attend editorial board meetings and "a meeting on the last Monday afternoon of each month with special guests."[26]

The editorial board of the *Spokesman-Review* in Spokane, Wash., includes a newsroom guest writer, a newspaper guest writer and a community guest writer.

A less formal arrangement has been used at the *Portland* (Maine) *Press Herald* and the Portland *Maine Sunday Telegram.* "We get our community input raw, from the street," editorial page editor George Neavoll said, "as members of the public join us nearly every morning for a free-flowing discussion of events in the news that day." He said, "We enjoy ourselves when we look our readers straight in the face, and they look in ours, and we talk directly with one another about things of mutual interest." The sessions are "sometimes rambunctious, often enlightening and always fun as a result."[27]

These boards are not universally seen as an answer to keeping in touch with readers. "Are newspapers now becoming some kind of public utility, subject to review by 'customers,' like citizen utility boards?" asked E.W. Kieckhefer, a retired editorial writer. "Yes, editors and editorial writers should be aware of what their subscribers are thinking and saying, but not necessarily for the purpose of having those thoughts dictate the newspaper's editorial policies."[28]

Freelance Columnists

Somewhere between guest writers and board-member contributors fall freelance columnists. Some newspapers use freelance writers to add to the voices, and range of voices, on editorial and op-ed pages. Others may see freelancers as a chance to save money on salary and benefits.[29] On the Madison., Wis., *Capital Times,* four freelance opinion columnists write twice a month. Eight freelance columnists—two writing each week—contribute to the Ogden, Utah, *Standard-Examiner.* The *Fort Worth* (Texas) *Star-Telegram* opens the Monday op-ed page to freelancers. Two retired staff columnists provide local perspective on a freelance basis on the *News-Journal* in Wilmington, Del.[30]

Pro-Con Arguments

One attempt to give readers the feeling that they were getting a fair debate on issues, and not just the newspaper's viewpoint, was a "pro-con" package that the editors of the *St. Petersburg* (Fla.) *Times* developed in 1971. They saw the package as a way to "reduce reader resistance to persuasion" without reducing the newspaper's commitment to its own viewpoint. The package contained a question and an explanation of the issue, "yes" and "no" arguments, a brief editorial stating the *Times'* position and a coupon on which readers could write and send in their comments.[31] The *Times* itself no longer runs this feature.

The *St. Paul* (Minn.) *Pioneer-Press* publishes pro/con articles on its op-ed page. In one issue, guest columnists debated whether cameras should be allowed in courtrooms.[32]

The Portland *Oregonian* asked whether the state liquor tax should be boosted to help offset a budget deficit, soliciting a "no" response from the executive director of the Oregon Brewer Guild and a "yes" response from the executive director of Rimrock Trails Adolescent Treatment Services.[33]

Media Critics (Reader Advocates, Ombudsmen)

The idea behind having a media critic (reader advocate, ombudsman, etc.) hired by the newspaper is that the person can benefit both the newspaper and its readers. The critic/advocate can serve the newspaper by providing a conscience and trying to uphold journalistic standards, and serve readers by listening to and considering their concerns. Once a week or so, the critic/advocate typically writes a column, generally carried on the editorial page, about good and bad practices or a journalistic issue. These columns, of course, are credible to the extent that the critics/advocates are knowledgeable, fair and free to write what they wish.

Although the original Swedish word "ombudsman" is considered to be gender-neutral,[34] use of the masculine-sounding name bothers some journalists who have been admonished in recent years to use, for example, firefighter instead of fireman. That may be why the *Chicago Tribune* and the *Oregonian* have a "public editor," the Minneapolis *Star Tribune* has a "reader representative" and the "On the Media" writer for the Denver, Colo., *Rocky Mountain News* has no title. The *Washington Post* has both a "media critic" and an "ombudsman." At one newspaper where the term "ombudsman" is used, the *Star-Telegram* in Fort Worth, Texas, editorial page editor Paul K. Harral said he preferred that title "because it is more neutral, since reader advocate implies the representative is only for the readers and sometimes readers are flat wrong."[35]

Several newspapers that were pioneers in this area (including the Louisville, Ky., *Courier-Journal* and the *Seattle Times*)[36] no longer provide this service, but the creation of an ombudsman position on the Spokane, Wash., *Spokesman-Review* in early 2002 brought the national count of media watchdogs to about 50, according to the Organization of News Ombudsmen.[37] The longest-serving, still carrying the title "media critic," has been David Shaw of the *Los Angeles Times*, who has been reviewing and commenting for more than three decades.

A survey of 32 newspapers found that a majority of both editors and ombudsmen thought that "[h]aving an ombudsman on staff influences the reporters and editors in a way that enhances fairness and accuracy." The primary advantages: providing direct access for readers, providing readers with "a voice" and showing readers "that someone will listen." The disadvantages: "shielding reporters and editors from complaints" and devoting efforts to "'too many kooks and regular callers' whose views may not be representative of all readers."[38] Kenneth Stark and Julie Eisele, who conducted the study, concluded, "It makes sense that a newspaper should have a solid and independent mechanism for feedback . . . to help restore virtue in the newspaper industry." They noted that other studies found that nearly eight out of 10 daily newspapers with more than 25,000 circulation lacked such a mechanism[39] and only 2.4 percent of all daily newspapers employed an ombudsman.[40]

The *Washington Post* has one of the longest-running ombudsman columns, with the writers serving two-year stints. One ombudsman, Michael Getler, handled a complaint from readers who thought they had received "rude treatment by the *Post*'s obituary desk." Getler concluded that "the desk seems like a pretty efficient operation, . . . [b]ut my sense is that this is a section that doesn't get much internal scrutiny."[41]

At the Minneapolis *Star Tribune,* reader representative Lou Gelford concluded that a story about "hundreds of black people" being taken to jail "for minor crimes" should also have included information about the warrants that were outstanding against these people.[42] In the *Rocky Mountain News* Dave Kopel (who carried no special title) chided his paper and the *Denver Post* for mislabeling counter-protesters at a Marilyn Manson concert as "First Amendment," "anti-censorship" advocates. In Kopel's view, no government censorship was involved. In the same column he also criticized the papers for ignoring a case of "actual censorship": the efforts of the Federal Communications Commission to keep radio stations from "playing Eminem's Grammy-winning song 'The Real Slim Shady.'"[43]

Other Newspapers' Opinions

Less popular than in previous days, when newspapers had fewer sources of diverse opinions, are reprints of editorials from other newspapers. The Wilmington, Del., *News Journal* uses the heading "What Others Say" for reprinted editorials, the *Denver Post* uses the heading "Other Views," the *Salt Lake Tribune* labels them "Another view" and the Newport, Va., *Daily News* calls them "A Sampling of Editorial Opinion." One Thursday morning, relying on Internet resources, the Portland *Oregonian* published portions of 11 editorials that commented on the State of the Union message that President George W. Bush had delivered Tuesday night.[44]

■ MAKING IT EASIER FOR READERS

Summaries

Editors have devised several ways to summarize information quickly for readers in a hurry. The *Detroit Free Press* began using a hammer headline for editorials as early as 1978: a large capitalized word or two followed by a summary sentence that continued on to a second line.

Some newspapers summarize conclusions in an insert in the editorial. The Wilmington, Del., *News Journal,* under a heading of "Where We Stand," summarized an editorial about a judicial candidate this way: "Mr. Lee's behavior was unseemly, but if he has done nothing wrong judicial officials should say so quickly and clearly." The summary was somewhat more specific than the headline on the editorial itself: "Candidate Lee deserves a swift opinion from judicial authorities."[45] An insert in an editorial in the Saint John, N.B., *Telegraph-Journal* stated: "We believe: Northern N.B. needs a realistic investment more than a new Sugarloaf." The editorial headline: "A more modest Games legacy. Spectacular developments have failed; more investments needed."[46]

The headline on an editorial in the Denver *Rocky Mountain News* said: "Under wraps: If review is positive, why not release it?" The insert was more specific: "The Issue: President's evaluation at Metro State. Our View: It was too expensive, too cozy and too secret."[47] The *Kennebec* (Maine) *Journal* went a step farther. In connection with an editorial on money for children's health care, a summary explained both the issue and how the paper stood:[48]

> **The Money Chase**
>
> THE ISSUE: Because Maine has done so well in using money supplied from the federal Children's Health Insurance Program, the state is eligible to receive funds not expended elsewhere—an amount that could mean millions of dollars to the state.
>
> HOW WE STAND: Officials will have time to reconfigure the program guideline before the funding is lost, but every effort should be made to secure as much of the leftover money as possible to meet identified needs.

Briefer, Easier-to-Read Editorials

To appeal to readers in a hurry, newspapers have tried various ways to present editorial opinions in brief form. Among respondents to a 1994 survey, 70 percent said they were writing shorter editorials than they had in the past and 65 percent said they were writing editorials that were easier to read.[49]

Many newspapers offer short comments on good or bad things that have happened. Under the heading "Cheers and Jeers," the *Sacramento* (Calif.) *Bee* offered a cheer to Gov. Gray Davis for seeking options to prevent an Indian tribe from taking over a struggling card room in the San Francisco Bay area and a jeer to Pulitzer Prize–winning historian Joseph J. Ellis for having "lied about his own military record."[50] The Nampa *Idaho Press-Tribune* offers space to readers to send in their own "Cheers and Jeers." One reader commended newspaper staff members for "trying to make their cheers and jeers more positive." Another reader offered a jeer over a tree and traffic sign that obstructed the view of a 35-mile-an-hour sped limit sign.[51] In brief comments written by staff members, the *Greenville* (S.C.) *News* awards a "thumbs up" or a "thumbs down," the Salem, Ore., *Statesman-Journal* names "This Week's Winners and Losers," and the *St. Paul* (Minn.) *Pioneer Press* carries a column titled "Sainted—Tainted."

In an Internet exchange on off-beat editorials, several editorial writers became involved in a contest to come up with short editorials. One cited Richard Aregood's three-liner written on the death of Spanish dictator Francisco Franco. The headline was "Adios Dictator." The editorial: "They say only the good die young. Generalissimo Francisco Franco was 82. Seems about right."[52] A writer who cited the editorial suggested that the last sentence was not needed.[53] Another editorial writer recalled that on the morning of the "Big Game" the University of Oregon was to play Oregon State University for the right to go to the 1995 Rose Bowl, the Eugene *Register-Guard* "used the entire editorial column for a one-line editorial: Go Ducks!"[54] Another participant in the exchange recalled that, when Northwestern University won a Rose Bowl game, an editorial in the student newspaper had simply proclaimed: "Roses." He also noted that editors of the University of Chicago student paper, not impressed, had responded with another one-word editorial: "Onions."[55]

Visual Aids

Visual devices also can help attract readers. The *Boston Globe*, for example, inserted a map in an editorial that discussed the need for "building strong connections between the South Boston waterfront and downtown [Boston]."[56] The *Reno* (Nev.) *Gazette Journal*, in an editorial about helping the Lear Theater, ran a picture of the theater.[57] The *Litchfield* (Conn.) *County Times* enlivened an editorial page with a large photo of a jack o'lantern carved from a pumpkin.[58]

When John Ashcroft was sworn in as attorney general, the *Detroit Free Press* wrote a "Dear John" editorial, the theme of which was expressed in one of the sentences: "Your new job will require you to rise above your history." The editorial was made to look like a letter. A thin-line box marked the edges of the supposed sheet of paper, which carried the *Free Press* letterhead. The letter was displayed at about a 10-degree angle, making it look as though it had been casually placed on the page.[59]

Internet Innovations

Two innovations already have been noted: the "have you ever cheated?" online poll on the *Atlanta Journal-Constitution*'s web page and the *Oregonian*'s use of the Internet to obtain quickly 11 editorials on the president's State of the Union address. In addition, Chapter 17, "Letters to the Editor," describes how editors are using the Internet to encourage web users to submit letters.

Among the most common features of online editorials is an option that allows readers to respond to an editorial online or pass it on to a friend. The reader can simply click on a spot that is labeled "Mail this story to a friend," "E-mail this article," "E-mail a letter to the editor" or "Send us comments about this article," and the article or response is immediately on its way.

The *Atlanta Journal-Constitution,* the Vancouver, Wash., *Columbian* and the *Roanoke* (Va.) *Times* are among newspapers that offer users guides to their opinion page writers and editors (including, in some instances, photographs).

Increasingly, editors are also providing readers with instant access to more information on the topics under discussion or to related web sites. The Denver, Colo., *Rocky Mountain News,* in an editorial titled "Freeing Sex Offenders," told viewers, "An abbreviated list of 374 offenders is available on RockyMountainNews.com, giving name, age, county and the offense for which each was convicted."[60] A Greensboro (N.C.) *News & Record* editorial titled "Klan propaganda not fit for library" told viewers that the KKK tape in question had been "identified as one installment of the group's 'weekly Internet TV show' (www.kukluxklan.org)."[61] The *Roanoke* (Va.) *Times*, in an editorial on "A catch-up plan for campus construction," provided viewers with one-click access to the web sites of the Virginia General Assembly, Radford University, Gov. Mark Warner and House Speaker Vance Wilkins.[62]

As a standard feature, the opinion web page of the *Rockford* (Ill.) *Register Star* offers the option of going to another page to view the newspaper's editorial agenda: "Our stance on issues and goals that we believe are critical to the short- and long-term health of the Rock River Valley." Readers also can check out "Our statement of principles."[63] To promote its web site, the Danbury, Conn., *News-Times* has run on its printed editorial page a 4-by-4-inch "advertisement" for newstimes.com, the newspaper's web site.[64]

■ BRINGING THE COMMUNITY ABOARD

Some newspapers have taken additional steps toward establishing relations with readers and the community. Some have actively recruited community members to contribute to the opinion page. Some have attempted to engage in a dialogue with the community. Some have set out to help their communities establish and carry out goals.

Civic or Public Journalism

To bring their newspapers and communities closer together, some editors have experimented with "civic journalism" or "public journalism." (Sometimes it is called "community journalism," but that term has traditionally been used to refer to weekly newspapers.) Because such journalism is not specifically defined and its nature varies widely from one newspaper to the next, it inevitably has become the subject of widespread debate and misunderstanding. How far should editors go to bring the community into the news and editorial processes of the newspaper? How far should editors go in providing leadership in the community?[65] A survey found that newspaper journalists' ideas about the proper role of "civic journalism" range from "provid[ing] information on alternative solutions" to "conduct[ing] town meetings to discover key issues."[66]

In 1994, in the midst of the debate over public journalism, the *Spokesman-Review* of Spokane, Wash., unveiled what it called "reinvented" opinion pages, announcing: "We have turned the majority of the space on these pages over to you—now do something about it." The newspaper named two interactive editors who (as the opinion editor, John Webster, explained in a *Masthead* symposium on "The Future") would "go into the community to recruit writers, speak before local civic groups and hold issue forums." Webster reported that, as a result, the number of lengthy guest columns had increased. Once a week the paper runs a reader-written "Your Turn" column.[67]

The *Spokesman-Review* received a grant from the Pew Center for Civic Journalism to (in Webster's words) "develop software tools that allow journalists to use e-mail and database technology to interact with readers." One of the databases contains several thousand names, mostly of people who have written letters to the editor. "We've used this tool with great success," Webster said, "to collect diverse, immediate commentary on major news developments such as a local land-use plan proposal and the war on terrorism as well as many smaller issues in the news."[68]

In Figure 11, page 326, is the result of a request for opinions on the war on terrorism. Early on the day the U.S. began its war in Afghanistan (a Sunday), Webster said that his staff sent out e-mail requests to 450 readers requesting comments. "Within a few hours we had received enough replies to fill Monday's letters page with public commentary," Webster reported. Talk about a quick turnaround! Twenty responses were printed. On another occasion readers were asked to comment on "the Legislature's debate over transportation improvements." Ten responses were printed.[69]

The *Spokesman-Review* also has created the opportunity for reporters, as described by Webster, "to develop electronic 'beats,' exchanging information via e-mail with readers and sources who have known interests and expertise." As examples, he said, the paper collects comments and sends out news to people in a specific sporting event, "such as our state's B Basketball tournament or Gonzaga University's next trip to the NCAA tournament."[70]

More Community Voices

The *St. Paul* (Minn.) *Pioneer-Press* set out to de-emphasize anonymous editorials and bring more community voices onto the page. But its editors also sought

Figure 11 Spokesman Review

Spokane, Wash. / Coeur d'Alene, Idaho — Monday, October 8, 2001 — Page A19

ROUNDTABLE

Letters

How to write? See "Keep in touch" at the bottom of this page.

READY, AIM, TYPE!

Editor's note: The Spokesman-Review asked several hundred readers by e-mail to give their opinions about the military and humanitarian campaign that was launched on Sunday. Here is a representative sampling of the responses:

Aim guns and butter with care

I think this "guns and butter" approach to Afghanistan is just right. Guns for the Taliban and butter for the Afghanistan people! However, I think it is going to be very hard to keep the butter away from the Taliban. They most likely will take it away from the Afghanistan people and keep it for themselves!

Also, I think the Taliban most likely will hide among the Afghanistan people when the going gets rough, how are you going to find them? Reminds me of the war in Vietnam, how do you find the enemy when they all look and dress alike?

James A. Rowland
Marcus, Wash.

Time for 'sleeping giant' to fight

People who are being fed aren't likely to consider you an enemy. The Romans conquered half the world using the same approach. As to more attacks in this country, yes I am concerned. Our economy is balanced on a thin knife edge and anything that upsets that balance can ruin a lot of businesses and lives. At the same time I support the president and his policies 100 percent. If we sat back and did nothing then the people who hit the World Trade Center have won. They have fired the first shot in this war. Let us follow the lead of our parents and grandparents who made true the quote from Admiral Yamamoto: "I am afraid that all we have done is wakened a sleeping giant and made him angry."

Stephen Higgins
Clark Fork, Idaho

Fight the bully, help the hungry

We have to attack them, they declared war on us. We can't just sit here and get beat up by a bully, we must show them that we don't stand for that. And why not help the starving people who didn't have anything to do with it while we are there? It sounds like a win-win situation to me. Will they attack us again? I never expected them to attack in the first place, so I can't say how I'd think about the probability of being attacked again. It's like being struck by lightning twice in one year. It's unlikely to be struck by lightning even once, but it happens every year, and some have been struck twice. So will it happen to us? Possibly.

Justin D. Naylor
Spokane

Flatten defenses, then lend a hand

Self-preservation and hunger is of paramount concern to the Afgan people, as it would be to any people that have been under decades of war and repression. Humanitarian aid in the form of food and medicine is a positive response from America. Nullifying the air defenses, and then targeting the terrorist camps and Taliban defenses should come first.

It would be a mistake to put Americans into harm's way delivering aid before these steps are taken.

Pete Larsen
Deer Park

Hit the enemy hard

Even if the attacks on Afghanistan fail to destabilize the Taliban government or deliver bin Laden, I believe that a strong military response to terrorist attacks against the United States is years overdue.

In our obsession with avoiding injury to "innocent people," in the wake of the slaughter of our Marines in Lebanon, the embassy bombings and the attack on the USS Cole, we have threatened and equivocated and ultimately made no use whatever of our awesome retaliatory powers. In the end, we have richly deserved the shameful epithet of "Pitiful Helpless Giant." I agree with the political/military analysts who in hindsight now declare that a furious and immediate military response to the truck-bomb slaughter of our Marines in Lebanon would have made it clear to the world that a heavy price must be paid by those who carry out, facilitate, or rejoice in such attacks. Failure to respond to this latest horror would have been an invitation to our enemies to accelerate the attacks with impunity.

Robert Barcus
Spokane

Condemn militant forms of Islam

I think the guns and butter approach in Afghanistan can work in the long term only if we press hard for a resolution of the Palestinian-Israeli conflict. Otherwise there is a big risk that terrorism will continue, particularly against the United States and Europe.

Obviously we must capture bin Laden and his close associates and bring them to trial. We must replace the terrorist-supporting Taliban with a more moderate Afghan government.

But recent verbal sparring between President Bush and Prime Minister Sharon, and continued Israeli-Palestinian fighting during the U.S. Afghan build-up, illustrate the risks of hoping that Israel and the unemployed, often hungry Palestinians can make peace without U.S. help. They need our help. Over-population and a displaced Palestinian population are huge problems.

Now that President Bush has envisioned a Palestinian State, he needs to move quickly to promote one, as Jordan's king advised.

Everyone, including all moderate Islamic clerics, needs to condemn militant Islam, as distinguished from mainstream and peaceful Islam. The idea of Jihad or "Holy War" is medieval, yet is still believed fervently by significant Muslim minorities. This is dangerous.

Matt Schaffer
Spokane

It's about time . . .

It is about time the world recognizes terrorism for what it is and takes some action to stop violent acts. Food for the refugees is good as long as it reaches those who need it, not local chieftains who will attempt to line their pockets.

Dennis Kuhl
Spokane

Defeat the enemy with generosity

I'm always concerned when my country starts dropping bombs on other people. It seems like we have attacked small, fairly helpless countries — Grenada . . . Panama . . . even Iraq and Vietnam hardly qualified as equal enemies. It's pretty hard to bomb Afghanistan back to Dark Ages, since it is already there.

However, the threat of additional terrorist attacks by bin Laden's group and others is very real and, like the threat of Hitler, cannot be ignored. I don't know if it will do any good, since we are trying to eliminate an idea from the mind of men (it's always the men!) who are willing to die for it, and don't care how many innocent people they take with them.

The people of Afghanistan are probably so numb after 30 years of war (not to mention all the wars before that) that they are too tired, too hungry and too terrified to care where the food comes from. But I think that we do much better with a carrot than with a stick.

Our greatest asset is the generosity and forgiveness of the American people. I've always believed we could defeat Castro in a few hours of generosity instead of trying to embargo his country. It wasn't Reagan or Star Wars that brought down the Soviet Union — it was Pepsi-Cola, McDonald's and all the other decadent trappings of free enterprise that showed up communism for the dismal failure it was. If we can get enough food and supplies to the people of Afghanistan without accidentally blowing up civilians, hurray for us.

Peggy Herbert
Spokane

Just bomb the Afghans

After listening to the news on the radio about the bombings in Afghanistan, I don't understand the aid that we are sending to them. We need to target the training arenas for terrorism and the high officials who are responsible.

The people of that country have been suffering for a long time under the regimes that have been in power, yet they stay loyal to them. If we are to truly send a message that terrorism will not be tolerated, we must concentrate on only that issue. Sending aid says that, yes, we will be bombing you, but watch for the incoming supplies to keep you going because we can afford it.

Shouldn't we be taking care of some of our own issues before we dole out millions to other countries? Let's take care of our sick, homeless, underpaid, and elderly Americans, as well as our budget, before we are unable to help anyone.

Brenda Cunningham
Spokane

We have to do it

Yes, I am concerned about our attack on Afghanistan. I'm sure it will invite more assaults on our country and our people. But I firmly believe we have to do it, and I also believe we will need to use ground troops before the thing is finished. I hate to see us get involved in Afghanistan, but after all, they didn't give us much choice. I'm not concerned about our war-making capability, but I am concerned about the Islamic world's interpretation of our actions. If the bad guys succeed in making it look as though we are attacking Islam, we are in for a long hard day.

Clayton A. Fouts
Clarkston

This is freedom's price

We have to show the terrorists and the world that we are going to walk our talk.

The guns and butter approach is evidence that this is a different war. In the past we usually made war, made peace and then delivered the humanitarian aid and helped to build up the devastated nations. This time we are doing it all at once. The United States has always helped other nations.

Additional terrorist attacks on the United States will most likely be entirely different than the attacks of Sept. 11. That's the scary part, not knowing what to expect. Perhaps our leaders have an idea of what to expect from information gained through intelligence sources.

This is a price we pay for peace. This is the price we pay to keep the world free.

Trudy Lundy
Spokane

No fan of Bush, but . . .

I do not, in general, favor use of military force. I am also no supporter, in general, of the policies of President Bush. I also believe that we are in part responsible for the existence of the repressive governement in Afghanistan.

That being said, I do believe that our country was attacked with the active support of the Taliban. If this is true, I support the use of force to deal with Osama bin Laden and his group and to help the people of Afghanistan if they wish to move toward a democracy.

If we could help the Afghan people rid themselves of oppression, deal with those who have planned and abetted criminal acts and inaugurate a foreign policy based on respect for diversity this would be, in my opinion, a justifiable use of military force.

Jack Sandberg
Nine Mile Falls

I'd enlist, if I could

I very well understand the president taking this action to try to impress upon those people that our actions are not against the Islamic people but against the Taliban al Qaeda and Osama bin Laden.

I support this action; and feel that the President is approaching this war very carefully, but very stridently.

As far as future terrorist attacks against the United States, I feel certain that they were planned even prior to the Sept. 11 attack. For Osama bin Laden to say that future attacks are in retaliation for our attack against Afghanistan is nothing more than an excuse on his part. He would have done it anyway.

Thirty years ago, I retired from the U.S. Coast Guard. If I were young enough, I would gladly volunteer for whatever assignment the military felt that I was suited for.

Paul E. Sapp
Spokane

If not now, when?

I favor aid to the longsuffering people of Afghanistan. I think it to be not only the right thing to do, but good policy.

To those who oppose military action, my only question would be, if not now, when? Should we not systematically destroy the threat posed by terror groups now as suggested by the President, or wait for the day when the real threat grows to include chemical, biological or even a nuclear bomb in a suitcase planted in downtown Los Angeles? There is no question these terrorist groups are actively trying to acquire such weapons.

As for additional terrorist attacks against the United States in response to military actions, it is the stated policy of these groups to engage in such attacks against Americans when and where they can. So what has changed? On Sept. 11 I don't recall us bombing anyone.

Richard L. Jones
Spokane

Do it right, this time

Yes, in fact we are totally at war. My biggest concern is that we learned from Desert Storm, and that this won't be a repeat of spending billions of dollars and not getting the job done.

As far as terrorists here in the United States, and the fear factor, I believe we all carry a bit of fear now, and we are all stakeholders in the attack on New York and Washington, D.C. If ever there was a time to stand together, it's now. They will come forward in all kinds of disguise and pretenses, and it's up to all of us to be on guard, no matter where we live or work. God Bless America.

Clay Larkin
Post Falls

Make terrorists pay

We must make the cost of terrorism so high that nations stop funding it and giving its perpetrators sanctuary.

R. P. Grunwald, M.D.
Valleyford

Unique in the annals of war

This two-pronged approach (bombs and bread) may be unique in the annals of war. I've never heard of it before. It's a way of saying that we have no quarrel with the long-suffering Afghan people, and in fact feel sorry for them. Their whole culture has been kidnapped by the evil Taliban and al Qaeda. Who knows? This could start a whole new precedent on how wars should be conducted. Hopefully the terrorist infrastructure can be rooted out with a minimal loss of innocent life.

Jack A. Jennings
Spokane

Violence in pursuit of peace

With the retaliation against Afghanistan, we have begun a war against people who hate. In my lifetime, this is the first occurrence of a war for peace. Can it succeed? Only if the people of the world — Americans especially — refuse to accept violence as a way of life.

Let us begin to be outraged at offenses against humanity anywhere in the world, and at the offenses that transpire each day on the streets of our cities and towns. Violence cannot be tolerated — domestic, gang related, incidental or terrorist.

It is only by changing what we accept in our society that these military attacks can result in victory.

As for the humanitarian efforts, let's all hope and pray that they will help the innocents affected by this horrible situation.

War with compassion. War for peace. We are in a new time, experiencing a new way of fighting against a new type of enemy. We need a new way. Let us keep the innocent people of Afghanistan, and all Muslim communities, in our hearts and our prayers. Maybe bringing in food and medicine is the way to let them know. this is a war against the extremists, not the nation.

I add my prayers to those of all the people of the world, and I continue to focus on an ultimate goal of a united world living in peace.

Jean M. Alley
Spokane

Bomb terrorist America

In his speech on Sunday as the attacks began, President Bush said "If any government sponsors the killers of innocents, they have become outlaws and murderers themselves."

In his press conference from the Pentagon, Secretary Rumsfeld said that "terrorism is a cancer on the human condition, and we will oppose it wherever it occurs."

By their own logic, our military forces should now begin targeting the Pentagon, the White House, the Capitol, and CIA headquarters in Langley, Va., to name a few. Those four places are where the policy of economic sanctions against Iraq was crafted, supported, and perfected over the past 10 years.

By conservative U.N. estimates, half a million Iraqi children have died over that period of time as a direct result of U.S.-led economic sanctions, and 5,000 more die every month. That didn't happen as an unfortunate mistake. It has been the deliberate policy of the U.S.-led coalition which enforces the sanctions to target the Iraqi water infrastructure. When children don't have access to clean water, they die. We know that. We're doing it on purpose.

We, by the very words of President Bush and Secretary Rumsfeld, are part of the international terror network. When will we get our punishment?

Brad Read
Spokane

Don't play politics

Let's keep politics out of the war. I think President Bush has given the terrorist community sufficient time to entrench itself and prolong whatever action he has planned. His "Declaration of War" was no more than verbalizing what the public wanted to hear. The fallacy that we will successfully fight and win a war against terrorism is akin to the war on drugs in its likelihood of success.

If we start down the road toward eradicating the world of all religious fanatics, are we any better than the Nazis were? That is the only road to a win in the war against terrorism in that region of the world.

Will our leaders have the guts to finish what they are starting? Doubtful, but it is not an election year so they will be less likely to do the popular thing.

As usual Uncle Sam is going to play both ends toward the middle to be both aggressor, and savior to the lands we choose to beat up on. How noble. Selectively kill bad guys and then feed their widows and children. The United States gets to pay twice.

We should stop betting on both sides and take a firm stand. Like, defend our land from home, instead of keeping our military in every corner of the world and angering other fanatics.

Robin Palachuk
Veradale

Doonesbury — By Garry Trudeau

Mallard Fillmore — By Bruce Tinsley

more imaginative ways to use its own editorial writers' talents. One way, as described by editorial page editor Ron Clark, was to assign editorial writers to "dig deeper into important subjects that require more illumination, analysis and informed opinion." Editorial writers would be encouraged "to work with the community, where appropriate, in the search for solutions to tough public problems."[71] As an example of in-depth research, Clark cited an editorial writer's signed analysis of the movement to reform academic tenure at the University of Minnesota and elsewhere. The article accounted for about 80 percent of the page, with the remainder devoted to letters. The absence of an editorial was not unusual.

More recently, according to Clark, and partly as a result of "the impact of restructuring," editorial writers have been producing more editorials and fewer in-depth analyses and backgrounders. Clark also noted that "a greater percentage of staff time [was being] devoted to selecting and editing letters, selecting and editing guest columns, improving our Web site, copy editing, page design, etc." During February 2002 the paper ran 25 editorials. On nine days no editorials were published.[72]

One feature that Clark said "has proven popular with readers and has added a lot of diversity to our pages" is a "Community Columnist" feature. Four years into the program, 200 readers had applied for the eight positions. One column is published each Sunday, with each writer appearing seven or eight times a year. Clark noted that recent groups included two Muslims, a college student, a female police officer and a senior citizen.[73]

Another innovation that has brought more community members onto the *Pioneer-Press* opinion page has been the "Sainted—Tainted" feature mentioned earlier. (See Figure 12, page 328.) Readers are asked: "Like to see someone, or something, Sainted or Tainted? Send us your nominations, briefly explaining your reasons." In this page the editorial board offered a "Tainted" item of its own ("World Trade Center says, 'You're not welcome.'")

Public Forums

When Andrea Neal became editorial page editor of the *Indianapolis* (Ind.) *Star* in 2000, she set out to find ways "to engage the community in dialogue."[74] With Channel 13 Eyewitness News (WTHR-TV), and supported by the Pew Center for Civic Journalism, the *Star* conducted a series of town halls. An October 2001 meeting on terrorism and homeland security attracted 400 people. A December 2001 meeting looked at top priorities for the coming state General Assembly session. As a result of meetings with the public, Young-Hee Yedinak, Eyewitness News special projects coordinator, said: "I'm a lot more attentive to what people are saying about small things going on in the community that add up to the bigger picture."[75]

Neal reported that after several sessions readers who had submitted letters to the editor said they found the editorial page "a lot more accessible."[76] Recognizing the importance of the forums in "gauging public sentiment on issues," Neal said that *Star* editorial writers purposely solicited "feedback *before* we formally [took] an editorial position" on issues considered at the forums. For more community input, the *Star* also named six local "ordinary citizens" to a community advisory board and recruited local writers to contribute on Tuesdays to "the lead column spot on the editorial page."[77]

Figure 12 **Pioneer Press**

ST. PAUL PIONEER PRESS ■ WWW.TWINCITIES.COM — SATURDAY, FEBRUARY 2, 2002 **13A**

OPINION

When people fall, Saints are there to help them back on their feet

SAINTED / TAINTED

Sainted: Dedicated, caring people who cared for me on Martin Luther King Jr. Day, when I fainted at the checkout counter at Roseville's Rainbow Foods. Thanks to whoever caught me, so I wasn't injured in falling. Thanks to a retired paramedic, who came immediately to my aid and cared for me until the paramedics arrived. Thanks to the team of paramedics, who quickly got me on the way to St. Joseph's Hospital. Thanks to the ER staff, who were wonderful. Thanks to Mary and other Rainbow employees, who responded so quickly to get help. How blessed I am to live in such a great city and community among so many good Samaritans.

DOROTHY JOHNSON
Roseville

Tainted: Those who scheduled the Orchid Show at the Como Conservatory during Winter Carnival. I looked forward to the show last Sunday. Thanks to the great weather and the great people of St. Paul who love their Winter Carnival, especially the snow slide and winter park, I could not get within sight of the Conservatory, much less find a parking spot. Please, next year schedule this important event a week before or a week after the Carnival. The orchid growers deserve an appreciative audience for their tropical displays in the middle of another Minnesota winter.

AUDREY LUHRS
South St. Paul

ST. PAUL PIONEER PRESS

Harold Higgins
Publisher/President

Vicki S. Gowler
Editor/Sr. Vice President

Ronald D. Clark
Editorial Page Editor

Steven Dornfeld
Associate Editorial Page Editor

Bernard H. Ridder Jr.
Chairman Emeritus

Sainted: The paramedics who so promptly and considerately came to my aid Jan. 24 at Aldrich Arena after the nasty fall I took on the ice. Also, kudos to the skaters who were able to maneuver me off the rink and attend to me until the paramedics arrived. Special thanks to Lorraine Eheim, who transported me to the clinic and waited while I received stitches, and then took me home and saw me safely inside. A big thanks you to Ed Oslund, who drove my car to my house and made another trip with some of my belongings. There surely are many wonderful people in St. Paul, and I am grateful for having met some of them.

CATHERINE SATRIANO
St. Paul

Sainted: The person who saw my purse on Highway 13, stopped and brought it into my condo office completely intact, but left no name. I am eternally grateful. I am a senior citizen and I can't imagine how I would have ever replaced everything.

CORDY VALLARINO
West St. Paul

Sainted: The players, fans and coaching staff at the Jan. 25 hockey game at Mariucci Arena, when Dan Welch of Hastings made his return to the line-up after a two-year absence. Dan showed great courage and humility in his pre-game interview, during which he talked about the difficulties that caused him to drop out of the University of Minnesota in his freshman year. He highlighted many of the pressures faced by young student athletes, most of whom will never earn a living in sports. During that night's game, when Dan made his first shot on goal, he received a standing ovation even though the puck hit the pipe and did not go in. The Golden Gophers went on to lose. No matter. Never have I seen such a display of good heart and generous spirit by so many at one time. Welcome back, Dan.

MIKE KLUZNIK
Mendota Heights

NOMINATE SOMEONE

Like to see someone, or something, Sainted or Tainted? Send us your nominations, briefly explaining your reasons.

Mail: Sainted & Tainted, 345 Cedar St., St. Paul, MN. 55101.

Fax: 651-228-5564.

E-mail: letters@pioneerpress .com.

World Trade Center says, 'You're not welcome'

TAINTED: The management and security guards of the Minnesota World Trade Center who, a week ago, would not let people stand on their steps at Seventh and Wabasha streets to watch the Winter Carnival Grande Parade. How inconsiderate. What an unwelcoming message that sent.

Pioneer Press Editorial Board

Tainted: Those who don't provide closed captioning on TV for the hearing impaired. I am writing this for my disabled mother in St. Paul, who is pretty much homebound. One of her disabilities is her hearing. She likes to watch TV. She enjoys some of the older programs that are not on during prime time that at one time did have closed captioning available, but now when she turns them on, they do not. My mother is also a consumer, just like the hearing person, and learns about products from the television sponsors. She will not be purchasing products from those sponsors that advertise during programs without closed captioning. Maybe those sponsors should realize the large group of consumers they are not reaching because of this problem.

S.C. DUMAN
Denver, Colo.

Sainted: A friendly, helpful young woman, name not known, who walked two blocks to call for help for an elderly lady whose car conked out on busy Thompson Avenue in West St. Paul on Jan. 25. She walked back again to advise that a tow truck was on the way. Thanks, angel in disguise, for caring.

MURIEL FRANDSEN
Roseville

Tainted: The 25 members of the U.S. Senate and House of Representatives, who took a whirlwind trip to inspect the prison in Cuba. Did it really take 25 people to put their stamp of approval on the prison's conditions? Wouldn't three or four OKs have sufficed, if needed at all? The 25 got a nice warm vacation (Cuba in January) at our, the taxpayers' expense. What a joke.

ELIZABETH BENNETT
St. Paul

Tainted: Chi Chi's corporate offices for closing its Maplewood location with absolutely no notice after more than two decades in business. The corporate e-mail response: "We needed to concentrate more in core markets where we can run a profitable business." Profitable? This location was always busy. To not at least notify customers of the closing was a poor business move, considering the decision to close was not made overnight.

LISA GRESSEN
St. Paul

Tainted: Those with no etiquette when parking on the street. It never fails that someone parks right in front of our sidewalk (and house), forcing my wife, who is pregnant, to go through the snow bank to access the side door of our van with our 1-year-old. This occurs even though the whole street is wide open, and there is only one other house on the street. There is always space on our street for people to park without parking RIGHT in front of our house, blocking our use of our sidewalk. Every weekend. Use some common sense when parking in the neighborhoods of St. Paul and don't park your cars in front of houses unless it is the only place left.

JIM SAMPAIR JR.
St. Paul

Tainted: The Minnesota Revenue Department. In an age when governments are trying to reduce paper work and simplify systems, they have managed to add one, and possibly two, forms to the income tax filing system. And they have managed to make one, the M1W, the most complicated form ever issued by a tax agency.

ART WILDE
Vadnais Heights

Tainted: The people at the Grande Day Parade who got in front of the rest of us who were on the curb and back (where we were supposed to be) and ruined our view.

SARAH WRIGHT
St. Paul

Dollar power

NICK ANDERSON, LOUISVILLE COURIER-JOURNAL

GARY MARKSTEIN, COPLEY NEWS SERVICE

STEVE BENSON, ARIZONA REPUBLIC

University needs to consider more than one side in the Mount Graham controversy

A University of Arizona astronomer claims the Apaches he spoke to had no objection to the Mount Graham telescope project. Now compare his undocumented hearsay with the 24 San Carlos and White Mountain Apache tribal spiritual leaders, who signed documents opposing that sacrilege.

Additionally, there are over 40 separate official San Carlos and White Mountain tribal government declarations of opposition.

Between 1990 and 2002, the San Carlos Council passed five resolutions against any permanent modification to the mountain, which would produce a serious violation of Apache traditional religious beliefs.

Finally, a University of Minnesota astronomer said he feels that there's "plenty of room" for everyone on the mountain (Jan 17 story). This statement is the equivalent of claiming it should be inoffensive to build a commercial complex in Arlington National Cemetery, on the Mount of Olives or Mount Sinai or any other sacred ground, just because there's "plenty of room."

I find it appalling that after centuries of systematic denial of tribal rights to land and religious freedoms that this issue is even a debate. It makes me sick to know that so many "centers for higher learning" can see nothing wrong with involvement in this project.

KELLY HERRMANN
Minneapolis

The writer is a University of Minnesota student.

LETTERS TO THE EDITOR

Avoid revenge

I want to be proud to say that Americans treat prisoners well, and that we are above torture and inhumane treatment. Poor treatment of prisoners will upset our allies, who might publicly embarrass us. They might refuse to be our allies in the future.

Our soldiers will, someday, be prisoners also. I would like to think that they would not be treated badly in revenge for the way we treated their soldiers. What we do in this war may affect what people believe about our country for many years to come.

DOROTHY JAMISON
Sandstone

Enron

In her Jan. 17 column, Laura Billings took a verbal slap at the Bush administration for not helping Enron Corp. when they were in financial trouble. Think of the whining she would have done if the administration had helped them in any way whatsoever. She would have yelped that it was a favor in return for political contributions. Did she want the government to help an evil corporation or not?

WILLARD L. TALBERG
Stillwater

It's good that the Enron bankruptcy is giving renewed impetus to the drive for campaign finance reform. Now let's hope it drives a stake through the heart of so-called "tort reform."

The issues are related. Tort reform is being pushed by the same right wing Republicans who are campaign finance reform's fiercest opponents. They like to trot out Rush Limbaugh-style anecdotes about how damage awards in civil suits have gotten out of control in America, but their real objective is to protect the Ken Lays of the world from the consequences of their misdeeds by capping the amount that plaintiffs can seek in civil lawsuits.

Not surprisingly, tort reform is high on the agenda of the same corporate America that can buy and sell politicians at will under current campaign finance laws. It's time to put a cap on campaign contributions, not on the damages shareholders, employees and consumers can win when they sue those whom Teddy Roosevelt — a Republican incidentally — labeled "malefactors of great wealth."

RICHARD BRODERICK
St. Paul

What crisis?

The Jan. 28 story showing that St. Paul has more middle-class residents than anywhere else also exposes the city's "affordable housing crisis" as the urban myth it really is. Of the 64 largest cities in America, St. Paul boasts the highest percentage of people who pay less than 30 percent of their income for rental housing. In the same study, the city ranks seventh in affordable home ownership.

The message is quite clear to those "advocates" of affordable housing: Stop playing the class warfare game. Stop inventing a phony crisis to further your social engineering agenda. My suggestion to the Planning Commission, City Council and Mayor Randy Kelly is to put forth a housing policy that seeks to improve the quality and quantity of housing at all income levels, rather than wasting time and resources to solve a phony affordable housing crisis.

GREG HAMMOND
St. Paul

Terrorist treatment

Not one Muslim who interprets the Shia has condemned the World Trade terrorists as vile murderers. Nor have they spoken against the countless Muslims who rejoiced at the massacre.

They do speak mildly of this action as being an aberration of Islam, even as they demand the terrorists now in custody be provided prayer rugs and copies of the Qur'an. Even letter writer Mohamed-Shiraz Mohamed suggests treating these thugs with "gentleness and righteousness" (Jan. 19).

No one wishes for peace and safety more than veterans who have been there, and the servicemen that are there now. Unfortunately, making nice with people lacking compassion and decency does not preserve freedom or save one from becoming a bearer of wood or drawer of water.

ROY THATCHER
Galesville, Wis.

SHANE MCCOY, U.S. NAVY

In this photo from the Department of Defense, Taliban and al-Qaida detainees in jumpsuits sit in a holding area under the watchful eyes of military police at Camp X-Ray at the U.S. Naval Base at Guantanamo Bay, Cuba, during processing to the temporary detention facility on Jan. 11.

When Philadelphia public schools were faced with a proposed state takeover, the *Philadelphia Daily News* held a public forum on school choice. Collecting the e-mail addresses of the 60 people who attended, according to Wendy Warren, the paper's "Rethinking Philadelphia" editor, the *News* created "something of an instant forum that we're in touch with by e-mail" to comment on public issues as they arose.[78]

OP-ED PAGES

The first op-ed (opposite-editorial) pages may have been produced by the *New York World* in the early 1920s. The executive editor, Herbert Bayard Swope, said he got the idea for an op-ed page when he found that, "in spite of our hard and fast principle," opinion kept creeping into the news columns. "It occurred to me that nothing is more interesting than opinion when opinion is interesting," he recounted later, "so I devised a method of cleaning off the page opposite the editorial page . . . and thereon I decided to print opinions, ignoring facts."[79] The page sparkled with the names of famous writers that Swope recruited: Alexander Woollcott, writing on books and theater; Harry Hansen, on books; Heywood Broun, on whatever he wished. Franklin Pierce Adams (better known as F.P.A.) wrote a witty, acerbic column called "The Conning Tower." The *World's* op-ed page was heavily oriented toward the arts and culture. (A 1942 book on newspaper editing credited the Louisville, Ky., *Courier-Journal's* editorial page and "page opposite editorial," or "op-ed" page, with setting one of the outstanding examples in design for editorial pages.)[80]

Although the idea and the name of the op-ed page have been around for a long time, the *New York Times* is generally credited with setting the example that has led to a substantial number of such pages in recent years. Harrison E. Salisbury, the first editor of the *Times'* op-ed page, said the idea emerged when editors were looking for something to attract readers from the *New York Herald Tribune,* which had just folded. The immediate aim was to present a wider diversity of opinion. The *Times* was also facing the need to raise subscription and advertising rates. The op-ed page was seen as an opportunity "to give the readers something extra for their extra money," Salisbury said. The *Times* moved its own columnists to the op-ed page, leaving room for more letters on the editorial page, and began to publish a variety of articles on the remainder of the page. Salisbury was given only three-quarters of a page; an advertisement occupied the remainder. He said he accepted the ad partly to anchor the page in the real world but also because he feared he would not have enough material to fill a whole page.[81]

When the *Los Angeles Times* joined the movement, according to David Shaw, the paper's media critic, it deliberately planned a less intellectual page than that of the *New York Times,* reasoning that readers got enough reporting on social issues in the opinion columns and from the columnists. "I'd especially like us to give our readers a clear feeling of what it's really like to live in Southern California," the op-ed page editor was quoted as saying. "I want personal experience pieces, stories that tell how it feels to drive the freeway and to suffer a death in the family and to be out of work."[82]

A 1994 survey of newspapers found that fewer than half had op-ed pages. The survey also found that op-ed pages generally were edited by the same person who edited the editorial page. "This greatly reduces the odds favoring an independent public forum disconnected from the agenda of the signature editorial page," the conductors of the survey concluded. In their view, while aiming for a balance of opposing points of view, the "op-ed page becomes the flip side of the editorial page, thereby limiting the possibility that an agenda driven primarily by public concerns will emerge."[83]

Writing in 1997, one syndicated columnist who appears on op-ed pages said that such pages no longer presented truly diverse views. Norman Solomon saw op-ed pages as presenting "variations of conventional wisdom—spanning only from avowed right-wingers to cautious liberals," in which "timeworn arguments resemble billiard balls bouncing between two rails." "No wonder," he added, "so many op-ed pages have a monotonous tone."[84]

My own examination of 165 or so editorial and op-ed pages, from 1999 to early 2001, tends to confirm, for many papers at least, what these critics were saying. On most papers the opinion writers were the standard syndicated columnists discussed and identified in Chapter 18, "Columns and Cartoons."

But there are bright spots. I came across outstanding examples of op-ed pages while judging the 2001 contest sponsored by a relatively new organization, the Association of Opinion Page Editors (AOPE). The page judged to be the best single op-ed page was a "Commentary" page in the *St. Louis* (Mo.) *Post-Dispatch*. The dominant article, "100 years haven't been enough," looked back at social conditions when the Missouri Association for Social Welfare was established. The author, Peter De Simone, concluded that "this little organization, MASW, has survived and helped the evolution of social policy in Missouri for 100 years because it's a long road to social justice and somebody has to do it. Things get mostly better, but sometimes worse." What is needed now, De Simone claimed, is a "new generation of leaders . . . determined to keep MASW going for another century because one century wasn't quite enough."[85] The article was dramatized by accompanying old-time sepia-colored artwork from *Leslie's* magazine depicting "Homes of the Poor." At the bottom of the page was an article by a middle school teacher who remembered how she had worked to win the "trust and respect" of a challenging 12-year-old. She had read in the morning paper that he had been killed crossing the street.[86] Also contributing to the page was a local columnist who wrote about "the mess baseball is in."[87]

Winning first place for theme op-ed page was the *Atlanta* (Ga.) *Journal-Constitution* for a sensitive, in-depth report titled "Southern kin, black & white." It was the story of two *Journal-Constitution* employees who discovered that they were "related through the legacy of slavery." Each wrote about how she felt at making this discovery and how she felt about the other person. Dominating the page, as dramatic as the women's accounts, was a reproduction of their common family tree accompanied by faint photographs of some of their ancestors.[88]

Judged the outstanding op-ed feature was "Eyes to the ground: The perils of the black student" in the *Hartford* (Conn.) *Courant*. According to Carolyn Lumsden, the *Courant's* commentary editor, the editorial board had been debating the reason for "the gap between black and white students on achievement tests" when a black member of the board "weighed in with his account of how a well-meaning professor had lowered the class standards just for him, without being asked." He was asked to write his account of the incident. He recounted how he had been made to feel "intellectually disabled or, at least, incapable of exerting the same mental rigor or rising to quite the same level of intellectual expectation as my white classmates." At the end of the article, the writer offered suggestions for the roles that parents, guardians and teachers might play in helping students develop confidence in themselves.[89]

The award for best series went to the *Rochester* (N.Y.) *Democrat and Chronicle*. Over a three-month period the "Speaking Out" page carried at least 13 articles written by local people (plus many letters) about the surprise announcement of a local hospital closing. The series began with an explanation by the CEO of the corporation that owned both that hospital and another, more thriving, local hospital. The casual reader might have thought that article would end the matter. Within four days, however, a piece by a local gynecologist appeared, describing how existing hospital facilities might be shifted around to save the hospital. In a few more days, more than a half page of letters appeared protesting the closing, as well as an article suggesting the Rochester Health Care Forum be used as "an umbrella to ensure the best possible outcome" to the hospital closing. Then came articles by the president of the county medical society, three state legislators, CEOs of two local businesses and health care professionals, among others. In the last article that was submitted as part of the AOPE contest entry, one legislator announced the formation of a Save the Genesee Committee, which would soon hold a meeting to discuss making "recommendations for restoring community control over our health care system." What started as an explanatory article, thanks to the availability of the *Democrat and Chronicle*'s op-ed page, evolved into a community dialogue on health care.

Among the newspapers that I examined for this edition, a few showed evidence of trying to bring outside voices to their pages, beyond the traditional syndicated columnists. The *Denver Post* carried a twice-a-week column by a local former newspaper editor, another local writer who appears three times a week and local guest writers under the label of "Colorado Voices." The *Rocky Mountain News* (also in Denver) ran a regular "On the Media" column by a local person. One article discussed the "Denver dailies' coverage of the Marilyn Manson concert, the protests and the counter-protests."[90] The "Viewpoints" page of the *Dallas Morning News* periodically carried a local political columnist. The "Forum" page of the Portland *Maine Sunday Telegram* ran a columnist on state and national issues. The "OpEd" page of the *Bangor* (Maine) *Daily News* ran a column by a political economist. The *Providence* (R.I.) *Journal* "Commentary" page carried a weekly column by a nature and outdoor recreation writer. Several papers ran editorial or op-ed articles written by their own editors and staff writers, some on a regular basis.

Frequently appearing on the pages were reprints from magazines or contributions from think tanks, foundations and other interest groups. The interest-group contributions generally are offered at no charge, but if they are responsibly presented they can be valuable alternative opinions. Reprints, of course, require prior permission to publish (perhaps at a price). Editorial writers discussed the problem of getting permission in an exchange on the NCEW e-mail discussion group. One suggestion was to establish a list of the magazines from which articles were most frequently published and arrange a quick way to get approval. Here is the initial list:[91]

American Demographics	*Commentary*
The American Enterprise	*Commonweal Magazine*
American Spectator	*Foreign Affairs*
The Atlantic	*Foreign Policy*
The Chronicle of Higher Education	*The Futurist*

Governing   *The New Yorker*
Harper's Magazine   *Policy Review*
Mother Jones   *The Progressive*
The Nation   *Public Interest*
National Interest   *Reason*
National Review   *Vanity Fair*
The New Republic   *Washington Monthly Magazine*

■ CONCLUSION

The principal purpose of innovation, whether in layout, content or telecommunications, should be to encourage readers to think more deeply about more subjects. The purpose of page design is to get ideas across to readers by attracting them and then holding their attention long enough to stir their thoughts. The makeup of the page itself cannot carry a message to readers, but it can help set the tone of the page. If an editor has a flamboyant editorial style, a flamboyant style of typography will help reinforce the message. Conservative typography will help reinforce a conservative, reserved editorial style.

Whatever style an editor chooses, page design must meet two criteria. The first is to distinguish the opinion pages from the news pages. Readers need constantly to be reminded of this distinction. Editorial columns can be wider than news columns. Body type can be larger. Headlines can use different typefaces. Heads can be centered instead of flush left. Sketches instead of photographs can be used. The page can be run in a distinctive and consistent position in the paper.

The second criterion is to present a page that will attract readers. The makeup should say that this is an important page and that the editors have put a great deal of time, effort and thought into it. Thus the page should be deliberately, carefully and attractively laid out. It should have enough life to it that it is not always the same day by day, yet it also must have enough consistency in page design to suggest that the same editors, with the same editorial philosophy, are producing it each day.

If editors can meet those two criteria, they can design their pages in any manner they wish. In the end, what really counts is what they say on the pages. The search for new ways to bring more, and more varied, viewpoints to the opinion pages also reflects an effort to keep the pages from becoming routine. Just as readers ought to be surprised from time to time by the appearance of an editorial page, so should they be surprised once in a while by the content. This means that editors must go beyond the traditional staff-written editorials, syndicated columns and cartoons, and letters to the editor. The possibilities are limited only by editors' imaginations and their ability to carry out their ideas, possibilities that may include the features discussed in this chapter—op-ed pages, guest columns, solicited contributions, boards of contributors, questions of the week, pro-con packages, visual illustrations and reprints from other publications as well as criticism of, and comment on, the press itself.

The purpose of all these efforts, of course, is to promote a greater exchange of ideas among readers and to convince readers that their newspaper is doing a thorough and responsible job of serving them. Even more important is actually to do a thorough and responsible job.

■ QUESTIONS AND EXERCISES

1. Examine the makeup of the newspapers in your area. Do you find it easy to distinguish editorial pages from news pages?

2. Does the liberal or conservative nature of the makeup reflect the liberal or conservative editorial policy of the page? Consider the size of headlines, the style of headline type, the use of white space or rules, and the horizontal or vertical nature of the layout.

3. Does the makeup of a specific newspaper change from day to day or remain the same? If it changes, what principles seem to be operating in determining the layout—the relative importance of elements, the readership appeal of the elements or whim? Does the layout change so radically day by day that the page has a disjointed character?

4. What could be done to improve the design of the editorial pages in your area?

5. Which newspaper do you judge to have the best design? Why?

6. Which newspapers in your area have op-ed pages? How often do they appear? Is there a difference between the material that appears on the editorial page and the material on the op-ed page? What seems to be the policy in determining what goes where?

7. Does the editor of the op-ed page seem to be trying hard to bring contrary and different views onto the page? Does the page contain surprises?

8. What devices does the editor use to try to encourage more participation by more people in the opinion pages? A pro-con package? A question of the week? A guest columnist? An in-depth analysis? Articles by experts?

9. Do any of the newspapers have media critics? If so, how free do they appear to be to criticize the newspaper?

CHAPTER TWENTY

The Editorial Page That May, and Must, Be

Truth crushed to earth, shall rise again;
The eternal years of God are hers
But, Error, wounded, writhes in pain,
And dies among his worshippers.
—WILLIAM CULLEN BRYANT [1]

"The prestige of the editorial page is done," wrote James Parton in the early 1870s after the deaths of Henry J. Raymond of the *New York Times,* James Gordon Bennett of the *New York Herald* and Horace Greeley of the *New York Tribune.* In a day when television viewers could *watch* and *listen* to the editorial comments of an Eric Sevareid, a John Chancellor or a Bill Moyers, why would they go to all the effort to *read* editorials in a newspaper? If Internet surfers, with the click of a mouse, can inundate themselves with opinions from everywhere around the world, why would they read two or three editorials in a morning newspaper?

Despite these supposed signs of impending doom, to paraphrase Mark Twain, the news of the death of the editorial page has been exaggerated. It has survived the deaths of the great editors and the passing of the TV commentators. There are several reasons why the printed opinion page should able to hold its own against the World Wide Web.

The first advantage of the opinion page is that it does *not* inundate the user. Web opinion-seekers are as likely to be confused as satisfied with the myriad "hits" they are overwhelmed with when they seek opinions on almost any subject. Without a lot of prior knowledge, how can seekers choose among all that material, let alone evaluate its credibility? Here is where opinion writers and editors provide a service. Editorial page editors perform a gate-keeper role. Some Internet users prefer to be their own gatekeepers, but others appreciate being able to turn to an opinion page and know that they will find a moderate number of editorials, columns, cartoons and letters on topics in which they are likely to be interested.

With this gatekeeping advantage goes a responsibility as well. Readers will continue to turn to the opinion page only if editors and writers have done their jobs well. This means that, in selecting topics, they must seek a balance between what readers think they want to know and what editors and writers think they should know. This responsibility also includes bringing to readers high-quality, well-written, well-edited editorials, columns, cartoons and letters. To achieve this standard, newspapers must provide sufficient financial and other resources to hire and keep good staff members and to obtain the editorial material necessary to produce a lively, stimulating, informative opinion page. In short, owners and managers must make a substantial commitment to guarantee that readers will get a first-class product for their investment of money and time. Throughout this book I have cited and reprinted top-notch editorials as examples of opinion pieces that have attracted, informed and stimulated readers. I also have noted how editors have brought a diverse range of opinion to their pages through letters, columns, forums, boards of contributors, ombudsmen, op-ed pages and civic journalism.

The second advantage lies in the community-based nature of the newspaper. I would do nothing to discourage newspaper editors from publishing news stories and opinion pieces on national and international subjects. (In fact, one area in which most newspapers are not fulfilling their responsibilities is providing adequate and meaningful international news.) Compared to television, cable and the Internet, newspapers are way ahead in being able to report and comment on local, state and regional topics. The circulation area of a newspaper, whether it's small-town Florence, Ore., or the state of Oregon, is where people live and where what happens affects them. Newspapers can provide more words on an opinion page, let alone the entire newspaper, than can a local news broadcast. It is a rare television station that offers editorials. In earlier chapters we noted how, on the local level, the *San Francisco Bay Guardian* campaigned for public power and how the *Los Angeles Times* helped focus attention on mentally ill street people. At the state level we saw how the *Rutland* (Vt.) *Herald* helped encourage a positive atmosphere while the Vermonters were debating what to do about carrying out a controversial state Supreme Court order involving same-sex unions.

The area-based newspaper traditionally has served the citizens of its community (or region or state) as a source of common information and as a forum for dialogue about, and resolution of, public issues. Unfortunately this community function is being threatened by a slow, steady increase in the percentage of people who choose not to buy a newspaper. It is also being threatened by the decision of some companies not to sell newspapers in certain "marginal" parts of their circulation areas. In looking at the effects of corporate ownership, we noted that some managers are purposely cutting back circulation in these areas to create a more attractive buying package for advertisers. If these trends continue—if owners, managers and editors allow them to—newspapers may eventually lose the advantage they have as community-based institutions.

In expressing confidence that the newspapers should be able to hold their own against the Internet, I do not intend to disparage electronic innovations. Repeatedly throughout this book, I have called attention to how newspapers are using the Internet—to obtain information, post their editorials, encourage letters to the editor and get feedback from readers. Editorial writers also are sharing ideas among themselves through a web site and e-mail discussion group sponsored by the National Conference of Editorial Writers. Instant access to information on the web can be particularly helpful to editorial writers who, at a 9 a.m. meeting, find themselves assigned an editorial that must reach the editorial page editor's computer by 3 p.m. Through the use of e-mail and news and opinion web sites, the writer can quickly come up with more than enough information and ideas to comment authoritatively and responsibly on a topic. In the years ahead editors no doubt will find new ways to share their editorial products on the Internet. But it is not likely that in the near future the computer screen will replace the printed page, certainly not as a hometown product—if only because readers like to clip and squirrel away printed reports on births, weddings, deaths and events, as well as favorite editorials, columns and cartoons.

Another thing going for the print media is the First Amendment. Because speech, the press and the right of assembly were the means of communication at the time the Bill of Rights was drafted, the First Amendment specifically guarantees freedoms in these three areas. Over the years, questions have been raised about how far free speech should be allowed on radio, television and cable, and now on the Internet.

Of course the guarantees and privileges that First Amendment bestows on the print media are not intended to make jobs easier or more profitable for reporters, editors, publishers or owners, or to give them competitive advantages over other media. Freedom of the press is intended to assure that citizens of this county have access to all the information they need to make intelligent political and social decisions. The responsibility for assuring that citizens get this information, and that they have ample opportunity to engage in public dialogue themselves, rests largely with the owners, the writers and the editors of the press. This is a heavy responsibility, but it can be an exciting and challenging one.

One task for future writers and editors is to find new and better ways to keep the editorial function of the press alive and healthy. This book is intended to help would-be writers and editors get started down the editorial path. The direction that path takes in the future will be decided by them. Who knows? Down that path may go modern-day Horace Greeleys, William Allen Whites or Eric Sevareids.

One final word: If you don't think there are solutions to local, state, national and international problems, don't go into editorial writing. You must believe that efforts of government, private agencies and individuals can make a difference in communities and in the lives of families and individuals. Editorial writing, at heart, is an optimistic business. Each new day, and each new editorial page, offers an opportunity to help make something better.

Endnotes

Introduction

1. David Shaw, "The End of Punditry," *Gannett Center Journal,* 3:1 (Spring 1989).

Section I The Why of the Editorial Page

Chapter I
The Editorial Page That Used to Be

1. Rollo Ogden, ed., *The Life and letters of Edwin Lawrence Godkin* (Westport, Conn.: Greenwood, 1972), p. 255.

2. James Parton, "Prestige," *North American Review,* 101:375–76 (April 1866) cited in Frank Luther Mott, *American Journalism* (New York: Macmillan, 1941), p. 385.

3. W.S. Burleigh, *Lostine Leader,* November 5, 1987, in Lloyd W. Coffman, *5200 Thursdays in the Wallowas: A Centennial History of The Wallowa County Chieftain* (Enterprise, Ore.: Wallowa County Chieftain, 1984), p. 48.

4. Ogden, *Life and Letters.*

5. Michael Emery and Edwin Emery, *The Press and America,* 6th ed. (Englewood Cliffs, N.J.: Prentice Hall, 1988), pp. 66–68.

6. Ishbel Ross, *Ladies of the Press* (New York: Harper, 1936), p. 29.

7. Ibid., p. 32.

8. Ibid., p. 37.

9. Roland E. Wolseley, *The Black Press,* 2nd ed. (Ames: Iowa State University Press, 1990), p. 25.

10. Ibid., p. 28.

11. Parton, "Prestige," p. 385.

12. Edward P. Mitchell, *Memoirs of an Editor* (New York: Scribner's, 1924), p. 109.

13. Harold E. Davis, *Henry Grady's New South* (Tuscaloosa: University of Alabama Press, 1990).

14. Hal Borland, *Country Editor's Boy* (Philadelphia: Lippincott, 1970), pp. 156–69.

15. Sally Foreman Griffith, *Home Town News: William Allen White and the Emporia Gazette* (New York: Oxford University Press, 1989), pp. 133–38.

16. Wm. David Sloan, Cheryl Watts and Joanne Sloan, *Great Editorials: Masterpieces of Opinion Writing.* (Northport, Ala.: Vision, 1992), pp. 178–79.

17. Harrison E. Salisbury, *Without Fear or Favor* (New York: New York Times Books, 1980), p. 26.

18. Quoted in Justin Kaplan, *Lincoln Steffens: A Biography* (New York: Simon & Schuster, 1974), p. 121.

19. Upton Sinclair, *The Brass Check* (Pasadena, Calif.: The Author, 1920), p. 22.

20. Quoted in Ferdinand Lundberg, *Imperial Hearst* (New York: Equinox Cooperative, 1936), p. 77.

21. Edwin Emery and Michael Emery, *The Press and America,* 4th edition (Englewood Cliffs: Prentice-Hall, 1978), p 329.

22. David Nasaw, *The Chief: The Life of William Randolph Hearst* (Boston: Houghton Mifflin, 2000), p. 263.

23. Emery and Emery, *The Press and America,* p. 329.

24. Richard Norton Smith, *The Colonel: The Life and Legend of Robert R. McCormick* (Boston: Houghton Mifflin, 1997), pp. 235–36.

25. Emery and Emery, *The Press and America,* p. 334.

26. Emery and Emery, *The Press and America,* p. 335.

27. Quoted in Nasaw, *The Chief,* p. 479.

28. Robert R. McCormick, *Chicago Tribune,* September 2, 1939, quoted in Jerome E. Edwards, *The Foreign Policy of Col. McCormick's Tribune, 1929–1941* (Reno: University of Nevada Press, 1971), p. 147.

29. Emery and Emery, *The Press and America,* p. 336.

30. W.L. White, "The Last Two Decades," *Emporia Gazette,* May 1940, quoted in William Allen White, *The Autobiography of William Allen White* (New York: Macmillan, 1946), p. 641.

31. Emery and Emery, *The Press and America,* p. 339.

32. Nathaniel B. Blumberg, *One-Party Press?* (Lincoln: University of Nebraska Press, 1954), p. 44.

33. Robert Lasch, "The Containment of Ideas," *St. Louis* (Mo.) *Post-Dispatch,* January 17, 1965, reprinted in Wm. David Sloan, *Pulitzer Prize Editorials, 1917–1979* (Ames: University of Iowa Press, 1980), pp. 139, 141.

34. William Safire, "New day of infamy," *New York Times*, Sept. 12, 2001; "Inside the bunker," *New York Times*, Sept. 13, 2001.

35. Maureen Dowd, "Liberties: Autumn of fears." *New York Times*, Sept. 23, 2001.

36. Frank Rich, "The end of the beginning," *New York Times*, Sept. 29, 2001.

37. Dan Guthrie, "When the going gets tough, the tender turn tail," *Daily Courier*, Sept. 15, 2001.

38. Quoted in Dave Astor, "A post-9/11 review of editorial cartooning," *Editor & Publisher*, 135:31 (Feb. 4, 2002).

39. Quoted in Ibid.

40. Associated Press, "Editorial cartoon generates outcry," *Arizona Republic*, Feb. 9, 2002.

41. Gilbert Cranberg, "Corporate ownership affects pages," *The Masthead*, 53:22 (Fall 2001).

Chapter 2
The Editorial Page That Should, and Could, Be

1. Alexis de Tocqueville, "A Newspaper's Value," cited in *The Masthead*, 28:29 (Winter 1976).

2. Robert Reid, "More Hell-Raising Editorials," *The Masthead*, 39:26–27 (Winter 1987).

3. Bruce B. Brugmann, letter to the Pulitzer Prize Committee, Jan. 30, 2002.

4. "Don't buy PG&E's lies," *San Francisco Bay Guardian*, Oct. 17, 2001.

5. Brugmann, letter to the Pulitzer Prize Committee.

6. "Public power's future," *San Francisco Bay Guardian*, March 20, 2002.

7. Buford Boone, cited in Johanna Cleary, "Lessons in Editorial Leadership," *The Masthead*, 40:46 (Summer 1988).

8. Hazel Brannon Smith, cited in Cleary, "Lessons in Editorial Leadership," pp. 49–50.

9. Bernard Kilgore, "A Publisher Looks at Editorial Writing," *The Masthead*, 6:47 (Spring 1954).

10. Quoted in Paul Greenberg, "Tyerman Sums Up," *The Masthead*, 17:23 (Winter 1965).

11. Quoted in Philip Geyelin, "Who Listens to Your Bugle Calls?" *The Masthead*, 30:9 (Summer–Fall 1978).

12. Elsa Mohn and Maxwell McCombs, "Who Reads Us and Why," *The Masthead*, 32:24 (Winter 1980–81).

13. Lenoir Chambers, "Aim for the Mind—and Higher," *The Masthead*, 13:20 (Summer 1961).

14. James J. Kilpatrick, "Editorials and Editorial Writing," *The Masthead*, 5:7 (Spring 1953).

15. Quoted in Kathryn S. Wenner, "No Wonder It Won a Pulitzer," *American Journalism Review*, 23:17 (June 2001).

16. "Politics and morality," *Rutland* (Vt.) *Herald*, Jan. 27, 2000.

17. "A conscientious start," *Rutland* (Vt.) *Herald*, Feb. 11, 2000.

18. "Leadership in action," *Rutland* (Vt.) *Herald*, April 26, 2000.

19. "A Death Foretold," *Lexington* (Ky.) *Herald-Leader*, Dec. 2, 1990.

20. *Los Angeles Times*, advertisement, *American Journalism Review*, 24:7 (May 2002).

21. Ernest Hynds and Erika Archibald, "Improved editorial pages can help papers, communities," *Newspaper Research Journal*, 17:19–20 (Winter/Spring 1996).

22. Kenneth Rystrom, "The Impact of Newspaper Endorsements," *Newspaper Research Journal*, 7:19–28 (Winter 1986).

23. Pew Center for Civic Journalism, advertisement, *American Journalism Review*, 24:1 (May 2002).

24. "What's happening in Pew projects," *Civic Catalyst*, Spring 2002, p. 10.

25. Ibid., p. 11.

26. Ibid., p. 12.

27. R.S. Baker, "The Editorial Writer: The Man in the Piazza," *Montana Journalism Review*, 15:18–19 (1972).

Section 2: The Who of the Editorial Page

Chapter 3
Anybody for Editorial Writing?

1. Robert H. Estabrook, "Why Editorial Applicants Aren't," *The Masthead*, 12:53 (Summer 1962).

2. G. Cleveland Wilhoit and Dan G. Drew, "Portrait of an Editorial Writer, 1971–88," *The Masthead*, 41:6–7 (Spring 1989).

3. David E. Klement, "Who we are and what we do," *The Masthead*, 50:6 (Fall 1998).

4. Ibid., p. 7.

5. Ibid., p. 8.

6. Wilbur Elston, "The Editor Goes Status Seeking and Image Hunting," *The Masthead*, 15:1–18 (Fall 1963).

7. Klement, "Who we are and what we do," p. 8.

8. Warren H. Pierce, "What Makes a Good Editorial Writer?" *The Masthead*, 10:23-24 (Spring 1958).

9. David Manning White, "The Editorial Writer and Objectivity," *The Masthead*, 4:31–34 (Fall 1952).

10. Hoke Norris, "The Inside Dope," *The Masthead*, 8:55–57 (Spring 1956).

11. Pierce, "What Makes."

12. Irving Dilliard, "The Editor I Wish I Were," *The Masthead*, 19:51–57 (Summer 1967).

13. Frederic S. Marquardt, "What Manner of Editor Is This?" *The Masthead*, 19:57–58 (Summer 1967).

14. Klement, "Who we are," p. 6.

15. Ibid., p. 6.

16. Evelyn Trapp Goodrick, "Comparison of Women and Men on Editorial Page Staffs," *The Masthead*, 42:3–7 (Fall 1990).

17. Rekha Basu, "Minority voices sound like one hand clapping," *The Masthead*, 45:8–9 (Summer 1993).

18. James H. Howard, "Feedback from Readers Helps Teach," *The Masthead*, 27:21 (Spring 1975).

19. Donald L. Breed, "Why Publishers Rarely Write Own Editorials," *The Masthead*, 14:21 (Fall 1962),

20. John H. Cline, "The Quest for 'Good Editorial Thinking," *The Masthead*, 18:17–18 (Fall 1966).

21. Editor in the West, "Not in That Newsroom," *The Masthead*, 18:7–8 (Fall 1966).

22. Lynnell Burkett, "Looking for arrivals from the road less traveled," *The Masthead*, 50:5–6 (Winter 1998).

23. Susan Nielsen, "You're a WHAT? Getting used to the job title takes a while," *The Masthead*, 50:6 (Winter 1998).

24. Ben H. Bagdikian, "Editorial Pages Change—But Too Slowly," *The Masthead*, 17:16 (Winter 1965–66).

25. Jonathan W. Daniels, "The Docility of the Dignified Press," *The Masthead*, 17:8–14 (Winter 1965-66).

Chapter 4
Preparation of an Editorial Writer

1. LeRoy E. Smith, "The Polls of Journalism Educators," *The Masthead*, 28:25–29 (Spring 1976)

2. Robert B. Frazier, "What Do You Read, My Lord?" *The Masthead*, 14:10–16 (Summer 1962).

3. Hugh B. Fullerton, cited in Jake Highton, "Perhaps It's Time to Abolish Journalism Schools," *The Masthead*, 40:33 (Winter 1988).

4. Highton, "Perhaps It's Time," p. 33.

5. Otis Chandler, cited in LeRoy E. Smith and Curtis D. MacDougall, "What Should Journalism Majors Know?" *The Masthead*, 27:28–32 (Spring 1975).

6. Smith, "The Polls of Journalism Educators."

7. Curtis D. MacDougall, "A Modern Journalism Curriculum," *The Masthead*, 28:30–34 (Spring 1976).

8. Don Carson, "The Goal: Aiming for Perfection," *The Masthead*, 28:34 (Spring 1976).

9. Anson H. Smith Jr., "Try an Inspiring Year at Harvard," *The Masthead*, 22:33–5 (Spring 1970).

10. Sig Gissler, "A Sabbatical: Too Sweet to Be True," *The Masthead*, 29:30–31 (Spring 1977).

11. Maura Casey, "Apply for the Pulliam Fellowship," *The Masthead*, 53:47 (Spring 2001).

12. "Milestones, awards, educational opportunities," *The Masthead*, 54:35 (Spring 2002).

13. Gloria Padilla, "Hechinger inspires," *The Masthead*, 53:10 (Fall 2001).

14. Kenneth Rystrom, "An Editor Returns to Campus," *The Masthead*, 29:12–15 (Winter 1977-78).

15. Fred Fiske, "NCEW goes to college," *The Masthead*, 54:15 (Spring 2002).

16. John H. Taylor Jr., "Eager students a treat at Columbia," *The Masthead*, 54:16 (Spring 2002).

17. Sue Ryon, "Minority Writers Seminar works," *The Masthead*, 52:36–37 (Summer 2000).

18. Sue Ryon, "Growth in Foundation is rewarding," *The Masthead*, 52:36 (Winter 2000).

19. Terrence W. Honey, "Our Ivory Tower Syndrome Is Dead," *The Masthead*, 23:26 (Summer 1971).

20. Jim Boyd, "First-class outfit, first-class program," *The Masthead*, 54:22 (Spring 2002).

21. David Sarasohn, "Two days in the U.N.'s glass building," *The Masthead*, 52:28 (Spring 2000).

22. Nancy Q. Keefe, "Israeli Trip: A snapshot of the conflict," *The Masthead*, 54:21 (Spring 2002).

23. Larry Evans, "Regional meetings reach more, cost less," *The Masthead*, 45:24–25 (Summer 1993).

24. Dick Mial, "Regional partnerships work," *The Masthead*, 53:33 (Summer 2001).

25. Frazier, "What Do You Read, My Lord?"

26. Robert B. Frazier, "The Editorial Elbow," *The Masthead*, 15:5–16 (Summer 1963).

27. James J. Kilpatrick, "Editorials and Editorial Writing," *The Masthead*, 5:1-3 (Spring 1953).

28. Irving Dilliard, "The Editorial Writer I Wish I Were," *The Masthead*, 19:52 (Summer 1967).

29. Suraj Kapoor and Janet Blue, "Editorial page editors still call the shots," *The Masthead*, 45:29 (Spring 1997).

30. David E. Klement, "Who we are and what we do," *The Masthead*, 50:6 (Fall 1998).

31. Nina J. Easton, "Thunder on the Right," *American Journalism Review*, 23:32–37 (December 2001).

32. Nina J. Easton, "Left in the lurch," *American Journalism Review*, 24:38–43 (January–February 2001).

33. Steve Snyder, "You call that liberal?" *American Journalism Review*, 24:71 (March 2002).

34. Lori Robertson, "Ethically challenged," *American Journalism Review*, 23:22–23 (March 2001).

Chapter 5
Who Is This Victorian 'We'?

1. J.G. Saxe, in *The Press*, cited in *The Masthead*, 21:20 (Summer 1969).

2. Fred C. Hobson Jr., "A We Problem," *The Masthead*, 18:18 (Spring 1966).

3. Robert E. Kennedy, "(signed) The editorial writer," *The Masthead*, 42:23 (Summer 1990).

4. Sam Reynolds, "Editorial Transubstantiation," *The Masthead*, 27:2 (Fall 1975).

5. Warren G. Bovee, "The Mythology of Editorial Anonymity," *The Masthead*, 24:26–35 (Fall 1972) and 24:54–65 (Winter 1972).

6. Robert Schmuhl, "Accountability through Initials," *The Masthead*, 39:31 (Winter 1987).

7. Lou Brancaccio, "A sign of the times at *The Columbian*," *Columbian*, Feb. 9, 2002.

8. Ernest C. Hynds, "Editorial Pages Remain Vital," *The Masthead*, 27:19 (Fall 1975).

9. Robert U. Brown, "Shop Talk at Thirty," *The Masthead*, 17:38–39 (Fall 1965).

10. Quoted in David Nasaw, *The Chief: The Life of William Randolph Hearst* (Boston: Houghton Mifflin, 2000), p. 385.

11. Richard Norton Smith, *The Colonel: The Life and Legend of Robert R. McCormick* (Boston: Houghton Mifflin, 1997), p. 151.

12. G. Cleveland Wilhoit and Dan G. Drew, "Portrait of an Editorial Writer," *The Masthead*, 41:4–11 (Spring 1989).

13. Anonymous, "Editors Say More Leeway on Group-Owned Papers," *presstime*, 2:36 (May 1980).

14. Calvin Mayne, "Gannett Company," in "Symposium, Yeah, What about That Monopoly of Opinion?" *The Masthead*, 26:14 (Fall 1974).

15. DeNeen L. Brown, "Journalists feel shackled by new owner," Washington Post Service, Jan. 31, 2002.

16. Brown, "Shop Talk at Thirty."

17. Kennedy, "(signed) The editorial writer."

18. George C. McLeod, "The Paper's Masthead Is the Byline," *The Masthead*, 23:13 (Spring 1971).

19. Ann Lloyd Merriman, "No to Signed Editorials," *The Masthead*, 23:14 (Spring 1971).

20. Michael J. Birkner, "Behind the Editorial 'We,'" *The Masthead*, 36:20 (Summer 1984).

21. Richard T. Cole, "Pursuing the Elusive Editorial Board," *The Masthead*, 42:24–25 (Summer 1990).

22. *Register-Guard*, n.d.

23. Anonymous, "Report of the 1972 NCEW Continuing Studies Committee," *The Masthead*, 25:37–39 (Spring 1973).

24. Ernest C. Hynds, "Editorial pages become more useful," *The Masthead*, 47:40 (Fall 1995).

25. David V. Felts, "Roosevelt's 'I' or Victoria's 'We'?" *The Masthead*, 28:20-21 (Fall 1967).

26. Quoted in James Parton, *The Life of Horace Greeley* (New York: Mason Brothers, 1855), p. 78.

27. Kenneth Rystrom, "Would You Quit over Editorial Stand?" *The Masthead*, 37:25–26 (Fall 1985).

Chapter 6
Relations with Publishers

1. Meg Downey, "Editors and Publishers Should Fight," *The Masthead*, 42:18 (Winter 1990).

2. Hugh B. Patterson Jr., "When Ownership Abdicates Its Responsibilities, Newspaper Suffers," *The Masthead*, 14:16 (Fall 1962).

3. Bernard Kilgore, "A Publisher Looks at Editorial Writing," *The Masthead*, 6:44 (Spring 1954).

4. Ibid.

5. Donald L. Breed, "The Publisher and the Editorial Page," *The Masthead*, 3:34 (Winter 1951).

6. Michael Zuzel, "Because I say so," *The Masthead*, 51:3 (Spring 1999).

7. Ed Williams, "The endorsement that wasn't," *The Masthead*, 51:5 (Spring 1999).

8. *Group Ownership Survey*, American Society of Newspaper Editors, April 1990, pp. 1–2.

9. G. Cleveland Wilhoit and Dan G. Drew, "Profile of the North American Editorial Writer, 1971–1979," *The Masthead*, 31:10 (Winter 1979–80).

10. *Group Ownership Survey*, p. 16.

11. David Demers, "Corporate Newspaper Structure, Editorial Page Vigor and Social Change," *Journalism and Mass Communication Quarterly*, 73:862 (Winter 1996).

12. Ibid., pp. 868–70.

13. Roya Akhavan-Majid and Timothy Boudreau, "Chain Ownership, Organizational Size and Editorial Role Perceptions," *Journalism & Mass Communication Quarterly*, 72:863–73 (Winter 1995).

14. Robert T. Pittman, "How to Free Editorial Writers," *The Masthead*, 22:11 (Spring 1970).

15. Gilbert Cranberg, Randall Bezanson and John Soloski, *Taking Stock: Journalism and the Publicly Traded Newspaper Company* (Ames: Iowa State University Press, 2001), p. 10.

16. Cranberg, *Taking Stock*, p. 9.

17. Cranberg, *Taking Stock*, p. 11.

18. Cranberg, *Taking Stock*, p. 12.

19. Gilbert Cranberg, "Corporate ownership affects pages," *The Masthead*, 53:22–23 (Fall 2001).

20. David Halberstam, *The Powers That Be* (New York: Knopf, 1979), p. 573.

21. Katharine Graham, *Personal History* (New York: Knopf, 1997), p. 450.

22. Jon G. Udell, *The Economics of the American Newspaper* (New York: Hastings, 1978), p. 62.

23. Donald L. Breed, "Why Publishers Rarely Write Own Editorials," *The Masthead*, 14:22 (Fall 1962).

24. Suraj Kapoor, John Cragan and Irene Cooper, "Publishers' and Opinion-Page Editors' Political Perceptions: A Comparative Analysis," *The Masthead*, 42:7–14 (Winter 1990).

25. G. Cleveland Wilhoit and Dan G. Drew, "Profile of an Editorial Writer, 1971–88," *The Masthead*, 41:4–11 (Spring 1989).

26. Robinson Scott, cited in Kilgore, "A Publisher Looks."

27. Wilhoit and Drew, "Profile of an Editorial Writer."

28. Downey, "Editors and Publishers Should Fight."

29. David Holwerk, "Conflicts Are Inevitable—and Even Desirable," *The Masthead*, 42:18 (Winter 1990).

30. Suraj Kapoor and Janet Blue, "Editorial page editors still call the shots," *The Masthead*, 49:27-29 (Spring 1997).

31. Ed Williams, "The endorsement that wasn't," pp. 5–6.

32. Kenneth McArdle, "The Real Pressure Is to Make Sense," *The Masthead*, 22:8–9 (Spring 1970).

33. Kilgore, "A Publisher Looks."

34. Ibid.

35. Hoke Norris, "The Inside Dope," *The Masthead*, 8:55 (Spring 1956).

36. Frank W. Taylor, "Relations with the Publisher," *The Masthead*, 2:21 (Winter 1950).

37. Houstoun Waring, "Fertilizer for the Grass Roots," *The Masthead*, 4:12 (Spring 1952).

38. Nathaniel B. Blumberg, "Still Needed: A School for Publishers," *The Masthead*, 22:16 (Spring 1970).

39. Alan Kern, "Publisher Conflicts Not Often a Problem," *The Masthead*, 42:20–22 (Spring 1990).

40. Phil Duff, "'Yes, but . . .': Should the Publisher Be Involved in Civic Affairs?" *The Masthead*, 37:3 (Summer 1985).

41. Mindy Cameron, "When the publisher becomes a political activist," *The Masthead*, 51:6–7 (Spring 1999).

42. C.G. Wallace (Associated Press), "Publisher is bad news for newspaper," *Oregonian*, March 26, 2002.

43. Curtis D. MacDougall, "Our Opportunity to Educate or to Sabotage," *The Masthead*, 22:10 (Spring 1970).

44. Sam Reynolds, "It's Time We Blew the Whistle," *The Masthead*, 29:45 (Winter 1977).

45. Steve Parrott and Steve O'Neil, "Wall between Editorial, News Necessary, Most Editors Agree," *The Masthead*, 41:16-18 (Spring 1989).

46. Ibid.

47. "Needs info fast—please," online discussion, Feb. 26–27, 2002, NCEW-L.

48. Steve Parrott and Steve O'Neil, "Wall between Editorial, News," p. 17.

49. Patterson, "When Ownership Abdicates," p. 16.

50. Sevellon Brown III, "Setting Editorial Policy—Editors vs. Publishers," *The Masthead*, 7:22–24 (Summer 1955).

51. William H. Heath, "Editorial Policy," *The Masthead*, 19:66 (Summer 1967).

Chapter 7
Relations with the Newsroom

1. Clifford E. Carpenter, "When Reporters Speak Up," *The Masthead*, 12:30–32 (Spring 1960).

2. Steve Parrott and Steve O'Neill, "Wall between Editorial, News Necessary, Most Editors Agree," *The Masthead*, 41:16 (Spring 1989).

3. Edward M. Miller, "Take a Managing Editor to Lunch," *The Masthead*, 22:31–33 (Spring 1970).

4. Wilbur Elston, "The Editor Goes Status Seeking and Image Hunting," *The Masthead*, 15:1–18 (Fall 1963).

5. Parrott and O'Neill, "Wall between," p. 16.

6. Ellen Belcher, "Election offers insights from other side of the fence," *The Masthead*, 49:8–9 (Spring 1997).

7. William J. Woods, cited in Anonymous, "Policies and Politics," *The Masthead*, 11:43–44 (Summer 1959).

8. Parrott and O'Neill, "Wall between," p.17.

9. Desmond Stone, "How Does the News Staff Dissent?" *The Masthead*, 23:24–26 (Spring 1971).

10. Rufus Terral, "In Conference," *The Masthead*, 3:30 (Summer 1951).

11. Parrott and O'Neill, "Wall between," p. 17.

12. David Nasaw, *The Chief: The Life of William Randolph Hearst.* (Boston: Houghton Mifflin, 2000), pp. 558–561, 576.

13. Kevin Cash, *Who the hell is William Loeb?* (Manchester, N.H.: Amoskeag, 1957), p. 295.

14. Fred A. Stickel, "To the People of Oregon," *Oregonian*, Nov. 1, 1992.

15. Nathaniel B. Blumberg, "The Case against Front-Page Editorials," *The Masthead*, 8:17–20 (Summer 1959).

16. James J. Kilpatrick, "Why Not Throw Outworn Traditions Away?" *The Masthead*, 6:1–5 (Spring 1954).

17. James C. MacDonald, "'News' and 'Opinion' Get All Mixed Up," *The Masthead*, 6:21 (Summer 1954).

18. "Symposium, The Role of the Ombudsman/Media Critic," *The Masthead*, 28:3–15 (Spring 1976).

Chapter 8
The Editorial Page Staff

1. Lawrence J. Paul, "Many Papers Wretchedly Understaffed," *The Masthead*, 24:1 (Spring 1972).

2. Don Shoemaker, "Mine, by Damn, All Mine," *The Masthead*, 3:10 (Fall 1951).

3. G. Cleveland Wilhoit and Dan G. Drew, "Profile of the North American Editorial Writer," *The Masthead*, 31:10 (Winter 1979–80).

4. Paul, "Many Papers," p. 1.

5. Wilbur Elston, "Writers Need Topics, Not Orders," *The Masthead*, 28:10 (Spring 1976).

6. Shoemaker, "Mine."

7. Michael Loftin, "Dodging the Daily Boulder," *The Masthead,* 35:6 (Summer 1983).

8. Karli Jo Hunt, "Read, Read, Read, Clip, Clip, Clip," *The Masthead,* 35:9 (Summer 1983).

9. John G. McCullough, "Consulting Some Other Oracles," *The Masthead,* 28:5–6 (Spring 1976).

10. Hugh B. Patterson Jr., "When Ownership Abdicates Its Responsibility, News Suffers," *The Masthead,* 14:18 (Fall 1962).

11. Pat Murphy, "Fie on Conferences," *The Masthead,* 28:8–9 (Summer 1976).

12. Guy Kingsley, "Give everyone a chance to voice views," *The Masthead,* 52:3 (Fall 2000).

13. "Presidential hot air," *Register-Guard,* Feb. 19, 2002.

14. "What's a College Worth?" *Register-Guard,* Feb. 23, 2002.

15. Gilbert Cranberg, "Skull Sessions over Lunch," *The Masthead,* 28:10–11 (Summer 1976).

16. John H. Taylor Jr., "Get back to hands-on control," *The Masthead,* 44:32–33 (Fall 1992).

17. "How we spend our days," *The Masthead,* 48:22–25 (Winter 1996).

18. David E. Klement, "Who we are and what we do," *The Masthead,* 50:7 (Spring 1998).

Chapter 9
Relations with the Community

1. Susan Hegger, "Credibility Depends on Being Fair and Appearing Fair," *The Masthead,* 44:9 (Summer 1992).

2. Norman A. Cherniss, "In Defense of Virtue," *The Masthead,* 18:4 (Summer 1966).

3. G. Cleveland Wilhoit and Dan G. Drew, "Portrait of an Editorial Writer, 1971–88," *The Masthead,* 41:9 (Spring 1989).

4. David E. Klement, "Who we are and what we do," *The Masthead,* 50:7 (Fall 1998).

5. Wilhoit and Drew, "Portrait of an Editorial Writer," p. 6

6. James J. Kilpatrick, "How the Question Came Up," *The Masthead,* 18:2 (Spring 1996).

7. Laird B. Anderson, "A Few Thoughts on the 'Ethics Thing,'" *The Masthead,* 41:8–10 (Fall 1989).

8. Paul Greenberg, cited in Sue Ryon, "Editorial Writers Face Classic Dilemma," *The Masthead,* 42:32 (Winter 1990).

9. Lewis A. Leader, "Journalism and Joining Just Don't Mix," *The Masthead,* 44:5 Summer 1992).

10. Susan Hegger, "Credibility."

11. Van Cavett, "If Your Paper Supports a Position, Then You Can Too," *The Masthead,* 44:7–8 (Summer 1992).

12. Charles J. Dunsire, "Stay Away from Causes That Could Become a Topic." *The Masthead,* 44:7 (Summer 1992).

13. David Boeyink, "Anatomy of a Friendship," *The Masthead,* 41:7 (Fall 1989).

14. National Conference of Editorial Writers, "Basic Statement of Principles," *The Masthead,* 53:40 (Summer 2001).

15. H. Brandt Ayers, "Does a Plane Ticket Buy Your Soul?" *The Masthead,* 28:4–5 (Winter 1976).

16. John Causten Currey, "Is It Better to Nurture Ignorance?" *The Masthead,* 28: 4-5 (Winter 1976).

17. Smith Hempstone, "Self-Righteousness Gives Cold Comfort," *The Masthead,* 28:5–6 (Winter 1976).

18. Richard B. Laney, "Code Gives No Real Guidance," *The Masthead,* 28:6–7 (Winter 1976).

19. Robert Estabrook, "Those All-Expense Trips," *The Masthead,* 4:39–41 (Fall 1952).

20. Catherine Ford, "Ethics Are Expensive, But They're Well Worth the Price," *The Masthead,* 41:4 (Fall 1989).

21. Mark Clutter, "Don't Be Churlish," *The Masthead,* 12:5 (Spring 1960).

22. Jack Craemer, "One Who Refuses Feels Lonely," *The Masthead,* 12:8 (Spring 1960)

23. John Alexander, "Newspapers Took Different Roles as Corporate Citizens," *The Masthead,* 41:6–7 (Fall 1989).

24. Quoted in Fred Brown, "Civil journalism: still hanging on," *Quill,* 89:11 (April 2001).

25. Jan Schaffer, "Tell us your journalism story," *Civic Catalyst* (Winter 2002), p. 2.

26. Chris Peck, "Future news: It's more than just the facts," *Civic Catalyst* (Fall 2001), p. 10.

27. Quoted in William F. Woo, "Public journalism and the tradition of detachment," *The Masthead,* 47:16 (Fall 1995). (Adapted from a speech delivered in the *Press-*

Enterprise Series at the University of California at Riverside.)

28. Jay Rosen, *Community Connectedness Passwords for Public Journalism* (St. Petersburg, Fla.: Poynter Institute for Media Studies, 1993), frontispiece.

29. William F. Woo, "Public journalism," p. 20.

30. Phineas Fiske, online discussion, "Re: Mike Gartner," April 22, 1997, NCEW-L.

31. Paul S. Voukes, "Civic Duties: Newspaper Journalists' Views on Public Journalism," *Journalism and Mass Communication Quarterly*, 76:765 (Winter 1999).

32. Camille Kraeplin, "Public journalism: Is it on editorial turf?" *The Masthead*, 50:20–21 (Winter 1999).

Section 3   The How of the Editorial Page

Chapter 10
Nine Steps to Editorial Writing

1. Vermont Royster, "Parsley and Pot-Boiled Potatoes," *The Masthead,* 8:38 (Fall 1956).

2. David Horowitz, "Racial McCarthyism on College Campuses," *San Francisco Chronicle*, March 26, 2001.

3. David Hernandez, "Daily Cal Editor Caught between an Ad and an Apology *San Francisco Chronicle*, March 15, 2001.

4. George Comstock, Steven Chafee, Natan Katzman, Maxwell McCombs and Donald Roberts, *Television and Human Behavior* (New York: Columbia University Press, 1978), pp. 318-28.

5. Werner J. Severin and James K. Tankard Jr., *Communication Theories* (New York: Hastings, 1979), p. 248.

6. Wilbur Schramm and William E. Porter, *Men, Women, Messages and Media*, 2nd ed., (New York: Harper, 1982), pp. 110–11.

7. Elsa Mohn and Maxwell McCombs, "Who Reads Us and Why," *The Masthead,* 32:21 (Winter 1980-81).

8. W. Phillips Davison, James Boylan and Frederick T.C. Yu, *Mass Media*, 2nd ed. (New York: Holt, Rinehart and Winston, 1982), p. 173.

9. Alexis S. Tan, *Communication Theories and Research* (Columbus, Ohio: Grid, 1981), p. 103.

10. Schramm and Porter, *Men, Women*, p. 188.

11. Tan, *Mass Communication Theories*, p. 149.

12. Henry M. Keezing, "Who Are Your Brothers?" *The Masthead*, 8:47 (Spring 1956).

13. James J. Kilpatrick, "Editorials and Editorial Writing," *The Masthead*, 5:5–6 (Spring 1953).

14. David Hernandez, "Daily Cal Editor Caught Between an Ad and an Apology."

15. David Horowitz, "Racial McCarthyism on College Campuses."

16. Joseph Anderson, "The Issue Is Racism," *San Francisco Chronicle*, March 26, 2001.

17. Bob Wieder, "Reparations Hustle," *San Francisco Chronicle*, March 26, 2001.

18. Tan, *Mass Communication Theories*, p. 140.

19. Schramm and Porter, *Men, Women*, p. 196.

20. Ibid.

21. Tan, *Mass Communication Theories*, p. 139.

22. Davison, Boylan and Yu, *Mass Media*, p. 190.

Chapter 11
Ten Steps to Better Writing

1. James J. Kilpatrick, "Editorials and Editorial Writing," *The Masthead*, 5:5 (Spring 1953).

2. Vermont Royster, cited in Harry Boyd, "They Write by Ear," *The Masthead*, 8:31 (Fall 1956).

3. R. Thomas Berner, "Let's Get Rid of Those Pesky Pronouns," *The Masthead*, 31:32 (Summer 1979).

4. Galen R. Rarick, "The Writing That Writers Write Best," *The Masthead*, 21:3–5 (Winter 1969-70).

5. Rudolph Flesch, *The Art of Readable Writing* (New York: Harper, 1949) and *How to Test Readability* (New York: Harper, 1951).

6. Francis P. Locke, "Too Much Flesch on the Bones?" *The Masthead*, 11:3–6 (Spring 1959).

7. "Countering racial, ethnic and religious profiling," *Quill*, 89:38 (November 2001).

8. Cited in "Words Have Disabling Power," *Roanoke Times & World-News*, August 23, 1992.

9. Judy E. Pickens, ed., *Without Bias: A Guidebook for Nondiscriminatory Communication* (New York: Wiley, 1992).

10. Kilpatrick, "Editorials and Editorial Writing," p. 4.

Chapter 12
Subjects That Are Hard to Write About

1. Creed Black, "Government Is Great, But—," *The Masthead*, 19:23 (Summer 1967).
2. Lauren K. Soth, "How to Write Understandable Editorials about Economics," *The Masthead*, 6:19 (Winter 1954).
3. Linda Seebach, "Yes, journalists can too do economics," *The Masthead*, 50:4 (Winter 1998).
4. Ibid.
5. Stein B. Haughlid, "Make international editorials relate to local issues," *The Masthead*, 48:8 (Spring 1996).
6. Joe Geshwiler, "Find the connection," *The Masthead*, 48:9 (Spring 1996).
7. Aubrey Bowie, "The Arts Need Same Zeal as Sewers," *The Masthead*, 41:23 (Fall 1989).
8. "The care and feeding of culture," Minneapolis (Minn.) *Star Tribune*, Oct. 7, 2001.
9. "Energize Oregon arts—Now's the time for Legislature to act," Eugene (Ore.) *Register-Guard*, April 14, 2002.
10. D. Michael Heywood, "Health Care Can Be Lethal to Editorial Writing," *The Masthead*, 43:8 (Fall 1991).
11. Susan Willey, "Journalism and religion," *Quill*, 85:29 (January–February 1996).
12. "Shooting preserves," Minneapolis, Minn., *Star Tribune*, April 18, 2000.
13. Tony Cavarno, "Knows what is right," June 2, 2001.
14. Quoted in Kathryn S. Wenner, "No Wonder It Won a Pulitzer," *American Journalism Review*, 23:17 (June 2001).

Chapter 13
Subjects That Are Deceptively Easy

1. James E. Casto, "Holiday of Headaches," *The Masthead*, 35:15 (Fall 1983).
2. "Pedestrian nightmare," *Providence* (R.I.) *Journal*, October 7, 2000.
3. Mike Heywood, "Earth Day," online discussion, April 17–18, 1997, NCEW-L.
4. Lauren K. Soth, "From Alpha to Omega," *The Masthead*, 20:3 (Spring 1969).
5. Richard B. Childs, "When You Can't Pass the Buck," *The Masthead*, 29:3–4 (Summer 1977).

6. Kyle Thompson, "A Wish List on Christmas Day," *The Masthead*, 35:17 (Fall 1983).
7. Ann Lloyd Merriman, "It Helps to Be Prepared," *The Masthead*, 35:6 (Fall 1983).
8. Elissa Papirno, "The Holiday Problem," *The Masthead*, 35:13–14 (Fall 1983).
9. Joanna Wragg, "Relying on Traditional Material," *The Masthead*, 35:9-11 (Fall 1983).

Chapter 14
Subjects That Are Neglected

1. David Jarmul, "Ain't Science Articles Fascinating?" *The Masthead*, 39:15 (Summer 1987).
2. David Jarmul and Leah D. Fine, "Science rare topic of editorial pages," *The Masthead*, 45:10–11 (Winter 1993).
3. Ben Bagdikian, "Editorial Pages Changing—But Too Slowly," *The Masthead*, 17:20 (Winter 1965-66).
4. Andy Rooney, "Editorial Pages Are Better Off without Humor," *The Masthead*, 43:9 (Summer 1991).
5. Nordahl Flakstad, "It's No Laughing Matter, But There's Still Room for Humor," *The Masthead*, 43:7–8 (Summer 1991).
6. Rick Horowitz, "Call Me Irresponsible?" *The Masthead*, 43:8 (Summer 1991).
7. Rick Horowitz, "He missed the point-but I'm the target," *The Masthead*, 45:8 (Winter 1993)
8. Mark L. Genrich, "Down with Fruitcakes," *The Masthead*, 39:5–6 (Spring 1987).
9. Joseph Plummer, "Use It Selectively," *The Masthead*, 39:10 (Spring 1987).

Chapter 15
Editorials on Elections

1. Elizabeth Bird, "Kingmaker or Informer?" *The Masthead*, 40:35–36 (Summer 1988).
2. Peter Lyman, "Elections and endorsements," *The Masthead*, 52:7 (Spring 2000).
3. "To Endorse, Or Not," *Editor & Publisher*, Oct. 26, 1996, p. 4.
4. "Paid Ads or Endorsements?" Letter to the Editor, *Daily News*, Longview, Wash., date unknown.
5. Ken D. Davis, cited in "Candidate Endorsements: Who, When and Why: A Complaint and a Reply," *The Masthead*, 20:19 (Summer 1968).

6. Dick Timmons, "Forget endorsements," *Editor & Publisher*, 147:9 (Aug. 10, 1996).

7. Hugh B. Culbertson and Guido H. Stempel III, "Public Attitudes about Coverage and Awareness of Editorial Endorsements," in Guido H. Stempel III and John W. Windhauser, eds., *The Media in 1984 and 1988 Elections* (Westport, Conn: Greenwood Press, 1991), pp. 187-99.

8. Peter Kohler, "FCC rules give pause to advocacy," *The Masthead*, 52:14 (Spring 2000).

9. Thomas J. Lucente Jr., online discussion, "Endorsements," Nov. 12, 2001, NCEW-L.

10. Jackman Wilson, online discussion, "Endorsements," Nov. 12, 2001, NCEW-L.

11. James G. Lakely, online discussion, "Endorsements," Nov. 12, 2001, NCEW-L.

12. Cited in "Candidate Endorsements: Who, When and Why."

13. Dave Kushma, "Plan carefully and enjoy the rewards," *The Masthead*, 52:9 (Spring 2000).

14. "To Endorse, Or Not," p. 4.

15. Jackman Wilson, online discussion, "Endorsements," Nov. 12, 2001, NCEW-L.

16. Michael Smith, online discussion, "Endorsements," Nov. 12, 2001, NCEW-L.

17. John H. Taylor Jr., online discussion, "Endorsements," Nov. 12, 2001, NCEW-L.

18. Mike Smith, Ibid.

19. Jeffrey M. Brody, Ibid.

20. Ronald D. Clark, "Assessing candidates," *The Masthead*, 52:8–9 (Spring 2000).

21. "Electronic report focuses on editorial front," *The Masthead*, 49:13-17 (Spring 1997).

22. "Electronic report," p. 15.

23. Ed Williams, "Skip exercises in editorial masochism," *The Masthead*, 45:7 (Spring 1993).

24. Richard Mial, "Small communities require careful endorsements," *The Masthead*, 52:12-13 (Spring 2000).

25. Frank Luther Mott, "Has the Press Lost Its Punch?" *The Rotarian*, Oct. 1952, p. 13.

26. Nathaniel B. Blumberg, *One-Party Press?* (Lincoln: University of Nebraska Press, 1954), p. 11.

27. George Comstock, Steven Chafee, Natan Katzman, Maxwell McCombs and Donald Roberts, *Television and Human Behavior* (New York: Columbia University Press, 1978), pp. 136, 319–28.

28. "Electronic report," p. 14.

29. Cited in Bruce Davidson, "A book for devout campaign workers," *The Masthead*, 52:17 (Winter 2000).

30. Fred Fedler, "To Endorse or Not to Endorse," *The Masthead*, 36:26 (Summer 1984).

31. Kenneth Rystrom, "The Impact of Newspaper Endorsements," *Newspaper Research Journal*, 7:19–28 (Winter 1986).

32. Kenneth Rystrom, "Apparent Impact of Endorsements by Group and Independent Newspapers," *Journalism Quarterly*, 63:449–53, 532.

33. Fred Fedler, Ron F. Smith and Tim Counts, "Voter Uses and Perceptions of Editorial Endorsements," *Newspaper Research Journal*, 6:20 (Summer 1983).

34. Ruth Ann Weaver-Lariscy and Spencer F. Tinkham, "News Coverage, Endorsements and Personal Campaigning: The Influence of Non-Paid Activities in Congressional Campaigns," *Journalism Quarterly*, 68:442–43 (Fall 1991).

35. Quoted in Robert Neuwirth, "Political quandary: Have publishers lost influence over editorial endorsements?" *Editor & Publisher*, 149:12 (Jan. 17, 1998).

36. Byron St. Dizier, "Republican Endorsements, Democratic Positions: An Editorial Page Contradiction," *Journalism Quarterly*, 63:581–86 (Fall 1986).

37. John J. Zakarian, "Speaking of Elections: Sacred Cows of the Highest Order," *The Masthead*, 25:3 (Spring 1973).

38. St. Dizier, "Republican Endorsements."

39. Robert J. White, "Endorsement Process Became an Election Issue," *The Masthead*, 43:6 (Spring 1991).

40. Douglas J. Rooks, "Given a Chance, Candidates Take Issues Seriously," *The Masthead*, 43:14 (Spring 1991).

41. Mindy Cameron, "Share the Process and Remove Presumptuous Arrogance," *The Masthead*, 43:8–9 (Spring 1991).

42. Cecilie Gaziano, "Chain Newspaper Homogeneity and President Endorsements, 1972–1988," *Journalism Quarterly*, 66:836–45 (Winter 1989).

43. John C. Busterna and Kathleen A. Hansen, "Presidential Endorsement Patterns by Chain-Owned Papers, 1976–84," *Journalism Quarterly*, 67:286-94 (Summer 1990).

44. Roya Akhavan-Majid, Anita Rife and Sheila Gopinath, "Chain Ownership and Editorial Independence: A Case Study of Gannett Newspapers," *Journalism Quarterly,* 68:59–66 (Spring/Summer 1991).

45. Quoted in Dorothy Giobbe, "Endorsements—Influential or irrelevant?" *The Masthead,* 52:9 (Spring 2000).

Chapter 16
Other Types of Opinion Writing

1. John Beatty, cited in Anonymous, "Broadcast Editorials: A Dying Breed in a Ripe Market," *Quill,* 80:37 (July–August 1992).

2. William L. Rivers, *Writing Opinion: Reviews* (Ames: Iowa State University Press, 1988), p. 24.

3. Steve Duin, "Bambi fawns as Godzilla trims the fat," *Oregonian,* Oct. 25, 2001; "Aimless and hapless in the face of adversity," *Oregonian,* Oct. 28, 2001.

4. Margie Boule, "A brother relives the pain after finding lost sibling," *Oregonian,* Oct. 23, 2001; "True or false? After Sept. 11, e-mail grabs imagination," *Oregonian,* Oct. 25, 2001; "Nonprofits choke on Portland schools' rent increases," *Oregonian,* Oct. 28, 2001.

5. Karen McCowan, "Gang has more business links," *Register-Guard,* Oct. 26, 2001; Charles Munger, "Purifying the 'public,'" *Register-Guard,* Nov.1, 2001.

6. Bob Welch, "The world is still imperfect," *Register-Guard,* Oct. 28, 2001; John Daniel, "Focusing the picture," *Register-Guard,* Nov. 1, 2001.

7. Laura Reina, "Why Movie Blurbs Avoid Newspapers," *Editor & Publisher,* Aug. 31, 1996.

8. Martin F. Kohn, "Slaves' story: Good history, labored drama," *Detroit Free Press,* Jan. 30, 2002.

9. Christine Dolen, "'Proposals' is second-rate Simon," *Miami Herald,* Jan. 29, 2002.

10. Melinda Bargreen, "Heart-wrenching horn solo uplifts Tchaikovsky's 5th," *Seattle Times,* Feb. 9, 2002.

11. Gerry Kowarsky, "1940s Radio Hour," *St. Louis Post-Dispatch,* Oct. 12, 2000.

12. Gordon Cox, "A long day's journey into grief," *Newsday,* Jan. 28, 2002.

13. Christine Dolen, "Proposals."

14. Douglas J. Keating, "Overlong play, obscure protagonist: Not much fun," *Philadelphia Inquirer,* Feb. 11, 2002.

15. Kyle Lawson, "Enthusiastic 'Brides' cast true to movie," Phoenix *Arizona Republic,* Jan. 9, 2002.

16. Marion Garmel, "'Tomorrow' dawns slowly before shining," *Indianapolis Star,* Jan. 29, 2002.

17. William L. Rivers, *Writing Opinion: Reviews,* (Ames: Iowa State University Press, 1988), p. 56.

18. Tim Bywater and Thomas Sobchack, *Introduction to Film Criticism* (New York: Longman, 1989). Other types of reviews include the genre, social science, historical and ideological/theoretical.

19. Ibid., p. 3.

20. Irving Wardle, *Theater Criticism* (London: Routledge, 1992), p. 4.

21. Ibid., p. 14.

22. Boyd A. Levet, "Editorials and the Business of Broadcasting," *The Editorialist,* 17:7 (Spring 1991).

23. G. Donald Gale, "The Need for Broadcast Editorials," *The Masthead,* 40:37–38 (Spring 1988).

24. Daniel H. Toohey, cited in Howard W. Kleiman, "Unshackled but Unwilling: Public Broadcast and Editorializing," *Journalism Quarterly,* 64:708 (Winter 1987).

25. David Spiceland, "Research finds broadcast editorials continue to wane," *The Masthead,* 46:15 (Winter 1994).

26. David Spiceland, "Survey examines broad cast editorials," *The Masthead,* 50:32 (Winter 1999).

27. Beaty, "Broadcast Editorials," p. 37.

28. Cited in Neil Heinen, "It's gloves off for broadcast laggards," *The Masthead,* 51:23 (Fall 1999).

29. Neil Heinen, Ibid.

30. David Spiceland, "Survey examines broad cast editorials," p. 32.

31. Tom Bryson, "Seek out, encourage broad casters." *The Masthead,* 50:34 (Fall 1998).

32. David Spiceland, "Survey examines broad cast editorials," p. 32.

33. Jill Olmsted, "Whatever happened to network commentary?" *The Masthead,* 44:8 (Winter 1992).

34. Tom Bettag, cited in Ibid.

35. Ibid., p. 9.

36. John Beaty, "Broadcast Editorials," p. 37.

37. Frank Stanton, cited in Kleiman, "Unshackled but Unwilling," p. 713.

38. Robert Logan, "TV vs. Print," *The Masthead*, 37:11–25 (Summer 1985).

39. Phil Johnson, cited in Ibid., p 19.

40. Lesley Crosson, cited in Ibid., p. 21.

41. Robert S. McCord, "Move from print to broadcast brings surprises," *The Masthead*, 46:15–16 (Winter 1994).

Chapter 17
Letters to the Editor

1. Kay Semion, "Masthead Symposium: Letters, Epistles and Cards," *The Masthead*, 53:4 (Summer 2001).

2. Barry Bingham Sr. in "Dear Sir You Cur!" *The Masthead*, 3:38 (Fall 1951).

3. Fred Holzweiss, "First letter leads to 90-plus per year," *The Masthead*, 53:19 (Summer 2001).

4. Suraj Kapoor, "Most papers receive more letters," *The Masthead*, 47:18-21 (Spring 1995).

5. "Creating a lively letters page," *The Masthead*, 53: 5-6 (Summer 2001).

6. "Letters Box Score," Eugene, Ore., *Register-Guard*, March 18, 2001.

7. "Letters Log," *Oregonian*, March 17, 2001.

8. Keith Carter, "Successful Letters Column Requires Ongoing Effort," *The Masthead*, 44:10 (Spring 1992).

9. Robert Bohle, "Just Running Letters Is Not Enough," *The Masthead*, 43:10–13 (Spring 1991).

10. Sue O'Brien, "Set priorities," *The Masthead*, 53:5 (Summer 2001).

11. O'Brien, Ibid.

12. Barry Rascovar, "Edit lightly," *The Masthead*, 53:5 (Summer 2001).

13. Dale A. Davenport, "Play up letters," *The Masthead*, 53:6–7 (Summer 2001).

14. Lisa A. Hoff, "Use empathy with writers," *The Masthead*, 53:6 (Summer 2001).

15. Irene Portnoy, "Go the extra mile," *The Masthead*, 53:6 (Summer 2001).

16. Rascovar, "Editing Lightly," p. 5.

17. Susan Nielson, "The envelope, please," *The Masthead*, 53:7 (Summer 2001).

18. Bill Williams and David Medina, "Why Women Don't Write," *The Masthead*, 53:8-9 (Summer 2001)

19. Williams and Medina, "Why Women Don't Write," p. 10.

20. Suraj Kapoor and Carl Boton, "Studies Compare How Editors Use Letters," *The Masthead*, 44:5–7 (Spring 1992).

21. Davenport, "Play up Letters," p. 6.

22. John R. Markham, "A Letter Is a Dangerous Thing," *The Masthead*, 5:18–19 (Fall 1953).

23. James J. Kilpatrick, cited in Markham, "A Letter Is a Dangerous Thing," p. 20.

24. Glenn Sheller, "Dogma if you do, damned if you don't," *The Masthead*, 46:25 (Summer 1994).

25. "To participate in these pages," Minneapolis, Minn., *Star Tribune*, Aug. 20, 2000.

26. "Letters Guidelines," Canton, Ohio, *Repository*, Aug. 11, 2001.

27. M. Carl Andrews, "Pity the Poor Editor without Letters," *The Masthead*, 20:12 (Fall 1968).

28. Carol Suplee, "A Problem," *The Masthead*, 39:32 (Winter 1987).

29. Kapoor, "Most papers receive more letters," p. 19.

30. Charles Towne, "The Trouble with Letters Is Editors," *The Masthead*, 28:9 (Fall 1976).

31. Wally Hoffman, "Keep a Balance," *The Masthead*, 40:5–6 (Spring 1988).

32. Phil Fretz, "Don't Run 'em," *The Masthead*, 40:6 (Spring 1988).

33. Marc Franklin, "Letters and Libel," *The Masthead*, 40:10–13 (Spring 1988).

34. Steve Pasternack, "Dear Editor—Print This at Your Own Risk," *The Masthead*, 36:5–6 (Spring 1984).

35. Clifford E. Carpenter, "The Letter Litter, Its Dangers and Potentials," *The Masthead*, 19:80 (Summer 1967).

36. Palmer Hoyt, "A Publisher Looks at Editorial Writing," *The Masthead*, 6:49 (Spring 1954).

37. Franklin Smith, "Who Elected the *Times?*" *The Masthead*, 23:34 (Summer 1971).

38. Andrews, "Pity the Editor without Letters," p. 13.

Chapter 18
Columns and Cartoons

1. Edwin M. Yoder Jr., "In 40 Years, a Sea Change," *The Masthead*, 38:12–13 (Fall 1986).

2. Joe Rodriguez, "Why I write columns," *The Masthead*, 51:24 (Summer 1999).

3. Sam G. Riley, *The American Newspaper Columnist* (New York: Praeger, 1998)

4. Ibid.

5. Michael Emery and Edwin Emery, *The Press and America*, 6th ed. (Englewood Cliffs, N.J.: Prentice-Hall, 1988), p. 368.

6. W.A. Swanberg, *Citizen Hearst* (New York: Scribner's, 1961), p. 483.

7. Riley, *The American Newspaper Columnist.*

8. Ibid.

9. Robert H. Estabrook, "Their Varied Views Are Important," *The Masthead*, 10:22–24 (Fall 1958).

10. Mark Ethridge, "The Come-Back of Editorial Pages," *The Masthead*, 18:28–32 (Summer 1966).

11. Yoder, "In 40 Years."

12. John Gioffo, "Art Buchwald: Common wisdom," *Columbia Journalism Review*, 40:92 (November–December 2001).

13. Scott Sherman, "The rise of the conservative voice," *Columbia Journalism Review*, 40:84–85 (November–December 2001).

14. Ethridge, "The Come-Back of Editorial Pages."

15. William Safire, "U.S. government stays quiet on Iraq's link to bin Laden," Eugene, Ore., *Register-Guard*, Oct. 23, 2001.

16. Yoder, "In 40 Years."

17. "Cal Thomas in select 500 club for columnists, " *Editor & Publisher*, 150:44 (May 8, 1999).

18. Dave Astor, "Mapping both sides of ideologic divide," *Editor & Publisher*, 153:28 (April 1, 2002).

19. Ibid.

20. Ernest C. Hynds, "Editorial Pages Remain Vital," *The Masthead*, 27:19–22 (Fall 1975).

21. Frank Wetzel, "Territorial Exclusivity Is Attached," *The Masthead*, 30:3–4 (Winter 1978).

22. Mark Fitzgerald, "Exclusivity Gets Upheld by Court," *Editor & Publisher*, December 28, 1996.

23. Lauren Soth, "Conflicts of Interest by Political Writer, Editor," *Des Moines Register*, Nov. 29, 1973.

24. National News Council, "Findings of the National News Council," *The Masthead* 26:53 (Fall 1974).

25. Robert Schulman, "The Opinion Merchants," *The Masthead*, 32:21 (Spring 1980).

26. Gilbert Cranberg, "What syndicates owe to their editors," *The Masthead* 47:36–37 (Fall 1995).

27. Gilbert Cranberg, "One-time disclosure misses the point," *The Masthead* 48:9 (Summer 1996).

28. Roy Paul Nelson, "Looking at history through cartoonist eyes," *Register-Guard*, March 3, 2002.

29. Robert Van Ommeren, Daniel Rife and Don Sneed, "What Is the Cartoonist's Role?" *The Masthead*, 36:12–15 (Spring, 1984).

30. Ommeren, Rife and Sneed, "What Is the Cartoonist's Role?" p. 14.

31. Chris Lamb and Nancy Brendlinger, "Drawing Conclusions: Are Cartoonists and Editors on the Same Page?" paper presented at the annual meeting of the Southeast Colloquium, Association for Education in Journalism and Mass Communication, Roanoke, Va., March 15, 1996, p. 22.

32. Ommeren, Rife and Sneed, "What Is the Cartoonist's Role?" p. 13.

33. Lamb and Brendlinger, "Drawing Conclusions," p. 23.

34. David Astor, "The battle, him and the 'Republic,'" *Editor & Publisher*, Oct. 29, 2001, p. 25.

35. Quoted in Signe Wilkinson, "Editors, cartoonists learn to coexist," *The Masthead*, 47:28 (Winter 1995).

36. Ibid.

37. Thomas Gebhardt, "A Gamble Paid Off," *The Masthead*, 40:7 (Fall 1988).

38. Jim Borgman, "No trench warfare," *The Masthead*, 40:8 (Fall 1988).

39. Dick Herman, "Facts Is Facts," *The Masthead*, 40:7–8 (Fall 1988); Paul Fell, "The Self-Imposed Limits of My Cage," *The Masthead* 40:9 (Fall 1988).

40. Draper Hill, "Cartoonists Are Younger—and Better," *The Masthead* 38:14–17 (Fall 1986).

41. Cited in David Astor, "Cartooning Views from Non-Artists," *Editor & Publisher,* July 13, 1966, p. 24.

42. Chris Lamb and Nancy Brendlinger, "Drawing Conclusions."

43. Quoted in David Astor, "Another Major Newspaper Fires a Political Cartoonist," *Editor & Publisher,* Oct. 29, 1994, p. 33, cited in Lamb and Brendlinger, "Drawing Conclusions."

44. David Astor, "Cartoonists without a Hometown Newspaper," *Editor & Publisher,* May 18, 1996, pp. 40–41.

45. John G. Finneman, *Drawing Fire: The State of Political Cartooning.* (Reston, Va.: American Press Institute, 1998), p. 8.

46. Cited in Alan Vitiello, "In defense of editorial cartoonists," *Editor & Publisher,* July 20, 1996.

47. David Astor, "Another Major Newspaper Fires a Political Cartoonist," p. 33.

48. Pat Oliphant, quoted in Finneman, *Drawing Fire,* p. 34.

49. Steve Benson, quoted in Finneman, *Drawing Fire,* p. 38.

50. Cited in David Astor, "Cartooning Views from Non-Artists," p. 24.

51. Stephen Hess, quoted in Finneman, *Drawing Fire,* p. 4.

52. Ibid.

53. Mark McGuire, "In times of crisis, comics leave some readers fuming," Eugene, Ore., *Register-Guard,* Oct. 29, 2001.

54. Maurice Horn, editor, *The World Encyclopedia of Comics.* (New York: Chelsea, 1976), p. 459.

55. Ibid., p. 154.

56. Bill Blackbeard and Martin Williams, eds., *The Smithsonian Collection of Newspaper Cartoons* (Washington, D.C.: Smithsonian Institution Press, 1977), pp. 328–33.

57. Eric Schmitt and James Dao, "A 'Damaged' Information Office Is Declared Closed by Rumsfield," *New York Times,* Feb. 27, 2002.

58. Jonathan Kandell, "Boss," *Smithsonian,* 32:89 (February 2002).

59. Gebhardt, "A Gamble Paid Off."

60. Fell, "The Self-Imposed Limits."

61. "Editorial Cartoonist Goes Audio/Fax," *Quill,* 80:4 (October 1992).

62. Ron Cunningham, "Want cartoons? Try asking for them," *The Masthead* 45:17-18 (Spring 1993).

63. Nicole Kirby, "Stability in the midst of change," *Community Newspaper Showcase of Excellence* (1995), p. 21.

64. A. Rosen, Discussion Session, American Press Institute, Columbia University, May 1972.

Chapter 19
Innovations in Design and Content

1. Ralph J. Turner, cited in Anonymous, "Professor Gives Tips on Improving Appearances of Editorial Pages," *SNPA Bulletin,* January 3, 1990.

2. Robert Bohle, "Most Pages Have Resisted Change," *The Masthead,* 38:18–21 (Fall 1986).

3. Quoted in Ibid.

4. John E. Allen, *Newspaper Makeup* (New York: Harper, 1936), p. 332.

5. Miles E. Tinker, *Legibility in Print* (Ames: Iowa State University Press, 1963), pp. 74–107.

6. Ernest C. Hynds, "Pages join design revolution," *The Masthead,* 48:19–21 (Winter 1996).

7. Susan Albright, e-mail letter to the author, April 23, 1997.

8. Cited in Ibid.

9. "Your View," Saint John, N.B., *Telegraph-Journal,* Sept. 27, 2000.

10. "What Do YOU Think?" Boise *Idaho Statesman,* Sept. 1, 2001.

11. "Cheaters unable to cover tracks," *Atlanta Journal-Constitution,* Jan. 17. 2002.

12. "Question of the Moment," Cleveland, Ohio, *Plain Dealer,* Aug. 11, 2001.

13. *Billings* (Mont.) *Gazette,* Aug. 16, 2001.

14. "Talking It Over," *Roanoke* (Va.) *Times,* Feb. 5, 2002.

15. "Golden Pen," Spokane, Wash., *Spokesman-Review,* Oct. 8, 2001.

16. "Journalism Interactive," *Civic Catalyst,* Summer 2001, p. 12.

17. "What Others Think," Vero Beach, Fla., *Press Journal,* Aug. 18, 1999.

18. "Question of the Week," Portland *Maine Sunday Telegram,* Sept. 24, 2000.

19. Sig Gissler, "A Forum for Our Readers," *The Masthead*, 23:31–32 (Spring 1971).

20. "Guest Opinion," Nampa *Idaho Press-Tribune*, July 12, 2001.

21. "Maine Magazine," Portland *Maine Sunday Telegram*, Sept. 24, 2000.

22. "Fresh Voices," *Newsday*, July 30, 2001.

23. "Reader's View," Boise *Idaho Statesman*, July 30, 2001.

24. "Talk Back," Idaho Falls, Idaho, *Post Register*, Aug. 8, 2001.

25. Richard Hughes, online discussion, "Editorial Boards," Feb. 5, 1997, NCEW-L.

26. "Advisory board seeks members," *News Journal*, Feb. 12, 2000.

27. George Neavoll, "Community input walks in the door every day," *The Masthead*, 47:7 (Summer 1995).

28. E.W. Kieckhefer, "Taking orders from customers runs contrary to great tradition," *The Masthead*, 48:16 (Summer 1996).

29. Dave Astor, "Free-lance column usage on the rise?" *Editor & Publisher*, 135:16 (March 4, 2002).

30. Ibid.

31. Robert T. Pittmann, "Ten Best Bets for Edit Pages," *The Masthead*, 23:33–34 (Spring 1971).

32. *St. Paul* (Minn.) *Pioneer Press*, Jan. 28, 2002.

33. Portland *Oregonian*, Jan. 4, 2002.

34. Kenneth Stark and Julie Eisele, "Newspaper ombudsmanship as viewed by ombudsmen and their editors," *Newspaper Research Journal*, 20:37 (Fall 1999).

35. Paul K. Harral, online discussion, "Ombudsman," Oct. 12, 2001, NCEW-L.

36. Kenneth Stark and Julie Eisele, "Newspaper Ombudsman."

37. "People and Places," *Quill*, 90:43–44 (January–February 2002).

38. Kenneth Stark and Julie Eisele, "Newspaper Ombudsman."

39. Gilbert Cranberg and Kenneth Stark, "Complaint department out to lunch," *Editor & Publisher*, Aug. 1, 1998, p. 32, cited in Kenneth Stark and Julie Eisele, "Newspaper Ombudsman," p. 47.

40. Barbara Marquand, "Watchdogs or PR flacks? The Rare Ombudsman," *Editor & Publisher*, March 7, 1998, p. 17, cited in

Kenneth Stark and Julie Eisele, "Newspaper Ombudsman," p. 47.

41. Michael Getler, "The art of the obit," *Washington Post*, Feb. 10, 2002.

42. Lou Gelford, "Report on arrest should have included information about outstanding warrants," *Star Tribune*, Aug. 20, 2000.

43. Dave Kopel, "Real censorship story was buried," *Rocky Mountain News*, July 1, 2001.

44. Portland *Oregonian*, Jan. 10, 2002.

45. Wilmington, Del., *News Journal*, Feb. 12, 2000.

46. St. John, N.B., *Telegraph-Journal*, Sept. 27, 2000.

47. Denver *Rocky Mountain News*, June 30, 2001.

48. *Kennebec* (Maine) *Journal*, Sept. 26, 2000.

49. Ernest C. Hynds, "Editorial pages become more useful," *The Masthead*, 47:40 (Fall 1995).

50. "Davis tackles gambling growth," *Sacramento* (Calif.) *Bee*, June 25, 2001.

51. "Cheers & Jeers," Nampa *Idaho Press-Tribune*, July 2, 2001.

52. Richard Aregood, "Adios, Dictator," *Philadelphia Daily News*, 1975.

53. John McClelland, online discussion, "Short Editorials," Feb. 5, 2002, NCEW-L.

54. Henny Willis, online discussion, "Short Editorials," Feb. 4, 2002, NCEW-L.

55. Howard Ziff, online discussion, "Short Editorials," Feb. 5, 2002, NCEW-L.

56. "Access to the channel," *Boston Globe*, Sept. 19, 2000.

57. "Lear theatre tour: Time to look, help," *Reno Gazette*, Sept. 19, 2000.

58. *Litchfield County Times*, June 25, 2001.

59. "Dear John," *Detroit Free Press*, Jan. 22, 2001.

60. "Freeing Sex Offenders," Denver, Colo., *Rocky Mountain News*, July 1, 2001.

61. "Klan propaganda not fit for library," Greensboro, N.C., *News & Record*, Jan. 18, 2002.

62. "A catch-up plan for campus construction," *Roanoke* (Va.) *Times*, Jan. 19, 2002.

63. *Rockford* (Ill.) *Register Star*, Jan. 18, 2002.

64. Danbury, Conn., *News-Times*, Oct. 6, 2000.

65. Paul S. Voukes, "Civic Duties: Newspaper Journalists' Views on Public Journalism,"

Journalism and Mass Communication Quarterly, 76:765 (Winter 1999).

66. Judith Sheppard, "Climbing down from the ivory tower," *The Masthead,* 47:7 (Fall 1995).

67. John Webster, "Spokane experiments with change," *The Masthead,* 48:14-17 (Fall 1996).

68. John Webster, email to Kenneth Rystrom, Feb. 14, 2002.

69. John Webster, letter to Kenneth Rystrom, Feb. 20, 2002.

70. John Webster, email to Kenneth Rystrom, Feb. 14, 2002.

71. Ron Clark, "Letting go of daily editorials," *The Masthead,* 48:12-14 (Summer 1996).

72. Ron Clark, email to Kenneth Rystrom, March 1, 2002.

73. Ibid.

74. Andrea Neal, "'Star' is conservative *and* balanced," *The Masthead,* 54:27 (Spring 2002).

75. Quoted in "What's happening in Pew projects," *Civic Catalyst* (Winter 2002), p. 11.

76. Ibid.

77. Andrea Neal, "'Star' is conservative *and* balanced,"

78. Quoted in "What's happening in Pew projects," p. 10.

79. Quoted in E.J. Kahn, Jr., *The World of Swope* (New York: Simon and Schuster, 1965), p. 260.

80. Quoted in Norman J. Radder and John E. Stempel, *Newspaper Editing: Makeup and Headlines* (New York: McGraw-Hill, 1942), pp. 332–33.

81. Harrison E. Salisbury, "An Extra Dimension in This Complicated World," *The Masthead,* 23:29–31 (Spring 1971).

82. David Shaw, "Newspapers Offer Forum to Outsiders," *Los Angeles Times,* Oct. 13, 1975.

83. Andrew Ciafalo and Kim Traverso, "Does the op-ed page have a chance to become a community forum?" *Newspaper Research Journal,* 15:51–61 (Fall 1994).

84. Norman Solomon, "Monotonous Tone of Op-Ed Pages Could Spell Trouble for Newspapers," *Editor & Publisher,* March 29, 1997.

85. Peter De Simone, "100 years haven't been enough," *St. Louis Post-Dispatch,* Nov. 26, 2000.

86. Ellen Berg, "He wasn't just another kid," *St. Louis Post-Dispatch,* Nov. 26, 2000.

87. Kevin Horrigan, "Sen. Seamhead and the coming baseball apocalypse," *St. Louis Post-Dispatch,* Nov. 26, 2000.

88. Tucker McQueen and Mae Gentry, "Southern kin, black & white," *Atlanta Journal-Constitution,* Dec. 10, 2000.

89. Okey Ndibe, "Eyes to the ground: The perils of the black student," *Hartford Courant,* Oct. 1, 2000.

90. Denver, Colo., *Rocky Mountain News,* July 1, 2001.

91. Phineas Fiske, online discussion, "Magazine Reprints," Feb. 24, 1997, NCEW-L.

Chapter 20
The Editorial Page That May, and Must, Be

1. William Cullen Bryant, "The Battle-Field," *Poems* (Philadelphia: Henry Altemus), p. 124.

Bibliography

Editorial Writing and Editorial Pages

Babb, Laura Longley, ed., *The Editorial Page* [of the *Washington Post*]. Boston: Houghton Mifflin (1977).

Casey, Maura, and Michael Zuzel, eds., *A Handbook for Editorial Writers*. Rockville, Md.: National Conference of Editorial Writers (2001).

Fink, Conrad C., *Writing Opinion for Impact*. Ames: Iowa State University Press (1999).

Hays, Robert G., *A Race at Bay: New York Times Editorials on "the Indian Problem."* Carbondale: Southern Illinois Press (1997).

Hulteng, John L., *The Opinion Function: Editorial and Interpretive Writing for the News Media*. Hayden Lake, Idaho: Ridge House (1973).

Kreighbaum, Hillier, *Facts in Perspective: The Editorial Page and News Interpretation*. Englewood Cliffs, N.J.: Prentice-Hall (1956).

MacDougall, Curtis D., *Principles of Editorial Writing*. Dubuque, Iowa: W.C. Brown (1973).

Rivers, William L., *Writing Opinions: Reviews*. Ames: Iowa State University Press (1988).

Rivers, William L., Bryce McIntyre and Alison Work, *Writing Opinions: Editorials*. Ames: Iowa State University Press (1988).

Sloan, Wm. David, *Pulitzer Prize Editorials: America's Best Writing, 1917–1979*. Ames: Iowa State University Press (1980).

Sloan, Wm. David, Cheryl Watts and Joanne Sloan, *Great Editorials: Masterpieces of Opinion Writing*. Northport, Ala.: Vision (1992).

Stonecipher, Harry W., *Editorial and Persuasive Writing: Opinion Functions of the News Media*. New York: Hastings (1979).

Waldrop, A. Gayle, *Editor and Editorial Writer*. 3rd ed. Dubuque, Iowa: W.C. Brown (1967).

Press Criticism

Bagdikian, Ben H., *The Effete Conspiracy and Other Crimes of the Press*. New York: Harper & Row (1972).

Blumberg, Nathaniel B., *One-Party Press?* Lincoln: University of Nebraska Press (1954).

Dunsmore, Herman H., *All the News That Fits: A Critical Analysis of the News and Editorial Content of the New York Times*. New Rochelle, N.Y.: Arlington (1969).

Efron, Edith, *The News Twisters*. Los Angeles: Nash (1971).

Ghiglione, Loren, ed., *The Buying and Selling of America's Newspapers*. Indianapolis, Ind.: R.J. Berg (1984).

Goldstein, Tom, ed., *Killing the Messenger*. New York: Columbia University Press (1989).

Irwin, Will, *The American Newspaper*. Ames: Iowa State University Press (1969). (First published in *Colliers*, January–July 1911.)

Isaacs, Norman A., *Untended Gates*. New York: Columbia University Press (1986).

Kovach, Bill, and Tom Rosenthal, *The Elements of Journalism: What Newspeople Should Know and the Public Should Expect*. New York: Crown (2001).

Lee, Martin A., and Norman Solomon, *Unreliable Sources*. New York: Carol (1990).

Patner, Andrew, *I.F. Stone: A Portrait*. New York: Pantheon (1988).

Seldes, George, *You Can't Print That*. Garden City, N.Y.: Garden City Publishing (1929).

Seldes, George, *Lords of the Press*. New York: Messner (1938).

Seldes, George, *The People Don't Know*. New York: Gaer (1949).

Sinclair, Upton, *The Brass Check: A Study of American Journalism*. 8th ed. Pasadena, Calif.: The Author (1920).

Squires, James D., *Read All About It! The Corporate Takeover of America's Newspapers*. New York: Times (1994).

Stone, I.F., *The I.F. Stone's Weekly Reader*. Edited by Neil Middleton. New York: Vintage (1974).

Cartoonists

Anonymous, *The Image of America in Caricature and Cartoon*. Fort Worth, Texas: Amon Carter Museum of Western Art (1976).

Block, Herbert, *The Herblock Book*. Boston: Beacon (1952).

Block, Herbert, *The Herblock Gallery*. New York: Simon & Schuster (1968).

Block, Herbert, *Herblock's Here and Now*. New York: Simon & Schuster (1955).

Block, Herbert, *Herblock's State of the Union.* New York: Simon & Schuster (1972).

Colldeweih, Jack, and Kalman Goldstein, eds., *Graphic Opinions: Editorial Cartoonists and Their Art.* Bowling Green, Ohio: Bowling Green State University Popular Press (1998).

Editors of the Foreign Policy Association, *A Cartoon History of United States Foreign Policy, 1776–1976.* New York: Morrow (1975).

Giglio, James N., and Greg G. Thielen, *Truman in Cartoon and Caricature.* Ames: Iowa State University Press (1984).

Hill, Draper, *Political Asylum.* Winsor, Ontario: Art Gallery of Winsor (1985).

Hill, Draper, *The Young Years, 1982–1985.* Detroit, Mich.: Detroit News (1986).

Lendt, David L., *Ding: The Life of Jay Norwood Darling.* Ames: Iowa State University Press (1979).

Lurie, Ranan R., *Nixon on Rated Cartoons.* New York: New York Times Book Co. (1973).

Mauldin, Bill, *Back Home.* New York: Sloane (1947).

Mauldin, Bill, *Bill Mauldin's Army.* Novato, Calif.: Presidio (1983).

Mauldin, Bill, *The Brass Ring.* New York: Norton (1971).

Mauldin, Bill, *Up Front.* New York: Henry Holt (1945).

Miller, Frank, *Frank Miller Looks at Life.* N.P., n.d.

Nelson, Roy Paul, *Cartooning.* Chicago: Regnery (1975).

Payne, Ralph Bigelow, *Th. Nast: His Period and His Pictures.* Princeton: Pyne (facsimile of 1904 edition).

Pett, Joel, *Rough Sketches.* Lexington, Ky.: Lexington Herald-Leader (1982).

Salzman, Ed, and Ann Leigh Brown, *The Cartoon History of California Politics.* Sacramento: California Journal Press (1978).

Columnists and Writers

Alsop, Joseph, with Adam Platt, *I've Seen the Best.* New York: Norton (1992).

Alsop, Stewart, *Stay of Execution: A Sort of Memoir.* Philadelphia: Lippincott (1973).

Baker, Russell, *The Good Times.* New York: Morrow (1989).

Baker, Russell, *Growing Up.* New York: New American Library (1982).

Breslin, Jimmy, *Damon Runyon.* New York: Ticknor & Fields (1991).

Burner, David, and Thomas R. West, *Column Right: Journalists in the Service of Nationalism.* New York: New York University Press (1988).

Carter, Joseph H., *Never Met a Man I Didn't Like: The Life and Writings of Will Rogers.* New York: Avon (1991).

Childs, Marquis, and James Reston, *Walter Lippmann and His Times.* New York: Harcourt, Brace (1959).

Ciccone, F. Richard, *Royko: A Life in Print.* New York: Public Affairs (2001).

Driscoll, Charles B., *The Life of O.O. McIntyre.* New York: Greystone (1938).

Fecher, Charles A., *The Diary of H.L. Mencken.* New York: Knopf (1990).

Fowler, Will, *The Young Man from Denver: A Candid and Affectionate Biography of Gene Fowler.* Garden City, N.Y.: Doubleday (1962).

Geyer, Georgie Anne, *Buying the Night Flight.* New York: Delacorte (1983).

Graham, Katharine, *Personal History.* New York: Knopf (1997).

Grayson, David, *American Chronicle: The Autobiography of Ray Stannard Baker.* New York: Scribner's (1945).

Griffith, Thomas, *Harry and Teddy* [Henry R. Luce and Theodore H. White]. New York: Random House (1995).

Heaton, John L., *Cobb of "The World": A Leader in Liberalism.* New York: Dutton (1924).

Hobson, Fred, *Mencken: A Life.* New York: Random House (1994).

Hopper, Hedda, and James Brough, *The Whole Truth and Nothing But.* Garden City, N.Y.: Doubleday (1963).

Hudson, Robert V., *The Writing Game: A Biography of Will Irvin.* Ames: Iowa State University Press (1982).

Kaplan, Justin, *Lincoln Steffens.* New York: Simon & Schuster (1974).

Klurfled, Herman, *Behind the Lines: The World of Drew Pearson.* Englewood Cliffs, N.J.: Prentice-Hall (1968).

Krock, Arthur, *Memoirs: Sixty Years on the Firing Line.* New York: Funk & Wagnalls (1968).

Krock, Arthur, *Myself When Young*. Boston: Little, Brown (1973).

Kurth, Peter, *American Cassandra: The Life of Dorothy Thompson*. Boston: Little, Brown (1990).

Lubow, Arthur, *The Reporter Who Would Be King* [Richard Harding Davis]. New York: Scribner's (1992).

Luskin, John, *Lippmann, Liberty and the Press*. University: University of Alabama Press (1972).

McMurry, Linda O., *To Keep the Waters Troubled: The Life of Ida B. Wells*. Oxford: Oxford University Press (1999).

Miller, Lee G., *The Story of Ernie Pyle*. New York: Viking (1950).

Mills, Kay, *A Place in the News*. New York: Dodd, Mead (1988).

Pickett, Calder M., *Ed Howe: Country Town Philosopher*. Lawrence: University Press of Kansas (1968).

Pilat, Oliver, *Drew Pearson: An Unauthorized Biography*. New York: Harper's Magazine Press (1973).

Pilat, Oliver, *Pegler: Angry Man of the Press*. Boston: Beacon (1963).

Reston, James, *Deadlines: A Memoir*. New York: Random House (1991).

Reston, James, *Sketches in the Sand*. New York: Knopf (1967).

Riley, Sam G., *The American Newspaper Columnist*. Westport, Conn.: Praeger (1998).

Ross, Ishbel, *Ladies of the Press*. New York: Harper & Brothers (1936).

Sanders, Marion K., *Dorothy Thompson*. Boston: Houghton Mifflin (1973).

Sokolov, Raymond, *Wayward Reporter: The Life of A.J. Liebling*. New York: Harper & Row (1980).

Steel, Ronald, *Walter Lippmann and the American Century*. Boston: Little, Brown 1980).

Steffens, Lincoln, *The Autobiography of Lincoln Steffens*. New York: Harcourt, Brace (1937).

Stone, Melville, *Fifty Years a Journalist*. Garden City, N.Y.: Doubleday, Page (1921).

Weiner, Ed., *The Damon Runyon Story*. New York: Longmans, Green (1948).

Yoder, Edwin M., Jr., *Joe Alsop's Cold War*. Chapel Hill: University of North Carolina Press (1995).

Editors and Publishers

Agran, Edward Gale, *"Too Good a Town": William Allen White, the Community and the Emerging Rhetoric of Middle America*. Fayetteville: University of Arkansas Press (1999).

Anonymous, *Gardner Cowles*. Des Moines, Iowa: Des Moines Register and Tribune (1946).

Anonymous, *Life and Labors of Henry W. Grady*. New York: Goldthwaite (1890).

Armstrong, William M., *E.L. Godkin: A Biography*. Albany: State University of New York Press (1978).

Baldasty, Gerald J., *E.W. Scripps and the Business of Newspapers*. Urbana: University of Illinois Press (1999).

Barrett, James Wyman, *Joseph Pulitzer and His World*. New York: Vanguard (1941).

Barrett, James Wyman, *The World, the Flesh and Messrs. Pulitzer*. New York: Vanguard (1931).

Becker, Stephen, *Marshall Field III*. New York: Simon & Schuster (1964).

Bigelow, John, *William Cullen Bryant*. Boston: Houghton Mifflin (1890). Reprint, New York: Chelsea (1980).

Bond, F. Fraser, *Mr. Miller of "The Times."* New York: Scribner's (1931).

Boswell, Sharon A., and Lorraine McConaghy, *Raise Hell and Sell Newspapers: Alden J. Blethen and The Seattle Times*. Pullman: Washington State University Press (1996).

Bower, Tom, *Maxwell: The Outsider*. New York: Viking (1992).

Bowman, Charles A., *Ottawa Editor*. Sidney, B.C.: Gray's (1966).

Bowman, Lowry, *Confessions of a Dark-Barker*. Abingdon, Va. (1992).

Braddon, Russell, *Roy Thomson of Fleet Street*. London: Collins (1965).

Bradley, Ben, *A Good Life*. New York: Simon & Schuster (1995).

Brands, H.W., *The First American: The Life and Times of Benjamin Franklin*. New York: Anchor (2002).

Brendon, Pers, *The Life and Death of the Press Barons*. New York: Atheneum (1983).

Brenner, Marie, *House of Dreams: The Bingham Family of Louisville*. New York: Random House (1988).

Brian, Denis, *Pulitzer: A Life*. New York: Wiley (2001).

Brown, Francis, *Raymond of the Times*. New York: Norton (1951).

Bruces, Charles, *News and the Southams*. Toronto: Macmillan (1968).

Carlson, Oliver, *Brisbane*. Westport, Conn.: Greenwood (1937).

Carlson, Oliver, *The Man Who Made News: A Biography of James Gordon Bennett*. New York: Duell, Sloane & Pearce (1942).

Carter, Hodding, *Where Main Street Meets the River*. New York: Rinehart (1952).

Cash, Kevin, *Who the Hell Is William Loeb?* Manchester, N.H.: Amoskeag (1975).

Casserly, Jack, *Scripps: The Dynasty Divided*. New York: Fine (1993).

Catledge, Turner, *My Life and The Times*. New York: Harper & Row (1971).

Chandler, David Leon, with Mary Voeltz Chandler, *The Binghams of Louisville*. New York: Crown (1987).

Chaney, Lindsay, and Michael Cieply, *The Hearsts: Family and Empire: The Later Years*. New York: Simon & Schuster (1981).

Chisholm, Anne, and Michael Davie, *Lord Beaverbrook: A Life*. New York: Knopf (1993).

Clarke, Ronald W., *Benjamin Franklin*. New York: Random House (1983).

Clough, Frank C., *William Allen White of Emporia*. New York: Whittlesey (1941).

Cochran, Negley D., *E.W. Scripps*. Reprint, Westport, Conn.: Greenwood (1972).

Coleridge, Nicholas, *Paper Tigers: The Latest, Greatest Newspaper Tycoons*. New York : Birch Lane (1993).

Cooney, John, *The Annenbergs: The Salvaging of a Tainted Dynasty*. New York: Simon & Schuster (1982).

Copeland, David A., *Colonial Newspapers: Character and Content*. Newark: University of Delaware Press (1997).

Cornell, William M., *The Life and Public Career of Hon. Horace Greeley*. Boston: Lee & Shepard (1872).

Cousins, Paul M., *Joel Chandler Harris*. Baton Rouge: Louisiana State University Press (1968).

Cox, James E., *Journey Through My Years*. New York: Simon & Schuster (1946).

Crockett, Albert Stevens, *When James Gordon Bennett Was Caliph of Bagdad*. New York: Funk & Wagnalls (1926).

Crouthamel, James L., *James Watson Webb*, Middletown, Conn.: Wesleyan University Press (1969).

Dabney, Virginius, *Pistols and Pointed Pens: The Dueling Editors of Old Virginia*. Chapel Hill, N.C.: Algonquin (1987).

Daniels, Jonathan, *They Will Be Heard: America's Crusading Editors*. New York: McGraw-Hill (1965).

Daniels, Josephus, *Editor in Politics*. Chapel Hill: University of North Carolina Press (1941).

Daniels, Josephus, *Tar Heel Editor*. Chapel Hill: University of North Carolina Press (1939).

Davies, Marion, *The Times We Had: Life with William Randolph Hearst*. Indianapolis, Ind.: Bobbs Merrill (1975).

Davies, Nick, *The Death of a Tycoon: An Insider's Account of the Fall of Robert Maxwell*. New York: St. Martin's (1992).

Davis, Deborah, *Katharine the Great: Katharine Graham and Her Washington Post Empire*. New York: Sheridan Square (1991).

Davis, Harold E., *Henry Grady's New South*. Tuscaloosa: University of Alabama Press (1990).

Downing, Sybil, and Robert E. Smith, *Tom Patterson: Colorado Crusader for Change*. Niwot: University Press of Colorado (1995).

Drewry, John E., *Biographies of Famous Journalists*. New York: Random House (1942).

Driberg, Tom, *Beaverbrook*. London: Weidenfeld & Nicolson (1956).

Duncan, Bingham, *Whitelaw Reid: Journalist, Politician, Diplomat*. Athens: University of Georgia Press (1975).

Durey, Michael, *"With the Hammer of Truth"* [James Thomson Callender]. Charlottesville: University Press of Virginia (1990).

Eagles, Charles W., *Jonathan Daniels and Race Relations: The Evolution of a Southern Liberal*. Knoxville: University of Tennessee Press (1982).

Escott, T.H.S., *Masters of English Journalism*. (1911). Reprint, Westport, Conn.: Greenwood (1970).

Evans, Harold, *Good Times, Bad Times*. New York: Atheneum (1984).

Felsenthal, Carol, *Citizen Newhouse*. New York: Seven Stories (1998).

Ficken, Robert E., *Rufus Woods, the Columbia River and the Building of Modern Washington*. Pullman: Washington State University Press (1995).

Frankel, Max, *The Times of My Life and My Life with The Times*. New York: Delta (1999).

Franklin, Benjamin, *The Autobiography*. Chicago: Scott, Foresman (n.d.).

Fyfe, Hamilton, *Northcliffe: An Intimate Biography*. New York: Macmillan (1930).

Gies, Joseph, *The Colonel of Chicago* [Robert McCormick]. New York: Dutton (1979).

Golden, Harry, *The Right Time*. New York: Putnam's (1969).

Guiles, Fred Lawrence, *Marion Davies*. New York: McGraw-Hill (1972).

Graham, Katharine, *Personal History*. New York: Knopf (1997).

Grayson, David, *American Chronicle: The Autobiography of Ray Stannard Baker*. New York: Scribner's (1945).

Griffith, Sally Foreman, *Home Town News: William Allen White and the Emporia Gazette*. New York: Oxford University Press (1989).

Guiles, Fred Laurence, *Marion Davies*. New York: McGraw-Hill (1972).

Haines, Joe, *Maxwell*. Boston: Houghton Mifflin (1988).

Hale, William Harlan, *Horace Greeley: Voice of the People*. New York: Harper & Brothers (1950).

Harris, William C., *William Woods Holden: Firebrand of North Carolina Politics*. Baton Rouge: Louisiana State University Press (1987).

Hearst, William Randolph, Jr., with Jack Casserly, *The Hearsts: Father and Son*. Niwot, Colo.: Roberts Rinehart (1991).

Heaton, John L., *Cobb of "The World."* New York: Dutton (1924).

Heuterman, Thomas H., *Movable Type: Biography of Legh R. Freeman*. Ames: Iowa State University Press (1979).

Hinshaw, David, *A Man from Kansas: The Story of William Allen White*. New York: Putnam's (1945).

Hoge, Alice Albright, *Cissy Patterson*. New York: Random House (1966).

Hoopes, Roy, *Ralph Ingersoll*. New York: Atheneum (1985).

Hough, Henry Beetle, *Country Editor*. New York: Doubleday, Duran (1940).

Jernigan, E. Jay. *William Allen White*. Boston: Twayne (1983).

Johnson, David E., *Douglas Southall Freeman*. Gretna, La.: Pelican (2002).

Johnson, Gerald W., *An Honorable Titan: A Biography of Adolph S. Ochs*. New York: Harper & Brothers (1946).

Johnson, Gerald W., *William Allen White's America*. New York: Henry Holt (1947).

Juergens, George, *Joseph Pulitzer and the New York World*. Princeton, N.J.: Princeton University Press (1966).

Kahn, E. J., Jr., *The World of Swope* [*New York World*]. New York: Simon & Schuster (1965).

Kansas City Star Staff, *William Rockhill Nelson*. Cambridge, Mass.: Riverside (1915).

Kneebone, John T., *Southern Liberal Journalists and the Issue of Race, 1920–1944*. Chapel Hill: University of North Carolina Press (1985).

Kroger, Brooke, *Nelly Bly*. New York: Times (1994).

Leapman, Michael, *Arrogant Aussie: The Rupert Murdoch Story*. Secaucas, N.J.: Lyle Stuart (1985).

Leidholdt, Alexander S., *Standing before the Shouting Mob: Lenoir Chambers and Virginia's Massive Resistance to Public School Integration*. Tuscaloosa: University of Alabama Press (1997).

Linn, W.A., *Horace Greeley*. New York: Appleton (1903).

Lundberg, Ferdinand, *Imperial Hearst*. New York: Equinox Cooperative (1936).

Maier, Thomas, *Newhouse*. New York: St. Martin's (1994).

Marberry, M.M., *Vicki* [Victoria C. Woodhull]. New York: Funk & Wagnalls (1967).

Marcosson, Isaac F., *"Marse Henry": Biography of Henry Watterson*. New York: Dodd, Mead (1951).

Markham, James W., *Bovard of the Post-Dispatch*. Baton Rouge: Louisiana State University Press (1954).

Martin, Harold H., *Ralph McGill, Reporter*. Boston: Little, Brown (1973).

Martin, Ralph G., *Cissy*. New York: Simon & Schuster (1979).

McEnter, James, *Fighting Words: Independent Journalists in Texas.* Austin: University of Texas Press (1992).

McFeely, William S., *Frederick Douglass.* New York: Norton (1991).

McKay, Floyd J., *An Editor for Oregon: Charles A. Sprague and the Politics of Change.* Corvallis: Oregon State University Press (1998).

Meeker, Richard H., *Newspaperman: S.I. Newhouse and the Business of News.* New Haven, Conn.: Ticknor & Fields (1983).

Mills, George, *Harvey Ingham and Gardner Cowles, Sr.* [*Des Moines Register and Tribune*]. Ames: Iowa State University Press (1977).

Mitchell, Edward, *Memoirs of an Editor.* New York: Scribner's (1924).

Montgomery, Gayle B., and James W. Johnson, *One Step from the White House* [William F. Knowland]. Berkeley: University of California Press (1998).

Morrison, Joseph L., *W.J. Cash: Southern Prophet.* New York: Knopf (1967).

Moscowitz, Raymond, *Stuffy: The Life of Newspaper Pioneer Basil "Stuffy" Walters.* Ames: Iowa State University Press (1982).

Munster, George, *Rubert Murdoch: A Paper Prince.* New York: Penguin (1985).

Nasaw, David, *The Chief: The Life of William Randolph Hearst.* Boston: Houghton Mifflin (2000).

Neuharth, Al, *Confessions of an S.O.B.* New York: Doubleday (1989).

Nixon, Raymond B., *Henry W. Grady: Spokesman of the New South.* New York: Knopf (1943).

Noble, Iris, *Joseph Pulitzer: Front Page Pioneer.* New York: Messner (1957).

Nye, Russell B., *William Lloyd Garrison and the Humanitarian Reformers.* Boston: Little, Brown (1955).

Ogden, Rollo, *The Life and Letters of Edwin Lawrence Godkin.* 2 vols. Reprint, Westport, Conn.: Greenwood (1972).

Parton, J., *The Life of Horace Greeley.* New York: Mason (1855).

Patner, Andrew, *I.F. Stone: A Portrait.* New York: Pantheon (1988).

Pfaff, Daniel W., *Joseph Pulitzer II and the Post-Dispatch.* University Park: Pennsylvania State University Press (1991).

Pierce, Robert N., *A Sacred Trust: Nelson Poynter and the St. Petersburg Times.* Gainesville: University Press of Florida (1993).

Potter, Jeffrey, *The Story of Dorothy Schiff.* New York: Coward, McCann & Geoghegan (1976).

Pride, Armistead S., and Clint C. Wilson II, *A History of the Black Press.* Washington, D.C.: Howard University Press (1997).

Pulliam, Russell, *Publisher: Gene Pulliam, Last of the Newspaper Titans.* Ottawa, Ill.: Jameson (1984).

Pusey, Merlo J., *Eugene Meyer.* New York: Knopf (1974).

Raper, Horace W., *William W. Holden: North Carolina's Enigma.* Chapel Hill: University of North Carolina Press (1985).

Reavis, L.U., *A Representative Life of Horace Greeley.* New York: Carleton (1872).

Richardson, James H., *For the Life of Me.* New York: Putnam (1954).

Rosebault, Charles J., *When Dana Was the Sun.* Reprint, Westport, Conn.: Greenwood (1971).

Ross, Ishbel, *Ladies of the Press.* New York: Harper & Brothers (1936).

Russell, Francis, *The Shadow of Blooming Grove: Warren G. Harding and His Times.* New York: McGraw-Hill (1968).

Russell, Phillips, *Benjamin Franklin: First Civilized American.* New York: Blue Ribbon (1926).

Schmitt, Jo Ann, *Fighting Editors.* San Antonio, Texas: Naylor (1958).

Scripps, E.W., *Damned Old Crank.* New York: Harper (1951).

Scripps, E.W., *I Protest.* Madison: University of Wisconsin Press (1966).

Seitz, Don Carlos, *James Gordon Bennett.* Reprint, New York: Beckman (1974).

Sharpe, Ernest, *G.B. Dealey of the Dallas News.* New York: Henry Holt (1955).

Shawcross, William, *Murdoch.* New York: Simon & Schuster (1992).

Sleeper, Jim, *Turn the Rascals Out: The Life and Times of Orange County's Fighting Editor.* Trabuco Canyon: California Classics (1973).

Smith, Richard Norton, *The Colonel: The Life and Legend of Robert R. McCormick.* Boston: Houghton Mifflin (1997).

Smith, Rixey, and Norman Beasley, *Carter Glass.* New York: Longmans, Green (1939).

Spender, J.A., *Life, Journalism and Politics,* 2 vols. New York: Stokes (n.d.).

Steele, C. Frank, *Prairie Editor: The Life and Times of Buchanan of Lethbridge.* Toronto: Ryerson (1961).

Steele, Janet E., *The Sun Shines for All: Journalism and Ideology in the Life of Charles A. Dana.* Syracuse, N.Y.: Syracuse University Press (1993).

Steffens, Lincoln, *Autobiography of Lincoln Steffens.* New York: Harcourt, Brace (1931).

Stern, J. David, *Memoirs of a Maverick Publisher.* New York: Simon & Schuster (1962).

Stoddard, Henry Luther, *Horace Greeley.* New York: Putnam's (1946).

Stone, Gregory N., *The Day Paper: The Story of One of America's Last Independent Newspapers.* New London, Conn.: Day (2000).

Storke, Thomas L., *California Editor.* Los Angeles: Westernlore (1958).

Streitmatter, Rodger, *Raising Her Voice: African-American Women Journalists Who Changed History.* Lexington: University of Kentucky Press (1994).

Suggs, Henry Lewis, *P.B. Young: Newspaperman: Race, Politics and Journalism in the New South.* Charlottesville: University Press of Virginia (1988).

Swanberg, W.A., *Citizen Hearst.* New York: Scribner's (1961).

Swanberg, W.A., *Luce and His Empire.* New York: Scribner's (1972).

Swanberg, W.A., *Pulitzer.* New York: Scribner's (1967).

Swanson, Walter S.J., *The Thin Gold Watch: A Personal History of the Newspaper Copleys.* New York: Macmillan (1964).

Tagg, James, *Benjamin Franklin Bache and the Philadelphia Aurora.* Philadelphia: University of Pennsylvania Press (1991).

Tebbel, John, *The Life and Good Times of William Randolph Hearst.* New York: Dutton (1952).

Teel, Leonard Ray, *Ralph Emerson McGill: Voice of the Southern Conscience.* Knoxville: University of Tennessee Press (2001).

Thomson, Lord, of Fleet, *After I Was Sixty.* London: Nelson (1975).

Tifft, Susan E., and Alex S. Jones, *The Patriarch: The Rise and Fall of the Bingham Dynasty.* New York: Summit (1991).

Trible, Vance C., *The Astonishing Mr. Scripps: The Turbulent Life of America's Penny Press Lord.* Ames: Iowa State University Press (1992).

Turnbull, George S., *An Oregon Crusader* [George Putnam]. Portland, Ore.: Binsford & Mort (1955).

Villard, Oswald Garrison, *Fighting Years: An Autobiography.* New York: Harcourt, Brace (1939).

Waldron, Ann, *Hodding Carter: The Reconstruction of a Racist.* Chapel Hill, N.C.: Algonquin (1992).

Waldrop, Frank C., *McCormick of Chicago.* Englewood Cliffs, N.J.: Prentice-Hall (1966).

Wall, Joseph Frazier, *Henry Watterson: Reconstructed Rebel.* New York: Oxford University Press (1956).

Wallace, Ernest, *Charles DeMorse: Pioneer Editor and Statesman.* Lubbock: Texas Tech Press (1943).

Watterson, Henry, *"Marse Henry": An Autobiography.* 2 vols. New York: Doran (1919).

Wells, Evelyn, *Fremont Older.* New York: Appleton-Century (1936).

White, William Allen, *Autobiography.* New York: Macmillan (1946).

Whited, Charles, *Knight: A Publisher in the Tumultuous Century.* New York: Dutton (1988).

Wilkinson, J. Harvie, III, *Harry Byrd and the Changing Face of Virginia Politics.* Charlottesville: University Press of Virginia (1968).

Williamson, Samuel T., *Frank Gannett.* New York: Duell, Sloan & Pearce (1940).

Wilson, Charles, *First with the News: The History of W.H. Smith 1792–1972.* London: Jonathan Cape (1985).

Wilson, R. Macnair, *Lord Northcliffe: A Study.* Philadelphia: Lippincott (1927).

Winkler, John K., *William Randolph Hearst: A New Appraisal.* New York: Hastings (1955).

Wright, Elizabeth, *Miller Freeman: Man of Action.* San Francisco: Miller Freeman (1977).

Newspapers

Andrews, J. Cutler, *Pittsburgh's Post-Gazette.* Reprint, Westport, Conn.: Greenwood (1970).

Angelo, Frank, *On Guard: A History of the Detroit Free Press.* Detroit, Mich.: Detroit Free Press (1981).

Anonymous, *The History of The Times: "The Thunder" in the Making 1785–1841.* Vol. 1. New York: Macmillan (1935).

Anonymous, *The History of The Times: The Tradition Established 1841–1884.* Vol 2. New York: Macmillan (1939).

Anonymous, *The History of The Times: The Twentieth Century Test 1884–1912.* Vol 3. New York: Macmillan (1947).

Anonymous, *The History of The Times: The 150th Anniversary and Beyond 1912–1948.* Vol. 4. New York: Macmillan (1952).

Anonymous, *The Lee Papers: A Saga of Midwestern Journalism.* Kewanee, Ill.: Star-Courier Press (1947).

Anonymous, *Pictured Encyclopedia of the World's Greatest Newspaper* [*Chicago Tribune*]. Chicago: Chicago Tribune Co. (1928).

Anonymous, *The Press (1861–1961).* Christchurch, N.Z.: Christchurch Press 1963).

Anonymous, *The Virginia Gazette 1775.* Chardon, Ohio: Block (1975).

Anonymous, *The WGN.* Chicago: Tribune Co. (1922).

Ayerst, David, *The Manchester Guardian.* Ithaca, N.Y.: Cornell University Press (1971).

Baehr, Harry W., Jr., *The New York Herald Tribune since the Civil War.* New York: Octagon (1972).

Baker, Thomas Harrison, *The Memphis Commercial Appeal.* Baton Rouge: Louisiana State University Press (1971).

Berger, Meyer, *The Story of the New York Times.* New York: Simon & Schuster (1951).

Berges, Marshall, *The Life and Times of Los Angeles.* New York: Atheneum (1984).

Braley, Russ, *Bad News: The Foreign Policy of the New York Times.* Chicago: Regnery Gateway (1984).

Bruce, Charles, *News and the Southams.* Toronto: Macmillan (1968).

Canham, Erwin D., *Commitment to Freedom: The Story of the Christian Science Monitor.* Boston: Houghton Mifflin (1958).

Catledge, Turner, *My Life and The Times.* New York: Harper & Row (1971).

Chamberlain, Joseph Edgar, *The Boston Transcript: A History of the First Hundred Years.* Boston: Houghton Mifflin (1930).

Chambers, Lenoir, and Joseph E. Shank, *Salt Water and Printer's Ink: Norfolk and Its Newspapers, 1865–1965.* Chapel Hill: University of North Carolina Press (1967).

Chapman, John, *Tell It to Sweeney: An Informal History of the New York Daily News.* Garden City, N.Y.: Doubleday (1961).

Claiborne, Jack, *The Charlotte Observer.* Chapel Hill: University of North Carolina Press (1986).

Coffman, Lloyd W., *5200 Thursdays in the Wallowas* [*Wallowa County Chieftain*]. Enterprise, Ore.: Wallowa County Chieftain (1984).

Cohen, Lester, *The New York Graphic.* Philadelphia: Chilton (1964).

Conrad, Will, Kathleen Wilson and Dale Wilson, *The Milwaukee Journal: The First Eighty Years.* Madison: University of Wisconsin Press (1964).

Copley Press, Inc., *The Copley Press.* Aurora, Ill.: Copley (1953).

Cose, Ellis, *The Press: Inside America's Most Powerful Newspaper Empire.* New York: Morrow (1989).

Cross, Wilbur, *Lee's Legacy of Leadership.* Essex, Conn.: Greenwich (1990).

Crouthamel, James L., *Bennett's New York Herald and the Rise of the Popular Press.* Syracuse, N.Y.: Syracuse University Press (1989).

Dana, Marshall N., *The First Fifty Years of the Oregon Journal.* Portland, Ore.: Binfords & Mort (1951).

Diamond, Edwin, *Behind the Times: Inside the New York Times.* New York: Villard (1994).

Douglas, George H., *The Golden Age of the Newspaper,* Westport, Conn.: Greenwood (1999).

Dyar, Ralph E., *News for an Empire: The Story of The Spokesman-Review.* Caldwell, Idaho: Caxton (1952).

Edelman, Maurice, *The Mirror: A Political History*. New York: London House and Maxwell (1966).

Edwards, Jerome E., *The Foreign Policy of Col. McCormick's Tribune*. Reno: University of Nevada Press (1971).

Ferril, Thomas Hornsby, and Helen Ferril, eds., *The Rocky Mountain Herald Reader*. New York: Morrow (1966).

Fredericks, William B., *Covering Iowa: The History of the Des Moines Register and Tribune Company 1849–1985*. Ames: Iowa State University Press (2000).

Gjelten, Tom, *Sarajevo Daily: A City and Its Newspaper under Fire*. New York: HarperPerennial (1995).

Gottlieb, Robert, and Irene Wolf, *Thinking Big: The Story of the Los Angeles Times: Its Publishers and Their Influence on Southern California*. New York: Putnam's (1977).

Goulden, Joseph C., *Fit to Print: A.M. Rosenthal and His Times*. Secaucus, N.J.: Lyle Stuart (1988).

Griffith, Louis Turner, and John Edwin Talmadge, *Georgia Journalism 1763–1950*. Athens, Ga.: University of Georgia Press (1951).

Grimes, Millard, *The Last Linotype: The Story of Georgia and Its Newspapers since World War II*. Macon, Ga.: Mercer University Press (1985).

Haig, Robert L., *The Gazetteer (1735–1797): A Study of the Eighteenth-Century English Newspaper*. Carbondale: Southern Illinois University Press (1960).

Halberstam, David, *The Powers That Be*. New York: Knopf (1979).

Hooker, Richard, *The Story of an Independent Newspaper: One Hundred Years of the Springfield Republican*. New York: Macmillan (1924).

Hosokawa, Bill, *Thunder in the Rockies: The Incredible Denver Post*. New York: Morrow (1976).

Keeler, Robert F., *Newsday: A Candid History of the Respectable Tabloid*. New York: Arbor (1990).

Kelly, Tom, *The Imperial Post*. New York: Morrow (1983).

King, Charles, *The Ottaway Newspapers: The First 50 Years*. Campbell Hall, N.Y.: Ottaway Newspapers (1986).

Kluger, Richard, *The Paper: The Life and Death of The New York Herald Tribune*. New York: Knopf (1986).

Lyons, Louis, *Newspaper Story: One Hundred Years of the Boston Globe*. Cambridge, Mass.: Belknap Press of Harvard University Press (1971).

MacNab, Gordon, *A Century of News and People in the East Oregonian*. Pendleton, Ore.: East Oregonian Publishing Co. (1975).

Martin, Douglas D., *Tombstone's Epitaph*. (1958). Reprint, Norman: University of Oklahoma Press (1997).

McClure, Kevin Michael, *The Great American Newspaper: The Rise and Fall of the Village Voice*. New York: Scribner's (1978).

McGivena, Leo E., et al., *The News: The First Fifty Years of New York's Picture Newspaper*. New York: News Syndicate Co. (1969).

McLaws, Monte Burr, *Spokesman for the Kingdom: Early Mormon Journalism and the Deseret News, 1830–1898*. Provo, Utah: Brigham Young (1977).

McPhaul, John J., *Deadlines and Monkeyshines: The Fabled World of Chicago Journalism*. Englewood Cliffs, N.J.: Prentice-Hall (1962).

Morison, Bradley L., *Sunlight on Your Doorstep: The Minneapolis Tribune's First Hundred Years*. Minneapolis, Minn.: Ross & Haines (1966).

Murray, George, *The Madhouse on Madison Street*. Chicago: Follett (1965).

Nevins, Alan, *The Evening Post: A Century of Journalism*. New York: Boni & Liveright (1922).

O'Brien, Frank M., *The Story of the Sun*. Reprint, Westport, Conn.: Greenwood (1968).

O'Donnell, James F., *100 Years of Making Communication History: The Story of the Hearst Corporation*. New York: Hearst Professional Magazines (1987).

Perkin, Robert L., *The First Hundred Years: An Informal History of Denver and The Rocky Mountain News*. Garden City, N.Y.: Doubleday (1959).

Price, Warren C., *The Eugene Register-Guard*. Portland, Ore.: Binfords & Mort (1976).

Pritchard, Peter, *The Making of McPaper*. Kansas City, Mo.: Andrews, McMeel & Parker (1987).

Pugnetti, Frances Taylor, *Tiger by the Tail: Twenty-Five Years with the Stormy Tri-City Herald.* Pasco, Wash.: Tri-City Herald (1975).

Rice, William B., *Los Angeles Star: 1851–1864.* Berkeley: University of California Press (1947).

Roberts, Chalmer, *In the Shadow of Power: The Story of The Washington Post.* Cabin John, Md.: Seven Locks (1989)

Roberts, Chalmer, *The Washington Post: The First 100 Years.* Boston: Houghton Mifflin (1977).

Robertson, Charles L., *The International Herald Tribune: The First Hundred Years.* New York: Columbia University Press (1987).

Robertson, Nan, *The Girls in the Balcony: Women, Men and The New York Times.* New York: Random House (1992).

Root, Waverley, *The Paris Edition: 1927–1934.* San Francisco: North Point (1989).

Rosenfeld, Richard N., *American Aurora.* New York: St. Martin's (1997).

Ross, Margaret, *Arkansas Gazette: The Early Years 1819–1866.* Little Rock: Arkansas Gazette Foundation (1969).

Salisbury, Harrison, *Without Fear or Favor: An Uncompromising Look at The New York Times.* New York: Times (1980).

Smith, J. Eugene, *One Hundred Years of Hartford's Courant.* Reprint, Hamden, Conn.: Archon (1970).

Talese, Gay, *The Kingdom and the Power* [*The New York Times*]. New York: World (1969).

Tebbel, John, *An American Dynasty: The Story of the McCormicks, Medills and Pattersons.* Garden City, N.Y.: Doubleday (1947).

Tifft, Susan, and Alex S. Jones, *The Trust: The Private and Powerful Family behind the New York Times.* Boston: Little, Brown (1999).

Toole, John H., *Red Ribbons: A Story of Missoula and Its Newspaper.* Davenport, Iowa: Lee (1989).

Turnbull, George S., *History of Oregon Newspapers.* Portland, Ore.: Binfords & Mort (1939).

Veblen, Eric, *The Manchester Union Leader in New Hampshire Elections.* Hanover, N.H.: University Press of New England (1975).

Vigilante, Richard, *Strike: The Daily News War and the Future of American Labor.* New York: Simon & Schuster (1994).

Wendt, Lloyd, *Chicago Tribune.* Chicago: Rand McNally (1979).

Wendt, Lloyd, *The Wall Street Journal.* Chicago: Rand McNally (1982).

Williams, Harold A., *The Baltimore Sun: 1837–1987.* Baltimore, Md.: John Hopkins University Press (1987).

Wolseley, Roland E., *The Black Press, U.S.A.* 2nd ed. Ames: Iowa State University Press (1971).

Wright, Elizabeth, *Independence in All Things, Neutrality in Nothing* [Legh Richmond Freeman]. San Francisco: Miller Freeman (1973).

Works of Opinion Writers

Abell, Tyler, ed., *Drew Pearson Diaries, 1949–1959.* New York: Holt, Rinehart & Winston (1974).

[Allen, Robert, and Drew Pearson], *Washington Merry-Go-Round.* New York: Liveright (1931).

Anderson, Jack, and James Boyd, *Confessions of a Muckraker.* New York: Random House (1979).

Anderson, Jack, with Daryl Gibson, *Peace, War and Politics.* New York: Forge (2000).

Brier, Warren J., and Nathan B. Blumberg, eds., *A Century of Montana Journalism.* Missoula, Mont.: Mountain Press (1971).

Brook, Alexander B., *The Hard Way.* Bridgehampton, N.Y.: Bridge Works (1993).

Buchwald, Art, *The Buchwald Stops Here.* New York: Putnam (1996).

Buchwald, Art, *Leaving Home.* New York: Putnam (1993).

Buchwald, Art, *Lighten Up, George.* New York: Putnam (1991).

Carter, Hodding, *The Angry Scar.* Garden City: Doubleday (1959).

Carter, Hodding, *Southern Legacy.* Baton Rouge: Louisiana State University Press (1950).

Carter, Hodding, *Their Words Were Bullets: The Southern Press in War, Reconstruction and Peace.* Athens: University of Georgia Press (1969).

Carter, Hodding, *Where Main Street Meets the River.* New York: Rinehart (1952).

Chadakoff, Rochelle, ed., *Eleanor Roosevelt's My Day.* New York: Pharos (1989).

Childs, Marquis, *I Write from Washington.* New York: Harper & Brothers 1942).

Cobb, Irvin S., *Exit Laughing*. Garden City, N.Y.: Garden City Publishing (1942).

Coblentz, Edmund D., ed., *William Randolph Hearst: A Portrait in His Own Words*. New York: Simon & Schuster (1952).

Davis, Richard Harding, *The Notes of a World Correspondent*. New York: Scribner's (1911).

Delaplane, Stanton, *The Little World of Stanton Delaplane*. New York: Coward-McCann (1959).

Fowler, Gene, *Timberline*. New York: Covici Friede (1933).

Fowler, Gene, *Trumpet in the Dust*. Cleveland, Ohio: World (1930).

Frazier, Bob, *Bob Frazier of Oregon*. Eugene, Ore.: Eugene Register-Guard (1979).

Fuller, Edmund, ed., *The Essential Royster*. Chapel Hill, N.C.: Algonquin (1985).

Golden, Harry, *For 2 Cents Plain*. Cleveland, Ohio: World (1943).

Golden, Harry, *Only in America*. Cleveland, Ohio: World (1944).

Goldsmith, Barbara, *Other Powers: The Age of Suffrage, Spiritualism and the Scandalous Victoria Woodhull*. New York: Knopf (1998).

Grady, Henry W., *Life and Times of Henry W. Grady*. New York: Goldthwaite (1890).

Greeley, Horace, *An Overland Journey from New York to San Francisco in the Summer of 1859*. Lincoln: University of Nebraska Press (1999).

Greeley, Horace, *The Reflections of a Busy Life*. 2 vols. Reprint, Port Washington, N.Y.: Kennikat (1971).

Harris, Julia Collier, ed., *Joel Chandler Harris: Editor and Essayist*. Chapel Hill: University of North Carolina Press (1931).

Harris, Sydney J., *Leaving the Surface*. Boston: Houghton Mifflin (1968).

Harris, Sydney J., *The Best of Sydney J. Harris*. Boston: Houghton Mifflin (1975).

Hearn, Lacadio, *Editorials*. Boston: Houghton Mifflin (1926).

Hearst, William Randolph, *Selections from Writings and Speeches*. San Francisco (1948).

Hosokawa, Bill, *Thirty-Five Years in the Frying Pan*. New York: McGraw-Hill (1978).

Hutchins, John K., and George Oppenheimer, eds., *The Best in the World*. New York: Viking (1973).

Kilpatrick, James J., *The Foxes' Union*. McLean, Va.: EPM (1977).

Knight, Oliver, ed., *I Protest: Selected Disquisitions of E.W. Scripps*. Madison: University of Wisconsin Press (1966).

Krock, Arthur, *In The Nation (1932–1966)*. New York: McGraw-Hill (1966).

Krock, Arthur, *The Editorials of Henry Watterson*. New York: Doran (1923).

Lampman, Ben Hur, *At the End of the Car Line*. Portland, Ore.: Binfords & Mort (1942).

Lampman, Ben Hur, *How Could I Be Forgetting?* Portland, Ore.: Binfords & Mort (1926).

Lippmann, Walter, *Early Writings*. New York: Liveright (1970).

Lippmann, Walter, *Public Opinion*. New York: Harcourt, Brace (1922).

McGill, Ralph, *No Place to Hide: The South and Human Rights*. 2 vols. Macon, Ga.: Mercer University Press (1984).

McGill, Ralph, *Southern Encounters: Southerners of Note in Ralph McGill's South*. Macon, Ga: Mercer University Press (1983).

McKabe, Charles R., ed., *Damned Old Crank: A Self-Portrait of E.W. Scripps*. New York: Harper & Brothers (1951).

Meyer, Karl E., *Pundits, Poets, & Wits: An Omnibus of American Newspaper Columns*. New York: Oxford University Press (1990).

Miller, Joaquin, *Selected Writings of Joaquin Miller*. Eugene, Ore.: Urion (1977).

Nichols, David, ed., *Ernie Pyle's America: The Best of Ernie Pyle's 1930s Travel Dispatches*. New York: Random House (1989).

Pickett, Calder M., *Ed Howe: Country Town Philosopher*. Lawrence: University of Kansas Press (1968).

Pyle, Ernie, *Ernie Pyle in England*. New York: McBride (1941).

Pyle, Ernie, *Brave Men*. New York: Henry Holt (1944).

Quinlen, Anne, *Thinking Out Loud*. New York: Random House (1993).

Riley, Sam G., *The Best of the Rest: Leading Newspaper Columnists Select Their Best Work*. Westport, Conn.: Greenwood (1993).

Royko, Mike, *For the Love of Mike*. Chicago: University of Chicago Press (2001).

Royko, Mike, *One More Time*. Chicago: University of Chicago Press (1998).

Royster, Vermont, *A Pride of Prejudices*. New
  York: Knopf (1967).
Safire, William, *Coming to Terms*. New York:
  Doubleday (1991).
Smith, Jack, *The Big Orange*. Pasadena, Calif.:
  Ward Ritchie (1976).
Stone, I.F., *In a Time of Torment*. New York:
  Random House (1967).
Stone, I.F., *The Truman Era*. New York: Vintage
  (1973).
Sulzberger, C.L., *A Long Row of Candles: Memoirs
  and Diaries, 1934–1954*. New York:
  Macmillan (1969).
von Hoffman, Nicholas, *Left at the Post*.
  Chicago: Quadrangle (1970).
Watson, Emmett, *Digressions of a Native Son*.
  Seattle, Wash.: Pacific Institute (1982).
White, William Allen, *Selected Writings of William
  Allen White*. New York: Holt (1947).
White, William Allen, *In Our Town*. New York:
  McClure, Phillips (1907).
Winchell, Walter, *Winchell Exclusive*. Englewood
  Cliffs, N.J.: Prentice-Hall (1975).
Yoder, Edwin M., Jr., *The Night of the Old South
  Ball*. Oxford, Miss.: Yoknapatawpha (1984).

Credits and Acknowledgments

*Grateful acknowledgment is made
for permission to use the following:*

Permission to reprint sections of articles from
The Masthead throughout the book: National
Conference of Editorial Writers.

Chapter 1
Robert Lasch, "The containment of ideas,"
St. Louis Post-Dispatch, January 17, 1965.
Reprinted with permission of the *St. Louis Post-
Dispatch,* copyright 1965.
Lenoir Chambers, "The year Virginia closed the
schools," *Virginian-Pilot,* Jan.1, 1959.

Chapter 2
Excerpts, Bruce B. Brugmann, letter to the
Pulitzer Prize Committee, Jan. 30, 2002.
Excerpts,"Don't buy PG&E's lies," *San Francisco
Bay Guardian,* Oct. 17, 2001.
Excerpts, "Public power's future," *San Francisco
Bay Guardian,* March 20, 2002.
Excerpts, "Politics and morality," *Rutland Herald,*
Jan. 27, 2000.
Excerpts, "A conscientious start," *Rutland Herald,*
Feb. 11, 2000.
Excerpts, "Leadership in action," *Rutland Herald,*
April 26, 2000.
Excerpts, "A death foretold,"*Lexington Herald-
Leader,* Dec. 2, 1990.
Excerpt, R.S. Baker, "The editorial writer: The
man in the piazza," *Montana Journalism Review,*
15:18–19 (1972). Reprinted by permission of
Montana Journalism Review.

Chapter 5
Lou Brancaccio, "A sign of the times at The
Columbian," *Columbian,* Feb. 9, 2002.
Excerpts from *Register-Guard* editorial (date and
title unknown).

Chapter 9
NCEW, Basic Statement of Principles.
Phineas Fiske, online discussion, "Re: Mike
Gartner," April 22, 1997, NCEW-L.

Chapter 10
"The sanctity of the confessional," *St. Petersburg
Times,* May 19, 1996.
W. Wat Hopkins, "A note about libel."

Chapter 12
Excerpts from "The care and feeding of culture,"
Star Tribune, Oct. 7, 2001.
Excerpts from "Shooting preserves," *Star Tribune,*
April 18, 2000.
"Get over it, Iowa, and move ahead," Jan. 20,
2002. *Copyright 2002, reprinted with permission by
The Des Moines Register.*
"Yet another big box for West Andover," *News &
Record,* Jan. 17, 2002.
"Utah's heavy tax burden," *Deseret News,* Aug. 7,
2000.
"Heat-sensing justice," *Register-Guard,* June 14,
2001.
"Open Utah courtrooms to TV news cameras,"
Standard Examiner, Aug. 8, 2001.
"Famine," Minneapolis, Minn., *Star Tribune,* Aug.
20, 2000. Reprinted with permission of the
Star Tribune.
"Belfast Flashpoint," *Boston Globe,* Sept. 9, 2001.
"As essential as any other sustenance," *Star
Tribune,* Oct. 7, 2001. Reprinted with
permission of the Star Tribune.
"Stem Cells," Cleveland, Ohio, *Plain Dealer,* Aug.
12, 2001. © 2001 The Plain Dealer. All rights
reserved. Reprinted with permission.
"Atheist makes her point," December 17, 2001.
The Oregonian © 2000–2002, Oregonian
Publishing Co. All rights reserved. Reprinted
with permission.
"Minor surgery," *Daily Camera,* June 29, 2001.
"Ancient remains need scientific inquiry,"
Bulletin, Sept. 13, 1999.
"Boise State starts on road toward big-time
sports," *Idaho Statesman,* Sept. 1, 2001.
"Put Schwinn back on a roll," *Denver Post,* June
28, 2001.
"Let states regulate amusement parks," *Oakland
Tribune,* June 17, 2000.
"Bigotry 101," Florence, Ore., *Siuslaw News,* Aug.
20, 2000.
"A charitable view," *Rutland Herald,* Feb. 9, 2000.
"Listening to Vermont," *Rutland Herald,* Feb. 9,
2000.

Chapter 13
Maura Casey, online discussion, "Earth Day,"
April 17, 1997, NCEW-L.
Michael Heywood, online discussion, "Earth Day,"
April 17, 1997, NCEW-L.
"Roy Drachman helped shaped today's Tucson,"
Tucson Citizen, Jan. 17, 2002.

"A hero, not a celebrity," *Sacramento Bee,* July 29, 1999.

"She'll be missed," *Independent,* Aug. 11, 2001.

"Kirsten," *Register-Guard,* June 21, 1997.

"Sorry, Boston," *Mercury-News,* Jan. 20, 2002.

"Region making progress," *Rockford Register Star,* April 29, 2001.

"The Assembly Game," *Richmond Times-Dispatch,* Jan. 11, 1997.

"A Legislative Goose," *Richmond Times-Dispatch,* Feb. 3, 1995.

Ron Dzwonkowski, "We still declare," *Detroit Free Press,* July 4, 2001.

"Our lives, our fortunes, our corn," *Omaha World-Herald,* July 4, 1995.

"King fought for all Americans, not just blacks," *Charlotte Observer,* Jan. 18, 2002.

"Candy cane memories," *Times Colonist,* Dec. 11, 1999.

Chapter 14

"Risking disaster," Cleveland, Ohio, *Plain Dealer,* Aug. 9, 2001. © 2001 The Plain Dealer. All rights reserved. Reprinted with permission.

"Not worth the risks," *Independent,* Aug. 10, 2001.

"When Fido goes unmourned," *Omaha World-Herald,* July 9, 2001.

"Trail of Mistakes," *Burlington Free Press,* Oct. 4, 2000.

"Oil's Spoils," *Columbian,* March 25, 2000.

"Snowmobiles don't belong in Yellowstone," *Daily Times-Call,* June 29, 2001.

"Welcome change," *Salt Lake Tribune,* Aug. 8, 2001.

Steve Woodruff, "City's pursuit of tapes is wrong," *Missoulian,* March 9, 2001.

"Protecting anti-abortion speech," March 29, 2001. *The Oregonian* © 2000–2002, Oregonian Publishing Co. All rights reserved. Reprinted with permission.

"Style and substance," *Boston Globe,* Oct. 1, 2001.

"How to play football in Eugene," *Bulletin,* Oct. 4, 1998.

"Way it is," *Keene Sentinel,* Oct. 6, 2001.

"A dry brow," *Keene Sentinel,* Feb. 4, 2002.

"An Ivy League jail," Sept. 8, 2000. *The Oregonian* © 2000–2002, Oregonian Publishing Co. All rights reserved. Reprinted with permission.

Chapter 15

Thomas J. Lucente, online discussion, "Endorsements," Nov. 12, 2001, NCEW-L.

James G. Lakely, online discussion, "Endorsements," Nov. 12, 2001, NCEW-L.

Jackman Wilson, online discussion, "Endorsements," Nov. 12, 2001, NCEW-L.

John H. Taylor Jr., online discussion, "Endorsements," Nov. 12, 2001, NCEW-L.

Michael Smith, online discussion, "Endorsements," Nov. 12, 2001, NCEW-L.

Jeffrey M. Brody, online discussion, "Endorsements," Nov. 12, 2001, NCEW-L.

Paul Akers, Editorial Page Editor, "and for attorney general," *Free Lance–Star,* Oct. 30, 2001.

Editorial Page Editors, "Elect Schundler," *Press of Atlantic City,* Oct. 30, 2001.

"Jerry Kilgore for attorney general," *The Virginian-Pilot,* Nov. 1, 2001.

"For governor, Mark Earley," *Roanoke Times,* Oct. 28, 2001.

"Edge to McGreevey," Oct. 28, 2001. The Times, Trenton, N.J. All rights reserved. Reprinted with permission.

Chapter 16

Excerpts from Howard W. Kleiman, "Unshackled but Unwilling: Public Broadcast and Editorializing," *Journalism Quarterly,* 64:708 (Winter 1987).

Myriam Marquez, "Make no mistake: Evil child abusers should die," *Orlando Sentinel,* Nov. 6, 1998.

Mary Pilon, "Censorship stunts teens' intellectual growth," *Register-Guard,* Feb. 4, 2002.

Douglas C. Lyons, "Church, state should serve different masters," *Sun-Sentinel,* July 31, 1999. Reprinted with permission of the South Florida Sun-Sentinel.

Joe Rodriguez, "City Hall's spending policies leave 10-year-old holding his nose," *San Jose Mercury News,* c. 1998.

John Moore, "Becoming American," *Denver Post,* Jan. 28, 2002.

Ralph Berrier Jr., "That ol' John Mayer ain't what he's going to be," *Roanoke Times,* Feb. 11, 2002.

Dan Hortsch, "Analyses lead readers to subject, don't tell them what to think," Feb. 10, 2002. *The Oregonian* © 2000–2002, Oregonian Publishing Co. All rights reserved. Reprinted with permission.

"Shifting from Dollars to Sense," *American Journalism Review,* Sept. 2001.

G. Donald Gale, "Student mistakes mock First Amendment."

Peter Kohler, "Melting pot or not?" Cablevision Channel 12, Jan. 25, 2002.

Neil Heinen, "It's not the heat, it's the stupidity," WISC-TV, Aug. 1, 2001.

Chuck Stokes, "Victims," WXYZ-TV, Sept. 14, 2001.

Chuck Stokes, "Voter mail—discrimination," WXYZ-TV, Oct. 18, 2001.

Mark Lowery, "CUNY tuition hike," Cablevision New York, Feb. 8, 2002.

"UW—does governing mean support?" WISC-TV, Feb. 6, 2002.

Duane Cardall, "Guns at university," KSL-TV, Feb. 28, 2002.

Chapter 19

Paul K. Harral, online discussion, "Ombudsman," Oct. 12, 2001, NCEW-L.

Richard Aregood, "Adios, Dictator," *Philadelphia Daily News,* 1975.

John Webster, e-mail to Kenneth Rystrom, Feb. 14, 2002, and Feb. 20, 2002.

Ron Clark, e-mail to Kenneth Rystrom, March 1, 2002.

Excerpts from Peter De Simone, "100 Years haven't been enough," *St. Louis Post-Dispatch,* Nov. 26, 2000.

Excerpts from Okey Ndibe, "Eyes to the ground: The perils of the black student," *Hartford Courant,* Oct. 1, 2000.

Phineas Fiske, online discussion, "Magazine Reprints," Feb. 24, 1997, NCEW-L.

Page from the *Washington Post,* Jan. 20, 1953. Copyright © The Washington Post.

Pages from the *Star Tribune,* Dec. 17, 2001, and Dec. 19, 2001.

Page from the *Oakland Tribune,* Dec. 17, 2000.

Page from the *Billings Gazette,* April 30, 2002.

Page from the *Missoulian,* March 8, 2001.

Page from the *Daily Times-Call,* June 29, 2001.

Page from the *Telegraph-Journal,* Sept. 28, 2000.

Page from the *Spokesman-Review,* Oct. 8, 2001.

Page from the *Pioneer Press,* Feb. 2, 2002.

Index

About the Author

Kenneth Rystrom has spent 20 years in the newspaper business and 20 years teaching journalism. He has written and edited editorials on the *Register* in Des Moines, Iowa, and the *Columbian* in Vancouver, Wash. He has taught editorial writing and other journalism courses at the University of Montana, Washington State University, the University of Redlands and Virginia Polytechnic Institute and State University. He received a bachelor's degree from the University of Nebraska–Lincoln, a master's degree from the University of California–Berkeley and a Ph.D. from the University of Southern California.

Rystrom has been recognized for his contributions to journalism, journalism education and scholarship. For his contributions to journalism and journalism education, he was awarded a life membership in the National Conference of Editorial Writers, an organization for which he has also served as president. For his scholarly work in journalism, he has four times received the Henry M. Grady Award. Upon his retirement, he was awarded professor emeritus status at Virginia Polytechnic Institute and State University. He is now living in Florence, Ore.